AF829245

"This will become the next 'go-to' textbook for off-the-shelf and up-to-date guidance that is relevant to the vast array of children, young people and adults who benefit from AAC."

Janice Murray, *Department of Health Professions, Faculty of Health and Education, Manchester Metropolitan University*

"The book is accessible and unique in its focus on explanations rather than on simply recipes on 'how to do it'. It provides accessible yet sound reasonings behind the choice of particular forms of AAC or sets of intervention strategies."

Gloria Soto, Professor, *Department of Speech, Language and Hearing Sciences, San Francisco State University*

"The text can fill an important gap in highlighting the lifetime impact of developmental disorders and the changing role of AAC across all life stages… I anticipate that it will become a key reference in most programmes where AAC is a curriculum focus."

Martine M. Smith, *Professor, Clin. Sp. & Language Studies, School of Linguistic, Speech and Communication Sciences, Trinity College, Dublin*

Augmentative and Alternative Communication for Children, Adolescents and Adults with Developmental Disorders

This book is about the possibilities and achievements of children, adolescents and adults who have developmental disorders that make their development of speech difficult or very delayed and who therefore need to develop communication and language with other means than speech. For some, the difficulties are temporary in childhood, others continue to communicate with alternative communication systems throughout adulthood.

This comprehensive and accessible volume offers guidance based on current knowledge about typical and atypical language development for all those supporting families and professionals involved with children, adolescents and adults who may benefit from using augmentative and alternative communication (AAC) systems.

The text covers all major issues and gives a thorough introduction to factors that are important when choosing communication systems, vocabularies of manual signs and graphic symbols. It guides the reader in assessment strategies, adaptation of the language environment, and the principles for teaching comprehension and use of AAC, sentence formation and conversational skills to individuals with different disabilities, including motor disabilities, intellectual disabilities, autism spectrum disorders and developmental language disorders. The volume also addresses the influence of AAC on speech development and the use of AAC to promote participation in various activities, including social media, and to reduce challenging behaviour.

The book will be essential reading for students and practising psychologists, speech and language therapists, special educators, teachers, physiotherapists and occupational therapists. The accessible guidance will also be helpful for the families of children, adolescents and adults who use augmentative and alternative communication.

Stephen von Tetzchner is Professor Emeritus of Developmental Psychology at the Department of Psychology, University of Oslo, Norway.

Harald Martinsen is Professor Emeritus at the Department of Special Needs Education, University of Oslo, Norway.

Kristine Stadskleiv is Professor at the Department of Special Needs Education, University of Oslo, Norway.

Augmentative and Alternative Communication for Children, Adolescents and Adults with Developmental Disorders

Stephen von Tetzchner, Harald Martinsen and Kristine Stadskleiv

Routledge
Taylor & Francis Group
LONDON AND NEW YORK

Cover image: Øivin Horvei and Astrid H. Støren

First published 2025
by Routledge
4 Park Square, Milton Park, Abingdon, Oxon OX14 4RN

and by Routledge
605 Third Avenue, New York, NY 10158

Routledge is an imprint of the Taylor & Francis Group, an informa business

© 2025 Stephen von Tetzchner, Harald Martinsen and Kristine Stadskleiv

The right of Stephen von Tetzchner, Harald Martinsen and Kristine Stadskleiv to be identified as authors of this work has been asserted in accordance with sections 77 and 78 of the Copyright, Designs and Patents Act 1988.

All rights reserved. No part of this book may be reprinted or reproduced or utilised in any form or by any electronic, mechanical, or other means, now known or hereafter invented, including photocopying and recording, or in any information storage or retrieval system, without permission in writing from the publishers.

Trademark notice: Product or corporate names may be trademarks or registered trademarks, and are used only for identification and explanation without intent to infringe.

British Library Cataloguing-in-Publication Data
A catalogue record for this book is available from the British Library

ISBN: 978-1-032-48140-1 (hbk)
ISBN: 978-1-032-48145-6 (pbk)
ISBN: 978-1-003-38763-3 (ebk)

DOI: 10.4324/9781003387633

Typeset in Times New Roman
by SPi Technologies India Pvt Ltd (Straive)

Contents

Figures

Manual signs and graphic symbols

Manual signs (mainly British)

Blissymbols

www.blissymbolics.org

Pictogram Ideogram Communication (PIC)

http://www.pictoworld.com

Picture Communication Symbols (PCS)

https://goboardmaker.com/pages/picture-communication-symbols

Widgit symbols

www.widgit.com

Aragonese Portal of Augmentative and Alternative Communication (ARASAAC)

http://arasaac.org

Overview of illustrations

Illustrations 1.10, 1.11, 2.1, 2.5, 2.8, 2.9, 2.10, 4.5, 9.2, 10.1, 10.2, 10.3, 10.4, 12.2, 12.3, 12.4 created by Øivin Horvei

Figure 1.9 Designed by Freepik.com

Figure 2.1 Bottom row: left image with permission of Ablenet, middle image with permission of Normedia, right image with permission of Tobii Dynavox

Manual signs performed by children drawn by Astrid H. Støren

Manual signs performed by adults and the childish adult sign drawn by Kristin Torp

Aragonese Portal of Augmentative and Alternative Communication System is created by Aragonese Centre of Augmentative and Alternative Communication and available at http://arasaac.org

Blissymbolics is created by Charles Bliss and available from Blissymbolics Communication International at www.blissymbolics.org

Pictogram Ideogram Communication is created by Subhas C. Maharaj and available at www.pictoworld.com

Picture Communication Symbols© are used with permission from Tobii Dynavox, www.tobiidynavox.com

Widgit Symbols© are used with permission from Widgit Software Ltd 2002-2024, www.widgit.com

Foreword

The background for this book is the many possibilities for communication and language development in children, adolescents and adults with severe developmental disorders who struggle with the development of speech. Most of them are able to develop language through other modes than speech when given the opportunity. Learning augmentative and alternative communication (AAC) is a significant achievement that enables them to compensate for or supplement their delayed or limited development of spoken language. However, similar to communication and language development in children with typical development, the development of AAC is a complex process that requires support and guidance from the language environment. Most people in society are not familiar with alternative language modes before they get involved with individuals who need AAC, as parent, sibling, peer, therapist, teacher or another role. However, with specialist support they are able to interact with and guide individuals who develop communication and language with alternative means and become members of an accessible language environment for individuals using AAC.

The aim of the book is to provide a foundation for achieving AAC competence to people who are engaged with individuals who may need AAC. It contains comprehensive information about the development of AAC in diverse groups of users with developmental disorders, the variety of alternative communication systems, and intervention strategies that can increase the communicative possibilities of individuals with limited spoken language. The extensive reference list enables readers to expand their insights and follow special interests related to developmental disorders and AAC.

The field of AAC has evolved significantly since the early start in the 1960s. Over the years, many new ideas and insights have emerged from research and practice, as well as from individuals using AAC and their families. Many people have contributed to the knowledge development within the field – too many to mention names. We have learned from publications on AAC, discussions in international and national conferences, and from collaborations with families who have a member who uses AAC. The international and national conferences of the International Society for Augmentative and Alternative Communication (ISAAC) have given us opportunities to share ideas with colleagues and families from around the World. Among others, the large international study *Becoming an Aided Communicator* (BAC) emerged from collaborations within ISAAC. The thoughtful and inspirational discussions in this group have been important for the current conceptualization of the acquisition of AAC as form of language development, and for the development of many of the principles and ideas presented in this book.

The present book may serve as an introductory text for students and practicing psychologists, speech and language therapists, teachers and special educators in school and preschool, physiotherapists and occupational therapists, care nurses, and other groups, as well as for families with members who have severe developmental impairments of speech and language, and to facilitate collaboration between different groups of professionals, and between professionals and families.

We express our thanks to Helen Pritt, Molly Selby and Shivranjani Singh at Routledge for their friendly and constructive collaboration and attention to details.

Stephen von Tetzchner, Harald Martinsen, Kristine Stadskleiv
Oslo, April 2024

Introduction

A significant minority of the population is unable to communicate fully through speech. They may be totally unable to speak, or their speech may not be sufficient to fulfil all communicative functions. They can achieve language competence but need an alternative language mode as a supplement to, or a substitute for, spoken language. Among them are children, adolescents and adults with motor impairments, intellectual disabilities, autism spectrum disorder, speech and language impairment, or other developmental or acquired disorders. The size of this group is not fully known (see Chapter 3) but studies suggest that the actual use of alternative means of communication is lower than the needs, implying that many children, adolescents and adults with limited speech do not get the means they need to reach their communicative potential (Andzik & Chung, 2022; Binger et al., 2021; Creer et al., 2016; Lillehaug et al., 2023).

The present book is mainly concerned with augmentative and alternative communication (AAC) for individuals who have *developmental* communication and language disabilities. There may be large differences between the consequences of congenital or early acquired impairments on the one hand, and of impairments acquired at a later age on the other. A congenital or early acquired impairment may make it difficult to develop skills which are only indirectly related to the impairment. For example, people who lose sight and hearing at an adult age can usually still speak and write, while individuals born deaf and blind rarely learn these skills. Many children with severe motor and speech impairments develop reading and writing disorders, while people who acquire comparable motor and speech impairments in adulthood rarely have such difficulties. Moreover, due to the diverse developmental experiences of the two groups, their everyday lives and social and societal participation may also differ. Inclusion of later acquired impairments would require a separate volume.

On language and speech

The distinction between language and speech is the very foundation of augmentative and alternative communication. Language consists of a set of symbols (words) representing people, things, places, ideas and so forth, and conventions for making sequences of symbols (word order) and modifying the symbols (inflections) to create different meanings. Language development is the process of learning to understand and use a language mode. The development may be typical or atypical (von Tetzchner, 2019a).

Most people develop vocal language, that is, language primarily produced in speech. Natural speech is the physical articulation of speech sounds. Spoken language refers to all languages produced in speech, such as English, Spanish, Norwegian and so forth (Paul, 1997).

DOI: 10.4324/9781003387633-1

Some electronic communication devices produce utterances with artificial speech output, constructed with the help of a graphic language mode (see Chapter 2). However, only the production of language with natural speech is referred to as speech development.

Language may be produced in non-vocal modalities, such as manual or graphic modalities. This makes it possible for children, adolescents and adults who have difficulties producing speech to use language (see Chapter 3).

Sign language includes all national languages produced in sign, such as British Sign Language, American Sign Language, Norwegian Sign Language, and so forth. The sign languages are natural languages that have evolved in deaf communities.

There are also several constructed manual sign systems that are much simpler than the natural sign languages, such as Paget Gorman and Seeing Exact English (see Chapter 1). These manual sign systems are part of AAC and are used by hearing individuals with little or no speech to fill the language functions. There are also manual letters, that is, hand shapes that represent the letters of the alphabet.

The graphic language mode includes letters and other written characters as well as graphic symbols. There are many different writing systems, such as Cyrillic and Roman alphabets and Chinese characters (Coulmas, 2022; Perfetti & Dunlap, 2008). Written language includes all language produced with letters or other written characters.

There are many different graphic symbol systems that vary in form, content and complexity (see Chapter 1). The symbols are combined to create utterances with different meanings. Graphic symbols are thus the words of the graphic communication systems, representing people, things, places, ideas and other content, as well as conjunctions, prepositions and other grammatical elements.

"Vocal" refers to the use of voice or speech while "verbal" refers to the use of words – language in any modality. All communication using a language mode is verbal, including written language and the non-vocal language modes applied in AAC, while communication applying gestures and other behaviours of the face, body, or voice (minus the linguistic content) is non-verbal (Hall et al., 2019).

The history of augmentative and alternative communication

Augmentative and alternative communication is a new area of practice and research but it has long roots. There have always been individuals with developmental disorders of communication, language and speech, and interest in the nature of these disorders and how to remedy them has been evident throughout historical time (Jakobson, 1968; Marx, 1967; O'Neill, 1980). The first reports of hearing individuals with developmental disorders and little or no speech using manual signs appeared more than 200 years ago (e.g., Itard, 1801; Lane, 1977). However, the constructed manual sign systems representing spoken language were originally intended for deaf people (Moores, 2010). There were occasional reports of non-vocal communication for hearing individuals with developmental disabilities and limited speech, but it took a long time before there were systematic materials and interventions involving non-vocal language modes for this group. Life without speech prior to the introduction of manual sign systems and graphic symbol systems is documented in a few early autobiographies written with assistance from family or friends (e.g., Deacon, 1974; Steenbuch, 1957).

In the 1970s, there was an increase in studies of manual signs and graphic or tangible symbols involving hearing individuals with autism spectrum disorder and intellectual disabilities (e.g., Berg & Sørhuglen, 1980; Deich & Hodges, 1977; Kiernan, 1977; Topper, 1975). Although

the sign languages of the deaf communities are not part of AAC, the strong sign language movement in the 1970s and 1980s contributed to the increasing use of manual sign systems as communication tools for hearing children with limited speech (von Tetzchner & Jensen, 1996; Zangari et al., 1994).

The first commercial communication boards with letters and written words appeared at the beginning of 1900. There were no graphic symbol systems, and parents of children with cerebral palsy would cut out pictures from magazines to make communication boards for their children (von Tetzchner, 1990). There were also reports of home-drawn symbols for communication boards. The communication board designed by McDonald and Schultz (1973) inspired later developments of communication boards with graphic symbols. Following the introduction in 1971 of Blissymbolics, the first formal graphic symbol system to be used for communication by individuals without speech, a range of graphic symbol systems emerged (von Tetzchner & Jensen, 1996). The complexity of Blissymbolics probably contributed to the general acceptance of graphic symbol systems as means of expressive language.

Most of the early studies focused on basic communication skills like requesting and less on more advanced communication functions and conversational skills. With the new possibilities that emerged from the general technological development, there was renewed attention to individuals who lack speech or have unintelligible speech due to motor disabilities (Peters & Kirstein, 1978; Vanderheiden, 2002). Many of these aided communicators had good cognitive skills and comprehension of spoken language, and, therefore, needed expressive means that enabled them to communicate more complex messages. The first scientific review of conversations involving aided communication contained 11 mostly unpublished studies (Kraat, 1985) and since then, thousands of studies have been published.

Today, AAC is used in most countries and there is a large number of manual sign systems and graphic symbol systems. The most common systems are presented in Chapter 1. In parallel with the emergence of new communication possibilities, specialized AAC services were established in many countries (e.g., Kalman & Pajor, 1996; Mendes & Rato, 1996; Zangari et al., 1994).

The *International Society for Augmentative and Alternative Communication* (ISAAC) was established in 1983 and ISAAC's biennial conferences represent an important international meeting place for sharing knowledge and discussing issues related to AAC. There are also several regular national and regional AAC conferences, such as the *Communication Matters Conference* in UK and the *Eastern and Central European Regional AAC Conference*. The journal *Augmentative and Alternative Communication* was established in 1985 and has remained the central scientific publication within the field, although studies of AAC have appeared in a wide range of scientific journals. Blackstone and Bruskin published the first textbook on AAC in 1986.

Individuals who need non-vocal communication systems differ

This book is concerned with the use of manual signs and graphic and tangible symbols in language intervention. The largest group of people who use manual signs are those who are deaf. However, deaf children acquire sign language in the same informal manner as most hearing children learn to speak. If they grow up in a signing environment, they do not need any special teaching to learn to sign. Consequently, the present book is *not* concerned with deaf people. The exception is deaf individuals who need a communication aid due to motor impairment making expressive signing very difficult or impossible (Lanphere & Terlektsi, 2023).

There are significant differences among people in need of AAC. The only thing they have in common is insufficient speech and a need for alternative language modes to substitute for or supplement spoken language. One subgroup is children who use AAC in the early years and then develop speech and do not need AAC anymore.

For individuals with a lifelong need for AAC, comprehension of spoken language and motor skills may determine their life course and the degree to which they will participate in ordinary social and societal activities. One subgroup do understand what other people say, and their need for alternative communication systems is mainly due to motor impairments that hinder speech. Motor disorders may also hinder other activities, making them dependent on assistive technology and assistance from other people. Another subgroup consists of people who struggle with both comprehension and production of speech, and whose language disorders are part of a more comprehensive impairment that also influences other intellectual and social skills (see Chapter 3).

Difficulties in communicating with other people may have widespread consequences and affect people in all phases of life and at all ages. In the pre-lingual period, communication difficulties may influence the interaction between children and their caregivers and the natural processes of enculturation. Parents of children with extensive communication disorders may have problems understanding their child's interests, likes and dislikes, and may be uncertain about what to do. The children risk losing the opportunities for natural learning which usually form part of any social environment. Most of what children learn as they grow up is co-constructed with more competent members of society: conveyed through shared focus, reactions from adults and other children, what others explain and tell them about things and seeing and hearing what others say and do. In this manner, children learn language and acquire the knowledge, values and norms of their culture (Nelson, 2007; Tomasello, 2003, 2020). Children with severe language and communication disorders will have less exposure than others to such learning opportunities. This emphasizes the need for early AAC intervention and follow-up through childhood, adolescence and adulthood.

From childhood and throughout life, feelings of self-efficacy, respect and worth are closely related to the ability to express oneself. The perception of oneself as independent and equal to others is related to the development of *communicative autonomy* – the ability to communicate about the things that are on one's mind, talk about one's thoughts, ideas and concerns, and use words to express one's feelings. When this ability is compromised, people may have difficulties making themselves "heard" and lose control over their own fate. They risk alienation and exclusion from the social world. They may experience that other people underestimate them, talk down to them and make decisions for them. On the other hand, other people may overestimate them, assuming they have an understanding and control of the situation that they do not have, and, hence, attribute meanness and bad intent to them rather than reduced ability to act and respond appropriately in social interaction. For people with the most severe disabilities, such negative experiences may – together with inconsistent and infrequent responses to their initiations and wants – lead to learned passivity and dependency on others, as well as frustration and depression. The aim of AAC intervention is to increase the individual's ability to communicate but also the understanding of people in the environment and their ability to adapt to the communication skills of the individual. Significant adults and peers in the environment usually need help and support in developing AAC competence. Thus, through the intervention, both the individual using alternative means of communication *and* the people in the environment should change.

Communication intervention may be crucial for all aspect of the individual's life. Providing AAC to children and adults with little or no speech may increase their quality of life and control over their own lives, as well as their self-efficacy and opportunity for feeling equal in the society. Moreover, for people with extensive motor impairments, language and communication may be easier to develop than other skills. For them, improved expressive language skills may have a dual function, enabling them also to participate more in all kinds of familial, social and societal activities.

The choice and implementation of AAC should thus be viewed in a broad perspective. The communication system provided should make a difference, increase autonomy and make the individual feel less disabled and more able to manage everyday life. The choice of communication system must, therefore, be based on the total situation of the individual. Most people who need AAC also need other forms of intervention. The provision of a new communication system should be coordinated with the whole range of services on offer: education, physical training, guidance and so forth. Communication and language intervention should not be isolated from other forms of intervention. In the same way as other modes of language and communication, AAC systems should function as a tool to be used in all aspects of life.

New communication systems and aids are regularly coming into use, and it may be difficult to obtain descriptions and evaluations of all of them. The various groups of people in need of AAC often require different communication systems. Although the newest model is not always the best, knowledge of what systems that are available is crucial in order to be able to make the right decisions. It is also necessary to know how to adapt the different systems and aids to the needs of individual users, and what kind of support they require.

Overview of the chapters

The chapters give a thorough introduction to AAC, the bases of early and later AAC intervention, and the development of AAC from early childhood to adulthood. The chapters present different aspects of AAC systems, AAC intervention and AAC development but their contents are interdependent and constitute a coherent whole.

- Chapter 1 presents the basic terminology related to AAC and gives an overview of the most common manual sign systems, graphic symbol systems and tangible symbol systems and their use with children, adolescents and adults in need of an alternative or supplement to speech.
- Chapter 2 gives an overview of communication aids, from communication books and boards to electronic devices with voice output, and the various ways of accessing and operating communication aids, including strategies for speeding up communication. The chapter presents principles for choosing communication aids, describes common features of aided communication and discusses how the use of communication aids may influence communicative interactions. It also presents AAC use with remote communication and social media, and other forms of assistive technology.
- Chapter 3 presents the principal groups of individuals in need of AAC, the differences between the groups and the considerable variation in skills and abilities within each of the groups. It further describes the main diagnostic groups – motor disabilities, intellectual disabilities, autism spectrum disorders and developmental language disorders – and discusses common problems related to communication intervention with individuals who have severe communication and language disabilities.

- Chapter 4 describes how to do a comprehensive assessment of individuals who may need AAC, observations, tests, checklists and interviews that may provide information that is important for the choice of communication system and vocabulary. The chapter highlights methods for assessing individuals who are difficult to assess because of severe motor, cognitive and communication impairments.
- Chapter 5 presents various intervention situations, including structuring, the organization of different training and communication situations, inclusion, and how to promote the use of AAC beyond training situations and create an AAC-supportive language environment.
- Chapter 6 presents the main principles for teaching AAC to individuals who develop different forms of AAC and are in different phases of AAC development. These include early and later intervention approaches related to comprehension and use of AAC, strategies for initiating AAC intervention, promoting joint attention and implementing structured overinterpretation and total communication, and a variety of implicit and explicit teaching strategies and evidence-based practices. The chapter discusses bilingualism in AAC and the effect of AAC on speech development.
- Chapter 7 presents principles and strategies for selecting and teaching an initial vocabulary for individuals who use less than 20–30 words, signs or symbols. It introduces the important distinction between communicative success and instrumental success.
- Chapter 8 presents the principles of vocabulary growth in AAC and strategies for supporting the acquisition of a varied vocabulary in individuals belonging to each of the three functional groups after they have learnt to use an initial vocabulary, emphasizing differences between the user groups as well as the need for individualization of vocabulary. It discusses how to organize vocabularies, the notions of core, basic and fringe vocabulary, strategies for teaching new manual signs or graphic symbols and supporting spoken words, ways of expanding the usage of already learnt and new vocabulary, as well as strategies used by individuals to construct meanings for which they lack manual signs or graphic symbols. The chapter also discusses the transition from graphic symbols to orthographic writing.
- Chapter 9 is about the transition from simple to more complex utterances, the principles and strategies for guiding children, adolescents and adults using AAC in constructing utterances with two or more manual signs or graphic symbols in everyday life, including strategies developed by individuals who use AAC.
- Chapter 10 is about participation in activities and how the use of AAC is embedded in social activities and events, including play and other child activities, as well as activities typical of adolescence and adult life, including social media. The chapter highlights the importance of social participation for communication and language development, presents strategies for promoting dialogues in play, shared book reading and other everyday activities, and how to support AAC development and social participation in times of pandemics, unrest and war.
- Chapter 11 is about the development of conversation skills, such as initiating, maintaining and ending conversations, discovering and repairing mistakes, and narrative skills. The chapter highlights strategies for engaging individuals using AAC in longer conversations with peers and adults, helping them to manage conversations, and increasing independent use of AAC in narration. The chapter also discusses strategies used by communication partners of individuals in the three groups.

- Chapter 12 is about supporting the language environment, promoting AAC competence in parents, teachers, peers and other significant people, and making the environment communicative accessible for children, adolescents and adults using AAC. It presents intervention measures for building up competence in parents, siblings and peers, teachers and other staff and other significant people in the environment.
- The short glossary explains central terminology related to AAC and AAC intervention.

Terminology

The research and practice related to the use of manual, graphic and tangible communication systems by hearing people with communication and language disorders is fairly recent and the terminology has changed over the years. The terminology used in this book is in accordance with the current professional literature (see von Tetzchner & Basil, 2011). The term "sign" is used about manual communication forms, while graphic and tangible communication forms are called "symbols". However, it should be noted that speech, graphic symbols, tangible symbols and manual signs are all symbols in the sense that they represent something else (Deacon, 2017; DeLoache, 2004).

The terminology used in this book to describe individuals using alternative means of communication follow international conventions. Individuals using manual signs are "signers". *Aided communicators* use some form of communication aid. The term "aided speaker" is reserved for children and adults who are using communication devices with speech output (aided speech), while a *natural speaker* is using speech in the typical manner. A *communication partner* may perceive a manual sign, "read" a graphic symbol, or interpret another mode of communication.

In this book, descriptions focus on the achievements of individuals using AAC, *what the individuals can do*. In professional reports or articles, it may be necessary to describe the individuals' degree of impairment in production and comprehension of speech, as well as in their production and comprehension of manual signs and graphic or tangible symbols. The term *non-speaking* is used to indicate that the individual lacks speech, while the term *non-verbal* indicates that the individual lacks any kind of language – spoken, manual or graphic. However, when describing individuals' development and use of other language modes than natural speech, it is most important to focus on their achievements and the related processes.

Most of the individuals who receive intervention to develop AAC are children, however, many adolescents and adults with developmental disabilities need support in using such communication systems. One reason for this is that many people with severe disabilities need communication and language intervention into adulthood – and some throughout their lives. Another reason is that in most countries, there are adults with developmental disorders who had an early need for alternative means of communication but who did not get the opportunity to learn such a system in childhood (Stancliffe et al., 2010). For simplicity, we use the term *individual* to refer to those who receive AAC intervention, unless it is clear from the context that it is a child, an adolescent, or an adult. For the same reason, we use the term *teacher* for all professionals involved in educating the individual. Thus, a "teacher" may be a nursery-school teacher, a teacher, a special educator, a care nurse, a speech and language therapist, a psychologist, and so forth. The term *significant people* is used to refer to family, friends, daily carers in sheltered housing and others who are close to the individual or

responsible for his or her interests. Significant people do not usually include teachers or other educators.

Notation

Writing about communication involving AAC requires special notational conventions. The notations used in this book follow von Tetzchner and Basil (2011) and are summarized in Table I.1.

Sign glosses are written in capital letters, for example, BOY RUN. The glosses of graphic symbols are both italicized and in capital letters, *BOY DRIVE FAST* (see also Figure I.1). Written whole words and ready-made sentences are underlined. Also S-p-e-l-l-e-d words are underlined. '*Sentences produced with a communication device with speech output*' are italicized and in single quotation signs.

Quotation signs together with an explanation in brackets are used to represent the meaning of different expressive forms, such as gestures, symbolic pointing, facial expressions, and so forth, for example, "no" (shaking the head) and "out" (pointing out of the window). Note that *symbolic pointing*, like pointing to graphic symbols, has a different function than ordinary deictic pointing. Deictic pointing is used to indicate the location or presence of somebody or something. Symbolic points, in contrast, function as word forms with a defined meaning or use – typically chosen because they are faster to produce than by spelling or

Table I.1 Summary of notational conventions

Utterance form	*Notation*	*Example*
Glosses of manual signs and gestures	Capital letters	MANUAL SIGN
Glosses of graphic symbols	Italicized capital letters	*GRAFHIC SYMBOL*
Glosses of tangible symbols	Capital letters and asterix	OBJECT* SYMBOL*
Spelled written words	Underline and hyphen	S-p-e-l-l-e-d w-o-r-d
Written words spelled with prediction and selection	Underline and hyphen of individual letters and letter clusters	c-a-catc-cat-cats
Written whole words selected individually	Underline each word	Individual whole word
Selections consisting of multiple word or a sentence (ready-made)	Continuous underline	Sentence with several words
Manual spelling (hand alphabet)	Capital letters and hyphen	B-O-Y
Naturally spoken utterances	Italicization	*Naturally spoken words*
Machine-produced digitized or synthesized speech (aided speech)	Italicization and quotation signs	'*Words and sentences spoken by a machine*'
Interpretation of other referring expressions	Quotation signs and explanation	"No" (shakes head) "I" (looks at door to own room) "Out" (looks out of window)
Interpretation of non-speech utterance	Quotation signs	DOG GONE = "The dog has run away"
Simultaneous production of two forms	Waved brackets	{PETER *Peter*} *is* {NOT *not*} *here today.*

indicating a graphic symbol or written word in a communication aid. For example, in a conversation with his father, an eight-year-old boy looked at the door to his room to say "I" instead of directing his father to turn pages in his communication book and locate the graphic symbol *I* (von Tetzchner & Martinsen, 1996).

Waved parentheses {…} indicate simultaneous expressive forms, for example speech and manual signs, or manual signs and graphic symbols. {HAPPY *I am happy*} means that the manual sign HAPPY is produced simultaneously with the naturally spoken sentence *I am happy*.

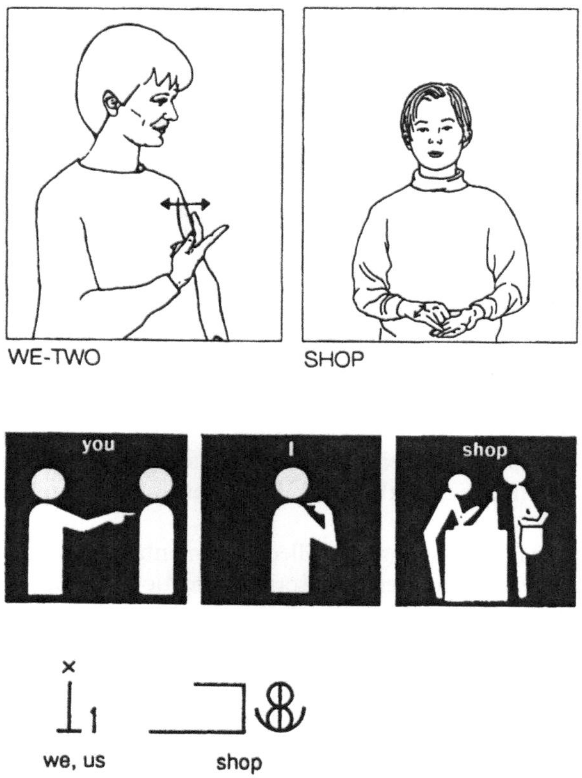

Figure I.1 WE-TWO SHOP (signs), *YOU I SHOP* (PIC) or *WE SHOP* (Bliss-words) may mean "We are going shopping".

Chapter 1

Augmentative and alternative communication

Speech is the most advanced form of human communication and the preferred mode for people with normal hearing. However, some individuals are not able to speak, no matter how much training they are given. For these individuals, some form of augmentative and alternative communication (AAC) will enable them to communicate. Others have more limited speech disorders. They may need an alternative form of communication while developing speech or in some situations to augment their communication and make their speech more intelligible to the communication partner. Thus, AAC can be a supplement to, or a substitute for, spoken language. The most common modes of AAC are manual signs, graphic symbols, tangible symbols, and letters and written words.

- ***Alternative communication*** is the means by which an individual who is not able to use speech can communicate in face-to-face interaction.
- ***Augmentative communication*** means supplementary or supportive communication. The word "augmentative" emphasizes the fact that intervention with alternative means of communication has a dual purpose: to promote and support speech and to ensure an alternative mode of communication if the individual does not develop the ability to speak.

All non-vocal communication systems are called "augmentative and alternative". The terms *sign system* and *symbol system* are used to describe collections of manual signs, graphic symbols and tangible symbols.

- ***Manual signs*** are performed with the hands. *Manual sign systems* are constructed systems with manual signs used as a form of AAC. *Sign languages* are the languages of signs used by deaf people. They are natural languages and *not* considered a form of AAC. The verb *to sign* refers to the production of both sign languages and manual sign systems.
- ***Graphic communication symbols*** include all graphically formed symbols, such as Blisswords, Picture Communication Symbols (PCS), Pictographic Ideographic Communication (PIC), and Widgit Symbols (WS).
- ***Tangible symbols*** are usually made of wood or plastic. They have distinctive shapes and surface textures that make them easy to distinguish with the tactile sense, for example, they may be made of silk or sand. They may also consist of small objects or models of objects.

The division between *aided* and *unaided communication* designates the two main modes of AAC.

DOI: 10.4324/9781003387633-2

- ***Aided communication*** includes all forms of communication in which the communicative expression exists in a physical form outside of the user. The expressions are *selected*. Communication folders, boards and books, electronic devices with speech output and other forms of communication aids belong to this category. Indicating graphic symbols, photographs or letters by pointing at them is included in aided communication because the graphic symbols, photographs or letters constitute the communicative expressions or are used in the utterance construction.
- In ***unaided communication***, the communicators are making the communicative expressions themselves. The expressions are *produced*. This chiefly encompasses manual signs, but hand alphabets and handwriting may also belong to this category. Blinking with the eyes to indicate "yes" and "no" is also a form of unaided communication. The same applies to ordinary pointing with hand or eye gaze and other gestures, because in these instances the pointing is the communicative expression.

The difference should be noted between the ordinary use of pointing in communication gesture and pointing to indicate graphic or tangible symbols. Ordinary pointing is used to indicate the location of something, usually with the index finger, but pointing can be done in many ways, including using an object or the gaze in an explicit manner, such as looking at something to produce a message or answer the question "Where is?" when the hands are occupied (Sargent et al., 2013).

The division between *dependent* and *independent* communication relates to how the alternative communication form is used, and the role of the conversational partner in formulating the utterances of the AAC user.

- ***Dependent communication*** means that an AAC user relies on another person to put together or interpret and formulate the meaning of what the AAC user expresses. Dependent communication is common with the use of communication boards with words and graphic communication symbols, but the partner may also need to interpret and formulate the meaning of keyword manual signs or "telegraphic" sign utterances.
- ***Independent communication*** means that the message is fully formulated in the alternative mode. For people using graphic communication, this may be achieved with the help of electronic communication aids where their sentences are presented on a screen or with voice output.

When the communication is in a dependent mode, the communication partner has a particular ethical responsibility to make every effort to ensure that it is the intended message of the AAC user that is formulated and not what the partner might want the user to say (Grove et al., 1999).

Manual signs

In most countries, there are two types of manual signs. The first type is the sign languages used among deaf people (Sandler & Lillo-Martin, 2017). These are named after the country, such as British sign language (BSL) or American sign language (ASL). Sign languages are *primary*, that is, not derived from a spoken language. Sign languages have developed naturally and have undergone change through contact with other sign languages, as well as with spoken

and written languages (Emmorey & Lane, 2000; Quinto-Pozos & Adam, 2020). They have their own grammar, with inflections and sign order (syntax) that differ from those of the spoken language(s) in the country (Napoli & Sutton-Spence, 2014). The sign languages of the various countries differ in much the same way as spoken languages do (see Figure 1.1). The topography (articulation) of the signs differs (Sandler, 2017), they vary in inflections and the sentences have different syntaxes (Fischer, 2017). There are also dialectal variations, between regions within the same country. The sign languages are not a form of AAC, but manual sign systems often borrow signs from the national sign languages.

The second type of manual signs are called *manual sign systems*. They are *secondary*, constructed to follow the syntax and grammar of the national spoken language(s). Accordingly, they differ from one country to the other and include, for example, *Signing Exact English* (Gustason et al., 1980) and *Paget-Gorman Sign System* (Paget et al., 1976). Manual sign systems are designed to represent the spoken language through signs and have never been used widely among deaf people because the inflections and syntax of spoken languages are not well suited to a visual and manual language (Scott & Henner, 2021). Manual sign systems are considered a form of AAC.

There are also tactile sign systems, mainly used with people who have combined visual and auditory impairment. The individual produces signs by moving the hands of the communication partner, and perceives the communication partner's signs by placing one or both hands on top of the hands of the communication partner and following the movements of the hand (Lindstrøm, 2019; Willoughby et al., 2018).

In intervention for hearing individuals with communication and language disorders, it is most common to use manual sign systems that follow the spoken language. Few hearing people are competent users of the national sign language prior to meeting an individual who needs manual signs as AAC in the family or at work. Because the manual sign systems follow the spoken language, they are easier to use together with speech. This is important because speech and manual signs usually are used simultaneously in AAC intervention (see p. 361). Moreover, the ability to learn foreign languages varies in the general population, and many people struggle when learning a new language. For persons using natural speech, it is easier to learn a manual sign system that closely resembles their spoken language than a sign language

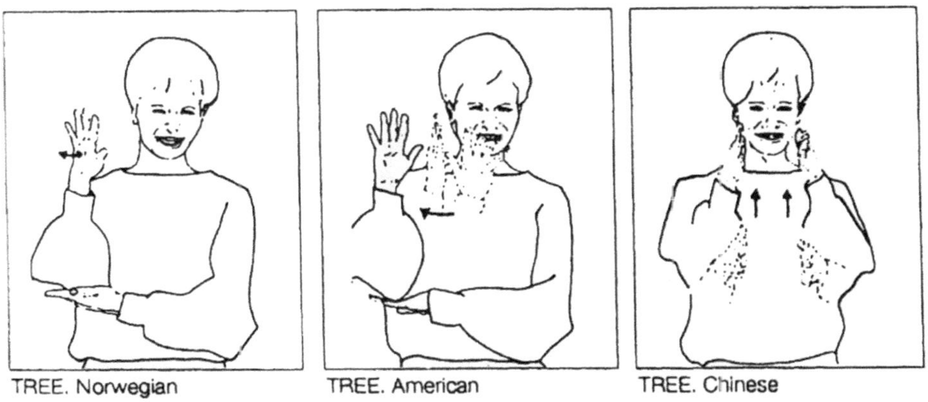

Figure 1.1 TREE in Norwegian, American and Chinese sign languages.

with a very different grammar. However, for people with a very good command of signing, a sign system that follows the spoken language would be less effective in use than a natural sign language (Scott & Henner, 2021).

Graphic communication symbols

Graphic communication symbols consist of an image and a written gloss under or above the image. They represent categories of people, animals, objects, actions, attributes, locations and so on. The image usually depicts one instance of the category represented by the symbol, for example a drawing of a small round ball to represent all objects belonging to the category "ball", independent of their size, colour and shape, or a drawing of a German shepherd dog to represent all animals belonging to the category "dog" (von Tetzchner, 2015). Graphic communication symbols are intended to have the same functions as spoken words, to be the individual's graphic words. It is crucial that parents and other people in a child's environment acknowledge the child's graphic communication symbols as graphic words, having the same functions as spoken words or signed words.

A number of different graphic communication systems have been used as AAC (von Tetzchner & Jensen, 1996), and only the most common systems are presented here. Nearly all of them belong to one of two mainly pictographic symbol groups: (1) white silhouette and gloss on black background, such as Pictographic Ideographic Communication, and (2) line drawings in black and white or colour and black gloss, such as Picture Communication Symbols. The Widgit Symbol System integrates graphic communication symbols and letters. There is one mainly ideographic system, Blissymbolics. In addition, Minspeak is included here, although it is not a traditional graphic system, but a set of graphic icons used to produce pre-coded words and phrases in synthetic speech. Links to each of the systems' websites are available in the Resources section at the end of the book.

Blissymbolics

Blissymbolics, the system of Bliss-characters, Bliss-indicators and Bliss-words, is a form of *logographic* or *ideographic* writing, that is, a writing system not based on phoneme-grapheme correspondences such as letters (Kessler & Treiman, 2015). Blissymbolics was originally constructed as an international written language inspired by Chinese characters (Bliss, 1965). The system was first used in 1971 in Canada with children with severe motor and speech impairment, who had severe difficulties in learning to read and write (McNaughton, 2003, 2014). Children who have severe articulation difficulties or little or no speech often have significant problems in learning an alphabetic written language (see p. 270). Their problems are related to constructing words from alphabetic letters and the children are usually able to learn to read words with logographic and ideographic characters, such as Bliss-words (Geschwind, 1972; Smith, 2005a).

The Blissymbolics system consists of a set of basic Bliss-characters, which can be used alone or in combination with other Bliss-characters. A Bliss-word may thus contain one or several Bliss-characters. Some Bliss-character combinations have become conventional Bliss-words. Blissymbolics Communication International, a non-profit organization that has the official rights, has adopted a number of fixed English glosses, or "translations", which can be adapted to fit different languages and cultures, today over 5,500 Bliss-words. A Bliss-character or Bliss-word may be used slightly differently in different countries, in the same way that a

word of a spoken language when translated may not have exactly the same usages and range of meanings in another language. When there is no conventional Bliss-word, it may be possible to construct several Bliss-words that correspond to the same spoken word. This variation reflects the flexible and creative nature of Blissymbolics. Any message can be formulated with Bliss-words.

- Bliss-characters are symbols that represent *semantic elements* that are combined and understood by analogy. For example, the Bliss-word *DEER* consists of *ANIMAL+HORN. HOME* is *HOUSE+FEELINGS. TOILET* is *CHAIR+WATER. HAPPY* is *FEELING+UP* (see Figure 1.3). When creating a new Bliss-word with several characters, the first character is the *classifier*, which indicates what type of concept it represents, for example a feeling or an animal. The following characters are *specifiers* that specify or narrow the meaning of the classifier, such as in *FEELING+DOWN* to construct *SAD* or *PERSON+GIVE+KNOWLEDGE* to construct *TEACHER* and *PERSON+RECEIVE+KNOWLEDGE* to construct *STUDENT* (Blissymbolics Communication International, 2020; Jennische & Zetterlund, 2015).
- In addition to the Bliss-characters that may correspond to a whole word, there are also a number of markers, called *indicators*, that constitute grammatical inflections and denote parts of language, such as *PAST-TENSE, PLURAL, THING, ACTION* and *ADJECTIVE.* By adding the indicator *ACTION*, nouns are transformed to verbs. *BOAT+ACTION* becomes (to) *SAIL*, and *BICYCLE+ACTION* is (to) *BICYCLE*. Similarly, *TIME+THING* becomes *CLOCK*. The systematicity is illustrated in the variations around *MOUTH*: *MOUTH+ACTION* becomes *SPEAK, MOUTH+EARTH* is *FOOD, MOUTH+LIQUID* is *DRINK, MOUTH−EARTH+ACTION* is (to) *EAT* and *MOUTH+MUSICAL-NOTE+ACTION* is (to) SING (see Figure 1.3). The grammatical symbols may support comprehension of grammar in spoken language and thus the transition to orthographic writing.

Other Bliss-characters are "strategic" in the sense that they change the meaning of a Bliss-word in a fundamental way or imply an instruction to the communication partner about the

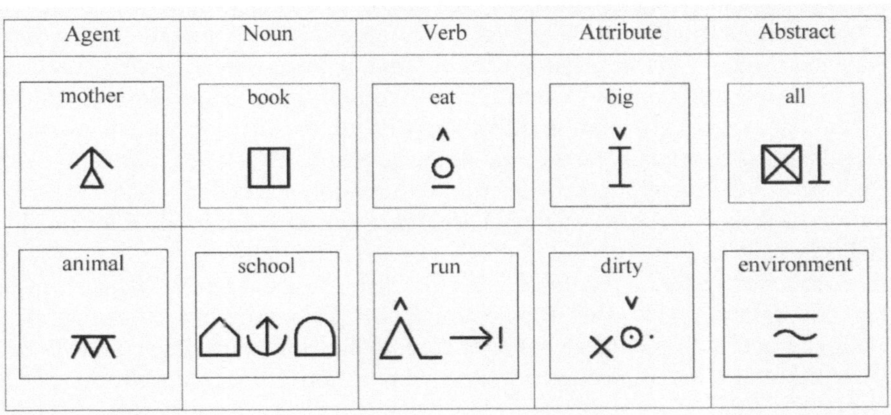

Figure 1.2 Bliss-words.

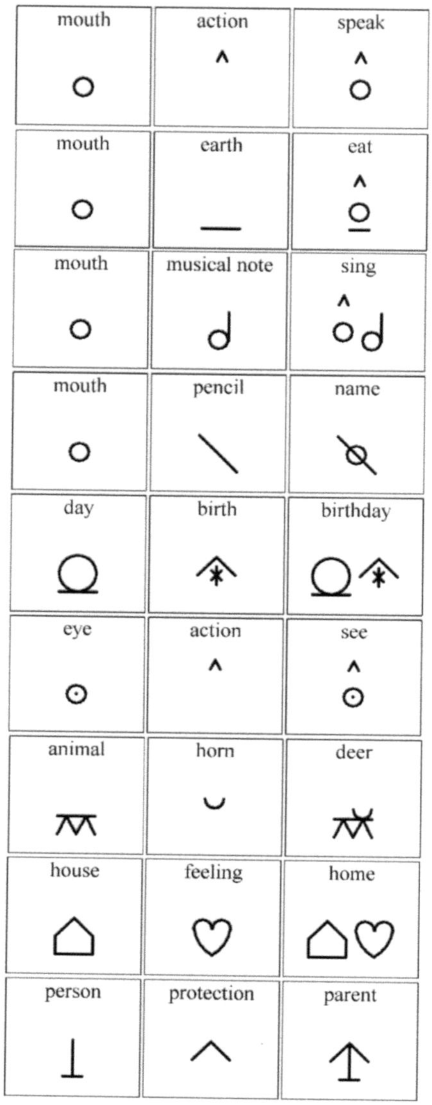

Figure 1.3 **Bliss-words with different markers and combinations.**

interpretation of a Bliss-word, such as SIMILAR-TO, SOUND-LIKE and LOOK-LIKE. The Blissymbolics system thus has a fairly complex construction, based on combinations of Bliss-characters, indicators and strategies with different functions. In addition, it is possible to combine Bliss-characters or Bliss-words with the alphabet. *GIRL+c* would indicate girl's name or a girl with a name beginning with the letter *c*, for example "Carmen" or "Catherine". It is quite common for interventionists to give different background colours to Bliss-words with glosses referring to different word classes. However, some Blissymbolics users complain that this limits the number of meanings of each Bliss-word and their creative use of the system (Kollar, 1999).

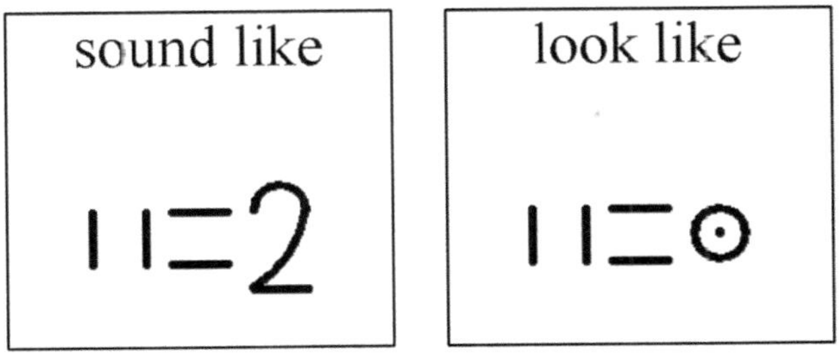

Bliss-words: *SOUND-LIKE, LOOK-LIKE*

Bliss-words may be joined together to form sentences. Bliss (1965) suggests a special syntax for Blissymbolics utterances, but in principle, any word order may be used. In most countries, the word order taught for Bliss-words will be close to the word order of the spoken language. However, this word order may not always be the most optimal for a graphic communication form (see Chapter 9).

Blissymbolics is a comprehensive and flexible system, which is necessary to enable the users to express the large variety of messages that are needed in human communication. Alphabetic systems have a small set of letters that together correspond to the speech sounds of the language. Bliss-words have a larger number of semantic elements. However, provided they get a systematic introduction to the Blissymbolics system, preschool-age children with normal vision and typical language and cognitive development learn the basic principles of the system quite fast (Jennische & Zetterlund, 2015; Krstic & Littorin, 2014).

Blissymbolics was the first graphic system to be used in many countries (McNaughton, 2003; von Tetzchner & Jensen, 1996) and it was one of the first systems to be used in communication devices with speech output (Hunnicutt, 1984; Olaszi et al., 2002). Over the years, there has been a decrease in the use of Blissymbolics. However, Blissymbolics is the most advanced system and the one that gives aided communicators who have difficulties using alphabetic script most communicative possibilities, whether it is on a communication board or in an electronic device with speech output (see Chapter 2). It is, therefore, important to provide Blissymbolics to those who are able to learn this system as early as possible.

It is sometimes said that conversational partners who can read do not need to know the child's Blissymbolics system, because the gloss is always written above the Bliss-words. This is true for the Bliss-words that exist on the communication board or device of the aided communicator. However, when an aided communicator combines Bliss-characters and Bliss-words to construct Bliss-words not found on the board, the communication partner must have sufficient knowledge of how the system works in order to interpret what the user has meant. Only then will they have full benefit of the system. Teaching the system to the family, teachers, peers and others that the aided communicator may meet regularly is therefore an essential element of intervention with Blissymbolics (and other systems) (see Chapter 12). Due to the inherent logic and system, Blissymbolics is quite easy to learn for an adult. On the other hand, the aided communicator must know what the partner is able to understand. Both utterance construction and interpretation can be difficult when the possible combinations are limited by the Bliss-words on the communication aid and the aided communicator's experience with constructing new Bliss-words. Both the creativity of the young aided communicator and the difficulties that partners sometimes may experience are illustrated in these examples:

A Swedish child was naming an animal drawing but did not have ZEBRA in his electronic communication device with speech output. In Swedish, *look* is *se* and *good* is *bra*. The child indicated SE+BRA (LOOK+GOOD) and the speech sounds produced by the device sounded like 'zebra' (Deliberato et al., 2018).

A ten-year-old boy told his teacher at school: MOTHER ALMOST COCA-COLA. The teacher asked questions but did not find out what the boy wanted to say until the boy's mother came to school later that day and told him that she had been angry with her son that morning. Then he understood that the utterance was intended to mean "Mother was angry", The boy used the bubbling over of the drink as a metaphor for anger.

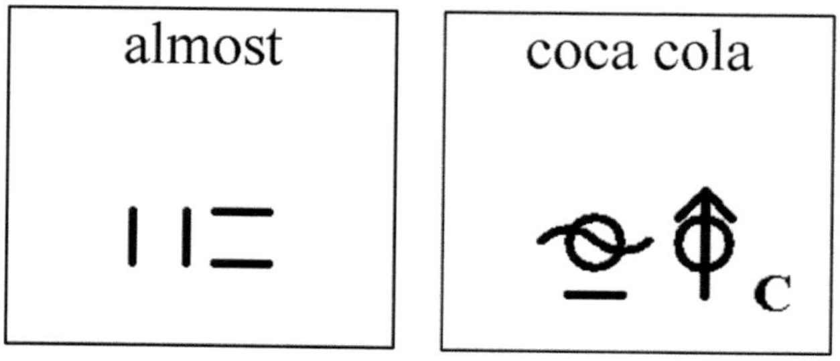

Bliss-words: *ALMOST, COCA-COLA*

The examples illustrate that the communication partner also needs to know the system and be creative in inferring meaning when conversations include more complex ideas and issues.

Pictogram Ideogram Communication (PIC)

Pictogram Ideogram Communication (often called pictograms) originates from Canada (Maharaj, 1980, 2022). This system was the first to replace the use of Bliss-words among people with severe intellectual disabilities and has been used much in Portugal and the Nordic countries. Pictograms consist of stylized drawings, which form white silhouettes on a black background. The strong contrast and limited details may make pictograms useful for children with cerebral visual impairments (Roman-Lantzy, 2007). The gloss is always written in white lettering above the image (see Figure 1.4). There are presently more than 2,500 pictograms (for an overview, see Maharaj, 2022).

Because pictograms are simpler than Bliss-words, both parents and professionals have found them easier to understand and use. However, the pictogram system is also less flexible and versatile than Blissymbolics. The vocabulary is relatively limited and not intended to be combined into more complex meanings, but it is possible to make simple sentences with pictograms (Maharaj, 2022). The relatively small vocabulary limits the meanings and sentences it is possible to construct, but when aided communicators who use pictograms need more vocabulary items, the pictograms can be supplemented with graphic symbols from other systems.

The use of pictograms has been of great benefit to many people, but it is important to change to a more advanced system or orthographic script when this is indicated by the cognitive and communicative development of the child.

Figure 1.4 Pictogram Ideogram Communication (PIC, pictogram).

Figure 1.5 Picture Communication Symbols (PCS).

Picture Communication Symbols (PCS)

Picture Communication Symbols (PCS, Johnson, 1981, 1985, 1992, 2001) originates in the USA. The system consists presently of approximately 40,000 vocabulary items. These are simple line drawings with the gloss written below or above the graphic representation (see Figure 1.5). Graphic communication symbols are usually in different colours but are also available in black and white. Children with cerebral visual impairments may benefit from symbols with high-contrast drawings. These have little detail, black background and drawings in yellow, pink, blue or green, which are the colours that are best perceived by children in this group (Roman-Lantzy, 2007). Today, PCS is the most widely used graphic system.

Aragonese Portal of Augmentative and Alternative Communication (ARASAAC)

The Aragonese Portal of Augmentative and Alternative Communication is a pictographic system with both line-drawing symbols and silhouette symbols (see Figure 1.6). The symbols

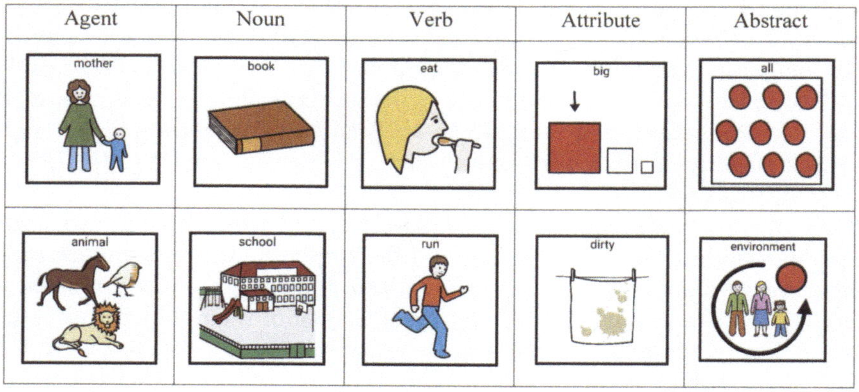

Figure 1.6 Aragonese Portal of Augmentative and Alternative Communication (ARASAAC).

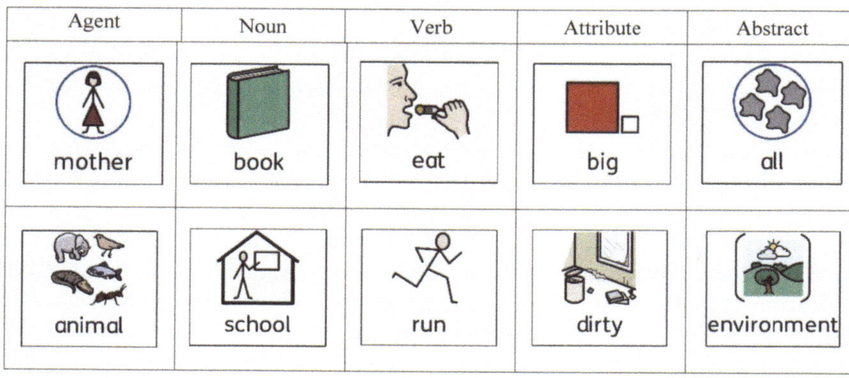

Figure 1.7 Widgit Symbols.

are available in colour and in black and white. The development of the system has been funded by Department of Education, Culture and Sports of the Government of Aragon, Spain (Paolieri & Marful, 2018). The graphic symbols and other materials can be downloaded in several languages (at present 19), including English, Chinese and Bulgarian (see Resources).

Widgit Symbol System (WSS)

The Widgit Symbol System has a long history and several names. It originated in the USA under the name of Rebus (Jones, 1979). A few years later, a British version appeared (van Oosterom & Devereux, 1985) which has been expanded into around 11,000 Makaton symbols (Grove & Walker, 1990; Walker et al., 2019). Rebus has also been integrated into the Widgit Symbol System (see Figure 1.7), which consists of more than around 20,000 graphic symbols (Detheridge & Detheridge, 2002; Detheridge et al., 2002). There is a subset of 2,400 graphic symbols with thicker image lines and other adaptations for individuals with reduced vision.

Widgit Symbols may be combined in different ways, for example, *STREET+LIGHT* becomes *STREETLIGHT*. There are some similarities to Bliss-words in the sense that some of the basic images can be combined into new meanings. For example, MOTHER is WOMAN with a circle around the image (see Figure 1.7). In addition, the pronunciation of the gloss may also be used productively. For example, *LIGHT* can mean both "bright" and "not heavy". This is a special feature of Widgit Symbols, which is somewhat similar to the Blissymbolics strategy *SOUND-LIKE*.

The Rebus system was originally designed to help people with a mild or moderate degree of intellectual disabilities to learn to read, and the emphasis was on using letters together with graphic images (Jones, 1979). The gloss of the graphic symbol was combined with one or more letters to form new words. When a graphic symbol is combined with a letter, it is the pronunciation of the two elements together that determines the new word form. The meaning of the graphic symbol plays no part. For example, c+*OLD* becomes "cold", p+*LIGHT* becomes "plight", and c+*AT* becomes "cat" (see Figure 1.8). This is different from the way Bliss-characters are usually combined with letters (see Blissymbolics section). Widgit has continued the focus on literacy, which is also apparent in Widgit's original choice of the name "Literacy Symbols". Widgit Symbols are often used together with Widgit's computer program SymWriter, where the user can combine Widgit Symbols and letters, as well as vocabulary from other graphic communication systems. Moreover, Widgit has several apps of varying functionality, which can be used in different communication devices (see Chapter 2).

Early studies found that the use of the Rebus system had a positive effect on reading skills (Kiernan et al., 1982), probably because it utilized the sounds corresponding to both glosses and letters. The letter strategies applied in the Rebus and Widgit systems place low demands on spelling skills, because the learner does not have to be able to read all the letters in a word. Investigations into the teaching of reading and sound recognition show that children with typical development in the initial phases of learning to read are able to pronounce the sound corresponding to the first letter or syllable in a word but may not be able to read aloud the sounds corresponding to the rest of the letters in the word. The Widgit System thus seems to utilize a midstage in the acquisition of reading and writing skills, and thereby, may enhance the further development of these skills (see p. 270). The reading-oriented strategies are a

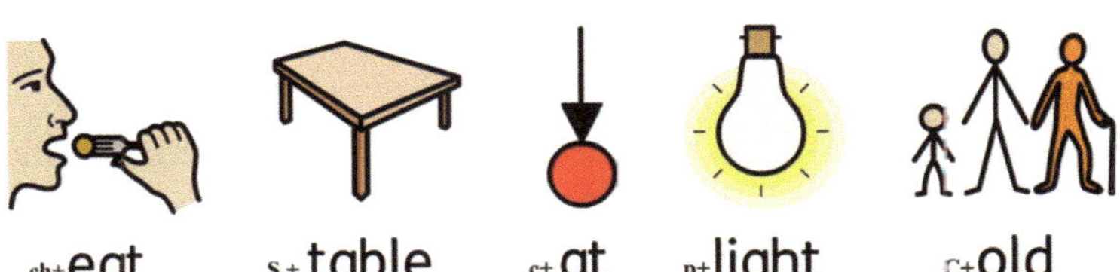

Figure 1.8 Widgit Symbols combined with letters.

strength of the system and the support of reading and writing seems to be the main focus of Widgit. However, Widgit Symbols may also be used in face-to-face conversations, and many of the strategies may be adopted with other systems.

Minspeak

Minspeak is a computer program with a system of graphic symbols – which Minspeak calls *icons* – that are used to produce pre-coded words and phrases (Baker, 1982, 1986). It is not a graphic communication system in the traditional sense but a coding system for operating the voice output of an electronic communication device, also called *semantic compaction*. For example, indicating BED produces *'bed'*, while sequencing BED with NOUN produces *'furniture'*, BED with VERB produces *'sleep'*, and BED with ADJECTIVE produces *'tired'*. The icons are similar to the graphic communication symbols of PCS and other systems in the line drawing group, and the graphic representations of the icons are selected to be associated with their meaning content (van der Merwe & Alant, 2004).

The semantic content and the order of icons in sequences have some similarities with the structure of the Blissymbolics system, and studies have found positive results of using Blissymbolics with the Minspeak program (Ferm et al., 2001). In Minspeak, the sequence of the icons is also part of the code and determines which pre-coded word or phrase that is said by the device. For example, with the sequence *MILK and HOT*, the device may say *'I want hot milk'*, while the sequence *HOT and MILK* may produce *'The milk is too hot'*. A combination may also lead to the articulation of a single word (see also Chapter 2).

Minspeak users are first taught the meaning of a limited set of icons (around 40–80) and then taught how to produce pre-coded words and phrases by combining the icons. The use of the Minspeak system builds on comprehension of spoken language and requires fairly good cognitive and linguistic abilities.

Pictures

Graphic communication symbols are the words of many aided communicators. Many of the communication symbol systems are pictographic but it is not the graphic representations but the usages and semantic meanings that constitute the essence of graphic communication symbols (von Tetzchner, 2015). It is therefore important to avoid calling graphic communication symbols "pictures" or their use as "communicating with pictures".

Pictures, here defined as non-system drawings and photographs, are commonly the first mode of graphic communication provided to young children. Infants are able to recognize things in pictures, but the understanding of pictures is a complex cognitive skill that emerges slowly (Troseth et al , 2004). Young children do not fully understand the relationship between pictures and reality, or the referring functions pictures may have in communication (Harris et al., 1997). The development of this understanding is delayed in children with intellectual disabilities (Stephenson & Linfoot, 1996). Picture comprehension is limited in many people with intellectual disabilities, and photographs are sometimes more difficult to comprehend than line drawings (Dixon, 1981; McNaughton & Light, 1989). If an individual who needs AAC does not seem to understand what pictures are supposed to represent, then there is little point in using pictures instead of graphic symbols from a communication system.

One reason often given for using pictures is that they can depict things that are familiar to the individual. However, recognizing objects and actions in pictures is not a goal in itself. The issue is whether the pictures help the individual to communicate better From this perspective, pictures have both advantages and disadvantages. A general interest in pictures may be an argument for using a pictographic system, providing that the "interest" does not only reflect that the child has learned "looking at pictures" as a fixed routine. If the child is interested in particular pictures, their usage will depend on what the child associates with the images. Looking at and reacting to pictures is not a *linguistic usage*, and using an image as a *word* may necessitate that the individual unlearns their original use of the image. Unlearning established reactions to familiar pictures may imply removing some of the individual's basis for social interaction, and this would seem neither necessary, nor wise.

Most children and adults are surrounded by pictures. When some pictures are supposed to function as an individual's vocabulary, it is necessary to distinguish between this use and how they are used ordinarily – to look at and as a cue to remember something, to talk about, as decoration or illustration, and so on. Pictures that are part of a vocabulary should be distinctive and clearly different from other pictures. The majority of the images in graphic communication symbols are selected on the basis of assumed iconicity (see below), and the pictorial content may sometimes be confounded with their intended function as word meanings. For example, children may have difficulties understanding that the human figure and the chair are not part of the meaning of the item *SIT* in PCS (Smith, 1996). At the same time, PCS, PIC and other graphic systems do have some special characteristics that may help aided communicators and communication partners distinguish the language functions of graphic communication symbols from the use of ordinary pictures: the written glosses help to highlight the semantic quality of graphic communication symbols. It is therefore more practical to use graphic communication symbols from a symbol system instead of non-system pictures.

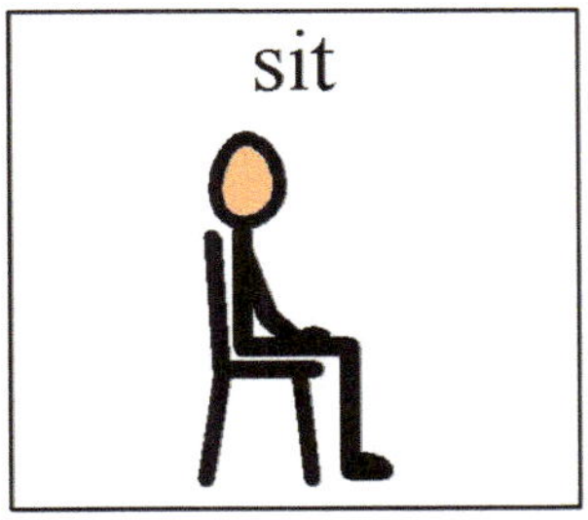

PCS: *SIT*

Further, the use of a graphic system may facilitate the teaching of naming, which is often difficult when a child is using a pictographic system. Parents and children with natural speech often sit together with a picture book and say the name of the things they see depicted in the book (Fletcher & Reese, 2005). This would also be a natural activity for young aided communicators and their parents, but instead of saying the name with natural speech, the children should use their communication aids. However, if (non-system) pictures on a communication board or in a communication device are similar to the pictures in the book, it may be difficult for young aided communicators to understand why they should indicate both the picture in the book and the picture on the communication board. The child may not perceive this activity as linguistic naming, but rather as a form of picture matching – an activity many children

with disabilities are used to doing as part of their training. The child may perceive the indication of a picture on the communication board as simply pointing at the picture and not as naming of the objects or activities depicted in the book, even if this activity is quite similar to how language is used when a parent and child are looking at a book together. The use of a graphic system instead of ordinary pictures may make the linguistic quality of the graphic symbol and its naming function clearer, and thereby support the aided communicators' use of an important language function.

A related problem with ordinary pictures is that people in the environment may not readily perceive them as the child's language. Aided communicators sometimes experience that they are not taken seriously when they communicate with pictures, and that people do not always understand that pointing at a picture means that they have something to say (Conway, 1986). This can also be a problem with pictographic communication symbols. Basil (1989) describes how some parents reacted as though their child had pointed at an ordinary picture when the child tried to communicate by indicating a graphic symbol. They began to talk about things in the image of the graphic communication symbol and what was happening there, instead of answering the child's utterance.

When making communication boards for young children and individuals with severe intellectual disabilities, it is common practice to use photographs of things in the child's own environment. For example, parents may take a photograph of the family car and use this photograph as a general way to say "car", thinking that it is easier for the child to recognize a familiar car than a car never seen before. However, this may make it difficult for the child to use the picture to talk about other cars than the family car. The picture is treated as a proper name, "Mummy and Daddy's car", instead of as a generic name for "car" that can be used to talk about all sorts of cars. If one imagines that photographs of a child's mother and father were used as *MAN* and *WOMAN*, that is, to talk about men and women in general, the problem with using pictures of familiar objects as representing general categories becomes even clearer.

The most important function of photographs on communication boards may be to represent names of persons (and animals). Because a name refers to a particular person, photographs fill this function well. The child may use the photograph to talk about his own mother and the graphic symbol *MOTHER* to communicate about other children's mothers or mothers in general (see Chapters 7 and 8). Moreover, the child is often present in the photograph when the photograph has other functions. This may make it difficult for the child to learn to use the photograph flexibly and for the communication partner to interpret the meaning and get to know how the photograph is used. If the photograph shows the child in a swing on the playground, it may refer to the location, the swing, the child or several other aspects, or it may refer to the whole situation. The presence of the child in the photograph may suggest that it is somehow about the child. However, communication should not only be about the aided communicator. It will be difficult for both the child and the adult to use a photograph with the child in a swing to communicate about other children or adults using a swing. In order to avoid these problems, it is better to introduce a separate photograph of the child, which then can be used together with one or more photographs or graphic communication symbols that denote objects, actions, activities and so forth. By having a separate photograph of the child, and a photograph or graphic symbol representing actions or other aspects of the situation instead of integrating them in one vocabulary item, it will be possible to change the action, activity, object and so on, while keeping the photograph of the child, as well as communicating about others by combining the photograph of another child or adult with graphic

communication symbols representing actions, objects, locations and so on. Furthermore, this may establish a foundation for the development of multi-item utterances even if the photograph of the child and the symbol denoting the activity at first are presented side by side (see Chapter 9).

Orthographic writing

Orthographic writing may be used in both the manual and graphic mode. There are several manual alphabets, but the one-handed international alphabet is the most used (see Figure 1.9). For individuals with good fine motor skills, spelling with a manual alphabet may be fast and efficient – and letters made by the hands are always available.

The graphic orthographic mode includes printed letters and words. Most aided communicators who have started to learn to read and write have the alphabet on their communication aid. Some may begin the transition from graphic communication symbols to written language by supplementing the graphic symbols with written words. Some communication aids contain mainly letters and written words. These are mainly used by individuals with relatively good comprehension of spoken language and expressive non-vocal language skills. Because spelling of words and sentences can take a long time for individuals with severe motor disabilities, communication aids often contain words and phrases in addition to single letters and common letter clusters. For aided communicators who have a limited vocabulary, the communication aid will consist mainly of single words (see Figure 1.10).

Figure 1.9 The international one-hand manual alphabet.

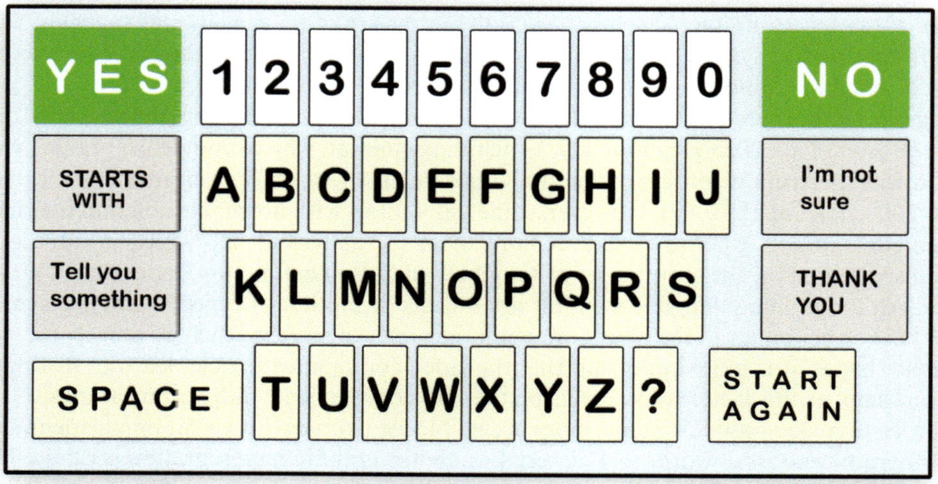

Figure 1.10 Communication board with letters and words.

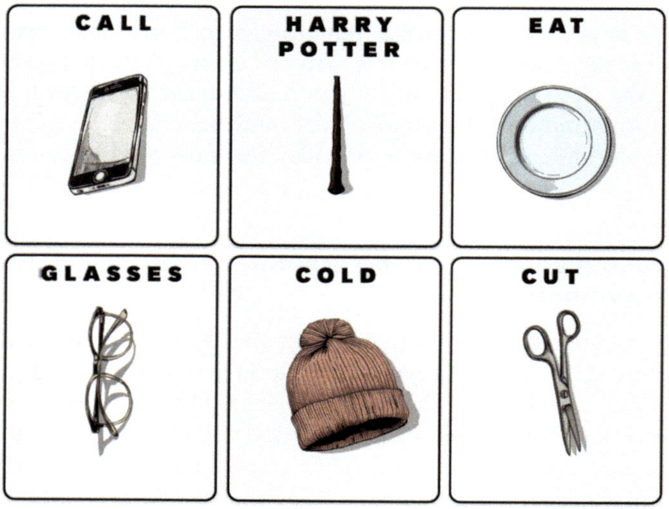

Figure 1.11 Tangible symbols.

Tangible and tactile symbols

Tangible symbols are usually made of wood or plastic, may have different forms and textures and can be physically investigated, manipulated and moved (see Figure 1.11) (Roche et al., 2014; Rowland & Schweigert, 2000; Sigafoos et al., 2008). Objects or models of objects used as symbols are also called "objects of reference" (McLarty, 1997; Park, 1997). Recognition of

tangible symbols is based on the tactile sense, and they are therefore often called "tactile symbols" (Aasen & Nærland, 2014). There is no clear distinction between tangible symbols, objects of reference and tactile symbols, and the terms are often used interchangeably. There is no comprehensive system but Trief and associates (2009, 2013) have developed a standard set of 55 tangible symbols.

Tangible symbols are mainly intended for children with visual impairment and little or no speech (Boster et al., 2023 Hagood, 2002), including children who cannot learn braille or who have autism spectrum disorders or multiple impairments (Aasen & Nærland, 2014; Lund & Troha, 2008; Trief et al., 2009). However, some individuals with normal vision find it easier to differentiate symbols when they can explore them tactually and haptically, in addition to visual inspection. For this group, a set of tangible symbols may function better than a graphic system. Although many tangible symbols are objects or models of objects, tangible symbols do not have to be similar to the object or action they refer to and may include non-iconic wood or plastic shapes. It is more important that the aided communicators can learn to distinguish between them, as this is necessary for using them to communicate different meanings.

In order to make graphic systems more accessible for people with visual impairment, making pictograms and Bliss-words in a material where the graphic representation is raised, like a *relief*, has been attempted, enabling the user to feel the pattern (Edman, 1991; Garrett, 1986; Isaacson & Lloyd, 2015). Volkswitch developed the *Bliss Tactile System*, using 3-D printer to produce relief Bliss-words (see Resources). These may be useful for people with reduced vision who can use touch to support visual perception. However, for people who rely totally on touch for discriminating between symbols, graphic symbols in relief may not be readily perceivable with the fingers. Many patterns that are easy to discriminate visually are very difficult to identify tactually. For this group, it is better to use a system that takes the possibilities and limitations of the visual impairment fully into account, and, instead, use tangible symbols with distinct forms and textures. Small objects may be relatively easy to recognize tactually and investigate through manipulation, provided the individual has enough experience to recognize the object.

Choosing between manual signs and graphic communication symbols

Comparing different sign and symbol systems is not an easy task. Within a country, it is practical to use a standard set of alternative communication systems. Students using AAC should never have to change system because they change teacher. As many people as possible should use the same systems, so teachers and other professionals only rarely have to learn a new system when children and adolescents using AAC arrive from other schools or institutions. Standard systems also make it more likely that children using AAC communicate directly and learn from each other. This also means that it is generally best to use national resources, such as British manual sign systems in the United Kingdom and signed Norwegian in Norway, and so on. The national set of graphic communication systems should reflect the heterogeneity among individuals who need AAC. It might consist of one system from the black and white silhouette group (e.g., PIC), one from the line drawing group (e.g., PCS or ARASAAC), one advanced ideographic system (Blissymbolics) and one writing-oriented system (Widgit Symbols). Minspeak or a similar program could also be part of a national set of communication systems, but Minspeak is not available in all languages. All graphic communication symbols should have a gloss in the language used in the individual's environment (sometimes

more than one). Before a new system is introduced, there should be convincing evidence that this particular system is actually needed; that it provides new communicative possibilities for users compared to the systems already in use. The use of a standard set of alternative communication systems also increases the likelihood that teachers and other professionals gain experience with these systems and get to know both their strengths and weaknesses. A standard set should never restrict the available vocabulary. If a particular symbol is missing, a new item may be created, or the system may be supplemented with symbols from other systems.

In order to find the best language mode for an individual in need of AAC, the choice of system should be based on knowledge about the characteristics of the child or adult, in particular motor skills and the ability to perceive motions, forms and pictures (see Chapter 4). Professionals should first determine whether the individual should begin with aided or unaided communication, or both, and choose between manual signs, a graphic symbol system and a tangible symbol system. If the individual needs more than one system, it should be decided which system(s) should be introduced first.

Manual signs or graphic symbols

Several factors are important for choosing between manual signs and graphic symbols, and the decision should be based on a thorough assessment (see Chapter 4). The individual's perceptual abilities need to be taken into account. Individuals with low vision may perceive the movements of manual signs more easily than the lines of graphic representations. The signing movements can also be understood kinaesthetically, as in communication among people with a combined visual and hearing impairment, where the conversational partners perform the signs with the other partner's hands. For some individuals, electronic communication aids with graphic communication symbols and synthetic speech output are helpful. Some individuals with intellectual disabilities will not profit from the use of graphic symbols; for others graphic symbols have a great attention value. Some individuals seem to benefit from being able to feel and manipulate the tangible symbols, but in general, little is known of how this may influence their learning and use.

One significant difference between manual signs and graphic symbols is that graphic communication symbols are selected, while manual signs must be produced. Manual signs therefore place greater demands on the user's motor abilities, as well as on attention and memory. Adept use of the arms and hands is necessary for manual signing. Children with severe fine motor impairments need aided communication. To perceive manual signs and graphic communication symbols, the individual has to be able pay attention to the communication partner and understand the communicative functions of the signs and symbols that the partner produces. In expressive communication, the demands on attention are somewhat different. Users of manual signs may need to be attentive to the communication partner or to the person, object or event referred to while they are signing. Users of graphic communication symbols have to pay attention to the communication board or device while they are communicating because they need to look for the graphic symbols they are selecting. This may make it difficult for them to attend to the communication partner and other aspects of the situation at the same time. If a child is using a set of individual graphic communication symbols, he or she has to find the symbol needed, before showing it or handing it to the communication partner.

Most children with autism spectrum disorders and/or intellectual disabilities who do not have severe visual, or motor impairments can usually learn both manual signs and graphic symbols. A small number of the children in this group do less well with graphic symbols and

better with manual signs (Tincani, 2004; van der Meer et al., 2014). Manual signs also have the advantage that they are produced with the individual's hands, while the graphic symbols need to be carried around. People in the environment are usually not familiar with manual signs but they can easily learn the moderate number of signs that these children learn to understand and use. Some children learn several hundred manual signs, but this may be over a period of a year or more. Motivated by the positive progress of the child, people in the environment do not usually have any problems keeping up with the child.

Other children within this group do better with graphic symbols (Hodges & Schwethelm, 1984; von Tetzchner, 2019b). One reason may be that the static images of graphic communication symbols are easier for them to perceive and attribute meaning to than the movements of manual signs. Another advantage of graphic symbols is that they can be used in electronic communication devices, which seems to give positive results for many children (van der Meer et al., 2014). There are also examples of children who have learned to use aided communication after manual sign teaching had been unsuccessful. A nine-year-old boy rapidly learned to use a tangible system, despite the fact that manual sign teaching beforehand had proved unsuccessful. Afterwards, he also learned to use manual signs (Deich & Hodges, 1977). This shows that learning one communication system may support the learning of other systems. One issue, however, is that graphic communication symbols are rarely used regularly by adults outside of restricted training situations. Even if graphic communication symbols can be used in joint activities with other children in preschool (von Tetzchner et al., 2005), there are usually very few people in the child's environment that the child can observe and from whom the child can learn to use graphic communication symbols.

When the child is not hindered by severe perceptual or motor impairments, it is not necessary to choose one communication mode and exclude the others. Graphic symbols and manual signs can supplement each other, as seen in the following examples.

Jessica was a preschool-age girl with normal hearing and cognitive abilities and comprehension of spoken language in the typical range but with severe expressive language disorders and great problems communicating with speech. Her family had started early to use manual signs and Jessica picked up new signs spontaneously from the environment in a typical manner. She was provided with an electronic communication device with graphic symbols and voice output for use in preschool and school with adults and peers who did not know signing, and with letters for teaching reading and writing. Both the parents and Jessica preferred the spontaneity and accessibility of signs over aided communication and continued signing in everyday communication. As most children with developmental language disorders, Jessica belonged to the developmental language support group and showed significant progress in spoken language (see Chapter 3). She continued to use manual signs to supplement her speech when she lacked a spoken word or her speech was not understood (Light et al., 2021).

A thirteen-year-old boy with moderate intellectual disabilities preferred using manual signs but was able to write short messages on a small electronic device, which he used when he met people who did not know manual signs. He had also learned to ask people first in writing whether they knew manual signs. If the answer was positive, he began to sign, which was quicker for him. If the answer was negative, he continued to write. He had approximately the same size of vocabulary in manual signs and in writing: a little over three hundred words (Reichle & Ward, 1985).

The core idea of total communication is to utilize *all* possible means. Many children who need AAC can learn both manual signs and graphic symbols, but some may prefer one of the modes or have somewhat different vocabularies in the two modes (Achmadi et al., 2014; Tincani, 2004). Many individuals who use aided communication at school and who, like Jessica, have sufficient fine motor skills, also use manual signs at home and with friends (Marshall & Goldbart, 2008; O'Neill & Wilkinson, 2020). They find that using both modes makes their communication more flexible and helps them cope better in more varied situations, and with different people. The positive impact of the total communication approach is further illustrated by a young autistic man who expressed himself in sentences in manual signs (his preferred mode of communication) as well as in graphic symbols. He could spell words on an electronic communication device with speech output and would make each letter with the one-handed international manual alphabet before hitting the key. There are thus many reasons why professionals should have both manual signs and a variety of graphic symbol systems as part of their teaching repertoire to support the development of language in children with little or no spoken language.

Manual signs

With regard to manual signs used in AAC, there is little evidence to suggest that one system is easier or more difficult to learn than others. However, there are individual signs that are easy to perform and others that are more difficult. Children may produce manual signs in a childish manner, similar to the childish articulation of spoken words by young children with typical development. For individuals with developmental coordination disorder (making the performance of voluntary actions difficult) or other forms of motor disability, the signs should be simple to perform. However, many of the manual signs in common use in a society are complex but can simplified so that individuals with fine motor problems find them easier to perform (Bonvillian et al., 2020a, b; Grove, 1990). This has worked well.

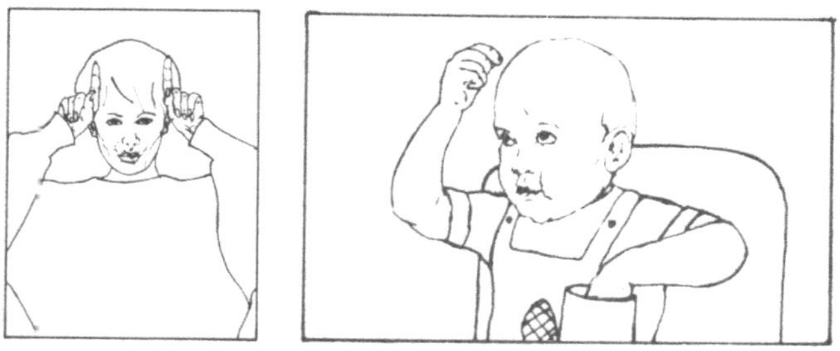

Manual signs: adult (adult), COW (child)

The manual sign systems that follow speech may reflect the inflections of the spoken language, and if these are included, sign utterances may become rather complex. The complexity is less dependent on the manual sign system than on the extent to which inflections are used. In the early stages of teaching, the use of inflections may not be necessary. However, children with intellectual disabilities can learn to make the meaning more precise by modifying the execution of the sign, for example by making smaller or bigger movements to indicate the size of an object (Rudd et al., 2007).

Graphic communication symbols

A number of factors may be important when choosing a graphic system for an individual who needs aided communication. Language and cognitive abilities will be decisive for selecting what kind of graphic system a child starts with. Blissymbolics, for example, place greater demands on cognition and language comprehension than pictographic systems like PCS and PIC, and it is common practice to start with a pictographic system.

Most aided communicators use graphic symbols in colour. However, when using pictographic material, it is necessary to assess the individual's ability to distinguish between the graphic representations. Colour blindness is common among children with typical development, especially boys (Simunovic, 2010), and a few individuals have a total lack of colour sight, achromatopsia (Haque et al., 2018; Sacks, 1996). Colour contrasts that the teacher may perceive as strong may not be visible to individuals with colour blindness. Sensory impairments are more common among individuals with intellectual disabilities than among individuals with typical development. They may be colour blind or for other reasons be unable to utilize colour information (Misra et al., 2019), and they may struggle with visual perception if there is too much detail (Ego et al., 2015). These individuals may need black and white graphic symbols with strong contrast. There may, thus, be different reasons for choosing a symbol system in black and white instead of colour, to ensure that the user will perceive and comprehend the differences between the symbols in the communication board or device. However, coloured symbols may be used as long as one makes sure that they are being recognized and identified by the individual who is taught to use them.

Over the years, there has been considerable discussion about the characteristics of graphic symbol systems and how easy or quick they are to learn (Barton et al., 2006; Fuller & Lloyd, 1987; Schlosser, 1997a,b). The choice is often between a pictographic or an ideographic system. Experimental studies have found that pictorial symbols from PCS are quicker to learn than Bliss-words (Alant et al., 2005; Clark, 1981, Mizuko, 1987) (see also Chapter 6). How easy it is to infer the meaning of a Bliss-word without instruction varies (Bornman et al., 2009; Krstic & Littorin, 2014). However, it is not certain that faster initial learning means that a graphic system is more useful in the longer term. Blissymbolics is the most advanced graphic communication system and although Bliss-words may take a little longer for three-year-olds to learn, Bliss-words may still be more functional in real-life communication than pictographic symbols.

There are experimental studies of how quickly individuals with little or no speech learn a few symbols and how they are remembered over a short time. However, there are no studies of how the graphic communication symbols of different communication systems function over time in the everyday life of young aided communicators. Also in typical development of spoken language, the growth of vocabulary is rather slow in the months after the first word appeared (Harris, 1992). The growth usually increases considerably towards the second birthday (MacWhinney, 2015).

Individuals with severe intellectual disabilities may have difficulties learning the Blissymbolics system. Experiments with teaching Bliss-words to individuals with intellectual disabilities have not been very successful, except when using only a limited number of simple Bliss-words. This user group may benefit more from learning a simpler and more pictographic system. It is children with relatively good cognitive abilities, speech impairments and reading and writing difficulties, who have gained most from the use of Blissymbolics (McNaughton, 2003, 2014). Also, the use of Blissymbolics may help autistic children with relatively good

cognitive skills to more advanced communication and concept development, and thus represents a positive educational opportunity for this group (Alant et al., 2013; Jennische, 1988).

Blissymbolics is comprehensive but not very complex, and the utility of the system depends on appropriate teaching (Jennische & Zetterlund, 2015). Children learning Blissymbolics usually have quite good comprehension of spoken language, and a common teaching strategy is to say the spoken word that the Bliss-word corresponds to, similar to second language teaching in general. However, for the children to gain a full understanding of the system, it is necessary to explain the meaning and functions of Bliss-characters, Bliss-indicators and Blissymbolics strategies, and show how they can be combined to construct new meanings. The simple naming of the glosses of Bliss-words by the teacher may suffice for the child to learn Bliss-words with only one Bliss-character or very simple combinations. To facilitate the learning of more complex and abstract Bliss-words, it is important that the teacher gives the child a thorough explanation of the meaning of each element and their function in the Bliss-word, such as the fact that *BIRTH* and *PARENT* both include the Bliss-character *PROTECTION* (see Figure 1.3) (Schlosser & Lloyd, 1997; Shepherd & Haaf, 1995). This will help the child to learn to construct different meanings and contributes to establishing competence in using the Blissymbolics system flexibly and creatively.

Interventionists sometimes try to make Bliss-words more pictographic by adding details that make them look like an exemplar of the category referred to, for example by drawing a door and windows on the image of *HOUSE*. The idea behind this was to make it easier for younger children and people with intellectual disability to remember individual Bliss-words (Raghavendra & Fristoe, 1990, 1995) but the added pictorial details interfere with the general principles of Blissymbolics. *Blissymbolics Communication International* does not recommend making Bliss-words more figurative, because this will reduce the flexibility and usefulness of the system. It may be better to start with a pictorial system like PCS or PIC and progress gradually to Bliss-words when a user appears developmentally ready for this.

For children of preschool age with good cognitive skills, the question often arises whether they should continue with the same pictographic symbol system or change to a more advanced system, such as Blissymbolics, Widgit Symbol System or Minspeak. Some children who would benefit from changing to Blissymbolics are not introduced to this system because teachers find the system too time-consuming for the child and themselves to learn and fear it will interfere with other activities. A teacher, who was interviewed about the education of a boy with severe speech and motor impairments when he was in the second grade, recalled a discussion when the boy who was using pictograms (PIC) was five years old:

> There was still a need for expanding his vocabulary and communicative competence. Then the issue of reading and writing was raised and his possibilities in relation to that. And how should we spend the time? If he were to learn Blissymbolics, how much time would be left for play? This was the real issue. If he could jump from pictograms to reading quite fast, before first grade, we would not spend the time on teaching Bliss-words. We would use it for play.
>
> (von Tetzchner, 1997a, p. 229)

Acknowledging the importance of play, the teacher cited above seemed to overlook the fact that for children with speech and motor impairments, language may be the key to participating in play as well as in conversations. Many young aided communicators with relatively good comprehension of spoken language are severely motor-impaired, and language is often their

best skill. They can use language to instruct others to perform actions they cannot do themselves, including play actions and other child activities (see Chapter 10). Supporting the development of the most advanced communication system that the child is able to manage, will therefore also give the child the best chance to participate in play and other social interaction. If aided communicators have to rely on systems that are less advanced than they are able to master, the consequence may be that they remain unnecessarily long at a plateau in their expressive language development while waiting for orthographic writing to be introduced. The individual who is able to spell may have access to an unlimited number of words without needing to remember every single one. However, children with speech and motor impairments are at risk of developing reading and writing disorders (Smith, 2005a). It may take several years from when they write their first spelled words to when they reach a level of spelling competency where they can spell most ordinary words easily (see Chapter 8). For this group, Bliss-words and Widgit Symbols are usually easier to learn than alphabetic writing and may be used as an intermediate step between pictographic communication symbols and orthographic writing. A lack of access to an advanced form of non-orthographic graphic communication may slow down their general language development.

The vocabularies of the graphic symbol systems may not suffice for each user. Even though a good deal of work has gone into selecting the symbols that make up the systems, their vocabularies should nonetheless be regarded as suggestions (see Chapter 8). The ideas, interests and needs of individual aided communicators should determine the selection of graphic symbols for their communication aids. If the graphic symbol system does not have an item corresponding to a meaning the individual wants in the aid lexicon, a new graphic symbol may be designed. To emphasize the linguistic function of graphic communication symbols, it may nonetheless be helpful if the homemade symbols resemble the graphic symbols already present in the communication system that the individual is using. However, there is no reason why graphic symbols from different systems should not be mixed. There is nothing magical about the systems that requires the use of one communication system only. There is a relatively limited number of pictograms in the PIC system, and it may be necessary to supplement them with symbols from, for example, PCS or ARASAAC. A child may use graphic symbols from several systems and when a new graphic symbol is needed, may prefer the symbol from one particular system. That makes the choice easy. If PCS and PIC become too limited for the user, Bliss-words may be placed among symbols from PIC or PCS as the beginning of a gradual transfer to the Blissymbolics system. Bliss-words generally have a wider use than PCS and PIC, and hence may become a more efficient and useful tool for the aided communicator. Bliss-words are more complex, but they build on the communication and language skills the user has acquired through the early use of PIC, PCS or other mainly pictographic systems.

Tangible symbols

For people who are not visually impaired, the most commonly used tangible symbols are probably *objects of reference*: objects and models of objects. They are typically selected among objects in the individual's environment and their meanings tend to be idiosyncratic (Bloom, 1990). However, it is often impractical for the child to carry objects around, making it less likely that the child will be using them outside training or routine situations. In addition, young children may have greater difficulty in understanding that an object symbolizes something other than itself than with a graphic representation (DeLoache et al., 1998). In order to avoid confusion with ordinary objects, it is usually an aim to change to graphic symbols or

manual signs as soon as possible, if the individual has sufficient vision. People with severe visual impairment need symbols (or signs) that may be discriminated tactually without visual support (Mathy-Laikko et al., 1989). Because there is no generally available tangible system, most schools and institutions create individually tailored sets, based partly on general assumptions about needs and knowledge about the individual user.

Usage in everyday life

When an assessment of factors related to the individual's abilities and learning does not indicate which manual sign or graphic symbol system is best suited for that individual, other conditions may be given more weight, such as specific aspects of the individual's environment. The family may not be positive to learning manual signs and may prefer graphic symbols – or vice versa. The desires for mobility, a large vocabulary, and being easily understood by many people are often contradictory when it comes to choosing an AAC system. What should be given priority depends on the individual who will use the system. For an adolescent who cannot read and write but has good cognitive and social functioning, many friends and relations, and often meets new people, a graphic system may be the most beneficial. For an autistic child or adolescent with intellectual disabilities who rarely has contact with people outside of their home, school or institution, manual signs may be the best choice. People in the environment can be expected to learn to comprehend and produce the adolescent's manual signs, and the adolescent will not have to remember to carry a communication board or device around at all times. The AAC system(s) provided to an individual may be decisive for his or her potential for communication with others. The choice of system(s) should be based on a thorough assessment (Chapter 4) and professionals need to be both creative and pragmatic to provide individuals who need AAC with communicative means that give them the best possibilities for social interaction and participation in society.

Chapter 2

Communication aids

The term "communication aid" is used to denote aids that help people express themselves and includes the tools and materials used for aided communication. These include non-electronic and electronic devices of variable complexity (see Table 2.1). Non-electronic communication aids may be made of paper, plastic or other solid material. Electronic communication aids may be devices designed especially for face-to-face communication or communication software used in standard computers, tablets or smartphones. Communication aids have been in use for a long time, but the development and use of communication aids have received special attention since communication aids based on computer technology came into common use (Hourcade et al., 2004; Vanderheiden, 2002). Since the year 2000, communication technology has become cheaper and more generally available (Tönsing et al., 2024a, b). Technology may be used in different ways for educational purposes and to facilitate learning of words and grammar (Cook et al., 2020; Morel & Spector, 2023; Shadiev & Yang, 2020). Such technologies may also be useful in educating children who use communication aids; however, electronic communication aids are not educational tools but tools for constructing language.

Communication aids should be both sturdy and transportable so they can be accessible in a variety of situations. Both non-electronic and electronic communication aids may be difficult for a toddler or young child, or for children and adults with limited muscle strength, to carry around. Individuals using wheelchairs usually find it easier to transport a communication aid, as the aid can be mounted on the tray or a pole on the wheelchair. Even though electronic devices with voice output give users access to a voice, and may give access to social media, some aided communicators prefer non-electronic boards or books in their everyday communication as these can withstand any type of weather, are often efficient in use, and may be easier to transport (Iacono et al., 2011; Smith et al., 2010).

Others prefer a combination, where they use electronic devices in some settings, for example, when communicating with less familiar communication partners, and non-electronic devices for quick and routinized everyday communication with familiar partners.

The function of all communication aids is to enable the users to express themselves in spite of limited speech, but there are considerable differences in the aids' physical form, operation, content and output. Choosing a communication aid for an individual should therefore be based on characteristics of the user, especially fine motor skills, an evaluation of the complexity of the layout, the usability of non-electronic and electronic aids, navigation within the aid to the place where a symbol is located, as well as the access method and output mode. In addition, there are some special issues involved in the use of communication aids, such as time usage, mobility and the role of the communication partner.

DOI: 10.4324/9781003387633-3

Table 2.1 Main classes and types of communication aids

Class	*Type*	*Description*
Non-electronic	Box	Container with individual graphic symbols, photographs, line drawings or objects, which can be handed over or shown to aided communicator or communication partner
	Folder	Folder with several pages, graphic symbols, photographs, line drawings, numbers and words on laminated cards attached with Velcro; can be handed over or shown to aided communicator or communication partner
	Board	Chart made of cardboard or another solid material; with graphic symbols, photographs, line drawings, objects, numbers, letters and words; organized with fixed locations.
	Book	Book with several pages containing graphic symbols, photographs, line drawings, numbers, letters and words; vocabulary organized with fixed locations; index page in front and tabs on each page to facilitate navigation
Electronic	Single message device	Simple device with one pre-recorded word or sentence; content may be changed by making a new recording; key to be pressed to produce message may be marked with a graphic symbol, photograph or line drawing
	Limited messages device	Simple device with two or a small number of pre-recorded words or sentences; content may be changed by making new recordings; keys to be pressed to produce message may be marked with graphic symbols, photographs or line drawings
	Mechanical device	Board with arrow or lights that can be operated by electric switches to indicate graphic symbols, photographs or line drawings
	Screen-based device	Electronic device with graphic symbols, photographs, line drawings, letters and words; operated by direct touch or switches to select or construct a message on a screen
	Electronic board with speech output	Dedicated communication device with touch keyboard or screen with graphic symbols, photographs, line drawings, letters and words; organized with fixed locations; output may be digitized or synthetic speech
	Computer-based device with speech output	Electronic device with dynamic display with graphic symbols, photographs, line drawings, letters or words; organized in domains with fixed locations; operated with eye-gaze technology, direct touch or switches to select or construct a message on a screen; output may be on screen or digitized or synthetic speech

Classes and types of communication aids

There are two main classes of communication aids: non-electronic and electronic. Within each class there are several types (Table 2.1). They differ in number of pages and vocabulary items and level of complexity (Figure 2.1). The number of vocabulary items will influence the child's ability to express different meanings. For young children, it is more difficult to choose one item from four than from two items. Selecting a graphic symbol in a larger communication folder or book takes more cognitive resources than making the same selection between four graphic symbols (this also applies to assessments, see Chapter 4). It is, however, important not to limit the child's communication unnecessarily. A communication aid should always contain as many vocabulary items as the child can practically manage in the situation.

The distinction between using non-electronic and electronic aided communication is not absolute. Most aided communicators who use electronic devices have a non-electronic device for use in situations where an electronic device is not suitable, in situations where it is likely they will need a more limited vocabulary, and as a backup in case of equipment failure.

Non-electronic communication aids

Non-electronic communication aids may be a box, folder, board or book with graphic symbols, drawings, photographs, letters, words, numbers or phrases (Table 2.1). Initially, children with severe intellectual disabilities may not have an actual communication aid but are shown two or three graphic symbols or photographs to choose between, for example, toys, foods or activities (see Chapter 7). At school, a child might choose between playing with a ball or looking in a book by selecting *BALL* or *BOOK* attached with Velcro to a piece of plastic or card, a frame, or another device for displaying graphic symbols. At home, the child may be given a similar choice between *BOOK* and *TV*, or between *BANANA* and *APPLE* when returning from school. This method of giving limited choices by displaying two or a few graphic symbols is most suitable for emerging aided communicators who cannot yet attend to many different symbols at a time – typically less than ten – and for communicators who benefit from physically handing over the graphic symbol to another person to make their communication message clear (see p. 184).

	Single symbols	Topic tables	Communication books/ dynamic displays
Paper-based			
Electronic based			

Figure 2.1 Non-electronic and electronic communication aids with different levels of complexity.

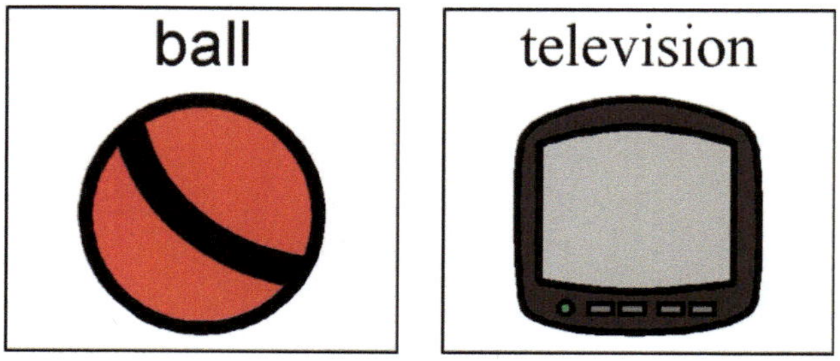

PCS: BALL, TV

For some children, the next step may be a *communication box*, which contains individual cards with graphic symbols or photographs. It is usually the adult who brings the communication box along for the child to use. The child may show or hand over the selected item to the communication partner. The adult may also use the same items to suggest limited choices to the child. One girl used a play suitcase for a period, which she would fetch when she wanted to ask for something (Figure 2.2). However, it is more common to use *a communication folder*, a booklet where graphic symbols are attached to the pages with Velcro. The child can show or hand over one or more items to the communication partner, or place them on a fold-out page where the messages are constructed (Figure 2.3). The adult can also take out items from the folder to suggest limited choices to the child.

When aided communicators are able to point to or otherwise indicate graphic symbols to express themselves, and begin to have larger vocabularies, communication is usually more efficient with *communication boards* or *communication books* – where the vocabulary items are in fixed places. Having the graphic symbols in fixed places on the communication board may increase communication speed because the users, to some extent, automatize the motor movements they use to navigate to the location of each item, in addition to knowing the image and gloss of the graphic symbol. For example, the standard Blissymbolics communication board contains around 400 graphic symbols, always organized in the same manner, independent of the language(s) spoken in the community (see Figure 2.4).

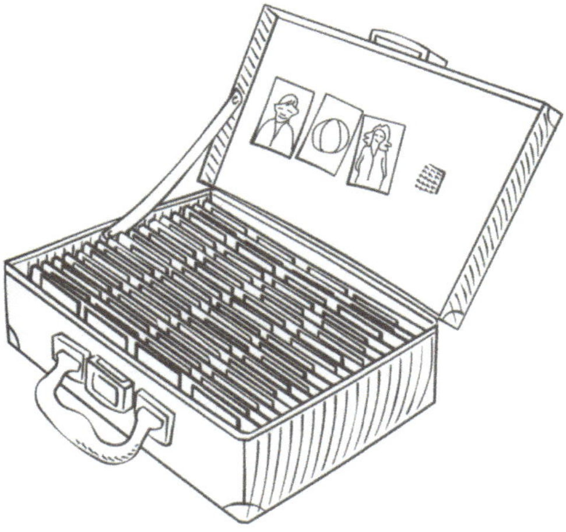

Figure 2.2 Play suitcase as communication aid.

Figure 2.3 Communication folder with fold-out page for message construction.

Having many vocabulary items on the board might give the aided communicator a good overview of the graphic symbols that are available. This may be a help in navigation, at least if the user has good eyesight and fine motor skills. However, if the graphic symbols are too small, they may be difficult for an aided communicator with fine motor impairments to access. One solution is to group the graphic symbols and then code each symbol within a group. For example, with colour coding, the individual first indicates which group of symbols the graphic symbol belongs to, and then the colour of that symbol in the group (see Figure 2.8 below). Another solution may be a board that only contains numbers or another form of *code* that refers to a list of words (the glossary). The codes may give aided communicators a means of expressing a larger number of graphic symbols, words, or phrases than they would otherwise be able to reach, but this system makes heavy demands on memory. Another solution again might be a communication book with several pages, and for some children their first communication aid is a book.

Communication is more than making choices. As the individual's aid lexicon grows (see Chapter 8), the items may need to be organized into a *communication book*. A communication book may have a few or many pages, and the vocabulary can be organized according to: (1) domains like "persons", "toys", "foods", "places" and "activities"; (2) pragmatic functions, such as "telling", "asking" and "requesting"; (3) word classes like "nouns", "verbs" and "adjectives"; (4) orthography, such as organizing verbs after the first letter of their gloss or (5) topic, such as organizing verbs after the body part most involved in performing the action. Many communication books use a combination of domains, such as the *Pragmatic Organization Dynamic Display* (PODD) (Porter & Cafiero, 2009).

In a communication book, the vocabulary items are in fixed places, the first page usually contains an index to the other pages, and each page has a tab marked with the index symbol (Figure 2.5). This helps the aided communicator (and the communication partner) navigate faster and more efficiently in the communication book. If the user needs help turning pages, all the pages may have navigation symbols like *FRONT PAGE* and *NEXT PAGE*. In some communication books, the pages on the left-hand side of the book have the same set of graphic symbols throughout the book, such as symbols for persons (e.g., *MOTHER, FATHER, TEACHER*), pronouns (e.g., *I, YOU, THEY*), feelings (e.g., *HAPPY, TIRED, PAIN*), and verbs (e.g., *PLAY, LOOK, FETCH*), while the pages on the right-hand side are different and contain vocabulary items for specific topics (e.g., *VEHICLE, DINOSAUR, BALLET*). This organization makes it easier to construct sentences. For example, *I* and *LIKE* are on the left page and *DANCE* and *TV* on different pages on the right-hand side, hence making it easy to produce sentences such as *I LIKE DANCE* or *MOTHER LIKE TV*.

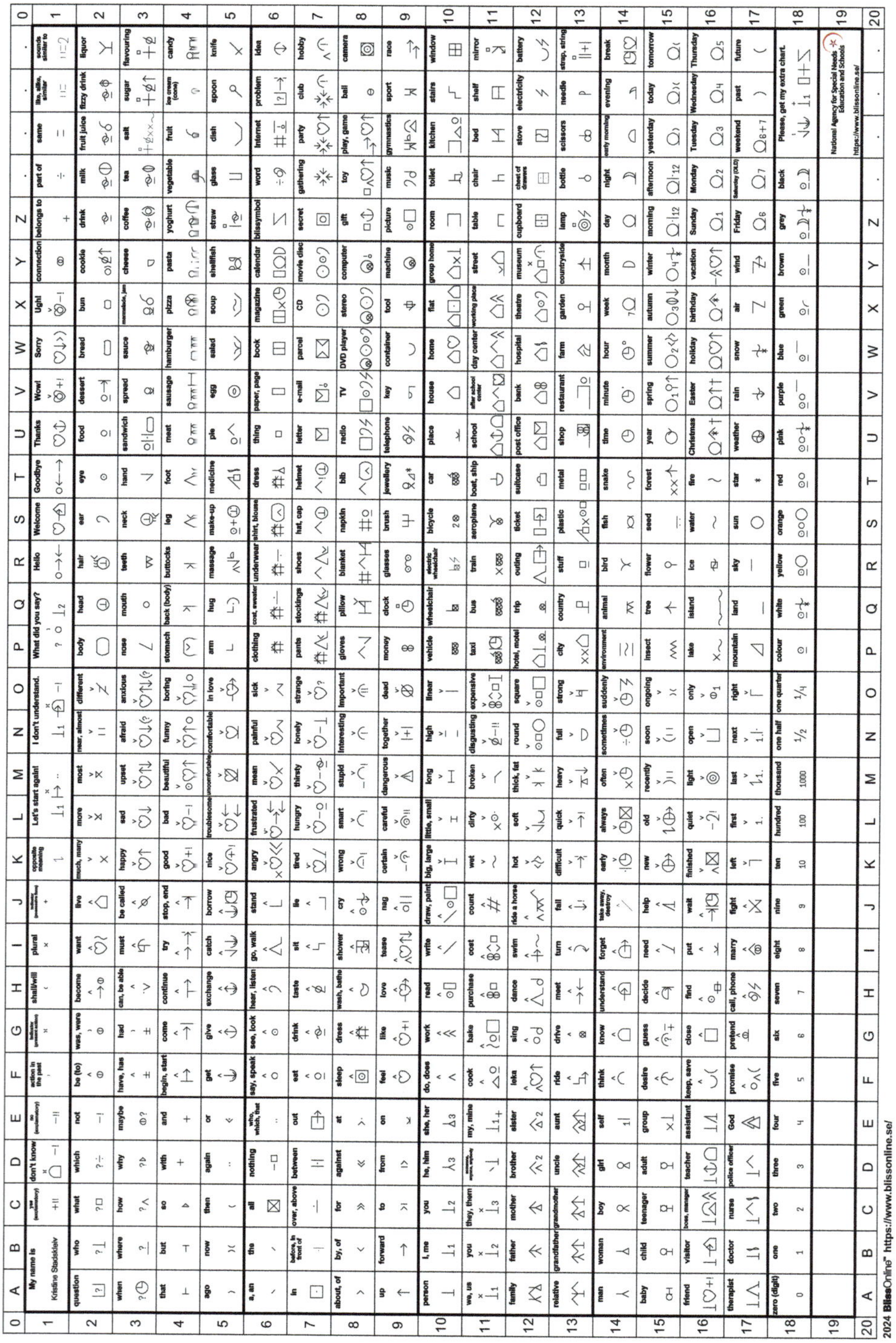

Figure 2.4 Communication board with Bliss-words.

Figure 2.5 Communication book with index tabs.

Electronic communication devices may have a similar organization. The communication book may be the child's main expressive means of communication, but it may also be useful for the child to have specialized *topical boards* in some situations, for example in school. In some situations, it may be more efficient for a young aided communicator to have a small board for fast access in specific situations and activities, such as when doing a "True" or "Not true" quiz (*YES, NO* and *DON'T KNOW*), or when an aided communicator with limited use of the hands is playing chess (letters A–H, numbers 1–8) or other games with peers. However, he or she may use the main communication aid when chatting with the players.

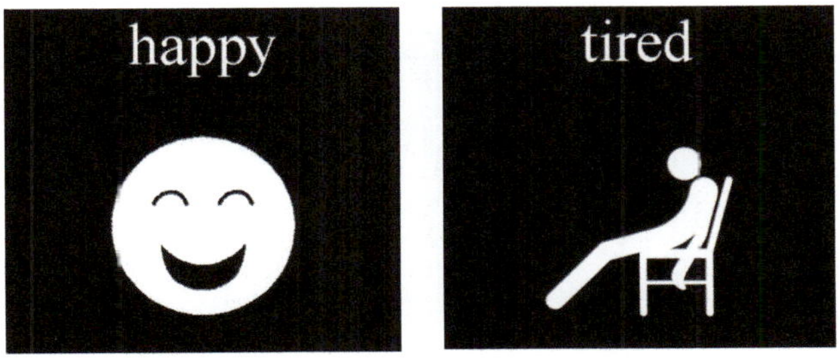

PIC: HAPPY, TIRED

WIDGIT: DANCE, FETCH, PLAY

Non-electronic communication aids are important for enabling expressive communication in individuals with limited or no speech but may also have some weaknesses. When the aided communicator is severely motor disabled, using a board or book for communication may be very time consuming. It may take several minutes to construct a short sentence with graphic symbols (Deliberato et al., 2018). When an aided communicator produces long utterances on a letter board using spelling, communication may break down because it is difficult for the communication partner to retain the earlier words in their memory while simultaneously registering the letters of the next word. The aided communicator may forget which words he or she has communicated while searching for the next letter, word or graphic symbol (see also p. 54). It may also be difficult for the communication partner to concentrate for an extended period on what the aided communicator is doing (Smith et al., 2010). In ordinary conversations, the communication partners may divert their gaze without it causing problems in following what is being said. In a conversation involving an aided communicator who is using a non-electronic aid, a moment of inattentiveness may cause the partner to fail to understand or misunderstand the aided utterance, leading to communication breakdown and frustration. However, it should be noted that the sustained attention needed in communication involving an aided communicator also functions to establish collaboration and closeness during the conversation (see Smith et al., 2010).

Electronic communication aids

There are several types of electronic communication aids, and most, but not all, use speech output (Table 22.1) Some electronic communication aids are referred to as "low-tech" as they have quite simple technology, such as switches or buttons, paper-based overlays and digitized speech output. Devices may contain a small number of messages pre-recorded in digitized speech, although devices with only one message have limited usability as they lack potential for further choice-making or selecting messages. The recorded messages can typically be activated by the individual hitting one or more buttons. Low-tech devices with several buttons may be used together with an overlay with graphic symbols or photographs. These devices may serve to guide the child towards the expression of context-based messages in a play activity, such as "the trolls come" or "the princess smiles", and thereby establish a foundation for developing independent use of a larger set of graphic symbols or photographs.

"High-tech" communication aids are based on computer technology and typically have touch screens and synthetic speech output. An important feature of some high-tech devices is

the possibility to use eye gaze technology to operate the communication aid (Griffiths, 2020; Karlsson et al., 2019). This is much faster than using switches to scan (see p. 47). High-tech devices include both dedicated communication devices and communication software and apps for use with tablets, smartphones and laptops. In some programs and apps, it is possible to choose a graphic symbol system, but in others the users may have to switch from, for example, PCS to Widget Symbols if they are changing the type of communication device. There are, however, attempts to harmonize graphic symbol systems and make them interoperable, meaning they can be used for text to symbol and symbol to text translations with ease (Draffan et al., 2020; Judge et al., 2023).

Semantic compacting is a special coding system that can be used in some high-tech communication aids. It requires synthetic speech and at present can be used with Danish, Dutch, English, French, German, Norwegian, Spanish and Swedish. The most common form is *Minspeak* (Baker, 1982, 1986). The user combines a limited number of graphic symbols (Minspeak icons) to produce pre-made utterances (see p. 21). Minspeak is therefore a system for word or sentence selection rather than construction. Minspeak is used in communication aids for individuals with motor impairment, as well as for individuals who have intellectual disabilities or autism spectrum disorder (Mathisen et al., 2009).

Blissymbolics is an advanced symbol system where the user can combine a core set of graphic forms to construct new meanings (see p. 13). It may be used in high-tech devices in the same manner as other graphic symbols. It is part of the *Concept Coding Framework* effort which would make Bliss-characters available on all computers worldwide (Lundälv & Derbring, 2012a, b). There is ongoing work towards coding Bliss-words in Unicode, the international standard for computer-writing (Unicode Consortium, 2020). When Bliss-characters or other graphic symbol systems are associated with Unicode code-points, they can be contained in ordinary files, sent by email and rendered in web pages. Any software that is Unicode-compliant will function with any language (MacKay et al., 2007).

Both low-tech and high-tech devices may be used with different user groups (Lancioni et al., 2019; Manzoor & Vimarlund, 2018; Sigafoos et al., 2016). The use of high-tech devices has increased as tablets and smartphones have become less costly, especially in interventions for individuals with little or no speech and no severe motor impairments. These devices have many advantages, but also have features that require attention. As with all electronic devices, there can be technical problems or the batteries may run out (Murray et al., 2020; Shepherd et al., 2009). Very few electronic communication devices are waterproof or can handle low temperatures. Many aided communicators are provided with low-tech communication devices because they are sturdy and easy to use, present the items clearly in bright light, and can have speech output in any language as the messages are recorded and thus do not require a speech synthesizer (see following section). However, all aided communicators using electronic communication devices need access to a non-electronic aid, to safeguard against situations where they may be hindered from expressing themselves due to lack of access to their electronic communication device. Furthermore, some children with autism spectrum disorder or intellectual disabilities have difficulties understanding that indicating symbols on a tablet has a communicative function, especially if they have been using the tablet for games or watching videos. For this group, communication folders or books where they can indicate or physically hand over graphic symbols to a communication partner may be easier to understand.

Digitized and synthetic speech

An important technological development in communication aids is the use of speech output. There are two forms of speech in communication aids: digitized and synthetic (Bendel, 2019; Venkatagiri, 2010).

- *Digitized speech* is natural speech that is recorded with the aid of a sound sampler and stored in the memory of a communication device. The sound sampler converts sound waves (an analogue signal) to numbers (a digital signal). The speech is stored in this digital form. Digitized speech is not language dependent, as any language can be recorded. Most electronic aids that use digitized speech are low-tech with limited vocabularies. The advantages of digitized speech are good sound quality and the possibility to record a voice that suits the aided communicator in terms of dialect, age, sex and so forth. The disadvantage of digitized speech is a lack of flexibility because each word must be recorded. A sentence may be strung together by selecting several single words, but sentence intonation would require that the whole sentence is recorded as one entity.
- *Synthetic speech* is made with software that contains a set of rules for the transferral of combinations of letters to speech (text-to-speech). These rules vary with the language and each language therefore requires its own software. A communication aid with synthetic speech is able to say everything the user writes or expresses with graphic symbols linked to written text. Synthetic speech may be a little more difficult to understand than natural speech, especially in noisy conditions. However, for most languages the quality of the synthetic speech is good and with regular use, communication partners become accustomed to it, just as people adapt to different dialects (Higginbotham, 2010; Pinkoski-Ball et al., 2012). Younger children and people who are not native speakers of the language that is synthesized tend to have more problems comprehending the speech output (Drager et al., 2010). General speech synthesizers give users few opportunities to vary the speech to reflect dialect background and a distinctive voice. However, it is now possible to create personal voices by blending general synthetic speech with a small sample of digitized speech from a sibling, peer or another voice donor (Chen et al., 2023; Creer et al., 2013; Westley, 2018), but child voices are a little more difficult to create than adult voices (Georgila, 2023).

The use of speech-generating communication aids has improved the communication of children and adults from all the user groups, including individuals with cerebral palsy, intellectual disabilities or autism spectrum disorders. Speech output has positive social consequences: the utterances produced are more similar to the language of people in the environment and the aided communicators do not have to wait to attain eye contact with the communication partner or use a bell or another attention-getting device before initiating an utterance. They can interrupt and begin talking in the same way as the other people who take part in the conversation. They immediately hear the utterances they produce and thus whether the words or graphic symbols they selected were the right ones, so they can swiftly correct any mistakes. However, synthesized voices in communication aids are somewhat flat as they cannot express emotions by different tones of voices (Pullin & Hennig, 2015). Another important advantage is that speech output makes it easier for aided communicators to communicate directly with one another, without the need for a person using natural speech to serve as interpreter and mediator.

Remote communication and social media

Language intervention has mainly been concerned with face-to-face communication. However, the technological development over the last decades has opened up new avenues for remote communication and getting the opinions of aided communicators to a larger audience through social media, blogs, podcasts and so forth (Buchholz et al., 2020; Hemsley et al., 2017; Smith, 2019). Many young aided communicators who use graphic symbols have never written a letter by themselves. A writing program for graphic symbols (combined with letters) can provide them with a whole new realm of opportunities (Parette et al., 2008) and may also support their development of writing skills (Hetzroni, 2013; see also p. 271). This may be useful for individuals with relatively good cognitive abilities who struggle with reading, but also individuals with intellectual disabilities enjoy sending letters with birthday greetings, messages and so forth (Hine & Arnott, 2002), as illustrated in Figure 2.6.

It is possible to write emails with graphic symbols (Sundqvist & Rönnberg, 2010) and as communication in messaging apps becomes more symbol-based, using text sparingly, even for mainstream users and audiences, this also opens up new possibilities for aided communicators. Video-telephony and web-based conference solutions, like Skype and Zoom, make remote communication with manual signs or aided communication possible (Buchholz et al., 2020; Grace et al., 2019). *Social media* on the Internet provides social meeting places via smartphone, tablet or computer (Lauricella et al., 2014; O'Keeffe, 2016). Many aided communicators with motor impairments have a strong wish to engage in social media (Hynan et al., 2015). Moreover, for aided communicators who may need a long time to compose a message, it is an advantage that conversations via social media are asynchronous rather than in real time. With social media, they can take the time they need and express opinions and communicate on a more equal footing with others (Caron & Light, 2017; Howery, 2018a).

Other areas of assistive technology

Many individuals who develop aided communication are severely motor impaired and need assistive technology in other areas (Cook et al., 2020; Lancioni et al., 2019; Oliver, 2019). The same modes of operation as in high-tech communication aids can also be used in teaching areas. In addition to serving as communication aids, technological devices may can be used for problem solving, environmental control, playing games and doing other leisure activities, and serve as educational tools. Environmental control, such as being able to open doors, turn music, audiobooks, television, the Internet and lights on and off, turn pages in a book, and so forth, may give the user increased *self-esteem* and *self-efficacy* (Bandura, 1997; Beauchamp et al., 2018). *Aided play*, where children perform play actions with the help of technology, may provide opportunities for independent activity and give children with motor disabilities and their caregivers a common interest to communicate about (see also Chapter 10).

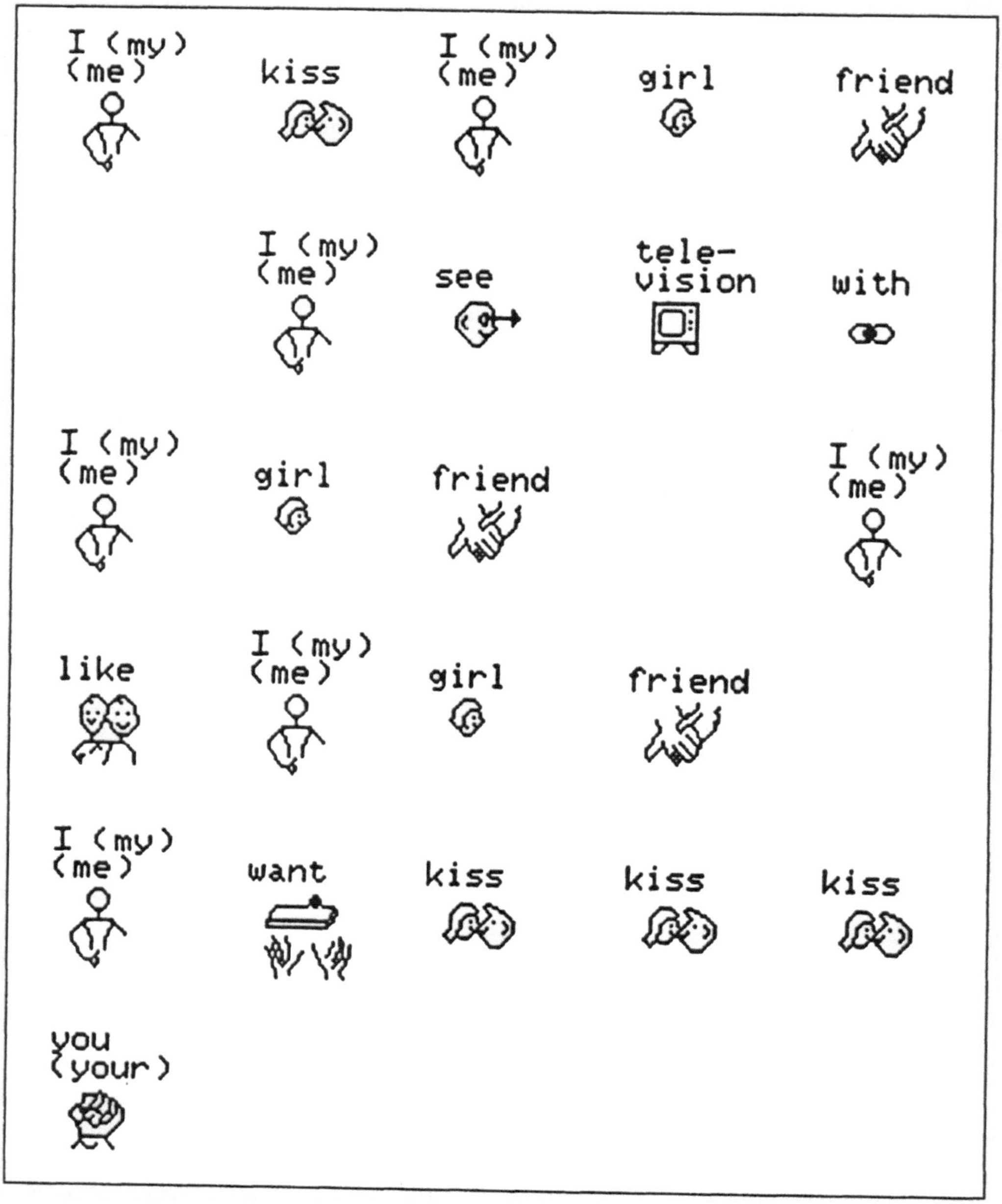

Figure 2.6 Letter to girlfriend written with graphic symbols.

Ken is 12 years old, with a diagnosis of cerebral palsy and a moderate degree of intellectual disabilities. He is unable to speak but has a good comprehension of spoken language. He uses a few manual signs and a communication board with Rebus symbols. He cannot spell. When Ken was given a computer with an adapted keyboard, it took no time at all before he began writing letters, especially to his girlfriend (Osguthorpe & Chang, 1987).

Educational software represents an important resource for students both with and without disabilities (Fernández-Batanero et al., 2022; Morel & Spector, 2023). Children with motor disabilities who use electronic communication aids can operate educational programs using the same modes of access. This may increase autonomy and more equal participation in school work, both individually and in groups, and in simpler and more complex learning environments (Dell & Newton, 2014; Woodward & Ferretti, 2014).

Electronic games have become a common activity for young people (Rideout, 2015), and individuals with severe motor disorders can operate some of the games with switches or eye-gaze control (Bekteshi et al., 2020; Cairns et al., 2019; Compañ-Rosique et al., 2019; Hassan, 2023). In fact, new technology allows individuals with severe disabilities to participate in some group games using just one switch (Bulgarelli et al., 2018; López et al., 2017). Computer games can be fun, and this is a good reason for playing them, especially for children who have limited access to ordinary toys. In addition, games can help the children develop skills that they may need later for operating communication aids (Hemmingsson et al., 2018). Many computer games apply synthetic speech, but games with artificial speech will not improve the child's ability to communicate. The games "speak" but do not engage the child in a dialogue. What the machine says has no communicative significance, and instead of fostering communicative skills, the stereotypical computer utterances may rather sustain a passive communicative style (see p. 73).

It is an advantage that computers and tablets can be used for a variety of activities. However, it is a definite disadvantage that aided communicators will be unable to communicate while they are using their device for other things. When children and adolescents are playing electronic games together or using a computer for other joint activities, there is usually a lot of communication going on. It is therefore important that aided communicators have a means for communicating while participating in a game or another activity, or opportunity to switch fast and independently between the game and the communication mode if their own device is used for gaming. Sometimes it may be preferable to use one device for communication and another for games. The same applies to school settings, where the child might need one device for working on school assignments and another for communication.

Access

The usability of the communication aid for the individual depends on the access mode. Access is the operation of the communication aid; the manner in which the aided communicator is constructing messages with graphic symbols, photographs and letters. Access can be direct selection or scanning. Both are complex tasks involving coordination of motor, perceptual and cognitive skills. For professionals, it may take a long time to find the optimal switches, keyboard or other access modes, especially if the individual's hand motor function is very variable.

- *Direct selection* means that the user points at or touches the graphic or tangible symbol selected on a board, book or screen, or they press a key on a keyboard. Direct selection may also involve moving the item that is selected to a particular position in a folder or a screen, or handing it over to the communication partner.

The use of scanning usually implies that the aided communicator is severely motor impaired. Scanning is either automatic or directed.

- In *automatic scanning*, some form of marker moves through a set of graphic symbols, photographs, letters or words. The aided communicator activates a switch when the marker is on the vocabulary item representing what he or she wants to communicate.
- *Directed scanning* is usually performed with two or more switches. One switch is used to move the marker through the set of graphic symbols, photographs, letters or words, and another switch is used to make the communicative selection.

There are several ways of organizing the scanning. Directed and automatic scanning can be either simple or sequential (Figure 2.7).

- *Simple scanning* is when all the items on the board or screen are scanned in one movement.
- *Sequential scanning* implies that each dimension is scanned separately. The user may first select a row and then the vocabulary item in the row that represents what he or she wants to say.

When an aided communicator has a large vocabulary, simple scanning can be very time-consuming. Sequential scanning is quicker and more efficient. With young children and individuals with intellectual disabilities it is natural to begin with simple scanning and progress to sequential scanning when the individual masters simple scanning. There are also dependent and independent forms of scanning, which can both be applied with simple or sequential scanning.

- *Independent scanning* means that the user directs or stops the scanning indicator without help from others. This is used on electronic devices that can be controlled with switches.
- *Dependent* or *partner-assisted scanning* means that the communication partner or another person points systematically at the board, book or screen. The aided communicator informs the communication partner or helper when she or he is pointing at the desired row, graphic symbol or word, for example by blinking with the eyes, becoming tense in the body or vocalizing.

Partner-assisted scanning may be used with both electronic and non-electronic communication aids, if the aided communicator is unable to operate the device independently, or when,

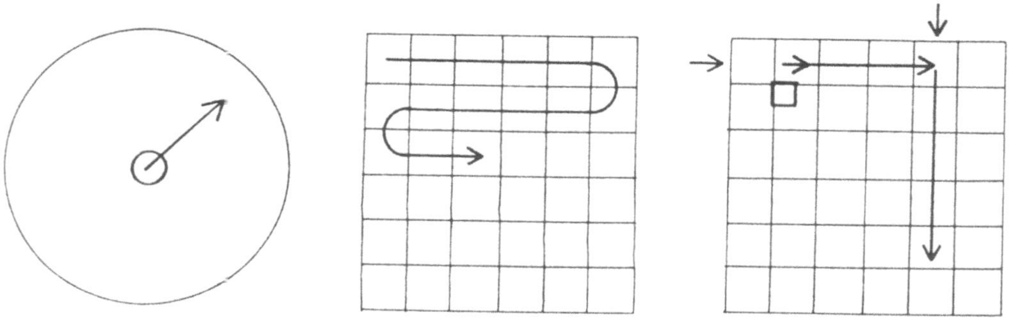

Figure 2.7 Simple and sequential scanning.

for example, the individual's communication aid cannot be mounted on the wheelchair tray during transport for safety reasons.

Direct selection

Direct selection usually involves touching, pressing buttons or keys on keyboards, different forms of pointing or handing over cards with graphic symbols. Direct selection with touch requires relatively good motor coordination and reach. Pointing does not necessarily imply an outstretched forefinger. Many individuals with motor impairment are unable to extend their forefinger, or to use it to point at all. It is important to be flexible and accept the form of pointing that the user can manage.

> Peter is 30 years old and has severe motor impairments. He likes to chat and can communicate efficiently about a range of topics with the Bliss-words on his communication board. However, he often experiences misunderstandings because the staff at the day centre insists that he should use his forefinger to indicate the Bliss-words. It is far easier for him to use the innermost joint of his thumb, a manner that his parents and siblings are used to at home. The staff's lack of flexibility hinders Peter's language use, causes him unnecessary frustration and reduces his quality of life.

For aided communicators who are unable to point with their hands, there are a number of other ways of pointing: eye gaze, a foot, a head stick, a lamp mounted on glasses or on the head that sends out a beam of light, or another part of the body.

There are different ways of using *eye-gaze* for individuals who have limited control over their body and hands. Many aided communicators with severe motor impairments are unable to use their hands or another body part to point but have good eye motor control. For them, *eye-pointing* can be an effective means of communicating ideas, wishes and other messages. Eye pointing (also called gaze pointing), may be used for indicating items in the same way as other forms of pointing but there are also coding systems designed especially for eye-pointing, such as E-Tran (Figure 2.8). Eye-pointing requires that the conversational partner is located in a position where he or she is able to follow the gaze of the aided communicator, and this will determine the overall structure of the conversational situation.

Eye-gaze technology can be used to operate high-tech communication aids (Griffiths, 2020; Vessoyan et al., 2023). The computer tracks the direction of the user's gaze and the user selects letters, words or graphic symbols by looking at them for longer than, say, half a second (Figure 2.9). Eye gaze may also be used with scanning, where the user blinks or moves the eyes when the cursor is in the desired position. Thus, the gaze may replace the functions of the mouse (Cognolato et al., 2018). The individual uses on-screen controls to operate different computer programs to communicate, play games, and so on (Hsieh et al., 2022). The development of eye-gaze technology has been important for individuals with severe motor impairments, because direct selection via eye-gaze technology makes message construction much faster than using switches. In the last decade, there has been a rapid development of this technology (Hemmingsson & Borgestig, 2020; Perfect et al., 2020). It has become more affordable as it now may be used with ordinary computers and tablets, but it is still expensive in many countries.

Using eye-gaze to point or operate a device requires good oculomotor control and the ability to fixate and direct the eye-gaze voluntarily (Cognolato et al., 2018; Sargent et al., 2013). This may be assessed with the *Eye-pointing Classification Scale* (Clarke et al., 2022).

Figure 2.8 E-Tran with colour coding.

Furthermore, even though eye-pointing may be a natural part of the communication repertoire of aided communicators, there is a significant difference between using eye-pointing to indicate occasional objects and events in the environment and using eye-gaze at the main mode of operating a communication device. Aided communicators are using the eyes for orienting and for expressive communication, and sometimes also for receptive communication. It can sometimes be difficult for the communication partner to know when the aided communicator is orienting in the environment and looking at things, eye-pointing at something (concrete or symbolic pointing, see below) or constructing a message in the communication aid. With time, training and practice, this will usually be a lesser issue, as both the aided communicator and communication partners become more experienced with the technology and familiar with the screen layout (Borgestig et al., 2017; Karlsson et al., 2019).

For individuals with intellectual disabilities and autism spectrum disorder who have sufficient fine motor skills, it may be useful to have a communication folder where they select graphic symbols by moving them. In the early phases of aided language intervention, it may be practical for the aided communicator to hand over the graphic symbols to the conversation partner and this also makes it easier for the child to understand the communicative function

Figure 2.9 Some electronic devices are operated with eye gaze.

of the symbols. Another strategy is to move the graphic symbols to a particular location (using Velcro to keep them in place), for example, an area of the communication board or a fold-out page in the communication folder (see Figures 2.2 and 2.3, p. 37-38). Communication partners can also use this as "conversation place" when they use keywords with vocabulary items from the aided communicator's system. This interactional strategy may promote true dialogue and the development of more reciprocal communication. Moreover, the possibilities for observing aided communication in others might help aided communicators overcome the gap between their own aided constructions and the spoken utterances of people around them. In electronic communication aids with screen output, the selected items are often moved to the top or bottom of the screen. This may help the aided communicator understand the functions of the graphic symbols and ensures that the conversation partner sees the message. Some individuals point very fast and may not adjust their pointing to the visual attention of the communication partner. Putting the items that are selected together may also be useful when the aided communicator is constructing longer utterances, because the words or graphic symbols remain visible until the utterance is completed.

Pointing or other ways of indicating objects, persons and locations *outside* the communication board is a common aided language strategy, which may compensate for a limited vocabulary in the communication aid and increase the speed of communicating. It saves time, because it may be faster to look at a person, an object or a place than navigating to the graphic symbol representing them in the communication book. Sometimes looking at or pointing to a person or object is *symbolic*: the person, object or place indicated is used to represent a category, as a symbol to stand for something else (Deacon, 2011; de Villiers, 2007).

For example, an eight-year-old boy looked at the door to his room to say "I". This was much faster for him than navigating to the pictogram *I* in his communication book, and well known among his usual communication partners (von Tetzchner & Martinsen, 1996).

Scanning and switches

Independent scanning implies that the aided communicator controls the aid by activating switches. There are usually one or two switches, but more switches may be used if necessary. A switch can be activated in different ways, for example with the hand, arm, foot, head, mouth, chin or eye muscles. There are switches that require little pressure and switches that can be treated roughly. Switches may be large or small. They can be shaped like a normal light switch, have a "tongue" through which the hand slips, or consist of a frame that a hand or foot is pushed into. Switches may also be activated by sucking and blowing, or by small contractions of the muscles. If the user has better control of the limbs, a joystick can also function as a switch (Cook et al., 2020; Ntoa et al., 2014; Steriadis & Constantinou, 2003). There is presently much research on brain-computer interfaces, which would allow individuals with little or no control of their bodies to operate high-tech communication aids and other electronic devices by regulating their own brain waves. However, the work is still at an experimental stage (Chang & Anumanchipalli, 2020; Peters et al., 2022).

The usefulness of the switches may determine how well an aided communicator learns to control the communication aid. There are many different types of switches, and adjusting the switch is often a difficult and time-consuming part of adapting communication aids for individuals with extensive motor disorders. Professionals often begin with the hand function, since this seems the most "natural", and then go on try other parts of the body, if use of the hand is not successful. However, experience shows that a majority of this group of users have best control of their heads, and for them it may be most effective to learn to use a head switch or head pointer first. The hand or foot may then be the first choice for switch number two. Although it is desirable that the individual is able to use the hands, it is more important to get started with aided communication and avoid frustration. Thus, when the individual's hand functions are uncertain, the best strategy may be to begin by using the head to activate the switch. If the individual later develops sufficient hand control, he or she can change to a hand-operated switch.

Professionals often try to find *the one* switch that functions best for the aided communicator. However, even the best switch may be arduous for the individual to learn to control and impossible to use over a longer time. The aided communicator may tire quickly and spend more resources on activating the switch than on the content of the communication. Although head switches may be a good start, over time they may cause strain to the neck muscles and dizziness. In addition, the general physical condition of the aided communicator may vary from day to day, and this may influence the ability to use different switches and thus to communicate. In order to reduce the strain on the user's muscles and make expressive communication as accessible as possible, it is therefore important for many aided communicators to have several switches, which are activated in various ways.

Directed scanning requires that the user is able to carry out repeated movements, while in automatic scanning, the user must be able to coordinate his or her own actions with the movements of, for example, a moving light. If independent scanning proves difficult, *partner-assisted scanning* might be the better solution. A human is more sensitive than a technical device. Dependent scanning only requires a change in facial expression or posture if the

communication partner knows the aided communicator well, and less physical effort may make it easier for the individual to focus on the content of the communication. Partner-assisted scanning is therefore often a good way of initiating the development of more varied communication with children who are dependent on scanning but who have not yet grasped an independent scanning technique, focusing on the content rather than the physical aspects of the aided communication. It may take a long time – sometimes years – from a child's first introduction to scanning to full proficiency (Jones & Stewart, 2004). There are several approaches to teaching scanning, including the use of games (Hemmingsson et al., 2018; Marina et al., 2012). The operation of the communication aid should be constantly adapted to the individual's present skills, and the vocabulary items in the aid regularly adapted to the individual's cognition and language (see Chapters 7 and 8). The aim is that scanning should gradually become as independent as possible. However, if it is impossible to find a movement that the individual can control consistently, and eye-gaze control does not function, dependent scanning may continue to be the best way for him or her to operate the communication aid. Furthermore, dependent scanning may also be a more relaxing communication mode with familiar communication partners than independent scanning, even for experienced aided communicators.

Keyboards

A keyboard is a common tool for operating a computer. Many electronic communication aids use an ordinary or adapted keyboard with letter keys, and some have extra keys for special functions. Adapted keyboards may contain words or graphic symbols, rather than letters only. For individuals who are unable to reach very far, there are miniaturized keyboards, and for individuals with imprecise hand movements, there are keyboards with larger keys or more space between the keys. The aim of the hand may be improved with a finger guide, a transparent plate with holes for the fingers over the keys. This can help the user reach the right key and also reduces mistakes and the physical effort because the user can rest the hand on the plate. Such a finger guide may also be used with tablets and devices with touch screens.

Adaptations may also include regulation of the sensitivity of the keys on the keyboard. Normally, the letter will be repeated if a key is held down, but this function can be turned off so that the pressure on the key must be released before that key can be activated again. It is also possible to adjust the time that the key must be held down before it is reactivated, so that the letter or graphic symbol is only repeated after the key has been held down for, say, two or three seconds. The operation of a computer often requires that the user is able to press two keys at the same time. This may be difficult or impossible for individuals with poor fine motor control and individuals who are able to use only one hand or who use a head stick. There is therefore software that enables the user to press one key after the other, to perform functions that usually require that two keys are activated simultaneously.

With the use of keyboards on touch-sensitive screens, aided communicators no longer have to divide their focus between the keyboard and the screen. Often a "dynamic" keyboard is embedded in the communication program or app, meaning that the surface of the "keys" on the touch-sensitive areas can be changed as easily as a screen page. Keyboards on touch-sensitive screens can be accessed both with proximal direct access (touching the screen) and with switches or eye-gaze technology.

Abbreviation and prediction

Many communication programs for high-tech aids include opportunities to use abbreviation and prediction.

- *Abbreviation* means that the user only needs to write a couple of letters and then press the space bar or another key to produce a word or a phrase, thereby saving key strokes and time. For example, the user writes c-a, and cat appears on the screen, or s-y-l or c-y-a to write "see you later" or t-b-c for "to be continued". Abbreviations are predetermined and may be individual, combining spelling and codes, or standard graphic symbols and graphic symbols representing phrases or sentences.

Abbreviations are common in ordinary text messages with smartphones but require that both the sender and the receiver know the abbreviation, for example that LOL means "laugh out loud" (Kemp, 2023; Partey et al., 2018). It is, in principle, the same function when aided communicators prepare some sentences or stories prior to a planned conversation. With electronic communication aids, they can integrate these sentences or stories into an ongoing dialogue with a few keystrokes. This makes it faster for an aided communicator to tell a friend about a trip to another city or jokes at a party, without slowing down the ongoing conversation too much (Waller & O'Mara, 2003), but preparation requires that the aided communicator knows the content of the upcoming conversation.

- *Prediction* means that the machine provides a suggestion to complete the word or for the next word as the user is writing (Vertanen et al., 2012). If the suggestion is not the right one, the aided communicator merely continues to write. If the word or graphic symbol suggested is correct, the aided communicator carries on to the next word or sentence by pressing the space bar or typing a full stop. The suggestions produced by the communication aid may be based on general word frequencies and the words used by the aided communicator. The machine remembers which words are used and suggests the most commonly used word that contains the letters the aided communicator has selected. For example, after m, the machine might suggest man, after m-o, more, and after m-o-t, mother. If mother is the word the user is writing, half of the key strokes needed for typing or saying '*mother*' have been saved. In some programs several alternatives will appear, and the user may either choose one of these or continue typing.

Word prediction has become increasingly common in mainstream applications, following development of artificial intelligence. Prediction in aided communication has been most common with orthographic writing but may also function to suggest the next graphic symbol in the utterance for aided communicators who are using graphic symbols (Hervás et al., 2020; Pereira et al., 2022). Abbreviations and prediction can be useful, but both systems are dependent on the words being fairly complex and that they are used often enough for the system to save time. Studies have found that some of the prediction systems save around half of the key presses, which both increases the speed of communication and reduces the energy demands (Garcia et al., 2014; Jordan et al., 2020). For aided communicators who indicate slowly due to motor impairments, but who move the gaze quickly, prediction can save considerable time. Individuals with good fine-motor skills who write text or select graphic symbols fast may only

be distracted by having to pay attention to the suggestions on the screen all the time, and this may considerably slow down their speed of communication.

Children with motor and speech impairments often have great problems with written language, even if they have good comprehension of spoken language (Smith, 2005a). For this group, prediction may serve as a writing prosthesis and educational tool for learning to write (McCarthy et al., 2015 Newell et al., 1991; von Tetzchner et al., 1997).

Advanced forms of prediction may include not only suggestions for words or graphic symbols based on what the user has already selected, but also selections according to pragmatic functions, the conversational setting and the emotional state of the user (Alm & Newell, 1996; Judge et al., 2015). Some communication apps use the geographical position of the aided communicator to adjust the displayed vocabulary (Garcia et al., 2016). For example, when the aided communicator is outside a bakery the display might show graphic symbols for things like *CAPPUCINO* and *BUN* alongside vocabulary such as *I, WANT, LIKE, PAY, PLEASE* and *THANK YOU*. The system builds on a rather simple presupposition regarding what aided communicators want to say in different settings, in the example above, requesting things to eat and drink. However, an aided communicator may want to talk about something entirely different in the bakery, for example that his young nephew is sad because he cannot eat buns due to gluten intolerance. Furthermore, the use of geopositioning raises concerns about the user's privacy.

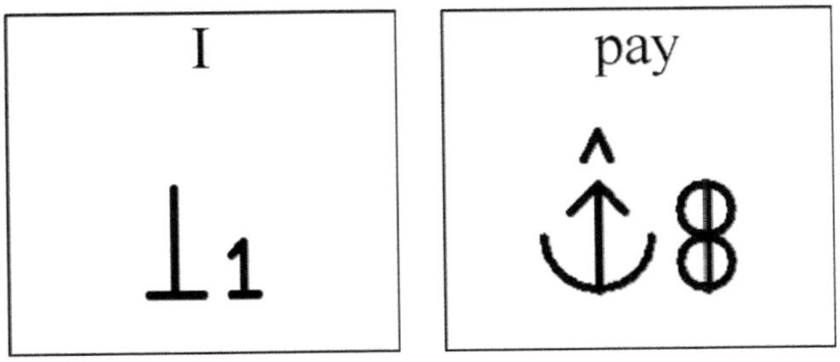

Bliss-words: I, PAY

In recent years, computer programs like ChatGPT based on artificial intelligence have emerged that are trained to follow an instruction in a prompt and provide a detailed response. They may be used to expand prediction functionality with large language models or advanced language models based on real language samples to create macros that work as frames in sentence prediction in particular situations to produce grammatically correct and complete sentences on the basis of one or a few graphic symbols (Lang et al., 2023). The predicted utterances may vary considerably, as illustrated in Table 2.2, and aided communicators express concerns that the utterances produced do not reflect their communicative intentions, that they may be too scripted and that all aided communicators may talk the same way. The technology based on artificial intelligence is promising for high-tech communication devices, but it is still being developed and its applications need to be further researched (Valencia et al., 2023).

Navigation

The use of communication books with several pages and electronic communication aids with dynamic displays require that the aided communicator has the skills needed to navigate in the

Table 2.2 Examples of predicted sentences from one-word answers to the question "Do you want to get pizza?" based on AI and macros. The bolded replies are the preferred ones (from Valencia et al., 2023)

Question	*Answer from aided communicator*	*Predictions*	*Evaluation*
Do you want to get pizza?	Later	1. I'm feeling pizza later, are you? **2. What time do you want to get pizza?** 3. Sure, let's get pizza 4. Ok, where do you want to go?	Extremely appropriate
	Eat	**1. I'm always up for pizza** 2. I'm sorry, I'm not hungry right now 3. I'm not hungry 4. I'm hungry	Very appropriate
	Work	**1. I'm sorry, I can't go out this afternoon** 2. I'm already at work 3. I'm busy with work today 4. I'm working today	Not at all appropriate

aid and construct multi-word or multi-symbol utterances. "Navigation" may be defined as the strategies used to reach a particular graphic symbol. The vocabulary in communication aids is often organized in domains and, hierarchically, in levels with gradually more specified content. For example, to say something about bananas, the aided communicator may have to manoeuvre through a hierarchy of levels to get to *BANANA*. In this example the aided communicator is using an electronic device.

1. Selects the domain *THINGS* on the index page, which opens a page with graphic symbols for different kinds of things.
2. Selects *FOOD* on the things page, which opens a page with graphic symbols for many sorts of food.
3. Selects *FRUIT* on the food page, which opens a page with graphic symbols for different kinds of fruit, including *BANANA*.
4. Selects *BANANA*.

A similar construction process may be applied with a communication book by first selecting the page with the tab *THINGS* (see p. 40), then the page with the tab FOOD, then the page with the tab *FRUIT* and finally indicating *BANANA*.

PCS: THING, FOOD. FRUIT, BANANA

This kind of organization is most common for communication devices with graphic symbols, as the alphabet can usually be displayed on a board or on one page in a display, although there may be some whole words and phrases in addition to the alphabet, which may require some navigation.

With larger vocabularies, it is usually faster to navigate in electronic devices than in communication books with many pages. In assisted scanning, too, it may be faster for the communication partner to operate an electronic device than a communication book with many pages. Aided communicators with large aid lexicons may thus have an electronic device even if they cannot operate itthemselves. If the output is visual, the message remains on screen until it is erased or replaced by new utterances. High-tech aids therefore place less demand on the attention of the communication partner. This may reduce the attentional stress of the aided communicator and the partner, and so make communication proceed more smoothly. This will also make it easier for the conversational partner to observe the aided communicator's non-verbal behaviour, such as facial expressions and posture, without losing the gist of the conversation. On the other hand, communication partners may be less engaged in the communication process if they have to wait too long for the language constructions of an aided communicator with severe motor disabilities using an electronic device (Smith et al., 2010).

Choosing a communication aid

Choosing a communication aid must be based on a thorough assessment (see Chapter 4). For individuals with fine motor impairments or cognitive challenges, operating a communication aid may require considerable effort and resources, and it is important to spend the time needed to choose the optimal communication aid (Murray et al., 2020). It can be challenging to find the best access mode(s). Seating and positioning, as well as trunk and head control, need to be assessed and optimized. It may take time for young aided communicators to learn to operate and navigate in the communication aid at the same time as they are learning the content and the organization of the aid's lexicon and the routes to different lexical items. In addition, many individuals with severe motor impairments become fatigued from controlling their limited range of movements and suppressing involuntary movements. They may need several communication aids and the opportunity to switch between access modes.

Communication aids are normally used in combination with manual signs, symbolic pointing, gestures and vocalizations. The goal of the assessment is to find one or several aids that best support the current communication skills of the individual, as well as the skills the aided communicator is expected to develop in the near and more distant future. Aided communicators should thus be provided with communication aids that give them the potential to develop new communication skills. For many children, their first communication system may not enable them to realize their communicative potential even in the relatively near future. Their communication systems may have to be updated or replaced regularly, representing smaller and larger discontinuities in expressive means (Smith-Lewis, 1994). Aided communicators change mentally and physically, and professionals should try other communication systems, aids or access modes if the individual's system does not appear to be optimal. This may imply changing from a communication book to an electronic device, but also from an electronic communication device to a non-electronic board when this is more functional for the aided communicator (see Iacono et al., 2013; Smith et al., 2010). It is important that the aided communicator feels comfortable using his or her communication aid(s) but also that other people can perceive the competence of the aided communicator.

It is often recommended that one should start by assessing the communication needs of the individual, list the communication aids that are suitable, and, with the use of elimination, find the communication aid that best suits these needs. However, most needs are shared by all humans: to be able to communicate with children and adults, with familiar and unfamiliar people, and with people who can and people who cannot read, in different situations and in different locations. These needs will therefore only partially determine which type of communication aid to choose. The individual's ability to use alphabetic script will be important for the choice of aid because spelling skills may give access to a communication aid with unlimited vocabulary and speech output (see also p. 269). However, the need to be able to write electronic or non-electronic letters, essays, reports and so forth will vary, and the need for a workstation for written productions may, to some extent, be considered independently of an aid for face-to-face communication.

It is important to distinguish between the selection of a graphic system and the selection of a communication aid. The individual's language skills and the communicative accessibility of the environment will be more decisive for choice of graphic system than for choice of communication aid. The choice of communication aid will depend on the individual's physical, cognitive and linguistic abilities, the physical design of the communication aid, how it can be transported and used, and how easy it is to learn to operate. For individuals living in areas with cold winters, for example, equipment must function under extremes of temperature and in rain and snow. For aided communicators on holiday in warm areas, at least some of their communication aids have to be able to withstand direct sunlight and high temperatures. Professionals have to make priorities and often difficult decisions when choosing communication system for a child or adult, or helping an aided communicator choose a communication system, which also reflect the fact that communication aids are still being developed (Elsahar et al., 2019; Kristensson et al., 2020; Sennott et al., 2019; Smith, 2019). Sometimes priorities and decisions have to change when new features are added to the available communication systems.

Age of aided communicator

It is generally recognized that children with little or no speech should get access to communication aids as early as possible, when possible at the same age as children with typical language development begin to speak. However, all kinds of assistive technology seem to be underutilized in the early years (Dugan et al., 2006; Romski & Sevcik, 2005). A main concern is that communication aids are generally designed for older children and adults, and not for children in their second year of life. This means that it may be difficult to make provisions for non-vocal "babbling" and the early language skills among children who develop aided communication. This may be one reason why there are few reports on aided language development in toddlers aged 2–3 years (Hemmingsson & Borgestig, 2020; Perfect et al., 2020; von Tetzchner et al., 2013). However, even high-tech devices can be implemented early, as demonstrated in this example.

> Lucas was severely motor impaired (tetraplegia) with very little use of the hands. He was provided with eye-gaze technology at 9 months, to support the development of play activities, making choices and social interaction with parents. At 15 months, he chose between 10 images of objects on a screen and between 30 images of objects at 21 months
>
> (Hemmingsson et al., 2018).

Lucas' expressive vocabulary of ten graphic symbols is within the typical range of vocabulary development at the age of 15 months.

Some researchers have introduced electronic devices with "visual scene displays" for young children instead of the usual displays with graphic symbols organized in a grid (Holyfield et al., 2017; Wilkinson et al., 2012). The visual scene may be a photograph or drawing of a room in the house, of the child playing with something, or of another common situation. The visual display has "hotspots" which activate an utterance with speech output when touched (Light & McNaughton, 2012a). When the child touches an object or something else located at a hotspot in the display, the device says the name of the object or another word relevant to the situation on the picture. For example, if the child points to a cake in the picture of a birthday party on the display, the device says '*cake*' or sings the birthday song with synthetic or digitized speech. Sometimes this is accompanied with a pop-up of the graphic symbol *CAKE*. There are usually several hotspots in the display. For example, in the birthday scene, touching the spot with candles might make the device say '*candles*', touching the spot with the child's mouth might make the device say '*blow*' with a sound effect of blowing, touching the spot of the child might make activate the child's name, and so on (Wilkinson et al., 2012). A serious problem with this approach is that the children are not given opportunities for learning words forms, that is, consistent physical ways of expressing certain messages, as they would be given in communication aids with graphic symbols in a grid layout (von Tetzchner & Stadskleiv, 2016).

(Light and McNaughton (2012a) claim that it is an advantage of visual scene displays that the pictures on the display include more of the language learning context. However, this appears to reflect a misconception of the concept "context". The image of the visual scene display is not a communicative context, the communicative context is the communicative situation of the aided communicator, which includes athe setting where the conversation is taking place, the topic of the prior or ongoing conversation, the communicative intentions involved, and so on. In the example above '*cake*' is produced when the child touches a particular part of a picture depicting a birthday party. This may lead the child to the unfortunate assumption that *cake* is only used in relation to birthday parties and thus hinder generalization and generative use of the word *cake*.

Infants with typical development may need several months to learn the use of their first 5–10 words (Harris, 1992). It is therefore also to be expected that young children learning to use graphic symbols will need some time to grasp their first graphic symbols. The full command of a word (in any mode) implies knowing both the form and the meaning or use of the word. There is no doubt that most children can learn to touch hotspots in a visual display. The problem is that the visual scene display replaces a grid with graphic symbols that will come to be the child's words, at least for the first years of life. By replacing a communication aid with distinct expressive communication forms, the use of visual scene displays may, in fact, make the acquisition of graphic symbol use more difficult (von Tetzchner & Stadskleiv, 2016).

Nonetheless, there may be a use for visual scene technology in play. The function of a visual scene seems quite similar to when infants and adults are looking together at picture books: the infant typically points at things depicted in the picture book and the adult then names them (Clemens & Kegel, 2021). Young children may enjoy producing birdsongs, animal sounds, songs or spoken phrases by touching a book page, a tablet display or an electronic device especially designed for this. However, there is no evidence indicating that substituting picture book interaction with an adult with eliciting words from a computer will enhance young children's language learning (Madigan et al., 2020).

Mobility

Children and adults communicate about many issues and in all kinds of situations. How aided communicators can take their communication system with them is always an important factor when choosing a communication aid. The aim is that they should have access to most or all of their expressive vocabulary at any given time. Individuals who use electric wheelchairs are usually able to transport fairly large and heavy aids. For children and adults who are able to walk independently but with some difficulty, it is essential that the communication aid is not too heavy or bulky. A folder or book containing graphic symbols or letters and words, a tablet or a thin board with graphic symbols or words on both sides, may be the best choice for this group, depending on the size of their aid vocabulary. Using plastic NeverTear printer paper instead of laminating ordinary paper can cut the weight of a communication book significantly, which is important in ensuring that it is carried around and used outside teaching sessions. Individuals with autism spectrum disorders and intellectual disabilities with little or no speech but good motor skills will usually be able to carry communication books and tablets, and may also benefit from using smartphones (King et al., 2020; Lancioni et al., 2019).

Aided communicators with severe motor impairments need to express themselves in different situations and not only when seated in a chair or wheelchair. They often want to communicate about something when they are lying in bed, on the floor or in the sofa, and it should therefore be possible to adapt the communication aid so the individual can operate it while lying down.

Issues related to transport often make it necessary for aided communicators to have more than one communication aid. They may have a quite bulky electronic communication device

Figure 2.10 Communication should be possible in many positions, including lying down.

with a large vocabulary, eye-gaze technology, synthetic speech output and a printer attached for use at home, in the classroom and for serious conversations with peers, and a communication board or a small, lightweight electronic communication aid or tablet with digitized or synthetic speech for use during breaks and outdoor activities.

Direct selection or scanning

It is the individual's ability to use the arms and hands that determines the choice of communication aid and strategies for indicating graphic symbols, letters, words and sentences. If the user has sufficient fine motor control, direct selection is quicker and easier than scanning, although the difference between using a joystick and direct selection can be fairly small (Lesher et al., 1998). A joystick has the advantage that it can be adjusted to the individual's motor function by increasing resistance in order to stabilize it so that the amount of force exerted makes no difference. However, a joystick requires fairly good fine motor control and sense of direction. Scanning makes higher demands on attention and cognitive resources than direct selection (Horn & Jones, 1996; Ratcliff, 1994). The choice between direct selection and scanning is determined by the individual's reach, accuracy when pointing, speed, ability to perform several controlled movements successively and activation strength. The individual's perceptual skills and ability to orient visually are also important for using both simple communication boards and electronic devices.

Vision

Visual perception is crucial for the use of communication aids. Visual impairment is common among individuals with motor impairments and developmental disabilities, and assessment of vision and the individuals' use of their visual resources is always necessary (see Chapter 4). If the aided communicator's field of vision is limited, or vision is severely reduced in one eye, it may be necessary to use only part of the communication board or display and to take this into consideration when placing the communication aid.

Children needing aided communication also have an increased risk of cerebral visual impairment, an impairment of visual perception following a brain lesion or malfunctioning, where there might be nothing wrong with the eyes or the posterior visual pathways (Blackstone et al., 2022; Ortibus et al., 2019). Children with cerebral visual impairment may profit from symbol systems with fewer visual details and clear contrasts, and it may also be considered in relation to how the pages in a communication book or device are set up – for example using a black background and leave some space between the symbols to make each symbol easier to identify. Individuals who are blind may use auditory scanning, but this is slow, and the constant repetition of words interferes with the general situational orientation. However, devices with speech output may be useful because they give the users immediate feedback from their own production. Communication aids for individuals who are severely visually impaired may have tactile markers and different surfaces to support navigation (Horton et al., 2017; Lancioni et al., 2016). It is very important that the graphic symbols have fixed locations on the board, so the aided communicator does not have to create new mental maps of the layout.

Reach and accuracy

Precise selection is necessary for aided communication to function. If the movements are imprecise, the communication partner may be uncertain or misunderstand the aided

messages. With the exception of gaze-pointing or the use of a beam of light or an arrow, direct selection requires that the individual is able to reach a sufficient number of graphic symbols or words. For example, individuals with muscular diseases often have limited reach. This may be remedied by using miniaturized communication books, screens or keyboards. A large smartphone sometimes functions better than a tablet or computer. Scanning with switches or a joystick is another way of increasing the individual's functional reach.

Direct selection also assumes a sufficient degree of accuracy. Many people with cerebral palsy have no difficulty in reaching things, but they may need rather large graphic symbols or words, or at least some distance between the items, because difficulties in fine motor coordination make it difficult for them to indicate in such a way that the communication partner can clearly see where they are pointing. Accuracy will also determine the choice of switch and the distance between switches. The placement of the vocabulary on the board is important, and sometimes only part of the board can be used.

Speed

The individual's potential speed of communication is a main focus when choosing a communication aid. Aided communication always takes longer than natural speech, but it is particularly individuals with severe motor impairments who may need a long time to select items when constructing an aided utterance (Deliberato et al., 2018). Scanning is a slow method and changing to direct selection with eye-gaze technology has increased the speed of communication for many aided communicators who had earlier used scanning. However, when the individual's head is moving involuntarily and other movements are imprecise, there may be many errors, and communication may be exhausting and time consuming. If it takes a long time from when a movement is initiated until it is completed, scanning may be the better solution because the individual can utilize the time the device is scanning and begin his or her own movement. The individual's speed will also determine the scanning rate of the aid, that is, how quickly the indicator can move from one item to another. For some individuals, assisted scanning may prove most efficient because the communication partner can adjust to the voluntary and involuntary movements of the aided communicator (see p. 96).

Repeated movements

The profile of the individuals' ability to press switches or keys will determine what type of scanning might function best for them. Directed scanning may be quicker than automatic scanning when the individual has difficulties with timing but is able to carry out several movements in rapid succession. Other individuals do better with automatic scanning because they have problems stopping after pressing a switch or key the right number of times. With electronic communication aids, it is possible to program delays and prevent the user from double-keying by only allowing the switch to react after a certain period of time has passed.

Strength

Access to communication aids always makes some demands on the user's strength and endurance. If an aided communicator is mainly pointing, there are relatively small demands on user strength, but the motor control involved in precise pointing may, over time, still sap the user's strength and energy. When the aided communicator has to press switches or keys to produce messages on a screen or with synthetic speech, this may require considerable strength.

Keyboards and switches may place different demands on activation strength. Some require a quite small pressure, while others require a considerable amount of pressure. With electronic equipment, the pressure needed can be adjusted but if the aided communicator has poor motor coordination, switches may have to be solid and require pressure and using them may be tiring.

Non-electronic and electronic communication aids

In discussions of principles for choosing communication aids, a distinction is often made between the need for a board or book and an electronic communication aid. However, focusing on this distinction may take attention away from how different communication aids may function for the individual. The functioning of an electronic device depends on many factors and more important than having access to an electronic device is having access to a communication aid at all. If economic resources are limited, communication books and boards made at home or at school can function well (Iacono et al., 2013).

It is sometimes claimed that in order to be able to use a technically advanced communication aid, a young aided communicator must first have mastered a communication board or book. It is often practical to start with a communication folder or book because it may help the teacher explain to the aided communicator and his family how the graphic symbols are organized in domains and levels, but there is little evidence for the claim that children should always start with a non-electronic communication system. There is reason to believe that an individual who has learned to use an electronic communication aid will also be able to use a communication board or book with direct selection or dependent scanning if the need should arise, for example, in case of technical failure or problems with the power supply.

However, advanced technology is often attributed a higher status compared to non-electronic communication boards or books. Many aided communicators, their family and friends and professionals seem to look at the use of communication software in computers, tablets or smartphones as the highest form of communication achievement. However, many aided communicators use their non-electronic communication boards or books much faster and more productively than an electronic communication aid. When choosing between several communication aids, it is therefore important to assess how they function for the user with different communication partners and in different situations (see Smith et al., 2010).

Speech output

An important feature of electronic communication aids is that they often have speech output which allows the user to hear a graphic symbol, photograph, letter or word spoken when they select it. This may have a positive influence on the conversation. Furthermore, it may help younger children and individuals with intellectual disabilities learn the relationships between graphic symbols and spoken words, and how the graphic symbols can be used for various communication purposes. The individuals' comprehension of spoken language is utilized fully and may contribute to their understanding of the ongoing events. For individuals with visual impairment, speech output may be crucial for learning to use the communication aid. The possibility of comparing one's own synthetic speech with what others say may facilitate the acquisition of new words. Speech output may therefore be as important for individuals in the early stages of language development as for those who have already developed more advanced language skills. Several studies have demonstrated the positive effects of using

communication devices with speech output for communicative interactions involving children with cerebral palsy intellectual disability and autism spectrum disorder (An et al., 2017; Lancioni et al., 2013; Savolainen et al., 2020; Schlosser & Koul, 2015; Tegler, 2020).

For individuals with some, although limited, comprehension of spoken language, it is vital that the basic operation of the communication aid is sufficiently explained and demonstrated, so the individual does not need a longer period than necessary before understanding how the aid functions, even if the growth of vocabulary is slow. This does not mean that the communication aid must be technologically simple. The functioning of a communication aid with speech output may be easier to learn to use than a non-electronic communication board or book because the communicative consequences of the individual's communicative actions may be clearer.

On the other hand, studies do suggest that gaining the full benefit of speech output may require some comprehension of spoken language. In a study by Romski and Sevcik (1996), it was the children with relatively good comprehension of spoken language (called "advanced learners") that seemed to benefit from the intervention with speech output devices. The children with poor language comprehension (called "initial learners") did not show the same progress, indicating that they might have needed a different approach. One reason may be that if the individual speaks – even when it is with the help of a machine – the conversational partners are likely to assume that the aided communicator understands what they say. The result may be that they fail to adapt their communication to the aided communicator's actual comprehension of spoken language and use fewer key manual signs or graphic symbols to accompany their speech. If Romski and Sevcik had used intervention strategies for this group that did not depend on comprehension of spoken language, the "initial learners" might have shown significantly better progress (von Tetzchner et al., 2004).

Price

In spite of the fact that the cost of technology in general has been dramatically reduced in the last 10 to 20 years, many electronic communication aids are still quite expensive, especially if they include eye-gaze technology (Hamid & Kristensson, 2024; Nerişanu et al., 2017). This is not an argument against using them, but their usefulness should be in keeping with their price. Some of them may have limited communicative functionality. For a child who communicates quickly and efficiently with graphic symbols on a communication board, an electronic communication aid with speech output does not necessarily mean an improvement in communication if that device is more difficult to operate and carry around (Iacono et al., 2013; Smith et al., 2010). On the other hand, for children who struggle with learning to read, a computer with synthetic speech may facilitate the acquisition of reading skills (Grunér et al., 2018; Stauter et al., 2019; see p. 271). If professionals can prevent the development of reading disorders in children without speech, price is hardly an issue.

Some characteristics of aided communication

The development of aided communication is a significant achievement that enables many individuals with little or no speech to communicate in large and small social events, but their communication also represents challenges compared to individuals using natural speech. Aided communicators are dependent on the aided language competence of people in the environment and the adaptation of the language environment to the abilities of the aided

communicators (see Chapter 12). Teachers have to provide adequate teaching and support for aided language development, but also to be good conversational partners. This requires that they have thorough knowledge about the special characteristics of aided communication, that is, how conversations may proceed when one partner is using a communication aid. There are many differences between conversations between people with natural speech and conversations where one of the participants is an aided communicator (or, on rare occasions, two or more). There are also significant individual differences between aided communicators and between operation and lexical content of the communication aids they use, but aided language construction will always differ in several ways from the articulation of natural speech. The communication partners will often have support functions, in addition to formulating their own messages and negotiating meaning. It is important that interventionists and communication partners are aware of these characteristics and try to minimize their potential negative influence on the communicative interactions. It is also important that regular and occasional communication partners get information about how the aided communicator would like his or her communication partners to behave (Midtlin et al., 2015).

Utterance construction

People who speak naturally do not ordinarily think about how they articulate the words they are saying, how they move their tongues and mouths, or how they make their vocal chords vibrate. Apart from those occasions when one is using an unfamiliar word or speaking a foreign language, articulation is an automatic process. Only occasionally does one stop and search for the word that best expresses what one wishes to say.

Operating a communication aid to construct utterances may be regarded as the functional equivalent of articulating sounds, but the physical production of utterances with communication aids is not an automatized process. In aided communication, it is useful to distinguish between *utterance construction* and *utterance production* (Trudeau et al., 2010). With electronic communication aids, there may be significant differences between the user's construction with graphic symbols and the visual or auditory production perceived by the communication partner. Utterance construction is a conscious action that requires considerable attention and cognitive effort, and it can be quite laborious to construct longer messages. Reduced motor coordination and involuntary movements can lead to mistakes. Also, imprecise movements may make it difficult for the communication partner to register the selections of the aided communicator's construction and understanding of the message, if the letter, word or graphic symbol is not presented on a screen or in synthetic or digitized speech. The result may be misunderstandings, breakdowns in communication and frustration. In addition, attention may be drawn away from what the aided communicator is actually communicating.

Time

The time needed to produce utterances is probably the most significant difference between natural speech and aided communication. Even if the communication aid is operated quickly, the production of graphic symbols or words will be considerably slower than the articulation of words in natural speech (Deliberato et al., 2018). The slow construction rate means that it takes longer for aided communicators to express what they want to say, than for communicators using natural speech. The time needed places special demands on the

communication partner (see the following example) and may hinder aided communicators in taking part in many communicative situations (Blackstone et al., 2007; Hanley et al., 2023; Howery, 2018a).

The time it may take to relay a simple message is illustrated in the following example from von Tetzchner and Martinsen (1996). Seven-year-old George communicated with eye pointing and dependent scanning. His communication book contained 845 pictograms, drawings and photographs. He and his father were going to start playing, but the father saw from George's expression that something was wrong.

F: *Here?* (Turning pages, asking for each page).
G: *BODY.*
F: *Body. Body?* (Turns pages).
G: Vocalizes and gets tense in the body.
F: *Hm? Was it not the body? What was it? Was it this one.*
G: "No" (eye movements).
F: *This one?* (Points at *CLOTHES*).
G: "Yes" (eye movements).
F: *Clothes.* (Indicates domain. The father turns the pages to the clothes pages). *And here?*
G: "Yes" (eye movement).
F: *What?*
G: *SWEATER* (gaze).
F: *Is it something with the sweater?*
G: "Yes" (eye movement).
F: *What?*
G: "Yes" (eye movement, probably prompts guessing).
F: *Are the sleeves too long?*
G: "Yes" (eye movement).
F: *Oh, they are. Yes.*

PIC: BODY, CLOTHES, SWEATER

In this successful communication, it took George two minutes to ask his father to pull up his sleeve. A child of his age using natural speech would have said the same in three or four seconds (Deliberato et al., 2018; Walker & Archibald, 2006). In the next example, the message took even longer to produce. Bob had a communication board with 50 graphic symbols and could make a few gestures. The conversational partner (John) was a male nurse (Kraat, 1985, p. 81).

B: *HOME.*
J: *Home? What about home? Is it something to do with your sister?*
B: "No" (Shakes head).
B: *DAY-OF-THE-WEEK.*
J: *Sunday? Monday? Tuesday?… Saturday?*
B: "Yes" (Nods).
J: *Something to do with home and Saturday?*
B: *MAN.*
J: *A man? Is there a special man who's coming?*
B: "No" (Shakes head).
J: *Shall I find out who the man is?*
B: "Yes!" (Nods emphatically)
J: *A relative? A friend? Someone at the hospital?*
B: "Yes" (Nods).
J: *Someone at the hospital. Let me see, a doctor, a therapist, a friend?* Can you give me some more clues?
B: (Looks at the top of John's head).
J: *Head. Part of the head. Brain. Does he work with his head?*
B: *COLOUR.*

PCS: WEEKDAY, HOME, MAN, COLOUR

The whole "conversation" consisted of over 100 exchanges and lasted for 20 minutes before John understood what Bob wanted to ask: "Can Carl (a coloured security guard) drive me home on Saturday in the hospital van?" These conversation excerpts demonstrate that the conversational partner may be decisive for how well aided communicators can express themselves.

Due to the slow production rate, as well as other factors, the total amount of language produced by aided communicators is considerably lower than that typically produced by natural speakers. There are few studies investigating this, but Beukelman and associates (1984) found that four adult aided communicators produced between 269 and 728 words per day during a period of two weeks. Similar numbers are not available for children, but interviews with parents and professionals indicate that the number of words and graphic symbols produced with communication aids may be even lower for children. This is in stark contrast to children with typical development who at an age between 3 and 12 years may produce 20,000–30,000 words in one day (Wagner, 1985). Moreover, aided communicators often do not have access to their communication aid in many everyday situations (von Tetzchner et al., 2018). Although the technological developments likely have contributed to increasing the average daily language production of aided communicators, it still means that children who use

communication aids have fewer and more limited opportunities for learning to express themselves than children with typical language development.

The role of the conversational partner

In most conversations with natural speech, the participants are equal. Both can formulate what they wish to say, and although negotiation of meaning is an inherent part of conversations (Elder & Haugh, 2018), individuals who can talk are not usually dependent on help from their communication partners in order to express themselves. Aided communicators experience a quite different situation. As in the dialogue excerpts above, they may need a *message interpreter and formulator* to produce coherent utterances on the basis of their incomplete and fragmented words and sentences constructed with letters or graphic symbols (Murray et al., 2018; Smith et al., 2018). The conversation partner may thus have to articulate both their own utterances and the utterances of the aided communicator (see Chapter 12). In fact, producing what George and Bob wanted to say in the examples above came out as the result of cooperative efforts between them and their communication partners, George's father and John. In typical language studies, this is often referred to as *co-construction of meaning* (Jacoby & Ochs, 1995; Kelly & Bailey, 2013). In fact, after 100 co-constructive conversational turns, John had yet to say anything of his own: he had merely interpreted what Bob had said.

In particular, when the aided communicator uses graphic symbols and has a limited vocabulary, the conversation partner has to interpret and formulate what the aided communicator wants to say. In order to speed up the often-slow pace of aided communication, the communication partner may start too early to try to infer what the aided communicator wants to say. In the example with George telling his father about his sleeve, the father's inferences were successful. The communicative goal was achieved much quicker than if George had had to construct a complete sentence, which would have been possible for him. Because Bob had a limited number of vocabulary items on his communication board, John's inferences were necessary for Bob to get the message across. Both partners were successful. However, partners who have the double role of interpreter and communication partner sometimes fail to pay sufficient attention to the constructions of the aided communicator or try to figure out the message on their own without waiting for the aided communicator to finish constructing the aided message, as in this conversation where a young aided communicator (A) using a device with speech output is starting to tell a peer (P) about a video where a girl in a wheelchair eats a banana and throws the peel away, whereupon a woman slips on the peel (Smith et al., 2018).

A: 'Stop'.
P: Stop a robber?
B: 'Girl'.
P: Girl … pushing a robber out the window?
A: 'Boy'.
J: A girl and a boy, a boy just dressed as a clown? At a circus?

The peer had not seen the video. He was dependent on information from the aided speaker, but his creative interpretations were far beyond the information given in the aided utterances. Communication partners are sometimes able to infer the meaning correctly based on minimal information, the context and what they think is a plausible scenario, such as inferring "banana" when an aided communicator constructs the utterance *COLOR EAT* at the

breakfast table. However, this might not work so well when the aided communicator is conveying something less expected and without situational clues. If the communication partner makes incorrect inferences, the production of the utterance may take more time instead of less, or even lead to a complete communication breakdown (Dahlgren Sandberg & Hjelmquist, 1996; Murray et al., 2018; Neuvonen et al., 2022a).

When adapting the communicative environment to aided communicators, special attention should be given to the strategies used by their communication partners (see Chapter 12). It is clear from the excerpts above that partners may both promote and hinder the possibilities of aided communicators for expressing themselves. For example, although inferencing – sometimes even guessing – may be a useful strategy for speeding up the communication, premature inferences may limit the communicative efficiency of aided communicators and slow down their message production and the co-construction process. A lack of sensitivity may be reinforced by the fact that communication partners often function as general helpers and may be unaware of how they influence the communication.

It should be noted that the problems described here are not with the aided communicator *or* with the conversational partner, but with their relationship. The potential of an aided communicator to self-express may be limited, while the communication partner may have difficulties understanding what the aided communicator intends to communicate. They both try to solve the communicative problem in the best possible way. However, this complementarity creates a relationship with uneven distribution of power, a condition that warrants ethical consideration. A moral requirement for *autonomy*, that is, an equal footing or right to expression, places an ethical imperative on the more competent communication partner to be sensitive to what is being expressed by the other and to strive to overcome the asymmetrical relationship and help the aided communicator create authentic messages (Grove et al., 1999; von Tetzchner & Jensen, 1999).

Chapter 3

Children, adolescents and adults in need of AAC

A large minority of the population with developmental and acquired disabilities need AAC because they have little or no speech, or their speech is unintelligible. The prevalence of individuals who need AAC temporarily or throughout life has been estimated to be between 0.4 and 1.2 percent (Creer et al., 2016; Scope, 2008; Light et al., 2003). In a study of individuals with diagnoses and individual characteristics that are indicative of insufficient spoken language, Creer and associates (2016) estimated the need to 0.5 percent of the total population in the United Kingdom, including both developmental and acquired conditions, but the authors suggest that this is a low estimate.

Three functional groups

Individuals who need AAC may be categorized into three main groups depending on the function the alternative communication system will perform, that is, whether the individuals need a means of expression, a supportive language or an alternative language. The groups are named the expressive language group, the language support group and the alternative language group. All three groups are characterized by individuals who either did not begin speaking at a typical age or who lost their speech skills at an early age as the result of disease or injury. The biggest differences between the groups, and the basis for distinguishing between them, are the individuals' spoken language comprehension and their prognosis for developing intelligible speech in the future.

The expressive language group

Children and adults who belong to the expressive language group have a large gap between their understanding of other people's speech and their ability to express themselves through spoken language. They may use manual signs, graphic symbols or letters. Within this group are individuals with motor speech impairments, for example associated with cerebral palsy, who do not have sufficient control of the speech organs to be able to articulate speech sounds intelligibly (dysarthria or anarthria). Individuals in this group often have motor impairments that affect all or most of their movements, making graphic communication systems the obvious choice. Some individuals have a comprehension of spoken language that is adequate for their age, but intelligence within the normal range is not necessary for inclusion in the expressive language group. Individuals with intellectual disabilities or developmental language disorder may also have a significant gap between what they understand of spoken language and

DOI: 10.4324/9781003387633-4

their ability to express themselves through speech. For example, some individuals with Down syndrome belong to the expressive language group (Launonen, 2019a).

For individuals who belong to the expressive language group, the purpose of AAC intervention is to provide them with a language mode that will become their *permanent* means of expression, that is, a means of communication they can use in all kinds of situations and for the rest of their lives. Because their understanding of spoken language is comparable to their intellectual level, comprehension is not usually a specific target of the intervention. However, they may need special education to compensate for lack of experience because they participate less in many natural learning situations (Batorowicz et al., 2014; Oates et al., 2011). The main focus of the intervention is the relationship between the spoken language used in the environment and the alternative language mode used by the individual. However, comprehension of manual signs or graphic symbols (e.g. PCS, PIC or Bliss-words) should be targeted in the intervention. Teaching of ordinary written language may also be part of the intervention (see p. 269).

The supportive language group

The supportive language group may be divided into two sub-groups: the developmental group and the situational group. Both groups may use either manual signs or graphic symbols, depending on the individual's abilities and the preference of the family.

For the *developmental group*, AAC is not a permanent means of communication. The primary aim of the AAC intervention is to support the early comprehension and expressive use of spoken language. Manual signs or graphic symbols will function as language "crutches" for the child on the way to a normal command of speech. The most obvious use of AAC as a developmental supportive language is with children who are expected to begin speaking but whose language development is severely delayed. Children with developmental language disorder belong to this group, as do many children with intellectual disabilities (Launonen, 2019a; von Tetzchner, 1984a; Wright et al., 2013). Some children need AAC because they are unable to speak for a limited period, due to disease or injury, for example tracheostomy following an operation on the larynx (Adamson & Dunbar, 1991; DeMauro et al., 2016). The general focus of the intervention for this subgroup is to make clear the relationship between speech and the alternative language form, as well as helping them solve social problems that may appear as a result of their limited speech. Comprehension of spoken language varies within this group and this affects to what extent comprehension training will be included in the intervention.

The situational group consists of children, adolescents and adults who can speak but who have difficulty in making themselves understood with speech alone. This sub-group resembles the expressive language group, but speech rather than an alternative communication system is their main form of communication. The degree to which they are able to make themselves understood through speech varies with how well people know them, the topic of the conversation and noise conditions in the conversation environment. For example, discussing experiences shared with the communication partner, individuals in this group may easily make themselves understood, while the communication partner may not understand a description of a film or a book he or she does not know. A child who is well understood in a small classroom may be nearly unintelligible in a train or on a street with normal traffic noise. In such settings and with unfamiliar people, individuals in the situational sub-group may need to supplement their speech with manual signs or letters, graphic symbols, or written words or

letters. Intervention for this group focuses on helping them learn when they need to augment their speech, how to monitor the comprehension of the communication partner and how to use AAC and communication strategies in different situations (see Chapter 11).

A child may have a diagnosis where speech development may be slow, but speech is likely to emerge. In the majority of instances, however, conditions will not always be this clear to begin with. For example, among children with Down syndrome, some develop very good speech, some develop speech that is difficult to understand, and some develop no, or very little, intelligible speech. Professionals will always support speech and hope that the child will develop intelligible speech, but only time will show whether this will be the case (de Almeida Barbosa et al., 2018; Launonen, 2019a).

Studies have found that children with language disorders have a higher incidence of mental health problems than children with typical language development and that children with emotional and behavioural disorders have a higher incidence of language disorders than children without such disorders (Burnley et al., 2023; Im-Bolter & Cohen, 2007; van Daal et al., 2007). A child's language disorders may cause misunderstandings, communication breakdowns and conflict in the family, and the difficulties and frustration related to the communication problems may create a difficult family situation. One aim of AAC intervention for this group is therefore to provide them with temporary linguistic means that may reduce the potential negative consequences of the language disorders.

The alternative language group

Individuals in the alternative language group develop little or no comprehension or production of spoken language and the alternative mode of communication is the language they will use for the rest of their lives. This is also the language form that other people will generally need to use in order to communicate with them. The aim is therefore to teach and guide individuals in this group to use an alternative mode of communication as their native language; their "mother tongue". Intervention will target both comprehension and production of AAC. People in the environment will always use speech simultaneously with manual signs or graphic symbols but the main goal is to create situations where the individual can learn to understand and use AAC even if he or she does not understand what is said. This means that professionals must establish an environment where the alternative language form is truly functional, where the situation gives cues to the meaning and use of the manual signs or graphic symbols.

The alternative language group consists of people with autism spectrum disorder, severe or profound intellectual disabilities and severe language disorders. In this group, there are also individuals with *auditory agnosia* or "word deafness" who have problems identifying and attributing meaning to sounds. They have normal hearing in the sense that they can indicate that they have registered a sound, but are unable to distinguish between speech sounds and, in severe cases, between, say, a child crying and a foghorn (Luchsinger & Arnold, 1965; Musiek et al., 2019). Some individuals in the alternative language group may have multiple disabilities that include motor disability.

Distinguishing between the groups

The main reason for distinguishing between the expressive, supportive and alternative language groups is to highlight that children who need AAC may follow different developmental

paths to whatever competence they achieve. The AAC training may have different aims, and the intervention will differ in each of the groups. Intervention goals should be formulated on the basis of the strengths and weaknesses of each individual, and the division into the three groups may be helpful when formulating these goals.

The importance of distinguishing between these groups is illustrated in a study by Romski and Sevcik (1996). They provided intervention with graphic symbols and communication aids with speech output to children with intellectual disabilities. Some of the children did better than others and showed what Romski and Sevcik called an *advanced learning pattern*; another group showed less progress and showed what they called a *beginning learning pattern*. The pattern names suggest that Romski and Sevcik regarded the two groups as being at different stages on the same developmental path. However, the main difference between the two groups was in their comprehension of spoken language. It is probable that in this study the children with good comprehension benefited more from intervention with a speech output communication device than the children who had less understanding of spoken language. The latter group might have made greater gains with training not based so much on spoken instructions (von Tetzchner et al., 2004). The two groups did not simply need different amounts of the same intervention but different learning conditions. For the children who showed a "beginning learner pattern," intervention based on spoken instructions and a speech output device may in fact have put them on a "wrong" developmental path. This emphasizes the necessity of adapting the intervention to the abilities of the individual.

The division into three functional groups does not imply that it is always easy to determine in which group a given individual belongs. It is difficult to distinguish between individuals who belong to the supportive language group and the alternative language group, or between individuals who belong to the expressive language group and the language support group. For example, Eric, a boy with Down syndrome, was for many years believed to belong to the expressive language group. He developed an advanced competence in manual signing, including a large sign vocabulary, inflections and complex syntax. He had great difficulties articulating spoken words and his speech remained unintelligible in spite of much encouragement and speech therapy. When Eric was 13 years old, he gradually began to speak more clearly and by age 17, speech had become his main expressive language form. He only used manual signs as support in situations where he lacked words (Launonen, 2019b; Launonen & Grove, 2003). Moreover, AAC may be useful also for adults (Holyfield et al., 2017). In the early days of AAC, it was observed that 40 to 50-year-old people with intellectual disabilities and autism spectrum disorder benefitted from AAC after failing to develop speech in spite of years of traditional speech training. For some of these people, speech gradually became their main form of communication. On the basis of the results of the traditional speech therapy – before they were provided with AAC – it had been reasonable to assume that they were incapable of developing speech, or even communication. However, the intervention with AAC showed that the potential was there but also that for them an AAC approach was needed for speech to emerge.

The most common diagnostic groups in need of AAC

Among individuals belonging to the three functional language groups, there are individuals with different diagnoses, and a diagnostic group can be represented in more than one of the three functional groups. Some individuals with cerebral palsy need a communication aid in order to be able to express themselves, others need a support or supplement because their

speech sometimes is difficult to understand, or require an aid for a shorter period of time. Some individuals with autism spectrum disorder begin speaking after having used manual signs or graphic symbols. Others never learn to understand or use speech but are able understand and use some manual signs or graphic or tangible symbols.

Motor impairment

There are several small diagnostic groups with combined developmental language and motor disorders who need AAC (Creer et al., 2016). Motor-impaired children with some functional speech may also have a need for permanent or temporary aids as supportive forms of communication.

It is, first and foremost, children and adults with cerebral palsy who have motor disorders that render them unable to use speech to communicate, but brain tumours and neuromuscular diseases may also be the cause. Cerebral palsy is a disturbance of posture and movement due to a non-progressive brain lesion acquired during early development (Rosenbaum et al., 2007). The reported prevalences vary from 1.5 to 3.4 per 1,000 live births, depending on the economic situation and country income (McIntyre et al., 2022). This group includes individuals who due to the motor impairments have insufficient control of the speech organs (tongue, mouth, throat, and so forth) to be able to articulate speech sounds normally (anarthria, dysarthria). They may be paralyzed or have spasms that make it difficult for them to control their articulation properly, which will make it difficult for people who do not know them well to understand what they are saying (Pennington, 2015; Pirila et al., 2007). Among children with cerebral palsy, about half have speech problems and a quarter are categorized as lacking speech, and this is especially frequent among children with dyskinetic motor impairments or those who are non-ambulatory (Andersen et al., 2010; Novak et al., 2012). Motor disorders that only affect speech are rare. Most of the children who have a severe motor speech impairment also have other impaired motor functions. They may experience varying degrees of reduced coordination of their arm and hand movements. Many are dependent on wheelchairs or crutches.

In many countries, every year a significant number of children are born with a motor disability that implies a need for AAC. The motor impairments will have a direct effect on the form of communication the children will be able to utilize. Most children with fine motor disabilities will need some type of communication aid.

Motor abilities – and impairments – influence children's development in many ways (Adolph & Hoch, 2019; Campos et al., 2000). The children's reflexes and involuntary movements may affect their attempts to react to both people and events that occur in their environment. For example, when a child with cerebral palsy reaches for an object or person, a sideways movement of the head associated with the tonic neck reflex may make the child's reaching movement look like a rejection, and adults might interpret this as the child not being interested in the person or object (Sigafoos et al., 2021). Children with cerebral palsy are often regarded as more alert and interested when they are tense than when their muscle tonus is low (Burkhart, 1987). This may be unfortunate because high muscle tonus leads to reduced motor control and may make the communication more difficult for an individual using AAC. Moreover, children who experience severe difficulties in mobility and speaking may develop a passive communicative style. This is not only a result of the children's disabilities but also reflect reactions of the environment. Training, feeding and hygiene take much time, and there are often few activities that the parents and the child can take part in together. When the children are

young, their parents may consider them to be happiest when they are passive. However, the influences are bidirectional: parents influence their children and children influence their parents (Sameroff, 2010; Zirpoli & Bell, 1987).

Smiles, crying and vocalization are *signals* that reflect the child's attentional and emotional state. Such signals are cues for adults' reactions to children and play an important role in early interaction (von Tetzchner, 2019a). The smiles and vocalizations of children with motor impairments may be unclear or inconsistent, and their crying may be more pervasive and deviant compared to that of other children. These signals may be difficult to understand for parents. Parents usually react to their child's crying and interpret it as an expression for different needs, depending on how long it is since the child ate, had the nappy changed, and so forth. Among children with motor disorders, crying is often caused by matters beyond the parents' control, such as muscular pains due to increased muscular tension, reflux and other gastrointestinal dysfunction (McKearnan et al., 2004; McKinnon et al., 2019; Vinkel et al., 2022). It may be difficult or impossible to calm the child, and the parents may become frustrated and feel inadequate. Long-lasting and frequent bouts of crying can be a source of constant irritation for the parents (Potharaju, 2022). When all this is taken into consideration, it is hardly surprising that parents of children with severe motor disabilities may feel that their children are happy when they are passive.

A child's comprehension of spoken language may be reduced compared to peers, even if the neurological basis for language development has not been affected. Children with extensive motor disorders lose a significant part of the varied language experiences that children usually learn from. Children with typical development in the pre-lingual period cry, laugh and take hold of and reach out for objects, make gurgling noises that may resemble words, and so forth, which make parents and other adults react and speak to the children, and thus indirectly guide them to language learning (Service et al., 1989). After the children have begun to speak, they develop language in a similar way by taking part in conversations with adults and peers. They receive comments about what they themselves say and do, and answers to their questions about objects and events they are interested in or wonder about. Children with motor disorders lose out on many of these experiences, and this may lead to reduced language comprehension and less knowledge about the environment (von Tetzchner, 2018).

Motor impairments may imply considerable restrictions on children's personal development. There are activities in which they are unable to participate and many areas where they gain only limited experience. Part of this limitation is not caused primarily by the motor impairment, however, but by the fact that, due to negative experiences, they come to believe they are unable to do anything – learned helplessness (Basil, 1992; Seligman, 1972). Later on they may no longer try to do things that they perhaps would have been capable of. They learn that they are incapable because others do things for them which they would be able to manage alone, given the opportunity to practice, the necessary aids, and sufficient time. The attitudes of parents, professionals and peers, which children with disabilities to a great extent assume themselves (Madge & Fassam, 1982), therefore play a significant role in forming their life and opportunities for personal growth.

Many children and adolescents with severe speech and motor impairments develop a responsive and passive communicative style. There is reason to believe that the foundation of this style is laid already at an early stage. Many of the children had "yes" and "no" as their main form of communication for many years – a kind of "Twenty Questions" with, say, eyes up for "yes" and down for "no". The introduction of graphic symbols and communication aids represented new opportunities for communication. However, it appears that many young

aided communicators do not easily initiate conversations even when they appear as though they have something to say, have learned to control their communication aid and are able to answer all sorts of questions. It may be difficult for children who, for several years, have had answering questions as their main or only communication strategy, to learn to use language in new ways. It is therefore important to find communicative expressions that the children can utilize to take the initiative, so that they do not learn that they must wait until others have asked them a question before they start to express themselves.

Cognitive level and language comprehension vary considerably among children and adults with speech problems due to severe motor disorders (Cummings, 2008; Stadskleiv, 2020). Many individuals in this group have a large gap between what they understand and what they can express in spoken language and thus belong to the *expressive language group*, others have similar difficulties with both comprehension and production. For some, an alternative communication system will be the form of communication that they understand best. Thus, among those with severe speech and motor disorders, there will also be people who belong to the *supportive language group* and the *alternative language group*.

Developmental language disorders

Children usually say their first words around the age of one but there is considerable variation. Some children are nine months, while others begin at 17 months or later. By the age of two years, the average vocabulary size is around 150 words, and children can have learned anywhere from 10 to 450 words (MacWhinney, 2015). Following the *vocabulary spurt*, defined as the first month in which a child's vocabulary increases by at least 15 words (Poulin-Dubois & Graham, 1994), word learning increases at a formidable pace. Estimates vary from an average of 5.5 to 9 words per day until the age of 18 years. Around six years of age, children usually comprehend between 10,000 and 15,000 words, and produce somewhat fewer (Anglin, 1993; Carey, 1978) (see also p. 235).

The estimates of language disorders in early childhood vary considerably, and as many as 25 percent of parents of four- to five-year-olds are concerned about their child's language development (McLeod & Harrison, 2009). Studies find that approximately 6–12 percent of all children show delayed language development or language impairment, and 1–2 percent have severe language disorders. About 7.5 percent of school age children show developmental language disorder (Calder et al., 2022; Paul, 2020). They need support but only a small minority needs AAC. Some children have problems with speech, others with the language itself. Some have mainly expressive disorders while others have global disorders of language processing, involving both comprehension and production. Receptive disorders are more severe than expressive disorders, and impaired comprehension will always influence expressive language. Purely expressive disorders will influence the language learning situation and hence to some extent the child's receptive skills. Language disorders are more common among boys than girls (Cummings, 2008; Weindrich et al., 2000). Children with developmental language disorders vary considerably in non-verbal cognitive abilities from intellectual disabilities to giftedness. The causes may be unknown or the language disorders may be associated with other developmental disabilities (Bishop, 2014, 2017).

There are several sub-groups with different developmental trajectories and associated disorders. Children with *phonological disorders* have difficulty perceiving and producing speech sounds, while children with *articulation disorders* have problems with the physical production of speech itself. *Grammatical impairments* involve problems with sentence formation and

conjugation (changes in verbs to show number, person, tense, and so on). *Semantic impairments* entail problems with the contents of language, and *pragmatic disorders* with the communication and use of language, such as understanding others' intentions, choosing topic, discovering and repairing gaps in the communication and maintaining a coherent conversation. Even children with good pronunciation and correct sentence structure may have poor understanding of how language can be used (Bishop, 2006; Cummings, 2014).

A notable sub-group appears to be children with *dyspractic traits*; that is, children who have difficulty in performing voluntary acts, especially those that require coordinated movements. These children may have significant problems in carrying out motor acts in a large variety of activities. Around one in 1,000 children presents with *developmental apraxia of speech*, also called *childhood apraxia of speech* or *developmental dyspraxia*. This is a neurological childhood speech sound disorder where the precision and consistency of movements underlying the speech are impaired in the absence of neuromuscular deficits, and may occur together with other neurodevelopmental disorders (Shriberg et al., 2019). The problems are related to motor planning, reduced ability to transform a phonological representation into motor speech commands, resulting in slow speech and inconsistent errors in speech sound production and prosody. Onset of speech is delayed, and vocabulary growth limited. Apraxia of speech differs from dysarthria because dysarthria is a result of known muscular impairments (McNeil et al. 2017; Terband et al., 2019). The lack of consistency in errors makes the child's speech difficult for others to learn to understand. Moreover, the lack of visible motor impairments makes the child's difficulties more difficult to observe. It is a persistent language disorder, and the speech problems may be part of a global language-processing problem. Language comprehension may be impaired at school age even if the articulation problems have been resolved (Lewis et al., 2004). Children with apraxia of speech may need many years of speech therapy, may have severe problems with learning to read and write and the condition may last into adulthood (Gillon & Moriarty, 2007; Lewis et al., 2023). Some individuals show minimal improvement following interventions that focus on articulation and remain severely disordered. Studies have found that children with apraxia of speech may benefit from using manual signs or graphic symbols to express themselves and support speech development, but the dyspractic problems may also make sign production difficult for them (Iuzzini-Seigel et al., 2022; Oommen & McCarthy, 2015). Electronic aids with speech output have proved useful for communication and supporting the child's speech development (Bornman et al., 2001; Lüke, 2014). Importantly, intervention should focus on speech production, non-speech oral motor training is not necessary or sufficient (Watson & Lof, 2008).

Most children with developmental language disorders will gradually begin to speak, even though their speech may be quite unintelligible throughout the preschool period, especially for people outside the family. When the children reach school age, most have begun to speak clearly enough so that even those who do not know them will understand them. Due to their delayed language development, however, the children will usually have a smaller vocabulary and often less knowledge of their environment than their peers. The extent to which this happens will depend on how the children function in other areas. Reduced knowledge is common in children with moderate or more severe developmental language disorders until they are well into their school years or later (Kan & Windsor, 2010; Wren et al., 2016, 2021).

In conversations with other children or adults, children with developmental language disorders may experience problems making themselves understood. The difficulties other people experience in understanding the children often make them give vague answers such as *yes, no* or *hmm* in response to the children's communicative efforts, and the children may not receive

an appropriate answer to their questions (Schjølberg, 1984). Adults may solve the problem of not being able to understand by taking control of the interaction with the child. Compared to parents of children with typical language development, parents of children with language disorders tend to give more commands and ask fewer questions (Blackwell et al., 2015; Paul & Elwood, 1991). This reduces the pressure on the adults to understand what the children are saying, but at the same time deprives the children of the chance of leading the conversation towards topics they are interested in. In addition to the fact that the children lose out on interactions typically enjoyed by children, poor intelligibility may reduce the children's participation in other ordinary social interactions. These interactions are natural learning settings and important for children's acquisition of language, concepts and general knowledge about society.

The problems that adults and other children encounter when they are together with children who have language disorders may lead to the children withdrawing from the interaction. Many preschool children with developmental language disorders are shy and timid in the company of others; both among adults whom they do not know and among other children. When they commence school, they often have problems establishing relations with other children. Some children develop *selective mutism*, which implies that they do not speak outside their family and home, and many of them have a history of language delay (Kotrba, 2015; Scott & Beidel, 2011). Other children with developmental language disorders may show behaviour disorders and appear disruptive (St Clair et al., 2011; Valera-Pozo et al., 2020; Willinger et al., 2003).

It is likely that the problems these children experience are an indirect result of the difficulties they experience in making themselves understood. Most social situations require proficiency in language. When they meet new people, young children are typically asked such questions as *What is your name?* and *How old are you?* and when they fail to give intelligible answers to these questions, their impaired language immediately becomes apparent. In some cases, children with poor articulation find speaking "clearly" and understandably to be such a strain that it also becomes more difficult for them to do other things. The speech disorder may then spread and become a more extensive problem.

Children with developmental language disorders are not usually taught an alternative communication system in order to provide them with a mother tongue. They typically belong to the developmental subgroup of the *supportive language group*, and for them, the aim of intervention with AAC is primarily to support their development of speech. Many in this group benefit from interventions with manual signs, graphic symbols and communication devices with speech output (Bornman et al., 2001; Lüke, 2014; Navarro et al., 2020; Oommen & McCarthy, 2015; von Tetzchner, 1984a).

The effect AAC may have on the children's conversational partners is almost as important as the direct effect on the children of learning AAC. Adults may overestimate or underestimate how much children with limited speech understand. When the children use *total communication* – manual signs or graphic symbols at the same time as they speak – it will help the adults to understand and reply meaningfully to what the children are communicating. For the children, this means that their interaction with adults may become more successful and meaningful. At the same time, it may be easier for adults to comment on what the children are doing and tell them about objects and activities that are happening, in the same way as they do when interacting with children with typical development. This increases the probability that the children will learn names of objects, how events are discussed, how objects are used, social rules and so forth. These are important foundations of language development (Nelson,

1996, 2007). Thus, when AAC intervention is successful, children in this group will have a larger vocabulary and more optimal conceptual development.

An important aim of AAC intervention is to develop further children's social skills and participation. Even after children have begun to speak clearly and make themselves well understood, there may be many social and interactional rules that they have not yet learned, with which their peers are familiar. Improving children's ability to make themselves understood and increasing their participation in valuable social interaction may make them less shy and timid, and thus help them to enjoy improved social interaction both with peers and with adults whom they do not know well.

Intellectual disabilities

The terminology used in connection with more extensive general disorders of development and learning is undergoing constant change. The *Diagnostic and Statistical Manual of Mental Disorders, Fifth Edition* (DSM-5) uses the term "intellectual disabilities" (American Psychiatric Association, 2013), while the *International Classification of Diseases for Mortality and Morbidity Statistics, Eleventh Revision* (ICD-11) uses "disorders of intellectual development" (World Health Organization, 2022; see Harrison et al., 2021). Traditionally, the group with intellectual disabilities included all children who were considered unable to benefit from ordinary schooling and therefore ought to attend special schools. Today, "intellectual disabilities" is used as a collective term for a range of different conditions with wholly different causes. Common to these, however, is the fact that the intellectual abilities of those concerned, and their chances of coping in society, are restricted and that the condition is observable during the developmental period.

ICD-11 includes four levels of intellectual disability, based on IQ and adaptive function. In mild intellectual disability, adaptive functioning and intelligence scores are two to three standard deviations below the age mean. For intelligence tests with an average of 100 and a standard deviation of 15, this corresponds to IQ 69–55. Moderate intellectual disability is defined as adaptive functioning and intelligence scores three to four standard deviations below the mean (IQ 54–40). In both severe and profound disabilities, intellectual functioning is more than four standard deviations below the mean (IQ 39 and lower). The Wechsler tests and other modern intelligence tests do not include a sufficient range to be able to distinguish reliably or validly between individuals with intellectual functioning who score in the lower part of the scale, below IQ 50 (Carlier & Roubertoux, 2014). Severe and profound disorders of intellectual development are therefore differentiated on the basis of the children's age scores on developmental scales or intelligence tests and their adaptive behaviour. The DSM-5 considers IQ to be an approximate expression of the ability to form concepts and to reason, and does not use IQ in the classification of intellectual disabilities. Instead, it describes conceptual, social and practical skills according to the same four levels of intellectual and adaptive functioning as used in ICD-11: mild, moderate, severe and profound. Intelligence tests continue to be important tools for assessing intellectual functioning but in DSM-5, also children who achieve a full-scale IQ of over 70 can meet the criteria for intellectual disability. Schalock and associates (2021) emphasize that intellectual disability is characterized by significant limitations in both intellectual functioning and adaptive behaviour and suggest that the best way to differentiate between different levels is to specify the need for support.

Caution is indicated in assessment of intellectual disabilities, especially for younger children whose test scores tend to be less stable (Schneider et al., 2014). In addition, one cannot use a full-scale IQ as a basis for the diagnosis when the profile is skewed and not all results are

in the low range. In such cases, the mean score may provide a false indication of both what the child masters and what the child is unable to do (Greenspan & Woods, 2014). For example, one 13-year-old girl scored average for her age on the non-verbal subscales but did not master any correct items on the verbal subscales. An IQ in the middle would give too low an estimate of her non-verbal skills and too high an estimate of her verbal skills.

Children with severe intellectual disabilities show a delayed development in most areas and the differences to typically developing children increase with age (Hall et al., 2005). Many show lower tolerance for novelty, complexity and uncertain situations, and have difficulties understanding social and emotional cues (Whitman et al., 1997). The incidence of motor impairment, sensory impairment, epilepsy, autism spectrum disorder, attention deficit hyperactivity disorder and other disorders is often several times higher among children with intellectual disabilities than among children in the general population (Carr & O'Reilly, 2016a, b). Moreover, even lesser visual or auditory problems may have greater consequences for individuals with intellectual disabilities than they have for others. Among those who have the most severe intellectual disabilities, compensating for the loss of vision or hearing may be problematic because eye glasses and hearing aids are easily broken and may cause injury.

A low IQ and poor adaptive abilities do not say all about an individual. Children with intellectual disabilities only share a general difficulty with learning, otherwise they are unique individuals with different aetiologies and developmental backgrounds. Regarding them as a homogeneous group would mask important differences in their possibilities and limitations and their needs for an adapted environment (Leonard & Wen, 2002). The overall score attained on an intelligence test may conceal differences to a far greater extent than reveal them. Even what may be called the ability to learn varies considerably among individuals with the "same" level of intelligence. It is difficult to predict language skills on the basis of the non-verbal intelligence or overall score on an intelligence test. The relationship between language and other cognitive abilities varies with aetiologies such as Down syndrome and Williams syndrome, and with the aspects of language measured, for example vocabulary or grammar (McGregor, 2017). Verbal skills are part of general intelligence tests but should be assessed separately. For individuals who achieve a score of more than 40–50, there is no connection between overall scores and the milestones in language development, that is, the time at which they begin to speak and the time they produce their first word combinations. Among people who achieve an overall IQ score lower than 40–50, it may be difficult, both practically and theoretically, to distinguish between poor language and communication skills and impairments in other cognitive functions. The performance on an intelligence test will depend on the test instructions being understood and this may not always be the case for individuals with poor communication and language skills. Poor language skills also prevent people from learning other abilities that are measured in intelligence tests. There is a clear statistical correlation between IQ and language skills among people with moderate and severe degrees of intellectual disability, but also some individuals with profound intellectual disabilities may develop basic language skills.

Individuals with intellectual disabilities constitute a heterogeneous aetiological group (Heikura et al., 2005). The largest single group with a known aetiology is individuals with Down syndrome. With an incidence of one in 720 live births, they make up about 6–8 percent of children with intellectual disabilities (Presson et al., 2013; Vissers et al., 2016). Compared with children with typical development, children with Down syndrome have a significantly delayed language development (Kent & Vorperian, 2013; Rondal, 2009). In one study, three-year-old children with Down syndrome used an average of 45 words, varying between 0 and 250 words. At the age of five, only one of the children had a mean length of utterance above

1.5 words, which implies that the children produced mainly one-word utterances (Smith & von Tetzchner, 1986). Children with Down syndrome spontaneously use gestures to compensate for lack of words (Bello et al., 2020). The acquisition of spoken language by children with Down syndrome is related to their development in other areas, and the extent to which they are able to interact with their caregivers. The children's participation in social interaction with others, and thus their opportunities for natural language and concept learning, is affected by the fact that they spend more time processing and reacting to sensory impressions than other children, and that they often have such a low level of activity that most of their interaction is controlled by adults (Ryan, 1977).

Other common syndromes involving various degrees of intellectual disability are Rett syndrome, Lesch-Nyhan syndrome, Fragile X syndrome, Williams syndrome, Cornelia de Lange syndrome, Prader-Willi syndrome and Angelman syndrome. In about half the cases, the cause of the intellectual disability is unknown, but new syndromes are constantly being identified (Abbeduto et al., 2019; Savatt & Myers, 2021). In this book, children with Down syndrome are often used to illustrate the category "intellectual disabilities". There are, however, considerable differences between diagnostic groups as well as individual differences among children with the same diagnosis, both with regard to their biological basis and their environment (Thomas et al., 2020). Each child follows a unique developmental pathway.

Owing to the great differences in functional levels and the high incidence of sensory and motor impairments, children with intellectual disabilities may belong to all the three functional groups. Some will belong to the *expressive language group*, others to the *supportive* or *alternative language group*. Many children with Down syndrome have a need for AAC while they learn to speak and thus belong to the language support group. Others continue to have difficulties speaking intelligibly and have a large gap between what they understand and what they can express with spoken language, and thus belong to the expressive language group. A smaller group have very little or no comprehension of spoken language and thus belong to the alternative language group (Clibbens, 2001; Launonen, 2019a). The most common form of AAC for children with Down syndrome is manual signs. Studies of intervention with manual signs, graphic symbols and electronic communication devices with speech output report positive results (de Almeida Barbosa et al., 2018; Foreman & Crews, 1998; Frizelle et al., 2023; Launonen, 2019a). In a study of children with Down syndrome who had early intervention with manual signing, at two years they had an average of 34 manual signs and four spoken words, at three years, an average of 93 manual signs and 17 spoken words, and at four years, an average of 108 signs and 128 spoken words, varying from 3 to 300 words. A comparison group who attended the same kind of early intervention but without manual signs, showed a slower growth of spoken vocabulary than the signing group – and, of course, hardly any manual signs (Launonen, 1996, 2019).

In principle, the aim of AAC intervention for children with intellectual disabilities is – as with children with developmental language disorders – to accelerate the acquisition of speech and increase the quality of interaction in the period before the children begin to speak. At the same time, through the AAC intervention a functional language mode will be secured for those who develop little or no speech, or whose speech remains very difficult to understand.

Autism spectrum disorders

Autism spectrum disorder is a severe neurodevelopmental disorder characterized by deficits in communication and social interaction and repetitive and restricted interests and behaviours (Lord et al., 2020). The core features of the diagnosis have remained stable since the first

description by Kanner (1943) but the diagnostic process has changed somewhat over the years (Happé & Frith, 2020; Volkmar & McPartland, 2014). Earlier subcategories like *infantile autism*, *Asperger syndrome* and *atypical autism* are no longer considered valid. In the most recent diagnostic tools, DSM-5 and ICD-11, "autism spectrum disorder" has become a collective term for a disorder that varies along a dimension in severity and need of help, with possibilities of specifying if the individual has intellectual disabilities or language impairment or is lacking speech. Many individuals with this diagnosis prefer to be called "autistic individual" rather than "individual with autism spectrum disorder" (Tan, 2018). The disorder emerges in childhood but the former requirement that symptoms should be present before the age of three years has been abandoned in the ICD-11 and the DSM-5, since many of the problems of children with autism spectrum disorders and relatively high cognitive and language functioning may not become apparent and the children remain undiagnosed until early school age or later. The defining characteristics of autism spectrum disorder will affect the individual's adaptive functioning, social and societal relations, education, work and quality of life. An autism spectrum diagnosis always implies that the individual needs some help and support, but also positive talent may be found among autistic individuals or individuals with autistic traits, including in art and mathematical abilities (Happé & Frith, 2010).

Initially, autism spectrum disorder was believed to be a rare condition, with an estimated prevalence of 4–6 per 10,000 (Lotter, 1966) but the prevalence has gradually increased to 15 per 1,000 (Baio et al., 2018). The increase in prevalence has been most prominent in the high-functioning group – those without intellectual or language problems that warrant an additional diagnosis (Wolff et al., 2022; Zeidan et al., 2022). The reason for the increase has been the subject of much discussion, and most researchers agree that it partly reflects an expansion of diagnostic criteria, earlier diagnosis, and increasing attention to the high-functioning children within this group and autism spectrum disorder as a lifelong condition. At least twice as many boys as girls have autism (Calderoni, 2023).

There is considerable aetiological heterogeneity among children diagnosed with autism spectrum disorder, in the emergence and developmental trajectory of both autism symptoms and other features (Lord et al., 2015). Researchers emphasize that there is no single explanation of the development of autism spectrum disorder and that there is more than one way for this condition to emerge (Happé et al., 2006). Individual differences are likely to reflect variation in genetic influences (Bishop et al., 2014; Persico & Napolioni, 2013), relevant brain mechanisms (O'Neill et al., 2020), and environmental influences (Emberti Gialloreti et al., 2019; Mandy & Lai, 2016). A diagnosis on the autism spectrum means that the child shows the characteristics that define this diagnosis. Besides these characteristics, the diagnosis says little about the child's functioning, feelings, thinking and behaviours, and how the autistic traits have emerged. The diagnosis alone is not enough to decide an intervention (Thapar et al., 2017).

Children with autism spectrum disorder also show considerable variation in non-verbal intelligence and other abilities (Ankenman et al., 2014; Hughes, 2009). Approximately two-thirds now score within or above the normal range on intelligence tests (IQ above 70) (Shenouda et al., 2023). Some have an even cognitive profile, while others are more skilled in some areas than in others (Wolff et al., 2022). Many autistic children are delayed in the development of joint attention skills and comprehension and use of non-verbal and verbal communication (Landa et al., 2013; Mundy & Bullen, 2022). Lack of joint attention skills is an important early indicator when screening for or diagnosing autism spectrum disorder (Kim & Lord, 2013; Stenberg et al., 2014). Autistic infants and children typically have poor command of gestures and their gestures may be difficult to understand (Mishra et al., 2021; Sarriá et al., 1996; Wu et al., 2024). This makes it difficult to establish joint attention and

create a shared context. However, they may look at another person in a seemingly demanding way, lead the person by the hand to something and then indicate by reaching or focused staring what they want the other person to give them or do. Older children and adolescents with limited speech may use deictic and affirming or rejecting gestures to supplement their limited speech (Valle et al., 2021).

Language skills vary from little communicative ability to advanced language skills. Some lack speech, while others talk incessantly (Rapin et al., 2009). Some autistic children understand and produce long and complex sentences but may have problems understanding when and how to use language. A considerable minority of autistic children show severe delays in speech development or fail to develop spoken language at all, even if they grow up in an adequate language environment and receive speech therapy. Autistic children who use less than three spoken words are often classified as "lacking speech" (Norrelgen et al., 2015). Children who are classified as "minimally verbal" may have as much as 30 spoken words and fixed phrases that they use communicatively (Tager-Flusberg & Kasari, 2013). Their rate of spoken language is usually very low and may include scripted phrases that have been extensively trained (such as "I want X"). Moreover, their spoken words or phrases are often restricted to particular contexts and may only be used for one or two communicative functions – typically trained requests or greetings with familiar adults. Some minimally verbal children may also use echolalic or stereotyped language without any evident communicative function. Many of these children are not only delayed but persist in having problems expressing themselves in speech. Anderson and associates (2007) found that nearly 30 percent of nine-year-olds who had been diagnosed with autism spectrum disorder before the age of three used less than five spoken words. In a Norwegian survey of 64 autistic children and adolescents, there was little evidence of progress in the quality of language from preschool age to early adulthood. The few exceptions to this rule were children who had been given systematic manual sign teaching (Kvale et al., 1992).

In the past, it was usual to say that about half of adults with autism spectrum disorder lacked functional speech. Today this number is significantly reduced and estimated at about 20 percent. About 30 percent remain minimally verbal (Koegel et al., 2019). However, due to the increased prevalence of autism spectrum disorder, the actual number of children without functional speech is still increasing. Most of the autistic children who learn manual signs or graphic symbols go on to acquire spoken words. Their first words typically correspond to the signs or symbols they have learned, indicating that these supported their speech development. A significant proportion of autistic children do not understand spoken language and never begin to speak. A graphic or manual communication system will become their main form of communication and alternative language. Autistic individuals may thus belong to any of the three functional groups.

Language comprehension among autistic individuals who lack speech or are minimally verbal varies: some have much better comprehension than their limited expression of spoken language, while others have little or no comprehension of spoken language (Rapin et al., 2009). Also intellectual abilities differ in this subgroup and some score in the normal range on non-verbal tests (Light et al., 1998; Schaeffer et al., 2023). Individuals who do not understand language may be considered non-verbal (without language), while individuals with little or no speech but some comprehension of spoken language are verbal but *non-vocal* because they understand but are unable to produce expressive language. All these groups may benefit from intervention with AAC. Although their linguistic means are not comparable to the spoken language of individuals with typical development, intervention with manual signs or graphic symbols can improve their communication skills significantly, and often can also improve

their spoken language (Dunst et al., 2011; Schlosser & Wendt, 2008). Even children with no comprehension of spoken language may learn to use manual signs or graphic symbols to communicate (von Tetzchner et al., 2004). Developmentally, the distinction between "non-verbal" and "preverbal" is important – "pre-verbal" means that the child is on the way to language, while "non-verbal" means that the child will not develop language (Tager-Flusberg & Kasari, 2013). However, they may not be easy to distinguish at an early stage. Most children with autism spectrum disorder who lacked verbal means in the early years may turn out to have been pre-verbal, because they later developed comprehension and use of spoken or alternative language forms.

Many autistic children react atypically to sensory impressions. Some do not react visibly to voices and may be suspected of being deaf. Even among cognitively high-functioning individuals with autism spectrum disorder, it can be difficult to know whether they are paying attention when being spoken to and interested in what is being said. Some are oversensitive to sounds: ordinary sounds may be troublesome and sometimes painful for them, especially in periods when they are stressed (Leekam et al., 2007; Robertson & Baron-Cohen, 2017).

A core characteristic of individuals with autism spectrum disorder is negative reactions – such as anger or anxiety – to uncertainty, such as when their daily routines are broken or changed unexpectedly (Helverschou & Martinsen, 2011; Jenkinson et al., 2020). They need predictability and structured teaching and visual support, which were introduced in the early programme Treatment and Education of Autistic and Related Communication-Handicapped Children, TEACCH (Mesibov & Shea, 2010; Mesibov et al., 2004), and have become central elements in most intervention programmes (see Chapter 5). Moreover, many autistic individuals have limited ability to occupy themselves. They may take part in a limited range of activities and carry on performing those same activities for long periods of the day over months and years. They may wander around aimlessly, twirl and spin things round like a whirligig, fill a basin with water, leaf through books, turn lights on and off, tap objects and listen to music, and show little or no interest in ordinary toys favoured by children with typical development. The structured approach of TEACCH may be useful for involving autistic individuals in activities (Park & Kim, 2018). Closely linked to the lack of self-initiated activities are the stereotypies and repetitive behaviours that are a core diagnostic feature. These include sitting and rocking, flipping with their fingers or objects they are holding, "filtering" light through the fingers, twining hair, waving arms, banging the head against objects and twisting the body, arms or hands into unusual positions. When frequent, such behaviours may be considered challenging by people in the environment (Goldman et al., 2009; Melo et al., 2020). Hence, for children with autism spectrum disorder, an important aim of AAC intervention is to guide them to take more part in more interactive and culturally acceptable activities.

For more than 50 years, AAC has been part of autism intervention. Most autistic individuals can learn both manual signs and graphic symbols. Until recently, manual signs have been the most common form of AAC for this group. Many studies have documented that autistic individuals who are without speech or are minimally verbal can learn to use manual signs (Bonvillian, 2019; Schwartz & Nye, 2006; Tan et al., 2014; von Tetzchner, 1984b; Webster et al., 1973, 2016). One early review includes 20 studies with more than 100 autistic individuals with little or no speech, aged 3½ to 23 years. About half of them had received speech training based on applied behaviour analysis without success prior to the sign intervention. All of them had learned some manual signs and the size of their vocabularies varied from 5 to 350 manual signs (Bonvillian et al., 1983). A small group of children do less well with graphic symbols and better with manual signs (Tincani, 2004; van der Meer et al., 2014). Manual signs have the advantage that they are produced with the child's hands, while the child

needs to carry the graphic symbolsaround. Other autistic children do better with graphic symbols (Deich & Hodges, 1977; von Tetzchner, 2019b). It is possible that for this subgroup, the static images of graphic symbols are easier to perceive and attribute meaning to than the movements of signs. Another advantage is that graphic symbols can be used together with electronic communication devices, which seems to give positive results for many children (van der Meer et al., 2014).

In the literature on AAC for autistic children, it sometimes may seem as if the Picture Exchange Communication System, PECS (Bondy & Frost, 1998, 2002), is the only training method used for this group. Although PECS's practice of handing over graphic symbols may be useful in the early phases – and is also used in other programmes (see p. 49) – this adult-oriented and reinforcement-based approach seems somewhat old-fashioned and often has limited results (Howlin et al., 2007; Logan et al., 2017). Autistic children may benefit from intervention with both manual signs and graphic symbols and from a variety of intervention strategies (see Chapters 5 and 6).

Experiences with teaching autistic children to use manual signs or graphic symbols are unequivocally positive, including those where training with manual signs or graphic symbols was implemented to improve the communication of children who had some speech. Not all autistic individuals acquired many manual signs or graphic symbols, but most of them learned a least some signs or symbols, often in a short space of time (Bonvillian, 2019; Deich & Hodges, 1977; Holyfield et al., 2017; Lorah et al., 2022; Nunes, 2008; Schaeffer et al., 1994; Schlosser & Wendt, 2008). Some exceptional individuals have a vocabulary of several hundred manual signs or graphic symbols and spontaneously use long sentences. It seems realistic to assume that even the cognitively lowest-functioning autistic individuals will be able to acquire spontaneous use of between five and ten manual signs or graphic symbols during one year's intervention. This may seem like a modest goal but even such a limited improvement in the individual's capacity for self-expression and understanding of others can have a great significance for everyday well-being, provide opportunities to learn social and practical skills and improve the general quality of life. And, although their initial development may be slow, most individuals in this very low-functioning subgroup continue to increase their vocabulary.

Rett syndrome

Individuals who have multiple impairments and profound communication disorders are at risk of being left out and not offered communication intervention. This group is here represented by girls and women with Rett syndrome, because it is the second most prevalent genetic condition implying severe or profound intellectual disabilities after Down syndrome. Rett syndrome is a neurological disorder that mainly affects girls, with a prevalence of about one in 20,000 births, that is, one in every 10,000 girls (Fu et al., 2020; Hagberg & Hagberg, 1997). In classic Rett syndrome, development is seemingly normal until the age of 6–18 months, but in retrospect it may appear as though the girls were more passive than other infants before the disease became apparent. At the age of 6–18 months, they begin to lose previously acquired skills. The circumference of the head is normal at birth but growth slows, and over time the circumference becomes below the normal average (Neul et al., 2010; Sandweiss et al., 2020). Epilepsy is common and may appear at any age (Henriksen et al., 2018). A number of girls do

not fulfil all the criteria for classic Rett syndrome but are still more similar to Rett syndrome than to other known conditions and are considered variants of the same syndrome or set of symptoms, including a congenital variant, an early seizure variant and a preserved speech variant (Hagberg & Skjeldal, 1994; Neul et al., 2010).

Rett syndrome is mainly related to mutations in MeCP2, a regulating gene on the X chromosome, but the syndrome is also associated with several other genes and not all individuals with a MeCP2 mutation show the features of Rett syndrome (Collins & Neul, 2022; Ehrhart et al., 2018). It is the course of development that determines the diagnosis, and a gene test alone cannot be used to determine if a girl has Rett syndrome (Chelly et al., 2006; Percy et al., 2018). The course of development varies considerably and not all of the characteristics occur to the same extent among all girls with Rett syndrome. It can be difficult to give a reliable early diagnosis, and many girls with Rett syndrome have received a different diagnosis prior to the Rett diagnosis (Davis et al., 2023). The typical age of diagnosis is two to four years, but some girls are diagnosed much later (Vilvarajan et al., 2023). Life expectancy is somewhat shorter than among women in the general population, but 70 percent will be older than 50 years and some reach more than 80 years old (Henriksen et al., 2020; Tarquinio et al., 2015).

During the first years of the disease, hand control deteriorates. Fine motor skills worsen and gradually the girls are no longer able to, for example, use a pincer grip to pick up things. One result of the girls' steadily deteriorating control over their hands is that they lose the ability to play with and manipulate objects. They may clutch at things with a "pawing" movement and grasp objects with their whole hand. It becomes difficult for them to get hold of things. They drop objects easily and if an object is placed in a girl's hands, it is likely to just slide through. This also means that girls and women with Rett syndrome have increasing problems occupying themselves and doing things on their own initiative, and thus become more dependent on others.

Most girls with Rett syndrome – though not all – develop a special hand stereotypy, where they rub their hands in a sort of handwashing movements, sometimes most of the day. Many also open and close their hands almost incessantly. Stereotypical handwashing movements are common also among other children with intellectual disabilities or autism spectrum disorder, but not to the extent that is typically found among girls with Rett syndrome. The handwashing movements have therefore become a "trademark" for the girls.

Rett syndrome

A core feature of Rett syndrome is dyspraxia: reduced ability to perform voluntary actions. It is apparent in the learning of new skills as well as in carrying out actions that the girls are familiar with. Even starting to walk or lifting a leg to climb stairs can take a long time, and they may need help in getting started. Dyspraxia increases with excitement, so when motivation increases, actions become more difficult to perform. It is commonly noted that girls with Rett syndrome function best in tranquil surroundings where they are under little pressure. Intervention is therefore aimed at helping the girls to perform actions, thereby lessening their frustration.

Girls with Rett syndrome appear severely intellectually disabled and the deceleration of head growth and low brain weight provide support for this impression (Armstrong, 2001; Pohodich & Zoghbi, 2015). Attempts to assess cognitive functions have shown that most girls and women with Rett syndrome – without regard to their age when tested – are not able to perform more advanced tasks than seen in one-year-olds with typical development and many of them obtain even lower age scores (Cass et al., 2003; Garber & Veydt, 1990; Olsson & Rett, 1987, 1990; Woodyatt & Ozanne, 1992, 1993). Some girls and women show better functioning. Interpretations of test results, however, should take into account that assessment of this group is extremely difficult and it is not at all clear which categories are best suited for describing the development of cognitive functions in girls and women with Rett syndrome (Berger-Sweeney, 2011; Byiers & Symons, 2012). Assessment of cognitive skills usually applies tasks that require hand use, such as building block patterns, reaching for hidden objects, moving objects and other manipulative skills, but the majority of girls and women with Rett syndrome have almost no functional use of the hands. It is possible to use the preferential looking method (Rose et al., 2013; von Tetzchner et al., 1996) or gaze technology to overcome the girls' lack of hand use (Ahonniska-Assa et al., 2018; Kurmanaviciute & Stadskleiv, 2017). However, it is important to distinguish between interpreting the girl's eye gaze as an index of attention and interest and regarding the gaze as a means of pointing. Pointing is a deictic gesture with communicative intent whether it is performed with the index finger, the eye or another body part (Tomasello et al., 2007). The intense staring observed in many girls with Rett syndrome may reflect interest but not necessarily communicative intent and an attempt to influence the mind of another (Sigafoos et al., 2011; von Tetzchner, 1997b; von Tetzchner et al., 1996; Woodyatt & Ozanne, 1992). One study found that when presented with two items, most girls with Rett syndrome looked longer at one of the items but they rarely displayed other behaviours indicative of a communicative intention (Urbanowicz et al., 2018).

Most girls and women with Rett syndrome never speak after the onset of the disease. They have no use of words at all and would be dependent on AAC to express themselves. If they had any words prior to the onset of the disease, these are usually lost (von Tetzchner et al., 1996; Uchino et al., 2001). The exception is the small group with the preserved speech variant but even in this group, speech is not normal, and its functionality varies considerably (Marschik et al., 2012; Renieri et al., 2009). In most cases, language comprehension appears to be absent or severely limited, although it should be noted that it is difficult for people with severe dyspraxia and great difficulty in expressing themselves, to show what they understand, and variation in comprehension may be wider than suggested by earlier studies (Wandin, 2020). Girls and women with Rett syndrome have a restricted behavioural repertoire but for those who can walk, the location they tend to move to might be used to infer their interests and preferences. They may touch or look at objects, or move towards a person, an object or a particular location. Movements often appear random but systematic observation may indicate that they are not (Sharpe, 1992). However, these movements may indicate *action*

intentions rather than *communicative intentions*. Most girls with Rett syndrome seem unable to direct or follow the attention of another person and engage in joint attention (von Tetzchner, 2006). Without joint attention skills, language acquisition will be impossible or extremely difficult (see p. 160) and most girls and women with Rett syndrome appear non-verbal and belong to the *alternative language group*.

There are some descriptive reports of aided communication intervention in girls with Rett syndrome (Sigafoos et al., 2011, 2023; Simacek et al., 2016; von Tetzchner, 1997b; Urbanowicz et al., 2018). Interventions have typically aimed to help the girl choose between two objects or activities. The choice is interpreted on the basis of which item the girl looks at and hence may not imply a communicative intention but rather an interest, and thus attention rather than joint attention.

However, even if the girl understands the use of aided communication, performance is not without problems. A simple motor movement such as pointing may be difficult for girls with Rett syndrome. If their attention is concentrated on the action, in this case the pointing, this may exacerbate the dyspraxia. When attempting to teach a girl to indicate an object, picture or graphic symbol, the teacher usually starts with the hands or the eyes. In order to reduce the effect of dyspraxia, it is important not to direct the girl's attention towards the movement itself, but rather towards the object or graphic symbol. This is also true when one attempts to assess the girl's preferences through their attentional focus. There are descriptions of gaze dyspraxia in girls with Rett syndrome, which may increase their difficulties and hinder social interaction with people in the environment. Moreover, it is vital to allow girls and women with Rett syndrome the time they need for visual and mental processing, even if this may take a long time. The choice of strategies should take into account their need for time to initiate contact and process and react to people and events in the environment (von Tetzchner, 1997b; von Tetzchner et al., 1996; Urbanowicz et al., 2018).

Some girls with Rett syndrome are able to touch or hit an object for a long time after they have lost most of the functional motor skills in the hand. A common intervention strategy is to guide the girl to hit a switch, which activates a device that produces a digitized word or phrase (Simacek et al., 2016). However, there are observations that girls with Rett syndrome have reacted positively to producing digitized speech, such as hitting a switch to produce '*chocolate milk*' or '*biscuit*' (von Tetzchner & Øien, 1989), but without any apparent expectations – for example looking for the object – indicating a communicative intent. Girls with Rett syndrome have also been guided to hit a switch to produce music but again this does not have to imply a communicative intent. Many girls with Rett syndrome are reported to like music but hitting a switch that starts the music does not require the intent to ask another person for music.

It is possible that some girls with classic Rett syndrome have a rudimentary understanding of spoken language. They may have established associations between some objects and word forms (von Tetzchner et al., 2002). This may suggest that some girls in this group – despite their limited understanding of language – have a gap between comprehension and expression and therefore may belong to the *expressive language group*. However, there is evidence that in typical development, the early object-word-relations are associative without understanding of the referential function of words (Werker, 2018a, b). Most girls and women with Rett syndrome seem unable to direct the attention of another person and establish joint attention (von Tetzchner, 2006). Without an ability to initiate and respond to joint attention, acquisition of referential language would be impossible or extremely difficult.

There are some anecdotal accounts of girls laughing at the right moment, showing interest when a person is mentioned, and so forth. Isolated outbursts of spoken words or sentences

have been described for some girls with Rett syndrome who belonged to the preserved speech variant, usually when they were febrile or excited about something, as in these examples:

> A girl with Rett syndrome was in town with her father. They stood for a long time waiting at a pedestrian crossing for the "red man" to change to green. Her father talked while the girl stared in fascination at the traffic light. During the evening meal that same evening the girl suddenly said *Red man* (Lindberg, 1987, p. 89).
>
> A girl with Rett syndrome had her grandfather to stay. When he came down to eat breakfast, she said clearly *Hi Granddad!* (Lindberg, 1987, p. 90).

However, it is difficult to use such events clinically. These may be examples of delayed imitation without communicative intent. They are single and unique events, and are not usually followed by similar events. They have no positive prognostic value and should not be taken as a sign of emerging speech (von Tetzchner, 1997b).

When communicative intentions appear to be lacking or are uncertain, which is common in girls with Rett syndrome, intervention may involve structured over-interpretation, which later may be extended to structured total communication (see p. 172). The aim of these strategies is to help the girls gain control over their environment and provide them with possibilities for indicating communicative intentions or possible interests, needs and preferences. Because of their limited use of the hands, manual signs are not suitable. Aided communication is therefore a natural choice, including objects, photographs or graphic symbols and different intervention strategies. Similar to other parents of children with severe disabilities, parents of girls with Rett syndrome may need help and guidance to see their daughter's preferences and interests, and to believe in what they are doing. This is also true for professionals who have little or no experience in working with girls or women in this group. Further, preferences and interests may change over time, for example in music taste. It is therefore necessary to observe girls and women with Rett syndrome and make new assessments regularly, although not very often.

For many girls and women with Rett syndrome, intervention with structured over-interpretation and total communication will not lead to spontaneous and independent communication. These strategies will still be useful for the girls and their families, because they may make a foundation for developing a shared lifestyle. Systematic over-interpretation may lead to a more predictable and understandable environment for the girls, and people in the environment may learn how they should best react in different situations. Even if a girl with Rett syndrome does not learn to express herself, this does not mean that she has not learned something. Over-interpretation as a part of the way of life implies creating a stable and predictable environment. Learning in both the girl and her parents is implicit in this approach (see Sameroff, 2009). Structured over-interpretation helps in maintaining what the girl has learned about routines and regularities in her environment, and may contribute to the girl's learning to influence the environment in other ways.

Some common issues related to communication intervention with individuals who have severe communication disorders

A number of problems often occur in intervention for individuals with severe communication disorders. These problems may be related to the fact that they need time to learn and have difficulties transferring acquired skills and knowledge to new situations, and that many

individuals with severe difficulties in communicating have become passive or dependent on others and may show behaviour disorders.

Learning takes time

One of the most common barriers in AAC intervention is that teaching and adaptation can be very time-consuming. Some children with very severe communication disabilities may take years to learn even seemingly simple communication and language skills, especially those with severe motor impairments and sub-groups of children and adolescents with intellectual disabilities and autism spectrum disorder.

Early short-term gains – which are most often reported in the research literature – may not reflect the potential long-term achievements. However, some professionals may take the child's progress or lack of progress as a measure of their own success, making them set unrealistic intervention goals and become impatient to see positive achievements. This may result in the intervention ending too early or other methods being tried instead. It is always important to evaluate the intervention strategies used (see Chapter 4) but this requires feasible short-term and long-term goals and that the strategies are implemented for long enough.

The length of time needed for intervention also has other consequences. One indirect consequence is the fact that the individuals who need the longest time to learn are also those who are most prone to experience discontinuities in the intervention (Smith-Lewis, 1994). They may have to change teachers or school, and the new teachers may have insufficient experience and knowledge of the students' understanding and capabilities. The new teachers may try to teach these students something they already know, or new ways of expressing things they can already express. They may not know which strategies have been tried and how the earlier teaching has been organized, or they may disregard AAC altogether. The result may be a lack of progress in learning and established skills may not be responded to and hence forgotten or "unlearned". Discontinuities and changes in an individual's intervention routines may cause frustration and lead to behavioural problems, which in turn will make the teaching and learning situation even worse.

There are examples where years of intervention for people with autism spectrum disorder and intellectual disabilities have been rendered worthless as the result of a change in, or the loss of, an educational programme (Kollinzas, 1983). The negative consequences are further aggravated by the fact that there is a significant risk that the skills acquired by the individuals with the lowest functioning will disappear altogether if intervention is not continued.

Generalization

A significant problem in AAC intervention is that communication and language skills are often taught in in one-to-one situations and the AAC skills are not transferred to other settings (see Chapter 5). For example, from the beginning, a lack of generalization from individual teaching sessions to everyday life has been a major problem in programmes for autistic children with intellectual disabilities based on applied behaviour analysis (Schreibman et al., 2015). A lack of communicative access and limited communicative participation in many everyday situations also make generalization of communication skills to settings outside the teaching situation a problem for individuals with age-typical cognitive skills (Lund & Light, 2007; von Tetzchner et al., 2018). When the problems of transferring knowledge and skills to new situations are seen in relation to the fact that the intervention takes a long time, it is

important that, in so far as it is practical, the teaching of communication and language takes place in everyday situations where one can be sure that the skills being taught will be useful for the individual (see Chapter 5 and 6). This further implies that time should be spent assessing the environment and finding situations where communication and language is functional and suitable for both teaching purposes and spontaneous everyday use. If teaching is planned in special sessions, it is important that there is a plan for transferring new skills to the different situations where they may be relevant. In line with a transactional model of development (Sameroff & Fiese, 2000), intervention should be integrated into the child's everyday life and parent training and involvement are necessary elements of this approach, together with teacher training and follow up and peer guidance in preschool and school (see Chapter 12).

Learned passivity and dependence on others

Early language intervention implies giving the child help and guidance. This may be essential but help and guidance may also represent a problem. Children who use AAC often become dependent on the help and may not be able to use their skills spontaneously. For example, young aided communicators do not have their means of independent communication available in many situations (von Tetzchner et al., 2018).

The dependence associated with language intervention is related to the learned passivity and dependence on others found in all groups in need of AAC. Many of the children who use AAC depend on others to interpret their utterances and help them formulate a coherent message. Early communication with limited expressive means may create habits and ways of adapting to communication that may be difficult to alter when a child or adolescent is later provided with new means of communication to express themselves. They may lack initiative, and it is not uncommon that children who have delayed language development ask their parents to speak for them when strangers approach them, even after their speech or AAC is well understood by others. For example, among autistic children who are unable to speak, the incidence of communicative episodes is low in comparison with other children, and it is particularly communication initiated by the children that is lacking. They may answer only when spoken to by others or take the "initiative" only after they have been prompted to do so. Even though it is not intended by the persons who plan the intervention, adult-centred teaching may contribute to increasing the child's dependence.

Behavioural disorders

Limited communication and language skills may impact all aspects of life. Individuals belonging to all the main diagnostic groups who have limited speech have an increased prevalence of emotional and behavioural disorders. They experience smaller and larger frustrating situations and life events, have fewer means for managing ordinary hindrances and may react to a difficult life situation with behavioural disorders and challenging behaviour (von Tetzchner, 2021a; von Tetzchner et al., 2019). They may attack others, destroy property, shout loudly, hit themselves or show intense repetitive behaviours. In severe instances, these actions may represent considerable risk to the health of the individual and others (Didden et al., 2012; Emerson & Einfeld, 2011; Fodstad et al., 2012).

Many factors may contribute to the development of challenging behaviour (see p. 128). It is often possible to demonstrate a relationship between limited communication skills and behaviour problems, and intervention leading to improvement in communication skills is

typically accompanied by a reduction in behaviour problems (Carr et al., 1994; Durand & Moskowitz, 2019). The primary reason for this improvement is probably that the individuals have become more proficient in gaining the attention of others to relay their wishes, problems and ideas, and thus perceive the world as more manageable and less unpredictable or threatening. They therefore have fewer experiences that lead to frustration, despair and anger. The individual may, for example, be able to express wishes to go out, get a break, obtain something, be comforted, chat, visit somebody, be left alone, and so forth (see p. 199). When the individual develops a larger communicative repertoire, he or she will have fewer negative experiences (von Tetzchner, 2004). However, communication intervention does not always lead to positive development unless the children find the training meaningful (Koegel et al., 1992). Training that does not make sense to the individual – for example, if the individual does not understand the functions of the actions he or she is required to perform – may in fact lead to an increase in challenging behaviour (Carr et al., 1996).

The prevalence of behaviour problems sometimes increases temporarily in the early phases of communication intervention. The individual may use the new skills to take very frequent communicative initiatives or refuse to participate in certain activities. As the individual's communicative competence increases further, negotiation becomes easier and behaviour regulation and self-regulation are improved. The important point is that behaviour problems or challenging behaviour should never be regarded as an obstacle to communication and language intervention, but rather as a positive sign that the individual has something to communicate but does not know how to do it in an intelligible manner. The communication intervention is thus very much needed.

Chapter 4

Assessment

Assessment is a foundation of all AAC interventions. The children, adolescents and adults who may need alternative means of communication are of all ages and differ in motor, perceptual, cognitive, communicative and social skills and abilities which constitute the basis for development of communication and language. Consequently, there will be large variability regarding type and scope of intervention. Optimal intervention for individuals with diverse diagnoses belonging to the three main groups in need of AAC (see Chapter 3) depends on a thorough assessment of both the individual's functioning and the physical and social environment.

The main aims of assessment are to reveal if an individual needs intervention and if it is decided that AAC is needed, what kind of AAC and intervention may be needed. The assessment is typically multi-disciplinary, covers many domains, utilizes a variety of methods, and may include both standard assessments and methods developed especially for assessing individuals who may need AAC. The assessments target different aspects of the individual's functioning and the environment, and how they relate to each other, but should be seen together and interpreted as a whole. The AAC pyramid presented below is a framework for guiding the process from identification to follow-up and new assessments (Stadskleiv, 2015).

This chapter discusses assessment in general but has a particular focus on assessment of individuals with disabilities that may make assessment difficult. They include younger and older individuals with severe cognitive impairments but also individuals with severe motor disabilities with cognitive skills as expected for their age. When individuals who may need AAC have better motor skills or cognitive abilities closer to the normal range, it is possible to apply most ordinary assessment methods.

The Individual Habilitation Plan is an important tool for "translating" assessment results into intervention that is adapted to the limitations and possibilities of the individual (Hesselberg & von Tetzchner, 2016). A plan for assessment and allocation of responsibility for the different parts of the assessment and the intervention are core features of the Individual Habilitation Plan.

The aims of AAC intervention are to promote the development of communication and language in individuals with little or no speech and enable them to be understood, understand others and communicate with different people (adults and children) in diverse settings and about a variety of topics physical, emotional and social needs, experiences, expectations, interests, ideas and so forth. Communication partners, settings and topics will vary from individual to individual, and change over time. The results of the initial assessment are the basis for deciding where to start and which skills, activities and situations should be focused on

DOI: 10.4324/9781003387633-5

first. Following this, regular assessments are needed to monitor developments in cognition, AAC competence and social participation.

Also individuals with the most extensive and complex disabilities tend to show changes in competence and may require AAC adaptations, adjustment of the environment and support throughout their lives (García et al., 2020; Iacono et al., 2019; Smith et al., 2020). This means that they need regular, although not always frequent, assessments throughout adult life in order to make sure that the adaptations and support are appropriate and reflect their current state, learning opportunities and life situation.

Most individuals who develop AAC require other forms of intervention, especially those with the more pervasive disabilities. This means that assessment must go beyond what is needed for the provision of AAC and that the results of the AAC assessment should be seen together with results of other assessments. The sum of the intervention measures that follow from the assessments should provide individuals with little or no speech with the best quality of life possible. Early assessment and assessment in childhood and adolescence are important for AAC development, but development and learning continue into adulthood and hence so does the need for assessment. The aim is that adults with developmental disorders using AAC should have the life-qualities that most adults take for granted: a home of their own, a job – or at least meaningful occupation – interesting leisure time and pleasure in the company of others, with family and carers but also with friends and romantic relations when possible. They should feel that they are agents in their own life and a sense of self-respect. A further aim of AAC assessment is to prevent individuals who need AAC losing these life-qualities.

Assessment and prediction

In evidence-based assessment, broad knowledge from theory, research and practical experience is used to decide the assessment procedures (Hunsley & Mash, 2007; Youngstrom et al., 2017). The basic assumption is that there are relations between the individuals' current characteristics and their responses to intervention measures. Professionals assess individual and environmental features that have been found to indicate that children may be likely – or not likely – to develop certain impaired functions. The assessment results are used to predict the likely future functioning of the child, both without intervention and with the implementation of certain intervention measures. Intervention is thus based on: (1) the prediction that the child's developmental trajectory will deviate from typical development if the environment remains the same without any special education or adaptation, and (2) the prediction that the child's development trajectory will be influenced in particular ways through intervention. These predictions about future functioning are a necessary basis for evaluating the effects of intervention measures. They may be correct or incorrect but they allow professionals to critically evaluate the possible effects of the intervention (Dombrowski et al., 2022).

The AAC Pyramid: A framework for assessment and follow-up

The AAC Pyramid of assessment (Figure 4.1) depicts the assessment process of individuals who use or may need AAC (Stadskleiv, 2015). Having early identification as the foundation of the pyramid highlights the importance of identifying a possible need for AAC and starting AAC intervention as early as possible. What "early" means will differ depending on the reasons for the need. For congenital conditions where the risk of speech impairment is well

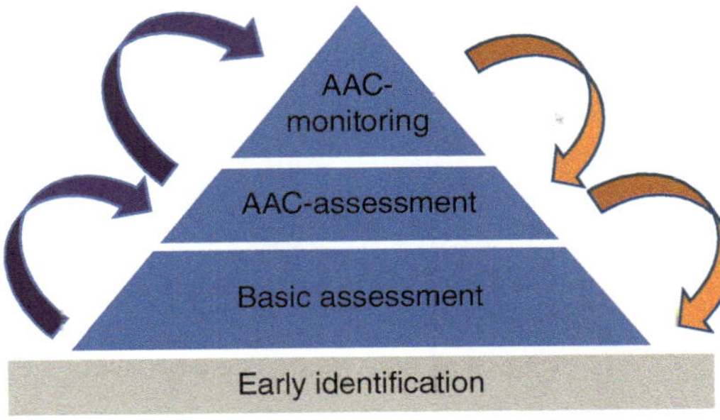

Figure 4.1 The AAC Pyramid of assessment.

known, "early" might mean starting intervention routinely in the first year of life, such as with Down syndrome or severe dyskinetic cerebral palsy, or after the child shows atypical developmental features. For acquired conditions, intervention should start as soon as the individual has sustained an injury or illness that implies a temporary or permanent need for AAC. For children and adolescents with degenerative conditions, AAC intervention might start while the individual still has speech, as the ability to learn new skills will also become negatively affected as the disease progresses (Tøssebro et al., 2019). Recognition of a possible need for AAC should elicit a comprehensive *Basic Assessment*, which will lay the basis for an *AAC Assessment*. This assessment evaluates the individual's communication skills and the potential usefulness of different AAC modes and intervention strategies. Through *AAC Monitoring*, with follow-up over time, the individual's comprehension and use of AAC are assessed, the intervention measures are evaluated and all or some of the earlier assessments are repeated. *AAC Monitoring* is important for all individuals who use AAC but particularly for children who need regular adaptations of their AAC interventions as they develop, learn new skills and take part in new social and societal activities.

The *Basic Assessment* includes the individual's daily functioning, somatic factors, motor functioning, perception, spoken language and cognition, as well as the family's need for support. Diagnostic evaluations regarding functioning and probable aetiology are often part of the basic assessment. For children with early acquired conditions due to disease or accident, the basic assessment may also include information about the child's functioning prior to the onset of the disease or the accident.

The *AAC Assessment* is informed by observations and builds on the results from the basic assessment. For example, information about motor and perceptual skills will contribute to determining what mode of communication that may be best suited for the individual. The *AAC Assessment* comprises communication mode, complexity of communication, ways of accessing communication aids and the comprehension and use of AAC.

AAC Monitoring is part of a general plan for follow-up, such as an Individual Habilitation Plan, which details all areas of intervention and the allocation of responsibility for different parts of the intervention. Regular meetings, where the family and professionals discuss and evaluate the intervention measures and the progress of the individual, are important for planning and evaluating transitions, for example from preschool to school, from primary to secondary education, or from the family home to a sheltered residence.

Assessment methods

There are various methods used in assessment, such as tests, classification schemas, checklists, interviews, questionnaires and observations, and each has benefits and drawbacks when used for assessing the functioning of individuals who develop AAC and relevant environmental factors. The choice of methods depends on what one needs to know, the motor, sensory, cognitive and communicative functioning of the individual, the formal skills of potential assessors and the availability of relevant instruments. One should not use instruments for the mere sake of assessment or habit, but because the information that may be gained from the instrument is considered necessary. For example, structured testing may provide information that is useful for determining the form and content of communication and language intervention, but before applying a particular instrument, it is still a good rule to make explicit how the test results will be utilized and how different results may influence the intervention plan. The results of assessments should have the potential to make a difference.

It is important to use methods that are appropriate culturally and linguistically, and for which the professionals who are doing the assessment have the necessary professional qualifications and certifications. National norms are important, especially for assessment of language skills. The use of tests without appropriate national norms is considered a breach of professional ethical conduct (Leach & Oakland, 2007). When planning an assessment, it may become clear to the assessor that relevant instruments with proper standardization are lacking.

A large number of tests, questionnaires and checklists exist and only a few commonly used instruments are mentioned in this chapter. Most of them are standardized in Great Britain or the USA; they may function as inspiration and be suggestive of the kind of information one can obtain with existing instruments. However, they should be substituted with similar instruments which have been standardized to the local language whenever possible. Some developmental scales for younger children and non-verbal tests may be possible to use across cultures but even then, norms should be used with care. On the other hand, many individuals with autism spectrum disorder and intellectual disabilities function so obviously different from their peers that the norms and questions about the magnitude of these differences are of little significance. The aim of the assessment is, first and foremost, to discover which abilities and skills the individual has and to build on these in the intervention.

Tests

A test is a set of tasks and a manual with a clear description of the population that the test is appropriate for and how the tasks should be administered (Roy & Chiat, 2022). Formal tests, also referred to as *standardized* tests, are normed. Norms mean that the tasks have been administered to a large representative sample of the population with whom it will be used, and the results of the standardization indicate what to expect at different ages (Sherman et al., 2022). Tests are usually standardized on a sample of children, adolescents or adults with typical development only (Neisworth & Bagnato, 2004).

Formal tests will have varying value in an assessment, depending on the individual who is assessed. Tests have the advantage that one knows the distribution of scores among typically developing individuals. This applies to both general intelligence tests and tests of specific abilities, such as language comprehension, memory span or gross motor skills. However, a

number of conditions may limit the use of ordinary tests with individuals who may need AAC. Typical test items require that the individual can answers questions, follow instructions, draw figures, construct patterns with blocks or repeat sequences of digits. This may imply that the individual can see, hear, understand spoken instructions and speak, as well as manipulate blocks or other objects. Many test items are scored according to time used or must be completed within a time limit, and even minor motor impairments may influence the time use. The task requirements may imply that the tests cannot be administered in the prescribed manner when assessing individuals with disorders of comprehension, motor impairments or reduced vision or hearing.

Testing must always take the individual's skills and abilities into consideration. Although tests are designed to be suitable for most individuals within a particular age range, it may still be necessary to accommodate or modify the test situation and test material to the abilities of the individual (Sireci & O'Riordan, 2020). For example, very few tests are designed for use with individuals who have severe motor impairments. In order to use the tests with these groups, testing procedures may have to be changed considerably: the instruction, the presentation method and what kind of answers that are required (Stadskleiv et al., 2022). The norms are based on the test being administered in the prescribed manner (Yin Foo et al., 2013). Testing with adapted procedures may involve modifications that imply that the test's norms cannot be applied and that the result cannot be interpreted in the ordinary manner (Sireci & O'Riordan, 2020). However, tests based on multiple choice without a time limit that only require pointing can be accommodated. When an individual is not able to point with a finger, others means of pointing or scanning may be used. For example, pointing may performed using the whole hand or eye-gaze. Scanning can be either with switches on a computer or partner assisted. In partner-assisted scanning the tester indicates each answer option in a systematic manner, which the individual then accepts or rejects (see p. 47). Studies have found that if only the answer mode is changed, and no other aspects of the test procedure, this accommodation will not influence test results (Fiske et al., 2020; Kurmanaviciute & Stadskleiv, 2017).

The same tests may be used in re-assessments and follow-up. It is therefore important not to tell the individual whether the answer is correct; that would make the test items useless for later assessments. The individual's efforts should be positively acknowledged, independent of whether they are responding correctly or not.

Raw scores, standard scores and age-equivalent scores

The raw score is the sum of the points the individual gets on a subtest. Standard scores are derived from the standardization of the test. They are based on the assumption that the scores have a *normal statistical distribution* in the population, that the scores are symmetrically distributed around the mean with a fixed percentage of the population within each standard deviation (see Figure 4.2). The standard score indicates the child's placement in relation to the statistical average and the score distribution in the standardization sample, or norm group, which should be the same as his peer group. Examples of standard scores are scaled scores with an age average of ten and a standard deviation of three, or the intelligence quotient (IQ), which has an age average of 100 and a standard deviation of 15.

In a normal distribution, 68 percent of the scores fall between +1 and -1 standard deviations from the age mean. This is often termed the *age-average range or normal area*. However, there should be a departure of more than two standard deviations from the average before it is regarded as significant. Most intelligence tests and many language tests have a mean of 100

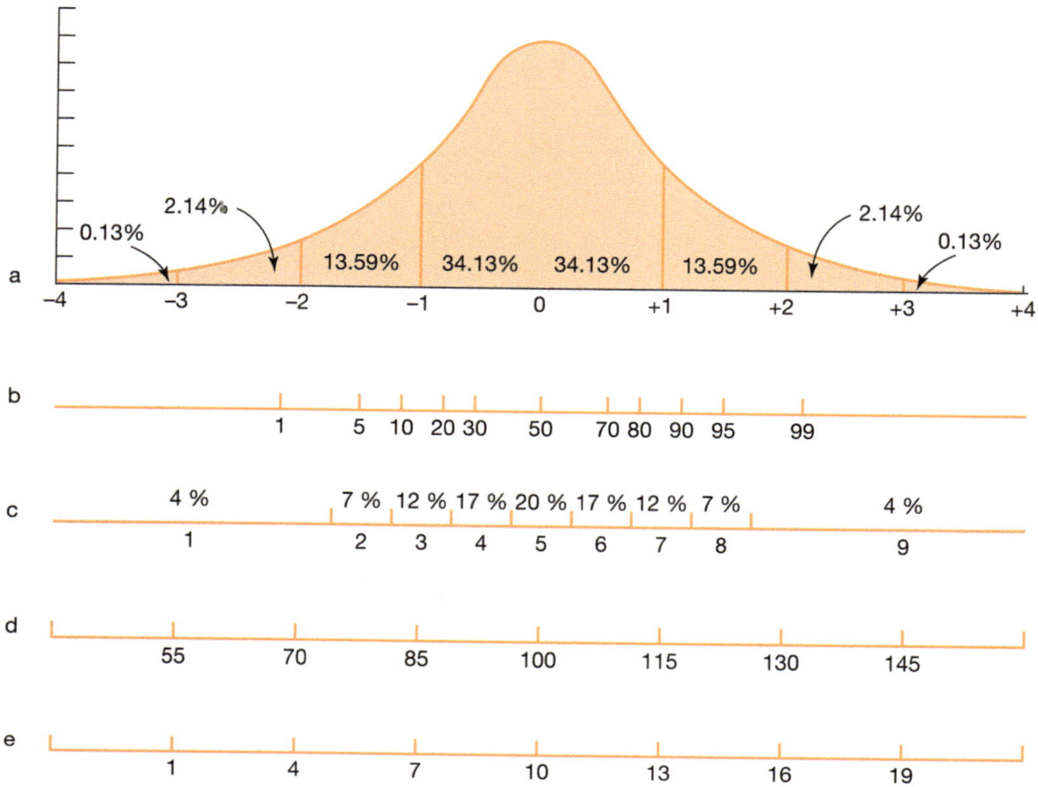

Figure 4.2 The normal distribution: a) with standard deviation, b) percentiles, c) stanine scores consisting of nine different scores or test categories and their percentage distribution, d) IQ based on the Wechsler test, and e) standard scores for Wechsler subtests.

and a standard deviation of 15 points. An IQ that is one standard deviation below the mean for the age group (IQ 85) is a low normal score, which is often used in clinical work as a threshold to identify the need for further assessment. The curve in Figure 4.2 shows that about 95 percent of the population have IQ scores between 70 and 130. About 2.3 percent score 70 or below and about 2.3 percent score 130 or above. If the individual obtains an IQ score below 70 on a test of general abilities (which is more than two standard deviations below the age mean) and also has significant delays in social and adaptive functioning, a diagnosis of intellectual disability might be considered (American Psychiatric Association, 2013; World Health Organization, 2022). However, many individuals have cognitive disabilities that are less severe, but still imply a need for follow-up at school.

For tests to be useful, the results must be interpreted and applied in a meaningful way. In educational settings, scores are often "translated" into *age-equivalent scores*. This may seem a straightforward way of describing an individual's level of functioning but may also give a wrong impression of the individual. For example, if a twenty-year-old man manages to solve similar tasks on a test as an average three-year-old, his functioning will nonetheless differ considerably from that of three-year-old children with typical development. Age-equivalent scores should therefore be used with caution (Connelly, 2013; Maloney & Larrivee, 2007). An age-equivalent score is a crude measure that may be indicate the level of complexity of tasks

that the individual manages to solve but it does not reflect the individual's experience or interests.

The advantage of standard scores is that they bring out the variation within a specific age group. Standard scores may be more informative than age-equivalent scores, as they indicate how the individual manages a given task, compared with others of the same age. However, most intelligence tests do not differentiate well when scores are more than three standard deviations below the age mean (IQ 55) because standardization samples do not usually include individuals in institutions and special schools (Neisworth & Bagnato, 2004). A pragmatic solution may be to use the standard score to indicate that it is a result in the low range and the age-equivalent score to describe the average age level of complexity.

Regardless of which format of scores is used to communicate the test results, such results should always be conveyed in an unambiguous but empathic manner (Hesselberg & von Tetzchner, 2016). It may be challenging for parents to learn that their teenager obtains scores in the low range, comparable to the difficulty level achieved, for example, by a ten-year-old or a seven-year-old. Professionals should emphasize how the results can be used in a positive manner to guide interventions and expectations of proficiency. In a clinical setting, focusing on skills that may be improved and how to support the individual's development will be more fruitful than merely stating the level of functioning and highlighting the deficits. Assessments should always seek to reveal both strengths and weaknesses that may be targeted in the intervention.

The professional who is doing the assessments should bear in mind that tests are not infallible, and that test scores can sometimes be misleading. For example, the first tasks on a test are usually quite easy and function to help the individual understand the nature of the tasks. If the first tasks on a test are too difficult for the individual, he or she loses this help into the task mode and may score lower than their capabilities might indicate. This is called a *floor effect*. If the scores do not go high enough, there may be *ceiling effects* because they do not differentiate well between children in the older age groups that the test is normed for. This can be seen by a flattening of the curve of scores in the higher age groups. One should also be cautious if the norms are based on a small sample or a very limited set of tasks. A small task set implies that minor differences in raw scores may result in age-equivalent scores that indicate a much lower or higher function than the standard scores (Maloney & Larrivee, 2007). It is therefore recommended to read about the development of the norms of the test one would like to use, as well as obtaining information about its reliability and validity. These are usually included in the test manual but may also be found in published articles.

Test profiles

Many children show a relatively even performance across domains, while others have a skewed test profile with more pronounced strengths and weaknesses. Some children are quick at solving puzzles, others are strong in language or particularly fast at mental arithmetic. To give an adequate description of children's cognitive and language functioning, it is necessary to assess their test profile (Fluss & Lidzba, 2020; Stadskleiv et al., 2018b). This requires assessment of a broad range of abilities in order not to draw wrong inferences. For example, if an individual scores in the low range on a test of vocabulary comprehension, this may be indicative of smaller than expected receptive vocabulary, a specific language impairment or a global cognitive impairment. It is therefore necessary to analyse the profile of test scores from multiple cognitive domains in order to draw conclusions about the individual's general level of

comprehension or other specific problems the individual might have. Uneven test profiles indicating problems in specific domains may co-occur with both typical cognitive functioning and intellectual disabilities (Toffalini et al., 2017). Similarly, even test profiles may be found at all IQ levels.

Dynamic assessment

The first assessment does not always give clear answers to the question of which intervention strategies may be best suited for the individual. This might be explored by applying a dynamic assessment approach (Barba-Colmenero et al., 2024; Boers et al., 2013; Valencia-Naranjo & Robles-Bello, 2020). Dynamic assessment seeks to assess the individual's *learning potential* – his or her capacity for learning – and uses tests in a manner that deviates significantly from the standardized procedure. Dynamic assessment should therefore be administered *after* static testing in the standardized manner is completed. It might include test guidance or experimental teaching where a teaching strategy is systematically tried out. The objective is to find out whether a particular task is within the individual's *zone of proximal development*, that is, whether the individual can increase independent proficiency from doing the task interdependently, with a teacher or another person (Haywood & Lidz, 2006; Tzuriel, 2021). Tasks within the zone of proximal development are tasks that the individual cannot do independently, but can solve together with a more competent person, *interdependently* (Vygotsky, 1962). If the task is too easy, it is within the individual's independent control and does not add any new knowledge. If the individual does not understand the nature of the task, it is outside the zone and seeing the teacher do it will therefore not advance the child's knowledge. New knowledge is developed through social collaboration, but this will only happen when the task is new, is understood and the teacher is able to give the right type and amount of help (von Tetzchner, 2019a).

Dynamic assessment has been found useful in identifying disorders and gaining insights into the developmental processes of communication and language, especially in linguistically and culturally diverse groups, such as in children and adolescents with a home language that differs from the majority language (Bamford et al., 2022; Hasson & Joffe, 2007; Hunt et al., 2022; Orellana et al., 2019). Dynamic assessment is also used to assess children with neurodevelopmental disabilities (Valencia-Naranjo & Robles-Bello, 2020) and to evaluate the effect of teaching on children using AAC (Binger et al., 2017; Gevarter et al., 2023b).

Classification instruments

Classification instruments have been developed to facilitate rapid characterization and communication about an individual's level of functioning in different domains (Shanmugarajah et al., 2021) (see Table 4.1). Classification instruments are not tests but consist of broad descriptive categories made by professionals with specialized knowledge. Classification scores are based on observation of the individual and information from significant others. An example is the *Gross Motor Function Classification Scale*, which is used to convey information about locomotion and postural control, typically completed by physiotherapists. The use of classification instruments is widespread in the care for individuals with cerebral palsy but may also be used with other groups. *The Eye-Pointing Classification Scale*, the *Visual Function Classification System*, the *Viking Speech Scale*, the *Mini Manual Ability Classification System*, the *Manual Ability Classification System*, the *Bimanual Fine Motor Function Classification*

Table 4.1 Classification instruments

Scale	*Acronym*	*Age (Years)*	*Domain*
Bimanual Fine Motor Function (Elvrum et al., 2017)	BFMF	3–18	Fine motor functions each hand separately
Communication Function Classification System (Hidecker et al., 2011)	CFCS	2–18	Expressive and receptive communication with known and unknown partners
Mini Eating and Drinking Ability Classification System (Sellers et al., 2022)	Mini-EDACS	1½–3	Eating and drinking abilities
Eating and Drinking Ability Classification System (Sellers et al., 2014)	EDACS	3+	Eating and drinking abilities
Eye-Pointing Classification Scale (Clarke et al., 2022)	EPCS	0–6	Looking behaviours related to eye-pointing in non-speaking children with cerebral palsy affecting their whole body
Gross Motor Function Classification Scale (Palisano et al., 1997)	GMFCS	1–6	Gross motor function
Gross Motor Function Classification Scale, Expanded and Revised (Palisano et al. 2008)	GMFCS E&R	6–12	Gross motor function
Mini Manual Ability Classification System (Eliasson et al., 2017)	Mini-MACS	1–4	Hand motor skills
Manual Ability Classification System (Eliasson et al., 2006)	MACS	4–18	Hand motor skills
Viking Speech Scale (Pennington et al., 2013)	VSS	4+	Intelligibility of speech is affected by motor impairment
Visual Function Classification System (Baranello et al., 2020)	VFCS	1–19	Functional use of vision, how vision is used purposefully to see, direct gaze, recognize and interact with and explore the environment.

and the *Communication Function classification System* are of particular relevance for AAC. All these instruments are constructed in a similar manner, with four or five levels. Level one describes the least impaired functioning and level four or five the most severely affected functioning (Paulson & Vargus-Adams, 2017; Rosenbaum et al., 2014). Many classification scales are available in several languages and may be downloaded for free (see Resources).

Information from significant people

Parents and other significant people are important sources of information about the individual and they usually have an important role in assessments. The individual's significant people are the caregivers, teachers and others who know the individual well. Their information may be collected through interviews, questionnaires and checklists (see following section). Conversations with parents and other significant people about the situation of the individual

are often a continuation of these instruments, but more detailed and directly relevant to the individual than similar information obtained from questionnaires and checklists. The information acquired from significant people is useful in assessing the skills and abilities of the individual, and also provides details about their own opinions of the individual and what he or she is able to do. However, information about the same issues from parents, professionals and the young person involved may differ significantly (Gudmundsson & Gretarsson, 2009; Rescorla et al., 2013; Seifer et al., 2004). It is therefore important to integrate information from different sources.

Checklists, questionnaires and interviews

Checklists and questionnaires have become common elements in assessment, both in screening and in assessment (see Table 4.2 for an overview). While tests measure the individual's performance in standard situations, checklists and questionnaires are completed on the basis of observations made by people who know the individual well. The difference between checklists and questionnaires is not absolute. Both consist of questions about the individual's skills, behaviour and everyday functioning, and about the environment. They are usually completed by parents or teachers, but checklists can also be self-completed by older children and adolescents. In addition, some checklists are used by professionals to structure their own observations.

Table 4.2 Some common checklists and questionnaires

Name and reference	*Acronym*	*Years; months*	*Domain*
Adaptive Behaviour Assessment System (Harrison & Oakland, 2015)	ABAS	0–89	Adaptive behaviour and skills
Behavior Rating Inventory of Executive Function (Gioia et al., 2000)	BRIEF	5–18	Executive functioning
Caregiver Priorities and Child Health Index of Life with Disabilities (Narayanan et al., 2006)	CPChild	5–18	Activity limitations, health status, well-being, and ease of care
Child Behaviour Checklist (Achenbach & Rescorla, 2000, 2001)	CBCL	1;6–18	Behavioural and emotional problems
Children's Communication Checklist (Wellnitz et al., 2021)	CCC	4–16	Communication, pragmatics and social interaction
Communication and Symbolic Behavior Scales (Wetherby & Prizant, 2002)	CSBS	0;6–2;0	Early communication and symbolic functioning
Communication Matrix (Rowland, 2004a)		0–2	Communication functions, observed by professionals
Communication Matrix for Parents (Rowland, 2004b)		0–2	Communication functions, observed by parents
Early Social Communication Scales (Mundy et al., 2003a)	ESCS	0;8–2;6	Non-verbal communication

(*Continued*)

Table 4.2 (Continued)

Name and reference	*Acronym*	*Years; months*	*Domain*
Family Impact of Assistive Technology Scale, (Ryan et al., 2019)	FIATS-AAC	3–18	Family functioning
Focus on the Outcomes of Communication Under Six (Thomas–Stonell et al., 2020)	FOCUS	1;6–6;0	Communication
Inventory of Potential Communicative Acts, (Sigafoos et al., 2000)	IPCA	(no age level indicated)	Communicative functions
Low Verbal Investigatory Survey (Naples et al., 2023)	LVIS	1–8	Communication and language
McArthur-Bates Communicative Development Inventories, third edition – Words and Gestures Form (Marchman et al., 2023)	MB-CDI	0;8–1;6	Comprehension and use of symbolic gestures, words and phrases.
McArthur-Bates Communicative Development Inventories – Words and sentences form (Marchman et al., 2023)	MB-CDI	1;4–2;6	Production of words, grammatical forms like plural –s, and word combinations like "mommy sock"
McArthur-Bates Communicative Development Inventories – CDI-III (Marchman et al., 2023)	MB-CDI III	2;6–3;1	Expressive vocabulary and grammar
Measure of Early Vision Use (Deramore Denver et al., 2022)	MEVU	(no age level indicated)	Use of vision in everyday activities, interactions and environments
Pediatric Evaluation of Disability Inventory Computer Adaptive Test (Haley et al., 2012)	PEDI-CAT	0–20	Functional skills
Pragmatics Profile of Everyday Communication Skills in Children (Dewart & Summers, 1995)		1–7	Pragmatic functions.
Psycho-Educational Profile (Schopler et al., 2005)	PEP	0:6–7	Skills and behaviours related to education and possible autism spectrum disorder
Responsive Augmentative and Alternative Communication (Broberg et al., 2012)	RAACS	1–5	Parents responsive style in interacting with their child who use AAC
Social Communication Questionnaire (Rutter et al., 2003)	SCQ	4+	Communication with focus on autism spectrum disorder
Vineland Adaptive Behaviour Scales (Sparrow et al., 2016)	VAPS	2–21	Communication, Self-help skills, social skills, and behavioural problems

A number of interviews and questionnaires are designed to describe perceptual, motor, social, language and everyday skills. *Vineland Adaptive Behavior Scale* or *Adaptive Behavior Assessment System* may be used to obtain an overview of everyday skills, language, cognitive and social skills. Achenbach's *Behavior Checklists* may be used to assess emotional and behavioural disorders from toddler age to old age (Achenbach et al., 2017). Other checklists measure life quality, characteristics of the environment and how parents and other significant people perceive their situation. Interviews may address many of the same issues as checklist and questionnaires but are usually more open, functioning more as a guide for topics to touch upon during the conversation.

Some checklists and questionnaires are meant to facilitate diagnosis. The *Autism Diagnostic Interview* (Rutter et al., 2003) is an interview that is used when considering a diagnosis of autism spectrum disorder. The *Vineland Adaptive Behavior Scales* and the *Adaptive Behavior Assessment System* are used in addition to tests of intelligence when diagnosing intellectual disabilities. These two instruments are used to obtain a comprehensive impression of the individual's functioning and coping in various domains, such as self-help skills, social skills, behavioural problems and communication skills. They contain concrete questions about the individual's everyday functioning, including management of dressing, eating, going to the toilet and so forth. The best interviews contain many questions about each particular domain, making it possible to draw up profiles.

Some interviews are structured like a questionnaire, with specific questions and a limited range of possible answers. Others are semi-structured with more open-ended questions, allowing the informants to elaborate and provide details, such as *Social Networks* (Blackstone & Hunt Berg, 2012) where significant people provide information about the individual's communication in everyday life, including use of AAC, communication partners and common conversational topics.

Interviewing significant people about an individual's functioning takes time. Many professionals therefore administer questionnaires instead of, or as a supplement to, interviews. Questionnaires can be completed by parents and teachers before testing and provide valuable information for planning the assessment process. Some instruments, for example the *Vineland Adaptive Behavior Scales*, have both a questionnaire version and an interview version. Other instruments only come as questionnaires, such as the *Children's Communication Checklist* and the *Caregiver Priorities and Child Health Index of Life with Disabilities*. Some questionnaires have specified answer options that the informants check off. For example, the *Focus on the Outcomes of Communication Under Six* and the *Family Impact of Assistive Technology for Augmentative and Alternative Communication (FIATS-AAC) Scale* consist of statements that should be rated on a seven-point scale, ranging from "always true" to "never true". The *Inventory of Potential Communicative Acts* contains open-ended questions, and the informants should provide examples of how the individual acts in different communication situations, such as when requesting an object or responding to a greeting.

Most checklists, interviews and questionnaires lack questions about how much and what type of help the individual needs in order to carry out specific actions and in which situations these are mastered. This information is important when planning intervention. The *Pediatric Evaluation of Disability Inventory* seeks to identify both functional skills and the individual's need for support. This is also one of the very few instruments that are recommended for use with individuals with severe motor impairment (James et al., 2014). *CPChild* takes the caregiver perspective into account by asking about both the functioning of the child and how the caregiver evaluates the importance of this function.

Systematic observation

Regardless of the individual's disability, systematic observation is always an important part of the assessment. The observations should comprise the whole individual and their everyday environments. The individual should be observed in different situations and activities, in the company of adults and peers, and alone. Play is a core activity for children and the child's play may be used as measures of development (Besio et al., 2018; Lifter et al., 2022). Play may also be an explicit goal of the intervention and used as a measure of intervention success (Kasari et al., 2021; Kelly-Vance & Ryalls, 2008). For children with motor impairment, performance on tasks where they use aided communication to instruct others to perform physical play actions may give information about both their aided language skills and the complexity of their play (Batorowicz et al., 2016).

Instruments

Observations are usually guided by the reasons for referral and the professional's questions about the individual's abilities and impairments. They may be relatively unstructured observation of the child in preschool or school, but there are also instruments for structured observations. Some of these are more like checklists, where the professional records instances of particular behaviours as they occur in the individual's natural environment, without any interference from the professional other than his or her presence in the room. For example, *Pragmatic Observational Measure* is used for observing children's everyday use of language (Cordier et al., 2014). Other instruments contain situations designed to elicit particular behaviours. For example, the *Autism Diagnostic Observation Schedule* (Lord et al., 2012) includes situations where it would be natural for the child to engage in joint attention or ask an adult for help, for example, with opening a glass jar of Lego blocks. To observe how the child communicates and engages with others in such situations is helpful for diagnostic purposes and provides valuable information for planning interventions. The use of this instrument requires certification.

Video

Video recordings are important for the documentation of interaction and communication skills of individuals with disabilities. A communicative action may last a short moment and disappear, while a video recording of the same event can be viewed many times. Several people may view a video together and look at specific sequences several times. Professionals can check information that crops up at a later stage, or circumstances they did not notice at the time of the video recording. The recordings also make it easier to document progress in children with slow development. Video recording may be combined with other assessment approaches. It is, for example, common to record sessions with the *Autism Diagnostic Observation Schedule*, as the scoring depends on careful observation of the child's use of gaze and other communicative and attentional behaviours.

Video recordings are also a good starting point for conversations between professionals and parents and other significant people, and for creating agreement about the individual's functioning. Parents can say whether the behaviour in the video is typical of the individual and can confirm or invalidate assumptions about what the individual can and cannot do. By

analysing video recordings, innovative ideas for new forms of intervention and communication situations may spring to mind.

Starting with basic information

When initiating an assessment, attention should be given to principal issues and finding out what is required in order to get intervention started. Among these issues is the question of the objectives of the language and communication intervention, for example, whether the individual is likely to need AAC as a means of expression, as a support for speech development, or as an alternative form of language (see Chapter 3). Even though it is often not possible to answer this question at the start, it helps to focus on what is likely to be the initial communication intervention. In addition, information may be required about social functioning, activity level, play, comprehension of everyday situations, self-help skills, general level of knowledge, visual, auditory and motor impairments, and behavioural problems. Once this basic information is in place, the full assessment should be planned and effected stepwise. The need for precise information will increase as the nature of the individual's problems gradually become clearer. Evaluations of the interventions that have been implemented are significant elements of the continuous assessment.

Parts of the assessment may take rather a long time. However, although assessment is important, it should not delay the implementation of intervention measures unnecessarily. There may be enough information to start intervention even before a formal assessment has started (Goosens', 1989). With children who have severe motor impairments, it often appears as though they are assumed to have other disorders, and for example language intervention may be postponed until the child has demonstrated understanding of spoken language. The communication aid is then used to *reveal* language skills instead of supporting their emergence.

At the start of an assessment, it is easy to ask parents about too much. This may lead to extra work and can sometimes make cooperation difficult. Professionals should therefore have a clear rationale for asking the questions they do and avoid situations where parents feel that they provide detailed information that is never actually used. The professionals should not focus so much on their own ideas that valuable information from parents and others is overlooked. It is recommended to include open-ended questions, such as *Is there more information you consider important for us to know about?* or *Have we addressed all issues that are important to you?*

Overview of the day

Before starting language and communication intervention, it is necessary to have an overview of the activities in which the individual participates. It gives an idea of the individual's strong and weak sides, and the kind of life he or she has. An overview of this kind is also the quickest way of gaining insight into the individual's existing intervention programme, and when and where intervention is taking place. In this way, new intervention measures can be planned so that they support domains that are not sufficiently addressed, without interfering with the individual's current positive activities. The overview should include all hours of the day and be so fine-meshed that most activities that occur during the course of the day are clearly discernible.

The *day clock* is a tool for professionals and caregivers that may inform the planning of intervention measures. It consists of many slots that are filled with activities that pertain to the particular individual (Figure 4.3). The information is collected through interviews with parents, professionals and others, depending on who is responsible for the activities at different times. A day clock should not be confounded with *visual support*, which is a tool for supporting an individual in managing activities and learning (see p. 149).

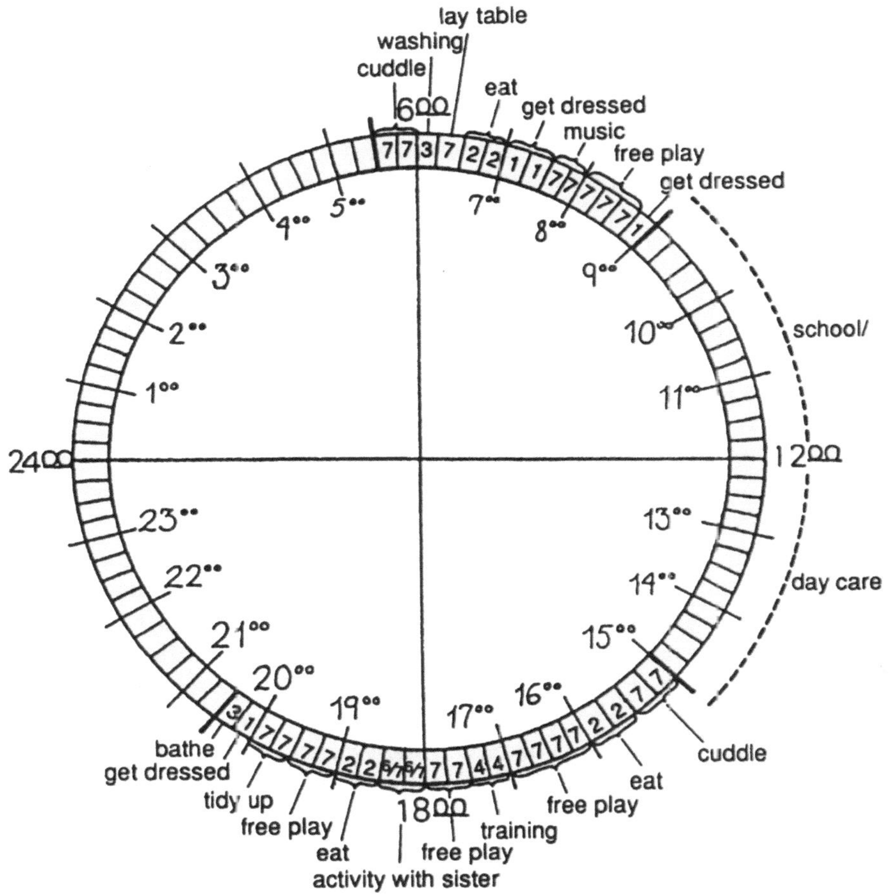

Situation	Code	Number	Time
Dressing/training	1	4	1
Eating	2	6	1.5
Washing/bathing	3	2	0.5
Training	4	2	0.5
Occupied alone	5	0	0
Occupied with children	6	2	0.5
Occupied with adults	7	20 (2)	5

Figure 4.3 Day clock for a ‘2-year-old autistic boy.

When completing a day clock, it is necessary to ask about a *typical* day. It is a good idea to begin by asking about the previous day. If this was not a typical day, then one should ask about the last day that was suitably typical. The slots of the day clock usually represent 15-minute intervals. This means that information is required about what the individual was doing and who was with him or her at every 15-minute interval on the day that is reported. Importantly, notes should be made about any variation that exists and about routines as well as rare but repeated events. It is also useful to ask whether any problems usually occur in each of the time slots, whether communication occurs, and if so, the type and manner of communication. It is often a good idea to make two day clocks – one for ordinary weekdays where preschool and school take up a lot of the day, and one for weekends, which are mostly spent with the family.

When planning communication intervention, it may be useful to produce a separate day clock for communication. This contains the times for training, situations where the individual regularly communicates and situations where he sometimes communicates. In this way, it will become apparent when the individual is not communicating. Studies have found that, in many common situations, young aided communicators do not have access to their communication aids (von Tetzchner et al., 2018). Both availability and use of communication aids in various settings should therefore be included in the day clock. Communication day clocks may integrate information from *Social Networks* (see p. 103), which gives an overview of the individual's use of AAC in everyday life, the various settings and communication partners.

A good day clock gives a comprehensive picture of the individual's existing intervention measures, activity level, activities that occur regularly and any problematic behaviour. This includes an overview of the individual's intervention, including daytime measures (nursery school, school, work or work-training), leisure activities and various forms of relief services. In addition, assessments and interviews provide information about self-help skills, self-occupancy and communication skills. When this information is pieced together with the routine tasks carried out by the family and other people in the environment, it provides a good understanding of how the existing total intervention seems to work.

Finally, the day clock is used to find times during the day that represent opportunities for communication and other skills that are being developed. As new activities are introduced, these are included in the day clock so that it always shows how the individual's current day is organized. Comparisons of day clocks from different periods give insights into how the individual is developing and the intervention is proceeding. Thus, day clocks may play an important role in the ongoing evaluation of the intervention.

Diagnosis

A diagnostic evaluation is always important. In principle there are two kinds of diagnoses: etiological and functional. The etiological diagnoses pertain to the cause of the impairments, such as a genetic anomaly or a brain injury. A functional diagnosis, such as autism spectrum disorder, intellectual disabilities or developmental language disorder, is based on observed behaviour (symptoms). Many individuals have both types of diagnoses. A diagnosis of Down syndrome implies that the individual has a whole or part of a third copy of chromosome 21. However, the cognitive level of individuals with Down syndrome vary considerably and degree of intellectual disability may be specified as mild, moderate, severe or profound (American Psychiatric Association, 2013; World Health Organization, 2022).

An accurate diagnosis of both the cause of an impairment and the functional level of the individual requires a comprehensive and multidisciplinary assessment process. This may include genetic analysis and assessment of neurological, sensory, motor and cognitive functions, as well as communication and language. When interviewing parents, it may be relevant to ask about their child's developmental history, such as milestones, age when they first noticed that the child developed differently compared to siblings or peers, and whether there are family members with similar challenges. The multi-disciplinary assessment necessary for diagnostic purposes also contributes valuable information towards the *Basic Assessment* in the comprehensive assessment described in the AAC Pyramid (see Figure 4.1). Both professionals and parents need an accurate diagnosis to make a prognosis, that is, evidence-based information about what they may expect on the basis of what is known about the typical developmental course and variation in children and adults with similar diagnoses.

There are several good reasons for emphasizing the necessity of an accurate medical diagnosis, even when this diagnosis does not have a direct bearing on the planning of intervention. For some children, a medical diagnosis may be necessary for providing appropriate medical treatment, but intervention is rarely a *direct* result of this diagnosis. Most intervention measures are general in the sense that they are provided to individuals who belong to highly different diagnostic groups. However, information stemming from a thorough medical examination, such as information about any pain, problems with feeding or elimination, and epilepsy can be important for a proper understanding of the individual's reactions and needs.

An important reason for procuring a diagnosis is that in many countries a formal diagnosis is a means of securing the necessary intervention. The diagnostic label makes it easier to get support for the urgency of the intervention. For parents and other significant people, the diagnosis can be necessary for obtaining realistic and tangible information about the individual's disorders. Information of this kind is also provided by parents of children with similar disorders and organizations, and through courses and Internet (see Resources). Associations for parents of children with disabilities arrange their own courses and also participate in courses that are open to both professionals and parents. The diagnosis is the basis for contact with all these various sources of information.

There are many examples where a correct diagnosis of children and adults with communication and language disorders helped produce more suitable forms of intervention and improved the planning of intervention measures for future needs. For example, a girl may prove to have Rett syndrome (see p. 84) rather than autism spectrum disorder, as was previously assumed, leading to changes in the intervention in several areas. For example, the diagnosis may well lead to a move away from manual sign intervention, based on the knowledge that the girl's hand motor skills are likely to deteriorate, to communication boards or devices and interpretation of the girl's looking behaviour. One may also try to establish a calm environment, because girls with Rett syndrome seem to function best in such conditions (Lindberg, 2006; von Tetzchner, 1997b). Another example may be a re-diagnosis of mild or moderate intellectual disabilities in individuals with severe speech and motor impairments who had been assumed to have severe or profound intellectual disabilities. Even when individuals are correctly perceived as fulfilling the criteria of a diagnosis of intellectual disabilities, their comprehension and potential for expressing themselves, may vary considerably. Individuals with very severe speech and motor impairments may only be provided with expressive opportunities for choosing between two objects, when they could have expressed themselves in multi-word utterances using graphic symbols if they had only been given the opportunity to do so (Deacon, 1974; Kildal et al., 2021).

The family's need for support, relief and help

A child with severe disabilities has a decisive influence on the life of all of the family (Seligman & Darling, 2007). Children bring joy and happiness to their family, but few parents are equipped to care for a child with severe disabilities and little or no speech. Assessment should include their need for information, training and follow-up to become able to support their child's communication and language development (see Chapter 12), as well as their work load and worries about the future, which often represent a great strain on families with children who need AAC (Allen & Shane, 2014; Saito & Turnbull, 2007). The *Family Impact of Assistive Technology Scale for Augmentative and Alternative Communication* (FIATS-AAC) includes items related to the emotional, social and economic consequences for the family of having a child developing aided communication, including family roles in caring for the child, the caregivers' energy and worries and the family's financial situation (Delarosa et al., 2012; Kron et al., 2018), and may also be used in follow-up to assess changes in the family situation (Ryan et al., 2018).

The degree of strain on a family, and which pressures are greatest, may differ based on which group the child belongs to. Parents of children with severe motor disorders usually experience a great deal of physical stress. Normal care and nursing are often time-consuming and require that the child is lifted and moved frequently (Fritz & Sewell-Roberts, 2020; Glenn et al., 2009). For parents of children with autism spectrum disorder, the pressures of always having to be present in order to prevent the child from doing self-injury, running away or damaging things, are often the greatest (Bonis, 2016; Ludlow et al., 2012). What many families of children in need of AAC have in common is that everyday tasks become considerably more time-consuming than for others, that contact with other family members and friends is reduced and that they are concerned about the future (Doak, 2021; Goldbart & Marshall, 2004; Saito & Turnbull, 2007).

The strains imply that the family both has a need for, and a right to, a reasonable amount of respite service. Assessment of parent worries and needs gives professionals the necessary insights into the family's life in order to provide the family with the support, resources and time needed for communication and activities with their child using AAC and for developing stable positive expectations about the future. The extent of the needs and planning of respite will vary with the family's organization and other duties, as well as the financial situation of the family. It is an integral part of a family-centred approach to intervention to assess the family's financial situation and give them the economic help and support they need and are entitled to, and ensure that they are informed of their rights (van der Mark et al., 2017).

The aim of family assessment is to reveal both the needs and the strengths of the family. The ability to cope with these pressures differs from family to family. In families where several individuals need much care and help (young children, sick or elderly family members), it is essential that resources are adapted to both the needs and the resources of the family. It is not reasonable to assume that everyone is equally resourceful and robust. Some families develop strength through caring for a child with disabilities (Tsibidaki, 2020; van Riper, 2007), while others have less strength. Experience shows that in many instances effective intervention measures are not implemented – even AAC – because they place too great a strain on families that are given insufficient support and help (Doak, 2021; Moorcroft et al., 2020; Resch et al., 2010). A good support system with relief services makes it easier to implement other measures. When families develop good coping strategies, these should be supported and included in the follow-up of the child and the family. This requires that family needs are sensitively and thoroughly assessed (see also Chapter 12).

Assessment should focus beyond immediate needs. Many families have a desire to fend for themselves and may say that they have little need for help. However, over time the strain may nonetheless become great, sometimes leading to burnout (Moorcroft et al., 2021). If the parents and other members of the family are given some time for separate activities, it may prevent burnout and be positive for the child using AAC and the whole family. Furthermore, respite is not only directed at the other family members. Being away from the family, especially spending time with peers, may promote autonomy and self-efficacy in older children and adolescents who use AAC (Tavares & Peixoto, 2003).

General issues

In this context, general issues include the individual's attention to people and things, knowledge about and interest in the surroundings, and self-help skills. The focus of the assessment is on activities and social participation. Assessment may include both observations of individuals in their natural environment and their responses to preliminary training.

Interest in people, objects, activities and events

A basic principle of AAC intervention is that all humans wish to communicate but not everyone is able to do so without assistance. It has often been said that motivation on the part of the individual is a prerequisite for the implementation of intervention, but this raises the question of what it means not to be motivated. Saying that an individual "lacks motivation" may indicate that he or she appears negative and unwilling. However, there is no reason to take this as an expression of a general reluctance to communicate, but rather as an expression of the fact that it is frustrating not being able to do so. Experience also shows that individuals become less reluctant and negative when they have acquired some communicative skills. This requires that the individual understands what the communication training is about and finds it meaningful. People are not likely to have a desire to communicate about anything and everything. If the intervention is to be successful, it is imperative that that the individual is taught to communicate about things, activities and events that he or she is aware of and interested in. Assessment for AAC intervention should therefore begin with an evaluation of the individual's interests and preferences related to people, things and activities. Only then can the initial communication intervention become meaningful from the perspective of the potential learner.

For individuals with severe intellectual disabilities, it is sometimes difficult to find things or activities that appear to be interesting to them, even for caregivers who know them well. This is a challenging condition for communication intervention and the initial communication training should include strategies for creating interest and awareness. A typical first step is to observe carefully what the individual is doing spontaneously. It may be that in the beginning, the only way to establish some form of interaction is to imitate the individual's behaviour and wait for a response. For example, if an autistic child seems particularly engaged when making a sound knocking an object repeatedly on the table, the adult may try to establish interaction by imitating his knocking. The adult should not repeat the knocking sound for very long, only long enough to get the child's attention. Then the adult might expand on this "knocking game" by introducing slight variations in rhythm, intensity and length, trying to establish joint auditory attention and promoting turn-taking skills. The next step might be to introduce a choice between objects that make different sounds. Note that the imitation in itself is not the purpose of this approach, it is only a means to get an interaction process started. It is

therefore important that the adult has plans for how to expand the activity, even if the expansions have to be very gradual, and the speed of progression slow, to avoid "mechanical" imitations that do not further the interaction and the individual's communicative development. Imitating the child's behaviour also means that the adult's actions are within the child's repertoire, increasing the likelihood that the child will pay attention to the adult and be interested in what she or he is doing (Contaldo et al., 2016; Heimann et al., 2006). Here, assessment and intervention activities merge.

Attention and initiation of interaction

Among individuals in need of AAC, attention and initiation of interaction with others vary widely, both within and between the three main user groups (see Chapter 3). Assessment of relevant actions is therefore important. Some individuals' manner of initiating contact and interaction can be so idiosyncratic that only people who know them well are able to understand their expressions. One result of this may be that the individuals become extremely selective with regard to those with whom they will attempt to initiate contact and interaction. In order to facilitate communication when an individual is using highly individualized means of expression, it is recommended to make a list of the communicative expressions that the individual is using. This may be kept in a book or electronically, for example with dedicated apps such as *KnowMe* or open-source resources such as *Book Creator* (see Beghdadi, 2019). A digital "expression bank" of the individual's communicative expressions has the advantage that it can include small video clips of the individual's communicative expressions, including the articulation of manual signs or the indication of graphic symbols. This makes it easier for others to learn to understand the individual's idiosyncratic manual signs, such as when a child signs MORE by thumping the left fist against the right arm or uses the thumb rather than the index finger for indicating graphic symbols.

Individuals with severe motor impairments may have limited means for initiating communication with others, even if their comprehension is relatively good and they belong to the expressive language group (see Chapter 3). Assessment should try out ways to facilitate communicative initiative, for example attaching a communication switch on the tray of the individual's wheel chair with a pre-recorded message like *I've got something to say*, which tells the communication partner to bring the individual's communication aid if it is not there and to start a conversation. There is significant variation among individuals in the supportive language group, but also in this group many individuals seldom initiate communication with others. Many individuals in this group are shy and timid when they meet unfamiliar people, others may appear negative and aggressive. They may develop an aversion to speaking, or, in extreme cases, develop *selective mutism*: they speak only to members of their close family and not in public settings like kindergartens or schools (Steffenburg et al., 2018; Steinhausen et al., 2006). Selective mutism is a form of anxiety and pressuring the individual to communicate may worsen the problem. Rather, an approach acknowledging all modes of communication as good communication is suggested, the teacher taking gradual steps to reduce the discomfort associated with communication failure and not making a big deal out of it when the child finally speaks (Standart & Le Couteur, 2003).

It is among individuals in the alternative language group, however, that assessment may reveal the most severe problems, both in terms of attention and initiation of communicative interaction with others. They generally have the poorest communicative, linguistic and social skills. They may not understand eye gaze, pointing or other cues to joint attention, or how to

use such behaviours to direct the attention of others and initiate joint attention (see p. 160). This group includes girls and women with Rett syndrome (see p. 84). For autistic children, adolescents and adults, problems in relating to other people are a diagnostic criterion. Initiation of communication and attention to others vary considerably within this group, however, and are dependent on the situation.

Self-help skills

Self-help skills include the ability to care for oneself: wash, dress, eat and so on. Such skills comprise a significant part of the individual's self-determination and are fundamental to a good quality of life. With the exception of very young children and individuals with very severe motor impairments, the majority of individuals in need of AAC possess some self-help skills. The assessment of these skills – including the amount of help needed – is therefore important for planning AAC intervention as well as interventions in other domains. In so far as it is possible, communication and language training should be integrated into self-help training in such a way that both forms of training are improved.

The individual's self-help skills are usually discussed in interviews with parents and other significant people, but it may also be useful to observe the individual in various everyday situations. The three main user groups have in common that adults and peers around them often believe that they can do less than they are actually capable of doing (Dada, 2019; Radici et al., 2022). Families and teachers may need to be made aware that individuals with severe motor impairments may develop *autonomy* and make their own decisions even if they cannot perform the actions themselves. They may apply "language for action", using aided communication to instruct others to perform most or all physical actions of everyday life. For individuals with better motor skills, structured interventions, including visual support such as daily schedules with graphic symbols and step-by-step illustrations of tasks, may help them develop both self-help skills and a sense of agency and control (see Chapter 5).

Self-occupancy

Social participation is a main goal of everyday life, but most people are not in interaction all of the time. Meaningful self-occupancy is an important aspect of everyday life and life quality. Many families find that the individual's inability to self-occupy poses considerable strain. The individual's participation in self-occupancy activities should therefore be assessed, as well as how intervention can help him or her develop a larger repertoire of independent activities. Language and communication intervention may increase the degree of self-occupancy, because improved self-expression may provide the individual with better opportunities for determining what she or he wants to do. Good communication and language intervention may also improve the individual's initiation skills and reduce dependency on others. For individuals with severe motor impairments, digital tools controlled with switches or eye-gaze technology may enable them to have independent access for example to music, video, television, games, print or audio books, emails, the Internet and social media (Hynan et al., 2014, 2015).

Self-monitoring

With age, children become better at regulating their thoughts and actions. They do not merely act but consider the context and adapt their actions to the situation. Executive functions

include abilities such planning and organizing, monitoring own behaviour, shifting rapidly between cognitive tasks and wilfully inhibiting automatic responses (Baggetta & Alexander, 2016; Miyake & Friedman, 2012). These cognitive functions are a foundation for planning and achieving everyday tasks (Blair, 2016; Carlson et al., 2013). They enable individuals to manage increasingly complex tasks, including, for example, planning and carrying out schoolwork or planning for and participating in a social outing with friends. Reduced executive functioning is associated with different diagnostic groups, including children with cerebral palsy, Down syndrome and autism spectrum disorder (Lai et al., 2017; Tungate & Conners, 2021; Weierink et al., 2013).

Executive functioning plays a role in the everyday functioning of all children, particularly in relation to learning and academic achievement (Baggetta & Alexander, 2016). However, for children using aided communication there are some special considerations. Children who use natural speech do not have to deliberately think about the articulation movements, while for aided communicators – particularly those using graphic symbols in communication books or communication apps on electronic devices – the construction of utterances requires conscious navigation through symbols organized hierarchically (see Chapter 2). This may imply that the individuals have fewer cognitive resources for executive tasks not related to utterance production (Stadskleiv et al., 2014). This double-taxing of executive functioning, for both the task itself and also utterance production, is important to consider when planning interventions and evaluating functioning. For ages 5 to 18 years, executive functioning can be assessed with the *Behavior Rating Inventory of Executive Function, BRIEF* (Roth et al., 2013)

Motor skills

Motor assessment is important because mobility and use of the hands are essential for most everyday activities. Many individuals who need AAC have severe motor impairments (see Chapter 3). There is limited correlation between mobility skills and manual skills, although this relation varies in subgroups of children with cerebral palsy (Carnahan et al., 2007). Gross motor skills are important for social participation, but use of the hands may be more decisive for choice of communication system and possible aids. Hand movements are assessed in order to determine whether or not the individual is able to produce intelligible manual signs, that is, to vary hand shape, articulation place and manner of the signs in such a way that it is possible for a communication partner to distinguish individual signs (see Bonvillian et al., 2020a, b; Grove, 1990). Manual skills are necessary for operating many communication aids but good eye movements and eye-gaze technology may allow the individual to access communication aids in spite of limited manual skills (Hoppenbrouwers et al., 2014; Karlsson et al., 2021).

It is evident that people with severe fine motor disabilities are unable to use manual signs, but assessment should also include less obvious disorders of motor coordination that may imply difficulties in performing manual signs (Cancer et al., 2020; Vaivre-Douret et al., 2016). Moreover, it is important to distinguish between difficulties in producing manual signs due to motor disorders and problems in following an instruction. For example, it may be difficult for a child with severe intellectual disabilities to understand the idea of imitating a hand form. When children have no apparent physical motor impairments, it may be practical to use their performance of actions related to everyday activities as a starting point (see Figure 4.4). The way they carry out these action will give cues as to how they can be physically involved in play and other activities (see Chapter 10), as well as how manual signs can be simplified to make it easier to produce them (see p. 29). It should be noted that many individuals with severe gross

Hand form		pull trousers up/down	pull shirt up/down	squeeze oranges for juice	palm on table, pick up pencil in fingers	put on sock	squeeze toothpaste onto toothbrush	hold brush handle when brushing hair	crumple paper	wipe table with cloth or sponge	turn key	pick up book from table edge
	1 squeeze	x	x	x	x							
	2 palmar						x	x	x			
	3 thumb adduction									x	x	x
	4 midposition of the forearm											
	5 thumb abduction											
	6 wrist movements							x				
	7 opposed grasp							x				
	8 pointing radial finger											
	9 release											
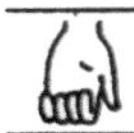	10 full supination											
	11 crossed finger											
	12 pointing ulnar finger											
Movement												
1 unilateral				x								
2 bilateral mirror		x				x						
3 unilateral across midline										x		
4 bilateral/one base–one mover							x					
5 bilateral two movers												
6 bilateral crossing midline												

self-feed using fingers/drink with cup														x		x			
self-feed using utensils			x											x		x			
turn steering wheel			x															x	
hold sandwich or finger foods				x															
hold jar of jam and twist lid				x															
turn knobs/dials				x															
comb hair				x		x										x			
brush teeth				x		x													
stir (contents in stable bowl)						x													
pouring from container into glass held by other hand																	x		
button/unbutton							x											x	
open and close zip on jacket							x												
dial phone number							x	x											
play instrument with keyboard							x	x											
use finger puppet							x												
wring wash cloth																		x	
tear paper																		x	
remove glove from fingers									x			x							
retrieve object from pocket									x										
throw ball up in air and catch										x									

Figure 4.4 Everyday activities for assessing motor skills.

motor impairments have somewhat better control of the hands and are able to produce some intelligible manual signs or gestures. Even if the number is very small, the signs or gestures may play an important part in the communication because they are always accessible to the individual. It is therefore always important to assess the individual's ability to produce signs and gestures and whether these are actually recognized by people in the environment (see also p. 362).

For individuals who develop aided communication, assessment of motor function also includes finding the optimal seating and positioning that will allow the individual to access the communication device (and other technical devices) most precisely and with as little effort as possible, whether this be via a keyboard, joystick, switches or eye-gaze technology. Individuals with extensive motor disorders rely on a stable sitting position in order to use their motor skills (Costigan & Light, 2010; Treviranus & Roberts, 2003). If it has been decided that the individual will use a communication aid, it is imperative to find the best possible access method. This is often a difficult and time-consuming task, but it is essential for individuals with severe motor impairment to be able to express themselves in the best possible way. There are some computer programs that are designed to assess motor functions, and there are also games and other programs that are designed to train individuals in the use of eye-gaze technologies or switches (Griffiths, 2020). If the indication method is unclear, the whole communication interchange will become unclear and hence also the language learning situation. There is often a tendency to focus on pointing with the hand but if the movement of the hand is difficult for the communication partner to read, it may be better to use other means of pointing or assisted scanning (see Chapter 2).

For individuals with severe motor impairments, many physical actions may cause strain when performed over time. The assessment should attempt to find more than one action or seating position, allowing the individual to vary between them and thereby reduce the physical strain.

Vision and hearing

Perceptual impairments are more common in all the diagnostic groups using AAC than in the population in general (Andersen et al., 2008; Emerson & Robertson, 2011; Herer, 2012; Hitoglou et al., 2010). It is therefore necessary to assess the individual's vision and hearing when selecting communication system and planning intervention. It is also vital that any perceptual problems are made known to all the assessors, so that behaviour and test results can be appropriately interpreted. However, it may be difficult to test the vision and hearing of many of the individuals who need AAC and assessment should therefore be made by experts in auditory and visual assessments.

There are "objective" tests for both vision and hearing, that is, examinations based on neurologically evoked responses that do not require cooperation on the part of the individual being examined. They can tell whether the eye and ear are intact and in working order and register whether stimulation of the visual and auditory organs reaches the brain (Creel, 2019; Picton, 2010). However, it is equally important to assess the functional use of vision and hearing (Ahmmed et al., 2022; Bennett et al., 2019). There are several instruments for assessing how individuals with developmental disorders are using their vision (Shanmugarajah et al., 2021) but a seemingly intact sensory organ is no guarantee that perception is normal. Many individuals with intellectual disabilities and autism spectrum disorder appear to have cerebral visual impairment, including children who use AAC (Blackstone et al., 2021; Ortibus et al., 2019).

Auditory or visual disturbances may be caused by agnosia, which influences the interpretation of the stimulation (Kaga, 2009; Riddoch & Humphreys, 2003). These disorders may be difficult to observe because the individual reacts to changes in stimulation, but the sense impressions are not being processed and perceived normally. Objective examinations should therefore be supplemented by observations of functional perception, that is, of how the individual uses vision and hearing in everyday activities, and in familiar and less familiar settings.

Communication and language

Assessment of communication and language in individuals with neurodevelopmental disorders requires a broad repertoire of assessment tools and strategies (Hamrick, 2023). The assessment should include comprehension and use of spoken language and alternative language forms, as well as non-verbal communication. The individuals' use of AAC will depend on whether people in the environment understand them. Assessment must therefore include communicative access and the competence and attitudes to AAC among significant people in the environment. This is particularly important when the intervention is well under way. A majority of children grow up in communities with more than one spoken language (Grosjean, 2022), including children who use AAC, some of whom are refugees (Brock & Thomas, 2021; Soto & Yu, 2014). Assessment of spoken language comprehension and use should include all the languages that are spoken in the child's environment.

Use

There are many tests that may be used to assess spoken language. One review found 76 standardized language tests for English (Denman et al., 2017). However, most individuals who are about to start learning an alternative communication system have little or no speech. The exception to this is children and adults who, because of motor disorders, have such unintelligible speech that it is only understood by the family and others who know them well. Many individuals are unintelligible even to their family. The initial assessment of the individual's use of communication and language prior to AAC intervention therefore mainly concentrates on other forms of communication than speech. The *McArthur-Bates Communication Development Inventories* (Marchman & Dale, 2023; see Table 4.2) is a detailed schema for registration of the child's use of common words and phrases, which exists in many languages. It has been used extensively in research with children with typical and atypical development, including delayed language (Heilmann et al., 2005), autism spectrum disorder (Charman et al., 2003), intellectual disabilities (Thomas et al., 2020) and cerebral palsy (Molinaro et al., 2020). It may be used with children being assessed for AAC but because the child will not use many spoken words the expressive part may be expanded to include the child's use of manual signs or graphic symbols (see Figure 4.6).

The communicative expressions initially used by children and adults in need of AAC vary considerably. Assessment of expressive communication should include all types of expression and early pre-verbal communication skills may be part of the AAC assessment. *Early Social Communication Scales* and *Social Communication Questionnaire* investigate the child's early use of pointing and other behaviours used in initiating joint attention (see Table 4.2). They are designed for screening children with suspected autism spectrum disorder, but observations of the child's early non-verbal communication are also useful for planning early communication intervention for children with other disabilities (Goldin-Meadow, 2020).

In some children with severe motor disorders, expressive communication may be limited to looking at things in which they are interested, vocalizing as an expression of wishes and interests, and crying or other signals of excitement. Sometimes the strongest expression of interest is a change in muscle tonus, for example that the child's body stiffens and stops making small movements. Other children and adults with severe motor disorders have relatively good comprehension of spoken language and may be able to express "yes" and "no", for example by moving the eyes up and down, blinking, nodding or shaking the head. If children and adults with developmental disorders communicate in such a way, even while an assessment is being made of which first communication aid would be most appropriate, this indicates that they will receive the communication aid at a much later age than is ideal. They have already developed considerable language comprehension and have probably needed communication aids to express themselves for a long time (see von Tetzchner et al., 2018).

Children who belong to the alternative language group can also have unusual forms of communication. For example, autistic children may approach an adult, take hold of the adult's hand and lead her to a place where there is something they want, or where a particular activity is usually carried out. This may, for example, be the refrigerator where a bottle of orange juice is usually kept. In instances of this kind, communication typically takes place in a succession of events. After the child and the adult have arrived at the refrigerator, the adult will open the refrigerator door and the child will reach out for the bottle of orange juice, perhaps at the same time saying *uh uh* or vocalizing in other ways.

Children who belong to the alternative language group may also use locations as part of their communication. There are children who are reported to sit down under the table when they want to go to the toilet, stand by the door to the kitchen when they are hungry, or sit down by their boots when they want to go outside. These activities may be interpreted as communicative signals, but because the individual does not address another person, the signals may be difficult to discover for parents or teachers in the midst of all the other daily tasks. Moreover, when an individual moves to a particular location this may not be always an expression of a communicative intention, like in this example of a girl with Rett syndrome (see also Chapter 3):

> A girl with Rett syndrome sometimes moves to the sink in the kitchen and stays there. When she is given something to drink, she drinks eagerly, suggesting that she is thirsty. However, she never addresses the adult or initiates interaction when she is sitting by the sink.

In this example, it seems as if the girl had associated the sink with drinking but she had not developed the ability to address someone to request what she wanted. In the following example, the girl's interest is easy for the mother to infer from the girl's behaviour:

> Kathryn is a nine-year-old autistic girl. She is unable to speak. When she hears her father drive the car into the garage, she often goes to the door and pulls at the door handle while she looks at her mother and vocalizes. When she is allowed to go with him, she smiles and looks happy. These actions were therefore interpreted as Kathryn's way of expressing that she wants to go for a drive with her father.

Children who have normal motor functions but who have not developed speech may use gestures in very different ways. Children with developmental language disorder or childhood apraxia of speech typically begin to communicate using pointing and conventional and self-created symbolic gestures (Capone & McGregor, 2004; Funayama & Nakajima, 2023).

Autistic children, on the other hand, tend to have poor mastery of gestures and other forms of non-verbal communication (Watson et al., 2013). It is still important to assess the way they use gestures and other forms of directive behaviours (Ellawadi & Weismer, 2014; Phillips et al., 1995). There are children who only use pointing when they have been taught to do so. Some children in the supportive language group and the alternative language group use idiosyncratic gestures in ways that resemble words or manual signs. In families with deaf children, these are called "home signs" (Napier & Leeson, 2016). They emerge in the interactions between the child and the family and do not resemble conventional signs.

> Geoffrey is an 11-year-old autistic boy. He beats the table with his fist to say "Daddy" (Steindal, 1990).

> A woman had created her own manual name signs for significant people. MOTHER was articulated by stroking the index finger and middle finger along the temple of her head. FATHER was articulated with the index finger at the jaw. AUNT-BEATE was articulated by taking grip of the ear lobe with two or three fingers. The name of the special teacher, ELLEN, was articulated with the index finger at the neck. Three other teachers had their names on the forearm. (See Figure 4.5)

Similar idiosyncratic expressions are common in the initial stages of speech development in children with typical development, often called *vocables* (Ferguson, 1978). A vocable is defined as a vocalization that has a fixed, recognisable acoustic form and a clearly defined use. Vocables have, however, no acoustic similarities with conventional words. *Vroomvroom* may, for example, be used about toy cars and tractors, and *uvuvuv* about birds, aeroplanes, flies and other flying things. Both vocables and the equivalent gestures that are used by children with language disorders have uses that do not correspond to specific words in the spoken language. The fact that children do not use the words in the same way as adults is, however, a general feature of their language, and is not only linked to the use of vocables (see p. 212). A one-year-old child may use *bow-wow* when speaking of dogs, cats and sheep (over-extension), or say *dog* only when his father points at a picture of a dog on his bib (under-extension). When assessing receptive vocabulary, one may go beyond the naming of pictures of animals and common objects, and observe comprehension in sentences and conversations.

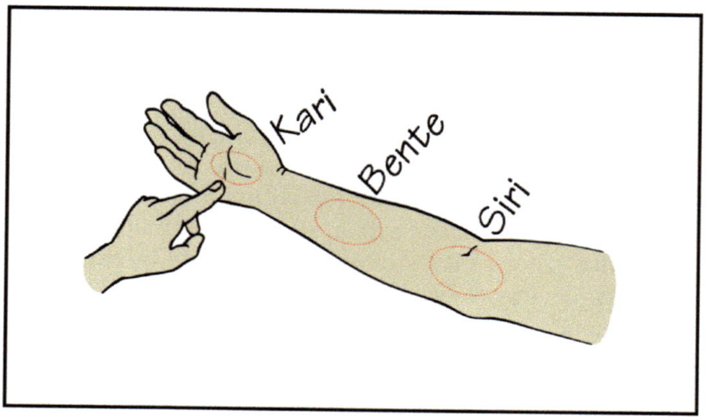

Figure 4.5 Home signs for names.

When the child has a low frequency of communication, descriptions given by parents and other significant people are often the most important source of information about a child's various modes of communication. A low incidence of communication means that usually only those people who are in close contact with the child have practical opportunities to know the form and extent of his communication. A problem for children with language disorders is that their idiosyncratic expressions, which is the communication mode they have that most resembles words, are often not recognized by teachers as "proper" communication. Parents also relate that they have not been believed when they told others about their child's idiosyncratic communication. Although the aim is that the individual should be understood by as many people as possible, it is important to register and acknowledge these expressions, which may later be replaced with more conventional expressions. The *Communication Matrix* may be a useful tool for registering children's very early communicative functions in any communication mode. The *Pragmatics Profile of Everyday Communication Skills in Children* may also be useful for registering uncommon communication expressions in children up to the age of around ten years. Both instruments contain questions about pragmatic functions, like greeting, requesting or naming, and how the individual manages them (see Table 4.2).

Use of AAC

When the assessment takes place after AAC intervention has been initiated, the individual's comprehension and use of the AAC system should be a natural part of the assessment. In early development, the assessment should include a description of how each manual sign, graphic symbol or tangible symbol is used by the individual (semantic mapping). It is possible to use various natural situations to elicit alternative language samples that allow a calculation of the individual's mean length of utterance, utterance structure and pragmatic functions (see Chapters 9 and 11). There are, however, no norms for language development with alternative means. The aim is therefore not to establish some kind of "alternative language level" but to understand the complexity of the individual's AAC constructions and form a basis for deciding the following steps in the intervention. This description is especially important for building on successful interventions and for providing new forms of interventions that may sustain the individual's development of more complex and precise ways of communicating.

For assessment of children who have developed a larger expressive AAC repertoire, listing of the vocabulary is not enough but formal tests of expressive alternative communication are lacking. There is a test of British Sign Language production (Herman et al., 2004) and a few other national sign language tests that may be adapted to other sign languages (Enns et al., 2016; Kanto et al., 2021; Mann & Haug, 2015). These may also inspire assessment of manual signs used as AAC, but the vocabularies and grammars of national sign languages are much more complex than the manual sign systems and the utterances produced by children using manual signs as AAC. Meuris and associates (2014) use a narrative format to get broader picture of the signing skills of individuals with intellectual disabilities using key word signing. The task of the individual is to retell a story that is first told by the assessor, both using a wordless storybook with pictures. Several scores are derived from the individual's narrative: number of different manual signs and words, number of spoken words, manual signs, and simultaneous signs and words, number of utterances, mean length of utterance and so forth. For assessment of manual sign use, Grove provides useful descriptions of manual sign production (Grove et al., 2019), multi-sign constructions (Grove, 2019a) and pragmatic functions

of signs (Grove, 2019b) in children with intellectual disabilities. Grove (2019a) emphasizes the need to include in the assessment how children are producing utterances combining manual signs and spoken language to establish a total language competence.

For children using aided language, the expressive tasks used in the *Becoming an Aided Communicator* (BAC) project might be used to elicit aided language constructions and assess graphic communication skills independent of spoken language (Table 4.3). The aim of many of the tasks is to assess the individual's ability to communicate something that is unknown to the other person. This is an important skill for individuals in the early phases of AAC development as well as more advanced users of manual signs and graphic symbols. The BAC tasks include naming of objects, describing drawings of pictured scenes and short video events that are unknown to the communication partner. Some of the scenes and videos are quite unusual, like a girl writing with a carrot or a man walking a pineapple on a leash, to avoid the partner inferring a common scenario from just one or two symbols. In other tasks, the child is instructing the partner to make a particular construction, such as building a tower or dressing a doll. The individual's instruction is based on a tower or doll that the individual but not the partner can see. In BAC Pragmatic Cartoons, the individual is shown sequences of pictures accompanied by a short dialogue and asked to provide the last dialogue turn. At present there are few tasks designed for assessing aided language use but those that exist may function as inspiration for creative interventionists. It is possible to develop new tasks of various complexities based on the principles of the BAC tasks. The tasks provide information about the individual's aided language constructions and strategies. This information is essential for intervention planning and assessment and intervention activities thus merge.

Table 4.3 Overview of comprehension tasks and production tasks used in the BAC study (see von Tetzchner, 2018).

BAC Task	*Material*	*Procedure*
Comprehension		
Vocabulary	One graphic symbol and four pictures	The individual is asked to indicate the picture that corresponds to the graphic symbol.
Sentence	One graphic sentence and four pictures	The individual is asked to indicate the picture that corresponds to the graphic sentence.
Sentence	One picture and four graphic sentences	The individual is asked to indicate the sentence that corresponds to the picture.
Sentence	A video and four graphic sentences	The individual is shown a short video and asked to select the sentence that best corresponds with the video. The individual is shown the video again after his or her first reply and offered the chance to maintain the original answer or indicate another sentence.
Symbol Order	One picture and four graphic sentences	The four sentences on each task contain the same graphic symbols but in different order. The individual is asked to select the one that fits best with the picture.
Story	Graphic story	The individual is shown a short story written in his or her own graphic system and asked ten yes-no questions about the content.

(*Continued*)

Table 4.3 (Continued)

BAC Task	*Material*	*Procedure*
Production		
BAC Naming	Drawings of objects	The task contains two training drawings and twenty task drawings. The child is asked to name each object on the drawing.
BAC Describing Without Naming	Drawings of objects	There are three training drawings and nine tasks. The drawing is hidden from the partner. The child is asked to describe the object in such a way that the partner can infer what it is.
BAC Pictured Scene Description	Drawings of situations	There are three training drawings and eight tasks. The drawing is hidden from the partner. The child is asked to describe the drawing in such a way that the partner can describe the content of the scene.
BAC Event Description	Short events on video	There are three training videos and fifteen tasks. The child is shown the video while the partner is out of the room. The child is asked to describe the video event in such a way that the partner can describe what is happening in the video.
BAC Pragmatic Cartoons	Sequences of drawings	There are two training cartoons with several pictures and twelve tasks. The dialogue in the cartoon is read to the child but the last turn is missing. The child is asked what the cartoon figure in the last picture says.
BAC Instructing and Constructing	Toys	The task of the individual is to instruct a partner to make a construction that is identical to a construction that can be seen by the individual but not by the partner. There are two training constructions and eight task constructions.

Additionally, the narrative format of Meuris and associates (2014) described for manual signs above can easily be adapted to aided language. The *Test of Aided-Communication Symbol Performance* (TASP; Bruno, 2010) is speech-based and may be used to assess some aspects of aided language in individuals who have used PCS for some time. In most of the tasks, the child has to indicate images from PCS representing single words spoken by the assessor or sequences of PCS images that represent spoken sentences. The test items require good comprehension of spoken language, visual perception and fine motor skills for finger pointing. For advanced aided communicators it is also possible to use verbal tasks that require answers with more than one word or graphic symbol, such as the verbal tasks in the Wechsler tests, as a measure of how well they express their reasoning and knowledge.

Comprehension

Comprehension of spoken language and alternative communication systems varies among individuals with little or no speech. Knowledge about an individual's ability to understand people in the surroundings will indicate to what extent he or she will benefit from spoken instructions and instructions with manual signs or graphic symbols in intervention. People in the environment of individuals who use AAC usually communicate using spoken language

and the instructions and strategies used by interventionists tend to be explicitly or implicitly based on assumptions about the individual's comprehension of spoken language. If the assumptions about language comprehension are not correct, the intervention strategies applied will not be optimal. Assessment of comprehension of both spoken language and alternative language forms is therefore crucial, but comprehension can be difficult to assess (Bishop et al., 2016). There are many examples of children and adults having been credited with good understanding of spoken language, while careful observation revealed that it was not the words they understood, but rather the gestures accompanying the speech or clues in the situation.

> Martin is a three-year-old autistic boy without speech. He is fond of orange juice and usually comes running when his mother shouts: *Come and have some orange juice*. As part of the AAC assessment, the mother was told to shout out in the same way as usual but sit still without moving. She was quite surprised to find that Martin did not react but carried on twirling a toy. A short while later she stood up, walked toward the kitchen table where the bottle of orange juice was standing and repeated the words. Martin came running immediately (Steindal, 1990).

Martin's lack of reaction indicated that he did not understand what the mother said. However, the fact that he reacted to the mother's gestures showed that he was observant and utilized other social cues and that he probably would have benefitted from much earlier access to AAC.

People with very extensive motor disorders may almost totally lack ordinary means of showing that they understand. Some have, for years, been underestimated in terms of what they understood of both speech and of what was going on around them. A serious consequence of underestimation is that the individual is not given the stimulation and the opportunities of development that ought to have been provided.

> Joe Deacon was severely motor impaired and had lived in various institutions for people with intellectual disabilities from the age of three. At age 24, he could vocalize but the staff regarded him as severely intellectually disabled and assumed that his unintelligible vocalizations had no meaning. At that time, a new man arrived in the institution. He had lived in the same institution as Joe in early childhood and was able to understand Joe's vocalizations. In a re-assessment of Joe's cognitive abilities, he functioned as interpreter. The man was intellectually disabled and could not answer the questions himself, only relay Joe's answers. The results showed that Joe was not severely intellectually disabled. Later, the two men allied themselves with two other inhabitants, a man with intellectual disabilities who was able to use a typewriter and a motor-impaired man who could spell. With the help of his friends, Joe wrote his autobiography, *Tongue tied* (Deacon, 1974).

Less dramatic forms of under-estimation – and over-estimation – may occur frequently (Mei et al., 2016, 2020). It is difficult to use ordinary systematic observation with this group because they may attempt to communicate rather infrequently. The observations would have to be so prolonged that it would be impractical to carry them out. However, systematic observation can be used advantageously at the same time as AAC intervention is started if it is carried out by people who are usually with the individual. The observations will then provide extra information about the individual's skills and form the basis for evaluation of the intervention.

The individual's expressive abilities will to some extent determine the methods that can be used to assess comprehension. For people who can speak or write and appear to have a reasonable vocabulary for self-expression, a good impression of their language comprehension may be obtained through conversations and by asking various everyday questions. It is much more difficult to assess comprehension when the individual has few words with which to show comprehension (Mei et al., 2020). The *McArthur-Bates Communication Development Inventories* for 8 to 18 months include a detailed schema for registration of the child's comprehension of gestures, common words and phrases (Marchman & Dale, 2023; see Table 4.2). For individuals who belong to the expressive language group and others whom one knows have some understanding of spoken language, ordinary tests can be useful tools, if the individuals have the motor skills that are necessary to carry out the task instructions. However, a number of tests or test items place considerable demands on motor skills. For example, in the *New Reynell Developmental Language Scales* (RDLS, Edwards et al., 2011) the child has to carry out instructions such as *Put the doll on the chair* or *Put all the pigs behind the brown horse*. Some tests of receptive language require minimal motor involvement; the individual shows comprehension of a spoken word by pointing out one picture among several others, like the *British Picture Vocabulary Scale* (BPVS, Dunn et al., 2009), the *Peabody Picture Vocabulary Test* (PPVT, Dunn, 2019) and tests with a similar format for assessing sentence comprehension, like the *Test for Reception of Grammar* (TROG, Bishop, 2003). These tests are available in several languages.

For many people with severe motor disabilities even pointing can be difficult to do in such a way that another individual can safely decide which of several alternatives the individual is pointing to. If physical pointing requires substantial cognitive efforts, this leaves fewer cognitive resources for problem solving and may reduce the number of correct replies. For individuals with good eye-motor control, eye-gaze pointing may be a good solution. Another alternative is to use assisted scanning, where the tester points to each answer alternative in an even manner, and the individual only has to reply when the tester indicates the right picture (Kurmanaviciute & Stadskleiv, 2017; Schiørbeck & Stadskleiv, 2008). When the child's responses are difficult to read, the assessor may need help to interpret the answers.

> Ida is five years old with cerebral palsy. She has severe motor impairments and no intelligible speech, and looks up with her eyes for "yes" and down for "no". A psychologist assesses her language comprehension and non-verbal cognitive abilities using assisted scanning. For each item, the psychologist indicates the pictures representing the answer alternatives with an even pace. However, Ida's expressions are difficult to read for people who do not know her well. Ida's mother is therefore helping to interpret Ida's expressions and telling the psychologist when Ida confirms the answer alternative that the psychologist is pointing at. The mother is sitting behind the psychologist and therefore cannot see what the psychologist is pointing at. She therefore does not know if the answer is right or wrong; she only looks at Ida and interprets her expression.

Due to Ida's motor impairments and their difficulties reading her expressions, some of the teachers in preschool had expressed doubt about Ida's cognitive abilities and thought that the mother maybe overestimated Ida's abilities. It was therefore important to do the testing in such a way that the mother could not influence the answers. Ida demonstrated abilities in the typical range. The teachers acknowledged that the results were valid, and this had a positive consequence for how they involved Ida in communicative interactions and activities.

A few tests are specially adapted to children with motor disabilities. *Computer-based Inventory of Low Motor Language Testing* (C-BILLT; Geytenbeek et al., 2010, 2014) measures vocabulary and sentence comprehension and can be answered using pointing, switches or eye-gaze equipment on a computer. This test is available in several languages.

Individuals with severe speech, motor and eye-motor or visual impairments are among the most difficult to assess. However, they may have a reliable manner of signalling acceptance or rejecting that may be utilized. For example, the first edition of *Illinois Test of Psycholinguistic Abilities* (Kirk et al , 1968) has yes-no questions like *Can boys eat?* or *Can parachutes paddle?* and such questions can be used to assess simple sentence comprehension, if the individual has some way of expressing "yes" and "no".

Assessment of more advanced language comprehension should not be based on vocabulary alone. Tests of vocabulary, like BPVS and PPVT, are based on knowledge of increasingly rare words. Individuals with little or no speech, especially those with severe motor disabilities, tend to have less varied language experiences than individuals with typical development. Their scores on a test based on increasingly rare words may reflect their lack of experience rather than their linguistic understanding and reasoning. For example, Lund (2015) describes a young man using aided communication who obtained a standard score of 77 on PPVT, well below the mean of 100. He was attending college and doing well, and the PPVT score therefore did not reflect his cognitive and academic functioning (Lund & Light, 2006). Grammatical knowledge may be less influenced by breadth of experience and TROG or other tests of sentence understanding may be a better measure of linguistic competence.

For individuals with limited comprehension, the best information may come in the form of tangible reports from significant people in the individual's environment. They have the advantage of a wealth of experiences gained from being together with the individual. It is also the significant people, and parents in particular, who, by spending so much time with the child or adolescent, have laid the foundations for both the usage and understanding of language and communication. The way children and adolescents with severe disabilities show their understanding can be very unusual and difficult for other people to discover. For young children, parents may complete checklists like the *McArthur-Bates Communication Development Inventories* (MB-CDI) (see Table 4.2). Adaptation of the MB-CDI is available in some sign languages (Caselli et al., 2020). The comprehension part of the *Word and Gestures Form* of the MB-CDI may be a good starting point for discussing vocabulary selection with parents although it should be noted that the MB-CDI contains a selection of commonly understood and used words and phrases that may not reflect special characteristics of the home language environment or the child's own interests. In a detailed diary study, the parents of one boy registered 341 words in the MB-CDI when he was 24 months old, but they had heard him use 679 words – 338 of these words were not part of the MB-CDI (Roy et al., 2015). The child's use of manual signs or graphic symbols may also be included in the form (see Figure 4.6) but the norms do not take the special situation of children developing AAC into account.

Parents of children with more severe disabilities are not always aware of the cues they use when interpreting their child's expressive communication, but systematic interviews can provide information about the individual's reactions. This information is important for planning the intervention and professionals should take the time needed when speaking with the family and others who are in close contact with the individual. As a starting point, one may ask such questions as: *Think of something you are quite certain that you can say to John or make him understand in another way. What is it John does that makes you sure that he has understood you?*

Category	Word	Shows comprehension	Word expressed with:			
			Speech	Manual signs	Graphic symbols	Other means
Animals	Cat	1	0	0	0	0
	Dog	1	0	1	1	0
	Cow	0	0	0	0	0
	Horse	0	0	0	0	0
Food	Bread					
	Jam					
Clothing	Sweater					
	Pants					
	Dress					

Indicate if the child shcws comprehension of a word and if the child expresses it with speech, manual sign, graphic symbol or in other ways. Mark words the child comprehends with 1, and words the child does not comprehend with 0. For each word, mark expressive modes mastered with 1 and the mode(s) not yet mastered with 0. If a child expresses a word in two or more moded, mark all with 1.

Figure 4.6 Expansion of MacArthur-Bates Communicative Development Inventory (MB-CDI) to include registration of other expressive modalities than speech. In this example, the parents indicate that their child comprehends *cat* and *dog*, expresses DOG with manual signs and graphic symbols, but not in speech, and does not comprehend or express the words *cow* and *horse*.

Questions of this kind can be asked in different ways and the professional's choice of words should be appropriate for the person who is asked.

In interviews, parents and other significant people initially may answer quite generally, saying things like: *I can tell just by looking at him*. General characterizations of the individual's language comprehension may well be correct but are nonetheless an insufficient basis for intervention. Follow-up questions are usually needed, such as *Yes, of course. But please describe it for me. What does he do? What does he look like when he is doing it? What is it he always understands?* or *What is it he only seems to understand now and again?* If the interviewer is patient, significant people will almost always be able to answer questions of this type. It is our experience that this is also true of people who are close to the cognitively lowest-functioning individuals.

Disagreement about the individual's level of functioning can make the collaboration around intervention difficult. The assessment should be the basis for a shared understanding of the individual's strengths and weakness. However, some parents feel that professionals are most centred on reducing their expectations as to the child's future development (Gohsman, 2021; Walter et al., 2022). An Individual Habilitation Plan based on a vision of the individual five years into the future, created jointly by the parents and the professionals, is a useful tool for overcoming such disagreements. The Habilitation Plan requires agreement on what immediate steps to take in order to promote development towards reaching the long-term goals – including AAC development. The discussion of these steps should make it easier to reach agreement about the child's strengths and weaknesses (Hesselberg & von Tetzchner, 2016).

Some degree of over-interpretation may be positive. Structured over-interpretation is a strategy for the early phases of intervention (see p. 172). However, the aim of the assessment

is to obtain the most correct impression possible of the individual's language comprehension. Overestimation implies that the language intervention will not be optimally adapted. It is particularly easy to overestimate the language comprehension of an individual who has some understanding of what is being said. For example, in a teaching or informal testing situation one might say: "Point at the red ball", whereby the individual points correctly. On the basis of this observation one may assume that the individual understands the whole utterance. In addition, one may also assume that the individual comprehends words that he or she understands in a given situation, in other, unrelated situations, too. In early phases of development, this is often not the case. Also informal tasks should be designed to minimize this problem, for example by having picture options that make it necessary to understand not only a single word, for example *ball*, but the whole phrase. This can be done by including pictures a *green ball*, a *red car*, a *red ball* and a *goal* as answer options. Similarly, in observations of sentence comprehension, it is important to ascertain that the child's reply is not based on an understanding of the individual words only, for example *dog, basket, in* and *lie*, but the whole sentence *the dog lies in the basket* by identifying the picture of that and ignoring pictures of a dog lying in front of a basket, sitting in a basket or lying in a bucket (see Geytenbeek et al., 2010).

Comprehension of words and situations

Understanding what is going on in communication does not depend only on the linguistic expression itself. Many conditions may contribute to the understanding of a situation and give cues as to what most likely is being communicated (see Chapter 8). The rattling of pots and pans in the kitchen may indicate that someone is preparing dinner, holding a coat may indicate that someone is soon to leave the house, and so forth. In addition, what is being said, often accompanied by eye contact, pointing and other gestures, also contributes to the understanding of the situation, even if what is being said is not in itself understood (like in the earlier example with Martin).

Some individuals show understanding only when they are together with certain people. This does not mean that they do not understand anything of what is being said, but rather that the understanding of individual words or phrases depend on the situation. This may be the beginning of a deeper comprehension of spoken words and manual signs or graphic symbols that emerges with increasing experience.

The fact that an individual's understanding of spoken words is linked to the use of gestures or other types of non-verbal communication is often not apparent in interviews with significant people. The communication partners may not be aware of making gestures or providing other communicative cues. Systematic observation of the communicative situations is therefore necessary when the information provided gives the impression that the communication is dependent on a situation or person. Documentation of such dependency can be a good starting point for further discussion about the intervention with parents and other significant people.

Information about how the parents and others evaluate the individual's comprehension has another important function: It provides insight into how people in the environment may interpret and react to the individual's signs of comprehension and the extent to which they try to adapt their own communication to support the individual's comprehension. This knowledge is useful when assessing the language environment and planning adaptation of the communicative environment to promote the individual's communication and language skills in the best possible manner (see Chapter 12).

Comprehension of AAC

Individuals using AAC experience a bimodal language situation (Smith & Grove, 1999). Most understand spoken language and manual signs or graphic symbols. Comprehension of spoken language is usually assessed but if the assessment takes place after AAC has been introduced, the individual's comprehension of his AAC system should also be included in the assessment.

The comprehension process can be very complex. Some individuals who use AAC understand spoken words alone; others only in combination with manual signs or graphic symbols. Some understand manual signs or graphic symbols alone; others need speech to support them as well. Some individuals understand only manual signs or graphic symbols in spite of years of simultaneous presentations of spoken words and manual signs or graphic symbols. As with speech, assessment should comprise the individual's interpretation of single manual signs and graphic or tangible symbols, as well as sentence constructions with two or more elements. For more advanced users of AAC systems, assessment may also include comprehension of metaphors, irony and other forms of figurative language, as well as of complex sentences presented in their own system.

There are tests of comprehension for some sign languages (Enns et al., 2016; Mann & Haug, 2015). The *British Sign Language Receptive Skills Test* and other sign language tests may, to some extent, be adapted to assess comprehension of manual signs used as AAC, but the vocabularies and grammars of national sign languages are much more complex than the manual sign systems used as AAC. Many key word signs differ from the signs of the national sign languages and the use of sentences is often limited in key word signing (Grove & Woll, 2017). There are adapted and normed versions of the *McArthur-Bates Communication Development Inventories* for British Sign Language (Woolfe et al., 2010), American Sign Language (Caselli et al., 2020), Spanish Sign Language (Rodriguez-Ortiz et al., 2020) and some other sign languages. The MB-CDI form may also be expanded to include scores for comprehension of manual signs or graphic symbols used as AAC (see Figure 4.6).

For children using graphic communication systems, tasks used in the BAC project also include comprehension of graphic vocabulary and grammar (see Table 4.3). The formats used are similar to BPVS, PPVT and TROG but measure comprehension of graphic symbols instead of spoken words (Figure 4.7). As with assessment of expressive aided language, new comprehension tasks may be created based on the principles of the BAC tasks (see Table 4.3).

Challenging behaviour

Individuals with severe communication and language disorders may experience many difficult situations and react with behaviours typically termed "problematic" or "challenging". They may scream, do damage, or cause injury to self or others (see p. 90). There may be different reasons for such reactions and in particular self-injury appears often in individuals with autism spectrum disorder and intellectual disabilities who have limited communication and language skills (Didden et al., 2012; Licence et al., 2020) – and in individuals with unidentified language disorders (Hollo et al., 2014). Collecting information about the presence of challenging behaviours should therefore be a part of the AAC assessment process.

Challenging behaviour may be reactions to frustration, lack of overview, insecure situations or complex demands, together with poor means to handle such situations (Oliver et al., 2022; Reyes-Martín et al., 2022; Rinaldi et al., 2022; von Tetzchner, 2004). Anxiety and depression

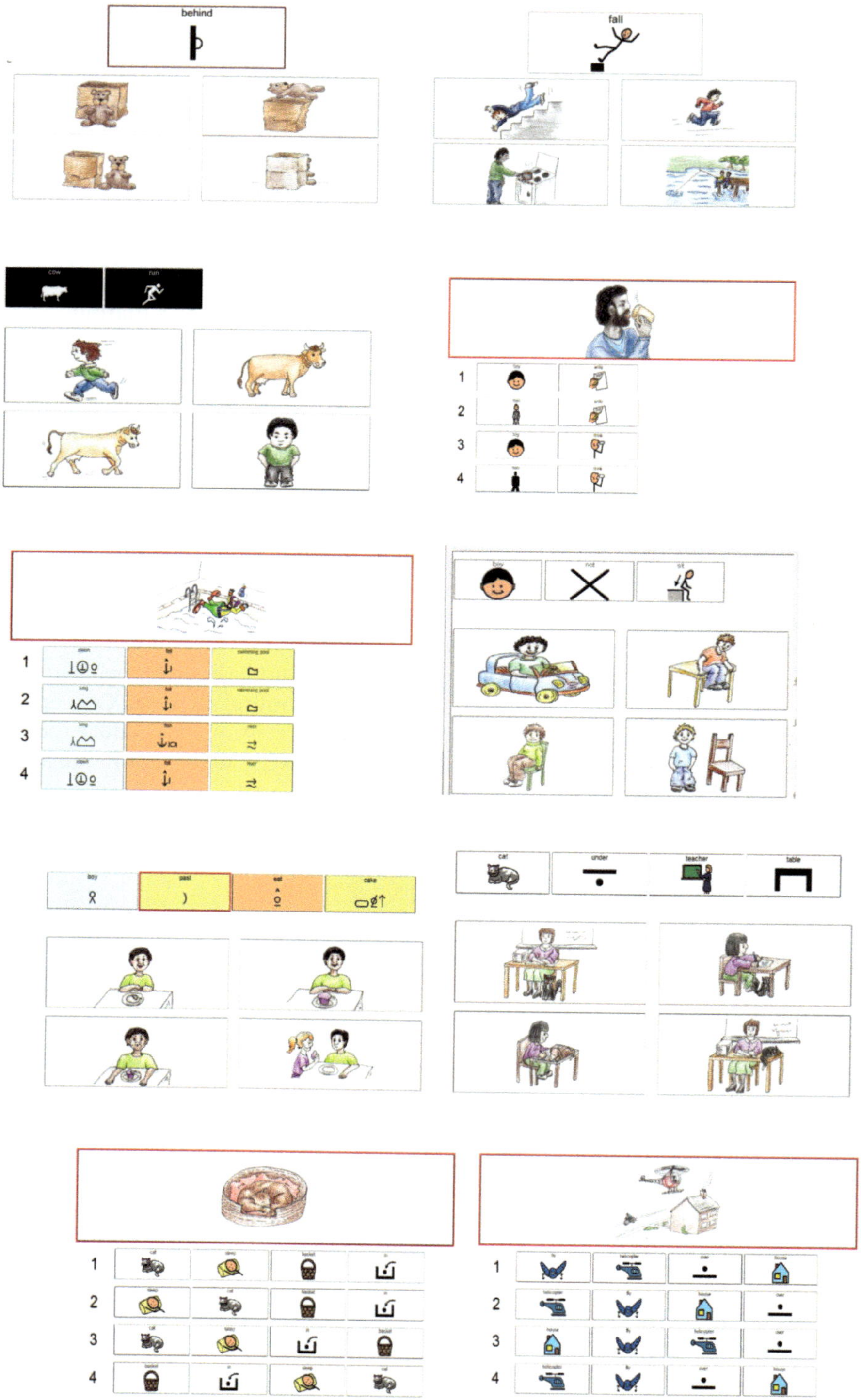

Figure 4.7 Examples of BAC comprehension tasks.

are common among individuals with autism spectrum disorder and intellectual disabilities, but symptoms may be atypical and difficult to recognize (Helverschou & Martinsen, 2011; Kerns & Kendall, 2014). A strong observed relationship between self-injury and communication skills indicates that self-injury may be related to the experiences of communication failures and suggests that early communication and language intervention may contribute to preventing the development of challenging behaviour (Bowring et al., 2017). Challenging behaviour reflects the subjective life of the individual, how she or he experiences and copes with everyday life, and his or her communication abilities and resources. Information about challenging behaviour may thus provide insight into the individual's interests, pleasures and fears. The objective of the assessment is to find out what the individual is interested in or concerned about, and why and when she or he may become frustrated. This may vary from situation to situation.

The observed relationship between challenging behaviour and language skills underlines the importance of providing individuals with means to express themselves, but also of revealing which circumstances elicit frustration, uncertainly and anxiety, and how communication skills may be supported to help the individual cope with such situations. In this way, AAC intervention may be a means to reduce frustrations and increase coping. The communicative competence of peers has been found to influence the individual's communication skills and thereby any challenging behaviour (Hofmann & Müller, 2021). The presence of challenging behaviour and persistent occurrence may indicate a lack of appropriate communication training, as well as whether the training is meaningful to the individual. Interventions with manual signs or graphic symbols can be non-optimal but it is particularly speech training without real communicative use of the words that seems to be frustrating and meaningless to the individual. For example, some reports describe a high prevalence of challenging behaviour in communication training based on the principles of applied behavioural analysis (Carr et al., 1996). A broader approach to communication assessment and intervention may reduce the probability of resurgence of challenging behaviour which often appears when communication intervention is terminated because the individual reacts less often with self-injury (Radhakrishnan et al., 2020). Reduced prevalence of challenging behaviour should thus not be regarded as an indication to stop the intervention but rather to continue intervention and expand the individual's communication skills

Assessment of communication partners and environment

The AAC competence of people in the environment will determine how well the individual is understood and whether there are people the individual can learn from. People in the environment must understand the individual's expressive communication, use a communication mode that the individual is able to understand, and communicate in such a way that the individual can learn new manual signs or graphic symbols and communication strategies through their conversations (see Chapters 11 and 12). The AAC competence of all the persons who are in regular interaction with the individual should be assessed, as well as the individual's opportunities to communicate in preschool or school, at the day centre or work, in leisure time, at home, and at respite and other forms of care. *Social Networks* (see p. 103) may be useful in this assessment.

The assessment may include significant persons' ability to recognize manual signs or graphic symbols, and how they would interpret a variety of utterances produced with manual signs or graphic symbols, or interpret the individual's communicative expressions on video. When the individual has acquired some communication skills, partner "testing" with special communication tasks may be useful, for example using BAC tasks to assess how the partner

understands the individual's description of a drawing of a scene that the individual but not the partner can see (Murray et al., 2018). Or the assessor may show the individual a video while the communication partner is in another room. The task of the partner – in interaction with the individual – is to find out what is on the video from the individual's utterances with manual signs or graphic symbols (see Neuvonen et al., 2022; Smith et al., 2018). (Similar tasks are used to assess the individual's ability to relay information). This type of dialogue gives insight into the communication partner's understanding of the individual's communication, and to the strategies the partner uses to find out what the individual wants to communicate. It also gives information about how the individual uses his manual or graphic vocabulary and other means of communication means to relay messages.

Even when people in the environment have appropriate skills, these skills are not always used. Both at home and in school manual signs may not be used frequently by adults (Launonen, 2019b; Rombouts et al., 2019) and partner use of keyword graphic symbols in everyday conversation may be rare (see p. 277). The assessment of people in the environment will provide insight into how they usually react to the individual's speech and alternative communication mode. It should also include information about what manual signs or graphic symbols people in the environment are using themselves, how they use them, and how often they use them in different situations. This is important information when planning to introduce new vocabulary items and sentence constructions. The assessment should include interviews with parents, significant people and other people about their attitudes towards the use of AAC, whether they agree with the individual's alternative communication form, and whether they are complying with the decision to use it. Without such loyalty, intervention will never be completely successful.

Assessment of the environment may reveal negative attitudes – often combined with a lack of AAC competence and relevant skills. This may imply that the professionals who are responsible for the intervention should provide better AAC training to people in the environment and use the time and resources needed to give them information about AAC and what their own competence may mean for the individual's development and life quality (see Chapter 12).

Evaluating the language intervention

The final step in the *AAC Pyramid* is *AAC Monitoring* (Stadskleiv, 2015). This is about continuity and change, about stability in intervention efforts and developmental progress. Regardless of how well intervention is planned in advance, it cannot be taken for granted that development will proceed as predicted. The implementation of AAC after assessment should therefore always be followed closely, with continuous evaluation of the intervention on the basis of the explicit objectives. The evaluation should be discussed beforehand and be part of the intervention plan right from the beginning. Planned evaluations help clarify the teaching objectives and make it easier to see the relationship between the different aims of the intervention. Because the evaluation is planned, the intervention does not have to be clearly inappropriate before it is adjusted or modified.

The evaluation should be as extensive as is practically possible and cover all relevant aspects of the individual's comprehension and use of AAC (Bean et al., 2023). It should cover the specific aims that have been set for the AAC intervention as well as the generalized effects of the intervention in terms of the total life situation, that is, whether the individual gets more opportunities to express wishes and ideas, participates in more activities, is more attentive during teaching sessions and in interaction with others, is more social, shows fewer

behavioural problems, and so forth. Monitoring should also include partner competence and communicative access of the environment.

There are several questionnaires designed to measure results of AAC interventions (see Table 4.2). The *Focus on the Outcomes of Communication Under Six* is designed for measuring growth in intelligibility, expressive language, social play, independence and coping strategies following interventions for children below the age of six. Parents rate 34 statements about the child's progress on a scale from one to seven, either from "1: Not at all like my child" to "7: Exactly like my child" or from "1: Cannot do at all" to "7: Can always do without help". Sum scores range from 34 to 238 and an increase in scores indicates a positive change (Cunningham et al., 2021). The *Family Impact of Assistive Technology Scale for Augmentative and Alternative Communication, FIATS-AAC*, measures how the introduction of communication aids influences the child's functioning and the family life (Ryan et al., 2018). Standardized instruments may not capture all aspects of a specific intervention; therefore, it is important to tailor the evaluation to the goals of each individual.

Specific goals

The intervention plan should state specific goals, and the evaluation should include information about the progress – or lack of progress – related to these goals, in particular the individual's acquisition and use of speech, manual signs and graphic or tangible symbols. This means a registration of the use of signs and symbols in everyday life and the development of other communication and language skills. The specific goals can be the use of new signs or symbols, sentence construction, pragmatic functions, contact strategies, a higher level of linguistic activity and so forth. In order to evaluate the effectiveness of the individual's language production, structured communication tasks may be useful (see p. 130). The tests, checklists and other assessment materials used in the assessment may also be used in the evaluations.

The individual does not always learn what was planned. Sometimes, the individual has learned another use of a manual sign or graphic symbol than the one that was planned. This is not always negative, like in this example.

> Giles is a 19-year-old boy with severe intellectual disabilities. He was taught the manual sign BREAD because he liked bread, but he quickly began to use this sign as a general call for help and to express that there was something he wanted. This usage of the sign was very functional for him and instead of forcing him to use the sign "correctly", the manual form of BREAD was redefined to mean "help". Everybody in his environment was informed about the idiosyncratic form of the manual sign HELP in Giles' vocabulary.

BREAD HELP

Manual signs: BREAD, HELP

This example emphasizes that one should not merely register "right" or "wrong" use but analyse what the individual's use reveals about the understanding of each manual sign or graphic symbol and pattern of use. One should never assume that the individual's use of a manual sign or graphic symbol is random, although it appears unusual, and rather establish useful fixed usages even if they were not the usages intended by the teacher. If, in the example above, the teacher had only told Giles that his use of BREAD was incorrect, insisting that the sign retain the conventional meaning she had tried to teach him, this would have taken away the communication function that Giles had actually achieved. By continually evaluating and reflecting on the situation, it is possible to adapt to an unexpected development when this is most functional. If the teacher thinks that it is important for Giles to be able to express "bread", there is always another sign that can fulfil that function, or the teacher can invent one. However, this pragmatic approach also requires that all communication partners are taught how Giles uses the signs. A personal sign dictionary is always useful and can be distributed to all persons who need it (see p. 269).

The same caution concerns the assessment of the communication of young aided communicators with good comprehension of spoken language. They often have a limited vocabulary, and use items in uncommon ways when lacking items to express a particular meaning (see Chapter 8). Information about these uncommon uses gives insight into the strategies applied by the aided communicator and writing down these uses will be useful when planning further vocabulary and aided language instruction.

The evaluation report should include the type and extent of help that the individual needs at any given time to accomplish a specific communicative act within or out of the teaching sessions. Teaching may be carried out in a number of ways and reduction of the amount of help the individual needs will always be an overall aim. Reports about intervention with manual signs or graphic symbols may merely indicate the number of signs or symbols that are being taught or are in use, often only what is going on in the training sessions. This may hide significant achievements by the learner. If the help level is included in the registration of sign or symbol use, the evaluation may show considerable progress, even if the individual has not yet begun to use new signs or symbols spontaneously, because the amount of help needed to initiate and reply to communication has been reduced. Inclusion of help level also directs the professionals' attention to the co-constructive processes underlying both typical and atypical communication and language development (Jacoby & Ochs, 1995; Solomon-Rice & Soto, 2011).

Generalized effects

The development of AAC does not happen in isolation. Different abilities and skills influence each other in the developmental process. It is therefore necessary to include other domains than communication and language in the evaluation. In general, those aspects of the individual's functioning and life situation that were included in the assessment before the intervention should also be included in the evaluation. New language skills bring with them new understanding of the surroundings and the acquisition of concepts and social skills in the broadest sense. Likewise, the experience with, and understanding of, different activities positively influence individuals' ability to understand the communication of others and to express themselves. Successful communication and language intervention will therefore have consequences for most types of activities.

Research shows that professionals may have limited knowledge about the individual's communication outside the educational setting (von Tetzchner et al., 2018). The evaluation of the

intervention should contain reports about the progress during training *and* about the individual's communication in the home and other non-educational settings. To what extent the individual generalizes what is learned to other settings and people is important information (see p. 89). It is especially important to register the individual's *spontaneous* use of manual signs or graphic symbols, including information about how the individual copes with communicative challenges and the type of help or guidance that people in the surroundings give when the individual spontaneously initiates communication using AAC. The individual may take communicative initiative and use manual signs or graphic symbols without help but only in the way they had been taught. Spontaneous use may also mean that the individual uses known manual signs or graphic symbols to communicate about other issues than those practised in training sessions or mentioned in messages from the school to the parents. Some utterances may perhaps be construed as "wrong" with regard to intervention goals, but they may represent genuine attempts at communication. It is important to note these attempts when they are not successful, too. The evaluation should thus contain information about the type of objects, activities and events each sign or symbol is used to communicate about, and whether they are used to communicate about other objects or activities than those that are part of the direct teaching. One needs to know whether the individual uses a manual sign or graphic symbol in a wider sense than the common use (over-extension), or in a more restricted way, that is, about a smaller set of activities and objects than is usual (under-extension) (see p. 212). Over-extension is usually easier to observe but under-extension is common in individuals with intellectual disabilities.

A coordination of language and communication intervention with other intervention goals implies that the results of the language intervention are seen in relation to the individual's development in other domains. The individual's mental network of semantic categories is likely to change over time and indications of this process may help professionals guide the individual's communication toward more conventional use of manual signs or graphic symbols. This will also make it easier for people in the environment to understand him or her. For children and adolescents with motor disorders, a core element of the assessment is the extent to which the intervention has led to more social participation and conversations, improved the individual's active participating in the classroom or at work, and the extent to which the individual has gained more control over the content of the conversations.

Information transfer when changing school, work or home

Many individuals who are developing AAC have a long-term need for intervention. Both established and new environments need to be organized in such a way that the individuals maintain established skills and continue to acquire new skills as they pass through the phases of the lifespan, from infancy to old age (Balandin & Morgan, 2001; Lund & Light, 2006; von Tetzchner & Stadskleiv, 2016; Wickenden, 2011c). For individuals who have extensive motor disorders, the technological development may lead to the construction of communication devices that imply new possibilities for communication and community participation. However, utilization of these possibilities requires that the individuals and people around them are informed about them and given instruction and training in how to use the new technology. In the alternative language group, the acquisition of new skills is often slow and the need for intervention is likely to persist throughout life. This means that the intervention and support will take place in different environments as the individual changes school, work and

residence. Children in the supportive language group, who are given AAC intervention for only a limited period of time, may also change their school or home environment.

An implicit aim of assessment is to create coherence in the individual's intervention and thereby in his or her life situation. When an individual who lives in an adapted environment is going to move, it is crucial that routines exist for the transferral of information from professionals who have been in charge of intervention to the professionals who are to assume responsibility. All too often, such routines are lacking, which may result in discontinuity in the teaching and skill loss or stagnation in the development of new skills (Smith, 2015; Smith-Lewis, 1994). The situation is illustrated in the following case history:

> Raymond is a 20-year-old man with intellectual disabilities. He attends a special education high school. He follows simple spoken instructions but he neither speaks nor uses any form of AAC. According to his reports, he received intervention with manual signs from the age of 13 years. By the time he was transferred to another school at the age of 16, he used EAT, WALK and TOILET, and was learning several new signs. When he was 18 years old, he was transferred to a new school and the notes that were transferred with him said that "he was in the process of learning to use manual signs". At the age of 19, Raymond changed school again. When he changed school again at the age of 20, the teacher sent with him a list of over 50 manual signs that the teacher had taught and comments as to how Raymond articulated them. There was no mention in the report, however, of Raymond using any of the signs spontaneously. After more than six years of teaching, Raymond did not use any manual signs spontaneously (Kollinzas, 1983).

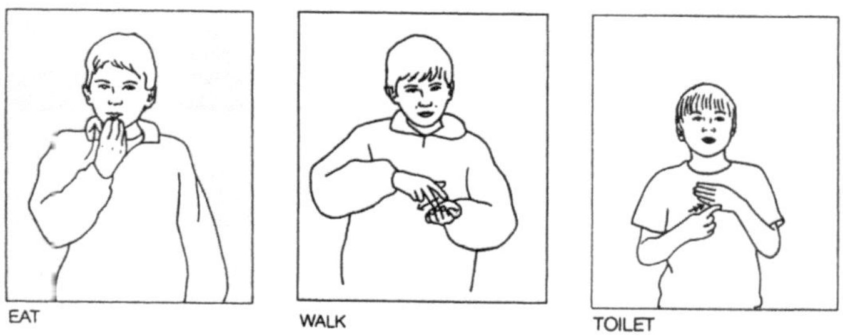

Manual signs: EAT, WALK, TOILET

There is every reason to believe that Raymond's lack of signing skills was related to his change of schools and the discontinuity he experienced in sign teaching. The *Communication Record* is designed for the registration and transferral of information about communication skills and teaching (Kollinzas, 1983). It contains information that *must* be included when the individual changes training environment, such as including information about the manual sign system or graphic symbol system used by the individual, the glosses of the signs and symbols that the individual is using or being taught, a description of how the individual articulates manual signs or indicates graphic symbols, and descriptions of situations in which each sign or symbol tend to be used (Figure 4.8). For children, adolescents and adults using aided communication, a description of their non-electronic or electronic communication aids and the access methods they use with their aids, should also be included.

COMMUNICATION RECORD

Name : Per Hansen
Age: 13;7
Instructor: Hans Larsen
Place: Vik school
Date: 2–10–88
Page: 2 of 4

Sign system	*Code*
Pictogram	P
Manual signs	H

Sign	**System**	**Execution**	**Situation information**
CHAIR	H	Normal	Performs the sign when the teacher shows the picture
TABLE	H	Normal	Performs the sign when the teacher shows the picture
KICK	P		Points himself in order to select the activity in the gymnasium
HORSE	H	Right hand between middle and ring finger	Executed alone when he knows he is going to ride
TOILET	H	Normal	Uses the sign spontaneously sometimes when he wants to go to the toilet. He is hand-guided to perform the sign when he is taken to the toilet
DOOR	H	Normal	Uses the sign spontaneously when he wants to go out
TELEVISION	P		Uses spontaneously at home when he wants to watch television
BOOTS	H	Indistinct	Not used spontaneously, the sign is hand-guided during dressing
SCARF	H	Indistinct	Not used spontaneously, the sign is hand-guided during dressing

Figure 4.8 The Communication Record.

The information in the *Communication Record* may help the staff in the new environment to develop realistic expectations of the individual – both achievements and limitations – and organize different parts of the environment to be as communicative accessible as possible. It will give the staff in the new setting some guidance from the staff who worked with the individual before the move and help to uncover the need for training of people in the new environment. External instructors and supervisors are often utilized in AAC intervention. The *Communication Record* makes it possible for the staff who are taking over to decide whether it is desirable and possible to use the same external consultants for AAC guidance and training in the new environment.

Some of the individuals with communication disabilities who have acquired some language skills may themselves be able to help in the training of people in new environments and new people who arrive in their environment, as shown in this case study:

> Isabel is a 13-year-old girl with Down syndrome. Her speech is unintelligible and she has an active vocabulary of approximately 70 manual signs. Her teacher has made a folder with drawings of all the manual signs she uses, with the signs' written glosses above the drawings. New signs are included in the folder as Isabel learns them. Isabel carries her folder with her wherever she goes. When new personnel or helpers appear, Isabel sits with them and works through the folder. She shows how the signs are articulated while the new helper struggles to learn them. This is a change of roles that Isabel clearly appreciates (Steindal, 1990).

It is unfair to the individual and a poor use of resources if what has been learned is not maintained and built upon. This would also increase the risk of frustration and negative emotional reactions. The transferral of information that can minimize the potential negative effects of a change in the individual's educational and living environment is therefore of great significance. For the people who were in charge of the individual's intervention before the move, completing the *Communication Record* should be a part of the planning of the transferral. For the people who take over the responsibility for the intervention, studying the individual's *Communication Record* is a way of getting to know the individual and a part of the entry assessment of the individual.

Putting plans into action: defining areas of responsibility

A thorough assessment is the basis of intervention plans. The quality of each intervention measure is to a large degree dependent on the presence and quality of other intervention measures and collaboration between different agencies. Without clear allocation of responsibility, it may be difficult to ensure coherence and continuity in the intervention. A lack of coordination is usually most evident in long-term intervention plans. The more extensive the individual's disorders, the greater the need for both long-term and short-term planning to ensure that the intervention measures provided are in proportion to the present and future needs of the individual. It is therefore crucial that each measure is seen in terms of the overall aim and that the Individual Habilitation Plan clearly defines who is responsible for the total intervention and each of the subdomains of the intervention (Hesselberg & von Tetzchner, 2016).

The need for coordination and planning is central in the education and care of individuals with severe disabilities. In many countries, *responsibility groups* have been established to fill this function. The groups are multi-disciplinary and which agencies that participate depends on the intervention required. Parents take part in the group meetings and together the group members should have a complete overview of the intervention, be able to initiate new measures and allocate responsibility, including financial responsibility and responsibility for coordinating the elements of the intervention and ensuring that they are seen in terms of a sensible long-term plan. There should be one person who knows the organization and all the measures well, who can act as *care manager* and whom the family and the other professionals involved can contact when action of some sort is needed. This person will take the initiative to discuss and implement the modifications indicated by the assessment and the evaluation of the interventions, manage the routines for presenting new initiatives and organize meetings when needed.

Chapter 5

Intervention situations

Children differ in their communication and language abilities (Kidd et al., 2018) but all children need a "Language Acquisition Support System" (Bruner, 1975). Children develop language through communicative interaction with adults and children in everyday situations. Children with typical language development grow up in environments with competent language users and engage in linguistic interactions for a variety of purposes, in different situations and with a range of communication partners. They acquire a broad linguistic competence and show communicative creativity and flexibility in all kinds of situations: at home, in school, in leisure activities, and so on. Most children do not need any language intervention; their language is adequate for their age and constitutes a basis for further language development. However, formal schooling brings knowledge and skills in many areas to all children and thus represents an important source of vocabulary growth (Nagy & Townsend, 2012).

The language acquisition support system should support the language development of children with little or no speech with alternative means of communication. The aim is to enable them to communicate in the same situations as children with typical language development. This presupposes that their environments are *communicative accessible*; that they have access to expressive means and that there are adults and peers in the environment who understand their mode of communication, who can answer them in a way that they understand and can learn from and who can guide them to develop AAC and be attentive to how speech and AAC are used by others and may be used by themselves (see Chapter 12). However, there are no societies where most people use AAC and where children can develop AAC only through ordinary everyday interactions with their parents and siblings, other adults and peers. They need situations where the language acquisition support system includes, but goes beyond, the informal scaffolding of language development in everyday activities. They need educational settings with sufficient resources and teachers who have the competence required for teaching AAC and can guide and support the children's comprehension and use of AAC. This may be an inclusive setting, a special education classroom or a mixture of settings.

Language learning – including the acquisition of alternative language modes – thus takes place in both formal and informal situations. This chapter is mainly about the settings where AAC is planned and taught. The reason for focusing on the intervention situations is that AAC training should try to get out of small special training rooms and into more varied settings, independent of training methods applied. Chapter 6 is about the variety of strategies that are used to support the acquisition of AAC. Chapter 10 is about how the support of AAC can be integrated into play and other activities, while Chapter 12 is concerned with how adults and peers in the environment can be made competent in AAC and thereby contribute to the individual's communicatively access. The chapters address different but equally

DOI: 10.4324/9781003387633-6

significant parts of the language acquisition support system of children developing alternative modes of language.

Communication situations

Language is part of most social activities and children learn language and communication through participation in various activities. In communication situations, there are two or more partners and at least one partner is attempting to relay information or engage in another communicative act directed at the other(s). Intervention with AAC may be conceived of as the construction of communication situations that can guide and support children's comprehension and use of AAC (Norrie et al., 2021; von Tetzchner & Stadskleiv, 2016). Language interventions typically include *direct teaching situations*, where the individual is taught comprehension and use of new communication forms, guided to discover *communicative problems* and helped to solve the problems with communicative means. For children in the alternative language group and the supportive language group, the first objective is to create a variety of language teaching situations that enable them to learn to use manual signs or graphic symbols with different partners. This means that in addition to the presence of the individual(s) who are learning and one or more communication partners, the intervention settings represent possibilities for establishing *joint engagement* around objects, persons, events, topics and so forth. The physical setting and ongoing activity provide clues to how speech and alternative language forms are used by others, by implicitly or explicitly directing the individual's attention toward certain aspects of the situation and ensuring uptake of relevant expressions from people in the environment. This provides the individual with some of the knowledge that is needed to establish a representational frame or schema within which the utterance may be understood in the situation. Thus, the features of the local environment matter (Mphahlele, 2020).

The expressive language group also needs AAC instruction but may have less need for basic language instruction than the other main language groups. For individuals with relatively good language comprehension, an important aim of the intervention is to organize the everyday environment so that it contains sufficient communication situations that support the individual's development and use of AAC. This includes providing the individual with an optimal number of manual signs or a set of graphic symbols that are accessible in all situations, and making it as easy as possible for communication partners to understand what is being expressed. Aided communicators in the expressive language group may experience many situations during the course of an ordinary day where it is difficult for them to communicate with others. In fact, studies show that young aided communicators with cognitive skills in the age-appropriate range do not have access to their communication aid in many situations that are considered good communication situations (von Tetzchner et al., 2018). An important aim of AAC interventions is to break down such barriers in potential communication situations, increase communicative access across settings and provide the individual with more opportunities for communicative problem solving and communicative interactions in activities outside educational settings.

The need for direct instruction is usually greatest among the younger children in the expressive language group, although older children and adolescents who use AAC will also need explanations and guidance in how to express complex ideas, construct longer utterances and develop new strategies, as they take part in more varied interactions and encounter more complex communicative challenges (Clarke et al., 2001; Smith et al., 2018). For this group, the AAC intervention sessions may be similar to other language courses in school.

Inclusion

A much discussed issue is where children with disabilities should get their education and training, and how their education should be organized in nursery school or school (Amor et al., 2019; Guralnick, 2005; Hayes, 2014). Educational inclusion may be defined as being a member of "a community of learners" (Rogoff et al., 1996) and sharing learning experiences and engaging in social interaction with children with and without disabilities. Segregated education is characterized by taking place in separate educational settings, such as special schools or units, where the students have little or no interaction with typically developing peers. However, inclusive intervention goes beyond education; inclusion should promote participation in the full range of social learning opportunities afforded by community participation (Felder, 2018; Guralnick, 2005).

A theoretical foundation of inclusion is that the context of learning matters. If the situation is identical over time, learning may be restricted. Teaching and learning are not isolated decontextualized activities; learning is *situated*, that is, grounded in the situation where it takes place (Jackson et al., 2010; Lave & Wenger, 1991). For children with disabilities or disorders, learning may require significant adaptations of the curriculum, of tasks, tests and experiences to make them accessible and of the physical and social environment. However, inclusive practice builds on the assumption that shared activities for students with and without disabilities naturally afford communication and negotiation skills and contribute to shared learning and understanding. The preschool and school environments are part of the language acquisition support system (Bruner, 1983), in both typical language development and the development of AAC.

Variation in context is important for language learning (Goldenberg et al., 2022). For children developing AAC, much of the language input comes from direct instruction and participation in educational activities (Leonet et al., 2022; Lynch et al., 2018). Usage-based theoretical approaches to language development emphasize the role of cultural and language experiences in a wide sense (Tomasello, 2003, 2016; von Tetzchner & Grove, 2003). Preschools and schools are children's most important social environments outside the home and inclusion is a recommended practice for children who develop AAC (Calculator, 2009; Soto et al., 2001). Inclusive preschool and school settings may offer varied communicative experiences for children developing AAC, in particular, communicative interactions with peers (Iacono et al., 2022; von Tetzchner et al., 2005). This requires that the language environment of the school is sufficiently adapted to the abilities and disabilities of the children using AAC (Brekke & von Tetzchner, 2003). Any one-to-one session should be comprehensible and meaningful for the child, support participation in the mainstream classroom and strengthen social interactions with adults and peers outside the training sessions. For example, the use of key-words with manual signs or graphic symbols by adults and peers in the environment supports an inclusive AAC practice (Cologon & Mevawalla, 2018). Inclusion may be the basis for AAC intervention, while communication and language skills enabled by AAC are a foundation for successful inclusion.

McNaughton (2003) raises the question of whether inclusive settings will provide sufficient language experiences for optimal development of children who use AAC. In particular, the planned aspects of AAC development may be difficult to manage in non-segregated environments, including explanations and demonstrations of the meanings and usages of manual signs and graphic symbols. Most children with severe disabilities need some one-to-one training or training in a smaller group, but this is not an argument for segregation in general.

Inclusion is not either/or; the education of children developing AAC may, rather, constitute a mix of inclusive and segregated activities. Degree of inclusion also varies considerably in non-segregated settings. Shared educational and other experiences and social interaction may be limited even if the individual attends a mainstream school (Qvortrup & Qvortrup, 2018). The abilities in different domains vary both within and between the diagnostic groups using AAC, and the individual's abilities may influence decisions concerning educational setting (see Chapters 3 and 4). However, inclusive participation is always an important aim of AAC intervention, and it is crucial to provide each child with the right blend of participation in shared activities with the class and training one-to-one or in a smaller group.

Inclusive education is important for the acquisition of academic skills but also for social functioning and *enculturation* in a broad sense – learning the ways and means of the culture – which is an essential part of children's development (von Tetzchner, 2019a). Inclusion implies active participation in a set of educational and other activities that constitute the foundation of meaning-making in nursery school and school, including play and social interaction during breaks and on the way to and from school (Batorowicz et al., 2006; von Tetzchner et al., 2005). Interaction with peers contributes to inclusion and the development of social and cultural knowledge and skills in ways that cannot be easily achieved by teacher instruction and adult-child interactions.

Organizing instructional situations

It is usually teachers and other professionals who decide which settings, objects and actions are relevant for promoting AAC at preschool or school and in the home. When choosing settings for intervention, professionals should start with discussing the child's current joint engagement and participation in situations that allow for various language practices. The day-clock may be a useful tool in this discussion (see p. 106). Educational situations and routines of daily living differ considerably, and intervention should be based on knowledge about how different aspects of these situations may fulfil supportive functions in language learning. Parts of the vocabulary are often used in certain situations and activities, and these may represent opportunities for the individuals to expand their AAC vocabulary and message construction. This may for example include names and descriptions of actions related to animals in picture books, such as TIGER RUN FAST or MONKEY CLIMB HIGH TREE. Situations should make it possible for the communication partners to direct the individual's attention towards relevant situational cues, and they should themselves have sufficient cues for interpreting the individual's expressions in a consistent manner, which helps in reducing frustration and misunderstandings. The situation should be so clear that whatever contribution the individual brings to the communication situation will be noted by the communication partners. The choice of situation and the content of the utterances will depend on the individual's cognitive level and AAC skills.

PCS: TIGER, FAST

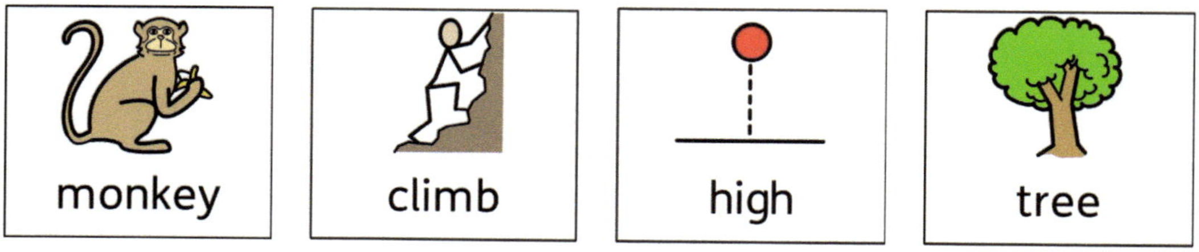

Widgit: MONKEY, CLIMB, HIGH, TREE

Independent of the main educational setting, it is usual to distinguish between *special training* and *training in natural situations*, also called *milieu teaching* (Kaiser & Wright, 2013). In special training the individual is taken out of the main classroom, alone or with a few other students. The teacher has formulated specific teaching procedures and goals. The communication mode, the manual signs or graphic symbols that are to be practised, the time and place for training, the people who will be present, and the material that will be used – everything is planned in advance. Natural situations include settings that the individual is usually part of, such as the home, preschool, school or playground. When intervention is in natural situations, the teaching of specific manual signs or graphic symbols take part in situations where it is believed or known that the individual will have a use for them.

There is no absolute dividing line between special training and training in natural situations. The degree of organization can also vary considerably when the teaching takes place in the individual's ordinary environment. It is therefore useful to distinguish between *planned* and *spontaneous* instruction in natural situations. In planned instruction, one or several teaching goals have been decided in advance. In addition to which vocabulary items or constructions that are going to be taught, the time, location, material to be used and the teacher may vary – but at least one of these has to be planned. If all aspects are planned, the only difference between planned teaching in natural situations and special training is in location: planned teaching takes place in a location where the individual usually spends his or her time. However, instruction that is so meticulously planned that it significantly alters the situation the individual is used to can hardly be called natural.

Spontaneous instruction is characterized by a relatively low degree of organization. It is generally a matter of being aware of the individual's use of specific manual signs or graphic symbols, and perhaps providing or making the individual aware of opportunities for using certain vocabulary items. In some cases, the instructional goal – for example, the use of a specific manual sign or graphic symbol – is decided beforehand, but instruction can also take place without this having been planned, merely because an opportunity suddenly presents itself. These examples illustrate different degrees of spontaneity and planning.

At fixed times Jack is taken to a room in his nursery school that is used for individual training. Two teachers bring fruit and practise the signs APPLE, BANANA and ORANGE. They take turns at teaching him. This is special training, in a segregated environment.

As part of his manual sign training, three times a day Jack is given the choice between an apple and a banana or between an apple and an orange. The training takes place in the part of the nursery school where the children usually eat, immediately before the ordinary meal. Jack chooses ten small pieces of fruit so that he is not too full before his meal. This instruction has a high degree of planning but occurs in his natural environment.

Every afternoon, the children eat some fruit in the nursery school. Because Jack is currently learning to sign APPLE, BANANA and ORANGE, his teachers have made sure

that the bowl of fruit contains only two types of fruit, and that these two are apple, banana or orange. This training has a small degree of planning and may be considered somewhat adapted spontaneous instruction.

In the afternoon, the teachers in the nursery school leaves a tray of fruit with apples, bananas and oranges on a table for all the children to eat. If Jack tries to make a sign or approach someone in order to get fruit, he is helped to use the signs. This is spontaneous instruction.

There will be similar modes of organization in intervention with graphic symbols. The degree of planning will also reflect the abilities and impairments of the individual. For example, there may be a need for a high degree of planning when the individual's motor impairment hinders spontaneous communicative attempts. The initial AAC intervention for autistic individuals may also require detailed planning.

It is not necessary to choose between spontaneous and planned instruction, and there is no contradiction between instruction in natural situations and special training. Special instruction and training in natural situations are often parts of the same intervention. In fact, many approaches represent blends of spontaneity and planning. Whether the teacher chooses to carry out training in planned situations in which the individual is not otherwise found, depends on the instructional goals. These are based on an assessment of the individual's abilities, preferences, interests and needs and on assumptions of how the goals may be most easily achieved. Teachers need to prepare planned instruction in the natural environment, just as in special training sessions, but instruction in natural environments usually has more potential for variation and spontaneity. Furthermore, one should plan for the possibility of spontaneous instruction by making sure that it is not only a special educator or a select few teachers who know about the intervention goals and strategies, such as focusing on signs for different types of FRUIT for Jack above. All the adults in Jack's daily environments should be taught his manual signs, so they can support him if an opportunity for spontaneous sign use arises. It is important to emphasize that skills will not automatically improve or be useful merely because the training takes place in the individual's ordinary environment. Teachers must formulate relevant teaching goals and ensure the motivation and attention of the individual. It is a requirement that the manual signs or graphic symbols that are trained should have a clear use for the individual or for significant people in the child's environment (see Chapters 7 and 8).

One important reason for training in the individual's ordinary environment is that professionals who are not directly involved in the training gradually get used to the fact that the individual is communicating. Unfortunately, it is not unusual that staff members in institutions and day centres – following a successful intervention – complain that the individual is communicating too much (Bird et al., 1989; Mitteer et al., 2020; Møller & von Tetzchner, 1996; Sidener et al., 2006). Beukelman and Light (2020) express concerns that individuals who use AAC lack access to and opportunity for participating in many social situations. The skills and attitudes of people in the environment may be barriers to the individual's use of abilities related to AAC (Baxter et al., 2012; Johnson et al., 2020). Such barriers are important to identify because they may reduce the positive effects of the intervention on the individual's autonomy and quality of life. Being present in a situation does not always in itself lead to optimal learning or better communication. The situation must provide the individual with sufficient overview and opportunities for initiating and responding with a mode of communication that he or she can manage.

Planning for generalization, maintenance and transfer of skills to new situations

The individual may have learned the correspondence between a manual sign or a graphic symbol and a spoken word, or the reference of a sign or symbol in a special training situation, but fail to use these skills in other situations. *Spontaneous use* and *generalization* of acquired communication skills are major objectives of all interventions involving AAC (Schlosser & Lee, 2000). Generalization of AAC may imply using manual signs or graphic symbols spontaneously to communicate about new objects and events, in new situations or with new people. Generalization may also involve using already learned manual signs or graphic symbols in combinations with new words, manual signs or graphic symbols. Spontaneous use means that the individual uses the manual signs or symbols without being prompted to do so. Spontaneous use may occur in both instructional situations and other situations. Teachers sometimes stop a child's spontaneous communication because the content is not part of the teacher's agenda. This may be appropriate when the focus is on the content but very often initiating communication is the primary educational goal while the actual content of the communication is less important. In particular, when the individual has little spontaneous communication, it is important to utilize rare spontaneous expressions by answering the individual and engaging him in further conversation when possible.

There has often been too little attention to generalization in language intervention, especially in behavioural interventions (Schreibman et al., 2015). The main emphasis has been on training of the form – the production of the manual sign and pointing at or handing over a particular graphic symbol. There seemed to be an assumption that generalized use would follow more or less automatically once the individual had learned to produce the manual sign or respond by indicating a graphic symbol, but studies have found that this is often not the case (Calculator, 1988; Schlosser & Lee, 2000). This was termed the "problem of generalization" (Shepherd, 1977). In recent years, there has been more emphasis on providing interventions in the child's natural environment, for example in naturalistic developmental behavioural interventions (Schreibman et al., 2015).

It is important to distinguish between generalization and the result of *teaching extended use*. If the individual, after having learned to use a manual sign or graphic symbol in one specific situation, is taught to use the manual sign or graphic symbol with new objects and actions, combinations, situations or people, this is teaching of extended use. Extended use does not necessarily reflect generalization but training extended use has been a common way to promote generalization. However, a less restricted teaching situation may lead to more generalization. In order to promote for example generalization of a manual sign or graphic symbol to new objects and events, it has been suggested that several different exemplars of the same class of objects should be used. For example, when practising the graphic symbol *CUP*, one should use cups of different shapes, sizes and colours. Degree of similarity between the

ARASAAC: CUP

image of the graphic symbol and the cup that is referred to is not important, because the aim is that the individual shall use the same symbol to communicate about the whole range of different cups.

Communication skills that are taught by only one particular teacher may not be transferred to other people. The generalization to new people may be facilitated if several people carry out the same training. Sometimes it is enough that two people carry out the training for the individual to understand that the communication skills acquired can be used in different situations. In one study, a teacher trained children with intellectual disabilities to say *hello* in the morning. The training functioned well but the children said *hello* only to the teacher who had taught them to say *hello*. The teacher had become an element of what was learned: say hello to this teacher instead of hello to any teacher. After an additional teacher began to take turns at the teaching, the children in the class began to say *hello* to the other teacher *and* to the whole staff of 20 people (Stokes et al., 1974). Varying the teachers may also facilitate the transfer of communication skills to new situations.

Many individuals who belong to the alternative language group or the language support group have problems transferring what they have learned in training sessions to new situations, autistic individuals especially may need help generalizing new skills (de Marchena et al., 2015; Su et al., 2019). Autistic children who have learned to use a manual sign or graphic symbol in a special training situation may not begin to use this spontaneously in new situations. Like the teacher above, the location may become part of what is learned. In addition, many individuals – especially in the alternative language group – need a long time to learn to communicate with manual signs or graphic symbols. These circumstances call for organizing the instruction in varied settings where the individual gradually spontaneous will use the skills he has learned.

When it has been decided that an individual's language instruction should take place in special training situations, it is essential to make plans in advance as to how to solve the problem of transferring the new skills to other situations. One method is to include elements from those situations where the communication will be used, that is, make the special training situation resemble more closely the natural situation. In order to do this effectively, one should have detailed knowledge of both the training situation and the situations to which the individual is more likely to generalize. However, during the planning of special training situations it may become clear that it is just as expedient to implement the instruction in the individual's natural environment without preliminary special training. Thus, planning for the transfer of skills to natural situations ensures that special training sessions are used only when there are strong arguments in favour of doing so.

In the same way as there are strategies for the transferral from special training situations to natural situations, there should also be strategies for making planned situations less organized. During the planning, it may become evident that the natural situations can be used for training with less organization than first assumed.

Duration and location of training sessions

The length of training sessions may vary. Intervention studies involving AAC tend to be short-term – a few hours' intervention over a few weeks – with limited learning goals (Langarika-Rocafort et al., 2021; O'Neill et al., 2018). For individuals who receive formal language instruction, for example in how to analyse graphic sentences and construct sentences with graphic symbols, the length may be a standard 45-minute class. When more basic

language and communication intervention is woven into, and becomes an integral part of the ordinary activities, the duration of the training sessions is likely to dictate itself. With planned training in natural situations, the sessions are usually short, say 5–15 minutes, and are repeated several times each day. It is more important that the individual – and thus the teacher – has true communicative success than that a vocabulary item is repeated many times during a short session. Also special training sessions for communication should be short but spread throughout the day. This is a further argument for training sessions in the individual's daily environment.

Sometimes it is consideration for the professionals' schedule that makes teaching situations too planned or organized.

> Kerry is a five-year-old autistic girl. She is training with a special teacher in natural situations. However, due to the special teacher's itinerary, the teaching takes place at fixed times. In order to reduce the dependence on his schedule, the special teacher uses much of his time to give Kerry's nursery school teacher and the assistant guidance in how they can utilize spontaneous situations and carry out short training sessions as part of or between other activities. As a result, the training is integrated into Kerry's daily life, Kerry receives more training, and the training is more varied in terms of content, times and persons. In turn, this will support generalization of the skills she learns.

Flexible training and teaching strategies, which, in so far as it is possible, utilize natural situations, place demands on the organization of the intervention. When professionals who are not directly connected to the individual's nursery school, school or daycare centre are responsible for the intervention, they have to work more indirectly, that is, by giving support and guidance to those who work in the individual's daily environment.

It is sometimes practical to have individual sessions that last longer but not so long that the individual becomes bored or tired. Moreover, the time of the intervention sessions may be varied to avoid creating unnecessary dependence on a particular time schedule. This may be useful also when the activities of the day are structured to support learning and self-regulation in individuals with intellectual disabilities and autism spectrum disorder.

Structuring

The terms "structure" and "structuring" are used in different ways and have no generally accepted definition. In relation to intervention, they are often used fairly loosely to indicate that the day's activities and events are planned, also where and when they will take place during the day. Structuring is a useful tool for organizing the activities in such a way that they support the development of comprehension and use of language and communication. A structure may be divided into three levels: *frame structure, situational structure* and *cues*.

Frame structure

The frame structure is the division of the day into different *situations*, that is, routines, events, activities, and so forth. A day always has a frame structure, whether it is planned or not. The first overview of the individual's ordinary day is the assessment of the frame structure that exists before AAC intervention is implemented (see p. 105). This describes how the intervention measures and other activities are spread out during the course of the day, how long the

different activities last and how much of the individual's waking day is planned. The assessment also gives information about routine activities that are repeated daily and how fixed the daily routines are. This is basic information for the evaluation of the individual's total intervention and the planning of language and communication intervention.

Weekdays can be more or less similar and the frame structure more or less dense. It is the individual's total life situation and need for training and adaptation that determine the content of the plan for the implementation of the current and future frame structures. An ordinary weekday should include intervention measures oriented towards future functioning, social interaction, everyday routines, leisure activities and periods of relaxation. What distinguishes a planned frame structure from a casual frame structure is the number of fixed activities included in situations that are repeated at regular intervals. The frame structure can be made denser by filling in the empty time slots with existing or new activities.

A planned and dense frame structure may be a useful tool for integrating language and communication training in everyday activities, particularly when the individual belongs to the alternative language group. For individuals who benefit from a dense frame structure, the overview should, in principle, consist of 15-minute slots, although some sessions may last shorter or longer than that. This means that for each 15-minute period of the day, the professional writes what is going to happen and the objective of each activity. In practice, the frame structure will not always be followed completely; some flexibility is needed in order to take into account unforeseen events and the school's or family's need for variation.

For individuals in the expressive language group, the assessment of the frame structure usually has another function as well as the planning of the training. Many in this group are severely motor impaired and much of their day consists of routines with limited variation. Care routines, such as morning care, dressing, change of positioning – for example from a wheelchair to a standing frame – managing medications, meals and transport, can take a long time. An important aim of the plan is to go beyond the routines and allow for new activities, variation and flexibility, and give the individual opportunities to influence the content of the day. Many individuals with severe motor impairments are not very mobile. They depend on a wheelchair and may need a helper to accompany them in their exploration of the environment, play and other activities. An assessment of the frame structure of children of school-age will typically reveal a need for help with leisure-time activities and social interaction with peers outside school hours. This form of help should be given high priority to avoid children spending all of their leisure time at home. This will support the children's opportunities for participating in social activities and develop autonomy and a positive self-image.

When assessing the frame structure of a child with disabilities, it may be a useful exercise to make a similar assessment of the frame structure of a similarly aged child living in the same environment. A comparison of their frame structures will show how they differ in activities and social participation and provide ideas for activities that can be introduced for the child with disabilities.

Situational structure

The situations that make up the frame structure have their own a built-in structure: the situational structure. The situations have varying degrees of organized contents and thus varying degrees of structuring. In situations with the least structuring, it is not decided beforehand where the individual will be, who will be present, or which activities he or she will participate in. In the situations with the highest degree of structuring, everything is decided in advance, based on a defined intervention goal.

A high degree of structuring enables professionals to be systematic. The objective of structuring is to make it easy for professionals to know what they should do in different situations; that is, how they should react, create expectations in the individual about what is going to happen, and organize for communication. Assessment of the situational structure gives a basis for planning adaptations and expansions of the communication and language training.

Cues

Knowledge of a word is not a simple association between a form and the reference; it implies knowing when to use the word and for what purposes. Learning a manual sign or graphic symbol thus includes situational features or cues. They enable a person to understand what another person is communicating. The description of the cues used in comprehension in a particular situation may be regarded as a third level of structuring. In planning language and communication intervention, it is often useful to ask how training situations can be created by building cues into ordinary situations or routines. Registration of cues is thus an important element of the communicative assessment of individuals who are starting to learn AAC.

In principle, there is an infinite number of possible cues, since communicative expressions may have many forms and varied functions and take place in different situations. In communication with individuals who are unable to speak, cues for their comprehension may be the actions they perform, their attention to objects or something that happens in the situation, knowledge about what the individual likes and usually does, cultural norms, and so forth.

> Angela is a twelve-year-old girl with Rett syndrome. When she heard her grandfather's voice from the room next door, she turned her gaze to a book, suggesting that she associated the voice with the book. People in the environment interpreted this as a signal that she wanted her grandfather to read to her – a common occurrence. In this situation, both the grandfather's voice and the girl looking at the book were cues that made such an interpretation reasonable.

Attention to possible contextual cues is particularly important when planning communication intervention for individuals with limited understanding of communication. In such cases, cues may be described in terms of over-interpretation, adults' tendency to react to child behaviour as though it had a communicative intent (see p. 172). Adults will search for possible cues to assume a communicative intent and react to the individual's behaviour as though he or she had this intent. Structured interviews with parents and other significant persons are usually the best way to investigate what cues they and the individual might be attentive to (see p. 100).

When relevant cues have been described, they become part of the planned situational structure. This means that, in addition to teaching the individual manual signs or graphic symbols, the situation is arranged so that it contains elements that make the use of the communicative expression reasonable and understandable for an individual with limited comprehension of speech.

Visual support

Visual support is an important element of structuring, which was first introduced in the program *Treatment and Education of Autistic and Communication-Handicapped Children* (TEACCH) in the 1960s (Mesibov & Shea, 2010; Mesibov et al., 2004). It has become a

standard element in most programmes for autistic children but also children with intellectual disabilities without an autism diagnosis may need structuring (Chiang & Kemp, 2019; Koyama & Wang, 2011). Structured visual support is behaviour support and not part of the communication training, although the graphic symbols the individual uses for communication may also be used in day schedules and other forms of visual support.

Visual schedules may be used to mark the frame structure, helping the child understand the activities and plan of the day, and prepare for the things that will happen (Figure 5.1). Visual schedules typically contain information about the activities that are going to happen, such as *PLAY, EAT, WORK* (train), or *READ* in kindergarten, and *SPORT, MEAL, ENGLISH CLASS, AAC CLASS, RECESS, or MUSIC CLASS* in school. They represent a timeline and hence function as an introduction to temporal understanding and time management. In addition to routines and activities, some individuals may need information about where they are going to be and who they are going to be with. Using visual schedules with two columns, one for information about activities and another for locations and persons, may be a good solution. They may contain the activities of the day in preschool or school, as well as chores and other home activities, leisure activities and activities with peers (Rutherford et al., 2020a).

Visual markers are used to mark transitions between educational settings, making these easier for the child (and for people in the environment). When the child is changing school, bringing the child's visual schedules to the new school facilitates the child's adaptation to the new school. If the individual is used to visual support, visual support representing the planned future routines of adult life with work or other day activities may help the individual's transition from school to adult life (Hart et al., 2021).

Transitions from one activity to another may be difficult for individuals with autism spectrum disorder and intellectual disabilities, especially when they are uncertain about what will happen. Visual support facilitates transitions and may contribute to reducing the confusion and anxiety that characterize many autistic children and thereby the risk for emotional and behavioural disorders and challenging behaviour (Meadan et al., 2011; Zimmerman et al., 2020).

Visual schedules may work well in general education classrooms (Banda et al., 2009). All children attending school have to learn the structure of the school year and the schedule of each week and day. They usually get a printed schedule to help them. However, studies find that many students with typical development benefit from the more detailed visual information provided to classmates with developmental disabilities (Rutherford et al., 2020b). The use of visual schedules thus supports inclusion. In many classrooms, visual schedules can now be integrated into technical solutions that all students use and benefit from, such as digital whiteboards and tablets.

Visual activity schedules mark the situational structure; the structure and organization of an activity or task the individual is going to do. The schedule may be a visual recipe or markers of the steps in the activity or task (Figure 5.2). Studies have documented that these schedules can help children with disabilities to learn, plan and perform school work, self-help skills

Figure 5.1 Visual schedule for a kindergarten day.

Figure 5.2 Example of visual activity schedule.

and other activities, and knowing when they are finished (Spriggs et al., 2017). The visual activity schedules show children how much they should do, and we have observed children sometimes use this information to negotiate with the teacher to obtain a smaller number of tasks. A major educational aim is that students willll become more independent in their school work. The use of visual activity schedules and other forms of visual support help students to more independent task work without reminders (Bryan & Gast, 2000; Knight et al., 2015). Also cognitively higher functioning children may benefit from visual activity schedules. Visual activity schedules may be presented on paper or electronically in tablets or computers. There are activity schedules in mobile phones and wearable electronic watches, which individuals can use when they meet challenges and need to perform incidental tasks by themselves (Jimenez-Gomez et al., 2021).

Although graphic symbols and manual signs are visual modes of communication, visual support is not part of AAC intervention. Visual schedules and other forms of visual support are commonly used with children who do not who need AAC (Brij, 2019; Bryan & Gast, 2000).

Structured or unstructured intervention situations

Structuring of the situation is one of the best tools in language and communication intervention, in particular for individuals with the most severe problems in language acquisition. The less self-initiated activity an individual has, the greater the need for a strict structure. A strict structure may support the development of self-initiated activity among individuals with severe disabilities and contribute to breaking up the passivity that very often characterizes their life. Another aim is that also people with extensive disabilities should achieve the greatest possible control over what happens with them, be able to take initiative in everyday life, and choose what they want to do. The easiest way to help them achieve this is to create a well-organized day with structured activities and teaching situations.

It has been suggested that structuring may hinder individual initiative and choice (McLay et al., 2019) but strategic and planned use of structuring should be made in such a way that it increases the individual's situational understanding, communication and level of activity, and provides a basis for more autonomous choices. Furthermore, with age the individual may become able to take an active part in the structuring process. In typical development, the ability to make a plan to reach a goal and monitor the progress evolves in parallel with the child's executive functioning (see p. 113). However, many children with severe motor impairments are not offered the natural and incidental opportunities that support this development, as they are physically incapable of performing the actions needed on their own. Parents and teachers may engage individuals in joint planning and monitoring of progress, and thereby promote their development of executive skills. Several of the strategies employed in expressive language teaching utilize structuring to foster communication and initiative. The frame structure is useful when giving the individual possibilities to choose between activities, while *the build-and-break strategy* utilizes the situational structure to create a need for communication. *Reactions to signal-elicited anticipatory behaviour* use the frame structure in a similar way (see Chapter 6).

It should be noted that structuring is a *helping condition* and not a goal in itself. Most people have a relatively structured existence. They get up in the morning, eat breakfast, go to school or work, eat dinner, watch television, and so on. However, the structure is fairly flexible; meals can be postponed, watching television may be replaced with a walk in the park, a trip to the cinema, an evening playing cards, a social gathering with friends, and so forth. A

similarly flexible structure is an ideal vision for people who receive intervention that includes structuring. The aim of structuring is thus to form a basis of the development of flexible behavioural patterns and the ability to make decisions. This means that the structure should be changed as soon as there is a basis for doing so.

Once a successful frame structure has been established, that is, when the individual seems to understand the activities of the day and is carrying them out well enough, it is probably time to begin dismantling the structure. For some individuals, all the situations throughout the day may be structured and the day proceeds with virtually no complications. The schedules may have remained unchanged for such a long time period that the individual and the people in the environment have no natural needs for communication in the daily routines. The routines have then lost their power as a support for communication. The visual schedules have become rituals and no longer help the individual build up new understanding of the environment. The individual may be so tied to the frame structure and the visual markers of the schedules that they hinder any development of new skills and choices instead of strengthening this development. The result of this unfortunate development may be called *learned dependence*.

However, the structure may fulfil many different functions. After the professionals have dismantled an over-routinized structure, the individual may still need visual schedules as an aid for *time management*. For example, a calendar may help the individual to understand why days are different, why there are weekdays, weekends and public holidays, or working days and vacations.

Edward is an 18-year-old autistic boy who has some understanding of spoken language. He enjoys going to school and when the weekly schedule is broken up by holidays and he is told that he is not going to school, he usually reacts with violent temper tantrums. It is difficult to quieten him and he may have to be constrained to keep him from injuring himself or others. Edward's mother then draws a calendar for him, in which she includes things she knows he likes. She uses images related to prominent activities to mark the days in the calendar (see Figure 5.3). To represent the days that he goes to school, she draws a picture of a bus, since he always looks forward to taking the bus. On some of his days off from school, he is allowed to drive his uncle's tractor, so the tractor becomes the symbol of these holidays. On Saturdays, they always wash the floor. On Sundays, they have egg for breakfast. Christmas shopping, the Christmas holidays and New Year's Eve are all represented with drawings that are easy for him to learn and understand. The calendar hangs in its designated place in the kitchen. Every morning, Edward, looks at it to find out what that particular day will bring. Each evening he crosses off the day that has passed before going to bed. Since Edward was given the calendar, his holidays have been much more peaceful. It appears as though it was important for him to know that he is going back to school, and that this part of his life is not over even when the holidays are long (Steindal, 1990).

Also other case histories suggest that a calendar should become an integrated part of the alternative communication means as soon as the individual starts to have expectations about event outside the immediate time frame (see p. 386).

Many autistic individuals with limited comprehension of spoken language react negatively when their routine activities are omitted or changed. The behaviour problems that may appear in such situations, can be prevented or considerably reduced if the activity is replaced with another, and the individual is informed about the change in a manner that he or she can

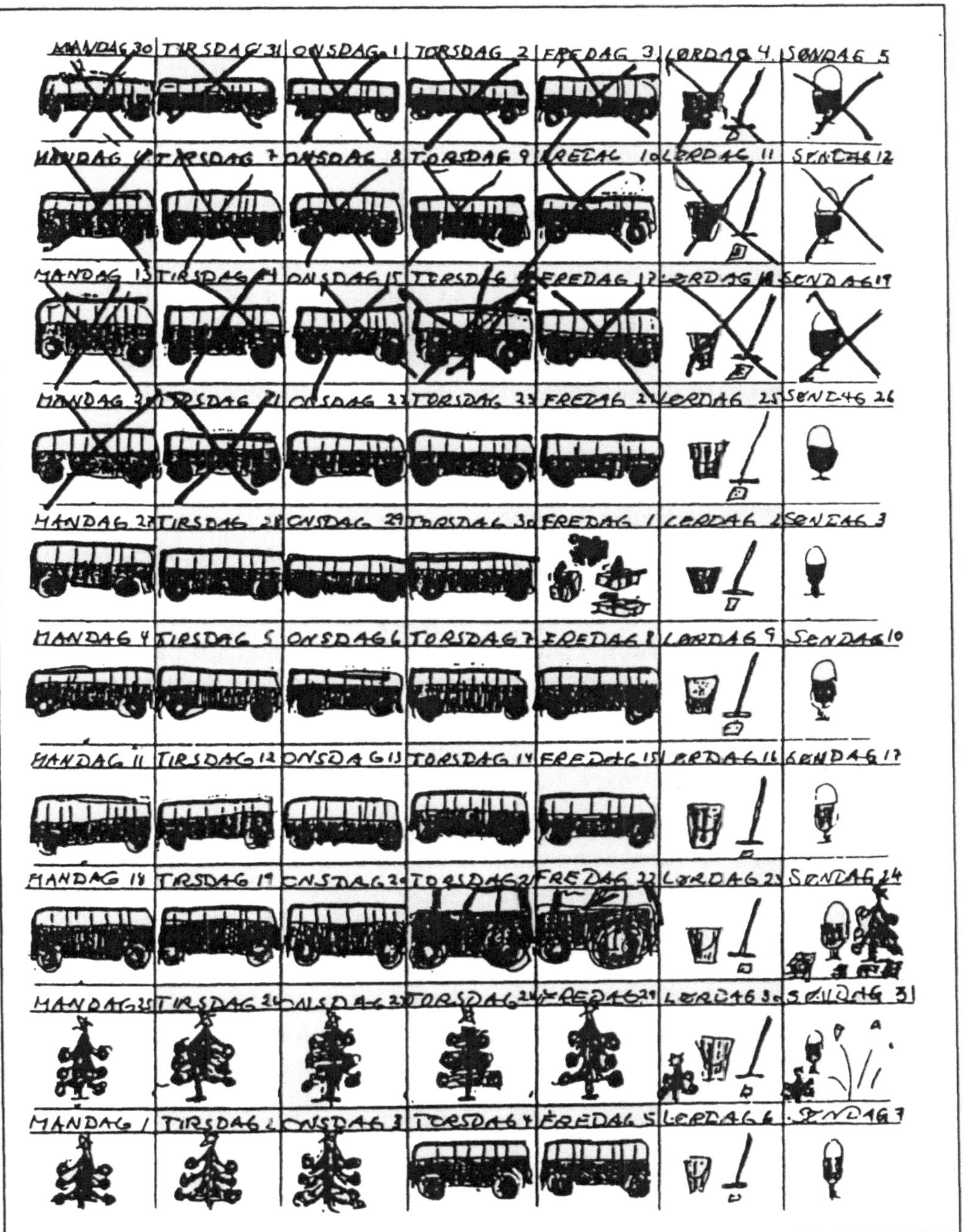

Figure 5.3 Edward's calendar.

understand (von Tetzchner, 2003). The changes may be indicated on the visual schedule of the day or on a calendar containing the activities of the day or the week. Both the routine activity and the replacement should be represented on the visual schedule or calendar. The graphic symbol of the activity that is omitted that day is marked with *NO*, for example in the form of a transparent red card with a black X, while a graphic symbol with a green arrow points from the omitted activity to the graphic symbol representing the activity that is replacing it (Hawkes, 1998).

Planned and unplanned language use

This chapter is about various settings for AAC interventions. Plans and structured situations are necessary parts of many interventions, but it is the conversations of everyday life that are the final target of AAC interventions. The situations are organized to make communication and language functions clearer to individuals with little or no spoken language and ensure that they become engaged in activities involving communicative problems that they are able to manage and learn from. Many of the strategies used in intervention situations, such as choice making and book reading, are also natural parts of everyday communicative interactions among children with typical development (von Tetzchner & Stadskleiv, 2016). The overall aims are thus that the individuals will have communicative access and become able to spontaneously use whatever language skills they have in both everyday situations and rarer events, that gradually they will need less structure and support, and that eventually, the planned intervention situations will no longer be needed.

Chapter 6

Intervention strategies

Finding a manual sign system or a communication aid and graphic symbol system that are suitable for the individual is just the start of AAC intervention. The individual must learn how the system works and can be used to engage in communicative interaction. The result for the individual should be better control of his or her life situation and an increase in self-determination and self-esteem. There are many ways to support the development of communicative functions and the comprehension and use of manual signs and graphic or tangible symbols. The strategies seek to elicit and guide communicative actions and will vary in the three main user groups, with individual differences in cognition, language and social skills, and with phases of development – from infancy to late adulthood. Chapter 5 focused on the teaching situations. This chapter gives an overview of strategies that may be applied in AAC interventions. Later chapters focus specifically on vocabulary selection, sentence construction, conversational skills, communication and language within activities, and the language environment.

What intervention strategies are used to promote communication and language in a particular child or adult will depend on their communication and language skills, and their perceptual, motor and cognitive abilities, as well as the intervention settings and the interventionists' theoretical framework and ideas about communication and language development. There is a universal agreement that interventions should be tailored to the abilities and challenges of each individual. The problems underlying the difficulties with communication and speech in children with, for example, cerebral palsy, autism spectrum disorder or Down syndrome require quite different approaches (see Chapter 3). Optimal intervention and developmental outcome will depend on the adaption of intervention goals and methods to both the abilities and the disabilities of the individual. Early intervention is important for children who need AAC and, for most of them, continued positive communication and language development will depend on the implementation of new strategies that follow their development and response to the intervention, and expand their existing competence. The strategies may be divided into three main sets.

1 *Early AAC teaching strategies* are directed at basic communication skills and the development of an initial functional vocabulary. They are mainly used in interventions for emerging communicators and individuals in the very early phases of language development, including adults who have shown little communicative progress. Many of the strategies presented in this chapter belong to this set.
2 *Further AAC teaching strategies* are introduced when the individual has learned the basic communicative functions and acquired a preliminary understanding of the

DOI: 10.4324/9781003387633-7

representational symbolic function of manual signs or graphic symbols. Although the support tends to be more explicit than in typical language development, many of the strategies in this set are inspired by the processes found in the informal scaffolding of typical language development.

3 *The formal AAC teaching strategies* are more similar to the strategies used in second-language teaching and formal first-language education of children and adolescents with typical development in mainstream schools, as well as in adult learning.

There is no absolute border between the three sets of strategies – they do not preclude one another, and they are often used in parallel. Some strategies may be applied to some extent along most of the developmental phases, including adulthood, such as "picture-book reading with naming" and "structured conversations" with different levels of complexity. The purpose of grouping strategies into three main sets is to bring out the fact that different strategies assume different individual competencies and presuppose varying degrees of professional planning and structure and knowledge about the learner. The strategies all have their strengths and weaknesses and may suit individuals with certain abilities and disabilities better than individuals with other abilities and disabilities.

The objective of this chapter is not to give ready-made "recipes", but rather to review the *intervention principles* and *methods* used in AAC intervention. Some of these principles and methods are based on theory, others on our own and others' experiences from research and clinical and educational practice. Parents' experiences with various approaches to AAC intervention are also an important source of information when planning interventions (see Chapter 12). The intervention aims and methods may vary considerably from individual to individual. Professionals should therefore have a large and varied set of methods, and their intervention decisions and choice of strategies should be governed by principles and experience, adapted to the individual and the practical circumstances and in line with the individual's overall intervention programme.

Evidence-based practice

Today, it is a requirement in most educational and health domains that intervention should be based on appropriate assessment and be evidence-based, emphasizing that there should be a research base to support the suggested functionality of an intervention programme (DeRosa et al., 2019; Kratochwill & Shernoff, 2004). Evidence-based practice is also strongly encouraged in the AAC field (Schlosser & Raghavendra, 2004; Smith, 2016). However, Schlosser and Sigafoos (2009) point out that empirical research support is not enough – evidence-based practice should also build on clinical practice and on the experiences of parents and other stakeholders.

Clinical research studies constitute an important basis for planning interventions, provided the results are relevant and valid. This is not always the case: an intervention strategy may function well for some individuals with a particular disorder but not for others. For example, several intervention programmes for autistic individuals are empirically supported in the sense that that there is research, which demonstrates positive results (Mesibov & Shea, 2010; Prizant, 2009). However, this does not mean that all of these programmes will be beneficial for all members of a diagnostic group. In fact, studies show that programmes in general are only effective for about half of the relevant population (Kasari & Smith, 2016). The average result may hide the variation within the group. Moreover, the strength of a programme may not be

in the remediation of core features of the disorder. For example, programmes based on applied behaviour analysis and discrete trial training typically show the largest gains in cognitive domains and the smallest in social skills, communication and language, which represent core deficits in autism spectrum disorder (Kasari & Smith, 2016; McGrew et al., 2016). One-to-one training may be positive for young autistic children with intellectual disabilities, while autistic children who are not intellectually disabled may benefit more from intervention integrated into the ordinary curriculum of the preschool or school. This emphasizes that interventionists must be able to evaluate and apply a variety of methods.

A sound evidence base is important for practice, but it is equally important to be aware of the limitations of research results, especially when planning intervention for a particular individual. A small, but statistically significant, difference between two groups receiving different treatments may have theoretical interest but limited application in individual intervention planning. Many AAC studies involve the teaching of a few vocabulary items, sometimes just one or two in different modalities (graphic symbol, manual sign, electronic device with voice output) (for example, Achmadi et al., 2014; McLay et al., 2017). A majority of AAC intervention studies were shorter than six weeks and long-term studies are rare (McNaughton & Light, 2015). The number of training trials in an experimental setting may say little about how this modality functions in everyday communication and thus may have limited practical relevance. Moreover, speed of first acquisition may not be indicative of how useful the material or method will be for the individual's long-term communication functioning.

Habit is a strong determinant of practice, but methods that have been used habitually for a long time do not always represent the best practice. On the other hand, new methodologies are sometimes overrated and used beyond the group who actually benefits from it. Teachers therefore need to make sure that they are familiar with the empirical and practical bases of the intervention methods that are generally used, and their own preferred intervention methods.

Initiating AAC intervention

For all individuals with disabilities, it is important that intervention is initiated as early as possible (Guralnick, 2011, 2017). Intervention in the three first years of life is typically considered early, although for children with intellectual disabilities, the first five years of life are considered the period of early intervention (Baker et al., 2016). An important argument for early initiation of communication and language intervention is the general agreement that there is a sensitive period for language acquisition. The brain is more plastic during the first few years of life, and it is easier for children of preschool age to learn language than it is for older children and adults (Kaiser & Roberts, 2011). The same arguments apply to intervention with AAC and there has been considerable focus on the early phases of AAC development for children with severe motor and cognitive disabilities (Branson & Demchak, 2009; Lorang et al., 2022; Romski et al., 2015; Smith & Hustad, 2015). All major intervention programmes for autistic children focus on communication and language and emphasize the benefits of starting early. Many of the programmes will initiate AAC if the children who are minimally verbal, or without speech, do not show significant progress in speech after a short period of speech training (Almirall et al., 2016; Tager-Flusberg & Kasari, 2013; Vivanti et al., 2017). Early intervention with manual signs or graphic symbols has a pivotal role in the prevention of challenging behaviour in autistic children with little or no speech (von Tetzchner, 2004). However, both for children with intellectual disabilities and children with

age-appropriate cognitive abilities, intervention with manual signs and graphic symbols is often initiated much later than the age when children usually start to speak (Kristoffersson et al., 2020; Muharib & Alzrayer, 2018; Tincani et al., 2006; von Tetzchner et al., 2018). One reason may be the presence of severe medical conditions, such as epilepsy, feeding problems or a need for ventilation, where the focus is on management of these conditions rather than initiating language intervention. For children with severe motor impairments, there is often an early focus on mobility. Professionals may also expect children with severe motor impairments to have other disorders and therefore delay the introduction of a communication aid until the children have demonstrated some comprehension of spoken language. Their communication aids are used to *reveal* language skills rather than to *promote* the development of such skills. Whatever the reason, late introduction of AAC is unfortunate for children's communication and language development.

A sensitive period implies a heightened susceptibility to environmental influences; the brain is particularly vulnerable to injury and at the same time capable of learning something more easily than during other developmental periods (Roth & Sweatt, 2011). There are two main explanations of sensitive periods. The first suggests that the potential to learn a language is determined by maturational factors, independent of experience, and hence functions as an independent timing device (Lenneberg, 1967; Newport et al., 2001). The second explanation is that learning and experience determine the development of neurological patterns in the brain. As these patterns become established, it becomes gradually more difficult to change them or to established new neurological patterns. The termination of the brain plasticity of the sensitive period has an important function, namely, to save resources and stabilize the functional neurological patterns that have been established, so they are not easily lost. If the brain has not received a particular stimulation by the time it is ready, development will proceed on the assumption that this stimulation is not significant in the individual's environment and that no systems or resources are necessary to process this type of stimulation. The brain's resources may rather be used for something else (Elman et al., 1996; Takesian & Hensch, 2013). This process makes it important to provide children with the language stimulation needed for developing neurological structures for processing language in a modality that is functional for the individual, and as early as possible. If language is not developed in the sensitive period, learning will have to utilize other existing neurological structures. This will make learning more difficult but still possible. Most humans learn one or more additional languages after the sensitive period, using the neurological structures they developed while learning their early developed language(s) (von Tetzchner, 2019a).

In addition to utilizing the sensitive period, early intervention supports better early parent-child interactions, attachment and more positive learning experiences for the child, and helps the child cope with educational challenges and social situations. The importance of including AAC in early intervention is illustrated in a study of two groups of children with Down syndrome. Both groups attended an early intervention programme based on the Portage Guide to Early Education (Cameron, 1986) and one of the groups in addition received manual sign intervention from age six months to three years (or longer). At eight years, the early signing group showed better social skills than the control group that did not have early signing intervention (Launonen, 2019a).

In line with the notion of a sensitive period for language development, studies of individuals with poorly developed language suggest that there appears to be an important dividing line around the age of four to five years in terms of speech acquisition. The proportion of the population of individuals with intellectual disabilities who develop speech seems to increase

very little after this age. The probability of children developing speech is quite low if they have not begun to speak before the age of five years and some have suggested waiting until after this age (Koegel et al., 2016). However, this observation only reflects a tendency in large groups. There are many documented cases of individuals who began to speak between the ages of six and twelve years, both with and without the use of AAC (Pickett et al., 2009). Launonen describes a boy with Down syndrome, Eric, who used manual signs throughout childhood, although he also received speech therapy from an early age (Launonen, 2019b; Launonen & Grove, 2003). Eric began to speak when he was twelve years old, and five years later speech was his main communication form.

Studies also document that there are many individuals without expressive language who were not been given opportunity to learn an alternative mode of communication in early childhood and who learned to use AAC at a later age (Andzik & Chung, 2022; McLay et al., 2015, 2017; Pickett et al., 2009).

Joint attention

Communication is a matter of influencing the mind of another. The intention behind a communicative act is to the direct the attention of other persons and make them aware of something for a purpose. This may be something in the immediate surroundings (e.g., a person or an object), a wish of the other to do something (e.g., get something or go away), or an abstract idea (e.g., the theory of relativity). In order to direct the attention of another person, attention must somehow be shared. It is not sufficient that two or more individuals look at the same object for attention to be joint; they must also be aware of each other's attention (Carpenter & Liebal, 2011). In this connection, "context" may be defined as the individual's perception of relevant physical, social and verbal aspects of the situation. *Shared context* may be defined as awareness of some of the same aspects of the situation, and joint attention activities are central in the acquisition and cultural shaping of this awareness. Shared attention, intention and context are prerequisites for language acquisition (Tomasello et al., 2005).

In the second half year of life, infants with typical development will start following the attention of other people, and somewhat later seek to direct the attention of other people towards something. Communication emerges as the children become able to engage in joint attention. Children use gaze, gestures and words to spontaneously initiate joint attention and respond to joint attention bids from others (Hansen et al., 2018). A child may initiate joint attention by directing her or his father's attention to a cat sitting in a window, and the father might smile and say *Yes, a nice cat*. An adult may use the child's attention and interests as clues to ensure that the child perceives relevant communicative expressions and lead the child's attention to those aspects of the situation that are relevant to what she or he is communicating, and the child may respond by following the adult's attention direction. There is often *joint action* in situations involving joint attention (Milward & Carpenter, 2018).

There are two main categories of communicative intentions: declarative and imperative or instrumental. In *imperative communication*, the intention is to make the other person do something, such as giving a toy or throwing a ball, or stop doing something. *Declarative communication* is based on an internal motivation to share experiences, making the other aware of something, for example, an interesting or scary animal, somebody wearing a nice dress, or a funny event taking place. In the professional literature, many equate declarative intent and joint attention (Yoder & McDuffie, 2006; Weisberg & Jones, 2019) but joint attention is also necessary for the development of imperative communication. If the child and the adult have

different perceptions of the purpose of the expression, the child is likely to misunderstand what the adult's expression is referring to and the adult will not understand the child's communicative attempts.

Declarative communication and imperative communication imply different reactions from the communication partner. For the child to have instrumental success, the other person must do what the child requests, for example, give the child the object she or he wants or perform a particular action. Declarative communication only requires that the adult somehow acknowledges the child's message without providing anything but a relevant answer. An appropriate response to the child's initiative to declarative communication might be a comment and a smile or another emotional expression, such as given by the father mentioned above, who smiled and commented the cat in the window that the child had pointed at. A child's declarative communication should thus not be met with the provision of objects or "rewards", but with communication that acknowledges the shared experience, such as showing awareness of the object or event indicated by the child and following up the child's comment in communicative interaction. A child expresses imperative communication when requesting a sweater from his or her mother, but may not have instrumental success because the mother answers *no*. However, the child will still have communicative success, because the request was understood.

In typical language acquisition, eye-gaze direction and deictic gestures usually play an important role as a means of establishing the object or event of attention, and later also in combination with symbolic gestures and words or signs. Activities with joint attention involving verbal communication provide children with cues to social events and interactions, and to both what the adult is communicating and how their own expressions are understood. Early joint attention skills predict later language development in both children with typical development and children with developmental disorders (Gulsrud et al., 2014; Mundy et al., 1990; Murza et al., 2016). Problems establishing both simple joint attention and a wider shared context may be a major obstacle to language learning, and such difficulties should be an early focus of language intervention.

Joint attention intervention

In early communication development, whether typical or atypical, it is mainly the adult partners who create *joint involvement episodes* (Schaffer, 1989). They (over)interpret the child's spontaneous expressions, utilize cues in the immediate setting and knowledge about the child and engage the child in social activities in which the use of spoken language or AAC may be embedded. Adults explicitly name persons, objects and actions which are meaningful within the child's environment and the culture in general, make some language forms more prominent than others and embed the conversation in non-linguistic features, which may implicitly direct the child's attention towards relevant contextual aspects, thereby creating "frames" for understanding and use of language (see p. 160). They interpret whatever the child expresses within such frames, so that the child implicitly gets to learn how these expressions are understood. The transition into language occurs as the child learns that words, manual signs or graphic symbols are used to refer to people, objects and actions. An essential part of this is that the child learns to interpret the situation in which the spoken words, manual signs or graphic symbols occur in a way that, to some extent, is similar to that of the adult. This implies a shared context where the child and the adult attend to some of the same aspects of the situation. A broader understanding of joint attention thus includes the child's and the

adult's contextual frames, which reflect their social and cultural knowledge. Also children with severe communication and language disorders bring to joint involvement episodes their assumptions based on earlier linguistic and non-linguistic experiences with people, activities and objects. As the children become more communicatively and linguistically competent, these assumptions will gradually play a greater role in their interactions.

Because joint attention is a prerequisite for language learning, in principle, all language interventions involve joint attention, including situations with teaching of comprehension and use of manual signs or graphic symbols. For the child to understand what is relevant to the communicative expressions being taught, the teacher must ensure the child's attention to both the expression and the relevant elements of the situation. Introducing explicit choices between objects or activities is one way of establishing joint attention, pointing at and naming objects or drawings is another. However, situations involving joint attention may also be non-verbal, such as when the adult or child shows objects or uses deictic gestures to initiate joint attention.

It is particularly autistic children who have problems with joint attention, but children with severe intellectual disabilities may also be delayed in developing joint attention skills, including deictic gestures (Smith & von Tetzchner, 1986; Stenberg et al., 2014, 2021). Autistic children tend to have more problems with declarative than with imperative communication, and declarative communication is the stated focus in most studies of joint attention intervention for autistic children (Murza et al., 2016). Studies have demonstrated that children who attend early intervention programmes with special focus on joint attention show better communication and language development than comparable programmes without a focus on joint attention (Chang et al., 2016; Kasari et al., 2006). Today, many early intervention programmes for autistic children include strategies for promoting joint attention skills, such as guiding the child to pay attention to the attention of others, to direct an adult's or a child's attention towards a toy or something else the child is interested in using by pointing or other gestures or spoken words, and to follow the direction of others who try to direct the autistic child towards something of interest (Hansen et al., 2018). The aim is usually to guide the child to engage in declarative communication, where the child directs attention to some object without an intention to obtain it. To achieve this, the adult may follow the child's lead, imitate the child's actions, comment and show engagement related to objects, people and events that the child appears interested in. Joint exploration and naming of toys or other objects are also typical declarative activities.

Play with two or more participants (a teacher or parent may be one of them) may be an ideal activity for promoting joint attention skills (see also Chapter 10). Many forms of play include attention direction both for requesting objects or actions (imperative communication) and for sharing an experience without implying a request (declarative communication). The intervention programme *Joint Attention, Symbolic Play, Engagement and Regulation* (JASPER) integrates activities with joint attention, shared affect, and imperative and declarative communication in social and symbolic play (Kasari et al., 2021). Studies of the JASPER programme found that the autistic children who were engaged in symbolic play showed the best communication and early language skills (Chang et al., 2016; Kasari et al., 2006).

Rewards and praise from the adult might make the child focus on what he or she can obtain by communicating and should be avoided when interventions aim to support the development of declarative communication. However, in some studies claiming to teach joint attention skills and declarative communication, the interventionists provided objects or activities contingent on the child's joint attention actions (rewards) or removed the child's toy if the child

did not comply to perform a joint attention action (punishment) (for example, Weisberg & Jones, 2019; Whalen & Schreibman, 2003). These studies appear to support imperative rather than declarative communication (see also p. 160).

The problems autistic children experience with non-verbal communication and joint attention are usually not permanent. With age, these children engage in a greater variety of situations involving joint attention even if they are less likely than other children to lead the attention of other people just to show them what has captured their own interest. Their early communication tends to be imperative with the intention to obtain something, rather than declarative with the intention to share an experience (Camaioni et al., 2003; Naber et al., 2008). However, most autistic children will come to understand and use spoken language, and some will become quite skilled in using manual signs or graphic symbols. It is important that the intervention is revised in accordance with the child's development. Training of joint attention skills and pointing may be useful in the early years but after this, the focus should on more advanced communication and language, and pointing will usually no longer be an intervention target (Gulsrud et al., 2014). This also implies that one should not expect a correlation between basic joint attention skills and language skills in school-age autistic children, even if they are minimally verbal (Pecukonis et al., 2019). Some individuals with profound intellectual disabilities, such as girls and women with Rett syndrome (see p. 84), may have persistent problems developing basic communication and joint attention skills (von Tetzchner, 1997b). This group may not benefit from play with implicit or explicit teaching of joint attention skills, but rather from interactions with emotional engagement and structured over-interpretation (see section 'Early strategies for promoting use of AAC').

Implicit and explicit learning and teaching

Most children develop their first language(s) through engagement in communicative interactions with adults and peers without any explicit teaching. Implicit learning takes place without conscious operations, without the individual trying to solve a communicative problem (Berry & Dienes, 1993). Implicit teaching does not seek to make learners aware of special learning strategies but rather seeks to demonstrate the use of particular words and grammatical constructions and to help the individual to use words and sentences in various communication situations. In explicit learning, on the other hand, the individual takes a meta-perspective and is aware the strategies he or she uses to acquire knowledge or skills. Explicit teaching utilizes the conscious operations of explicit learning (Baron & Arbel, 2022; Ellis, 2008). Implicit and explicit teaching both assume an active learner, but the cognitive operations and basic skills involved in these two learning forms differ.

The distinction between explicit and implicit learning and teaching conditions parallel some of the differences between strategies used in ordinary first-language and second-language learning and teaching of children with typical development (Rebuschat, 2015). In first-language acquisition, implicit learning is primary, while explicit learning and teaching strategies mainly belong to school. Explicit learning strategies and teaching are more prominent in second-language acquisition, although implicit learning and teaching also have a place (Ellis, 2008).

The distinction between explicit and implicit learning and teaching strategies is important when planning intervention for children with developmental language disorders (Ebbels, 2014). It is also fundamental to AAC intervention and directly related to the division of individuals in need of AAC into three main groups (see Chapter 3). For the expressive language group,

conditions often resemble second-language learning and teaching: a main focus of the intervention is the relationship between the spoken language used by communication partners and people in the environment in general, and how the individual expresses meanings with other means. Because there is a large gap between the individual's comprehension and expression, the teacher can use spoken instructions to explain how new manual signs or graphic symbols can be used and where in a communication aid a new symbol can be found, thereby also making the organization of the vocabulary explicit. Early strategies are often explicit although they may result in implicit learning and knowledge of language. The individual's construction of utterances with AAC may in itself constitute an implicit learning situation. Explicit strategies utilize the asymmetry in knowledge both of speech and the alternative language mode that exists between the learner and the teacher. In explicit learning, being able to form hypotheses and follow certain strategies in solving communicative problems may be most important.

At the other end of this dimension is the alternative language group. The aim of the intervention for individuals in this group is to promote a first language, a *mother tongue*. Figuratively, implicit language learning may be described as the individual's exploration of new territories without knowing where he or she is going. This necessitates implicit strategies, because the individual does not have the means for learning from explicit teaching. The individual has to learn to follow the attentional directions of others and to direct other people's attention for diverse purposes. In autistic individuals, problems following the attention of other people and directing others' attention are a prominent feature of their disorder (see Chapter 3). Implicit teaching strategies promote the development of skills that may increase in functional value and – for children with some comprehension of speech – make them aware of the relationships between language forms (speech, manual signs, and tangible or graphic symbols) and their usage. This means that the content of implicit teaching must be functional and relevant to the immediate situation.

A child belonging to the expressive language group may be taught to perform the manual sign or point to the graphic symbol that corresponds to a particular spoken word, a "translation" strategy typical of second language teaching. This strategy will have little meaning for children who do not understand spoken instructions. In spite of this, such instructions are frequently observed in interventions for individuals belonging to the alternative language group. Following the instruction would require skills that individuals in this group do not have. It may be noted, however, that as individuals become more proficient in the use of their alternative communication system, this system may be utilized for explicit teaching.

For children who belong to the supportive language group, emphasis may be on explicit or implicit teaching strategies, depending on their comprehension of spoken language and the communicative functions to be taught.

Usages of manual signs and graphic symbols

Comprehension and use are complementary aspects of language competence, and either or both may be addressed in language interventions, including interventions involving comprehension and use of manual signs or graphic or tangible symbols (see p 128). In *comprehension training*, it is the teacher or a conversational partner who produces manual signs or indicates graphic or tangible symbols. The aim is that the individual learns to recognize and understand the functions of manual signs or tangible or graphic symbols, to indicate an object or perform an action, to answer what has been expressed, or to demonstrate their understanding in another way. The aim of *expressive training* is to enable the individual to use manual signs or graphic or tangible symbols for various communicative purposes.

AAC intervention involves three types of usage of signs and symbols: signal, command and expressive. *Signal signs and symbols* are used to give information about subsequent activities and events to the learner. In interventions with children who are in an early phase of communication development and have limited comprehension of spoken language, many of the signs or symbols taught in comprehension training will be signals. The teacher may either hand-guide the individual sensitively to articulate a manual sign or point to a graphic or tangible symbol, or the teacher may perform the manual sign or point at the graphic or tangible symbol. A sign or symbol may be used to signal the arrival of a person.

Philip is 23 years old with profound intellectual disability. He lives in a community unit, where his father usually visits him on Saturdays. Before the father enters Philip's room, one of the staff members helps Philip to sign FATHER while simultaneously saying the word *father*.

If the individual is using graphic communication, showing a photograph of the father would fulfil the same function.

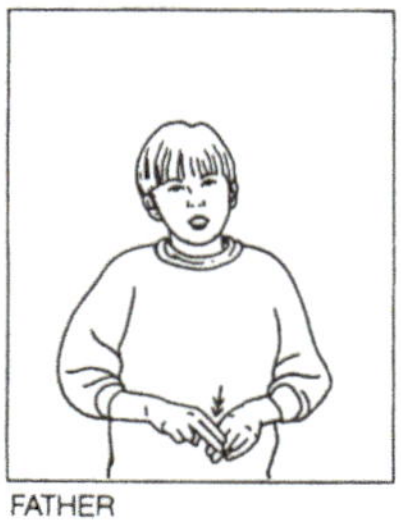

Manual sign: FATHER

The idea behind the signalling function is to support the individual's development of self-regulation. The aim of teaching signal signs and symbols is thus to prepare the individual for the next activity or event. When the individual is sensitively guided to sign or indicate a graphic symbol, he or she is both becoming aware of and learning to express what will happen. FINISH is useful for making the individual aware that an activity or event is terminated or has come to an end.

The main function of *command signs and symbols* is other-regulation. The communication partners use them to either tell the individual to carry out an activity or to stop doing one. NO, WAIT, CONTINUE and STOP may be particularly useful for regulating the actions of an individual.

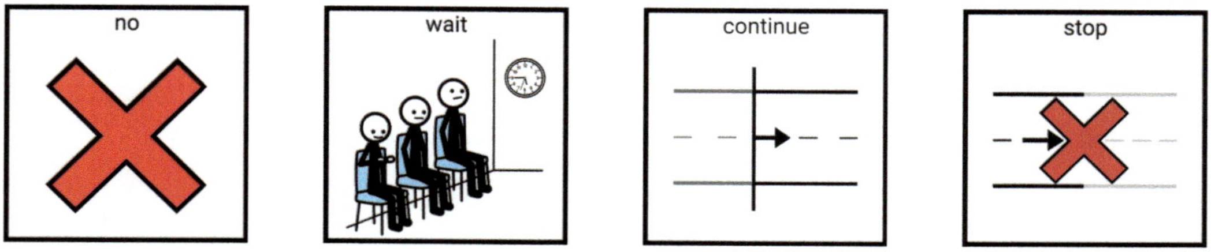

ARASAAC: NO, WAIT, CONTINUE, STOP

David is a seven-year-old autistic boy. He can stand for long periods of time switching the light on and off. His teacher signs STOP while saying *stop* emphatically in order to make David refrain from what he is doing.

Signal and command signs and symbols are initially not taught expressively. It is not an aim that the individual should learn to use command signs early, but he or she may soon find some of them useful. For example, it has often been reported that NO and FINISH are generalized and used spontaneously by individuals in the early phases of AAC development.

Expressive signs and symbols are used by individuals when they address another person to achieve a particular goal, inform about a specific event, comment on an activity, and so forth. The training focuses on how manual signs and graphic symbols may be used, including how the individual can use them to initiate communication with potential conversational partners. The conversational partner must be able to understand the manual signs or graphic symbols and answer or react appropriately to them. During training, the individual may be given help to articulate manual signs or select and indicate graphic or tangible symbols, but only the amount of help that is necessary. Help should be reduced as soon as possible.

Mary is a 14-year-old girl with severe intellectual disabilities. She likes to listen to dance music and is taught the manual sign MUSIC in special training sessions. There are two teachers. The tablet that is used for streaming music is placed on the table, out of her reach. When she stretches to reach it, one of the teachers guides her hands sensitively to perform the manual sign MUSIC. The other teacher gives her the tablet and she is allowed to listen to one dance melody.

In this kind of training, teachers often play very short melodies in order to carry out many training trials during each training session. However, this is an unusual use of music and may frustrate the individual. The music is not a reward but a result of a successful communicative request. It is better to use the music time to expand the communication related to the activity, for example, commenting on qualities of the melody, such as GOOD, SWEET, FAST or SLOW, or engaging the child in singing or dancing. Leading the individual into ordinary activities is an integrated aim of communication and language intervention.

PCS: GOOD, SWEET

Early intervention strategies for promoting AAC comprehension

Individuals need to understand their own AAC systems. The type of comprehension training to be implemented will vary with the individual's comprehension of spoken language. Intervention directed at the individual's comprehension of signs or symbols may take place in natural situations or in special training sessions (see Chapter 5).

Natural situation strategies

Many individuals with profound communication disorders have little overview of what their day will bring in terms of activities and events. They may rarely initiate activities and they are often taken from one activity to another by a teacher without being informed what is going to happen in a communication mode that they understand. Many autistic individuals react to uncertainty regarding what is happening with anxiety or fear. They may become passive and inactive or strongly oppose moving when someone exposes them to new activities.

> Martin is a three-year-old autistic boy. Every time he has to change activity in the nursery school and go to another room, he throws himself on the floor, kicks his legs and cries. It often takes a long time to quieten him down. His day at nursery school is marked by these problems (Steindal, 1990).

When signal signs and visual schedules with graphic symbols representing activities (see p. 165) were used to introduce changes, Martin's strong emotional reactions to change were gradually reduced.

Some individuals have difficulties deciding and expressing what they want to do, and it should at least be made clear to them *what* is going to happen. Days in preschool or school typically contain many routine activities that occur in the same place, at the same time of the day and in the same order. These can be signalled with manual signs or graphic symbols and may also be marked on a visual schedule (see p. 149). This may be called *signal-controlled frame structuring*. However, activities outside routines should also be signalled when possible.

While visual schedules mainly function to regulate the actions of the individual, signal signs and symbols are part of daily interactions and comprehension training. The aim is that the individual will learn that certain manual signs or graphic symbols precede specific activities and events and thus that they have a signalling function. The signs or symbols are selected so they are easy for the learner to recognize and distinguish from each other. They are presented just before the activity begins but in such a way that the individual has a little time to prepare for the change, even when it is not part of the daily routines. It is also practical to use a sign or symbol to indicate when an activity is ended, for example, FINISH. In principle, these markers may have any form: conventional manual signs performed together with the individual, guiding his or her hands if necessary, graphic symbols, objects that are used in the activities, and so forth. It is best to use manual signs or graphic symbols when this is possible as these may lead the individual towards the acquisition of a larger communication system. However, in the early phases of intervention, objects are often used to symbolize different activities.

PIC: FINISH

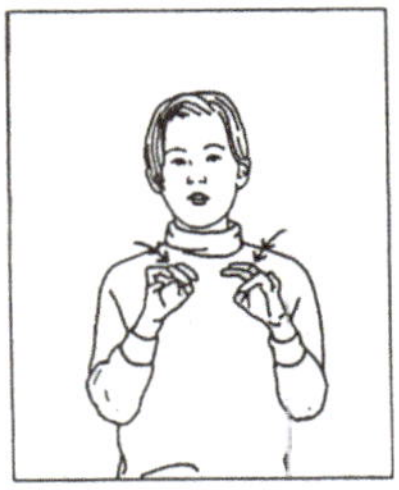

Manual sign: FINISH

There is usually most focus on signalling of positive events, but signal signs and symbols may be used to inform about both positive and negative events.

> John is a 10-year-old boy with multiple disabilities who likes to go for trips in his wheelchair. Before the adult goes out with him, John is guided to indicate the symbol *WALK*.

> Marie is a 17-year-old girl with profound intellectual disabilities. She has very bad teeth and is often at the dentist. Before she visits the dentist, who is situated in the building next door, she is helped to sign DENTIST.

Widgit: WALK,

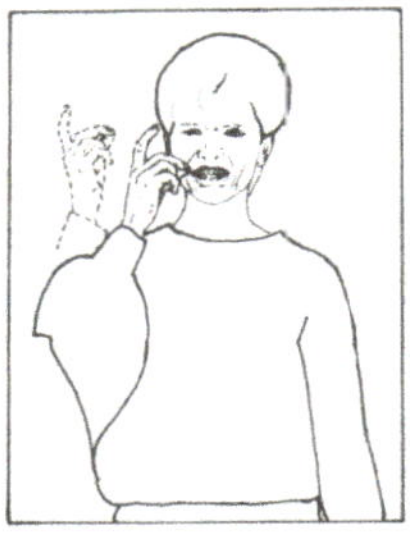

Manual sign: DENTIST

Like many other people, Marie was afraid of visiting her dentist and she sometimes showed anxiety when she was walking towards his office. It was therefore important that she knew when she was and was not going there, so she did not worry without reason. Because she was informed every time she was going to visit the dentist, she stopped showing anxiety when she

walked in the direction of his office but was not going to the dentist. As she gradually understood what the sign signalled, she began to protest when a member of staff signed DENTIST, but she nonetheless came along – albeit reluctantly.

The clearest indication that a sign or symbol has begun to have a signalling function for the individual is that he or she begins to show anticipation of what is going to happen. In individuals with the most severe intellectual disabilities, this may manifest itself in the individual straightening up, becoming more excited, or showing increased muscle tonus when the sign or symbol is presented. The individual may look or begin to move in the direction of the place where the signalled activity will take place, or where relevant things are kept. Such reactions may also be used as indicators that the individual associates the signs or symbols with certain events.

It is important that the signal signs or symbols being taught are presented immediately before the signalled activity or event. Manual signs can be made at any time. If the teacher or carer is using graphic symbols, having a set on a key chain will ensure that the graphic symbols are readily available when needed. If too much time passes between the presentation of the sign or symbol and the activity or event to take place, distracting events may interfere and make it difficult for the individual to understand the relationship between the sign or symbol and the activities or events they signal.

Hannah is a seven-year-old girl with intellectual disabilities. She was led by the hand to feel her bathing costume as a signal that she was going swimming. She was then dressed, accompanied to the bus stop, waited 10 or 15 minutes for the bus, sat on the bus for about 20 minutes, walked for five minutes, went to the changing room, undressed, put on her bathing costume and finally went swimming. However, she was often reluctant to go even if she clearly enjoyed being in the water when she got to the swimming pool. It might have been difficult for Hannah to understand that the bathing costume signalled a visit to the swimming pool. The routine was therefore changed. She was showed the graphic symbol *BUS* before leaving the house and then a photograph of the swimming pool when she left the buss. The bathing costume was introduced when she was in the changing room and the assistant was getting ready to help her undress.

ARASAAC: BUS

On the other hand, when teaching the function of signal signs or symbols it is also important that they are not presented too late. For example, it is not very informative to use the graphic symbol *FOOD* to tell an individual that he or she is going to eat when they are already seated at the table. The symbol is redundant, and thus meaningless, because it does not signal a change in the situation. The fact that the individual is going to eat has already been conveyed

through a large number of natural markers: the food is on the table, there is a smell of food, the individual is wearing a bib, and so forth. The graphic symbol should be presented just before the individual enters the room, or, at the very latest, before he or she is seated at the table.

Once an individual has learned a signal sign or symbol, the interval between the presentation and the activity may gradually be lengthened, which, over time, may enable the individual to communicate about activities that are not taking place immediately. This will also lay the foundation for the individual to either ask for things that are not visible, or express a wish to participate in activities that are not usually taking place at the time of asking. The reactions of the individual to signal signs or symbols will also inform the use of visual schedules.

In the example above, it might have been possible to use a more detailed visual activity schedule (see p. 150). The advantage of showing Hannah individual symbols was that these would also be used in other activities. In signal-controlled frame structuring with visual schedules, the fixed order of the various activities is a crucial element in the intervention. The individual should, preferably, have learned the signalling function of the graphic symbols in the context of the particular situation before they are presented independently for other usages. The individual should also have demonstrated some understanding of what the graphic symbols signal before they are used to review the activities of the whole day. If this is done too early, it may be difficult for the individual to learn the signal function of each symbol.

Structuring is a means to support learning of communication, but communication and structure should not be confounded. The use of signal signs or symbols in order to provide an individual with a better understanding of the environment is not dependent on frame structuring. Manual signs or graphic or tangible symbols may be used to signal activities and events, even though the events do not occur daily or at the same hour every time. They may be used with all activities and events that are repeated sufficiently often for the individuals to be able to learn to understand the signs or symbols. Using signal signs or symbols in daily routines and other situations where the same activities or events occur in the same order is especially useful because the fixed event order and the use of signal signs or symbols have a mutually enhancing effect Signalling facilitates the individual's understanding of everyday situations and this understanding facilitates the learning of signs and symbols.

In environments where manual signs are implemented, people tend to use signal signs also outside planned situations (Rombouts et al., 2019). This is less common with graphic or tangible symbols. The communication aid may not be available in many situations (von Tetzchner et al., 2018) and even when available, it may not be practical for the teacher to use. "Aided language stimulation" has become a common element in the teaching of graphic symbols but is used more in training sessions than in the general environment (O'Neill et al., 2018). However, when people in the environment also use graphic or tangible symbols when communicating to individuals with limited comprehension of spoken language, this may add to the individual's learning from unplanned experiences. In order to promote the individual's understanding that graphic symbols have corresponding spoken words, people in the environment should use graphic symbols together with speech whenever this is practical. In this way, the individual may associate the graphic symbols and words with different situations and learn that symbol-word correspondences may depend on the context. For individuals with a limited understanding of spoken language, the simultaneous use of graphic symbols and speech by people in the environment may also make it easier for them to understand the words that are being spoken.

Special training strategies

A common form of comprehension training is to present the individual with a manual sign or graphic symbol together with an object or action, for example, BALL and pointing at a ball, while simultaneously saying the gloss of the manual sign or graphic symbol. Another common strategy is where the teacher performs a manual sign, or points at a tangible or graphic symbol, and asks the learner to point to the corresponding object or picture, pick up something or perform an action. The teacher tells the learner whether the response is correct, thereby guiding the learning by trial and error.

Manual sign: BALL

In this type of comprehension training, the individual has to find the correct item among several objects or pictures. The positioning of the pictures or objects should vary, so that the individual does not merely learn to pick up the object or point at the picture that occupies one particular position.

> Dan is a 15-year-old boy with intellectual disabilities. A ball and a spoon are placed in front of him on a table. The teacher says *Give me the ball* while performing the sign BALL. Dan gives the ball to the teacher (Booth, 1978).

This is similar to ordinary testing of vocabulary, except that the individual's response may be guided or corrected if wrong.

This kind of comprehension training is less common in interventions with graphic or tangible symbols than with manual signs. One reason may be that manual signs must be performed each time they are used, while graphic and tangible symbols can be present the whole time. The teacher may become used to accompany his or her speech with manual signs during training sessions, but not with pointing at or showing tangible or graphic symbols. Another reason may be that many tangible symbols are miniature objects and graphic symbols are stylized drawings. Many teachers seem to assume that the individuals understand them immediately without training. In fact, comprehension of graphic symbols is usually given little attention in textbooks on AAC (for example, Beukelman & Light, 2020). However, it is the decision to use the image and gloss of a graphic symbol to represent something specific and refer to that in communication that gives the graphic symbol its function. The written gloss emphasizes the linguistic function. If the individual does not understand the symbolic function, the image on a graphic symbol is just an image. The symbolic function of each graphic symbol must be learned, in a similar way that children who develop spoken language must learn new vocabulary (von Tetzchner, 2015).

Aided language stimulation – where communication partners produce graphic keywords or graphic sentences without asking the individual to imitate them – may be considered an immersion support of aided communicators' comprehension of their own graphic system (O'Neill et al., 2018). Besides this, many aided communicators may have little experience with receptive graphic language (von Tetzchner, 2018; von Tetzchner & Grove, 2003). However, many of the strategies used in traditional speech and language therapy may also be used with AAC, such as shared book reading, where the adult is using manual signs or graphic symbols to present the story or name animals, objects and actions in the picture book (Sennott & Mason, 2016; Trudeau et al., 2003). Structured conversations, where the adult is using a copy of the child's communication system, may also support comprehension of more advanced graphic language use (see Chapter 9). Such conversations may be part of structured play or other joint activities (see Chapter 10).

Early strategies for promoting use of AAC

There are many ways of teaching the use of manual signs and graphic symbols. Most of them may be used in both special training and natural environments.

Structured over-interpretation and total communication

Parents and other adults typically tend to name what children are attentive to and often react to infants' actions as if these were communicative at an earlier age than it is reasonable to assume that infants have communicative intentions (Woodward & Markman, 1998). Over-interpretation theory suggests that these adult reactions help guide infants to engage in communication (Lock, 1980). This theory is the basis for the use of structured over-interpretation to support communication development in individuals with limited language comprehension. "Structure" means that it is a planned strategy, where some of the individual's spontaneous actions or movements are attributed communicative functions, and thus it takes advantage of what the individual is capable of and interested in. The aim is to help individuals with severe and profound disabilities to gain more control over their environment through significant others' systematic interpretation of certain behaviours as communicative and indicative of intentions related to the individual's interests, needs and preferences.

In structured total communication, individuals have some means for expressing their communicative intentions, including speech, conventional and idiosyncratic gestures, manual signs, graphic symbols, photographs, tangible symbols or objects. The basic idea behind total communication is that function is more important than form, and that for people with limited communication means, all modes of communication are valid and should be acknowledged (Purwowibowo et al., 2018).

Structured over-interpretation may help individuals with little or no communication to express themselves if they have the potential for developing such skills. It will support their communicative development if the actions are interpreted in the same manner by all who are involved in their care, including the family, the school and the respite care. It is always a goal to move from structured over-interpretation to structured total communication as soon as possible. However, for some individuals with profound intellectual disabilities, neither structured over-interpretation or other forms of intervention are likely to lead to spontaneous, self-initiated and independent communication. Even so, for these individuals and their carers, systematic over-interpretation may be of value and form a basis in the building up of an individual lifestyle (von Tetzchner, 1997b). The organization implied in structured

over-interpretation may lay the foundations of an everyday life for the individual with a better overview of the physical and social environment, and thereby a better understanding of what is happening. For people in the environment, structured over-interpretation may result in the accumulation of knowledge about how best to interpret the behaviour of the individual and react to him or her in different situations. It may thus contribute to a responsive and predictable environment for the individual, and, at the same time, to establishing a set of strategies that may be used by all significant people in the environment.

Watch, wait and react

This strategy is part of *structured over-interpretation*. The aim is to transform casual actions produced by the individual into signs by reacting to them as communicative, although it is not clear – sometimes even unlikely – that the individual's actions have communicative intent. The teaching may take place in unstructured situations and nothing special is done to encourage specific activities or actions. The individual is observed – watched, meaning that the teacher remains observant and sensitive to what the individual is doing. As soon as the individual makes a movement that may be recognized if repeated at a later stage, the teacher reacts to this movement as though the individual has performed a specific manual sign.

This strategy is best suited for intervention with individuals who show little self-initiated activity. It may have several positive effects. For example, there is reason to believe that the passivity that often characterizes children with poor language and communication skills is related to the fact that they, to a lesser degree than other children, display behaviour that causes reactions from others (Ryan, 1977). The watch, wait and react strategy makes it more likely that the individual's actions will cause a positive reaction, which in turn may stimulate the individual's activity level and initiative to communicate. The individual's actions and the teacher's reactions may thus have a transactional effect, leading to new actions and more learning opportunities for the individual. The new actions may be ascribed similar communicative functions, continuing the positive spiral of development. For this to happen, the actions reacted to by the teacher should, to begin with, be expressions that are indicative of the individual being attentive and motivated. This also increases the likelihood of the individual becoming aware of the relationship between what is happening in the situation, his own activities, and the reactions of people in the surroundings.

> Harold is a four-year-old boy with severe intellectual disabilities. He is passive and shows very little self-initiated activity. He likes to be lifted up and rough-and-tumble play. Sometimes he beats his chest. It is decided that his parents and the nursery school staff should attribute the meaning "I want to play" to this action. Each time he beats his chest, an adult lifts him up and initiates rough-and-tumble play.

Watch, wait and react represents a positive strategy for people in the environment but it has clear limitations. The expressions may be idiosyncratic and not easily recognized as communicative by people who are not involved in the intervention. The person who administers the intervention has little control over when the selected action will occur and can run the risk of having to wait for a long time before it is repeated. The individual has to be attentive and the reactions from others must be able to catch his interest. Interventionists may secure these conditions to a certain extent by selecting actions that the individual performs relatively often and basing the attribution of meaning to the action on information about the individual's interests and preferences.

Reacting to habitual behaviour

This strategy is part of *structured total communication*. It is most suitable for individuals who have some degree of self-initiated activity, but the activity is lacking in functionality. For example, reacting to habitual behaviour may be useful with children and adults who tend to wander aimlessly around in the room when left on their own, kick walls and furniture, hit a table if they pass one by, or pull objects down from shelves. The strategy requires that the teacher knows what the individual is interested in and what he or she will do in a given situation. The objective is to make a non-functional activity communicative and socially acceptable. In order to achieve this, the teacher must produce an intervention situation where it is possible to elicit certain actions and utilize them for teaching the use of manual signs or graphic symbols.

> Andrew is an eight-year-old autistic boy who uses a few manual signs. He has a tendency to empty any handbags he can get his hands on. He is placed in a room where a man is sitting with a handbag and nothing special is happening. The teacher follows Andrew as he walks around the room. As soon as he reaches for the bag, the teacher guides Andrew's reaching hands to form the manual sign HANDBAG. He is then given the bag by the man who is sitting there.

A similar situation could be used to teach Andrew a general sign, such as GET or GIVE, if the teacher had decided that learning these signs would have been more useful for Andrew in relation to the manual signs he had already learned. When a similar procedure is applied with graphic symbols, the individual is given a card with a graphic symbol and hand-guided sensitively to give or show the graphic symbol to the other person, such as the man with the handbag in the example above.

Widgit: GET, GIVE

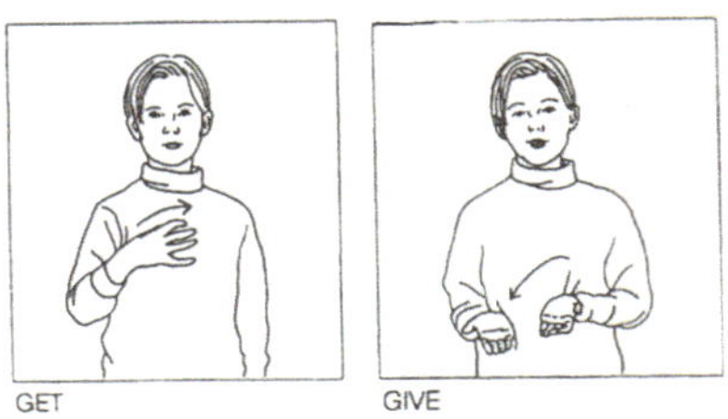

Manual signs: GET, GIVE

The purpose of this strategy is to give habitual behaviour that has previously been non-functional a communicative function by systematically reacting to the behaviour as though it was communicative. The strategy builds on the assumption that individuals will relate their own actions to the reactions of the communication partners. For the strategy to succeed, it is therefore essential that the individual is aware of both his or her own behaviour and the reaction of the other person, and that this will cause him or her to want the reaction to be repeated.

Many individuals with autism spectrum disorders and intellectual disabilities show behaviour problems (Emerson & Einfeld, 2011). It is an advantage of the strategy of reacting to habitual behaviour that it can be based on behaviour that people in the environment usually regard as a problem. Because the individual is taught a manual sign or graphic symbol that can help him or her to cope with a difficult situation, the intervention is also likely to lead to a reduction in the problem behaviour (see p. 128). Another advantage is that the teacher will be able to decide the time of the teaching by planning a situation in which the behaviour tends to occur habitually. This provides the teacher with control over the teaching of manual signs or graphic symbols, which will ensure a sufficient number of spontaneous repetitions.

Build-and-break chains

In this strategy, the teacher first constructs and implements a chain of activities that the individual is or becomes motivated to carry out. The teacher then obstructs one of the activities so that it is impossible to complete the chain without help (Carter & Grunsell, 2001). When the individual shows confusion or frustration, he or she is immediately guided to produce a manual sign or indicate a tangible or graphic symbol, led to the obstructed activity and thereby resumes the behaviour chain. This strategy can be utilized among individuals with varying levels of activity and is especially suitable for people who need to learn to do things on their own initiative.

The strategy usually begins with implementing a behaviour chain, but may also be used with untaught, naturally occurring chains (routines), provided that the individual is sufficiently motivated in the situation. A song can constitute a very short chain.

> Linda is a six-year-old girl with multiple disabilities. She likes songs and the teacher has introduced *Wheels on the bus*, which she sings with her every morning. They started with one verse, then added several verses with joint movements indicating GOING ROUND. After three weeks, when this small chain was well established, the teacher stopped singing and held Linda's hand without moving after the first verse and waited for Linda's reaction. The graphic symbol *SING* was placed on magnetic whiteboard next to the chair. When Linda tried to move her hands, the teacher said *sing*, pointed at *SING* and started singing again.

PCS: SING

A jigsaw puzzle can also be a chain.

Carl is a ten-year-old autistic boy. He has learned to complete a simple jigsaw-puzzle when the pieces are placed just in front of him, from left to right. Carl has learned to take the pieces in the left-to-right order, one after each other. The chain is broken by placing the pieces out of his reach, so that Carl needs help to get hold of them. There are two teachers. One is behind Carl and helps him, while the other sits in front of him and tends to the pieces. As soon as Carl discovers he is missing one of the pieces of the jigsaw-puzzle (preferably not the first piece), he reaches for it without getting hold of it and looks at the teacher sitting in front of him. The helper guides his hands to perform the sign PIECE. Then the other teacher gives him the piece of jigsaw-puzzle he needs.

PIECE

Manual sign: PIECE

The same procedure could be implemented with graphic symbols. One way of doing this might be to make the individual learn to follow a visual activity schedule (see p. 150) and leave out an element to break the chain. These types of situations could also have been used to introduce MORE, as a way of asking for repetition or more puzzle pieces or other things.

The underlying idea is that breaking the chain creates a "problem" for the individual that can be solved with communication. It is essential that the individual has learned the chain and is motivated to carry it out before it is broken for the purpose of teaching him or her to use manual signs or graphic symbols. This can be a difficult task for the teacher. One way of ensuring the individual's motivation is to begin by breaking the chain when the last link in the chain precedes something that the individual wishes to do. For example, if the individual likes to go for a drive, the fixed routine of getting dressed before going for a drive can be interrupted. In this case, going for a drive is signalled and added to the dressing chain but getting dressed does not always involve a drive. Sometimes it is possible to use humour and surprise to break a chain, for example, looking high and low for a missing graphic symbol that can be used to communicate what is missing and "repair" the chain.

Olga is five years old with severe motor-impairment. She likes doll play in the preschool and especially enjoys doing a morning routine where the doll wakes up, gets out of bed, washes in a bathtub, eats breakfast and goes to the toilet. She cannot do the doll actions herself but uses the gaze to point at the objects she needs in the different stages of the morning routine. After having played this several days, the teacher "forgets" the bathtub, and when Olga seems confused after the doll is out of bed, the teacher helps her to find *BATHTUB* on the board with graphic symbols representing objects and actions that are part of morning routines.

Similar procedures could have been done with chains related to other forms of doll play, such as dressing, making a simple meal or taking the bus. Doll play is used much in AAC intervention with children (see Chapter 10). However, in this connection, it is not the doll play but the breaking of a chain of actions that is the main element.

The build-and-break chain strategy implies that the teacher frustrates the individual in reaching a goal. The overall aim is that the individual experiences a need for communication and comes to understand that using manual signs or graphic symbols can be a useful way to solve the communicative problem. It is vital that the frustration the individual is subjected to – in the eyes of the learner – appears to be the result of situational circumstances. It should not appear to be produced by the conversational partner, who should act as a helper. Otherwise, the individual may be confused about the role of the partner, and may react as if being teased or punished without a reason.

Reacting to signal-elicited anticipatory behaviour

The basis of this strategy is that the teacher has constructed a frame structure in which familiar activities and events occur in a fixed order and are signalled with manual signs or graphic symbols. When the individual's actions suggest understanding of what is going to happen, his or her anticipatory reaction may be used to introduce new manual signs or graphic symbols. If the anticipatory reaction is an action that is suitable for such a use, it may be attributed a meaning and function as a sign, or the teacher may mould the individual's hands to form a manual sign or to point to a graphic symbol immediately after he or she has shown the anticipatory reaction.

The use of this strategy assumes that the activity or event that the individual has anticipated will follow naturally once the individual has reacted. In practical terms, this means that the teacher establishes a behaviour chain by introducing a manual sign or graphic symbol between the reaction and the activity. The chain will end with the individual doing the activity that the sign or symbol refers to.

> Elaine is a 19-year-old autistic girl. She enjoys basket-weaving. Elaine has become familiar with this situation, which is signalled with WORK. When the teacher says *work* and simultaneously signs WORK, Elaine looks in the direction of the shelf where the basket-weaving materials are kept. The moment Elaine directs her gaze towards the shelf, the teacher guides her hands to make the sign MATERIAL and immediately fetches the materials Elaine needs.

This is one example of the use of frame structure, where a manual sign is used to signal a group of activities. There may be various activities pertaining to "work" that are suitable for producing a situation in which the individual will gradually learn to use manual signs or graphic symbols to choose between different activities.

When an individual displays signal-elicited anticipatory behaviour, several basic conditions essential to the success of the teaching are already present: the individual is attentive, motivated for the action in question and has an understanding of what the situation entails. This makes it easier for him or her to learn to understand and use the manual sign or graphic symbol. In addition, the teacher has control over what is going to happen and is able to use the structuring as a tool to encourage active participation in individuals with a limited behavioural repertoire.

Structured waiting

As a way of making life easier for people with disabilities, many family members and professionals try to anticipate their needs and wishes and give them what they require without having to express it. However, by doing this they may also remove one aspect of the situation that makes communication necessary. The result may be that the individual is not given opportunities of taking the initiative in situations where this would otherwise have been natural. This may create a form of *learned passivity*.

In order to promote self-initiated communication, the teacher may introduce time delays before reacting to the individual in natural teaching situations, as well as in incidental teaching (see p. 186), when she believes that the individual may use a *known* manual sign or graphic symbol. Structured waiting – also called *expectant time delay* – implies that the teacher or another person waits a little while for the individual's action before they take the turn, make prompts or help the individual to perform a manual sign or indicate a graphic symbol (Leung, 1994; Liber et al., 2008). The waiting is called structured because it is part of a plan, and the length of the delay is decided beforehand. It is usual to begin with a short interval and gradually increase the time to approximately ten seconds. It is possible to wait even longer, but longer periods of waiting do not seem to lead to more self-initiation among people without severe motor impairments (Foxx et al., 1988). Among individuals with severe fine motor coordination problems who have difficulties pointing at graphic symbols, it may be necessary to wait considerably longer (see Deliberato et al., 2018).

> Jay is a seven-year-old boy with intellectual disabilities. Before exercising the teacher takes him to the changing room to change clothes. He needs help with the buttons on his trousers. The teacher holds her finger on a button but waits ten seconds before she, on the occasions Jay needs it, helps him performing the manual sign HELP.
>
> Jay used to push a small scooter together with his physiotherapist as a means of training his arm muscles. The physiotherapist will stop with regular intervals, wait ten seconds for Jay to perform the manual sign PUSH, before she helps him to perform the sign if that is needed (Oliver & Halle, 1982).

When the teacher waits before giving help, this gives the individual time to act and thereby increases the chances that the individual will take the initiative to communicate. This may make him or her more active and decrease the risk of learned passivity. Waiting before prompting the individual may also help the teacher notice when prompts are no longer needed, allowing for more ordinary communicative interchanges. Studies have found that individuals with intellectual disabilities needed less time to learn new manual signs when structured waiting was included in the teaching (Liber et al., 2008). These findings suggest that giving the individual more time to initiate communication before giving help is likely to make the intervention more effective.

Structured waiting can also be very important for individuals with severe motor impairments who belong to the expressive language group, but for a different reason. The motor impairment means that it takes them a long time both to answer and to take the initiative, and when the communication partner waits, this gives them sufficient time to prepare their utterance. Individuals with intellectual disabilities who belong to the other two main groups can also be relatively slow communicators, due, for example, to low processing speed, and therefore need time both to respond and to show initiative. Structured waiting thus has a double

function. It creates a need for communication in the learner and slows down the communication partners, making them more aware that they should not give help unless it is absolutely necessary. Intentional postponement of help may be used even with very young children.

Further AAC teaching strategies

These strategies imply a transition to more direct teaching activities and a greater emphasis on self-initiated communication and language.

Providing choices

This is the most common strategy. It may be used in both natural and special training situations, and with all the three main groups. Making choices is a typical early training activity and also part of an individual's everyday communication. The choices may be between foods, drinks, toys, activities, instruments, books and so on, depending on the interests and preferences of the individual (see also Chapter 7 and 8).

Making choices is positive for the individual. Arranging a choice situation is relatively easy for the teacher to do and for the learner to understand. It is therefore a practical way to start guiding an individual into using AAC. In interventions with individuals in the supportive language group or the alternative language group, guided choice-making is important for teaching them that they can influence their own activities, that they do not only have to follow instructions but have choices. Choice-making focuses on the individual's agency and self-determination, and thus represents a significant elaboration of the signalling, where manual signs and graphic or tangible symbols are used to inform the individual of already determined events and activities. For individuals in the expressive language group, highlighting choices may contribute to preventing learned helplessness and show them that they can achieve a particular goal by using manual signs or graphic symbols.

Many children with severe motor impairments have difficulty chewing and swallowing. Eating may be an activity they do reluctantly or not at all. For these children, asking them to choose between different types of food may not be the best strategy. On the other hand, it can be advantageous for this group of children to achieve better control over meals in terms of when the next bite of food will be consumed and when they want to drink. The choice may not about *what* they should eat but rather *when* a helper should put it into their mouth, for example, using *MORE, WAIT* and *STOP*.

Fulfilling spontaneous wants

As a strategy, fulfilling spontaneous wants may be introduced both in parallel with, and as a continuation of, providing choices. Conditions for requesting are also relatively easy for the teacher to arrange and for the learner to understand. It is particularly important that the intervention focuses on teaching individuals to express their own wishes and on reducing dependency on prearranged choices. Spontaneous requesting is more active than making a choice and supports the individual's personal agency – even if the situation is planned beforehand. Requesting may be used in special training situations but is most practical in natural situations. It is an aim for all three groups, that they discover that they can get something or do something which is not planned by the teacher or other adults. Like making choices, fulfilling spontaneous wants may contribute to preventing learned helplessness and frustration.

Creating communication situations related to fulfilling a desire to carry out a particular activity should be based on knowledge about the individual's interests and likes and dislikes. The teacher should organize a situation which contains a particular object that she or he knows the individual likes or which is typically used in the individual's preferred activity, such a puzzle or blocks that can be used for building something. The teacher arranges the situation and waits until the individual shows in some way that he or she wants the object, moulds the individual's hands into the appropriate sign or points at the relevant graphic symbol, and then gives him or her the object. Similarly, when the individual starts to get the things or initiate the activity, the teacher helps himor her to perform the appropriate manual sign or point at the relevant graphic symbol, and then lets him or her use the object or engage in the desired activity for a while.

Fulfilling wants can involve both implicit and explicit teaching and learning. With implicit teaching, the guiding procedures are made without explicit instruction, like in the examples below.

Henry is a seven-year-old autistic boy. He likes to crank the ladder on his toy fire-engine up and down. The teacher walks together with Henry and makes sure that they pass the fire-engine. When Henry clearly looks at the fire-engine, stops or reaches for it, the teacher moulds his hands into the sign CAR, whereupon Henry is given the fire-engine.

Manual sign: CAR

Elaine is a 43-year-old woman with multiple disabilities, who is using a wheelchair for mobility. She is fond of coffee, which she drinks with a straw, but she never takes initiative to get coffee. She can press keys with graphic symbols on an electronic communication device with speech output, but only does this when asked to do so. The teacher has put COFFEE into her device aid and places herself near Elaine with two cups and a coffee pot. When Elaine looks at the teacher, she approaches her and helps Elaine to press the key with *COFFEE*. The machine says *'coffee'* and the teacher pours Elaine a cup of coffee.

PCS: COFFEE

In Elaine's case, it was not the production of the word that was the focus of the intervention but her initiative to communicate, which seemed characterized by prompt dependence. Prompt dependence occurs commonly in individuals with intellectual disabilities (Brown & Cariveau, 2022; Gorgan & Kodak, 2019). Elaine pressed the keys on the communication device when prompted to do so but did not use this skill to communicate on her own initiative. The teacher began to wait until Elaine addressed her by looking at her. Then she guided Elaine to use the speech device. The aim was to make her aware of how she could use it to communicate that she wants something, without prompts from others.

With explicit teaching, the functions of the manual signs or graphic symbols. and how they can be used spontaneously to get or do something, will be explained to the individual.

> John is six years old and has severe motor disabilities due to cerebral palsy. He attends an inclusive preschool. He has a communication book with graphic symbols, but the vocabulary is limited and the book is rarely used. Both the teachers and the peers tend to ask *yes/no* questions – providing him with a sequence of choices. In the afternoon, the children have fruit or snack and for each of the items, the teacher will ask John if he wants it or not. John only shakes his head for "no" and smiles for "yes". To increase John's initiative and active communication, his teacher revises the vocabulary and tells both the other teachers and his peers to make sure that John has the communication book when they ask what he wants, and only use yes/no questions when John lacks vocabulary.

Many individuals with limited comprehension of spoken language, who are taught manual signs or graphic or tangible symbols, generally take part in few activities and may appear to like few things. However, limited interest is not the only reason why an individual may ask for the same things and activities, sometimes over many years. Those who plan the teaching sometimes show little imagination and creativity, failing to address the individual's need for exploration and variety. There are familiar people, toys and games, household objects, food, sweets, fruit, clothes and shoes, musical instruments, electronic devices such as tablets, gymnastics, outdoor activities and so forth. A craft session may naturally include requests such as DRAW, PAPER, CUT and GLUE. A physical activity may be to DANCE. Looking at a MAGAZINE may be enjoyable. With age and the acquisition of new skills, preferences and interests will also change in individuals with severe or profound intellectual disabilities. This implies a need for both new activities and new manual signs or graphic symbols, which in turn will promote the individual's language development. Teachers and other professionals should always take the individual's current development level and learning into account and help him or her to request and participate in new activities.

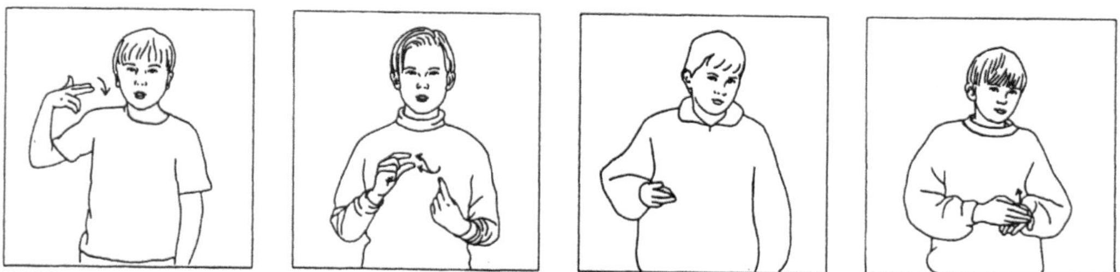

DRAW PAPER CUT GLUE

Manual signs: DRAW, PAPER, CUT, GLUE

Sometimes the manual signs or graphic symbols taught refer to things that are easily available in the environment. If an individual can reach an object, there may be little need to ask somebody for it, and the individual may not discover the usefulness of the signs or symbols that are being taught. In fact, the individual may not understand why the teacher demands that he or she should hand over a graphic symbol or perform a manual sign. There are several ways to manage such circumstances and make the communication intervention more meaningful to the individual. An open shelf located high up on the wall may be practical. Because the shelf is open, any object placed there is visible, reminds the individual about it and may elicit a wish to get hold of it. Because it is high on the wall, it cannot be reached without assistance and a natural solution will be to ask somebody to get it. It is thus a problem that the individual can solve with communication. It should be emphasized that the aim of this strategy is not to make it difficult for the individual to get something, but to help him or her to understand that an object out of reach, even out of sight, may be obtainable with the help of manual signs or graphic symbols.

Mari is a six-year-old autistic girl with profound intellectual impairments. Her communication aid is a miniature doll suitcase that contains about 20 strips, each with four photographs or pictograms. She is doing various activities together with a teacher in the main room of the preschool. Mari puts *PUZZLE* next to *MARI* (a photograph of herself) in the lid of the suitcase. The puzzles are located in a different room. Mari and the teacher therefore transfer *MARI PUZZLE* to a "memory strip" and bring this along when they go to fetch the puzzle (von Tetzchner et al., 2004).

PIC: PUZZLE

Early vocabularies often comprise many manual signs or graphic symbols for foods and drinks, because parents and teachers usually know what the individual likes to eat and drink. It is usually quite easy to create situations with choice-making for teaching vocabulary items like MILK, BISCUIT, JUICE and SAUSAGE. However, it is not always practical to start teaching manual signs or graphic symbols for food at mealtimes. If the individuals can make themselves understood by pointing at the desired food, one risks reducing the functionality of the communication skills that the individual already possesses, as well as ruining a situation that the individual likes. The teaching may be carried out in the location where the meals are usually served, but a short while before the meal begins. Once the individual has learned to use some manual signs or graphic symbols in this situation, these can be introduced carefully during real meals. However, if the desired things are accessible and the individuals make themselves understood with pointing or in other ways, they should not be asked to use a sign or a graphic symbol in the natural environment, only in teaching sessions where AAC is

expected or required. One way of making the individual need AAC is to "forget" to put something the individual likes and often eats on the table, and use this ploy to guide him or her towards using manual signs or graphic symbols to obtain the wanted foods during ordinary meals. This further demonstrates to the individual that signs and symbols may be used for getting something that is not in the immediate situation. Thus, AAC becomes a tool the individual can use for changing the situation in a positive manner. Getting food was used in the example above but many things may be used to fulfil the individual's wants and food names should not constitute a too large part of the early vocabulary. Fulfilling wants may also include teaching MORE as a request, where the individual is guided to indicate a wish to continue eating, playing, listening to music, or doing some other activity.

Widgit: HOT-DOG, MORE

Manual signs: FOOD, JUICE, SAUSAGE

Addressing the communication partner

For communication to be successful, somebody has to notice the individual's attempts to communicate. Addressing the communication partner, or establishing joint attention and engagement, is a core element of communication and therefore also a main target in communication intervention. The strategies that are described here aim to support the individual's spontaneous communicative initiative at the same time as learning to use AAC. This means that it is an integrated element of the teaching that individuals who are developing AAC should learn to address other people when they want to communicate something. Taking communicative initiative and addressing potential communication partners are basic conversation skills (see Chapter 11).

Many children with severe disabilities make frequent communicative initiatives even if they have problems acquiring spoken language. They may vocalize, gesture or lead the communication partner by the hand. Some children with severe motor impairments are unable to produce any vocalization and may therefore have problems attracting the attention of others when they want to communicate something (see p. 43). If they use an electronic communication device with speech output, they can say something with the aid to get attention or take the turn. If they have a communication board or book, they may have a bell or a small electronic device that says *"Hello"*. If they don't have access to the communication aid, they might have a small device that says *"I want my communication aid"*. For some children, it can be difficult to find an appropriate attention-getting device and they may only be able to initiate communication if the person they want to address is being attentive to them. One solution might be a wristband with a text indicating that they want access to their communication aid, so they can look at it when they want to initiate a conversation.

Some autistic children seldom make attempts to address others or try to make contact without paying attention to where they are looking. For this group it is necessary to apply intervention strategies that makes it clear to them that they need to get the attention of the other person in order to communicate successfully. This may imply that the visual attention of another person becomes a cue to performing a communicative act. For individuals who use manual signs, an objective of their training may thus be to ensure that they get the visual attention of the other person before they begin to sign. For individuals who use graphic communication, training may include the handing over of graphic symbols or photographs to the communication partner. This is a basic strategy of the *Picture Exchange Communication System* (PECS, Bondy & Frost, 2002), but in PECS it is mainly applied in training sessions and with limited developmental scope. However, handing over graphic symbols might be a useful strategy in the natural environment. For children and adults who have problems with addressing others and initiating communication, it is important that the addressing has a true communicative function and is part of an intervention where the individual solves meaningful communicative "problems" and achieves diverse communicative goals – both in special training and in natural situations.

Teaching expression and comprehension of AAC

The aim of AAC intervention is to provide individuals who have limited spoken language with better means both to express themselves and to understand what other people are communicating. In usage training, individuals are taught to express themselves to others. In comprehension training, they are guided to interpret and react to manual signs or graphic symbols that other people are using when communicating with them.

In reality, most communication and language interventions involve both comprehension and expression. However, different theoretical and practical arguments are presented for giving priority to either comprehension or expression in early intervention. Priority of comprehension training is often based on the assumption that children must understand words, manual signs or graphic symbols before they can be taught to use them. From this point of view, it is natural to begin with comprehension training and assume that manual signs or graphic symbols will be used once they have been understood. In general, measures of language comprehension slightly exceed measures of production but there is considerably variation (Bornstein & Hendricks, 2013). Studies show that in typical development, comprehension and use tend to develop simultaneously and complement one another.

Sometimes a child's use of a word or sign may appear more advanced than their comprehension of that same word or sign; at other times comprehension develops first (Bates et al., 1988; Hendriks, 2014). Autistic children may appear more impaired in language comprehension than in expressive language (Hudry et al., 2010). Naturally, children must have heard the word or seen the sign before they can use it, but children may use a word or sign productively (not necessarily correctly) before it is well understood. A child's apparent early comprehension of a word or sign may reflect an association between an object or category and a word or sign form, without understanding of the referring function of the word (Werker, 2018a). Moreover, the meaning and use of words are not instant or static but develop gradually and dynamically (Vihman, 2018). When children have learned a new word, they may soon start trying out new usages (Barrett et al., 1991). They talk to learn (see Chapters 7 and 8).

The time allocated to training is often limited, making it necessary for the teacher to make priorities. It is usually best to give more time to expressive teaching. There are several arguments for this. An individual's understanding of other people's use of a manual sign or a graphic symbol may not make him or her use that sign or symbol in the same way, while teaching the use of a manual sign or graphic symbol always gives information about what the sign or symbol refers to when used by other people. When others react to the manual signs or graphic symbols used by the individual, these reactions will, over time, help the individual to understand how the signs and symbols are understood and used. It is therefore more likely that expressive teaching will support comprehension than that comprehension training will lead to expressive use. In line with this, one study found that comprehension training did not lead to increased use in children with developmental language disorders (Leonard, 1981). In another study, a group of autistic children who had been taught to use manual signs showed better comprehension and use of manual signs than a comparison group that had only been taught sign comprehension (Watters et al., 1981).

In a study of children with Down syndrome, Romski and Ruder (1984) found that simultaneous use of manual signs and speech did not produce better results than teaching with speech only. This finding is unusual because studies of intervention with keyword signing generally have reported very good results with this group (Clibbens, 2001; Launonen, 1996, 2019a). What distinguished this study from other studies is that the children were not encouraged to use signs. It was the teacher who either used simultaneous signs and speech, or speech alone. This study gives support to the assumption that motor performance may play a role in the acquisition of manual signs and emphasizes how important it is that learners produce the signs themselves.

Another significant reason for giving priority to expression over comprehension in intervention is that expressive training directly teaches individuals how they can influence their surroundings. In comprehension training, it is the teacher who takes the initiative, while the individual provides answers or carries out instructions. A lack of communicative initiative is a common problem among individuals with little or no speech, and expressive training aims to shift the communicative initiative to the individual. In the education of aided communicators with severe motor impairments in the expressive language group, it is typically the teachers who are active most of the time, because the students' aided communication tends to be very slow (Deliberato et al., 2018). A focus on expressive communication in the classroom gives these students more possibilities for formulating and expressing what they learn, which is important for understanding and remembering the subjects that are taught, as well as for providing a basis for topical conversations. Finally, giving priority to expressive teaching is

supported by the emphasis in developmental psychology on the active role of learners in knowledge acquisition (Nelson, 2007; Piaget, 1950; Tomasello, 2019).

Giving priority to teaching expressive language, however, does not mean that comprehension training has no place in intervention. It is important to monitor the individual's comprehension of their own communication mode used by others (Dada et al., 2021). Especially after the individual has acquired a good number of manual signs or graphic symbols, it may be useful to teach expressive use and comprehension of the same vocabulary items simultaneously. It should also be an integrated part of the intervention that the communication partner uses the individual's communication system. Studies have found that children with various disorders who have little or no speech may benefit from partners using keyword signing (Bonvillian et al., 2020a; Grove & Launonen, 2019) or aided language stimulation (Dada & Alant, 2009; O'Neill et al., 2018). One large study of minimally verbal children demonstrated the importance of expression training with a speech-generating device, but also found that the children benefitted from observing the teacher using the device (Romski et al., 2010). There are also some individuals who benefit most from comprehension training with signal signs or symbols, such as girls and women with Rett syndrome, who have limited ability to perform voluntary movements and very restricted means of expression (von Tetzchner, 1997b).

Finally, an individual's language comprehension is important when selecting vocabulary. It is usually quicker for the individual to learn to use manual signs or graphic symbols that correspond to familiar spoken words than signs or symbols corresponding to unknown words(-Clarke et al., 1986). Understanding of the relevant aspects of the situation, a shared context, will facilitate the acquisition of manual signs and graphic symbols. Also children with typical development tend to use new words first in familiar situations – in line with Slobin's language acquisition principle: new forms are first expressed in old functions and new functions are first expressed with old forms (Slobin, 1973). For example, Bloom (1973) describes how her daughter initially said *car* only about the cars she saw from the window at home. Similarly, it is usually best to begin teaching manual signs or graphic symbols in routines or other situations that are familiar to the individual, where he or she may have some cues to attribute possible functions to the sign or symbol.

Incidental teaching strategies

In "incidental teaching" or "milieu teaching", the place and time for the training has not always been decided upon in advance, but much of the content of the interactions is planned (Hancock et al., 2016; Hart & Risley, 1982; McGee, 2022). The teacher uses potential communication situations in the individual's natural environment that occur more or less "incidentally" (see Chapter 5). The teacher usually knows what objects or activities the individual is interested in and has planned teaching manual signs or graphic symbols related to these interests, but without having decided exactly when and where the teaching should take place. It is possible to implement incidental teaching without the teacher knowing for sure what the individual is interested in. The teacher will try to create situations where it is likely that the individual will want something, and then wait for the expression of interest to appear. Incidental teaching may thus be similar to the *watch, wait and react* strategy, but usually more elements are planned.

> Eric is a six-year-old autistic boy. He stands in front of a closed cupboard and performs all the manual signs he knows, some of them several times. When the teacher opens the

cupboard, Eric reaches out for a toy airplane that is inside the cupboard. She quickly hand-guides Eric to make the manual sign AIRPLANE, and then gives him the toy.

Manual sign: AIRPLANE

Claire is a ten-year-old girl with intellectual disabilities. She holds a book in her hand and stands looking at her teacher. The teacher hand-guides her to indicate the graphic symbol READ, then follows Claire to the sofa where they sit down, and the teacher reads for Claire.

PCS: READ

Betty is an eight-year-old girl with multiple impairments. She has a small vocabulary of graphic symbols on a communication board placed on the wheelchair tray. One day, during the morning circle time at school, she looks intently at the pages of the large calendar that one of the children is allowed to tear yesterday's page off each morning. The assistant fetches the pictogram *TEAR*, puts it together with the other pictograms on Betty's communication board and helps Betty to point to it. The teacher then brings the calendar to Betty and, with help from the assistant, Betty tears off the page.

Incidental teaching has several advantages. It provides more teaching opportunities and greater situational variety than one-to-one training in a special room. This is important because in word learning, children need to generalize to both new exemplars and new situations (Sandhofer & Schonberg, 2020). Moreover, most of the training takes place in familiar environments and situations where the individual is interested in something, implying a need for expression. The individual may, in fact, be trying to *solve communicative problems*, like the children in the three examples above.

Incidental teaching may imply different levels of planning. Teachers and other adults may utilize unplanned situations where individuals seem to want something, search for something

or in other ways show that they have something to say. Teachers may also prepare for incidental teaching by placing cues related to things and activities that the individual can obtain using AAC; both things and activities that represent new vocabulary and familiar things and activities that he or she already has the expressive means to request. Using already acquired vocabulary may remind individuals that they can obtain something with communication, and thus implicitly prepare them for using communication to solve the problem of getting something specific in the environment, and thereby acquire new vocabulary. Similarly, the teacher may arrange events that the individual might want to communicate about, possibly something that is unusual or breaks positively with ordinary routines (see p. 304). This means that incidental teaching can be used with children in different phases of AAC development. It may be used with new manual signs or graphic symbols and signs or with symbols that are known to the child or are being practised, depending on the situation. However, utilizing an unplanned situation for incidental teaching requires that relevant vocabulary is easily accessible, that is, that the person in charge of the incidental teaching knows the manual signs that are needed and has easy access to taught and untaught graphic symbols that may be used in the situation. Providing opportunities for incidental teaching thus does not imply that the teacher should not plan or be prepared, rather the opposite, as the teacher needs to be open to an array of possible communicative scenarios.

Professionals sometimes find it difficult to teach manual signs or graphic symbols that are not part of the planned programme. The teacher may have limited knowledge of the child's communication system, although this is not usually the cause of the problem. It should not take very long for the teacher to learn a few new manual signs or have a reasonable large set of graphic symbols easily accessible. Moreover, when the target of the individual's interest has been discovered, it may be a good strategy for the teacher to take him or her along to look in the manual sign dictionary or to go through the graphic symbols together to search for the sign or symbol that is needed. The individual might find the joint search for the vocabulary item interesting and share the joy expressed by the teacher when the right manual sign or graphic symbol has been found (see also Chapters 7 and 8).

There are instances when the individual's acquisition of new manual signs in the training sessions had appeared to have stopped, and where the introduction of incidental teaching was like turning on a "sign tap". The reason for this may be that the sign teaching had taken place in the same situation which lacked cues for distinguishing the meanings of the signs. The situational variation of incidental teaching makes the use of each sign clearer to the individual. It is also possible that the teaching situation itself had become monotonous and ritualistic, and therefore no longer contributed to the acquisition of new signs. This explanation is supported by the fact that unexpected events have been found to have a positive influence on children's attempt to communicate (McClenny et al., 1992). This highlights the functional difference between communication in routines with some variation or with identical repetitions only.

This presentation of incidental teaching differs somewhat from many other descriptions in the professional literature. In much of the literature, incidental teaching is presented as *an opportunity to establish a teaching situation*. Despite the fact that the teaching begins with a communicative initiative from the individual, the goals are decided upon in advance and the teacher uses methods typically employed in special training, such as prompting, imitation, repetitions and so forth (McGee et al., 1999; Warren & Kaiser, 1986). These strategies may interrupt the natural flow of the communication and turn the "spontaneous" conversation into formal teaching. The approach seems to be founded on the behaviour analytic

assumption that the function of the environment is to provide reward and feedback to children imitating and performing trained behaviours, and to interpret and formulate in spoken language the non-vocal utterances produced by the children (Reichle et al., 2021). In the present approach, the aim of incidental teaching in varied situations is to guide the individual to solve meaningful communication problems and experience communicative success. Although basic learning mechanisms like classical and operant conditioning may have a role when designing intervention for people with profound intellectual disabilities and severe autism spectrum disorder, restricting intervention to this approach may hinder professionals in taking advantage of other aspects of situations involving AAC. For children who are less cognitively and linguistically impaired, conditioning is not likely to be a central element of the intervention.

Naming

Naming contains elements of both comprehension and use. Giving names to people, objects and events is a core linguistic activity, particularly for children in the very early phases of language acquisition. In typical early naming situations, children and parents play or look at picture books together, ask for and give the names of things, animals and persons. In interventions involving AAC, manual signs and graphic symbols are used to name people, objects and animals. The teaching often takes place in special sessions, where the individual learns to point at graphic symbols or perform manual signs that correspond to persons, objects and actions, without involving other usages of the signs or symbols. The teacher may name real objects or drawings of objects and then show these to the learner and ask *What is this?* The individual should answer by producing the correct manual sign or graphic symbol (Fischer, 1994; Kagohara et al., 2012).

> Peter is four years old. He is severely motor impaired, uses Bliss-words and shows good comprehension of spoken language. He is sitting together with his teacher in the nursery school. She has different objects lying around her, and points at objects or pictures of objects while simultaneously speaking their names. Peter points at the corresponding Bliss-words on his communication board as the teacher says the words. Sometimes, they change roles. Peter uses Bliss-words to names objects and the teacher has to point at the right object.

> Kate is a 14-year-old autistic girl. She uses a number of manual signs and a few spoken words. She is sitting with her teacher, who points at various objects, signs WHAT while simultaneously saying *What is that?* Kate then produces the appropriate manual sign, with some help when necessary.

Manual sign: WHAT

Naming is important in many everyday situations, such as when the individual is exploring some part of the environment together with the teacher, for example, when they are walking or using a wheelchair in a park or forest, travelling by bus, gardening or collecting flowers.

Naming is a typical declarative communication activity (see p. 160). The function of the manual sign or graphic symbol is not to request something but to provide information spontaneously or on request. In naming, there may be positive acknowledgement, but learning names is useful in itself and there is no need for praise or other rewards.

Naming usually requires that the individual has developed some competence, that is, shows communicative success in using manual signs or graphic symbols to attempt to obtain objects or participate in activities. Naming may also be useful when the individual is asked questions, but this is not the main goal of the initial intervention. For learners who have relatively good language skills, naming is a good method of acquiring new manual signs or graphic symbols in special training sessions that can be used in other situations and for diverse purposes.

In AAC intervention, naming is often used to relate spoken words to manual signs or graphic symbols, and naming is therefore mainly used with children who have some comprehension of spoken language (Stephenson, 2009a). However, in children with typical development, early naming is not based on knowledge of another language form but on shared attention to something. The adult or child may name something they attend to or say the name to direct the attention of another person towards something. Manual signs and graphic symbols may be used in similar ways, to name prominent and interesting parts of the environment, without reference to spoken words.

Structured conversations

Communication is by nature reciprocal, and the conversation is a natural unit in language research and intervention. Conversation is both a goal in itself and a means for learning vocabulary and sentence constructions. Both typical and atypical communication and language skills are best acquired within communicative interactions where the child as well as the communication partner contribute to the conversation (see Chapter 11). Early conversations may be related to joint activities and involve longer exchanges of turns with preferences and choices within the activity, including choices the teacher makes. For example, conversation with positive negotiations related to the individual's food wishes may incidentally appear during an ordinary meal in the preschool (see p. 247). Many early conversations are structured around different forms of play: questions, suggestions and comments are usually integrated elements of construction play and role play in groups (see Chapter 10). For young aided communicators with severe motor impairments, structured conversation around diverse everyday and societal topics may increase their general knowledge, support their aided language development and give them a greater repertoire of issues to communicate about. For young AAC users with autism spectrum disorder and intellectual disabilities, conversations may be structured around material they know or are interested in exploring, and thus contribute to their concept formation and social understanding. For example, a 17-year-old autistic boy was always eager to converse about his special interests: boats and airplanes. Conversations may take place during outdoor activities, on bus trips, during visits to shopping centres or museums and so on. When preparing structured conversations with an individual using AAC, the teacher should make sure that the activity, material or topic is appropriate for the individual's vocabulary, and in addition have some new vocabulary ready

in case there are possibilities for introducing new manual signs or graphic symbols during the conversation.

Structured conversation with AAC may support all aspects of language development: vocabulary, sentence construction, conversational skills, pragmatic functioning and so forth (Luckins & Clarke, 2021; Soto & Clarke, 2017). Strategies related to the different aspects are described in the following chapters. As the individual develops greater competence, more and more of the intervention sessions will take the form of a structured conversation.

Preparatory training

Some intervention approaches build on the assumption that there are prerequisites, certain skills that should be mastered before communication and language intervention can be implemented. These interventions therefore often begin with the teaching of skills, knowledge or activities that the teacher regards as preconditions for language acquisition. One example is the requirements that the child has object permanence and has reached Piaget's sensory-motor stage 5 or 6, an idea that was soon rejected (Chapman & Miller, 1980; Shane & Bashir, 1981). The ability to imitate has also been regarded as a necessary precursor to language acquisition (Piaget & Inhelder, 1969; Skinner, 1957; Tomasello, 2005). The assumption that such fundamental preconditions must exist in order for a child to develop language has little empirical basis, however, and has often led to inefficient teaching and hindered the acquisition of communication skills in individuals with severe and profound disabilities. There are many examples of individuals who are unable to do some tasks usually acquired in Piaget's sensory-motor stage 5 or 6, but who have nonetheless been able to develop some language skills (Romski et al., 2003; Rowland & Schweigert, 2003). Matching has been regarded as an important skill for learning graphic symbols but seems to be useful for some individuals rather than necessary (Franklin et al., 1996; Stephenson & Linfoot, 1996). Furthermore, if matching is restricted to a limited set of objects and symbols, that are repeated frequently, it may soon become just an activity and not a means for expanding the child's concept formation and understanding of language.

Another type of suggested prerequisite conditions have to do with the practical implementation of language intervention and establishing a «readiness repertoire» before initiating a structured programme. Some skills or activities are regarded as necessary, or extremely advantageous, if language teaching is to be effective. One example of such a skill is being able to sit still on a chair in front of a table for a short period of time. Other examples are the ability to be attentive, look at the teacher and follow directions (Lerman et al., 2016). Motivation to communicate has also been emphasized by some authors as a practical prerequisite for AAC intervention (Bryen & Joyce, 1985; Light & McNaughton, 2014). However, it may be virtually impossible to distinguish between a lack of motivation and a lack of communicative opportunity: the individual may be unable rather than unwilling. As the individual may be unable to refute the assumption of a lack of motivation, it is not warranted to make this attribution. Finally, the belief that an individual is lacking in motivation may reduce the teacher's motivation to introduce AAC – which may have disastrous consequences for the individual.

Teaching skills and activities that may support language development and contribute to a more effective language teaching at a later stage can be positive. This is in line with an approach where different intervention measures are regarded in relation to each other within the

framework of a dynamic system, where different skills merge into gradually more advanced competence (Perone & Simmering, 2017). But teaching of such skills should not be at the expense of communication activities. They may be a part of the total intervention without being necessary requirements for starting intervention with AAC. If there is a need for training such skills, this may take place in parallel with the language intervention, and without leading to an unnecessary delay in the individual's acquisition of communication and language skills.

There are a number of theoretically and practically justified conditions that have been given special attention. These include *eye contact, direction of gaze, attentiveness, sitting still, behaviour chains, imitation* and *motor skills*.

Eye contact

Early in life, infants are attentive to the eyes of other people (Bertenthal & Boyer, 2015). Eye contact, where people look at each other's eyes, is a core element of face-to-face interactions and the communicators' attention and gaze patterns may influence the course of the conversation (Conty et al., 2016; Massé et al., 2017). Autistic children tend to be less attentive to the gaze of others than infants with typical development (Jones et al., 2008). In intervention involving autistic individuals, training of eye contact in social interactions is often a primary aim (Rapp et al., 2019). However, there is no support for the assumption that the establishment of eye contact is a necessary precondition for language acquisition. In fact, children with very little or no vision may show typical development of language (Pérez-Pereira & Conti-Ramsden, 2020). In addition, a too-strong focus on eye contact may create difficulties in AAC intervention, because it is difficult to look another person in the eyes and simultaneously look at one's own or the other's manual signs, attend to graphic symbols on a communication board or device, or pay attention to relevant things in the environment.

Gaze direction and attentiveness

What people are attending to is important social information from infancy through to old age. Where infants are looking is an important clue to their attention, and many experimental studies use gaze direction to investigate how infants perceive the environment (Eckstein et al., 2017; Slone et al., 2018). In addition, many aided communicators with severe motor disabilities learn to eye point symbolically to things in the environment or to use eye-gaze to operate an electronic communication device (see p. 48).

The justification for training gaze is mainly practical. Gaze direction is regarded as an expression of attentiveness and especially autistic children are trained to direct their gaze at something that is important in the situation, for example, a person or an object (Hustyi et al., 2023). It is particularly autistic individuals with intellectual disabilities in the alternative and supportive language groups who are given training in gaze direction and attentiveness, but individuals in the expressive language group have sometimes been taught to look at objects they want before they are given access to a graphic communication system.

Being able to initiate and respond to joint attention is a fundamental prerequisite for an individual's success in language learning. Paying attention to another person may be a prerequisite for the individual's use of a manual signs or graphic or tangible symbols to be perceived as communication (see p. 160). Severe motor impairments may include eye movements, making use of the gaze difficult even for children with good cognitive skills. When autistic children

look in another direction than they are pointing, their pointing may not be perceived as communicative (Sarriá et al., 1996). Individuals with extensive motor impairments may not be perceived as communicating because the potential communication partners are not sure when the individuals are attentive. They may lack the physical ability to hold their head up, change the direction of gaze, and so forth. There are useful programmes for training motor-impaired individuals to operate electronic devices with their gaze (see p. 46). However, "dry" training of the gaze, for example, with praise or edible rewards (Hustyi et al., 2023) in advance of introducing AAC to children without motor disabilities may not be particularly productive. The understanding of how to initiate contact and get the attention of another person is best developed in functional contexts. Similarly, it can be futile to teach an individual to direct the gaze at another person unless it is clear why this has a purpose. "Reinforcing" such a behaviour, for example, by giving the individual small pieces of chocolate when he looks in the right direction, may only cause greater confusion. Both attentiveness and communicative initiative are easier to bring out in an actual communication situation than by special training. Moreover, in typical language development, talking about something the child is already attentive to seems to promote word learning better than when the adult first tries to direct a young child's attention to something before it is named (Masur, 1997). There is reason to believe that the principle of following the child's attention is also valid for early AAC development.

Looking at objects that are referred to is often a part of a conversation. The teacher may use the individual's gaze as a first indicator of choice or attentiveness, and as a basis for helping the individual to express a particular meaning with manual signs or graphic symbols. The gaze may also be used to indicate "yes" or "no", for example, by looking at the partner's "yes hand" or "no hand". In interventions with graphic symbols, the teacher may point first at the object to direct the individual's gaze towards it, and then try to move the individual's gaze onwards to the graphic symbol (Berg, 1998). If the individual is learning eye pointing or the use of a gaze-operated communication device, the gaze is part of the "articulation" of the communicative expression. This may require some special training (see p. 49) but the teacher should try to guide the individual's use of the gaze also in everyday communication settings.

Sitting still

Some interventionists spend considerable time trying to make the individual sit still in a chair by a table for a certain length of time, especially individuals with intellectual disabilities and autism spectrum disorder (Arthur et al., 2023; Cook et al., 2023; Ivy & Schreck, 2016). It may also be a goal in interventions for over-active children with less extensive disorders belonging to the supportive language group. In interventions with AAC, the teacher may train the individual to sit still and to follow for example, the command SIT.

It can be useful to teach an individual to sit at a table, because it may give better access to the large number of activities that tend to take place at the table, such as painting, building with blocks, doing jigsaw puzzles and so forth. These activities have their own value and may also be utilized in communication and language intervention. However, training in sitting still is not justified on the grounds of communication intervention, but rather by the objective that the individual should take part in table activities. In communication intervention, training the individual to sit still is often impractical, because the teacher may have to undo what the individual has learned. The intervention implies that the learner carries out certain actions and articulates a manual sign or points at a graphic symbol. Training the individual to sit still may

be a digression, implying extra work and delay of the implementation of communication and language intervention. It may be better to adapt the intervention to the individual's behaviour, like in the example below.

> Tracy is a six-year-old autistic girl. Her chief interest was running in the corridors at school. The first manual sign she was taught was therefore RUN. When Tracy started to move towards the door in order to get out into the corridor to run, she was gently stopped and guided to sign RUN before she was allowed to leave the room. There were many opportunities for the teacher to repeat this and Tracy started to use RUN spontaneously from the very first day. The teaching continued in the gymnasium with the signs JUMP and CLIMB (Steindal, 1990).

This example shows that restlessness can also be an expression of interest that may be utilized positively in the intervention.

At the beginning of an AAC intervention, some individuals may be anxious and distressed because the situation is new to them. They do not know what is going on, what to expect or which demands will be made of them. As they gradually become familiar with the situation, they will come to have expectations of the situation and understand what is expected of them. Then, their distress is also likely to disappear (Schaeffer et al., 1994).

Behaviour chains

Behaviour chains are the main element in the strategy "build-and-break chains" (p. 175), but they also have other uses. When starting language intervention for individuals with autism spectrum disorder and severe intellectual disabilities, the teacher often finds that they participate in few activities and have few experiences that they can communicate about. One way to approach this is to introduce behaviour chains, that is, several actions that are performed consecutively (Bancroft et al., 2011). A simple behavioural chain might consist of fetching building blocks and building a small tower. Learning to ride a bicycle involves a chain of advanced motor skills. The teaching of behaviour chains often includes the use of signal signs or symbols. The goal of introducing behaviour chains is to increase individuals' opportunities for communication and support the development of independence and understanding of their own environment. In the case of individuals with profound intellectual disabilities, not all the behaviour chains will be identified with manual signs or graphic or tangible symbols. It can be practical to use behaviour chains that have been established before, without involving any signs or symbols, as training proceeds and the individual's use of manual signs or graphic symbols is expanded.

Imitation

Imitation is the deliberate execution of an action performed by another person, and is rooted in social learning (Tomasello, 2005). Imitation training has been argued for both as a prerequisite for further learning and as a skill that is functional in itself (Deshais et al., 2022; Schreibman et al., 2015). The assumption that imitation is a necessary prerequisite for learning has led to an emphasis on teaching of imitation as a "meta-skill", that is, as a general ability to follow the instruction: *Do as I do*. This type of meta-skill usually appears quite late in development, however, and the first actions children imitate are actions they have already

acquired. One-year-old children can imitate someone combing themselves with a comb but will refuse to comb themselves with a toy car. Even children who are a good deal older can appear fairly frustrated if they are asked to do the same as, for example, someone who places her hand on her head (Guillaume, 1971). It is an important developmental milestone when children begin to try to imitate actions they have not acquired earlier and imitation thus becomes a functional aspect of the learning process. Imitation is not random: children imitate actions more often when the actions have a clear goal, have an effect on something or trigger an action, than when the action has no clear objective, such as just moving an object in a circle (Elsner, 2007). However, imitation may not be a suitable strategy for teaching new skills in very early development.

Imitation training may sometimes appear more functional than it is. In the preliminary stages of imitation training, children are often given help in performing the action they are supposed to imitate. When they are able to imitate this action later, this is taken as an indicator that they have been taught to imitate. However, another interpretation may be that the children have learned to perform the particular *action*, rather than imitation as a general ability. Although the imitation training appears to have been successful, in the sense that the individual imitates the presented actions or sounds, this does not necessarily mean that they will generalise the skill and begin to imitate signs or words that other people are using. Imitation taking place in interaction in natural environments is more likely to generalize (Ebbels, 2014).

The fact that imitation is not a prerequisite for language acquisition has been fully demonstrated by children and adults with extensive motor impairments. Many individuals who are barely able to imitate any action nonetheless develop the ability to solve problems, good comprehension of spoken language and use of language through graphic symbols or writing. Also individuals with severe intellectual disabilities who failed to learn to imitate have learned to use graphic symbols or manual signs.

Several studies show limited effectiveness of imitation compared to other strategies in speech training (Ebbels, 2014; Gibbon & Grunwell, 1990; Nelson et al., 1996). There are few studies that have compared imitation and sensitive hand guidance in the teaching of manual signs. Iacono and Parsons (1986) used these two strategies in intervention with three adolescents aged 11–15 years with severe intellectual disabilities. Two of them had never been taught manual signs. The third adolescent had been taught to use the sign DRINK several years earlier but had never used the sign spontaneously. In an evaluation of their imitation skills, one of the youths (F. L.) imitated six out of ten gestures, while the other two did not imitate any of them. The study was designed so that the manual signs BISCUIT and DRINK or BISCUIT and LOLLIPOP were first taught using imitation. Then imitation training was continued with one sign while the other was taught with hand guidance. Finally, both of the signs were trained with hand guidance. The results demonstrate clearly that imitation was not a good intervention strategy for these adolescents (Figure 6.1). Even F.L. who had imitated six of the ten gestures, did not learn from the imitation training. All three benefitted from sensitive hand guidance.

These results receive support from a study where seven preschool children were taught to imitate spoken words and manual signs and were hand guided to give graphic symbols to the trainer in communication intervention. After 20 sessions, six of the seven children did not imitate speech or manual signs, but had rapidly learned to hand over graphic symbols. Moreover, during training with vocal and manual imitation, the children showed frequent behaviour problems, while few such behaviours were observed during the training of graphic

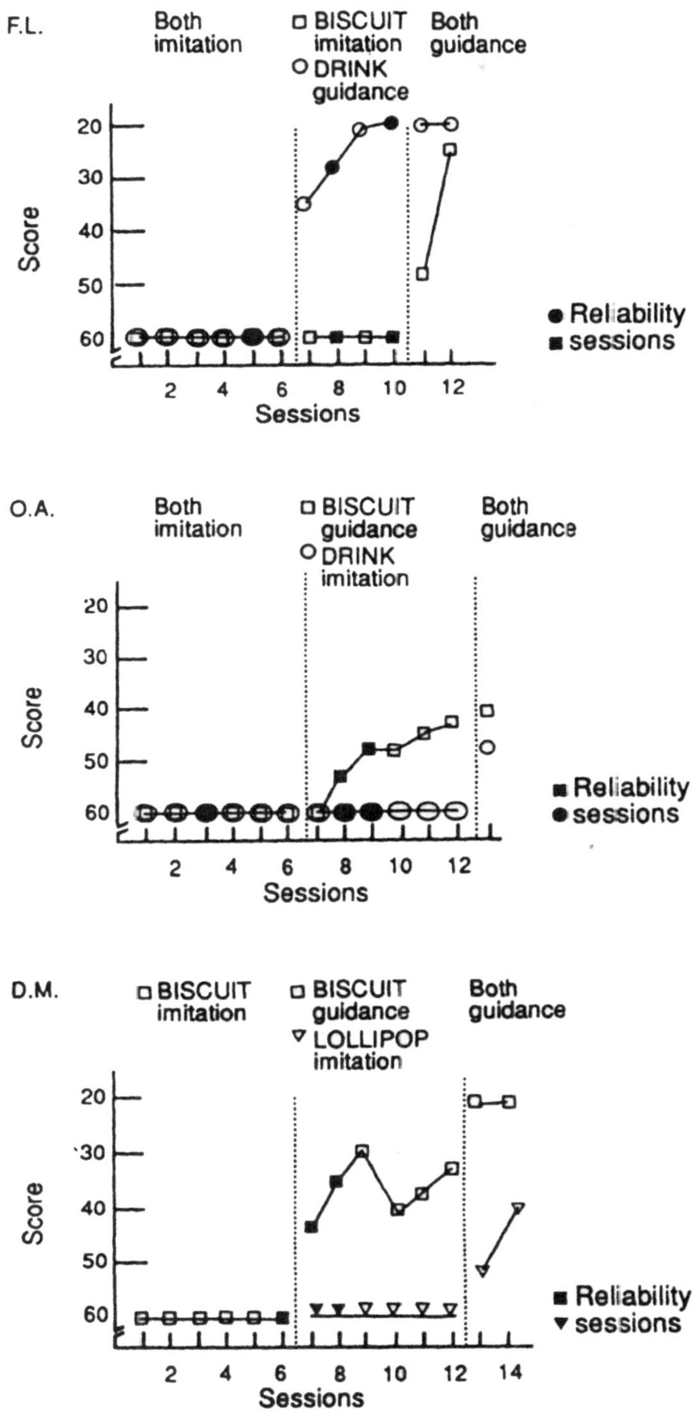

Figure 6.1 Learning curves with teaching based on imitation or hand guidance. The lowest score is 60, the highest 20 (from Iacono & Parsons, 1986).

symbols with hand guidance. The seventh child learned to imitate spoken words and manual signs and to give graphic symbols at similar rates (Bondy & Frost, 1998).

Requesting a child to imitate is a way of eliciting a particular behaviour. There are other ways of eliciting children's behaviours which may be more meaningful, such as in play, daily routines or during household activities. Many children observe their parents doing chores and may try to do some of the same actions. When a child presses a button the way Daddy did, the action is not necessarily imitated directly, but the result of having discovered new action possibilities afforded by the object (Yang et al., 2010). The assumption that being able to imitate for practical reasons is to a large extent a legacy from traditional speech training, where imitation of speech sounds is a major element. It is difficult to carry out speech training without the imitation of sounds because it is not easy to form the lips, tongue and other parts of the individual's speech organ in order to guide him or her to articulate a specific word. One of the great advantages of AAC systems is that imitation is not necessary, because help and guidance in pointing at or handing over tangible or graphic symbols, or articulating manual signs, can be given in other ways.

However, this does not mean that imitation should be avoided in intervention. Imitation *can* be a useful strategy, provided the individual is aware of what imitation is about and understands the function of imitation in the training. Many children and adults with autism spectrum disorders and intellectual disabilities imitate spontaneously. Others in this group imitate only when prompted to do so. It is important to utilize individuals' skills but in such a way that the skills acquired with imitation become spontaneous and independent of the initiative of the communication partner.

Motor skills

All language production implies some sort of action. Preparatory motor training has been given particular emphasis in the intervention for children with motor disorders. Fine motor skills may be necessary for operating a particular communication aid independently, but some electronic aids can be operated with eye gaze or minimal movements if the individual has stable seating (see Chapter 2). Sometimes a professional may demand that the individual is proficient in one specific way of operating the aid before being provided with a communication aid. An individual with moderate motor impairment may be able to activate switches with the hands or the head. However, when the control of the operating movements requires a lot of the individual's attention and other cognitive resources, there will be fewer cognitive resources for the language learning process (see p. 298).

When promoting the construction of utterances in children and adults with motor impairment, it may be necessary to distinguish between training of motor skills and training of language. The training of the motor skills that are needed to operate a communication aid should be integrated in the teaching of the communicative use of the aid, although not in the same activity when the cognitive load needs to be kept low. This can be done by allowing the individual to use a device to play games or carry out environmental control or other activities that require the same physical actions. At the same time, the individual can use the graphic communication system in dependent mode (see p. 47), so that he or she becomes acquainted with the function of graphic symbols without the aided strain of having to focus on motor performance. For example, if the individual is given a communication aid that utilizes automatic scanning, the communication aid can first be used with dependent scanning, where the communication partner points systematically and the individual indicates when the partner is

pointing at the right column and the graphic symbol or word. Parallel to this, but in other situations, the individual may train to operate automatic scanning. Some, but not all, may learn to manage independent scanning and unite their motor skills and language competence. For others, dependent scanning may continue to be the best way of using aided communication (Smith et al., 2010).

It may be practical to use games for motor training but using the individual's communication device for gaming may also cause problems. People in the environment may think of the device as entertainment and suggest that the individual use it for this when he needs something to do, instead of engaging in communication with him. This may reduce the use of the device for communicative purposes, especially when there is a lack of partners who will engage actively in conversations with the aided communicator. It may be better if the individual has one device for communication and another device for environmental control, play and gaming.

Formal education of AAC

Formal AAC teaching strategies are needed for individuals who have a quite advanced signed or aided language level, and usually also good comprehension of spoken language. The education is about the individual's language mode(s) and includes explanations of the structural qualities of the manual or graphic systems he uses, and how different messages may be expressed in these systems. Literacy may be part of the formal education for both emergent and competent spellers. As a school subject, AAC will be comparable to the teaching of the majority language in schools. Teaching may include all aspects of language, including how to adapt to different formal and informal situations and communication partners. It may also include poetry, songs and similar cultural expressions with manual signs or graphic symbols. Literacy beyond spelling may also be a topic for aided communicators using written language. The teaching of AAC requires knowledge about the individual's AAC system and AAC in general but builds on the general pedagogical abilities and skills of teachers.

For example, individuals who are learning more advanced graphic systems like Blissymbolics need to learn how Bliss-words correspond to spoken words and this may best be done by using spoken language to explain the system and how the graphic semantic elements indicate the meaning of Bliss-words (see p. 13). A typical way to approach this would be that the teacher first uses speech to explain the Bliss-word or Bliss-construction and then checks how well this has been learned by asking the individual to answer questions or perform instructions given in Bliss-words.

The formal education related to the individual's AAC mode of communication is also important because it signals an acceptance of this mode as language, supporting his or her development of an AAC identity, positive self-image and self-determination.

The problem of facilitating techniques

The use of facilitating techniques is very controversial. Such techniques do not really belong in a textbook on AAC but because they continue to receive considerable attention (Beals, 2020), they are included to make clear how they differ from the ordinary, uncontroversial forms of AAC intervention. The common term "facilitated communication" is avoided here because the messages are not produced by the individual who is facilitated but originate in the facilitator.

Facilitating techniques were first reported in Denmark to demonstrate "hidden skills" and to some extent in the USA in the late 1960s and early 1970s but became more known through influence from Australia in the 1990s (von Tetzchner, 1997c). Facilitating techniques consist in a helper (the facilitator) physically assisting an individual with severe communication impairment (typically related to autism spectrum disorder) in pointing at a traditional communication board with letters, pictures or graphic symbols, or in typing on an electronic communication aid or a computer. However, unlike ordinary sensitive hand guidance, the facilitator is not supposed to have any part in the construction of messages. The facilitator may provide hand-over-hand assistance, holding the hand of the individual and typically isolating the index finger for pointing. This kind of help is given also to individuals who seem to have the mechanical motor skills necessary for pointing independently and who may do so on other occasions. The facilitator may hold the arm or sleeve, or place a hand on the shoulder, leg or elsewhere on the individual with disabilities. She or he may slow down the individual's movements, make him or her withdraw their hand from the board and avoid obvious mistakes. In addition, the facilitator may provide verbal prompts and encouragement (Crossley, 1994).

Facilitated techniques are controversial because a large number of studies have found that the messages produced with facilitation originate in the facilitator and not in the individual (Hemsley et al., 2018; Schlosser et al., 2014). Moreover, there are several instances where messages produced with a facilitator have included accusations of sexual or physical abuse by the individual's parents or others (Boynton, 2012; Palfreman, 2012). The accusations were later refuted but still meant considerably harm to those involved. The overriding and very urgent issue is thus how these utterances are generated. There are three possibilities: (1) the messages originate in the mind of the individual with disabilities, and may or may not indicate an understanding of language and communication that is apparent only when the individual is given sensitive hand guidance by a facilitator; (2) the messages are produced by facilitators without them being aware of this, or (3) the messages are consciously produced by facilitators in order to somehow meet their own ends (von Tetzchner, 1996a, 2012).

The fact that some individuals with severe communication impairment may be able to express themselves together with another person is not disputed. This is uncontroversial and of little interest if the individual communicates as well or better via other means. The controversial claim of proponents of facilitating techniques is that they have revealed undiscovered communication and spelling skills in individuals with no or minimal instruction (see Biklen, 1990; Crossley & Remington-Gurney, 1992; Peña, 2019). Through the years, there are occasionally reports about individuals with severe motor and speech disabilities who are found to have better cognitive and linguistic competence than assumed by people in their environment, such as the story of Joe Deacon (see p. 123). However, the claim that such unexpected abilities have been revealed with facilitating techniques is refuted by empirical studies (Hemsley et al., 2018; Schlosser et al., 2014). A large number of studies have been designed to evaluate the use of facilitating techniques and investigate the method of production of the messages that are claimed to indicate unexpected linguistic competence in individuals with disabilities. The aim of the studies makes the basic design quite simple: all that is needed is a communicative situation with facilitation, where the disabled individual is given information that the facilitator does not know or can guess and thus cannot be its source. In these studies, spoken or written messages are relayed to the individual, which the facilitator can also see or hear in some of the trials, and are given a different message or no message in other trials. In some studies, earphones are used to provide auditory screening, while other studies use visual screening in

order to hide cards with words or sentences, pictures or objects from the view of the facilitator. In some studies, the individual has been told something or shown an object or a video without the presence of the facilitator, and then asked to relay information about this with facilitation from the facilitator. The studies have overwhelmingly demonstrated that the messages produced with facilitation only reflected the information given to the disabled individual when the facilitator was given the same information. If the facilitator was presented with a different message from the disabled individual, the output reflected the message presented to the facilitator rather than the message presented to the individual with disabilities. Moreover, after having participated in an evaluation procedure, sometimes as part of a court case, many of the facilitators told that they were not aware of their own influence on the messages, quite similar to the phenomenon of "automatic writing" (Todd, 2012; von Tetzchner, 1996a, 2012). They also expressed serious concern about the accusations they have been involved with as facilitators (Boynton, 2012).

The existing evidence thus clearly demonstrates that facilitating techniques usually reflect the thoughts and attitudes of the facilitators. The controlled studies show that the facilitators tend to attribute attitudes and skills to the individual that he or she does not possess. Facilitating techniques tend to be directive rather than supportive, and it seems considerably easier to demonstrate "unexpected" influence from facilitators than from the individuals who are exposed to facilitating techniques (Chan & Nankervis, 2014; Schlosser et al., 2014). Intentional sensitive hand guidance is a useful tool in AAC intervention, while facilitating techniques have no place in AAC interventions for individuals who are minimally verbal or lacking speech.

AAC in bilingual environments

Bilingualism is defined as proficient use of two or more languages (de Houwer, 2021). The prevalence of bilingualism and multilingualism increases with immigration and bilingualism is very frequent in today's societies (Bialystok & Werker, 2017; Grosjean, 2024). There are children in need of AAC in all societies and growing up in a bilingual society or with a home language that differs from the official language(s) of the country is as prevalent among children who use AAC as among other children (Tönsing & Soto, 2020).

The impact of bilingualism on cognition and language has been debated but today the general view is that bilingualism may be an advantage rather than a problem (Bialystok et al., 2022). In line with this, bilingual and monolingual children with autism spectrum disorder or intellectual disabilities show similar development, both in early and later childhood (Gonzalez-Barrero & Nadig, 2019; Petersen et al., 2012; Reetzke et al., 2015). However, children with developmental disorders seem to have less access to bilingual education and resources than bilingual children without such disorders (Kay-Raining Bird et al., 2016). The same is true for children who develop AAC. Studies in different countries found that families with a minority language background with a child who is using AAC were not given AAC resources in the home language (Alder, 2017; Frick et al., 2023; McCord & Soto, 2004). The following situation, described by a teacher, is not unusual:

> What's for sure is that [the students] feel bilingual. I'm thinking about a boy, whose family is Romanian, so of course they speak Romanian with him. [...] At school, he feels like he

> speaks Castilian, because he has some friends who speak it, and he feels like he speaks Catalan, because we speak it with him. [...] But his AAC system is in Catalan.
>
> (Salisbury, 2022, p. 33)

Moreover, the reduction in AAC services during the Covid 19 pandemic was more pronounced in the bilingual than in the monolingual population (King et al., 2022).

In many studies, professionals do not seem to have regarded language background as important in interventions with AAC. For example, Romski and Sevcik (1996) mention that one of the children in their study came from a Chinese-speaking family but maintained that this did not have any significance for the study because the family spoke English when they talked to this child. Several case studies also describe how professionals working with children from minority language backgrounds disregarded the children's need to communicate with the family using their home language (Lund & Light, 2007; McCord & Soto, 2004). Knowledge about strategies that support the use of AAC in bilingual environments is therefore limited. Professionals' intervention planning for this group requires both innovation and creativity.

The question of whether the family should speak only the majority language or both the home language and the majority language is often raised in discussions about special education for children from a bilingual background. Parents are often advised by professionals to speak only one language to their disabled child, the same as is used in school, as illustrated by this Chinese mother of a three-year-old autistic child:

> And that speech therapist would say, uh, the way we talk, in two languages, affects his language development. She kept insisting to us that it wasn't the problem of having or not having one–on–one therapy but that we need to speak English at home.
>
> (Yu, 2016, p. 428)

The advice was based on the belief that it is easier for children who struggle with language to learn only one language, that the child may be confused and that the home language will interfere with learning of the majority language. However, these beliefs are not supported by research: there is no evidence that children with autism spectrum disorder and intellectual disabilities are negatively affected by a bilingual situation (Dai et al., 2018; Drysdale et al., 2015; Lund et al., 2017; Peña, 2019; Yu, 2013, 2016). On the contrary, failing to provide opportunities for learning both languages in the early sensitive period of language learning may hinder an optimal language development and social functioning (Lim et al., 2019; Moore & Pérez-Méndez, 2006; Yu, 2013).

A main aim of intervention for bilingual children using AAC is that the communication system should function as a bridge between the spoken languages in their environment. If the child has some comprehension of spoken language, the intervention should try to make clear to the child what words or phrases the manual signs or graphic symbols correspond to in each of the spoken languages. If the child is using communication boards with graphic symbols, professionals can make people in the environment aware of the child's bilingual competence by writing the gloss of one language above and the gloss of the other language below the image of the graphic symbol. The same may be done with photographs, drawings and other graphic material. Many electronic devices with speech output may include several languages but functional use of this requires some adaptation (Frick et al., 2023). The devices may not

be used in the home if the vocabulary has not been adapted to the home language situation (McCord & Soto, 2004).

Any graphic system may be adapted to a bilingual situation, but Blissymbolics may be particularly well suited for bilingual children with some comprehension of spoken language. The system is available in many languages and new graphic symbols are always developed by an international group. Moreover, when the child is using Bliss-words, this may help parents who use a minority language to improve their knowledge of the majority language, as illustrated in the example below.

A bilingual teenager with severe motor impairments joined a project that focused on aided language development with Blissymbolics. At the beginning of the project, the mother felt insecure using Norwegian and she was therefore given a standard Blissymbolics board with both Norwegian and Arabic glosses. The introduction of the Blissymbolics symbols and the availability of Arabic and Norwegian glosses helped her to improve her spoken Norwegian. At the end of the project, the mother no longer felt the need for an interpreter in the AAC sessions.

When people in the environment are using the same manual signs in keyword signing or graphic symbols with glosses from both languages, this may help the child become aware of the similarity between words with the same meaning in the two languages. There should also be a dictionary that includes all relevant modes of language, for example, British and Arabic manual signs if – in a rare situation – both of them are used in the child's environment. Sign bilingualism may result if the individual is exposed to different manual sign systems.

It is always a goal of the intervention that the child should have AAC skills that are useable both in the home environment and in school, and that the family should experience AAC as beneficial in everyday communication as soon as possible. This implies providing the family and other significant people with the competence they need for the environment to be bilingually accessible to the child, with special concern for the family's spoken language and for code-switching between languages (King & Soto, 2022). When adapting AAC to the abilities of the child and the bilingual situation, the culture that is also reflected in the activities and the communication patterns in the family should be taken into account. In families who are from another part of the country, or from a foreign country, these may be different from what the professionals are used to. Intervention decisions belong to the family and the decisions they make should in turn influence the selection of vocabulary and routines for promoting development and use of AAC in the child's home (see Chapter 12).

The effect of AAC on speech development

Lack of speech is a major concern for parents of children with developmental disabilities who have little or no speech, and to promote speech is a major reason for introducing AAC. At the same time, parents may be reluctant to initiate intervention with manual signs or graphic symbols because they worry that this may hinder their child's development of spoken language (DiCarlo et al., 2001). It is understandable that parents may have this concern. It is therefore important that they are informed that there is no report of manual signs or graphic symbols hindering speech development. In fact, some parents of children with typical development use manual signs before their children begin to speak to promote the children's cognitive and language development (Acredolo & Goodwyn, 2000; Seal & DePaolis, 2014).

Many children with cerebral palsy and motor disability develop intelligible speech, some after an early period with aided communication (Hidecker et al., 2018; Kristoffersson et al., 2020). There are children with severe motor impairments who struggle with articulation and some never develop the oral motor control that is needed for to speech production. They continue to need AAC to be able to express themselves.

Many studies have demonstrated a positive influence of intervention with manual signs and graphic symbols on speech development in individuals with autism spectrum disorder or intellectual disabilities (Cott, 2008; Dada et al., 2021; Dunst et al., 2011; Millar et al., 2006; Schlosser & Wendt, 2008). One study found that a seven-year-old autistic girl used more spoken words and learned the words much faster with simultaneous sign and speech intervention than with training with speech alone (Carbone et al., 2006). Romski and Sevcik (1996) found increased speech intelligibility in children with intellectual disability after the introduction of graphic symbols and communication devices with digitized speech output. Other studies report positive effects of aided language stimulation on speech comprehension (Elmquist et al., 2019). Bondy and Frost (1998) found that most of the two- to five-year-old children who were trained with graphic symbols using the Picture Exchange Communication System (PECS) acquired spoken language, although this intervention approach did not seem equally effective for children with severe and profound intellectual disabilities. The following case study illustrates how speech may follow the introduction of graphic symbols, and the complexity of the acquisition process.

Robert received a diagnosis of autism spectrum disorder at the age of three. He had no comprehension or production of speech and his prognosis for speech development was regarded as uncertain but generally poor. He had learned a few manual signs but signing progress was slow. Intervention with graphic symbols and photos (persons) was therefore initiated when he was three-and-a-half years old. After a short training period, he started to use graphic symbols spontaneously and to combine them into multi-symbol utterances, with himself or another person as agents in the utterances. The staff always used speech together with the graphic symbols and to maintain his already acquired signing skills, they continued to augment their speech with manual signs. The number of manual signs used by Robert also increased somewhat after the introduction of graphic communication.

About one year after the initiation of graphic symbols Robert slowly began to speak. His first spoken word was *Mamma* (Mama) at the age of four years and eight months. When he was five years old, he began to imitate some animal sounds that the teacher played for him during training. He also produced some animal sounds when looking at photographs of animals but not necessarily the sound that corresponded to the animal on the photograph. At this age, he also started to attempt to imitate words and even if he was usually not very successful, the intonation often resembled the word he tried to imitate. Formal and informal assessments indicated that his comprehension of spoken language was still limited. At five years, he reacted to his own name. When assessed with the Reynell Developmental Language Scales at the age of six years, he understood some single words but failed on even simple sentences. He was easy to test and simply did not seem to get the meaning of the sentences. At this age, he sometimes collected several graphic symbols and photos before starting to construct the utterance on the fold-out page of his communication book (see p. 38), showing that he had planned the whole utterance. The graphic utterances Robert constructed were thus more complex than his comprehension of spoken sentences.

> The intervention with graphic symbols and manual signs seemed to help Robert understand the functions of the words others were saying. At the age of eight years, he had become a speaking child, but his speech was often unintelligible even to people who knew him well. He struggled with making himself understood and became very frustrated when he did not succeed. The graphic symbols were still used in visual schedules which was part of the intervention based on the Treatment and Education of Autistic and Communication-Handicapped Children (TEACCH) programme and at this age he probably would have benefitted from continuing with graphic symbols to support his speech. At sixteen years, his speech had developed and was generally intelligible, but his voice often sounded forced. (von Tetzchner, 2019b).

Robert's development towards speech is in accordance with the general assumption underlying total communication that all vocal and non-vocal language modes support each other. Intervention supporting the development of an expressive graphic language structure may therefore augment the comprehension and production of both manual signs and spoken language. Robert's achievements demonstrate that children can develop relatively complex expressive language skills independent of speech comprehension and that these skills may later facilitate the comprehension and use of spoken language.

Other studies report similar findings: that young children with autism spectrum disorder or intellectual disabilities began to speak or improved their speech following intervention with graphic symbols (Carr & Felce, 2007; Nunes, 2008). Children with partially intelligible speech showed improved language after intervention using speech-generating devices (Luckins & Clarke, 2021). Moreover, some individuals with little or no speech who had not benefitted from traditional speech therapy began to speak after first learning to use manual signs or graphic symbols (Casey, 1978; Romski et al., 1988). Some children began to speak between the ages of six and twelve years after having used AAC (Pickett et al., 2009). Research thus gives firm support to the assumption that communication skills in different modalities have a positive influence on each other. Starting with manual signs or graphic symbols does not mean that speech is abandoned. On the contrary, AAC intervention means that one tries to support the individual's speech in all possible ways!

The fact that speech and alternative forms of communication may support one another, implies that AAC may be taught at an early age without fear of negative consequences, and thereby prevent the potential negative effects of poor expressive means. That access to alternative communication early in life may have such a function is evident in a study of children with Down syndrome who had very early intervention with manual signing. On average, they showed better communication and social skills at eight years than a comparable group of children with Down syndrome who did not have early signing, even if the differences in spoken language measures were reduced at this age (Launonen, 2003, 2019a).

Thus, AAC intervention never means to opt out of speech. In fact, failing to provide AAC to children with no speech or very delayed speech development can sometimes result in less speech because the children do not receive the communicative support that they may need in speech development. Sigman and McGovern (2005) found, in general, small developmental changes in the spoken language from preschool to adolescence in children with autism spectrum disorders and intellectual disabilities.

In spite of the positive influence of AAC intervention on speech development reported in many studies, there will always be children who do not learn to speak. Children with severe

motor impairments may lack the physical basis for speech production but there are also children who are not motor impaired who do not develop intelligible speech (e.g., Ganz et al., 2008; Schwartz et al., 1998; von Tetzchner et al., 2004). For these children, an early onset of intervention with AAC will mean fewer negative experiences and ensure an optimal path of communication and language development. For children who do not develop speech, lack of access to AAC can be dramatic, because they may have no way of making themselves understood and conveying what they want, feel and think. AAC is thus a tool to support the development of spoken language but also the acquisition of knowledge, communication and interaction in children who do not develop spoken language.

Terminating intervention with AAC

For some individuals with extensive motor disabilities or other severe disabilities, AAC remains their main form of communication (see p. 71). They will need comprehensive AAC intervention throughout childhood and adolescence to reach their highest level of communicative and linguistic competence. For some this will be orthographic spelling. Individuals using electronic devices may need regular updates on equipment and instruction. Some adults with developmental disorders need support through the lifespan, adapted to their age and development (Balandin & Morgan, 2001; Iacono et al., 2013; Rombouts et al., 2017).

The answer to the question of when to stop AAC intervention for individuals without severe motor disabilities is simple: when the individual communicates well in all situations with speech alone. However, use of manual signs and graphic symbols is often terminated too early, sometimes just at the time the child starts to say his or her first words. For many children who had lacked speech, it was the support from manual signs or graphic symbols that made speech development possible, as in the case of Robert mentioned earlier. If the support is taken away, this may also reduce a further positive development of spoken language. Instead of stopping the intervention with manual signs and graphic symbols when a child utters the first spoken words, teachers should observe what the child is struggling with the present time and try to support those aspects of the child's language development. Maintaining the use of AAC as long as it is needed to support optimal language comprehension and use will ensure more communicative interaction and participation in social situations and fewer frustrations for individuals who develop speech very late, sometimes with onset in early adolescence (Pickett et al., 2009).

For some individuals, manual signs and graphic symbols remain their main form of communication and ensure an optimal path of communication development and reduce the risk of negative experiences in spite of the lack of speech. This is illustrated in an extraordinary case study, covering more than 40 years, of a man who had been introduced to manual signs in preschool and who at the age of 50 used a combination of manual signs and spoken words representing different word classes, and produced sentences with up to five elements. His speech was very difficult to understand but the manual signs made his spoken words more intelligible (Webster et al., 1973, 2016). Without the manual signs, his communication would have been much more limited, with serious risk of frustration and challenging behaviour.

Speech is the primary language mode of humans. The overall aim of language intervention is that all individuals should develop speech. Thus, AAC is an important tool for promoting the development of speech but also an alternative or supplement to speech for individuals

whose speech remains unintelligible or is lacking. Both too-late onset and too-early termination of AAC are common To promote optimal language development, AAC intervention should start as soon as it becomes clear that the child is at risk of severe communication and speech problems and should be maintained as long as the individual has problems understanding spoken language and/or producing intelligible speech. Starting early and maintaining the use of AAC as long as it is needed will contribute to more communicative interaction and participation in social situations, fewer overwhelming challenges and a better quality of life throughout the lifespan.

Chapter 7

The first signs and symbols

Words are the basic building blocks of language. To learn a word, children need to delineate and distinguish word forms and understand how the meaning and use of the word differ from the words they have already learned. In the early phases of language development, children learn the *references* of words and to use them to communicate about people, animals, objects, actions, events and so on. However, word learning is far more than linking a word form to a thing or action or a conceptual category. Children must come to understand the relevant communicative actions when words are used, the intent behind the words others say, such as why they name something or comment on an event. Most words are *polysemous*, meaning that they have more than one possible interpretation (Carston, 2021; Samuelson & McMurray, 2017). For example, the word "hot" entails quite different meanings depending on whether it is used to refer to a stove or to a topic. *Disambiguation*, removing uncertainty of the meaning, is an important aspect of word comprehension and hence also of language learning, usually with the help of contextual features (Agirre & Edmonds, 2007).

This chapter covers the first 30 or so manual signs or graphic symbols, while the next chapter presents the further growth of vocabulary. The first manual signs or graphic symbols introduced to an individual are special because they are chosen to form the basis of the individual's ability to self-express and to understand how signs or symbols may be used. The aim of this chapter is *not* to provide a recommended list of early words but rather to present the principles that should be applied when choosing an early vocabulary for a child with little or no speech. Children with typical development learn most words from informal interactions with adults and peers. They are exposed to a large number of words and the content of their early vocabularies varies considerably (Bloom et al., 1994; Nation, 2015; Tardif et al., 2008). Also, children who use AAC hear many words spoken to themselves or others – which they may or may not understand – but which they may not have the means to express. Children who communicate with manual signs or graphic symbols usually have few people from whom they can learn in informal interactions. They have limited exposure to AAC and thus few possibilities for learning new vocabulary from observation (von Tetzchner et al., 2018). The vocabulary is chosen by adults and introduced in more or less planned situations. For children who use AAC, it is usually the professionals and the parents who decide which lexical items are given priority and thus, to a large extent, also what the children may be able to express.

Comprehension of spoken language and intellectual abilities vary among children with little or no speech, as well as the age when they are first introduced to manual signs or graphic symbols. At one end are children with little or no comprehension of spoken language when AAC is introduced (see Chapter 3). For this group of children, manual signs or graphic

DOI: 10.4324/9781003387633-8

symbols may be their first introduction to symbolic communication. Although they are older, their communicative functioning and early vocabularies may be similar to those of young emergent speakers with typical development. The aim of the first manual signs or graphic symbols may be to guide the children to make simple choices between toys, songs and other interesting things and activities, and to understand daily routines. Teaching of the first manual signs or graphic symbols may take some time, while later vocabulary items generally take less time to learn. At the other end of this dimension are a group of children with language comprehension and cognitive functioning within the typical range for their age group or higher, for whom AAC fulfils a long-time need. Children in this group are usually given access to expressive means at a much later age than children with typical development begin to speak (von Tetzchner et al., 2018). Their early manual or graphic vocabulary should reflect their more advanced competence and aim to give them more control of communicative situations. Most children who need AAC have communicative and cognitive abilities between these two groups. For children with severe motor impairments, their motor skills may influence how easy it is for them to use the expressive means available, but some show a "vocabulary spurt" almost from the first day they are introduced to graphic symbols.

The choice of the first vocabulary is also important because a well-functioning early vocabulary will facilitate the acquisition process. A main principle is that the first vocabulary items should be chosen on the basis of their general usefulness for individuals, taking into account their interests, desires and needs. The parents and the teachers should make sure that the early vocabulary consists of manual signs or graphic symbols that they know – or have good reason to believe – can be used to communicate something the individual will wish to express. A focus on the individual's interests ensures motivation and attentiveness and makes it easier for the individual to understand the purpose of communication and in time also the purpose of the AAC intervention. The significance of these advantages cannot be overestimated. The intervention should seek to strengthen the child's motivation, attentiveness and understanding of the usefulness of communication but these are factors that sometimes appear to be lacking in the education of individuals with the most extensive communication and language disorders.

There is a general agreement about the usefulness principle but somewhat less agreement as to what is useful. Usefulness from the perspective of people in the environment seems sometimes to be placed before that of usefulness for the individual, focusing on vocabulary related to care and compliance. However, items such as SLEEP or WASH may be more useful for the individual in doll play than in real life. Children need care but it may be easier to relate early communication to play and other interesting activities. In the early phases of AAC development, usefulness for the individual implies that he or she is able to initiate participation in activities and request desired objects. Useful vocabulary items in this sense are also those that are most easy to teach.

The activities and things that are chosen will depend on the individual's abilities, living conditions and interests, but vocabulary items related to play, such as DOLL, TRAIN and ACTIVITY-BOARD are common (see Chapter 10). Also, fruits, foods and drinks are common in early vocabularies, such as WATER, APPLE and BREAD. However, if, for example, APPLE and BANANA are introduced as an early choice, it should be important to the individual to be able to express this choice. Moreover, the vocabulary items should be useful in various situations throughout the day, not only for requesting material brought for training by the teacher.

For individuals who have some speech and belong to the supportive language group, there may be specific objects or activities that are difficult to ask for, or situations where the individuals in this group find it difficult to make themselves understood. If arguments over toys occur frequently, which is quite common among younger children, MINE, YOURS, HIS/HERS may be useful. FIRST may be used in the sense "I had it first" or "I have the first turn". There are also situations where signs or symbols for emotions such as ANGRY, CRY and SAD have proved useful for children with a difficult temper. However, although infants and toddlers with typical development can recognize and express a range of emotions, including joy, interest and anger (Lewis, 2008), comprehension and use of emotion words tend to appear relatively late (Doost et al., 1999; Grosse et al., 2021) and can be very difficult to teach. It may be difficult for children with intellectual disabilities or autism spectrum disorder even to understand that words may refer to emotions. Emotion words should therefore only be introduced as part of the early vocabulary for children with a good comprehension of spoken language.

Manual signs: FIRST, ANGRY, CRY

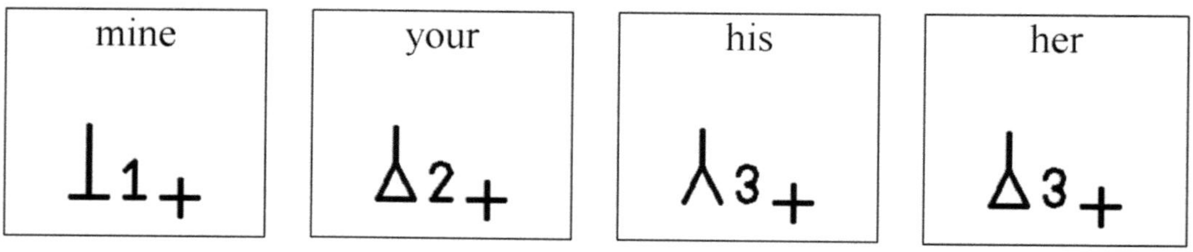

Bliss-words: MINE, YOUR, HIS, HER

Many individuals who belong to the expressive language group have a fairly good understanding of spoken language. The main purpose of the first vocabulary items for this group is therefore not to teach them how these are used, but to instil them with a sense that manual signs or graphic symbols are useful for expanding their expressive communication. Parents and teachers often say that communication boards are not used in spontaneous communication (Moorcroft et al., 2019; Salminen, 2001). One reason may be that the graphic symbols placed on communication boards do not reflect the user's competence and interests, and hence do not encourage use. Many early communication aids had a very limited use, like the one in Figure 7.1.

Figure 7.1 A communication board with YES, HOME, TOILET, DRINK, NO.

People in the environment may express a strong wish for the individual to learn one or more specific signs or symbols. They have a need to understand and to make themselves understood, and the usefulness of the vocabulary should also be seen in terms of their needs. Parents and other significant people in the children's environment should be able to explain to the child what he or she is allowed to do, what is dangerous and how he or she should behave. STOP, GO-AHEAD, ENJOY, NO and WAIT – but also HOT and DANGEROUS – may be useful for people in the environment. They also need to be able to communicate to the individual what is going to happen. Behavioural problems and anxiety experienced by individuals with severe communication problems are often related to their lack of understanding of what other people want them to do and why (South & Rodgers, 2017; von Tetzchner, 2004). Individuals in the alternative language group should be taught signal signs or symbols which may make the daily routines easier and reduce misunderstandings and conflicts (see p. 165).

The early AAC vocabulary is often related to daily routines. However, it is essential that communication itself does not become just a ritual but leads to an improved communication situation for the individual. Although manual signs or graphic symbols for foods and drinks may be appropriate for the initial phase of AAC intervention, they are sometimes unsuitable because they do not lead to increased communication. If individuals already have a means of expressing clearly to the people around them that they want particular things, the purpose of using a conventional sign or graphic symbol to express the same meaning may not be evident to them. The individual may, for example, use eye gaze to point at foods on the table, which may be faster than indicating a symbol on the communication board. Most individuals will need to learn the names of such things but that may wait until a later phase of their language development. The first manual signs or graphic symbols should improve the learners' possibilities for directing the attention of communication partners towards activities and objects of interest which they cannot easily indicate without using AAC.

Existing communication

Most individuals have at least some rudimentary communication skills when AAC intervention is initiated, sometimes in the form of unusual and idiosyncratic expressions. These communication skills should be observed and taken into account when selecting manual signs and graphic symbols. The idiosyncratic communication expressions have usually developed through interaction between the individual and the family, and it may have taken many years

to establish meanings of sounds, gestures, facial expressions and so forth that the family and other significant people are able to understand. Intervention should build on the existing communication, but not by trying to make individuals express in new ways things they are already capable of communicating. For example, if a boy smacks his lips to express that he would like some raisins, RAISIN should *not* be part of the first vocabulary taught to him, because RAISIN is already part of his expressive communication. If the teacher had chosen to teach the boy the manual sign or graphic symbol RAISIN, this would mean that the boy would have to unlearn an already established communicative practice. The sign or symbol may have no meaning for him, or he might attribute a different meaning than "raisin" to it. In such instances, it may be better to begin with teaching other signs or symbols. The aim of the first vocabulary is to *expand* the communication and promote the development of *more* skills, not only to change the form of the expressions the individual already has.

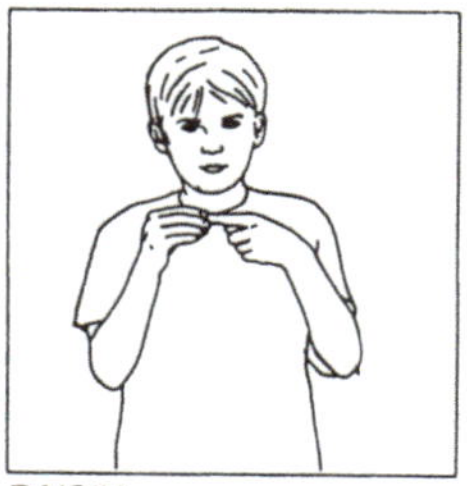

Manual sign: RAISIN

It is thus an important element of the first intervention to make parents and teachers aware of and able to understand the communicative expressions that the individual already possesses. It is only at a later stage, when the individual has learned to use a number of manual signs or graphic symbols that the individual's idiosyncratic communication forms can be replaced with conventional manual signs or graphic symbols. Moreover, it is not always necessary or advisable to replace all idiosyncratic communicative expressions with conventional ones. Sometimes an unusual expression simply reflects the expressions that the individual is able to produce which are possible for others to recognize. Individuals who develop aided communication will typically continue to use symbolic eye-pointing, gestures, body movements and vocalizations as part of their communication (Collins & Marková, 1999; Deliberato et al., 2018).

Fast mapping

The first time that children with typical development hear a word, they must – without any awareness on their own part – form an initial assumption about the word's meaning and use. This first attribution of meaning to a word form is called "fast mapping" (Dollaghan, 1985). Fast mapping is necessary for the child to be able to recognize the same word later and make use of it in other situations. It allows the child to start turning an unknown word form into a known one by creating a mental representation of its form and use, such as *cat* referring to a small four-legged animal. Without this first attribution of meaning, the word would appear to be new every time the child hears it. Fast mapping may lead to a quite correct understanding of the word's meaning and general use but for most of the early words, fast mapping merely

provides the child with sufficient clues to form a reasonable initial understanding of their meaning and start using them. After the fast mapping of a word, which may or may not be correct, there is a slow process of gradually determining what the word may refer to and learning its various senses (Samuelson & McMurray, 2017). The complexity of a word and its meaning will influence the fast mapping, and children with developmental language disorders have more difficulties with fast mapping and learning new words than children without language disorders (Alt & Plante, 2006).

The principle of fast mapping applies to the development of spoken language comprehension among children with little or no speech, and the learning process will be similar for comprehension and use of manual signs and graphic symbols. The individual has to form a mental representation of the physical features of the manual sign or graphic symbol and its use. The efficiency of AAC intervention will depend on the professionals selecting a first vocabulary of signs or symbols which can be taught by creating communicative situations with contextual clues to the meaning of the sign or symbol that the individual can attend to and understand.

Over-extension and under-extension

The use of words takes time to learn. In early language development, the word use of children with typical development may be broader, narrower or different from how the same words are used by adults. The *extension* of a word is all the exemplars that can be represented by that word. Over-extension means that a word is used beyond its conventional meaning, for example, when children say *woof-woof* about both cats and dogs. At the age of 16 months, Dromi's daughter Keren used the term *broom* for all items stored in a particular cupboard in the kitchen (Dromi, 1993). Under-extension means that words are used in a narrower sense than usual. The word may be correct when it is used but it is not always used when it would be appropriate (Griffiths, 1986). When Keren was between 12 and 15 months, her white toy elephant was the only thing she called *elephant*. She never said *elephant* when playing on a small slide with the shape of an elephant, or when her mother showed her toy elephants or pictures of elephants. Dromi observed approximately the same number of over-extensions and under-extensions in her daughter's early vocabulary. This illustrates that the use of a word is not static. Over time, the language environment usually provides children with sufficient clues to correct their inaccurate comprehension and use of the words. Over-extension and under-extension is part of the language learning process, and over-extension and under-extension should also be expected in children developing manual signs or graphic symbols. Teachers should therefore seek to provide communication experiences that may help the child learn the extension of the manual signs or graphic symbols.

General and specific vocabulary

The use of manual signs or graphic symbols may be *specific*, that is, refer to basic categories of objects and actions. Other signs or symbols represent more general or broader *classes* of objects, activities or events. COFFEE, JUICE, WEAVE and SEW may be regarded as specific signs or symbols, while DRINK and WORK are general. For example, WORK is often used to indicate both training, sewing, weaving and cutting grass. MORE may be considered specific when taught as a request for continuation or repetition of an activity or getting more of something.

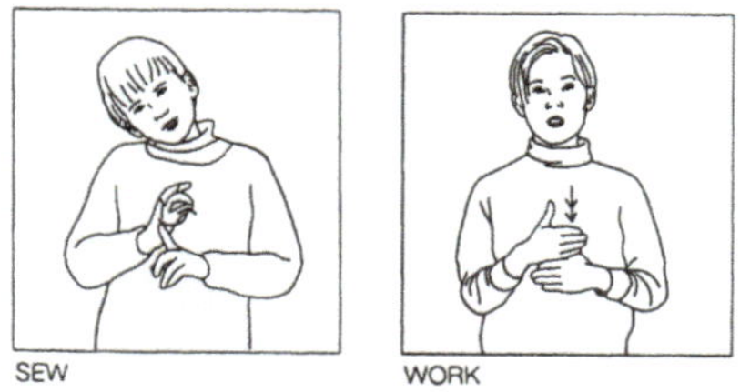

Manual signs: SEW, WORK

ARASAAC: COFFEE, WEAVE

For children in the alternative language group and some in the supportive language group, the first expressive manual signs or graphic symbols should be *specific*, to avoid delineation problems that may arise later, when the individual is taught new signs and symbols. For example, the individual may interpret a general sign as more specific than the teacher had intended, in a way that either partially or totally corresponds to the use of a specific sign or symbol, such as taking OUT to mean "swing" rather than representing any activity located outside. If an individual is taught to use DRINK and is given juice each time he or she signs DRINK, they may implicitly assume that DRINK means "juice". It may be difficult to understand why water or milk is offered when they sign DRINK. In order to teach JUICE, the teacher may have to chain DRINK and JUICE together to form a sentence or introduce a communication routine where the individual begins by signing DRINK, the teacher asks WHAT and the individual is guided to answer JUICE (or WATER). However, this procedure may become unnecessary complex and laborious at this stage of vocabulary development, and there may be misunderstandings and frustrations. It is more relevant when the individual has learned a somewhat larger vocabulary. A similar situation may arise when the individual gets a variety of drinks when he or she expresses DRINK. It may be difficult to understand why expressing DRINK results in different drinks. Learning a specific manual sign or graphic symbol after the introduction of a general sign or symbol may thus sometimes involve the unlearning of what has been learned. The risk for such misunderstandings is great, especially among autistic individuals who may interpret the situation differently and use other cues than the teacher assumes. They may have a tendency to perceive general signs or symbols as referring to something specific they are interested in and therefore are particularly attentive to in situations where the manual sign or graphic symbol is used. In this early phase, the teacher may rather present a choice, for example, between juice and milk.

Most children in the expressive language group and some in the supportive language group are provided with AAC at a later age than their peers with typical development start to speak,

and their comprehension of spoken language may be within the typical range for their age. They may benefit from getting an early vocabulary consisting of a mix of general and specific items.

Signal signs and symbols can be either specific or general, but they are often used to signal a general situation, such as *EAT* before all kinds of meals, *SPORT* before physical activities, or *MUSIC* before music therapy and other musical activities.

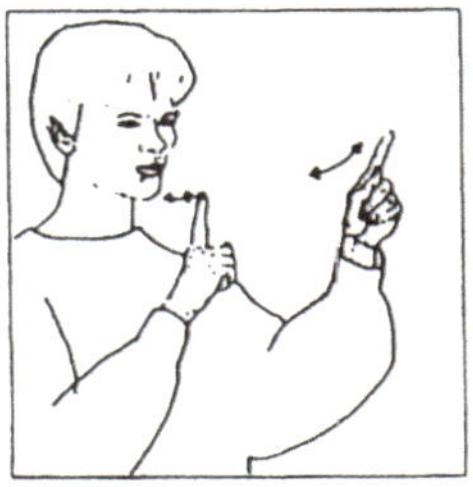

MUSIC

Manual sign: MUSIC

Communicative success

A major goal when selecting an early vocabulary is that the individual should experience communicative success and a feeling of being understood. The individual should become able to address others to express wants and thoughts and influence people in the environment in a way that is socially acceptable. This means that the individual has to learn what usages particular signs or symbols may have. A communicative act is successful when a specific communicative intention is understood by the communication partner (see p. 160). In the early phase of intervention, the individual will usually get the object or activity that the manual sign or graphic symbol represents (and thus also obtain instrumental success), because it is easy to teach and a practical way of making the child aware why the sign or symbol makes a difference.

When teaching early vocabulary, each manual sign or graphic symbol must have a different consequence, to avoid a situation where the individual interprets all of them as variations of one general meaning. The individual should never be given a piece of chocolate, a potato chip or other forms of reward or praise for performing – for example, for producing the signs or symbols BALL, BOAT or SCISSORS when these objects are present during training. The individual may be obedient and do what the teacher expects but instead of learning the different meanings, he or she may learn that BALL means "chocolate" when there is a ball on the table, that BOAT means "chocolate" when there is a boat on the table, and that SCISSORS means "chocolate" when there is a pair of scissors on the table. Thus, what the individual learns is that there are several ways of obtaining chocolate, depending on the situation. Being given a reward (chocolate, chips or something else) makes it difficult for the learner to understand the specific connections between the use of BALL and the category "ball" or the act of rolling or throwing a ball, between BOAT and the category "boat" or playing with a boat in the bathtub, and between SCISSORS and the category "scissors" or the act of cutting paper – or other acts related to these objects. When edibles, praise or other kinds of rewards are used, the child may be more attentive to the reward than to what the sign or symbol is meant to refer to.

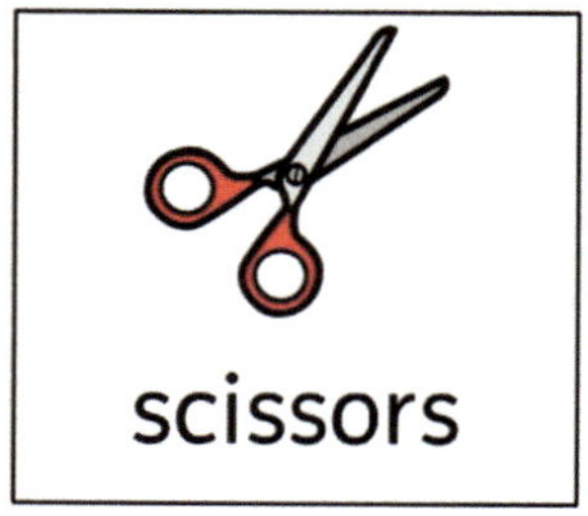

Widgit: BOAT, SCISSORS

The provision of this kind of reward is based on the assumption that the behaviour in itself is meaningless or non-communicative. To teach the individual the meaning or communicative use of a manual sign or graphic symbol, the teacher should demonstrate communicative usages that are related to *the referring function* each sign or symbol is meant to have, not to rewards that are used with many different signs or symbols. However, when the individual is using signs or symbols more frequently – also outside teaching sessions – it is not always possible or desirable that the individual gets what the sign or symbol refers to. The communicative success is still the same: being understood. A child may express joy when getting a piece of chocolate after having communicated CHOCOLATE to his father, but the chocolate is not a reward for communicating, just one of several possible answers to his request. The answer to the request may be "no" or the child's wish for chocolate may be fulfilled because it is time for the Saturday sweet, because he asked nicely for it, or maybe because his father thought he deserved it for having finished his homework.

Communicative success (being understood) is more important than instrumental success (getting what one wants). It is therefore important that the communication partner makes it clear that she or he has understood the sign or symbol, even when the answer is that the individual does not get what was asked for. It is worth noting that many individuals with autism spectrum disorder or severe intellectual disabilities often accept a graphic *NO* more readily than a spoken *no* (see p. 292). One possible explanation may be that the voice expresses emotions more strongly than a graphic representation – a spoken *no* can be quite emotional after a few repetitions. The result may be that the individual becomes excited or agitated, and therefore has problems following instructions or managing the situation in other ways.

A primary objective for individuals with good language comprehension who belong to the expressive language group is that they should be able to initiate conversation and other forms of interaction. In addition, even the first manual signs or graphic symbols should be useful in a variety of situations and for conversations about many topics. For children in this group, many early signs and symbols are general, such as *COME, HELP, LOOK, PLAY, GOOD, BAD* and *TALK*. However, with many general vocabulary items, there is still a risk that the individual may remain responsive and passive, and that the activities he or she takes part in are chiefly decided by others. The individual's development of independence and autonomy depends to some extent on being able to take the initiative in deciding activities and conversational topics. Specific words like *BOOK, COMPUTER, DOLL* and *LORRY* may also be useful early vocabulary for children in the expressive language group but it is important that the signs or symbols are not used only to ask for something, but also to comment and talk about persons, things and actions. Finally, for this group, the early vocabulary may include

items related to social conventions, such as *HELLO* to greet people, *THANK YOU* when receiving a gift, and so on. Such symbols contribute to making people aware that ordinary social conventions also apply to children in this group, provided they have the necessary expressive means.

ARASAAC: COME, GOOD, BAD

PCS: HELLO, THANK YOU

Repetitions

Being engaged in meaningful communicative interactions supports language development. For all three groups, it is an aim that the individual has opportunities to use the first manual signs or graphic symbols fairly frequently. For the alternative language group and supportive language group, the potential communication settings selected should be repeated often enough for the manual signs or graphic symbols to be learned, including situations where an adult can remind the individual to use AAC if he or she does not do this spontaneously. For example, swimming and horse riding are often activities children enjoy and SWIM and RIDE may therefore be used as signal signs or symbols. However, SWIM and RIDE are not well suited for the early phase of expressive language teaching, because such activities usually occur only once a week, or even less. When training takes place in the individual's natural environment, the best strategy is to start with manual signs or graphic symbols that can be used in routines and other activities that occur several times a day. However, many professionals start with names of food and other objects and activities that children and adults do not usually talk about very often, with too few natural opportunities for repetitions. In special training and planned teaching situations, the teacher has control over how often the signs and symbols will be used. Some individuals may benefit from situations that give them the

possibility to learn manual signs or graphic symbols through intensive or mass practice – but not so intensive that the individual becomes bored.

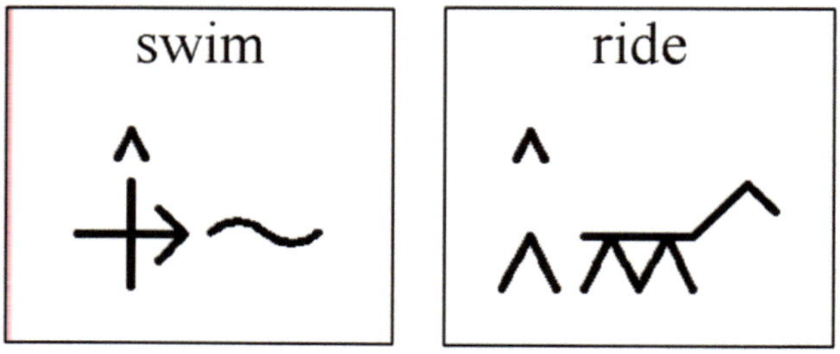

Bliss-words: SWIM, RIDE

Note that repetition does not mean that the educational situations should be identical – there should also be variation. For example, if the child is given binary choices between songs, the songs may vary from a pool of five to ten songs. For example, one time the child may be given a choice between *WHEELS ON THE BUS* and *ITZY BITSY SPIDER*, and the next time between *ITZY BITSY SPIDER* and *ROW, ROW, ROW YOUR BOAT* (for further expansion, see Chapter 8). To ensure that the child does not indicate the same position every time or make random choices, the teacher should observe if there is a song that the child really seems to enjoy, and then place the graphic symbol representing that song in different positions. If the child does not appear happy with the choice he or she has indicated, the teacher should still sing that song, and then guide the child to choose the other song the next time and observe if the child appears happier with that choice (the child's unhappy expression may have had other causes than the choice of song). The signs or symbols representing ordinary activities and objects that the individual enjoys are usually easy to introduce several times in the natural environment.

Studies have demonstrated that how often adults use words will influence the early vocabulary of children with typical and atypical development (Harris, 1992; Rowe et al., 2009). Graphic symbols and manual signs should therefore also be used sufficiently often by people in the environment to support and expand what the individual has learned in structured teaching (see Chapter 12).

Motor skills

Fine motor skills are necessary for producing manual signs (Meier, 2019). The individual must be able to perform manual signs in such a way that the communication partner can recognize them, and teachers should not attempt to teach manual signs to individuals who lack the necessary motor skills. Moreover, if individuals have great difficulties in producing manual signs, they may use many cognitive resources to manage the articulation of the signs, leaving less for the construction of meaning. The functional use of manual signs is more important than their articulation, provided they are intelligible to the communication partner (see Chapter 12).

In the same way as the spoken language of toddlers may be difficult to understand, young children's manual signs may be articulated in a childish way. Many individuals in need of

AAC are clumsy and manual signs of adults may also be difficult to recognize (Møller & von Tetzchner, 1996). It is particularly the distinctiveness of hand shapes that tend to disappear when manual signs are articulated in a childish or clumsy manner The communication partner may, for example, confuse the early articulation of signs like FOOD and DRINK. The individual may sign both of them just by moving the hand to the mouth, without producing the specific hand shape that is required for each of these signs. It may therefore be more practical to teach THIRSTY rather than DRINK as an early sign, since THIRSTY has a different place of articulation. In this way, both signs may be taught without placing too much emphasis on their hand shape. It is the function and not the articulation of the manual signs that should be emphasized, especially when teaching the first signs. CAR and MILK are also common early signs that are difficult to distinguish from one another. In order to increase the physical difference between the signs, MILK can, for example, be articulated with the hands close to each other and CAR with the hands further from each other. Another possibility may be to use DRIVE instead of CAR because DRIVE is easier to distinguish from MILK than CAR, for both the signing individual and for people in the environment.

Manual signs: MILK, CAR, DRIVE, DRINK, THIRSTY

It is not always possible to substitute complex manual signs with signs that are easier to perform. Another strategy is to simplify the articulation of manual signs (Bonvillian et al., 2020a, b; Grove, 1990). However, this may not always make them easier to learn. It may be useful to change to graphic symbols but some individuals with severe communication disorders find it easier to learn manual signs than graphic symbols, even though the motor requirements for graphic symbols are lower than for manual signs. It appears as though the motor patterns – which are distinctive for each sign – help some individuals distinguish between manual signs. This requires that the signs are different enough in terms of motor articulation. When manual signs are simplified, it is important to keep the elements that help the individual distinguish the signs from each other.

There are no fixed rules about what distinguishes manual signs that are easy to learn from those that are difficult, but studies give some cues as to the type of simplifications that should be made. The hand shapes should not be too complex or require that the fingers are placed in unusual positions. Signs that the signer can see are easier than signs that are not visible to the signer. Symmetrical signs, that is, signs where both hands perform the same movement, are easier to learn than asymmetrical signs, where the hands have different movements. Manual signs where the hands touch the body are easier to learn than signs where the hands are not in contact with the body. As might be expected, signs with two or more movements are more difficult to learn than signs with only one movement (Bonvillian et al., 2020a; Grove et al., 2019).

The primary motor requirement when using graphic symbols is the ability to point at the symbols in such a manner that it is clear to the communication partner which symbol is

indicated. The individual's fine motor skill may determine how the graphic symbols are indicated, by pointing with the hands, the feet, a head pointer, eye-gaze and so forth. It is important that the indication is as simple as possible, so that the individual can experience positive mastery with the first vocabulary. Any form of pointing may be difficult and strenuous for children with severe motor impairments. They may benefit from assisted scanning in this early phase but scanning also requires some kind of motor action for accepting or rejecting the graphic symbol indicated by the person doing the scanning. When the individual gets an electronic device, this may be gaze-operated (see Chapter 2).

People in the environment are usually unaccustomed to communicating with someone who is communicating using graphic symbols. When the aided communicator can indicate the graphic symbols reasonably quickly, the communication partners may be less likely to always take the initiative. For some children, the communication function may become clearer if they hand over the graphic symbol to the communication partner, but this requires better motor skills than pointing.

Perception

The individual's ability to perceive sensory impressions will determine the choice of both system and individual manual signs and graphic symbols (see p. 116). Individuals with a significant visual impairment may have difficulty in distinguishing between and identifying manual signs used by others, unless they are signing in a deaf-blind mode where the communication partners are articulating the signs with the communication partner's hands (Willoughby et al., 2018). Sight is also an aid when learning expressive manual signs. Visual acuity will determine the size of the graphic symbols and choice of individual symbols. Reduced visual acuity may make it difficult for individuals to identify graphic symbols which have very detailed images or distinguish between graphic symbols that resemble one another. Some need tangible symbols (Roche et al., 2014).

It is not only visual disorders in the usual sense that are of significance for visual perception. *Cerebral visual impairment* interferes with the ability to interpret visual information (McDowell, 2023; Ortibus et al., 2019). *Visual agnosia* due to brain damage may make it difficult to process and interpret visual sensations and recognize even common objects (Farah, 2004; Humphreys & Riddoch, 1987; Sacks, 1987). *Stimulus over selectivity* may make it difficult to distinguish between graphic symbols, because the individual uses only one or a few of the available cues when identifying an object (Lovaas et al., 1979; Ploog, 2010). If the attributes that an individual uses as clues for recognizing a particular person or object have been changed, the individual may fail to recognize them. Stimulus over selectivity is common among individuals with profound intellectual disabilities. If an individual is suspected to have this condition, one should select graphic symbols which do not share many visual features and hence are less likely to be mixed up by the individual. If an individual has problems noticing the differences between graphic symbols, it may be necessary to simplify them or change their form or colour. Early graphic symbols should thus be as different as possible, both in form and content. It is important to utilize whatever understanding the individual has of spoken language and also to take the words' acoustic features into account. For example, individuals with developmental language disorders may have difficulties distinguishing between words that sound alike (homonyms). Care should therefore be taken not to choose early manual signs or graphic symbols that correspond to similar sounding words. One may change the written glosses of the graphic symbols to reduce their sound similarity.

Iconicity

Iconicity is the resemblance of manual signs and graphic symbols to what they represent. The resemblance may seem straightforward but the relationship between iconicity and the acquisition of vocabulary is complex (Ortega, 2017; von Tetzchner, 2015). It is a general assumption that iconicity may facilitate the acquisition of both manual signs and graphic symbols (see also Chapter 1).

- *Iconicity* means that there is a resemblance between the performance of a manual sign or the image of a graphic symbol, and obvious features of the object or action they are used to refer to.

Iconicity is measured in terms of *transparency* and *translucency*.

- *Transparency* indicates the ease with which people who are unfamiliar with the manual sign or graphic symbol are able to infer their meaning from the sign's shape and movements or the image of the symbol, such as the circular movement of the manual sign BALL and the round image of the graphic symbol *BALL*. Transparency is sometimes called "guessability" although it is not really guessing, but inferencing based on visual clues.

BALL

Manual sign: BALL
Widgit: BALL

- *Translucency* indicates the ease with which one can perceive a relationship between the shape and movements of the manual sign or the image of the symbol and their meaning when the gloss is provided, such as the manual sign HELP or the Bliss-word SHOWER.

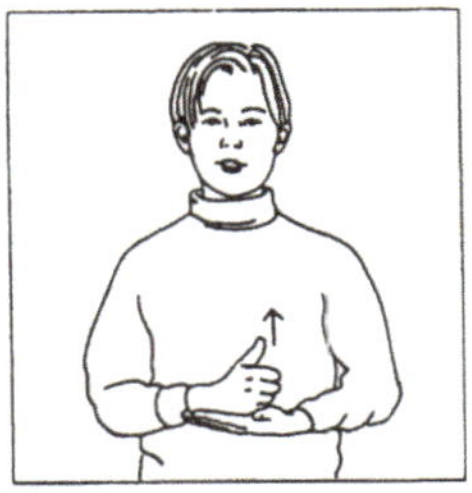
HELP

Manual sign: HELP

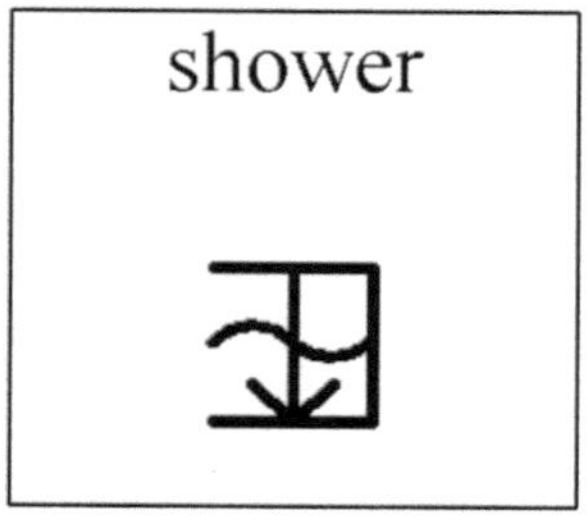

Bliss-word: SHOWER

- *Opaqueness* means that no relationship is perceived between the movements of the manual sign or the image of the symbol, and their meaning even when the gloss is known, such as the Lexigram *DIRTY*.

Lexigram: DIRTY

A manual sign or graphic symbol can be translucent even if the relationship perceived is not the true relation between the meaning and the form. For example, GIRL in American sign language is highly translucent because many people perceive a connection between the way the sign is performed – the thumb is stroked across the cheek – and the fact that girls have soft cheeks. The movements of the sign actually originate from the fact that girls in the USA early in the last century wore bonnets that were held in place by a ribbon attached under their chin. The stroking movement indicates the bonnet ribbon (Klima & Bellugi, 1979).

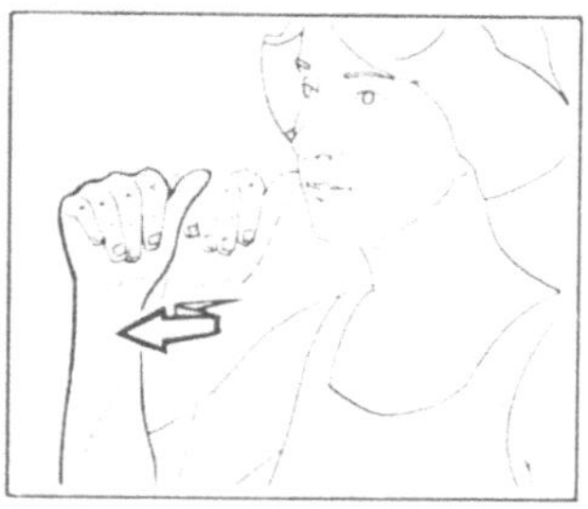

Manual sign (ASL): GIRL

Manual signs

Iconic manual signs include clues to the movements of actions (pantomime) or the physical appearance of things (e.g., shape) represented by the signs (Caselli & Pyers, 2017). The relationship between iconicity and the acquisition of manual signs depends on the diagnostic group being studied, and whether transparency or translucency is used as a measure of iconicity (Meuris et al., 2014).

Studies have found that transparency plays a role in the learning of manual signs among college students with typical development (Baus et al., 2013; Lieberth & Gamble, 1991). This is not surprising, because transparency implies that one does not need to know the signs to infer their meaning. For adults and older children with typical development, transparent signs will always yield a higher recognition score than opaque signs, whose glosses cannot be readily inferred and therefore have to be remembered. Moreover, signs that are transparent for some people – for example, college students – are not necessarily so for others – such as young children with language impairment. MILK originates in milking movements and the sign was perhaps fairly transparent to children in the first part of the last century because many had seen a cow being milked by hand. Today, only a few children would associate MILK with milking by hand without being told about the origin of the movements of the sign – making the sign translucent rather than transparent.

Studies of manual sign *recognition* have found that signs that are rated high in translucency are remembered better than signs rated low in translucency (Griffith & Robinson, 1980). This is to be expected since the meaning of many highly translucent signs may be possible to infer when one knows what aspect of the referent that is included. With regard to the *use* of manual signs, research has not found that translucency is important for the ease with which people with severe intellectual disability learn signs (Trasher & Bray, 1984).

The differences that exist in the perception of translucency are evident in a study of 100 signs for objects in American sign language (ASL) that are often used in the teaching of people with intellectual disabilities. A group of six-year-old children with typical development rated only one of these signs (TELEPHONE) as being highly translucent. A group of hearing college students and a group of deaf adults rated 26 of the signs as being highly translucent. The hearing children and students gave about half of the signs a low translucency rating, while the deaf adults rated only 16 signs as being of low translucency (Griffith & Robinson, 1981). The higher translucency scores of the deaf adults probably reflect that the experienced signers had more associations to the signs than the children and adults with little or no signing experience. The fact that iconicity is related to experience and culture is also illustrated by a study where native French signers rated signs from French sign language as more transparent than signs from German sign language. The German signers rated signs from German sign language as more transparent (Occhino et al., 2017). Another study found that hearing Italian non-signers were better at inferring the meaning of signs from Italian sign language than deaf signers from other countries (Pizzuto & Volterra, 2000).

It is not surprising that university students benefit from translucency when remembering signs. Perceiving a relationship between form and meaning makes it easier for them to recall a particular sign, and it is a common memory technique to establish such relationships (see Klima & Bellugi, 1979; Luria, 1969). The fact that college students may be able to infer the meaning of an unfamiliar sign from its iconic features does not always seem to make the sign

TELEPHONE (American Sign Language)

Manual sign: TELEPHONE (ASL)

easy to learn for children or adults with more limited cognitive resources. When individuals with intellectual disabilities do not learn manual signs that appear translucent any quicker than non-translucent signs, this may be due to the fact that they lack the cognitive abilities needed to utilize such similarities. They may fail to notice a relationship between the articulation of the sign and a specific aspect of the object or action represented by the sign. Studies have not found associations between transparency rated by adults with typical development and the recognition (Miller, 1987) or production (Trasher & Bray, 1984) of manual signs among individuals with intellectual disability. However, Goosens' (1983) found a positive correlation between transparency and recognition of manual signs when the individuals with intellectual disabilities had rated the transparency of the manual signs.

Iconicity seems to be of little help in recognizing manual signs among young children with typical development (Baus et al., 2013; Miller, 1987). Deaf children below the age of three do not learn more iconic manual signs in their early development than one would expect on the basis of the share of iconic signs found in American sign language. Perceiving and utilizing the iconic features of signs may thus require metalinguistic abilities that young children do not have (Ortega, 2017). Older deaf children seem to benefit more from iconic clues to meaning than younger children (Bonvillian et al., 1983 Ortega, 2017). Iconicity seems to have greater impact on action signs than on signs representing object attributes (Hodges et al., 2018). Some researchers argue for selecting iconic signs for individuals with severe disabilities (Bonvillian et al., 2020a) and manual sign systems intended as AAC tend to have a higher share of iconic signs than sign languages (Rombouts et al., 2020). However, although iconicity may play a role in sign learning, the results from the studies above may imply that the iconicity of manual signs is not an important feature when selecting an early sign vocabulary for very young children or individuals with severe intellectual disabilities. The usefulness of the sign in the individual's everyday life is more important than iconicity (Meuris et al., 2014).

There is thus limited support for the assumption that iconicity facilitates the acquisition of the first manual signs in young children with intellectual disabilities. However, iconicity does seem to facilitate recognition and production in older children and adults. Choosing iconic manual signs may therefore help communication partners who are starting to learn signs to remember and to recognize what the signs are supposed to express (Baus et al., 2013), and, thereby, contribute to creating a responsive and communicative accessible language environment. For this reason, iconic signs should be chosen when there is a choice of manual signs that otherwise seem equally functional and easy to learn for the individual.

Graphic symbols

When assessing iconicity in graphic symbols, pictorial resemblance is more evident. Most of the graphic systems consist of more or less stylized drawings (see Chapter 1). *Pictographic* symbols, where the images are similar to exemplars of the category they represent are often highlighted as important features that support the child's learning or reduces the need to learn (Drager et al., 2004; Light & McNaughton, 2012a; Renner, 2014). There are also symbols that are not pictographic in a strict sense but portray an object or action that is usually associated with what the symbol is used to refer to, such as various versions of the graphic symbol *HELP*. This way of constructing graphic symbols is called a *metonym* strategy, and metonymic symbols are often termed *ideographic*. Many such symbols are a natural result of the fact that many words are not easy to depict.

Roughly speaking, pictographic symbols are transparent, while ideographic symbols are translucent. The Bliss-words *HOUSE* and *TREE* are regarded as pictographic, as are the Widgit symbols *CRY* and *BALL*. The Bliss-words *FEELING* and *PROTECTION* and the Widgit symbols *LARGE* and *SMALL* are examples of ideographic symbols. Most pictograms (PIC) and PCS are pictographic, but, for example, the pictograms *HOME* and *FRIEND* and *HELP* in PCS are ideographic. Although this has not been much studied, there is reason to believe that iconic graphic symbols that represent object categories tend to be transparent, while iconic graphic symbols representing actions, spatial relations or other more abstract categories tend to be translucent. While iconicity in manual signs is often related to actions, iconicity in graphic symbols is more often related to object features. There are probably relatively more iconic graphic symbols representing objects than graphic symbols referring to other categories (see symbols from different graphic systems in Chapter 1). However, the image selected to represent, for example, the category "dog" is a prototype (Rosch, 1978) and may differ considerably from the appearance of many dogs (von Tetzchner, 2015).

Bliss-words: HOUSE, TREE

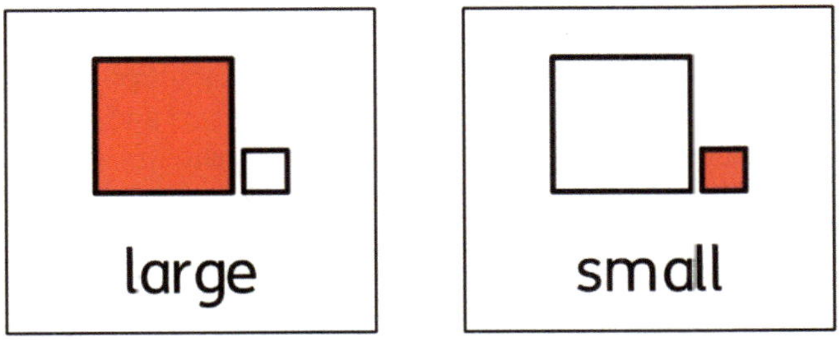

Widgit: LARGE, SMALL

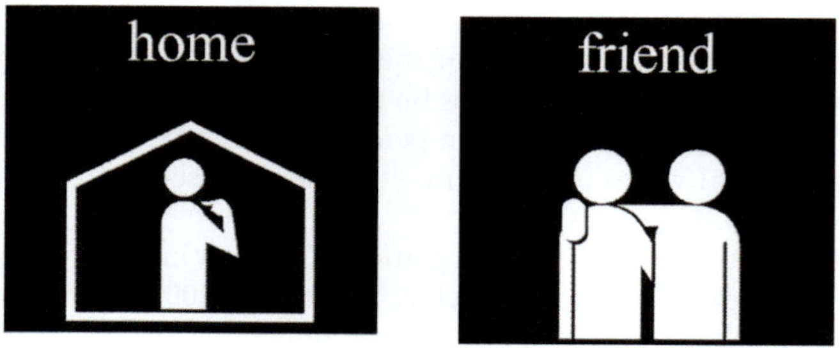

PIC: HOME, FRIEND

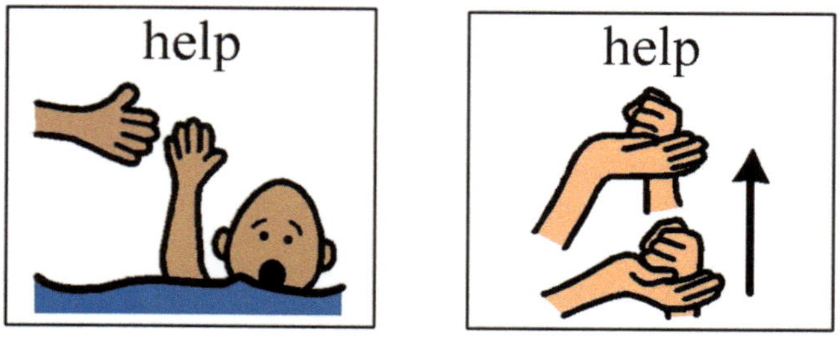

PCS: HELP

There are few comparisons of graphic symbols within a single system. Many studies use simple association tasks, where participants are taught to associate a graphic symbol with a spoken word. Using this method, Fuller (1997) found that the glosses of translucent Blisswords were easier to remember than the glosses of less translucent ones. Comparisons of different systems show that systems with more iconic symbols are quicker to learn than systems with many non-iconic symbols. Widgit symbols (Rebus) are easier to learn than Blisswords. However, speed of learning may not be the best measure of the functionality of a graphic symbol in everyday life.

In some electronic communication aids, one graphic symbol may represent a whole sentence. To infer the content of sentence glosses is more difficult than to infer one-word glosses, even when the choices are limited. In a study where school children with typical development were matching 36 sentences to a graphic symbol (PCS), only a few of their answers were correct. Moreover, their answers varied considerably, indicating that the children used different aspects of the graphic representations as cues to the symbols' meanings (Haupt, 2001). This indicates that for individuals in the alternative language group and the supportive language group, the first graphic symbols should represent single words (see also Chapter 9).

Based on comparisons of systems, it may seem as if iconic graphic symbols should be chosen in the first phases of intervention. However, individuals with severe intellectual disabilities do not always understand what the image of the symbol is supposed to represent and characteristics such as distinctiveness (being perceptually different from the other graphic symbols taught) may be more important than iconicity (Stephenson, 2009a). This implies that figurative differences – which seem prominent to most people because they convey meaning – may not be clear to individuals who do not understand the content of the image. For example,

some individuals may not notice the difference between *FORK* and *TOOTHBRUSH* in PCS because they are unaware of the functions of these object and do not take notice of the fact that there are prongs on the fork and bristles on the toothbrush. Many individuals with profound intellectual disability have difficulty in perceiving this type of difference, perhaps also because they have cerebral visual impairment, stimulus over selectivity or poor visual scanning strategies (Serna & Carlin, 2001).

In children with typical development, recognition of objects in pictures appears early, while recognition of actions appears later (Simcock & DeLoache, 2006). However, many individuals with intellectual disability are delayed and have difficulties in recognizing objects in pictures (Stephenson, 2009c; Warburg, 2001). One should be even more cautious about taking their perception of other sorts of pictorial content for granted. It may be difficult to represent, for example, actions and prepositions with pictures in an unambiguous way. If individuals do not understand that the graphic symbol represents an action, or is supposed to signal one, they may perceive it as depicting an object. The pictograms *RUN*, *JUMP* and *STAND* may just as easily be perceived as three images representing "man" or "human". The pictorial similarity between the symbols make them appear more similar, which is more likely to confuse the learners than to help them (Oxley & von Tetzchner, 1999). Moreover, the communication partner may assume that the individual's communicative intention when using the symbol is apparent in the image of the graphic symbol and focus on the image rather than on its possible functions as a referring expression. However, while the image in *DOG* in the PCS system is to be taken quite literally, for the symbol (to) *EAT*, parts of the image, like the spoon or face, should be ignored if the act of eating does not involve a spoon or if the eating agent is a dog or another animal (von Tetzchner & Oxley, 2013). This type of abstraction may not be evident, either for the young emergent communicator or the communication partner.

An important aspect of pictorial competence is the understanding of the relationship between the content of an image or a video, and reality (von Tetzchner, 2019a). This type of understanding is essential for the use of graphic symbols and develops more slowly than the ability to recognize things on pictures. In one study, toddlers saw an adult splash ketchup onto a toy pig. Each child was then shown three photographs: one of a clean pig, one of a pig with a white patch on its neck and one of a pig with a splash of ketchup, and asked which of the pictures most resembled the pig. Despite the fact that the pig with ketchup stood right in front of the child, the children below two years seemed to respond fairly randomly to the question (Harris et al., 1997). Recognition of an object or action in a picture is only the first step in the development of pictorial competence, but this may be sufficient for the early learning of using graphic symbols for communication.

The results demonstrate that picture recognition and pictorial competence should not be taken for granted in intervention with graphic symbols, although this is not an argument against the use of iconic graphic symbols in early teaching. Many factors influence the use of graphic representations as symbols. It is likely that iconic features will facilitate learning of graphic symbols for individuals who have developed the necessary understanding of pictures, and language comprehension may also influence how the individual learns to use images as symbols (Stephenson, 2009b). However, if an individual with intellectual disabilities is unable to utilize the figurative content that was the reason for the teacher's choice of a particular graphic symbol, the symbol will not be perceived as iconic to the individual and the presence of features that are iconic for people with typical development may not make learning easier for this individual. However, it is still possible for the individual to learn to use iconic graphic symbols for communication, provided the symbols selected by the teacher are easy for the individual to discriminate. As long as the individual is able to distinguish between the graphic symbols, it may be advantageous to use iconic symbols, because this may contribute to people in the environment reacting appropriately to an individual's use of them.

The wish to illustrate and make clear the meaning of the symbols can sometimes produce very unfortunate results. *YES* and *NO* are often selected as early graphic symbols for children who have some comprehension of spoken language and can understand simple questions. However, in PCS and other graphic communication systems *YES* and *NO* are illustrated with a smiling face and a sad face, which do not correspond at all well to the use of these two words. The emotional expressions are clearly misleading when used in reply to questions such as *Are you sad? Are you angry? Did he go? Is it raining?* or *Is it broken?* The consequence may be that the individuals will perceive *NO* as negative and *YES* as positive. There is also reason to believe that the communication partners will take notice of, and even mirror, the emotional content of the face drawings, and use them as cues to whether the individual is happy or sad, and only ask questions where the answer *YES* implies joy and positive wishes. Also the pictograms *YES* and *NO* are usually associated with something positive or something negative. It is better to use the *YES* and *NO* in PCS and other graphic systems that contain neutral images.

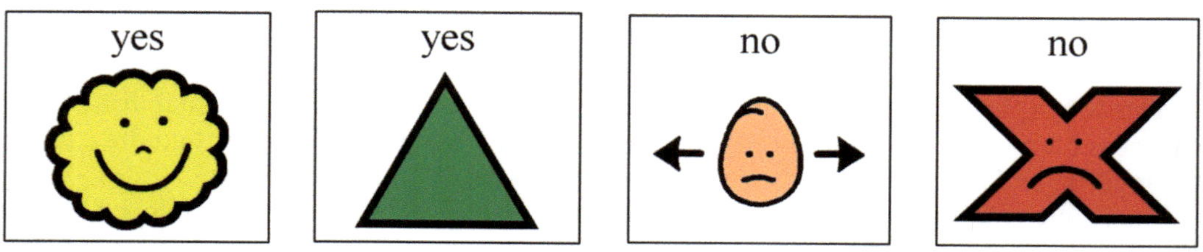

PCS: YES 1, NO 1, YES 2, NO 2

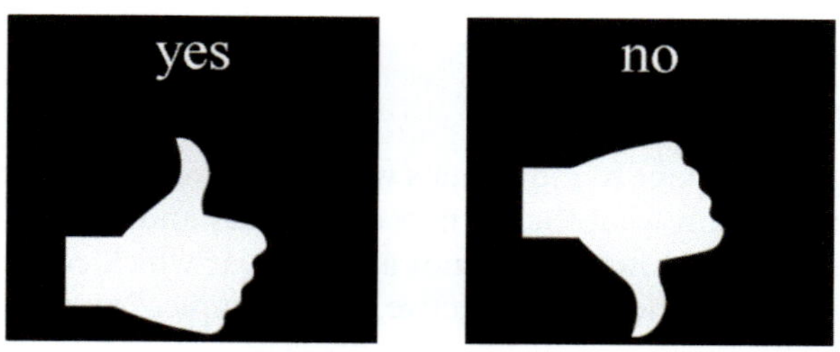

PIC: YES, NO

Graphic vocabulary development requires distinctive graphic forms with particular meanings and usages. Some researchers recommend the use of "visual scene displays" for young children (see p. 58). However, communication aids with this kind of display do not contain vocabulary with a clear form and thus fail to give the children opportunities for learning graphic symbols, that is, consistent physical ways of expressing certain meanings. Visual scene displays are therefore *not* recommended for use with children. Graphic symbols on individual cards in folders or in communication books, boards or electronic devices organized in a grid layout will function better when introducing the child to a graphic mode of communication (von Tetzchner, 2015; von Tetzchner & Stadskleiv, 2016).

Tangible symbols

There is not much research into the role of transparency and translucency of tangible symbols or "objects of reference" (see p. 25). For individuals who are blind and rely on tactile identification, the features that are used in recognition, and which would make some tangible symbols transparent or translucent, may be different from the ones used in visual recognition (Isaacson & Lloyd, 2015; Pérez-Pereira & Conti-Ramsden, 1999). Objects used as signal symbols or expressive symbols for activities are thus typically closely related to the activity that they are meant to refer to. They are often used only in relation to that activity, such as using a cup to ask for, or to be told, that there will be something to drink (Roche et al., 2014). Miniature models of real objects, including toys, may also be used as tangible symbols. However, such models may not be immediately recognizable for an individual who is visually impaired. For example, a 19-month-old blind child started to move his own legs when his mother tried to draw his attention to the legs of a small toy giraffe (von Tetzchner & Sedberg, 2005). Blind individuals may depend on learning what the models are supposed to represent, for example, that the toy car represents the vehicles that are used for transport. These tangible symbols are thus translucent rather than transparent. It may be better to apply a metonym strategy and use a part of the object which the individual can perceive by touch, such as shoelaces to refer to shoes, or part of a seatbelt to refer to a car.

For individuals who can see, or who have been able to see and thus have the ability to make mental images based on visual features, transparency and translucency may be somewhat similar to graphic symbols. For older children and adults with severe intellectual disabilities, it is possible to use tangible symbols with non-figurative forms and surfaces that are easy to distinguish, and which may represent different functions.

The iconicity of objects is often taken for granted. However, toddlers with typical development have difficulties understanding the symbolic functions of objects – that they represent something else (see p. 32). Thus, unless the individual has visual impairments, graphic symbols may be the best choice for early vocabulary.

Simple and complex concepts

In the early teaching of language to individuals with extensive communication disorders, it is necessary to take into account what the learners can understand of the manual signs and the graphic or tangible symbols. However, it is not always clear which concepts are difficult and which are easy from an educational perspective. For example, "mummy" and "daddy" can hardly be regarded as particularly difficult concepts. They are common early words among children with typical development, but it may nonetheless be difficult to teach comprehension and use of the manual signs or graphic symbols MUMMY and DADDY to an individual

with limited comprehension of spoken language, because it is difficult to create teaching situations where their communicative function is clear to the individual. It may be a better strategy that significant people in the child's environment just use the manual signs or graphic symbols MUMMY and DADDY in everyday settings when this is natural.

Instead of classifying concepts as simple or difficult, it may be better to seek to identify circumstances that make such concepts either difficult or easy to teach. In their guidelines for selecting early vocabulary, Lahey and Bloom (1977) emphasize "ease of demonstration" when choosing first words. They mention the difficulties related to demonstrating mental states as an argument for excluding words that express feelings when choosing a first vocabulary for children with language disorders.

The guidelines presented by Lahey and Bloom were mainly intended for children with delayed language development and less extensive disorders. Lahey and Bloom appear to assume that children with communication disorders are able to learn by observing other people, and ease of demonstration may thus be interpreted in a fairly literal sense. This is the case for many individuals with relatively good comprehension of spoken language who belong to the expressive language group, but for children with more extensive communication and language disorders, "ease of demonstration" for the first manual signs or graphic symbols is a question of designing implicit teaching situations, that is, situations that make the relationship between the sign or symbol and changes in the situation as clear as possible (see p. 163). When teaching signal signs and symbols, this means that the relevant cues in the situation must be prominent and clear. When starting to teach expressive manual signs or graphic symbols, the objects and activities they refer to should be reasonably similar in function or design from time to time, enabling fast mapping (see p. 211) that makes it possible for the individual to recognize situations where they can be used and, over time, learn their function.

It is essential that the content of the first manual signs and graphic symbols are not so similar that they may be mixed up. However, determining whether two signs or symbols are similar in terms of content is not always an easy task. "Similarity" may imply that both belong to the same basic category or that one is a sub-set of the other. For example, MILK and JUICE are both a form of DRINK. APPLE and BANANA are FRUIT, while POTATO and SAUSAGE are DINNER. All of these are FOOD. In the early phases of intervention, it is common that the teacher uses two or three things from the same category in a given situation, but using signs and symbols that represent a subgroup of a category represented by another early sign or symbol should be avoided. FOOD and DRINK are often used as signal signs or symbols while other manual signs or graphic symbols representing specific foods are being practised, but FOOD and DRINK are not used in such a way that the other food signs and symbols function as sub-categories of them. The meaning of FOOD might just as well be described as "eat" or "You may have something to eat now". Similarly, when used as a signal, DRINK may be translated as "You may have something to drink now". In this way, FOOD and DRINK denote *activities* within which manual signs or graphic symbols representing specific foods or drinks may be used (see also Chapter 8).

When the teaching of manual signs or graphic symbols is first initiated, the individuals will not learn a general use that is similar to how the word corresponding to the gloss of the sign or symbol is used among competent language users. Competent users apply words like *sausage* in a variety of combinations: *smoked sausage, sausage roll, liver sausage*, and so on. Individuals with communication disorders first learn a *limited usage* of the signs and symbols. The way, for example, SAUSAGE is introduced as an early vocabulary item, its meaning may best be translated as "I want a hot dog". Using SAUSAGE to say "There is a sausage" or combining SAUSAGE with RED to say "I want a red sausage" may be learned much later, or

not at all (see Chapter 9). Word learning is a gradual process that depends on whether the sign SAUSAGE has been used in situations that are functionally different. For example, one individual mixed up TROUSERS and SHIRT after practising these manual signs in the same situation (Doherty, 1985), which indicates that he perceived them as similar in some way. He had not been able relate each of them to the particular routine of putting on either trousers or a shirt. Instead, both signs may have come to mean "clothes" in a dressing routine. The situation in which the dressing had taken place may not have contained sufficient cues for the individual to be able to distinguish between them. When an individual, even after some time, seems to confuse two manual signs or graphic symbols, the teacher may either attempt to change the teaching situation in such a way that the individual becomes aware of relevant cues for distinguishing between their use, or discontinue the training of one of the signs or symbols and introduce another sign or symbol that is easier for the individual to distinguish from the other items that are taught. If one sign or symbol is omitted, the sign or symbol that remains will – at least in the beginning – comprise what was common for the two items. Such a sign or symbol will still be useful.

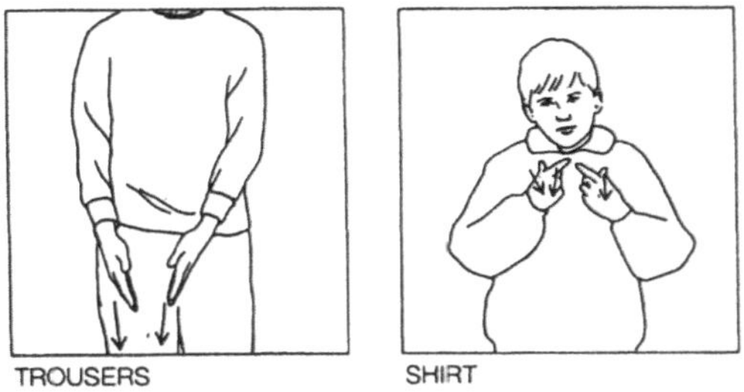

Manual signs: TROUSERS, SHIRT

Another way of finding words with a conceptual content that may be easy to learn, has been to register the words used by young children with typical development (see p. 259). It has been assumed that these words correspond to concepts that individuals with limited communication skills have or are in the process of developing, and therefore are also the most suitable ones to teach as first word, signs or symbols, even if the individuals with extensive communication disorders acquire language when they are much older. However, it is important to emphasize that the choice of vocabulary should take the individual's age into account. The vocabulary items chosen for older children and adults with intellectual disabilities should be different from those that young children with typical development usually learn. The complexity of the concepts represented can still be quite similar to those of younger children.

On the basis of their assumptions about what children usually express in early language development, Lahey and Bloom (1977) list six rules for choosing first words.

1 *Object words* (objects, people and places) can be chosen relatively freely, based on the situations in which the individual takes part.
2 *Relational words* (verbs, adjectives, prepositions, etcetera) should be chosen so that they can be used with all or a large number of objects.
3 Avoid *words for inner states* (including emotions) as these are difficult to demonstrate, and thus to teach.

4 Avoid *Yes* and *No* as expressions of affirmation and denial. *No* can be used to express other important conditions.
5 Avoid pronouns as they are usually acquired at a later stage. Use *mummy* and *daddy* and people's names instead.
6 Avoid *colours* and *opposites (big–small)*. Use only one element of such pairs because opposites are acquired at a late stage and may confuse the child. It is better to use the word *not* instead, for example, *not-big* instead of *small.*

Most of this advice make good sense. However, in this early phase of language development one should not link the difference between object words and relational words with word classes. Word classes are defined on the basis of the words' functions in sentences. As long as an individual is not combining words to make sentences, there is little sense in saying that a manual sign or graphic symbol belongs to a specific word class (see Chapter 9). Thus, JUMP and WALK may not be regarded as belonging to a different word class from ICE-CREAM and GRAPE unless they have different functions in utterances with two or more signs or symbols. Depending on the communication situation, ICE-CREAM may be interpreted both as referring to the object "ice-cream" and the action "eating-ice-cream". JUMP may be used both as a noun, "a jump", and as an action, "to jump".

The suggestion of Bloom and Lahey to use "no" to express rejection or refusal, non-existence, cessation of an activity and a ban on a particular activity, seems to be academically motivated. In the early stages of teaching, NO should be avoided as an expression of non-existence since adults should be able to use NO in order to deny the individual an activity or thing without being misunderstood. For example, if a child expresses CHOCOLATE and the teacher answers NO, the child may perceive this as meaning that there is no chocolate. If at the same time, there is a bar of chocolate on the table, or the child has seen the teacher put a bar of chocolate in the cupboard, this may lead to the belief that he or she has not been understood and therefore the child continues to repeat CHOCOLATE. Because the child is used to being misunderstood, this is a reasonable assumption to make.

It is useful to be able to express the non-existence of an object, especially if the individual notices that a particular object is missing. However, GONE may be a better choice than NO. It is questionable, though, whether GONE will be used any differently than GET, GIVE or HELP. These manual signs and graphic symbols may also be used to obtain something that is not present in the immediate situation. It is a matter of finding out which sign or symbol is the easiest to teach, and GONE may well prove to be the most appropriate sign to include in the early vocabulary.

GONE

Manual sign: GONE

ARASAAC: GET, GIVE, HELP

What to expect in the early phase

The expectations to the first phase of AAC intervention will differ, depending on which of the three main groups the individual is assumed to belong to, and on the aims of the teaching (see Chapter 3). Many individuals who belong to the expressive language group have a relatively good understanding of spoken language at the start of the intervention and they are therefore expected to learn quickly. However, it may still take some time before the learner begins to use the first manual signs or graphic symbols spontaneously, which is always the aim of the intervention. Children in the supportive language group will also be expected to make rapid progress, since many in this group are able to use some spoken words and have some comprehension of spoken language. The individuals in the alternative language group have the greatest difficulties and represent the highest degree of uncertainty in terms of progress. Most individuals acquire some communication skills when they are taught to use graphic symbols or manual signs, but there is significant variation in both content and size of vocabulary.

Even when the training functions well for the learner and takes place in the individual's natural environment, it may take several months before manual signs or graphic symbols are used spontaneously. In particular adults with severe communication disorders may have a long history of learned dependence, helplessness and passivity that have to be won over before they become able to use their vocabulary spontaneously. For individuals with profound disorders, it is important not to have too great expectations and to continue the training for long enough to allow the individual time in which to learn. Also when the intervention goes well and the individual begins to speak, AAC intervention should not be terminated immediately. There are many examples of children with autism spectrum disorders and intellectual disabilities who, after they have started to speak, continue for some time to use manual signs or graphic symbols to help find the words they wish to say. For example, Bondy and Frost (2002) describe the development of graphic communication and speech in a boy of preschool age. The first speech sound appeared six months after intervention with PCS was initiated, and the first word another six months later. After 16 months of intervention, the boy began to use less graphic communication. Two months later he used an equal number of graphic symbols and spoken words, and 24 months after starting graphic communication, he used 200 words and no graphic symbols. This means that there was a quite short period from the first spoken word to the discontinuation of graphic communication. However, the boy still increased the number of graphic symbols by 50 percent in this period, before speech took completely over.

In a study of children with Down syndrome, Launonen (2003) found that parents and professionals often stopped using manual signs as soon as the children said their first word around the age of three years, but many of the children continued to use manual signs to

support their speech when they lacked words two years later when they were five years old. Other observations show that adolescents with Down syndrome who speak naturally, sometimes use sign to support their speech when they lack a particular word.

If teachers terminate AAC intervention too early, and significant people in the individual's environment stop responding to and using manual signs or graphic symbols, this may reduce the individual's communication, increase the risk of behavioural problems, and hinder the continuation of positive progress in communication and language development.

Chapter 8

Further vocabulary development

The construction of a functional vocabulary is the foundation of AAC intervention. Functional means that the individual has access to a vocabulary that allows him or her to develop their cognitive and language skills and participate in varied social and societal activities. After the initial phase of vocabulary development when individuals are able to use 20–30 manual signs or graphic symbols (see Chapter 7), their learning becomes more varied and complex and the character of the intervention changes. The basic intervention aims are the same for the main user groups: (1) to teach new vocabulary items and strategies, (2) lay the basis for the production of sentences (see Chapter 9), and (3) promote participation in conversations (see Chapter 10). However, these aims will have a different emphasis in the three user groups. The individuals belonging to the alternative language group need a general expansion of the vocabulary but also more focus on vocabulary items that may facilitate the construction of simple sentences. The content of the vocabulary expansion in the developmental subgroup of the language support group will depend on their speech development and which vocabulary items at the time best supplement and support their spoken language development, while individuals in the situational subgroup need vocabularies that help make their spoken language more intelligible to the communication partners. Individuals in the expressive language group will need to develop a more flexible vocabulary, enabling more varied meanings that match and support their cognitive level and comprehension of spoken language.

For many individuals who belong to the alternative language group, the teaching of the first vocabulary functions as a test period because the course of development may be difficult to predict – some may need a long time to learn an early vocabulary. Once the individual has learned the first manual signs or graphic symbols, the teaching may become more flexible. The somewhat larger communication repertoire gives the teacher greater freedom to choose between various teaching situations and strategies (see Chapters 5 and 6). However, this also places new demands on teachers and others who are responsible for vocabulary selection. Expansion of the vocabulary usually represents both a continuation and a break with earlier strategies. The content of the vocabulary changes with the individual's age and social and cognitive functioning, independent of the communication mode that is being used. It is therefore particularly important that the teacher formulates long-term vocabulary goals and strategies for providing vocabulary that can sustain the acquisition of future language skills.

The lexicon of the communication aids determines which subjects the aided communicator will be able to discuss and what kinds of conversations are possible (see Murray et al., 2018; Neuvonen et al., 2022b; Smith et al., 2018). The literature on aided communication emphasizes that the graphic symbols in a communication book or an electronic device should be chosen on the basis of what is functional for the aided communicators in their particular

DOI: 10.4324/9781003387633-9

environment. However, there is still much emphasis on graphic symbols for care, nursing and so forth, despite the fact that most children and adolescents who develop aided communication seldom engage much in conversations about care, nursing or similar topics. Instead, they need graphic symbols they can use for a variety of communicative functions and in diverse situations and symbols that reflect their general learning and interests, as well as allowing them to converse about different topics.

Calculating the size of vocabularies

Size is basic to discussions about vocabulary selection. When counting spoken or written words, there are several options (Nation, 2015). A *lexeme* is a word with its various inflections; for example, *boy* and *boys, run, runs* and *ran, or big* and *bigger* represent three lexemes. The reason for counting lexemes rather than individual word forms is that children do not have to learn each inflected word form. When they have learned the basic inflection patterns, they do not have to learn each word individually. If they know one word form, they also know the other members of the lexeme, except for words with irregular inflections, such as *go* and *went*. A *lemma* is the word that is chosen to represent the lexeme, for example, to search for in dictionaries. The lexeme contains several words within the same word class. A *word family* includes all inflections and derivations and may thus contain several related lexemes. *To run* and *a runner* belong to different lexemes but the same word family.

Like the first spoken words in typical development, the first manual signs and pictographic graphic symbols are individual forms. However, the Blissymbolics system has indicators that function like morphological markers, which can turn a noun into a verb (action) or adjective (attribute) (see Chapter 1). For example, *MOUTH* with different indicators may represent *FOOD, EAT, EDIBLE* and *SPEAK* (see p. 15). *MIND* can be the basis for referring to different semantic classes: a thing (*BRAIN*), an action (*TO THINK*) or an attribute (*THINKING*), like in a thinking person. *MOUTH* and *MIND* may be regarded as the lemmas of two graphic symbol families.

Widgit Symbols and Minspeak have ways of modifying the meaning of a graphic symbol (see Chapter 1). Most graphic systems do not have any inflections or ways to mark grammatical morphemes. However, as aided communicators become more proficient, their use of graphic symbols becomes more flexible and the symbols more polysemous – representing more than one meaning. For example, *KETTLE* may be used to express both "kettle" and "to cook". Thus, for more advanced aided communicators, the graphic symbols in their communication aid may function as lemmas and represent lexemes or word families, rather than the narrower meaning indicated by the image of the graphic symbol.

Each of the 1000 simplified signs suggested by Bonvillian and associates (2020a, b) are used to express several related meanings (see p. 253). Their glosses may be regarded as lemmas of manual sign families.

The expressive vocabulary of manual signs or graphic symbols will typically be much smaller than the average vocabulary of typically developing peers, who know an average of 4,000 word families (see following sections) at the age of six and 11,000 at the age of 13 (Brysbaert et al., 2016; Nation, 2015). The smaller pace in the acquisition of manual signs or graphic symbols – even among those whose comprehension is comparable to peers – has consequences for the selection of vocabulary. Vocabulary acquisition with alternative means is not just a scaled-down version of typical language development – many aspects of the process are also qualitatively different.

Organizing the selection of vocabulary

Some manual signs or graphic symbols will have a place in most vocabularies as vocabulary items that enable the user to express needs, preferences and interests The early vocabulary often consists of items referring to food, objects and activities that the individual likes, together with manual signs or graphic symbols representing acceptance or rejection, such as YES and NO or LIKE and DISLIKE. Further vocabulary should be based on both general usability, items most individuals will need regularly and vocabulary items adapted to the communicative opportunities, interests, thoughts, feelings and needs of each individual. Selection may be done by examining situations in which the individual usually participates or would like to participate, favoured videos and television programmes, the manual sign dictionary on the Internet or the manual of the graphic symbol system the individual is using, other lists of signs or symbols, ordinary dictionaries and books that have recently been read to the individual. It is important that the vocabulary is not decided by external AAC professionals only. They may have solid competence in AAC but may not be familiar with the individual's everyday life and communicative interactions outside school (von Tetzchner et al., 2018).

It is practical to establish a vocabulary working group representing the main parts of the individual's everyday environment. The number of people in the group will vary but it should neither be too many, nor too few. There should be at least one professional with good AAC competence, for example, a speech and language therapist or a special educator. Other typical members may be the class teacher or work manager, a parent, a relief staff member, residential staff and other people who have a significant role in the individual's life. A peer may be helpful in bringing in special vocabulary items that are used often by the peer group. The working group should meet regularly to discuss new manual signs or graphic symbols, based on up-to-date information about the individual's development, learning and change of activities and interests. It is a dialectical process: new activities may lead to a need for new vocabulary and new vocabulary items may help initiate positive changes in the individual's activities and social participation.

For children using manual signs, some signs may become less used as the children grow older, while other signs naturally become more frequent. For individuals using graphic symbols, due to the time it can take to locate the graphic symbol needed, it may be necessary to limit the size of the vocabulary in the communication aid somewhat to keep it as efficient as possible. Synonyms may be avoided as well as different graphic symbols representing the same meaning. Sometimes, it may be practical to remove some of the early symbols from the communication aid to make it easier to navigate. For example, when transitioning from preschool to school, some graphic symbols may be less relevant as they were closely connected with activities and persons in the preschool. However, they should remain available to the individual in some way. In an electronic communication device, such "old" vocabulary items may have a special folder and graphic symbols on paper may be kept in a separate book or box. The individual may enjoy looking at these items later together with the parents, siblings, a long-time friend or a teacher, reminiscing about earlier days, activities, people and symbols.

Finally, each time the working group has decided certain changes to the vocabulary, they should assign responsibility for implementing the changes in the vocabulary to members of the group connected with the child's different environments, such as the home, preschool or school, and respite. This will ensure knowledge about the vocabulary and consistency in communication across the child's environments. With manual signs, this may imply teaching the new signs to both the individual and to significant adults and peers in the individual's environment (see Chapter 12). Including parents and other family members actively in the vocabulary

selection and implementation strategies will increase the likelihood of AAC being used in the individual's home environment.

One particularly useful strategy is "Kerstin's Method", named after special teacher, Kerstin Hellberg. The members of the vocabulary working group gather in a room, supplemented with other persons when needed. Each member is given small pieces of paper, on which they write the gloss of a manual sign or a graphic symbol that they think should be implemented at the present time, each word on a separate piece. These may be items for an initial vocabulary or suggestions for supplementing the individual's existing vocabulary. After each member has finished writing their suggestions, the pieces of paper with vocabulary suggestions are put in domain heaps on the table, or in small boxes with labels, such as "people", "actions", "activities", "food", "toys", "attributes" and so forth. Some items may have been proposed by several group members. After the duplicates have been removed, the group goes through the suggestions and decides which ones to include in the individual's training at the present time. The unused items will be kept and taken into consideration in future vocabulary discussions.

To further ensure that the manual signs or graphic symbols will be useful, the individual should be involved as much as possible in the process. This is especially important for older children, adolescents and adults with relatively good language comprehension, but attempts should also be made to involve younger children or older individuals who are intellectually disabled. The individual should be involved both in vocabulary selection and in the organization of the graphic symbols in the communication aid. Knowing the location is necessary in order for the individual to be able to navigate through the device and use the symbols independently at a later time. As part of language lessons, the teacher and the individual should discuss words and their corresponding graphic symbols, as well as when and how the graphic symbols can be used. Discussions of this type also give teachers insights into the individual's comprehension of spoken language and life situation, as well as cues to how conditions could be better adapted to him or her. As far as possible, the individuals should be allowed to choose graphic symbols for themselves. If there are graphic symbols the adult believes are important for the individual, these can be presented on another occasion, perhaps with the phrase: *I have a useful graphic symbol for you.*

The alternative language group

Very limited understanding of spoken language does not necessarily mean that the individual will remain minimally verbal. Even individuals with no understanding of spoken words may develop a considerable vocabulary of manual signs or graphic symbols (von Tetzchner et al., 2005). There are several ways of expanding the vocabulary. One major goal is that the individuals should be able to communicate in as many situations as possible. The teacher may seek to integrate the individual's manual signs or graphic symbols into new topics and situations and help him or her to use them for diverse purposes throughout the day. This approach may be called *surface-oriented.* When children with typical language development learn the names of new things, they want more than just the name: they want to know what it is, what it does and how it does it, thereby gaining new knowledge and relevant vocabulary (Harris et al., 2011). In line with this, one may introduce new manual signs or graphic symbols in situations where the individual is already using AAC, so that he or she will learn to use more signs or symbols within the same topic or domain. This approach may be called *domain-oriented.* A domain-oriented expansion of vocabulary provides a basis for deeper knowledge than surface-oriented vocabulary expansion. A domain-oriented strategy may support the development of

conversational skills because the vocabulary gives the individual opportunities for saying more when engaged in conversations about the subject.

> Jack is a 36-year-old man with intellectual disabilities. He is interested in birds, especially those in the park, and often asks the staff if he can go to the park and look at the birds. He uses the manual sign BIRD and the domain "birds" is expanded with DUCK, SPARROW, BLACKBIRD, WING, BEAK and FLY and some colour names.

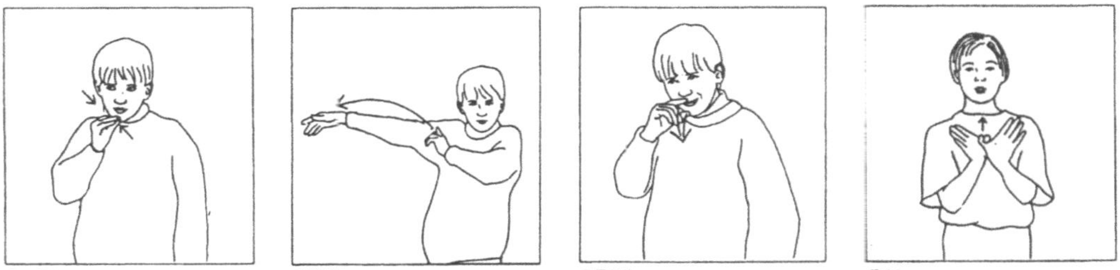

DUCK WING BEAK FLY

Manual signs: DUCK, WING, BEAK, FLY

The strategy of reacting to signal-elicited anticipatory behaviour (see p. 177) may also be useful for guiding Jack to use more utterances. The teacher first uses BIRD as a domain sign to initiate a bird activity and then gives Jack a choice of two or more activities within the domain. Making choices will be expressive training.

> Irene is a 15-year-old autistic girl. She is fond of crafts and is being taught embroidery and knitting. Her craft lessons are initiated with WORK. Then her teacher brings out a basket of materials and she is given the choice between SEW and KNIT.

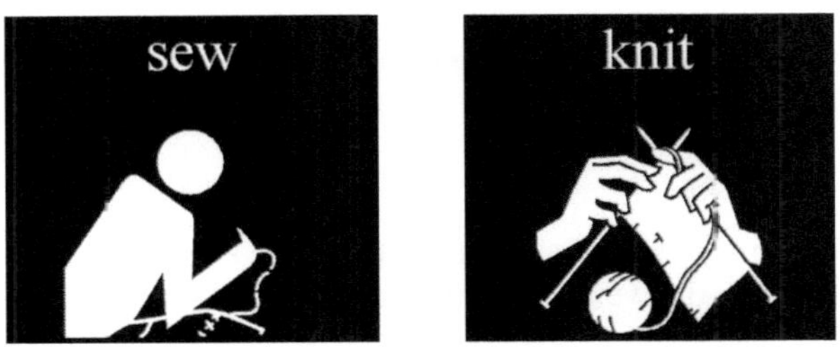

PIC: SEW, KNIT

This form of domain-oriented approach may be used in situations where the individual wants something or wishes to do something but can also be used in naming.

> Ivan is 20 years old and severely intellectually disabled. He has very little intelligible speech and communicates mainly with pictograms and photographs for person names. He attends a day centre and enjoys excursions with other people. The teacher takes photographs on the trips which he shows to Ivan on a computer screen and uses these to teach Ivan to name people and objects using pictograms and photographs.

One important quality of domain-oriented teaching is that it helps the individual delineate the usage of the manual signs or graphic symbols. Because several signs or symbols become

related to the same activity or situation, it is necessary to delineate the use of each manual sign or graphic symbol. This initiates the addition of new vocabulary and will increase the possibility that the individual will be engaged in longer social interactions within familiar activity frameworks (see also Chapter 10).

There is no contradiction between surface-oriented and domain-oriented expansion of vocabulary. A combination of these two strategies usually gives the best result. If the teachers rely only on the surface strategy, this may give the individual a large vocabulary of activities, but there is a risk that communication will only happen before and not as part of the activities. On the other hand, if the teachers rely only on the domain strategy, focusing on a few topics, such as "body parts" or "fairy tales", this might give the individual a good vocabulary for communicating about these topics but not about anything else. People in the environment may be enthusiastic at first, but they may soon get tired of talking about the same things every time. Thus, neither the individual nor the people in the environment may want to talk about the selected topics all the time, but the manual signs or graphic symbols the individual has been taught may make it difficult for him or her to talk about other things. It is always an aim of the expansion that new vocabulary should contribute to an individual having more interesting things to communicate about.

Contrast and exclusion

Children with typical development seem to assume that different word forms also have different meanings – new words lead to new usages (Clark, 1992; Schmidt et al., 2016). This observation has given rise to contrast and exclusion strategies as a means of introducing new manual signs or graphic symbols to individuals with profound intellectual disabilities (Wilkinson et al., 2009). An important objective of comprehension training is to make the individual aware that it makes a difference which manual sign or graphic symbol the teacher presents. When only one sign or symbol is presented at a time, some individuals may attend to the sign as a simple movement or the graphic symbol as a physical object in itself and not as a symbol representing something else. With contrast strategies, two graphic symbols and the objects they refer to are presented at the same time. Initially, one symbol should represent an object or activity that the individual has shown a clear preference for, and another symbol an object or activity in which the individual has shown less interest – but not aversion.

> Tim is a 14-year-old boy with profound intellectual disabilities and motor impairments. He is able to grasp and hold an object with his left hand. He enjoys playing the drum when a drum stick is put into his hand and the drum is on his lap. He has not shown interest in the triangle when this was offered during circle time. In order to teach him *DRUM*, the graphic symbol was first presented together with the drum, then *TRIANGLE* was shown with a triangle. The instruments were then hidden from his view while *DRUM* and *TRIANGLE* were placed in front of him. The first time, he reached for *TRIANGLE* and was given the triangle. He looked at it but seemed somewhat unhappy and the teacher therefore asked if he wanted to choose again. The graphic symbols and the instruments they referred to were shown again. The instruments were hidden, and *DRUM* and *TRIANGLE* were put in front of Tim. This time he reached for *DRUM* and got the drum. This was repeated a few times daily on the following days, the teacher presented *DRUM* with other instruments in which Tim had shown little interest. When Tim, over several days, had chosen *DRUM* during circle time, he was offered choices where both objects were appealing to him, such as *DRUM* and *TAMBOURINE*.

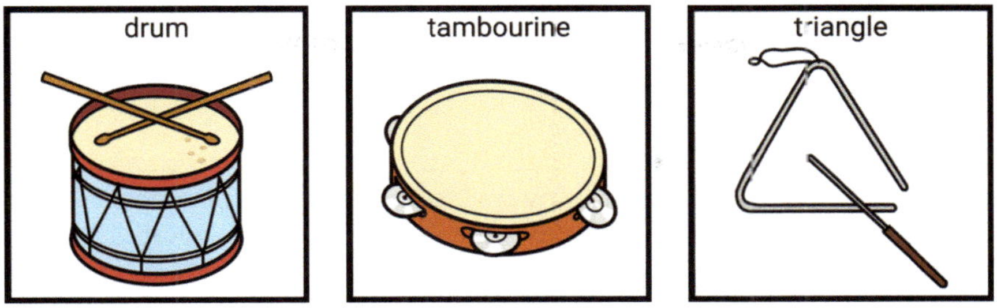

ARASAAC: DRUM, TAMBOURINE, TRIANGLE

Awareness of contrasts in symbol content is also the basis of exclusion strategies. The manual sign or graphic symbol representing a new toy, or another interesting object, is presented together with a familiar manual sign or graphic symbol. Individuals should infer that they must try to make the new sign or choose the unknown graphic symbol to obtain the new object, because they already know what the familiar sign or symbol will get them. Exclusion may also be a useful strategy for teaching HELP or WHAT by presenting new, attractive objects together with objects with which the individual is already familiar. The aim of teaching HELP or WHAT is to make it easier for the individual to understand that he or she can learn the sign or a symbol that represents something that they do not know how to express and which cannot be pointed at in the present situation. Some children with a small vocabulary of signs or symbols may try all of them in such situations.

If the tendency to perceive contrasts between word forms is a robust phenomenon also in individuals with intellectual disabilities and no speech, this will be of great practical and theoretical significance. It implies, for example, that when individuals appear unable to distinguish between the use of two manual signs or graphic symbols, it may be due to an inability to distinguish between them in production or because the categories they are meant to refer to are not distinctive enough to the individual. It is also conceivable that previous teaching employing the use of praise and other general forms of reward with many different signs or symbols has led to the unlearning of a "natural" tendency to perceive and use them differently, because they all are met with the same communicative consequence (see p. 162).

Parents often use contrasts when they explain the meaning of words to children with typical development: *This is large and that is small, This is green and that is red*, and so forth (Tribushinina et al., 2013). Contrasting vocabulary is a strategy that may be useful throughout the acquisition process and used in intervention (Davies et al., 2023).

> Dana has Down syndrome and is 2½ years old. She has little speech, and her family is using keyword signing together with speech. Dana is using about 30 manual signs and understands twice that number. The family is expanding their use of signs and has started to highlight signs that represent contrasts, like FAST and SLOW, LARGE and SMALL, HAPPY and SAD, and ON and OFF, in play and other activities involving objects and actions (Dark et al., 2019).

Attention to contrasting words is always important when selecting vocabulary and contrasting terms should be included as soon the individual appears to benefit from this.

Person names

Naming persons is a basic function of language that appears early in typical development (Hall, 2009). Family members, peers, teachers and other people constitute the individual's social environment. Also individuals with autism spectrum disorders and profound intellectual disabilities show person preferences. Parents typically have a strong wish that their child should have some way of expressing "mama" and "papa", as well as the names of siblings and other family members. People in the environment tend to talk with AAC users about what they are doing, and some intervention programmes focus mainly on training expressive graphic utterances with *I-WANT* or *I-SEE* (e.g., Bondy & Frost, 2002). It is important to break such limitations imposed by the training programme and expand the number of people and events the individuals can communicate about. Individuals using manual signs or graphic symbols need vocabulary items to address or communicate about other people and things they are not doing themselves. Also, individuals with intellectual disabilities and autism spectrum disorders are usually interested in who is present and what people in their environment are doing. Some use much of their time to communicate about others when given an appropriate vocabulary and opportunity to use AAC for this purpose. In sentences, names typically express the semantic roles of "agent" (the person performing the action) or "patient" (the person who is the recipient of the action). Names are therefore particularly important for promoting the construction of sentences in AAC (see Chapter 9).

It is often difficult to find good ways of teaching people's names, because the use of a name may have few immediate communicative consequences. It may be difficult for individuals with severe intellectual disabilities and autism spectrum disorder to understand what name signs or symbols refer to and how they are used. One way to start may be that people in the environment use manual signs or graphic symbols to name people in as many situations as possible, for example, when someone is coming or leaving, somebody is doing something unusual, or when the individual is going to do something together with a particular peer or teacher. In professional settings, it may be useful to have a wall board that indicates who is and who is not present. However, this is visual support rather than AAC (see p. 149).

In preschools, schools, day centres and sheltered houses, changes in staff members are often important events. Many individuals have their favourites such as people to whom they become particularly attached. In schools and institutions, the staff is often changed without telling the individuals and it can be difficult for them to get an overview over which staff members are or are not present. The absence of a particular staff member whom the individual expects to be present may, for example, be perceived as punishment if the individual attributes the absence to something he or she had done before. Autistic individuals find it difficult to anticipate events and lacking information about what is going to happen may lead to anxiety and panic reactions (Kerns & Kendall, 2014). Also people with severe intellectual disabilities may have difficulties knowing who is present and understanding why someone is not there. Active use of names with the individual's AAC system will ensure that the individual most of the time is informed about which members of staff that are present. In practical terms this may be done by each member of staff informing each individual that they have arrived, and by using names together with manual signs or graphic symbols for activities, thereby expressing both what the individual should do and who he or she should be with when doing it. When the individual knows who is present, this may increase the likelihood of communicative initiatives. Moreover, exposure to names in a mode they can use themselves may guide individuals to understand that people have names.

If the individual is using manual signs, each staff member and others in the environment should have a sign name. Hearing people often use the first letter of their name with the hand alphabet when they present themselves to deaf people who use sign language. However, it may be better to construct a manual sign name because several persons may have names starting with the same letter. Moreover, some letters may be difficult to sign for individuals with reduced fine motor skills. Signs may instead be constructed using salient personal attributes – such as having a beard, a moustache or long hair, or being especially tall or strong. In graphic communication, the name sign is usually a drawing or a photograph of the individual. Tangible symbols might, for example, be a distinctive form made in wood or a model of something which relates to the individual, such as a toy car to name the "driver".

For individuals with somewhat more developed language skills, the name signs or symbols are important for engaging in conversations about other people. For individuals with somewhat more developed language skills, the name signs or symbols are important for engaging in conversations about other people, like Bodil who had a vocabulary of 150 graphic symbols and photographs, and about 50 of these were third-person names (see p. 338). However, communication aids usually only have personal names of people with whom the individual has a close relation. This may be sufficient for younger children and individuals with very limited expressive abilities. However, in addition to having personal name signs and photographs that allow them to talk about familiar people, most individuals using AAC need signs or symbols for the role or relation in general. For example, a child may have a photograph of their own mother but also the graphic symbol *MOTHER* to be able to talk both about the mother of a peer or mothers in general. In addition to personal names, many individuals need personal pronouns, such as *I, YOU, HE, SHE, THEY* and *WE*.

Expanding use

Expanding the use of manual signs and graphic symbols may be as important as increasing the size of the vocabulary. Expanding use means applying one particular sign or symbol to communicate about different exemplars of the same object, several performances of the same action, in different situations and with other manual signs or graphic symbols in sentences. When teaching expanded language use related to setting the table, the objects and actions are varied systematically. For example, *PLATE* can be used to refer to large and small plates, as well as plates with different colours. JUICE may be practised in different meals and the pattern varied by using different glasses, cups and types of juice (APPLE, ORANGE, TOMATO). Later, individuals may learn to use graphic symbols in figurative ways, such as saying that *HE HAVE JUICE* to express that a person has respect and authority.

Widgit: TOMATO, PLATE

Expanded use also means that the manual signs or graphic symbols are used in new ways. When the individual seems to have understood how to use a particular sign or symbol to obtain something, it may also be used for naming and commenting. Note that this does not mean that all manual signs and graphic symbols referring to objects and actions have to be used first for requesting the objects and actions. One should rather try to introduce commenting and naming as early as possible to prevent the individual from inferring that manual signs or graphic symbols are always for requesting something (see p. 179).

Commenting on something without wanting it is a fairly advanced communicative skill for some autistic individuals, but others enjoy sitting together with adults naming people, objects and activities, often using a picture book. It may be difficult to design situations that invite a commentary, but unusual and funny situations are often suitable.

> Billy is three years old and minimally verbal. The teacher had attempted to teach him to name a ball, but he showed no interest in the task. One day a helper crept behind the teacher, who sat opposite Billy, held a large ball above the teacher's head and pretended she was going to drop it. When Billy saw this, he pointed excitedly at the teacher and vocalised what sounded like *ball* (Halle et al., 1984).

Naming of objects is often taught as a response to WHAT, meaning "What is that?" It may not make immediate sense to the individual to answer this question, but this activity is common in early child-adult interactions and most individuals are likely to learn this as a social routine. One of the main aims of teaching naming is that the number of manual signs or graphic symbols the individual can use to obtain something will increase without training the individual to ask for something with the new manual signs or graphic symbols. Naming is therefore a more economical and practical way of teaching new vocabulary that may be used for different purposes.

However, naming should not be taught only as an answer to WHAT but also in interactions involving other communicative functions than requesting. Moreover, the teacher should try to create reciprocal interactions, where the teacher and the individual take turns, each directing the other's attention to objects or activities that they want to know the name of, or to ask for comments on events that are taking place. Learning to use WHAT gives individuals a tool to ask what different things are called and hence to follow their own minds when communicating. The things individuals ask about give other people insights into their attention and interests in general but also when something interesting suddenly appears in the natural environment

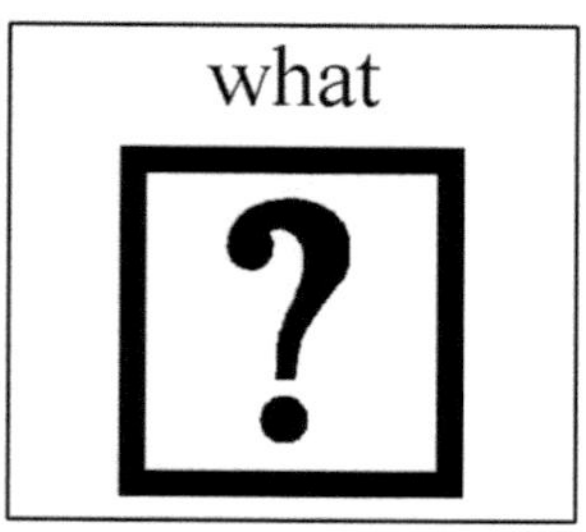

PCS: WHAT

Andrew is out for a walk in the park with his teacher. A helicopter flies overhead. Andrew points at the helicopter and signs WHAT. The teacher shows him how to perform the manual sign HELICOPTER.

HELICOPTER

Manual sign: HELICOPTER

Interactions beginning with the individual signing WHAT are generally good for teaching and learning. The interaction is based on the individual's wish to gain information about a person, an object, an action, an event or an activity. The individual's WHAT signals interest and motivation to learn a new manual sign or graphic symbol. The individual's use of WHAT may gradually lead to a more user-centred growth of vocabulary, even when the severity of the individual's disabilities makes it difficult or impossible to discuss vocabulary selection with him or her. If the individual, on occasions, asks about the manual sign of new objects or activities, it is a good idea to have a comprehensive sign dictionary available whenever possible. Likewise, for individuals using aided communication, the teacher and the family should try to have a box with many graphic symbols or a computer program available whenever it is practical.

The supportive language group

Individuals in the supportive language group may benefit from many of the strategies of the alternative language group, as well as those of the expressive language group (see following section), depending on their cognitive abilities and comprehension of spoken language. For the developmental subgroup, the use of AAC represents an intermediate phase of development. The role of AAC is to support the individual's development of spoken language and provide a means of expression until speech is sufficiently developed. The selection of vocabulary will depend on (1) what words the individual is most lacking at the moment to cope in everyday life, including in education, and (2) which manual signs or graphic symbols best support the spoken words that the individual is currently on the way to learning. The selection of vocabulary will thus reflect the individual's progress in speech comprehension and use, as illustrated in this example.

Per was three years old with severe developmental language disorder. He occasionally said something with some similarity to Norwegian words, but most of his speech was unintelligible even to his parents. This made him frustrated and he frequently reacted with temper tantrums. At assessment, he scored around the one-year level on the receptive scale and somewhat below this level on the expressive scale. He communicated by way of pointing, which he used excessively. He liked cheese very much but could not say the word in an intelligible way. OST (cheese) was therefore one of the first manual signs taught to him and he used it without help two weeks after it was first introduced. At this time, OST was

> accompanied by a slight aspiration, something like /p'/. Six weeks later, /p'/ was replaced by /lop'/. It took another eight weeks before Per said /ost/. Two days later, he stopped using OST, the sign had fulfilled its function (von Tetzchner, 1984a).

After six months of manual sign intervention, Per had gained one year in both receptive and expressive language. He produced more recognizable words, and he had started to combine words into sentences. Per's speech was easier to understand, and his signs helped the parents decipher what he was saying. With fewer frustrations related to not being understood, his temper tantrums disappeared.

The intelligibility of the speech of individuals in the situational subgroup will depend on their physical state and the sound level in the surroundings, as well as how familiar the other person is with their speech. The vocabulary should be selected to help individuals to make their utterances easier for others to decipher, by supplementing the speech with manual signs or graphic symbols. Individuals who are learning to spell may use key letters from the hand alphabet or small boards with letters and words as cues for the listener who do not recognize the words they are trying to say.

Keywords with manual signs or graphic symbols are typically used by adults in the environment to direct the individual's attention toward specific things, support comprehension using signs or symbols simultaneously with speaking, and provide opportunities to see their own language mode used by others (Dark et al., 2019; Meuris et al., 2015; see also Chapters 6 and 12). However, both children and adults in the language support group may benefit from using keywords to supplement their speech, if it is difficult for others to understand. For children, the keywords may also support the development of spoken words that they are in the process of learning. Manual signs or graphic symbols may help them to actively try to solve communicative "problems" (see p. 140). For adults, keyword signs or symbols may be a strategy across the lifespan if their speech remains difficult to understand for many people (Dark et al., 2019). Literate adults may spell part or the whole of unintelligible words with manual or printed letters.

The expressive language group

The expressive language group is very heterogeneous. Some are severely intellectually disabled and even if their main problem is a lack of expressive means, they may benefit from some of the same vocabulary as individuals in the alternative language group. Other individuals who belong to this group have cognitive skills in the typical range, or a mild or moderate degree of intellectual disabilities. It is not primarily cognitive disabilities that are the cause of their need for expressive means but the significant gap between comprehension and expression of spoken language.

In this part, the focus is on vocabulary development in individuals in the expressive group who have a relatively good comprehension of spoken language and who express themselves using graphic symbols. Ideally, this group should have an expressive vocabulary that gives them communicative possibilities comparable to those of their peers with typical language development. However, in the literature on aided communication, descriptions of vocabularies of more than 1,000 graphic symbols are rare. Individuals using electronic communication devices may have access to a large vocabulary but the time they need to search for symbols may limit their active use of this vocabulary. Even if the graphic symbols in the aid lexicon are regarded as representing word families (see p. 235), the size of the active vocabulary is likely to be far below the average of 4,000 word families of typically developing six-year-olds or the 11,000 word families of 13-year-olds (Nation, 2015; Sorell, 2015).

Some individuals in the expressive group use manual signs as their main form of communication. They have good manual motor skills and do not have the same problems with access to a large vocabulary. However, they depend on communicative access, that is, on people in their environment who understand and use manual signs, and who can teach them new signs. Professionals may apply some of the same strategies as with graphic symbols when increasing a manual sign vocabulary, aiming to expand the number of topics as well as the depth of conversation the individual can engage in. A combination of surface strategies and domain strategies may function best when helping individuals in this group to increase their vocabulary.

Expanding situations

Many individuals who belong to the expressive language group are severely motor impaired. They have limited mobility and tend to have a much narrower range of communicative and other experiences than their peers with typical development (von Tetzchner et al., 2018). In order to expand their use of graphic symbols, they must be given opportunities to engage in a variety of activities (see Chapter 10). Preschool and school constitute an important part of all children's social environment, but they are even more important for children and adolescents with motor impairments, who tend to participate less in leisure-time and outdoor activities with peers outside school hours. The teaching of communication aid use is often planned with the requirements of nursery school and school in mind. There are children whose vocabulary is mainly based on the schedule of their school day. All children learn many general words when they attend school as well as new vocabulary related to mathematics, geography, chemistry and other school subjects (Nagy & Townsend, 2012). English-speaking children learn between 3,000 and 5,400 word per year in 12 years of schooling. American school books for grades 3–9 contain about 88,500 words (Nagy & Anderson, 1984). Most children do not know all of these words and some of the words they might only encounter once in their lifetime (Beck et al., 1987). Analysing the words, Marzano (2012) identified around 15,000 unique words that would be necessary for basic literacy in the major school subjects from kindergarten to grade 12. Knowledge of this vocabulary is equally important to aided communicators and their peers.

On the other hand, teachers may also, to some extent, free themselves from the classroom and seek to expand the individual's situational repertoire. This is not always an easy task and may challenge the professionals' powers of innovation and imagination. Young helpers – siblings and peers – can play a core role in expanding aided communicators' participation in situations with peer activities if they get help and guidance in how they can adapt the communication environment to the individual (see Chapter 12). A good strategy is to involve peers in "language for action", where the aided communicator instructs peers to do the physical actions of the activity. Importantly, when the peers perform the actions, they also learn the individual's vocabulary and the graphic symbols become a shared means of communication. It should be noted that in this context, the aim of the social participation is vocabulary development. Participation in peer activities is also a goal in itself and the individual's vocabulary may contribute to increasing participation (see Chapter 10).

Access to communication aids is often limited outside of school and special teaching situations, even for aided communicators with comprehension of spoken language within the typical range (von Tetzchner et al., 2018). For an extended environment to lead to expanded understanding and use of symbols, the individuals must have access to their communication aids whenever it is needed. Any limitation in access is likely to mean a reduced active vocabulary.

AAC with the cultural basis around which many child activities are built. However, most parents of children using communication aids say that they do not have the aid available at the bedside and even if they do, it is not used much during bedside talk (von Tetzchner et al., 2018). Studies show that book reading where the adult engages in conversation with the child about the characters in the story, what they are doing and what is happening to them, and about the child's feelings during story reading, positively influences word learning and language development (Clemens & Kegel, 2021; Flack et al., 2018). However, the child's active participation in these situations requires relevant vocabulary and that the communication aid is available. Moreover, there are occasions where it is very important for children to be able to communicate at night. The reason a child cries and is restless may simply be that he or she is thirsty. If the child is able to say so and is given something to drink, everyone can get to sleep. However, the child may also cry because of a nightmare or an ailment.

> Kari was a nine-year-old girl with cerebral palsy who was using Bliss-words. One night she fell out of bed and awoke crying. Her mother came but Kari was inconsolable. In the light from a flashlight (in order not to disturb Kari's sleeping sister), Kari used her Bliss-board to explain that she had dreamed that she was able to walk and had tried to get out of bed, only to crumple to the floor. It was important for Kari to share her dream and for the mother know what her daughter was thinking and feeling, to be able to talk with her about it, and to comfort her knowing the reason for her distress (McNaughton, 2003).

Sometimes it may take parents a long time to find out what the matter is. The result can be a lack of sleep and perhaps grumpiness the next morning. Some graphic symbols on the wall or on a stand beside the bed may help reduce the number of sleepless nights and make the child feel more secure.

Vocabulary selection and access

The actual design of the communication board and the number of graphic symbols it can contain depend on the individual's motor skills and the method used for access (see Chapter 2). If the aided communicator is using direct selection, it is important that the symbols are not too small or placed so closely together that the communication partner often misunderstands which symbol the individual is pointing at. Since there is a limit to the number of symbols that can be placed on a surface, the vocabulary should at all times be adapted to the user's motor and linguistic abilities in the best possible manner. This may imply that the teacher or caregiver has to swap symbols instead of just adding new ones, especially in boards or books. If new graphic symbols are just added, the aid lexicon may become too large for efficient navigation and the communication book too heavy for practical use. With electronic aids, there is practically no limit to the number of graphic symbols it can contain, but too many symbols may be impractical because it may take a long time for individuals to find the symbols needed to construct the messages, or they may not find the symbols at all.

There is limited knowledge about how different vocabularies influence communicative interactions, but the aid lexicon sometimes gives the individual few means to communicate about things that interest them. In an experimental task, it proved almost impossible for a boy to tell his mother that the teacher had a toy crocodile in her pocket, even though the boy had good comprehension of spoken language and was eager to tell about the crocodile. His communication aid contained no useful symbols for constructing this message although both he and the mother tried hard, the mother did not manage to infer what he wanted to say

(Hagemoen et al., 2004). Carlson (1981) describes a girl who began to use her communication board only when the vocabulary was changed.

Vocabulary should be useful but there are no general rules for how a vocabulary should best be constructed to support the development of communication and language competence. On a general level, a combination of surface and domain strategies (see p. 237) seems to be the best approach. Surface-oriented expansion may increase the number of topics, but not the length of conversations because the vocabulary is meant for introducing new topics rather than sustaining the topic in a conversation. The domain-oriented strategy gives depth, but topics may become repetitive and communication partners bored (see Chapter 12). It is therefore important that the individual gets vocabulary items that contribute to communicative flexibility and making him or her an interesting communication partner. The combined approach makes it possible for individuals to talk about new issues but also to go deeper into each topic. This may help them to establish an equal footing in conversations and maintain the conversation in such a way that the conversational partner does not lose interest.

The vocabulary items that are visible on a communication aid are important for the conversational partner's appraisal of the individual and may determine which topics the partner will introduce. Communication partners sometimes treat aided communicators as though they function at a lower level than they actually do (Basil, 1992; Wickenden, 2011a). If some graphic symbols on the communication board appear childish, this may strengthen this tendency. Such symbols should therefore be replaced as the aided communicator "grows out" of them. For example, it may be necessary to remove TEDDY when the aided communicator becomes an adolescent, even if typically developing adolescents and adults also occasionally talk about teddy bears. However, their knowledge of the word is not visible and is not perceived as an expression of their cognitive level.

Even when the individual has a communication book with several pages or an electronic communication device with an unlimited number of pages, there will be limits to how large the vocabulary can grow and still have a structure that allows functional navigation. Speed of access depends on the organization of the vocabulary and the aided communicator may need time to find the intended items and construct utterances. If an individual is able to choose between four graphic symbols on three consecutive levels, this gives a vocabulary of 64 symbols. Three levels with 16 symbols on each page (plus some keys for navigating) give the individual access to 4,096 symbols (16 x 16 x 16). With 24 symbols on each page, the total number is 13,824. An individual with good fine motor control should be able to reach each symbol quickly, but an individual with severe motor impairments might take considerably longer to reach each symbol. Also, among individuals using eye gaze technology or other forms of direct selection, there are large differences in speed, accuracy and effort needed to operate the device. One minute or more to indicate one graphic symbol is not unusual (Deliberato et al., 2018).

One major issue is to organize the symbols so that the individual is able to remember their position at any given time without other visual support than the view of the communication page displayed on the screen. There will be a total of 256 different screens (16 x 16) in a search structure with three levels of 16 symbols each, and 576 screens with 24 symbols on each page. Some communication systems apply a combination of thematic and alphabetic organizing principles. The initial level consists of domains like *PEOPLE, FOOD* or *LOCATION. FOOD* leads to a subpage with different categories of edibles, including *FRUIT*, which leads to subpages where the content is organized alphabetically: *APPLE, APRICOT, BANANA, CLEMENTINE* and so forth. Although this brings consistency into the manner in which the graphic symbols are organized, it will be most functional when the individual can recognize some letters and is able to listen out the first sounds of the glosses.

PCS: PEOPLE, LOCATION

The vocabulary structure in a communication aid should not only evolve with the child's cognitive and linguistic development, but also remain as stable as possible. The vocabulary should allow the child to retain the navigating strategies developed and continue to build on them. When describing the individual's everyday life, the teacher should try to find central *domains* that may promote more profound conversation. For younger children, domain symbols such as *SHOP, BABY, CAR, DOCTOR* and *DOLL* may be used in conjunction with role playing, games and other activities. Older children and adolescents may need vocabulary domains related to their special interests, such as *SPORT, POP MUSIC, FILM STAR, ANIMAL, COMPUTER, GAME* and *BOOK*, school *(HISTORY, MATHEMATICS, GEOGRAPHY*, and so forth) or work (MEETING, SEND, READ, DISCUSS). If the individual is using a communication board, he or she may get smaller boards for specific topics, as well as for small talk with peers in school, in the youth club, on the school bus, at the movies and so on. However, he or she should always have access to their general vocabulary.

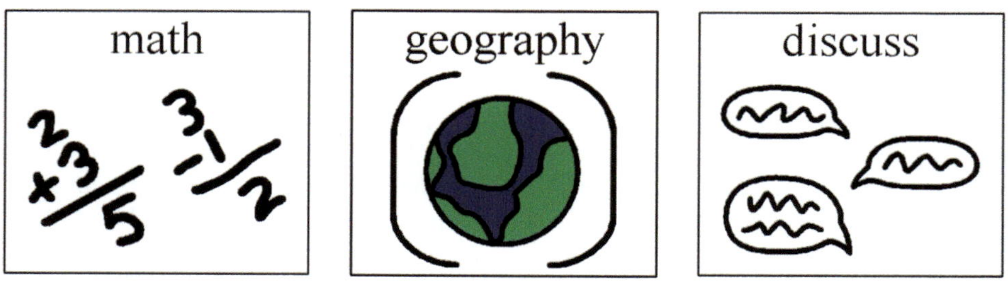

PCS: MATHEMATICS, GEOGRAPHY, DISCUSS

When creating domain-oriented vocabulary structures, the teacher may include both graphic symbols that the individual knows and symbols not yet known. The vocabulary should not only reflect what a child or adolescent has learned but also provide them with possibilities for independent exploration of the use of new graphic symbols, in the same way as speaking children are trying out the meaning of words they have only recently heard (Nelson, 2015). In this way, the aid lexicon may in itself support the individual's development of expressive and receptive vocabulary. In addition to adding new symbols that the individual has been observed to need, there should be a major revision of the vocabulary, for example, four times a year, so that the individual is not unnecessarily restricted by the existing vocabulary. At the same time, it is important that the overall structure of the aid is maintained, and that the graphic symbols remain in the same domain and have relatively fixed locations, so that the user does not have to develop new search strategies or waste time searching for

familiar symbols. One way of ensuring this, is to leave open positions for new items in the communication aid. The aided communicator should always be informed about changes in the vocabulary and be involved as much as possible in the revisions.

The introduction of additional domain-based communication boards or pages in electronic communication aids may also have a positive effect on the communication partners. Positive revisions may make it more probable that the individual will take part in varied linguistic experiences. Adults, as well as peers, who see the new communication boards, may begin to discuss new topics when they talk with the aided communicator. A domain board or page with interesting vocabulary may make more people want to initiate conversations with the individual.

Expanding vocabulary use with combinations and polysemy

Active AAC users will regularly be involved in conversations where they need to relay meanings for which they do not have a graphic symbol or manual sign. They therefore need to find ways of using the signs or symbols they have to express their intended meaning. Vocabulary selections need to take this into account. Intervention should include teaching of strategies that can help manual signers and aided communicators to get beyond the conventional use of their signs or symbols to increase the meanings they can express. This is one reason why general frequency of use may not be the most important feature when selecting vocabularies.

The lexical items on a communication aid do not only represent words but are also tools for making another person infer particular meanings. When the individual does not have or cannot find a graphic symbol with the exact meaning, the most common strategy is to give the communication partners more clues, typically by combining two or more symbols to construct meanings that usually would be expressed with a single spoken word, like in this creative example.

> Luke is a 13-year-old boy with dyskinetic cerebral palsy. He has no natural speech and uses an electronic communication aid with speech output. One morning his mother told him that she had a back pain when she woke up. Luke replied *"physio tractor"* with his speech-generating device. His mother, believing that he had said tractor by mistake and said *Yes, I should visit a physiotherapist*. Luke repeated *"physio tractor"*. His mother then understood that Luke suggested that she should visit a chiropractor. He combined a semantic strategy (*"physio"*) and a phonological strategy (*"tractor"* is sounding similar to the last part of *chiropractor*). When asked about it, Luke confirmed his intention and the construction.

Similar strategies may be used by individuals who have a limited vocabulary of manual signs.

Table 8.1 shows some examples of spontaneous strategies used by young aided communicators who were asked to name objects, for some of which they did not have an exact graphic symbol. Providing a superordinate category or the name of a similar object were common strategies, such as *ANIMAL* for "dog" or *AIRPLANE* for "helicopter", but the partner would need additional information to be able to infer what the aided communicator was referring to. Similarly, *BIG+ROUND* for "wheel" is smart but would be easier to understand if presented together with *CAR*. *HEN* to name a feather would need *PART-OF* or something similar. Many of the strategies require co-construction of meaning and a communication partner

Table 8.1 Some common strategies used by aided communicators when they are lacking a graphic symbol with the exact meaning (based on Deliberato et al., 2018)

Strategy	*Object to be named*	*Example*
Similar term	Helicopter	*AIRPLANE*
Superordinate, more general term	Scissors	*TOOL*
	Dog	*ANIMAL*
Subordinate, more specified term	House	*HENHOUSE*
Metonym, exemplar	Boy	*ROBERT*
Perceptual feature	Wheel	*BIG ROUND*
Function	Spoon	*EAT*
Related item	Feather	*HEN*
Phonological similarity	Wheel	BIL+JUL (CAR+CHRISTMAS, Swedish: Wheel = hjul)

who puts together the different pieces of information. The partners usually ask questions to narrow down the meaning to be inferred. The constructions reflect that aided utterances in conversational interactions are often the result of joint efforts between the aided communicators and the natural speaker (see Chapter 11).

Combining elements is an inherent element of the Blissymbolics system. Bliss-characters (with classifiers and specifiers), Bliss-indicators and strategic symbols are combined to construct Bliss-words that express more specific meanings (see Chapter 1). In one study, five-year-old Yehonathan constructed the Bliss-word CAR+TOGETHER+MAN to say "taxi" (Soto & Seligman-Wine, 2003). At the age of seven years, Kari indicated THINK+SLEEP to say "dream" and DIFFICULT+THINK to say "problem" (McNaughton, 2003). The communication book or device usually contains a number of conventionalized Bliss-words but the essence of the Blissymbolics system is that the individual can express a similar variety of meanings as in spoken language by combining the various Bliss-elements.

There are similar strategies in Widgit Symbols (see Figure 1.8, p. 20) and in principle, the symbols in any graphic system could be combined to form new meanings. The pictograms *HOUSE+LETTER* may mean "post office", *HOUSE+SPORT* may mean "gymnasium" and the Widgit symbols *MAN+LIGHT* may mean "electrician" if the individual does not have graphic symbols that refer to these concepts. When Sander was seven years old, he combined CHURCH+BOOK to say "Bible" (Brekke & von Tetzchner, 2003). However, such constructions may also be true metaphors, as when a child indicated *LEG BED+ROOM* to say that his leg was "sleeping".

Polysemy

Polysemy means that a word has more than one meaning or sense. Polysemy is a general characteristic of language that makes the use of words more flexible and creative (Carston, 2021). Also manual signs and graphic symbols may be used to express more than one meaning. Each of the 1,000 simplified signs suggested by Bonvillian and associates (2020b) are used to express several related meanings. For example, DRAW may also mean "drawing", "art", "artist", "design", "illustrate" or "sketch". AGAIN may also mean "frequently", "habit", "often", "once more", "practice", "regularly", "repeat", "routine" or "usually".

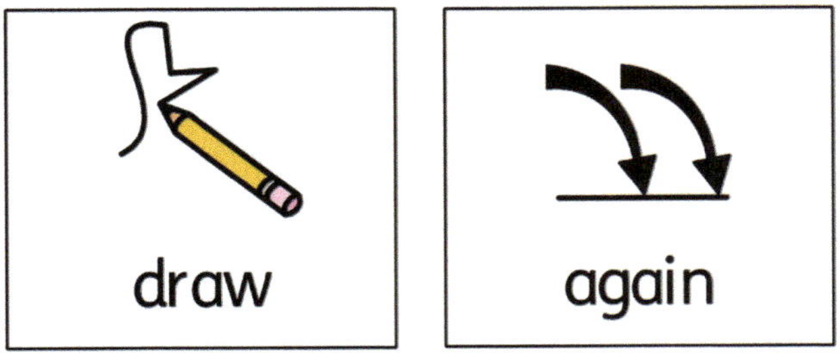

Widgit: DRAW, AGAIN

Polysemy of graphic symbols may be based on *metonymy*. A metonym may use an instance to represent a larger category (for example, a poodle to represent "dog") or a characteristic or something associated with a person or an object to communicate about to them. In such instances, the meaning expressed by the aided communicator can be quite different from the written gloss on the symbol. A good example is Sander's use of *PISTOL*. In a vocabulary discussion with his teacher, Sander had requested *PISTOL* on his communication board. He used it to express both the literal gloss meaning "gun" and to say "dangerous", a meaning for which he did not have a graphic symbol (Brekke & von Tetzchner, 2003). In another study young aided communicators were asked to name different objects. One child used *DIE*, another child *THING PERSON DEAD* and a third child *CATASTROPHE* when they intended to name the drawing of a gun (Deliberato et al., 2018).

Sander extended the use of *JACKET* to include the meaning "visit". One day, Sander used the pictogram *TOES* to tell the teacher that his father has a bad back. The background for his use of this symbol was that the father, who was a tall man, would lie on the sofa with his feet stretching outside the sofa when his back hurt. The toes would become a very salient feature of this situation. Sander's creativity and use of such idiosyncratic associations sometimes made him difficult to understand and the staff in preschool and school sometimes needed help from the parents to interpret these kind of utterances (Brekke & von Tetzchner, 2003).

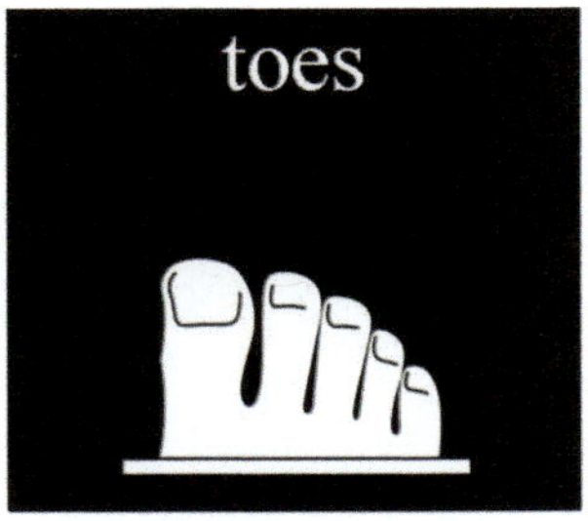

PIC: TOES

For individuals with limited vocabularies, active use of polysemy and metonymy represents important strategies for increasing the expressive vocabulary. The sometimes rather idiosyncratic associations underlying the use of graphic symbols probably reflect that many of the conversations of children using aided communication are routines where the partners know what the aided communicator will say (see p. 339). To be able to use these strategies both with partners they know well, and with less familiar children and adults, aided communicators need insights into what constructions particular partners will be able to understand. The teacher should engage the individual in a variety of conversations and discuss how each graphic symbol alone or in combination with other symbols may be used to express different meanings. The meanings that the individual often expresses using graphic symbols in unusual ways should be included in the individual's personal graphic symbol dictionary (see p. 133).

Another common strategy is to indicate an element in the image of the graphic symbol. For example, Sander pointed at the cross in the drawing on the pictogram *HOSPITAL* to say "Red Cross" (Brekke & von Tetzchner, 2003).

The strategies for vocabulary construction increase the meanings the individual can express and thus make it difficult to estimate the real size of the expressive vocabulary of individuals who use the Blissymbolics system or similar strategies with other communication systems to construct new meanings by combining graphic symbols.

The use of combinations, polysemy and metonymy sometimes place considerable demands on the communication partner, especially when the aided communicator is relating something that is unknown to the communication partner (Murray et al., 2018; Neuvonen et al., 2022b; Smith et al., 2018). The partners need to know the lexicon that the individual has access to in the communication aid and the strategies used to construct new meanings. In addition, both imagination and empathy are useful when trying to infer what the individual is saying. Even relatively uncomplicated statements are sometimes difficult to communicate. One girl used the graphic symbols of different clothes to indicate colours, because she had no symbols for colours in her communication device and the images on the clothes symbols had different colours. To recognize that this was the child's strategy required that the partner knew about the missing colour symbols and was able to look beyond the literal meaning of the images and glosses and of graphic symbols indicated by the girl.

These examples illustrate how important it is that teachers do not only see the individual's use of manual signs or graphic symbols as "correct" or "incorrect" based on the training they have given. When a young aided communicator uses a graphic symbol in what seems to be an incorrect or unusual way, teachers and other communication partners should try to identify the intention behind the symbol use. Aided communicators rarely select graphic symbols randomly; the symbols they use reflect that they are actively trying to create their own meanings, as in the examples above.

To have optimal use of their system, aided communicators should have graphic symbols representing grammatical and strategic functions, such as *PLURAL*, *ACTION* and *LOOK-LIKE* in Blissymbolics, and instruction in how to use these symbols. Some of the strategies children apply spontaneously when they use pictograms or PCS are included among the Blissymbolics strategies, but they have also been observed among children who had not been introduced to the Blissymbolics system. This demonstrates that children are creative and use the skills and whatever means they have available to resolve communication problems.

People who communicate regularly with individuals who use AAC should have sufficient education to support their vocabulary constructions and development (see Chapter 12). However, the individuals should also, as far as possible, learn to use their communication systems in such a way that they can also communicate with partners who do not have prior knowledge of their system.

Ready-made vocabularies

It is time-consuming to create an AAC vocabulary and many professionals have limited experience with this task. Since the very beginning of AAC intervention, efforts have been devoted to create ready-made vocabularies for manual signs or graphic symbols that will be useful for many individuals in need of AAC, and for both children or adults (Fried-Oken & More, 1992; Fristoe & Lloyd, 1980; Walker, 1976; Wilson, 1980).

In principle, all graphic communication systems represent a selective vocabulary. Their sizes vary from about 1,500 to 40,000 lexical items, most are much smaller than the vocabularies of children and adults developing spoken language (see p. 235). Most companies that manufacture electronic devices with communication software produce ready-made vocabularies, often several different ones for individuals who function at different language levels. A ready-made vocabulary for children may be useful for getting started but it may represent a communicative straitjacket if it is not revised in accordance with changes in the individual's general development, language, interests and social participation. Also adults are likely to need support to revise or expand their expressive repertoire (Andzik & Chung, 2022; Bosse & Wilkens, 2016; Holyfield et al., 2017).

Some of the early vocabularies, such as the Makaton Vocabulary (Grove & Walker, 1990; Walker et al., 2019), were designed for manual signs. Bonvillian and associates (2020b) present a set of 1,000 manual signs that have been simplified for ease of production and polysemy (more are planned). However, most ready-made vocabularies are made for graphic symbols.

Core and basic vocabulary

In discussions about AAC vocabulary, especially related to aided communication, some researchers point to the fact that in general, a relatively small number of words constitute a large part of what people say and write. In general English texts, the 700 most frequent word forms make up 70 percent of the text, and the most frequent 2,500 word forms make up 80 percent. The most common definition of core vocabulary is based on frequency only, usually calculated from transcripts of a large corpus of spoken conversations or books and other written material, but word frequencies vary with age (e.g., preschool children, adolescents, elderly people), demographics (e.g., working class, cultural elite, immigrants) and the conversational contexts or written material included (Lee, 2001).

Other definitions of core vocabulary are based on general usability and less on frequency. They include, for example, words that are most general, or unmarked, or central to the language, hypernyms or superordinate terms that can substitute for more specific words (birds, furniture), words that are cognitively basic or most salient, or words that, in their most general sense, have the most widespread usage across a wide range of genres (Lee, 2001). These definitions of core vocabulary thus represent a blend of frequency and usefulness across a variety of situations.

When based on frequency, core vocabularies contain mainly function words. Function words constitute a closed class which, in English, has about 300 words, including pronouns (she, they), articles (a, an), determiners (this, that), prepositions (in, under, to), auxiliary verbs (to be, to have) and conjunctions (and, but). The class is called closed because new function words are rarely created. Function words are also called relational or grammatical because their functions relate to the meanings of the other words in the sentence (Bryesbaert et al.,

2016; Montag et al., 2018). Although function words are very frequent in adult speech, including child-directed speech (see p. 357), most of them are not among the early acquired words (Bates et al., 1995). A few function words are often learned quite early, like *here* and *more*, but the meanings of most functions words are complex and difficult to learn. Throughout childhood and adolescence, most of the growth of the vocabulary consists of open class words, many of which, over time, tend to appear rather infrequently (Montag et al., 2018). The part of the vocabulary that is not considered core is often called *fringe*. This vocabulary consists mainly of content words: nouns, verbs, adjectives and adverbs.

The fact that a limited number of frequent words constitute a large share of ordinary speech and text has made researchers raise the question whether AAC users could communicate efficiently using a relatively small number of core words (van Tilborg & Deckers, 2016; Witkowski & Baker, 2012). This is also reflected in the search for standard vocabularies that may be used by many individuals (see following section). In the field of AAC, the term "core vocabulary" is mainly used to describe a smaller vocabulary of words that are useful across communicative situations, topics and communication partners. The size of this vocabulary is usually assumed to be 200-400 words, but some describe vocabularies with as few as 23 words (Laubscher & Light, 2020; van Tilborg & Deckers, 2016). Snodgrass and associates (2013) suggest that the core vocabulary in AAC should form a basis of the communication of the user, vary little over time, be useful to most individuals and allow for communication that is important and relevant to the individual. However, importance and relevance to the user would imply an individually adapted vocabulary rather than a general vocabulary based on frequency and general usability. The term "core vocabulary" is thus used about quite different vocabulary sets. "Basic vocabulary" may be a more accurate term because the choice of vocabulary items is based on different consideration and not only on frequency. This term will be used here when the vocabulary is not only, or mainly, based on frequency.

Most of the words in general core vocabularies are function words that belong to a closed class and represent a very small part of the average-sized vocabulary (Lee, 2001). Most interventionists emphasize the importance of providing individuals who use AAC with a vocabulary that allows them to express all kinds of ideas, needs and feelings in a variety of everyday situations. For AAC users to be able to converse in some depth and express more than basic needs, their vocabulary has to be useful in many communicative contexts. A communication aid with an disproportionate share of graphic symbols corresponding to frequent general terms may not contribute to the individual's development of independent conversational skills, because he or she will depend on the communication partner to formulate questions and comments to identify the relevant topic, object, theme or action. The result may be a conversation mainly based on yes/no questions and answers (see Chapter 11). The basic AAC vocabularies have fewer function words, but many items based on general usability may not allow for sufficient specificity in message construction. Lexical items from general core vocabularies should therefore not constitute a large part of an AAC vocabulary. On the other hand, a vocabulary that contains only content words, may make it difficult to construct complex utterances.

The content of the basic vocabularies suggested for AAC varies considerably. Even if the smallest vocabularies are excepted, only a few words are found across all the suggested vocabularies, reflecting differences in the participants' ages and demographics and the conversational situations where the language use was sampled (Laubscher & Light, 2020). Unlike the large general core vocabularies, where 80 percent of the 100 most frequent words are function

Table 8.2 Common words in basic AAC vocabularies (from van Tilborg & Deckers, 2016)

Vocabulary items	*N*	*Vocabulary items*	*N*
To be, am, is, was, were, aren't, wasn't, weren't	15	To see, saw	10
To go, goes, going, gonna, went	15	We	10
No, not	14	And	9
That	14	Because	9
All	13	Here	9
To have, has, having, had, haven't	13	Just	9
To want, wants, wanted	13	She	9
I	12	Still	9
Then	12	The	9
To come, comes, came	12	They	9
A	11	Time	9
He	11	To do, doing, don't, did, didn't, does, doesn't	9
It	11	What	9
There	11	For	8
To know	11	Hello, hi, hey, ey	8
Yes. yea, yep	11	Oh	8
You	11	OK, okay	8
But	10	On	8
Can, can't	10	People	8
Good	10	So	8
In	10	This	8
My, mine	10	To	8
To eat, eating	10	To make, made	8
To like	10	To take, took	8
To look, looking	10	Two	8
To say, says, said	10		

N indicates how many lists include each item. The table contains the vocabulary items that are shared by 8 or more of the 15 word lists. See the text for further description.

words, half of the basic vocabularies suggested for AAC consist of nouns, verbs, adjectives and adverbs, and the relative proportion of content words increases when more words are included.

Fifteen basic vocabularies suggested for AAC are compared by van Tilborg and Deckers (2016), based on observations of children and adults, ranging from toddlers to elderly people, with typical development and various disorders, and containing a total of 1,852 words. Among these, 637 words were unique (appeared in one list only); 51 words appeared in more than eight of the word lists; and 24 of the 51 words were represented in eight or nine of the 15 word lists (Table 8.2). The 51 words are considered by van Tilborg and Deckers as core vocabulary. Only two lexemes were present in all word lists: *to be* and *to go* in various versions (*am, is, was, were* and *goes, going, gonna, went*). The lack of overlap between the vocabularies indicates that a core or even a basic vocabulary for everybody may not be the best solution. However, a moderately sized list of commonly used words may be a good resource when starting to build up a larger vocabulary of graphic symbols, both for younger and for older aided communicators.

Beyond a basic vocabulary

Comparing vocabulary lists can be a good strategy when selecting vocabulary for individuals using AAC. Many of the content words included in basic AAC vocabularies may be useful from quite an early age. For children in the early phases of language development, very few function words will be useful (Smith, 2014). In typical development, function words increase with age but at a very limited rate. There is a general agreement that the vocabulary in a communication aid should have a balance between basic vocabulary and fringe vocabulary (Laubscher & Light, 2020; Stuart et al., 1997; van Tilborg & Deckers, 2016). This means that both frequently and less frequently used words should increase as the vocabulary of the child is expanded. The total vocabulary should include both an increase in the small vocabulary of frequently used words, and in a somewhat larger set of basic vocabulary, together with words that reflect the individual's educational level and prominent conversational topics in society, and words that reflect the individual's special interests and life situation. With few content words, the communicative context and most of the ideas and issues of the conversation must be derived from the situation or be implied. This requires that the communication partners have considerable shared knowledge or that the conversation is kept on a superficial level. However, relaying unknown information to others is an essential language function that depends on the individual's vocabulary (Murray et al., 2018; Neuvonen et al., 2022b; Smith et al., 2018).

The words reported to be common among children with typical development may be a good resource when selecting AAC vocabulary. The *McDonald-Bates Communication Development Inventory* (see p. 117), which is based on parent reports, has been suggested as a basis when planning a vocabulary for aided communicators in early phases of language development (Laubscher & Light, 2020; Soto & Cooper, 2021). However, even the quite large vocabulary of this inventory contains only common words found in the early vocabularies of many children with typical development and does not reflect the individuality and the many words found only in some early vocabularies. For example, at the age of two years, one child had used as many words not mentioned in the inventory as those registered in the inventory (Roy et al., 2015). Soto and Cooper (2021) suggest a Spanish starting vocabulary of 218 words which they extracted from two Spanish lists of words used in experiments with young children and the Spanish version of *McDonald-Bates Communication Development Inventory* (which overlaps about 80 percent with the American version) as a resource when selecting vocabulary for young aided communicators in a Spanish-speaking environment. About 86 percent of the words are from the open classes, including 103 nouns, 47 verbs, 11 adjectives and 13 adverbs. There are 22 animal names, 15 person terms, 13 foods and drinks, nine body parts, three clothes, two activities and one time word. The rest of the words in the list belong to the closed class and consist mainly of pronouns, articles, prepositions and numerals. It is a quite varied vocabulary, but Soto and Cooper emphasize that the initial vocabulary should be supplemented with vocabulary items that reflect the child's family background, culture, living situation and personal interests.

The Blissymbolics system (see p. 13) has a standard vocabulary of about 400 items, which can be adapted and expanded to the individual user. The standard vocabulary is not a basic vocabulary but includes many common words which may be combined with Bliss-characters, Bliss-indicators and other Bliss-words to create new vocabulary items as needed (Blissymbolics Communication International, 2020). The standard vocabulary is well designed for vocabulary growth, without the number of lexical items growing so large that finding or constructing Bliss-words takes so long that it becomes a major hindrance to communication. The standard

Blissymbolics vocabulary may also represent a useful resource when selecting vocabularies for individuals using other graphic systems (see Resources).

Although general vocabulary lists are useful resources, it is necessary to take into account that the semantics of graphic symbols in a communication book or an electronic device are different from a spoken vocabulary. Children with typical development learn a lot of words that they use quite infrequently, and which may not be included in a communication book or device as the search process would take a long time and lot of a young child's cognitive resources. Choices and requests for activities are central in the intervention, so children with such a large graphic vocabulary would probably have more vocabulary referring to activities, maybe also clothes (for communication related to both personal dressing and doll play) and fewer animals. Children with limited use of the hands would need a vocabulary that enables "language for action", that is, instructing others to perform the physical actions they cannot do themselves (see Chapter 10).

Many communication books are designed so that the pages on one side repeat the same content; a basic set of graphic symbols that are often used in combination with other graphic symbols. The pages on the other side are all different and contain the main part of the vocabulary (see Figure 2.5, p. 40). This larger vocabulary can, for example, be organized according to domain (see Chapter 2). The purpose of this set-up is to make it easier for the individual to construct multi-word utterances. This implies that the selection of items for the "basic" page is somewhat independent of the total vocabulary. All other common or frequently used words would have to be placed on the "main" pages. The content of the basic page is quite stable, although it may change a little as utterance complexity increases, but it is limited to one page. The main vocabulary will increase in accordance with the individual's cognitive and language skills and social participation. Similar solutions are possible in electronic communication devices.

When considering the balance between the basic and the main vocabulary for individuals using communication aids with graphic symbols, there are concerns which do not apply to individuals who speak or sign. The number of graphic symbols will be much smaller than the number of words most individuals who speak have access to, even for aided communicators with age-appropriate comprehension of spoken language. The most difficult task in vocabulary selection may not always be to find graphic symbols to include, but rather to decide which can be left out at the current time without losing too much communicative flexibility. For more advanced aided communicators, the vocabulary on the basic page should also include strategic vocabulary like *SOUNDS-LIKE, SIMILAR-TO* or *TYPE-OF* to instruct and provide communication partners in co-construction of utterances with additional clues. Such terms may be needed more often by aided communicators than by individuals using natural speech. Another implication is that meanings which are relatively easy to construct by combining vocabulary items already in the communication aid should not be selected as individual items, unless they are used very often. Even relatively frequent lexical items in the general vocabulary of natural speakers might have to be omitted.

The Makaton Vocabulary is a programme originally designed for teaching manual signs to individuals with intellectual disabilities, and later also for teaching graphic symbols (see p. 19). The Makaton Core Vocabulary contains vocabulary items that were regarded as the foundation of the programme, and which were supposed to be introduced first. At present, it consists of about 450 items with a wide variety of glosses, from MUMMY and DRINK to ALWAYS and BECAUSE (Walker et al., 2019). The Makaton Core Vocabulary is thus basic rather than core. It consists of nine vocabulary stages and the individual should learn vocabulary in the stage order, although not necessarily all items in each stage (Grove & Walker, 1990). The first

Makaton Vocabulary was based on observations of the communication of adults with intellectual disabilities living in institutions, and although child-oriented vocabulary items have been added, the adult perspective still seems prominent. There are many items missing that children might well need, while the vocabulary has many items associated with cleanliness and self-help, for which children may have limited use. The first stage includes, for example, NURSE, DOCTOR, BED, TABLE, WHERE, HERE, SLEEP, WASH, BATH and PLEASE. Stage 2 contains, for example, BREAD, BUTTER, TEA, FIRE, CLEAN and DIRTY. There are no words for toys, and few vocabulary items clearly related to play. The care vocabulary and BED can be used in doll play but clothes are lacking (Grove & Walker, 1990). KNIFE, FORK and SPOON may be useful both in play and when preparing for meals. When Makaton was first introduced, the vocabulary, the stages and the teaching procedures were met with considerable criticism (Byler, 1985; Kiernan et al., 1982). Although it has since been revised, the main structure is the same (Walker et al., 2019).

The Makaton Resource Vocabulary consists of over 11,000 items from various domains, such as "activities for adults", "animals, transports and vehicles", "dance", "drama", "human body parts, function, senses and emotions", "meal times", "medical", "work and leisure", "plants and trees", "summer games and international sports events" and "weddings". The Makaton Resource Vocabulary may be a useful tool, especially when planning the expansion of a manual or graphic vocabulary for adults with intellectual disabilities, independent of the manual sign or graphic symbol system that is used.

The importance of going beyond the basic vocabulary to find suitable manual signs or graphic symbols is demonstrated in the following example.

> Gerda was a 36-six-year-old woman with cerebral palsy who was unable to read and write. She had recently been given a board containing 24 Bliss-words. The board was, in effect, her first expressive vocabulary but her language comprehension suggested that she could use a far larger expressive vocabulary. She was given an electronic communication aid with speech output and chose her vocabulary herself together with a team of professionals. Once she had begun to use some symbols, the team produced a description of her environment and made a communication diary. Together with the team of professionals, Gerda reviewed four standard vocabularies.
>
> After this process, the total number of graphic symbols on Gerda's board was 240. Most of them were of a general nature, chosen on the basis of their presumed frequency of use. Symbols corresponding to words that were used infrequently were avoided. The selection of symbols was thus in line with the needs that a basic vocabulary is supposed to meet. A comparison with 11 standard vocabularies showed that none of them contained all the 240 symbols on her board, even though some of the vocabularies were fairly extensive. Most of them covered well below 50 percent of her symbols. Neither did the total of all the vocabularies – 2327 different words – cover what was regarded as her basic vocabulary needs (Yorkston et al., 1989).

There has been much effort invested in making vocabularies that are generally suitable in intervention with AAC. There are, without doubt, some manual signs or graphic symbols that will be represented in the vocabularies of most individuals using AAC, although this will differ somewhat between age groups, making vocabularies that are generally suitable seem to be an impossible task. However, together with other word lists, such vocabularies may constitute useful resources when professionals, together with significant people and the individuals themselves, when possible, are selecting a vocabulary of manual signs or graphic symbols.

Twenty-four principles for a developmental and balanced vocabulary

The function of an early vocabulary is to guide the individual into social interaction, communication and language use (Chapter 7). When selecting the vocabulary beyond the first 30 or so manual signs or graphic symbols, the aim is to enable communication in line with the individual's abilities and interests and the ecology, culture and social conventions of his or her environment. The very early vocabulary builds on the individual's interests, preferences and likes and dislikes, and often focuses on choices of things and activities. The growing vocabulary enables choice-making, but equally important are the possibilities for engaging in conversations about people, events, ideas and general issues related to the everyday life of the individual and society at large, in the family, in preschool or school, with peers and in other situations. The 24 principles presented below in an unprioritized order are derived from the issues discussed in this chapter. They mirror the many usages of language, the diversity of issues people talk about, and the special considerations involved in selecting vocabulary for children, adolescents and adults using AAC. The content of the individual principles will vary with age and may be applied somewhat differently with individuals in different developmental phases of language development.

In the population with typical development, the vocabulary continues to increase throughout the life span. From ages 20 to 60 years, people learn, on average, a new lexeme every second day (Brysbaert et al., 2016). Although many individuals who develop alternative means of communication may not reach a comparable level of receptive and expressive language, all individuals who use AAC should be expected to engage in new activities and expand their vocabulary in childhood and adolescence, and also as they grow older. The continued selection of manual signs and graphic symbols should strive to provide a vocabulary that balances the basic and broader content and facilitates communication about as many topics and for as many purposes as possible.

Provide vocabulary adapted to linguistic and cognitive abilities and age

The vocabulary should reflect the cognitive abilities of the individual and contain manual signs or graphic symbols that are comprehensible and learnable for him or her. However, it is important not to exclude signs or symbols that are abstract and may take longer to learn. Relevance and usefulness in communicative interaction and social participation are more important than speed of acquisition. Also individuals with typical development acquire words that they need to hear and use in different situations before the words are fully understood.

For many users of AAC, the intervention seeks to narrow the gap between what they understand and what they can express. The individual's comprehension is therefore important for the selection of vocabulary. This does not mean that the individual has to show comprehension of the corresponding spoken word before a manual sign or graphic symbol is introduced. Learning to use manual signs or graphic symbols may support both comprehension and production of spoken language, but comprehension of the corresponding word may decide *how* the manual sign or graphic symbol is taught (see Chapter 6).

The vocabulary should reflect the age of the individual and appear age-appropriate even if they are intellectually disabled. This is especially important when selecting vocabulary for aided communicators, where communication partners typically adapt their own language and conversation topics to the graphic symbols they see on the communication aid.

The selection of vocabulary for children and adults may have quite different functions. Both need a vocabulary that enables them to solve current and new communicative "problems". However, for young children, the focus of vocabulary growth may be to support their acquisition of new vocabulary. Adults may also need opportunities for learning new vocabulary but, in general, the vocabulary growth levels out and it may be more important to establish a vocabulary that optimizes the adult's communication and participation in everyday life.

Provide a varied vocabulary

A varied vocabulary is important for expanding the communication of individuals but also for their general competence and quality of life. Variation applies to both vocabulary content and word classes.

For individuals who are still mainly using manual signs or graphic symbols to make choices, the vocabulary should not only represent small objects like dolls, toy cars and balls, but also large objects (SWING, TREE), activities (WALK, PAINT), places (PARK, KITCHEN) and people (names and roles). The vocabulary may include contrasting qualities, like LARGE or SMALL, RED or BLUE, SWEET or SALT (snacks), FAR or NEAR, and SHORT or LONG (about things, time, and so on).

For individuals with more advanced communication skills, in addition to including manual signs or graphic symbols representing many domains and knowledge areas, a varied vocabulary should include grammatical signs or symbols (PLURAL, PAST-TIME). GET, LOOK, PLAY and HELP may be used in connection with many objects and activities and may also facilitate the acquisition of new manual signs or graphic symbols.

Provide early means for expressing likes and dislikes, yes and no

YES and NO may be very useful signs or symbols but answering yes/no questions requires that the individual understands the questions. This may not be case for many individuals in the alternative language group. In general, YES and NO are not suitable in the first phase of intervention for people with limited comprehension of spoken language (see also Chapters 7 and 9). To them, NO may mean "rejection", "non-existence", "cessation of action" or "denial of activity" (Lahey & Bloom, 1977). Most individuals have a way to express rejection when AAC is initiated, which means that priority should not be given to teaching NO as a new expression in the early phase of AAC intervention. To express "non-existence", GONE may be more suitable, since NO is used by others as a means of denying the individual an activity. STOP is better than NO to express that an activity should cease. WAIT may indicate a temporary stop or delay. Moreover, it may be difficult for the teacher to design good teaching situations for "rejection" and "non-existence". Finally, YES and NO are dependent on the initiative of others – somebody has to ask a question. This may lead to a responsive style but YES and NO are still important for confirming or rejecting the partners' inferences or interpretations.

Provide vocabulary that is relevant to the individual's activities

Conversations are always embedded in activities (see Chapters 10 and 11). Social participation is an implied goal of all AAC interventions and relevant vocabulary is the "ticket" to participation in joint activities. The vocabulary should allow the individual not only to choose an activity but to be an active participant and communicator within the activity. For example, when building a house with Lego, the individual may need house-building vocabulary (WINDOW, ROOF) as well as vocabulary for making stories during the house building (BRICK, GIVE) or when some toy figures move into the house (COOK, SLEEP). When attending a football match, relevant vocabulary might be SHOOT, OFF-SIDE, ON-SIDE, REFEREE, WIN, LOSE, TACKLE, SAVE, RIGHT, YES, NO, GOOD, BAD, CHEER and numbers. For individuals attending school, access to vocabulary for school subjects is necessary. Work may also imply learning new vocabulary.

Introduce new vocabulary items in utterances with familiar vocabulary

Getting to know a new vocabulary item is more than learning its manual sign or graphic symbol. Familiar vocabulary may function as cues to the meaning and use of the manual sign or graphic symbol. Introducing a new sign or symbol in utterances with familiar vocabulary may therefore give the individual broader information about the person, object, action or location referred to, and hence a deeper conceptual knowledge of the new item (see Chapter 9).

Provide vocabulary for likely future activities

Selection of new vocabulary means providing access to manual signs or graphic symbols that the individual has not yet been using. Vocabulary selection is thus about the future. It implies a prediction of which signs or symbols will best promote the communication and participation opportunities of the individual. This prediction should be the outcome of a collaborative process involving people from the main parts of the individual's language supportive environment. For individuals with limited abilities and skills, evaluating the existing vocabulary and needs for new vocabulary items should always be part of the planning of new activities. For individuals with more advanced abilities, vocabulary selection may reflect progress in school (for instance new vocabulary related to mathematics or social sciences at the start of a new school year) or changes in work duties (e.g., COPY, LETTER).

Provide vocabulary for issues of special interest to the individual

Most people have particular interests and topics that they are especially knowledgeable about. Children may know a lot about dinosaurs, cars or games, and this knowledge may be clues for providing new vocabulary items (domain strategy), as well as general vocabulary that is needed when communication about these and other preferred domains. This vocabulary may also function to show the competence of the individual.

Provide sufficient vocabulary referring to actions

Verbs constitute the second largest word class and verbs are important for the expression of many meanings, including relating the actions of people and animals. Verbs may also function to define the relationship between people and things and are thus important for sentence construction (Lahey & Bloom, 1977; Tomasello, 1992). New vocabulary items referring to actions tend to make children seek relevant information about the actions (Janakiefski et al., 2022).

Provide vocabulary that is needed in descriptions: adjectives, adverbs and prepositions

Descriptions of people, things, locations, actions and events can involve all parts of the vocabulary but it is important to make sure that the individual has vocabulary that is specific to descriptions, such as characteristics of people (TALL, KIND), things (SOFT, EXPENSIVE), relative locations (BEHIND, UNDER), actions (SLOW, HARD) and events (FUNNY, DANGEROUS) (Murray et al., 2018; Neuvonen et al., 2022c). This vocabulary may also include places, like PARK, HOME, SCHOOL, ZOO, BEACH or HOSPITAL.

Provide vocabulary for amounts and numbers

These include manual measures, like KILO, LITRE and METRE, relative indications of numbers and sizes, like MANY, FEW and MORE, as well as digits 0 to 9 to communicate numbers. These vocabulary items are important in school and useful in time management and when instructing others.

Provide vocabulary referring to positive and negative emotions

Naming emotional states is a core element in human interactions in general and in narratives of real and fictional events. Three-year-olds with typical development have limited emotional vocabulary but they can usually say that somebody is happy or angry because of something. Many emotional terms are difficult to teach and individuals with limited communication skills may have few emotional terms. However, they may learn vocabulary items like HAPPY, FUN and SAD. Doost and associates (1999) found that ten-year-old children with typical development knew, on average, eight words for positive emotions (joy, happy, nice), seven words for sad emotions (unhappy, lonely, sad), and six words for scary emotions (scared, horrible, angry). Articles about the development of emotional words may be used as a resource for selecting emotional vocabulary (for example, Grosse et al., 2021; Shablack & Lindquist, 2019). The need for varied emotional words increases in adolescence and book reading is found to support the acquisition of emotional words among adolescents (Dylman et al., 2020).

Provide names, not only name-photographs

Names are needed to address people or to talk about them. With manual signs, it is common to use the first letter of the individual's name with the hand alphabet letters as the name. When the individual uses a manual letter, communication partners have to guess among relevant individuals whose name begins with that letter. If the individual has started to learn to spell, more letters can be added, or a feature of the person (*B TALL, J DOCTOR*) can be used to specify the person.

For individuals using graphic systems, the name is usually a photograph of the person. That may work well as long as only people in the proximal environment are named and their number is limited. Individuals with more advanced language skills who communicate about people who are not represented with a photograph in the communication aid – neighbours, politicians, sports people, actors and actress, historical persons, rock stars and so on – need items representing common names like JOHN and MARY. These might be items with the gloss only (letters) or with an image that the aided communicator selects for persons with that name. Sometimes, it may be possible for the individual to indicate NAME SAME-AS and then indicate a photograph of a person, when referring to a person who has the same name as somebody with the photograph in the communication aid.

Who I, ME and YOU refer to is often implied in the context, but these terms can be useful for teaching the individual to relate different actions to the communication partners, as well as for supporting children in including peers in activities. The manual signs I and YOU are often easy to learn because they imply pointing at the person who is referred to (oneself or the communication partner). In graphic communication (and speech), it is more difficult to demonstrate the meaning of *I* and *YOU*, because the referent of the symbol depends on who is expressing it. It may therefore be better to use personal names instead of pronouns in the early phases of intervention with graphic systems.

Pay attention to possibilities for polysemy

Most spoken words will have more than one meaning, and the meaning or sense may depend on context. Polysemy is important in AAC as it increases the range of meanings the individual can express. Bonvillian and associates (2020a, 2020b) consider it part of the simplification of manual signs that each sign may be used to express several related meanings. Graphic symbols are sometimes used to relay meanings that are quite different from the literal meaning indicated by the image, but which are easy to understand, such as Sander's use of *PISTOL* to say "dangerous" (in addition to "gun") (see p. 254). The PCS system has two symbols with the gloss HELP, one with the metonym image indicating "help me do something," another with an image indicating "save me". Both are common senses of "help" and it seems unnecessary for an aided communicator to have both symbols as they take up double space. To make the vocabulary as flexible as possible, one should try to select graphic symbols with an image that may facilitate the partners' inferences of different meanings or senses based on the communicative context.

Provide vocabulary for seeking information

Exploration is a basic human function and children and adolescents with both typical and atypical development are curious and actively seek information in their exploration of the world (De Simone & Ruggeri, 2022). Question words like WHAT, WHERE, WHO, HOW, WHEN and WHY are linguistic tools for getting different types of information. Individuals who use manual signs or graphic symbols are often asked many yes/no questions, which require only a simple YES or NO from them. Partners may encourage individuals to construct longer utterances by using question words, and learning question words may help the individuals to inquire about names as well as functions of things they are interested in. Being able to seek the information they want makes individuals less dependent on others and may contribute to increasing their self-efficacy and sense of agency.

Provide vocabulary for kindergarten and school

Select general vocabulary for preschool and school attendance and items that enable the individuals to communicate about whatever subjects they learn at kindergarten and school, including subjects and tasks that are much below their age level.

Provide vocabulary for common issues

Many individual and group conversations with peers concern everyday activities, issues in the news, music and sports events, films, crime, politics and so on. True communicative participation requires sufficient vocabulary to describe the issue, for example, that a politician supports a tax reform or that a band will give a concert in London next year, as well as opinions about the reform or concert.

Provide vocabulary for time management

Much communication is about events, and time is a core element of events. Time vocabulary is needed in many types of conversations, as well as for relating events and stories, placing past and future events on a time line (YESTERDAY, WEDNESDAY) and avoiding misunderstandings about time (see Bodil, p. 386). Being able to understand and express time is important for the individual's self-regulation. Time management is an inherent element in structuring (see p. 147) and communicating about time may be part of the individual's internalization of everyday routines and structures. Time vocabulary may further support the ability to negotiate time and length of a task or an activity and thus the individual's development of autonomy.

Early time management may include terms like FIRST and THEN or BEFORE and AFTER to indicate sequences of activities, later being able to say TIME WAIT or FIRST EAT, THEN HOMEWORK may be useful. Time vocabulary may also be used when a teacher or parent is using visual schedules, but it is not enough that the adult is communicating these terms. Individuals with intellectual disabilities should also learn to construct utterances involving time, both to relate events and as a means to regulate themselves. Calendars can be designed to reflect the individual's understanding of time.

Select vocabulary items that enable combinations

Combining vocabulary allows the individual to construct a greater diversity of meanings and get more out of the aid lexicon. Combinations may be used (1) to express meanings where vocabulary items are lacking, and (2) to construct sentences. Both enable the individual to communicate more specific and complex messages. Provide lexical items that may be used in vocabulary construction, including manual signs and graphic symbols referring to relations and grammatical features, and teach strategies needed for constructing new vocabulary items. Many of them may be found in the Blissymbolics system.

Provide vocabulary for narratives

Narratives are true or fictional stories that involve actors, actions, things, places and time sequences (see Chapter 11). It is not a particular set of manual signs or graphic symbols that are needed, selecting vocabulary for narratives rather implies ensuring that the individual has a broad vocabulary that enables him to relate uncommon actions and events, and which prevent co-constructed narratives from becoming repetitive social routines without any new content. However, vocabulary items such as AND, BEFORE, BECAUSE and THEN can function to establish sequences of actions and coherence and may be part of the individual's basic part of the vocabulary.

Provide strategic vocabulary

This includes vocabulary items that may have particular uses in co-construction and in guiding the communication partner towards correct inferences. These vocabulary items may function as cues for partners to infer the individual's intended meaning when this differs significantly from the literal meaning of the gloss, such as SOUND-LIKE or SIMILAR-TO. These items are not referring to, or part of, sentence construction in themselves but help the communication partner interpret the aided construction and formulate the utterance in spoken language and in the individual's language mode when possible.

Provide key words that the individual is struggling with

The function of key word manual signs or graphic symbols is often to help the individual develop spoken language. People in the environment should therefore expand their own repertoire of key word signs or symbols in line with the individual's language development and select vocabulary items corresponding to spoken words that the individual is in the process of learning.

Pay attention to communicative successes and failures

Both communicative successes and failures may indicate that the individual has a need for specific vocabulary items. If a child, after a long negotiation, manages to explain that he or she has seen a bear in the zoo, this implies a need for BEAR but also other animal names because his or her efforts may indicate a special interest in animals. It is more difficult to use communicative failures because what the individual wanted to express was not resolved. However, there may still be clues in the failed negotiating of meaning which may be used when providing new vocabulary. It may also be useful to make "communicative problems" that are potentially solvable, to observe if the individual has the vocabulary and strategic means to solve them.

Make sure that the vocabulary items are used with some frequency

Some degree of repetition is important for vocabulary learning. Many words are used only rarely by the individual and the teacher and the family may need to ensure that all vocabulary items are repeated within a reasonable time frame. Use in different situations facilitates learning the extension of vocabulary items, while refreshment of use is important for memory and maintenance. With graphic symbols, people in the environment should take special notice of indicating both graphic symbols that the individual has recently started to use and graphic symbols the individual has not used for some time. This will remind the individual when the graphic symbol can be used and refresh the memory about its location.

Select vocabulary for peer interactions

Children and adolescent are word learners but also word inventers. They have their own vocabulary items and expressions that are not usually used by adults, or with different meanings and senses. For individuals using AAC, the peer vocabulary is important for inclusion, participation in peer conversations and social identity. Peers with typical development may be engaged in the selection of graphic symbols and choice of image and gloss.

Individual dictionaries

An individual sign and/or symbol dictionary should be started as soon as the AAC intervention is initiated. In the manual sign dictionary, the translations or glosses (lemmas) of the manual signs should be listed alphabetically, including all potential meanings. It should indicate which signs are being taught, and which are being used, understood, or both. The dictionary should also contain a description or drawing of how the manual signs are ordinarily performed and how the individual performs them (Kristoffersen & Troelsgård, 2010).

Dictionaries of graphic symbols should contain a description of how the individual indicates the symbols and navigate the communication aid and whether fixed combinations of symbols are used to express lexical meanings that are not represented on the board (see p. 252). Dictionaries for tangible symbols should contain drawings of the symbols and describe how they are selected.

Some of the information may be available to all potential communication partners, while other parts should only be available to selected persons. It is therefore necessary to find a way to share the information in a secure manner. This may be a designated and password-protected storing device, or an app designed for making such overviews and lists, which have this as a built-in feature.

There should be two or more copies of the dictionaries. The individuals' own copies should be with them at least in all their ordinary environments. For individuals using electronic communication aids, the dictionary may be located in the aid as well as in backup storage. With the help of the dictionary, a peer or adult who starts interacting with the individual can quickly get an idea of which manual signs or graphic symbols he or she uses and understands. If the number of sign or symbol combinations grows large, the dictionary will also help people in the environment to keep up to date on which manual signs or graphic symbols the individual has learned, or is in the process if learning.

The dictionary may also represent a basis for new ideas of expanding the individual's sign or symbol use. For example, the teacher may look at the manual action signs in the dictionary and try to find signs referring to objects or attributes that can be used together with the actions signs. Similarly, the teacher may look at object symbols in order to find action symbols or other symbols that may be used when communicating about these objects. Both of these approaches are domain-oriented strategies. The dictionary also makes it easier for the teacher to ascertain whether there are new actions, objects, attributes, persons, places or ideas for which the individual may need manual signs or graphic symbols. The teacher may organize the vocabulary in Excel or another program with semantic or linguistic category markers (agent, action, object, attribute and so on), which help to get an overview of the individual's vocabulary structure and whether there are too many or too few of some types of words.

The dictionary is also useful for the individual and when possible, the dictionary should be made together with the individual. It may be divided into domains or other categories that make it easy for someone who is unable to read to locate particular manual signs or graphic symbols. The dictionary will become a type of reader, which the individual can be proud of. Because the written glosses are listed together with the signs, it may also be useful when an individual who communicates mainly with manual signs needs to communicate with people who do not know manual signs (see p. 28).

From graphic symbols to orthographic script

For most children, reading and writing are academic and leisure skills. They learn to read and write at school and written language is a key element in most of the school's activities. For children without intelligible speech who use graphic communication, orthographic writing represents the highest level of competence. With spelling, many of the problems related to vocabulary growth are solved. Writing may fill a broad range of communicative functions, in education and entertainment as well as in face-to-face conversations. Hence, the teaching of reading and writing should always be part of AAC intervention as long as there is even a small chance that the individual will acquire functional reading skills.

Today, general reading and writing instruction focuses on the ability to identify and blend speech sounds (phonological awareness), the relationships between letters and sounds, word meaning, reading comprehension and reading fluency (Arciuli & Bailey, 2021). Ordinary reading and writing instruction has often yielded limited results for individuals using AAC, because they struggle with one or more of these or other related skills (Stauter et al., 2017). Functional reading and writing skills are rarely achieved by individuals in the alternative language group. Some individuals in the supportive language group have difficulties acquiring these skills (Smith, 2005a) and many severely motor-impaired individuals in the expressive language group with large expressive vocabularies of graphic symbols systems acquire literacy slowly. Reading and writing skills may be achieved as late as in the teenage years and some stop at an early stage and never achieve functional literacy (Dahlgren Sandberg, 2006; Dahlgren Sandberg et al., 2010; McNaughton, 2003). However, there is considerable variation: there are also children who learn to learn read and write with ease in spite of their limited speech, and some children develop reading and writing when this is not expected (Ferreira et al., 2007).

The use of graphic communication systems may facilitate the understanding that print conveys meaning, but, to a lesser extent, that words are built up of letters (Bishop et al., 1994; Rankin et al., 1994). The mere presence of a written word above or under the image in the graphic symbol is not sufficient for an individual to learn to read (Blischak & McDaniel, 1995), as illustrated in this example.

> Rudi and the special teacher were glueing cards with Bliss-words and written words on the doors of the school. Rudi was shown the correct Bliss-word on a list and had to find the corresponding Bliss-word card. He did this correctly even with complex Bliss-words and Bliss-words he had not yet learned. Suddenly, he chose *SCHULHOF* (school yard) instead of *SCHAUKEL* (swing). He was prompted to change his choice but was very confident that he was right, pointing at the word printed at the card. Both words began with Sch and Rudi had paid attention only to these initial letters, revealing that he was in a very early stage of reading (Gangkofer & von Tetzchner, 1996).

Thus, the transition from graphic symbols to orthographic script does not usually happen automatically, written language needs explicit teaching (Stadskleiv, 2020).

The large differences in literacy development indicate a need for varied and creative instructional strategies. Oral language development is usually considered a basis for learning to read (Lawrence & Snow, 2011; Suggate et al., 2018). Research has demonstrated a close relationship between problems with articulation and reading and writing disorders (Liberman, 1999; Snowling & Hulme, 2021). However, a connection between impaired articulation and reading and writing disorders does not mean that such disorders must always appear in the absence of speech, only that poor articulation skills make individuals vulnerable to such disorders. It is not known what distinguishes AAC users who learn to read from the ones who struggle more, but individual abilities may influence the acquisition of reading and writing in different ways.

Children with motor impairments may experiences other challenges than children with autism spectrum disorder. The methods used to teach literacy are also of importance (Barker et al., 2012; Sevcik et al., 2019; Yorke et al., 2021).

Older autistic individuals with limited speech may benefit from adapted instruction of letter-sound correspondences, although information about progress into further reading is lacking (Caron et al., 2023). The teacher may guide the individual to indicate the letters corresponding to the sounds the teacher says and engage him or her in small conversations where he or she spells simple and gradually longer words in contexts that are meaningful to the individual. Individuals with good fine motor skills may use both print letters and the manual alphabet (see p. 24). Because the manual alphabet is always available to the individual, it may become functional in everyday situations and provide increased opportunities for using spelling for communication.

Children with little or no speech typically need assistance to develop *phonological awareness* and *graphemic awareness* (Dessemontet et al., 2019; von Tetzchner et al., 1997). Phonological awareness may be promoted through rhyme and other forms of sound play, but these activities are not readily available to children without speech (Ferreira et al., 2007). However, access to a computer with synthetic speech output in preschool may give them the opportunity to learn to vocalize and blend sounds before reading instruction is initiated. By activating the keys on a physical or digital keyboard, the children can "babble" with synthetic speech, play with the sounds and incidentally or intentionally produce some words. It is the beginning of learning phoneme-grapheme correspondences, even if the children have not yet started formal letter instruction. Note that the aim is that children explore the sounds elicited by individual letters and letter sequences on their own; copying should not have a strong role.

An extension of this approach may be an alternative to ordinary reading instruction for children with little or no speech (Elbro et al., 1996; McCarthy et al., 2015). Instead of teaching reading first, the children start with writing. The computer pronounces with synthetic speech the letter sequences that the child writes (whether they are real words or not). The computer thus performs what the children with unintelligible or no speech find most difficult – sound blending, that is, pulling together sequences of sounds corresponding to letters and articulating words. Children with reading and writing disorders do not usually have problems recognizing spoken words. They may learn to write because the feedback from the computer's speech output forms a basis for correcting spelling mistakes and ascertaining the correct spelling. This technology may be combined with programs that check spelling so that English words like *near* and *build* are not written n-e-r and b-i-l-d, although in casual conversations, being understood by the partner is more important than correct spelling. The computer or electronic communication device should be available at all times so that the children can practise using words and making narratives on their own in a comparable way to children who develop natural speech (see Nelson, 2015).

Studies indicate that such an approach may yield positive results for both children using AAC and speaking children with reading disorders (Grunér et al., 2018; McCarthy et al., 2015; Schlosser & Blischak, 2001). It may, in fact, be the most efficient means to prevent disorders of reading and writing in children with little or no speech. In the 1980s, electronic communication devices were less common than today. However, most of the severely speech and motor-impaired children in Sweden, who at that time could read and write well, had access to computers with synthetic speech while learning to read (Hjelmquist et al., 1994). *Predictive systems* (see p. 53), both alone and in combination with synthetic speech, are useful tools for children with difficulties learning to read (Newell et al., 1991; von Tetzchner et al., 1997). Young people with fine motor impairments find that prediction increases their spelling speed (Atterström et al., 2023).

Early reading instruction for individuals with limited speech often spends much time on teaching sight words (Mandak et al., 2018; Ruppar et al., 2011). For children with little or no speech, starting with writing rather than with sight words or other forms of reading without spelling, emphasizes that for them written language is a means for communicative expression.

The potential of spelling for face-to-face communication is a strong incitement for individuals using AAC to learn to write. In some children, the acquisition of reading and writing skills begins to accelerate when they become aware how they can use letters to solve communication "problems". For example, Sander really started to focus on reading when he discovered that he could use the letters to clarify meaning. From the start, instead of drilling Sander in spelling, the teacher showed him how he could use letters to supplement Bliss-words and express more meanings than with his Bliss-words alone. Sander soon used letters to distinguish between colours using the Bliss-word *COLOUR* together with r for "red", b for "blue", y for "yellow", and so on. The dialogue below illustrates how Sander (S) used letters when he was 12 years old. He was communicating with the teacher (T) about a class trip and the teacher interpreted his utterances (Brekke, 2001).

S: TRIP CLASS PLACE+a *FAMILY*+y.
T: Class trip to Akavik.
S: WE PAST-TIME DRIVE CAR+t
T: We drove taxi.
S: I AND TEACHER PAST-TIME JOURNEY BOAT.
T: I and the teacher travelled by boat.
S: I SIT c-o-s-y+*ONE.*
T: I sat in the cosy bag ("bean bag").
S: EAT+s *DRINK*+a-o-a *AND* w-t.
T: We ate sausages and drank Coca Cola and water.

The literacy education was based on Sander's language competence with graphic symbols, similar to "talk-based reading instruction". However, in this context, the "talk" was use of graphic symbols (Schulerud, 2002). For young aided communicators, the acquisition of literacy skills may thus both build on and be a continuation of their communication with the graphic symbols.

Letters may be used in different ways to moderate the meaning of graphic symbols (see Chapter 1). In Blissymbolics and Widgit Symbols, letters are part of the system. The Widgit system contains several useful strategies that are intended to support the acquisition of orthographic writing (see p. 19). For example, a Blissymbolics user may indicate *PET*+c to say "cat", and a Widgit user may indicate s+ON to say "son". Strategic Bliss-characters based on correspondence with speech sounds may support the development of phonological awareness and Blissymbolics may also be used in other ways to support the development of literacy (Ottem, 2001). These orthographic strategies do not require the use of Blissymbolics or the Widgit system but can be applied with other graphic communication systems. However, there is a need for developing procedures and training strategies for the transition from graphic systems to orthographic script (Sevcik et al., 2022; Yorke et al., 2021). Because it often takes a long time before aided communicators who are learning to read master spelling well enough to rely on spelling only, there will be an extended period where they integrate graphic symbols and letters.

Even if individuals are able to use orthographic script as their main form of communication, with the freedom of expression this implies, it is still necessary to apply those strategies that are best suited to the communication form they use. For individuals with severe motor disabilities it is sometimes faster to select a graphic symbol than to spell. In this case, it is not the short words that take little time to spell that need to be represented with graphic symbols, but rather symbols with long glosses that are used relatively often. For many aided communicators, a blend of graphic symbols, letters and words may constitute the fastest and most precise language use for a period. The individual's use of letters may also help communication partners infer the meaning of his or her utterances and partners my support and encourage this blended strategy.

In spite of their problems learning to read and write, many of the children using AAC spend less time than their peers with actual reading instruction in the classroom (Doneski-Nicol & Bartz, 2018). They have fewer literacy experiences, such as being read to and discussing the text with the parents, and are given a less active role in such activities (Dahlgren Sandberg, 1996; McNaughton, 1998). However, such differences have not been found to distinguish good and poor readers among children with limited speech. Although it is important to increase the literacy experiences of children in this group, it is rather more fundamental problems with the processing of written text that inhibit their development of reading and writing skills and need to be overcome (von Tetzchner, 2010).

Lastly, the teaching of reading and writing is often initiated late and many children with severe disabilities have limited independent access to books and magazines. For children who do not learn to read or whose progress is very slow, it is crucial that they get access to information in other ways than through reading and have the necessary means to express and discuss the knowledge they gain in school, so that they are not unnecessarily hindered in knowledge development and academic achievement. Many textbooks and other books are available in audio versions, and text-to-speech computer programs can present text in synthetic speech. Many literacy activities – such as text messaging and electronic mail – may be performed with graphic symbols (see p. 42).

Chapter 9

Sentence formation with manual signs or graphic symbols

This chapter presents the foundations of sentence formation and strategies for promoting the use of utterances with two or more manual signs or graphic symbols. The transition from single words, signs or symbols to sentences makes children's language more efficient and is an important milestone in both typical and atypical language development. Most children with typical development start to make utterances with two or more words in the second half of their second year of life (Bates et al., 1995). This means that making sentences is not a very advanced skill and that children using manual signs or graphic symbols should be encouraged to construct sentences at an early stage, in line with their intellectual abilities.

The function of sentences is to express relations between two or more language elements within a particular communicative context. The message *Daddy car* is qualitatively different from *Daddy* and *car* produced separately – which may or may not be related in some way. *Daddy car* expresses a definite relation between "Daddy" and "car", although the nature of the relation may vary according to the context. The individual may intend to express that daddy owns a car, stands by a car, will be coming or going in a car, sits in a car, likes cars and so on. Sentences thus usually comprise more precise statements than individual words and reflect more elements of the shared focus of the communication partners.

Sentences are needed to get beyond simple requests and communication about the here and now. Utterances with two or more elements can specify persons, objects, actions, ideas and attributes, relate events in the past and the future, express more varied content and expand expressive possibilities, semantically and pragmatically. Sentence comprehension and production require a shared way of indicating the relationship between the elements in the sentence. In the development of spoken language, relations between sentence elements are indicated by word order, inflections and grammatical words.

Even children's early utterances with one or two words express a variety of relational content (Table 9.1). In fact, many of the early one-word utterances are holophrases in the sense that they represent an intention that adults would use more words to express (Barrett, 1982). *Mommy* may mean "mommy, come here" or "mommy, don't do that," and *ball* may mean "give me the ball" or "where is the ball?" Adults typically infer the children's intentions from situational cues. The transition from utterances with one word to utterances with two and more words tends to happen gradually. The child must have a sufficient vocabulary and good enough cognitive and productive control to plan and articulate two or more words within the same intonation frame (Herr-Israel & McCune, 2011; Peters, 1995). There are large individual differences with regard to when this happens. Some children use syntactic constructions at 15 months of age, others are two years old before they start to use sentences, and a few are even older (Rescorla & Schwartz, 1990; Zambrana et al., 2014). Ramer (1976) found that the time

DOI: 10.4324/9781003387633-10

Table 9.1 Typical relations in early utterances with one or two words (based on Bloom & Lahey, 1978)

1.	Existence The utterance refers to an object in the situation and the child looks or points at it, touches it, or picks it up, saying for example: *ball, there, there ball* or *that there.*
2.	Non-existence Some object does not exist in context, or the child does not see it, but there is some reason to expect it to be there or look for it. The child may say *no* or *gone*, or the name of the object with rising intonation (like a question) and look for it.
3.	Recurrence An object – or a similar one – which has disappeared reappears, or an object similar to an existing one is brought into relation with the first object. The child may say *more, again* or *another.*
4	Disappearance Some object has been in the context and then ceases to exist. It may suddenly be hidden from view, vanish or evaporate of its own accord. Children may say *all gone, away* or *bye-bye*. A girl pointed to the sun disappearing behind a cloud and said: *Gone.*
5.	Action The utterance refers to an action where the aim of the action is not to change the location of the objects or persons. Marte looks at the sandwiches: *Taste! Eat!*
6.	Possession The utterance refers to a possessive relationship between a person and an object. John takes the ball: *Mine!!*
7.	Attribute The utterance refers to a quality or characteristic feature of an object. Marte points at the jam: *Strawberry. Red.*
8.	Negation The child denies the identity, condition or event that is expressed in another person's utterance, or in the child's own preceding utterance. Mamma offers a glass of milk to Anders asking: *Want milk?* Anders shakes his head and says: *No.*
9.	Rejection The utterance expresses that the child refuses an action or rejects an object. Mamma says: *Don't you want milk?* Anders pushes the glass away: *No.*
10.	Locative actions The utterance refers to an action that aims to change the location of persons or objects. Anders places a doll in a chair: *Sit!*

from children's first two-word utterance until 20 percent of their utterances had two words or more, varied between 1½ and 9 months. Deaf children using sign language start to use sentences around the same age as hearing children do, provided they have an appropriate signing environment (Lillo-Martin & Henner, 2021; Rinaldi & Caselli, 2009).

Children who use AAC tend to continue to use utterances with single signs or symbols for an extended period, and the partners continue to use mainly situational cues to infer the children's communicative intentions (Binger & Light, 2008; Soto & Clarke, 2017; von Tetzchner & Grove, 2003). Many individuals with autism spectrum disorder and intellectual disabilities who use AAC systems are delayed in making the transition to longer utterances and some never learn to use sentences. Children with intellectual disabilities who develop speech may also continue to use mainly one-word utterances for longer than children with typical development and have a relatively larger spoken vocabulary when they start to produce sentences (Thurman et al., 2022). Often, AAC is initiated relatively late and the developmental course of individuals using AAC may not be directly comparable to individuals with intellectual disabilities who develop spoken language. Studies show that individuals with autism spectrum disorder and intellectual disabilities can learn to understand and produce sentences with manual signs (Bonvillian & Blackburn, 1991; Grove & Dockrell, 2000; Grove, 2019a; Launonen & Grove, 2003) or graphic symbols (Finke et al., 2017; Nigam et al., 2006; Wilkinson et al., 1994). Moreover, studies indicate that the semantic relations found in the sentences of children in this latter group are comparable to those produced by younger children with typical development.

There may be several reasons why some individuals mainly use utterances with one sign or symbol. Neurological impairments may hinder the individual's acquisition of relevant cognitive and linguistic skills. However, many individuals with severe intellectual disabilities produce spoken sentences (McLean et al., 1999). Moreover, although a vocabulary below 300 words has been said to limit sentence formation in children with intellectual disabilities (Bates & Goodman, 1997), the children's pragmatic abilities, such as talking about things, themselves and others, are more predictive of their later sentence formation than vocabulary size (Foster-Cohen et al., 2021). It is not clear what distinguishes children with intellectual disabilities who use multi-sign utterances from those who use single-sign utterances only (Grove, 2019a; Grove & Dockrell, 2000).

Many children in the expressive language group with good comprehension of spoken language tend to produce short graphic sentences and many of them use mainly single symbols (Binger & Light, 2008; Soto & Clarke, 2017; von Tetzchner & Martinsen, 1996). All children need opportunities for learning to express themselves in sentences, also young motor-impaired aided communicators with good comprehension of spoken language. This may be illustrated with a six-year-old girl with comprehension of spoken language in the typical range but lacking speech. When, as part of a study, she was communicating with her father and mother, only 12 of her 114 utterances produced with PCS contained two or more symbols, one utterance contained four graphic symbols (Smith, 2003). It was not the speech impairment that hindered her development of multi-symbol utterances but rather a lack of experience with constructing sentences. If she had not been motor impaired, she would probably have been speaking in long sentences. The same could be said about the majority of children with intellectual disabilities, autism spectrum disorder and severe language disorder who use communication aids. Thus, there must be other reasons why they mainly produce one-symbol utterances. Children with motor impairments using graphic symbols, in particular, need time to select and indicate each symbol. A small aid lexicon and the interaction patterns in dialogues between natural and aided communicators will also, to some degree, determine the structure of the utterances produced by the aided communicators (Jagoe & Smith, 2016; Smith et al., 2018).

The early vocabulary of children using AAC may function quite well for communicating about the here and now, but not so well for producing sentences. To promote the development of sentences, interventionists need to provide individuals with the manual signs or graphic symbols they need for constructing sentences (see Chapter 8), to teach them strategies that are useful for sentence construction and to engage them in activities that may elicit longer utterances (see Chapter 10). For younger children, symbolic play is a fertile activity for language development (Creaghe et al., 2021) and various forms of play have been utilized to teach sentences with graphic symbols (Binger & Light, 2008). When individuals start making longer utterances and communicate about events in the past or the future, they will need signs or symbols for objects and actions that are not usually present and that are not primarily related to themselves. They need vocabulary denoting attributes such as LARGE, FAST, WET and RED, spatial relations such as ON, IN, ABOVE and UNDER and temporal terms such as FIRST, THEN, TOMORROW and YESTERDAY. People are central agents in the social environment and person names are therefore an important part of the individual's vocabulary. The teacher's selection of signs or symbols belonging to different categories may, to some extent, depend on the sentence types the individual is learning. However, even when the individual has a relatively advanced linguistic competence, the teacher should select the manual signs or graphic symbols that are thought to contribute most to improving the individual's communication opportunities, social function and overall situation.

In addition to direct teaching, people in the environment using the child's mode of communication are the main source of information about sentence construction. However, people who use keyword signing seldom use two (or more) syntactically connected signs together with speech (Grove, 2019a; Grove et al., 1996; Rombouts et al., 2019). Communication partners have mainly used graphic symbols simultaneously with speech during teaching sessions (Drager, 2009; Romski & Sevcik, 1996) but more recently aided language modelling or aided language stimulation where partners indicate keyword graphic symbols when speaking have become more common (Douglas et al., 2023; Jonsson et al., 2011; Sennott et al., 2016). However, to support sentence construction, it is important that people in the environment expand their keywords to "keyword sentences" in their everyday interaction with individuals who are using manual signs or graphic symbols (see Chapter 12).

AAC intervention should guide the child to construct sentences with a variety of meanings. To achieve an optimal competence, the individual needs help from adults in developing sentence structure. From a usage-based perspective on language development, children's own constructions also constitute a basis for their sentence development (Tomasello, 2009a). Individuals who use AAC are also creative, and teachers should support the communicative creativity of the individuals.

Strategies for supporting sentences with signs or symbols

The main aim in teaching sentences with manual signs or graphic symbols is to make individuals aware of the meaning of each manual sign or graphic symbol and how they influence the meaning expressed with the sentence. They need answers to questions like those below.

- How does the meaning of a sentence change when a particular manual sign or graphic symbol is added?
- How does the meaning of the sentence change when a sign or symbol is removed from the sentence?
- How does the meaning of the sentence change when a sign or symbol is replaced with another?
- Which signs or symbols can take the same position in the sentence?
- Which sign or symbol should be added in order to express a particular meaning or change a meaning in a particular way?
- How can signs and symbols be modified to change the meanings?

Intervention should seek to guide the individuals to answers to these questions, and the teachers to try to teach sentence formation and use in different ways. Their strategies and the individuals' sentence learning are based on observed consistency and variation in sequences of signs or symbols in communicative interactions, and the related contrasts and similarities in meaning. The same information will support comprehension of sentences with manual signs or graphic symbols.

Pivot strategies

In the early stages of typical language development, certain words are used more frequently than others and these are often combined with other words. The words of this class have been termed "pivots" (Braine & Bowerman, 1976). Within child language research, pivots have received special attention because their relatively fixed position has been seen as an emerging sensitivity to word order and the beginning of sentence structure or syntax.

- In *Gone milk, Gone dog* and *Gone cake, gone* is a pivot.
- In *Me down, Doll down* and *Shoe down, down* is a pivot.

Pivots do not have a general fixed position, but a pivot tends to be used in the same position by the individual child. Some appear always at the front, others at the end of the utterances of a particular child. Some children may use a word as a pivot at the beginning, others may use the same word as a pivot at the end of the sentence. In addition, there are many early two-word utterances with combinations of non-pivot words, and pivots are also sometimes combined (Tomasello, 2006).

Some manual signs and graphic symbols are better suited to form sentences than others on the basis of their referents and relevance in the individual's environment (see Chapter 8). These may be selected as pivots in sentence construction based on a pivot intervention strategy. They may help the individual both to acquire new signs or symbols, and to combine signs or symbols to form sentences.

Pivots may, for example, be introduced in play in the form of action signs or symbols that can be combined with several objects, such as EAT APPLE, EAT BANANA and EAT BREAD, or object signs that can be used with a variety of action signs, such as SEE BALL, GET BALL, THROW BALL, ROLL BALL and KICK BALL. Signs and symbols like FINISH, GET, GONE, HAVE and GIVE may also be suitable as pivots: FINISH WORK, FINISH JUMP, BALL GONE and BALL GIVE. CARRY and SIT can be combined with many objects names: CARRY MILK, CARRY SACK, SIT CHAIR and SIT FLOOR. Wilkinson and associates (1994) identified *WANT, PLEASE, MORE, THROUGH, HELP, YES* and *NO* as pivots, but these were not used in a fixed position by each child, and hence did not have the fixed distribution that gives the syntactic quality to pivots.

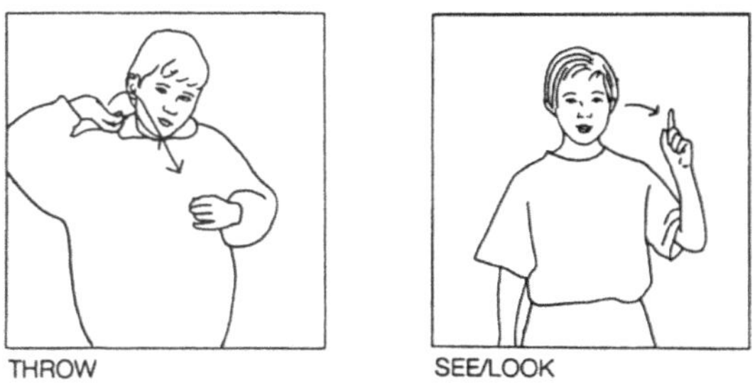

Manual signs: THROW, SEE

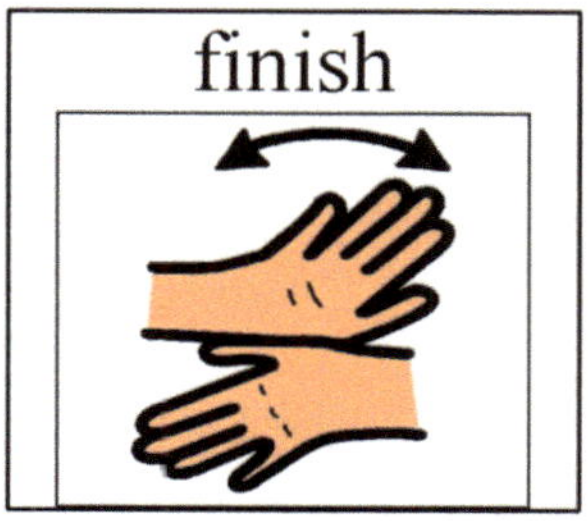

PCS: FINISH, CARRY

Pivot-oriented intervention thus has two main aspects. First, it implies a priority for signs and symbols that may be easy to combine with other parts of the child's expressive vocabulary, including deictic gestures. Pointing to an object or location is common in early speech development (Goldin-Meadow & Alibali, 2013) and may also be used together with manual signs or graphic symbols. Pointing and CAR may express "there car", "that car" or "give car". Shaking the head and CAR may mean "no car". Second, when selecting new manual signs or graphic symbols, those which can be combined with the child's pivots may be given some priority. It should be noted, however, that the pivot-oriented vocabulary selection strategy implies only that awareness of the pivotal function influences the choice of signs and symbols. Whether a particular sign or symbol will function as a pivot will depend on the child's actual use of it. It is sometimes useful to combine lexical items outside the pivot class. Pivot selections may help individuals organize their expressive language but if they do not appear to understand the function of the sign or symbol order, this may wait until later. The primary aim is to guide the individual to construct utterances with more than one manual sign or graphic symbol.

Formulas

Children are creative language users. In early typical language development, children reuse sentence constructions that have worked for them in the past when solving communicative challenges. These constructions thus function as formulas or frames for expressing similar meanings (Theakston & Lieven, 2017; Tomasello, 2006). Because children using AAC tend to have a relatively small language repertoire they may utilize the same utterance patterns in different situations. Learning I GET APPLE and I GET BOOK to request an apple or book may lead to the development of the formula I GET X, where X can be APPLE, JUICE, BOOK, BALL and so on. Other common early formulas are WHERE X, LOOK X and WE X. The formula X DO may be used to specify the person who should do something. X Y may be a formula where both the person and the action to be performed are open. When people in the environment make the same sentence structures with keyword manual signs or graphic symbols, this supports the individual's learning of the formulas.

Formulas are useful in the early phases of language development but if the individuals have only a limited number of formulas, their expressive communication would become rather stereotypical. Individuals should therefore be exposed to a variety of sentence constructions and experience how they *contrast* in meaning, and why sentence construction A is chosen

Widgit: WHERE, GET

rather than sentence construction B in certain situations. Formulas make it possible to exploit previously established sentence structures while the principle of contrast encourages the use of new grammatical constructions. Teachers (and other adults) should seek to make explicit to individuals using AAC how the sentence meaning changes when the formula and individual manual signs or graphic symbols are changed. They should also be guided to expand the formulas – in line with the questions on p. 277.

Semantic roles

The sentences produced with manual signs or graphic symbols may not always follow the grammar of the spoken language around the individual. To support sentence construction with manual signs or graphic symbols, interventionists may instead use other tools for analysing the sentences. Semantic roles (also called thematic roles) have been used to analyse early child language and may also be useful when analysing and supporting the early language of individuals using AAC (Tönsing, 2016).

Semantics is about the meaning of words and sentences (Chandler, 2002). Action words (verbs) have a prominent place in analyses of sentence meaning. The semantic roles indicate the relations the other words have to the main verb in the sentence. Semantic roles are thus about who acts, on what, with whom, where and so on. The roles emphasize the importance of selecting manual signs and graphic symbols that represent actions to support the individual's sentence construction. Table 9.2 defines the most common semantic roles and shows examples of semantic roles typically found in children's early utterances with 2–3 words. Note that many of these early utterances are describing events rather than requesting things.

The early sentences of children with typical development consist mainly of content words without inflections, like: *Doll sit, Sit chair, There Teddy, Teddy gone* and *Cat eat*. The sentences comprise a small number of semantic roles, typically Agent and Entity, and reflect the child's attentional focus and interpretation of the situation. However, when people in the environment interpret utterances of young aided communicators, they tend to assume that the aided communicator is the Agent. They expect less communication about other people's actions, although these actions are often most prominent in the environment. When the Agent is implied in this way, it is difficult to make the individual aware of the possibility of making somebody else the Agent in the utterance, for example, asking a peer or an adult to do something: JOHN THROW, MARY SING.

Table 9.2 Semantic roles that are common in early children's utterances with 2–3 words

Agent:	The one who performs the action
Action:	The action
Patient:	Whom or what something happens to
Location:	Where the action takes place or something is moved to or from
Possessor:	The one that owns something
Possession:	What is owned
Entity:	Object or person with separate existence
Attribute:	Characteristic of the entity
Demonstrator:	Pointing or indicating something
Agent + Action	*Baby cries*
Action + Patient	*Pulls wagon*
Agent + Patient	*Baby food*
Action + Location	*Sit chair*
Entity + Location	*Chair basement*
Possessor + Possession	*Mama glasses*
Entity + attribute	*Big tree*
Demonstrator + Entity	*There apple*
Agent + Location + Time	*I school today*
Agent + Action + Patient	*Doggie eat food*
Agent + Action + Location	*Man sits car*
Action + Attribute + Entity	*Cut big flower*
Demonstrator + Possession + Possessor	*There scissors Mama*

ARASAAC: SING, THROW

The semantic role of each manual sign or graphic symbol in a sentence is based on the function it has in the particular communicative context. It is therefore an important part of strategies based on semantic roles that the individual gets several lexical items that can fill each of the semantic roles. Studies show that individuals with autism spectrum disorder and intellectual disabilities can produce early sentences using AAC (Table 9.3).

In early intervention with aided communication it is common to have the child in photographs intended to represent activities, objects or situations. That makes it difficult to

Table 9.3 Sentences with manual signs and graphic symbols reported as used by children with autism spectrum disorder and intellectual disabilities

Manual signs

Lisa, three years, Down syndrome
CAR DRIVE FAST
DANGER PLAY ROAD
HURT *Lisa* CAR UNDER

Eric, five years, Down syndrome
MAN PLAY-ICE-HOCKEY
DOG ANGRY BARK YOU I AFRAID
CHOCOLATE DELICIOUS BUY SHOP
BOOKS BOOKS BOOKS BOOK "lots of books"

Ted, six-and-a-half years, autism spectrum disorder
DADDY EAT
GO SCHOOL
MOTHER CAR
FATHER HAIRCUT
EAT CAKE
MORE CAKE
NO FOOD
NO GO

Boy, school age, autism spectrum disorder
NO MOTHER CAR PLAY SCHOOL

Boy, school age, autism spectrum disorder
PAPER HEAD (request to play peekaboo) (the only two-sign utterance in nine months)

Eric, 12 years, Down syndrome
WANT I SWEET WANT BAR CHOCOLATE
PLAY-GUITAR I WANT GUITAR ELECTRICITY (topic comment structure)

Ana, 13 years, Down syndrome
BREAD CAKE SWEET PICK-UP DRINK PICK-UP

Asha, 14 years, intellectual disability
SLEEP GET UP BROTHER
GOOD FILM THAT FILM GOOD

Yayesh, 16 years, Down syndrome
WALK REACH CUDDLE HOT

Graphic symbols

Yvette, five years, motor and intellectual disabilities
TROUSERS PULLOVER "doll" (looks at doll)

Magda, seven years, motor and intellectual disabilities
CASETTE-PLAYER STORYBOOK
SHOWER WASH HAIR COMB

Alex, ten years, intellectual disability
ALEX SWIM BUS DRIVE ALEX SHIT! BROKEN DOWN BUS

(from Basil & Soro-Camats, 1996; Bonvillian & Blackburn 1991; Fulwiler & Fouts, 1976: Gangkofer & von Tetzchner, 1996; Grove 2019a; Heim & Baker-Mills, 1996; Launonen, 2003, 2019a; Launonen & Grove, 2003; Wilkinson et al., 1994) differentiate the Agent from the semantic information the photograph is intended to relay. The meaning may be interpreted as "child swing" instead of "swing", or "child drink" instead of "drink". Without being aware of it, the adults may promote the child's learning of the formula "child X" instead of "(Semantic) Agent X". In order to avoid this problem and make children more aware of the Agent role in their utterances, one should rather introduce a separate photograph of the child (Agent) together with one or more photographs or graphic symbols that may represent Action, Entity or other semantic roles. In line with this, the use of graphic symbols like *I-WANT* and *I-SEE* – which are central, for example, in the approach of the Picture Exchange Communication System (Bondy & Frost, 2002) – is not recommended (see also p. 84).

A semantic role strategy was applied when teaching the use of graphic symbols to "Robert", a four-year-old boy with autism spectrum disorder (von Tetzchner, 2019b). His communication book contained about 100 graphic symbols and photographs. They had Velcro on the back and the book had a fold-out "conversation page" where both he and his communication partners placed the graphic symbols (see Figure 2.3, p. 38).

At the beginning of the intervention, a photograph of the boy was always placed at the beginning of the graphic utterances, making him the Agent. However, the photograph of the boy would not really function as a semantic Agent until he could choose different Agents according to the communicative intent and context. As part of the teaching, a photograph of Robert (representing his name) was from time to time replaced with the photograph of another person, to signal a change of Agent and make Robert aware of the semantic function of the person photographs. For example, in order to make him aware that he could ask a particular person for help, Robert was given interesting toys that he had not yet fully learned to use on his own. Robert liked to play with Flip-flop – a "pipe" for blowing a ping-pong ball into the air – but was unable to blow the ball into the air himself. Kari, the teacher, used this to introduce *KARI* (photograph of herself) as Agent instead of *ROBERT*.

> Robert placed *FLIP-FLOP* after *ROBERT* which, as usual, was in the first position on the conversation page of the communication book. The teacher placed the ping-pong ball on the pipe and put it into Robert's mouth. He tried to blow, not very successfully, and pushed the hand with the pipe back toward the teacher. She replaced *ROBERT* with *KARI* saying: *Kari will blow*. She started to blow into the pipe, making the ball dance in the air above it. She then changed the names (photographs) again and gave the pipe to Robert.

One of the first clear indications that Robert had understood the semantic role of the Agent in the utterances appeared in the situation below.

> Robert took out *ACTIVITY-BOARD* and placed it to the right of *KARI*, which happened to have been left on the conversation page. Kari started to play with the activity board. Robert watched for some time, looking puzzled but smiling. He then took away *KARI* and placed *ROBERT* on the conversation page. Kari answered by putting *NO* (a red card with a black cross) on top of ROBERT. She then put *ROBERT* into the book again and *KARI* back on the conversation page and continued playing with the activity board for a while. Robert then took *ACTIVITY-BOARD* away and replaced it with *BARREL*, another toy he liked very much but was unable to operate himself. Kari showed great enthusiasm, made a lot of noise, and opened and closed the barrel. Robert watched, laughing and smiling.

The use of person photographs to indicate Agent before Action or other semantic roles may be used as part of the intervention from the start, also when an individual has not yet understood their function. Robert in the example above was unable to make sentences when his communication book was introduced. Because the person photographs were always there, he used symbol sentences *before* he had learned to construct sentences by himself. It represented a form of "talking to learn" which is an integral part of language acquisition in children with typical development (Bruner, 1983; Wells, 2009). They begin to use sentences they hear and adjust the meanings they attribute to them in accordance with the answers they elicit from their communication partners.

In Robert's utterances, the photograph of himself or another person was usually placed as semantic Agent in the first position on the conversation page, while the sequence of the other photographs and graphic symbols varied. Sometimes Robert just placed them in the order in which he found them when going through his communication book. Robert would sometimes take two person photographs from the same page of his communication book, place them next to each other on the conversation page, search for an action symbol and place it next to them, for example, *OLAV KARI EAT*. This shows that he had planned a relational utterance but did not yet use a fixed symbol order. The vocabulary items Robert selected spontaneously gave the teacher insights into his thinking and helped her guide his grammatical development.

A variety of strategies may be used to help children produce manual and graphic sentences with different semantic roles and of varied complexity (Bruno & Trembath, 2006; Rudd et al., 2007; Tönsing et al., 2014). Interactions with several persons at the same time is a useful way to teach Agent in natural settings, such as circle time. This makes it necessary to communicate about actions that can be performed by different persons, with several objects and in several ways, for example, SAM JUMP, TEACHER JUMP, SAM SLIDE and OLAV SLIDE. Such descriptions with manual signs and graphic symbols may be used both during an activity and when communicating about the activity and making narratives afterwards (see Chapter 11).

Verb constructions

The introduction of verbs is central in teaching sentence construction with manual signs and graphic symbols. Verbs constitute an anchor for the relational meanings of semantic roles and the acquisition of verbs is essential and has a cascading effect in the development of grammar (Ellis & Ogden, 2017; Horvath & Arunachalam, 2019). Action verbs are the organising element for expressing intention and represent an early conceptual frame for sentence construction because there is implicitly someone performing the action and somebody or something that is the recipient of the action (Tomasello, 1992, 2003). Verbs also express static states, such *to be* in the car or *to feel* happy. Making the implicit elements explicit affords the extension of verbs with other elements and the construction of sentences. For example, the verb *to kick* implies that someone is kicking and that something is being kicked, for example, a boy kicking a ball. As utterances get longer, more implicit elements become explicit, like in *The boy kicks the red ball through the neighbour's bedroom window*.

In the early phases of language development, children's action words may not reflect a linguistic understanding of verbs. According to Tomasello (2003), they are "verb islands", conceptual constructs based on isolated action words with a basis in specific activities. The verbs are "islands" of intentional actions, and the child learns to relate these actions to specific people, locations and objects. Thus, *draw* in *Pencil draw* is not the linguistic word class verb, but the expression of an action, or intention, that goes with "people who draw" and "objects to draw with", as well as colours and paper. Similarly, *Feel happy* implies that there is a feeling

	DOG	GIRL	MAN	BIRD	WHALE
CRY					
SWIM					
LAUGH					
FALL					
SLEEP					
FLY					

Figure 9.1 Example of matrix for combining graphic symbols representing Agents and Actions.

state and that somebody is feeling. What kind of sentences children construct will depend on the verbs they know and the actions and states they are trying to express. This emphasizes the importance of providing individuals developing AAC with a variety of verbs and related vocabulary (Savaldi-Harussi & Soto, 2018), and of creating activities where the verbs can be used (see Chapter 10). As the individual acquires more verb island constructs, these become reorganised into more abstract sentence constructions. Verb island constructs are both an experiential foundation and models for the individual's later sentence constructions.

Tomasello thus relates language learning to the performance – or imagined performance – of actions and activities. One important implication of the theory is that in order to promote the individual's use of sentences with several manual signs or graphic symbols, intervention should attempt to increase children's communication in situations where intentions can be expressed with verbs that may be combined with signs and symbols referring to nouns that are contextually related to these verbs. This may include a *matrix strategy* where signs or symbols representing a set of actions are combined, for example, with signs or symbols representing a set of objects (Nigam et al., 2006). Tönsing (2012) used vocabulary based on semantic roles in matrix training, such as *CRY, LAUGH* and *FALL, GIRL'S* and *BUNNY'S, NOSE, TUMMY, PANTS, CAR* and *TEDDY*, and *DIRTY* and *BROKEN*. The matrix may also be used to show contrasts, and signs or symbols that go together and do not go together (Figure 9.1). It should be emphasized that combinations of the sign or symbol sets selected in matrix training should also be useful in conversations during the individual's play or other activities of daily life, such as sentences with cartoon figures or toy animals as Agents and FALL, BITE, SPLASH, STRETCH and TICKLE as Actions (Gevarter et al., 2023a). Utterances with Actions like DRAW, PUSH and WASH and Entities like BALL, CUP and CAP may also be integrated into play.

Manual signs: DRAW, PUSH

PCS: FALL

Understanding the extension of actions referred to is more difficult for individuals in the early phases of language development than reference to objects. Utterances with familiar objects may be useful contexts for verb teaching and learning in both typical and atypical language development (Horvath & Arunachalam, 2019). Early vocabularies of graphic symbols tend to contain more objects than actions and the familiar symbols referring to objects may facilitate learning of verbs. Rather than focusing on graphic symbols in isolation, interventionists should present symbols for actions, states, persons, places, objects and so forth, in varied sentences and within diverse situations.

Sign or symbol order

Word order is a common way in many – but not all – languages to mark the relationship between the words in a sentence. *John gives the key to Mary* describes a different event than *Mary gives the key to John.*

Studies have shown that many individuals with intellectual disabilities who develop alternative means of communication produce manual sign or graphic symbol sentences with different orders. Grove and Dockrell (2000) found that children with intellectual disabilities who produced utterances with two or more manual signs, generally had subject before verb but that the sequences were less consistent with objects and verbs. In some of their sentences, the verb came before the object, in other sentences the object came before the verb. When teaching graphic sentences, teachers tend to place the symbol for the person doing the action first and the symbol for the person who is the receiver of the action last, like *JOHN GIVE APPLE MARY*. However, there are different ways to use symbol order and the actual symbol orders used by children and adults vary (Binger et al., 2017a, b; Sutton et al., 2004). Most teachers try to promote sequences that are similar to spoken sentences in the environment, but the word order of spoken language is not always appropriate when producing graphic sentences (von Tetzchner, 2021b).

Some individuals have difficulties understanding why one order is better than another in the situation but may still construct utterances with two and more signs or symbols (Rudd et al., 2007). Even if a fixed sentence structure may be practical and help the understanding of the communication partners, individuals who do not use a fixed order should still be encouraged to construct utterances with more than one sign or symbol. The teacher might work on sign or symbol order in teaching sessions by contrasting the meaning of different word orders. In training sessions, the teacher and the individual may have fun trying to act out MOUSE CATCH CAT and CAT CATCH MOUSE, TEACHER ASK STUDENT

QUESTION and STUDENT ASK TEACHER QUESTION, or the somewhat surrealistic MOUSE EAT CHEESE and CHEESE EAT MOUSE. However, the teacher should not correct the individual's sentences at all times. It is more important that the individual learns to combine manual signs or graphic symbols into more complex meanings than that they are produced in a fixed order. Many factors may determine the sequence of manual signs or graphic symbols produced by individuals in real communication situations. Also, children in the expressive group with good comprehension of spoken language – including grammar – may show considerable variation in sign or symbol order. For this group, the significance of word order will be part of their explicit school education.

ARASAAC: MOUSE, CAT, CATCH

Horizontal and vertical structures

When children with typical development are just starting to use sentences, they produce one-word utterances which follow each other and are related to the same event, like in this example from Bloom (1973). Allison (one-and-a-half years) hands her father a peach and a spoon.

Daddy.
Peach.
Cut.

The intended meaning may be something like "Daddy, can you cut the peach". Successive one-word utterances differ from "true" multi-word utterances in that they are not expressed within the same sentence contour. Scollon (1976) describes the relations between words in such sequences as *vertical structures*. When making the utterances below, Brenda, one year and seven months, holds a shoe up to Scollon.

mama
mama
mam
s
sis
su?
sus

Brenda's vertically structured utterance may be interpreted as: "This is Mama's shoe". The many repetitions probably reflect the great effort Brenda put into the production of this meaning. A similar utterance with *horizontal structure* may have been *Mama shoe*. In sentences with vertical structures, the words are separated from each other in time, and sometimes also by utterances from the conversation partner which are unrelated in meaning. However, if the individual speaks slowly due to dysarthria, the utterance will still be perceived as horizontal.

In typical development, the relational use of words interspersed with pauses, that is, of successive utterances in vertical structures, represents a transitional stage between one-word and two-word utterances. Utterances with vertical structures are important developmentally because they demonstrate that children may relate words meaningfully to each other before they have learned to express them within the same sentence intonation. When children are young, adults often say something in between children's single-word utterances. Scollon shows that a child's utterances may be related thematically even if the utterances inserted by the adult are not.

Vertical structures may be observed in children who produce manual signs with pauses between signs, but producing longer utterances is particularly difficult for young aided communicators with severe fine motor impairments. Utterances produced by children using communication aids often have a vertical structure, with a relatively long time between the graphic symbols in the utterances. The utterances are often interspersed with the partner's interpretation, as in this example where six-year-old Yvette and her mother are playing with dolls (Smith, 2003).

Y: *TROUSERS* (waiting for feedback).
M: *Trousers.*
Y: *SWEATER* (waiting for feedback).
M: *Sweater.*
Y: "Doll" (looks at doll on the table).
M: *Doll.*

Yvette's utterance consisted only of nouns but still represented a relational meaning within the activity, which the mother interpreted to mean: *Put trousers and sweater on the doll.* The action "dress" or "put" was implicit.

Vertical structures reflect the co-constructive nature of children's early language, both in typical (Jacoby & Ochs, 1995) and atypical development (Brekke & von Tetzchner, 2003; Neuvonen et al., 2022c). Parents and other adults facilitate the use of relational sentence structures by helping the individual in the formation of sign or symbol sentences. Vertical structures are important from an intervention perspective because many individuals use mainly utterances with one sign or symbol and start using longer utterances very late. Utterances with vertical structures imply a possibility of relating two or more signs or symbols to each other even if they are not produced as one coherent utterance. It may sometimes be useful to guide the individual to indicate *END* when he or she has finished constructing the utterance, and for the communication partner to be sensitive to the individual's indications of sentence completion. For children using electronic devices with speech output, saying the full sentence after having produced the individual words may be one way of marking the end of the sentence.

In addition, the sequences of single-symbol utterances of young aided communicators tend to have a time-related narrative structure rather than a relational sentence structure where the utterance relates persons, objects, actions, places and so on (see Chapter 11). To promote the construction of relational sentence structures, it is important to give young aided communicators enough time and to encourage them to comment the topics they introduce.

Chaining strategies

Behaviours, actions and events may be linked to the manual signs or graphic symbols representing them through communicative chaining. Communication chains may have both a narrative-oriented (temporal) and a relation-oriented (conceptual) foundation. Narrative-oriented chains typically consist of actions that may follow each other, such as READ (then) OUT, or EAT (then) WALK, which are not really sentences. In children with intellectual disabilities, this type makes up 30–40 percent of their utterances (Grove & Dockrell, 2000). Relation-oriented chains typically comprise sentences with actions, things, attributes and places, for example, BUY APPLE or WALK FOREST. Note that these chaining strategies are about constructing sentences, not visual support (see p. 149).

Sentences may also be produced by chaining specific signs or symbols with more general ones. For instance, OUT may first be used as a signal sign or symbol to indicate that the individual is going outside (se p. 165), while SWING and WALK are taught as expressive signs or symbols. These may then be combined to inform the individual that he or she is going out for a walk or on the swing: OUT WALK or OUT SWING. Individuals may be asked to tell which of these they want to do. Later on, OUT X may be used as a formula to construct OUT SHOP, OUT VISIT and so on. Because signs or symbols with a general meaning are usually produced before specific ones, such chains may help the individual develop sentences with a topic and comment structure (see next section) and approaching a pivot structure. Chains may also be expanded beyond two signs or symbols by adding more links in the chain, for example, OUT CAR SHOP, OUT PLAY SWING or OUT VISIT GRANDMOTHER. By adding a person, the chain may further be used for communicating about other people, for example, JOHN OUT PLAY or I JOHN OUT SHOP.

One objective of using chaining to teach individuals to use sentences is that they should also be able to communicate about sequences of activities that are not taking place at the time of conversation and which include objects that are not part of the here and now. This may enable the individuals to take the initiative to ask for objects that are not present in the situation, refer to events that are not currently taking place, describe more specifically actions and activities they want to do, and give them a better grasp of what has happened and is going to happen, contributing to both increased self-determination and more coherence in the individuals' life.

Topic-comment

There are also non-grammatical ways of using sign or symbol order that may be useful. The topic-comment structure is often considered a basic language construction where the topic is the theme that one wants to communicate something about, while the comment is what one wants to say about the topic (Bambini & Torregrossa, 2010). For example, in *Ball gone, ball* is topic and *gone* comment. Presentation of the topic establishes shared attention on some aspect of the situation, from which the listener can understand the comment (von Tetzchner, 1985). In the example below, the child repeats the topic *look* (directing the mother's attention to an event he wants her to see) until the mother acknowledges the shared attentional focus, and then presents the comment *Oy* (Martinsen & von Tetzchner, 1989).

Child: *Look!*
Lock!
Mother: *Yes, look there.*
Child: *Oy* (expression of excitement).

If the child had said *Oy* without establishing the focus for joint attention first, it might have been perceived as reflecting the child's state instead of the child's evaluation or interest in an event.

A topic-comment structure thus implies that the individual first presents the topic and then comments or specifies something related to the topic. The topic may contrast sentences containing the same manual signs or graphic symbols. For example, in RED DRESS, the colour red may be the topic, and DRESS may refer to an object with that colour. In DRESS RED, dresses are the topic and red the comment, referring to the colour of a particular dress. The topic-comment construction ensures the shared attention of the communication partner, makes it easier to infer what the individual is trying to communicate and reduces the likelihood of misunderstandings. It may take time to construct a graphic sentence like *FOOTBALL BOOK*. When *FOOTBALL* is the first symbol, it functions to make the conversational partner aware that the individual is going to say something about football. The next symbol, BOOK, may lead the partner to infer that the individual has a new book about football. In the example below, Cathy (C) and the teacher (T) were looking at photographs. Cathy got very excited and produced the manual letter J and the sign FRIEND.

C: J FRIEND.
T: *You and John are friends.*
C: FINISH.
T: *Yes, John has finished school.*

When John had been established as topic, Cathy signed FINISH to indicate that that he had finished something. She could also have added SCHOOL but the teacher inferred that this was about school. If Cathy had started with FINISH, the teacher might have interpreted it as Cathy wanting to stop looking at photographs or finishing something else. A topic-comment strategy may thus increase the likelihood that the communication partner's inferences and interpretations will be correct.

The topic-comment structure is typical of language used by people who have different native languages and therefore difficulties in communicating with one another. When they communicate regularly with one another, they may develop a small shared language with elements from both languages. Such languages are called *pidgins* and are mainly used for trading (Khan & Akter, 2021). Because a topic-comment structure is used in situations where people have limited shared language competence, this strategy is also well suited to people who use AAC with partners who are not familiar with AAC. It represents both a strategy for initiating a conversation or introducing a new subject, and a means for the AAC user to gain control over the content of the conversation. At the same time, it is an economical strategy, enabling the use of fewer words, which also makes the strategy useful for individuals who construct utterances slowly (von Tetzchner, 1985; Woll & Barnett, 1998).

Children who are developing aided communication often produce only a graphic symbol representing the topic and leave it to the communication partners to provide the comment (von Tetzchner & Martinsen, 1996). However, the topic-comment structure requires at least two manual signs or graphic symbols, in a vertical or horizontal structure. Intervention based on topic-comment structures guides the individual to direct the attention of the communication partner to the topic or domain and then to make a comment about it. A child may indicate *BALL* to make the adult focus on it and then *KICK* to make the parent kick the ball in aided play (see Chapter 10). Indicating *BALL* first increases the probability that the adult will kick the ball, compared to indicating *KICK* first, even if *Kick ball* is the comparative spoken sentence. When it takes a long time for children to indicate a graphic symbol, this may constitute a more efficient strategy than utterances with the structure of the spoken language, because it contributes to joint focus with the communication partner on a relevant *cue*, that is, something the children find relevant for what they want to communicate (von Tetzchner, 1985).

The aim of sentence instruction is to help the individual to make sentences that relay the intended message in an efficient manner (Gibson et al., 2020). One way of analysing a conversational situation is to attempt to identify the *critical words* related to the communication situation, that is, the words that are necessary for relaying the particular message intended (Bjerkan, 1975). This highlights what information the partner needs for a message to be understood and which elements the utterance must contain in order to be comprehensible to others. Reaching an agreement about topic may involve negotiations or clarifications about the critical information in the message (Neuvonen et al., 2022c). Individuals using aided communication may also apply a proximity principle, placing related symbols close to each other to make the utterance less ambiguous, for example, the symbol representing an attribute close to the symbol for the person or thing to whom it is applied (Sutton et al., 2004). Communicative competence thus includes both understanding what another person may consider critical, and relaying one's own perspective. Intervention strategies based on critical words or critical information may help parents and professionals choose manual signs or graphic symbols that maximise the individual's ability to construct messages that are understood by the partner. It may also contribute to adapting the communication situation in such a way that it becomes evident to the individual what the critical information is, and that critical signs or symbols should be included in the sentences.

Sentence instruction for individuals who use AAC tends to focus on the sentence structure of spoken language (Binger et al., 2020; Savaldi-Harussi et al., 2019). Utterances based on a topic-comment structure, or the proximity principle, may differ from what people in the environment might think good language should be like. It is important for children who use AAC to learn the structure of spoken language as well as possible, and to use it in formal situations. However, efficiency is more important than "correctness" in everyday communication. To ensure individuals who use AAC have an optimal way of communicating, it may be necessary to consciously break down the assumptions people in the environment may have about "good" sentences in everyday situations.

Negation

Children's early expressions are often modified by negation (Bloom, 1998) and ways of constructing sentences with negation may also be introduced early for children using AAC. In early intervention, it may be most practical to introduce negations that do not reflect what the children want to do because they usually have some non-verbal means to express rejection or "don't want". Such negation forms may also be difficult to teach because this, at least for a period of time, would imply frequently offering the individual something he or she does not like in order to make him or her reject it (see also Chapter 6). When the use of negation is not linked only to the individual's actions, it will be easier to promote the use of multiple Agents. Teachable negations may, for example, be "not here" and "do not".

Negation does not have to be linked to a person's actions. Using a *contrast* approach, the teacher may present pictures where persons and animals are or are not doing something in particular. The individual is guided to describe the difference with negation, for example, CAT SIT and CAT NOT SIT, TALL TREE and NOT TALL TREE, or BICYCLE and NOT BICYCLE. Instructions and role play may also be useful when teaching negation. Sentences with NO are often needed in storytelling, for example, when relating about a dog that climbs on the table or does other things dogs are not supposed to do (see Chapter 11).

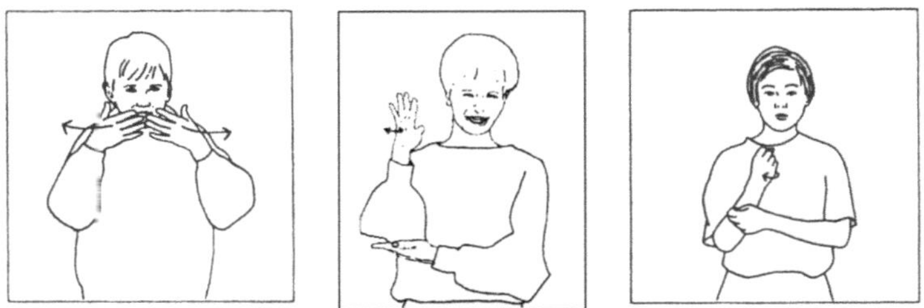

Manual signs: CAT, TREE, NO

In the example with Robert above, Kari introduced a graphic *NO* (a red card with a black cross) which was used to express "no" or "not". Robert seemed to understand and accept the graphic *NO* better than the spoken *no* or signed NO, and he quickly started to use *NO* himself. He made sentences with three items, like *KARI NO SOUP* (for lunch) where *NO* was put on top of *SOUP*. The way Robert used it, *NO* often had an inflectional quality because he put it on top of another graphic symbol to modify it, but he also used *NO* alone.

Fill-in strategies

In interventions based on semantic roles, the use of sentence structures with a frame and fill-in slots is a common strategy (see Figure 9.2). This is often used for teaching particular word orders and may also be useful for making the semantic roles of graphic symbols explicit. Robert constructed his sentences on a fold-out conversation page (see p. 38) and a place to construct graphic symbol sentences may be a prerequisite for applying fill-in strategies in planned or non-planned natural settings, where communication may be afforded by the visual presence of a popular toy or a favourite food out of reach. An incomplete sentence may be laid out on a conversation page together while the individual is watching. The individual is then encouraged to provide the rest of the information and complete the sentence, for example:

OLA EAT ?
? EAT CARROT
? EAT CHOCOLATE
OLA READ ?
DOLL ? RED
? CAP

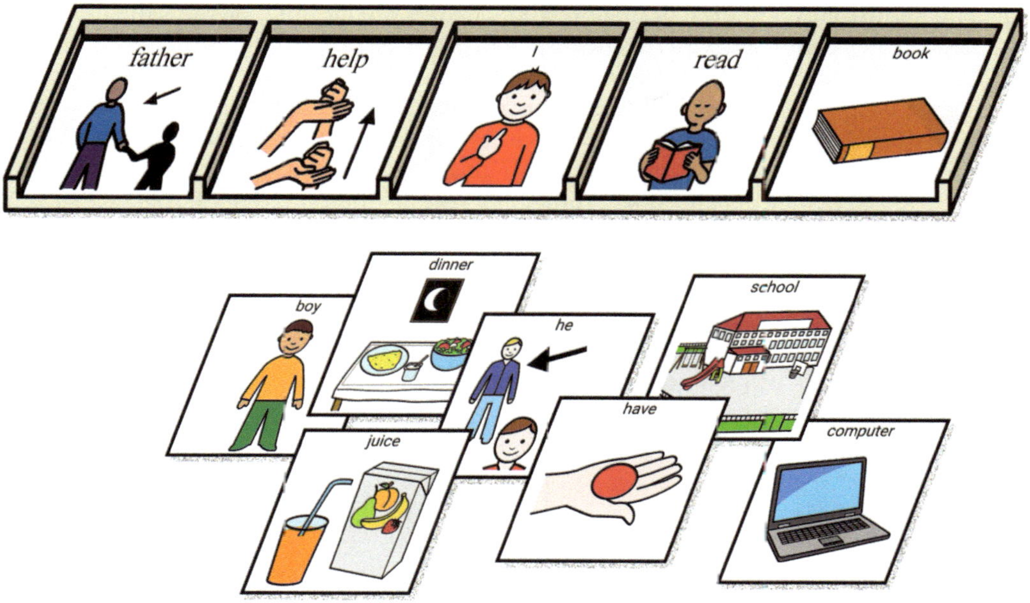

Figure 9.2 Frame for sentence construction.

If the individual does not respond, or seems at a loss, the teacher may help by presenting two or three graphic symbols to choose from, for example, different books or doll clothes that might be red. It is important that the individual solves the "problem" even if he or she gets a great deal of help. However, if the individual still does not complete the sentence, the teacher may choose a graphic symbol while demonstrating the function of the symbol that is inserted as clearly as possible. For this kind of strategy to be used, the individual should already have demonstrated relevant skills and the ability to make similar constructions in more structured settings. It is also important that the individual experiences the "missing" symbol in the utterance as a communicative act that originates in his or her own interests and needs, and not as some game he or she performs to please the teacher. Fill-in tasks may also be used in a reverse manner in comprehension, where the teacher gives instructions and descriptions by placing a new graphic symbol into an empty slot in a frame with symbols the individual already knows (see p. 166).

Visual Manipulative Communication (Arnesen & Wergeland, 1994) is a fill-in system for teaching sentences. It consists of a plastic frame with slots and cards with graphic symbols and colour codes that fit into the frame. Cards with graphic symbols for persons and animals are marked with blue, actions with red and objects with white. All graphic symbols with the same colour code can be placed in the slot marked with that colour. The individual is taught to make sentences by placing cards with graphic symbols in the slot that is marked with the same colour. In the early phases of training, the teacher places most of the graphic symbols in their slots. The individual only has to fill in one, and later two, graphic symbols to complete the sentence. Later, the individual may construct full sentences with graphic symbols, using the colour codes to support symbol order. An important element of the teaching is that the teacher demonstrates how each graphic symbol changes the meaning of the sentence. Fill-in strategies may be combined with the use of a matrix (see p. 285).

Also the *Picture Exchange Communication System* (PECS) includes some strategies for training sentence building. The individual constructs each sentence from a small set of graphic symbols selected by the teacher, usually about 3–7 graphic symbols (Bondy & Frost, 2002; Brady, 2000). The sentences start with *I-WANT* or *I-SEE*, for example, *I-WANT APPLE* or *I-SEE CAR* and can be expanded to express different attributes: *I-WANT RED APPLE* or *I-SEE BIG CAR*. However, teaching sentences that only include a few starters with the individual as Agent in the sentence limits the content of the sentences unnecessarily. Bondy and Frost designed PECS for children with autism spectrum disorder with the assumption that autistic children will not communicate about other people:

> The next phase of PECS involves teaching simple sentence structure, such as "I want… cookie." It should be noted that "I want" is a single icon, as at this point there is no one else to whom the child would refer; thus, at the moment, an isolated "I" would have no discriminative context.
>
> (Bondy, 2012, p. 791)

Although autistic individuals may have difficulties understanding the motives behind other people's actions and how they feel and think, they can still learn to describe what other people are doing. Such descriptions may, in fact, be an important basis for them to learn to communicate about other people's thoughts, feelings and motives. Also autistic individuals are interested in communicating about what people they know are doing and feeling and relating when somebody is doing something funny, exciting or strange.

Colour coding is the most common way to mark word classes or semantic roles in teaching graphic symbol sentences. However, it is not evident that colour coding in general is of benefit to aided communicators. Because communication aids usually have a relatively small lexicon of graphic symbols, it is important to expand the use of each lexical item as much as possible. One way to expand the expressive vocabulary is to use the same graphic symbol for different syntactic classes. Instead of using colour codes for teaching symbol sentences, it may be better to focus less on the restricted literal (or pictorial) meaning and let the communication context determine how each symbol should be interpreted – similar to interpretations of homonyms in spoken language (Piantadosi et al., 2012; Trott & Bergen, 2020). Communication becomes more flexible and versatile if, for example, a pictogram sometimes represents an object, and at other times an action or a location. The Blissymbolics system has special markers for making a noun into a verb, such as *SONG* into (to) *SING* (see below). Communication boards with Bliss-words often have background colours indicating word classes, but older and more competent users sometimes ask for the colours to be taken away because they feel the codes limit their communication (Kollar, 1999). Also simplified manual signs may represent meanings that correspond to words from different word classes (see p. 253).

Inflections and grammatical signs and symbols

The functions of inflections are to modify the content of words and sentences and make clear the relations between the words in the sentence, for example, who is performing the action and who is the receiver of the action. In English, plural is mostly marked with *–s* and past sense

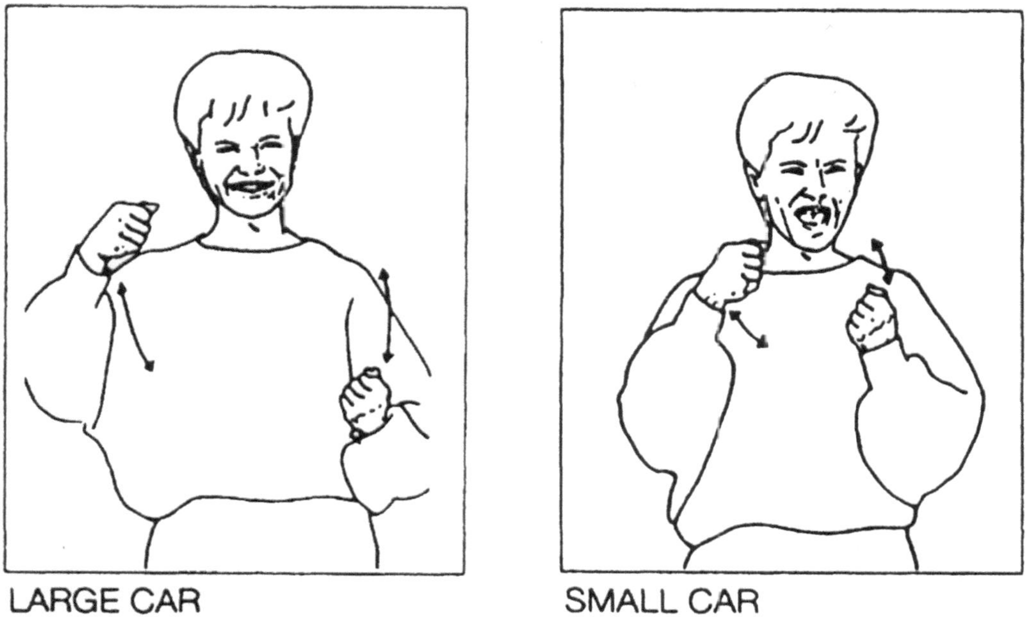

Figure 9.3 Modifications of manual signs: LARGE-CAR and SMALL CAR.

with *-ed*. Studies show that aided communicators may benefit from inflection training (Binger, 2008; Savaldi-Harussi et al., 2019) but this is strongly linked to spoken and written language. Individuals who use manual signs or graphic symbols may have different ways of marking plural, past tense and other modifications.

Inflections are an integral part of sign languages, often in the form of an analogue modification of the sign movements (Fischer, 2000; Napoli, 2019). This means that the articulation of signs is changed in order to make explicit a particular characteristic of the action or object that the sign refers to, for example, the size of a car: SMALL-CAR or LARGE-CAR (see Figure 9.3). Such inflections are rarely reported in signing of individuals with intellectual disabilities and language disorders who are using manual signs, and use of inflections do not seem to be a common goal of the sign teaching for this group. Intervention is often only focused on individual keywords without the continuation to sentence structures that should follow (Grove, 2019a). Grammatical modification of sign movements thus represents a much unused potential in intervention.

In spite of the lack of formal instruction and few other signers to learn from, investigations have found that many hearing children with intellectual disabilities combine two or more signs and modify their manual sign movements analogically to express more precise meanings (Bonvillian, 2019; Grove, 2019a; Rudd et al., 2007). RUN may be performed in a fast manner to say "run fast" and APPLE with amplified movement to say "large apple" (Grove & Dockrell, 2000; Launonen & Grove, 2003). In order for a sign modification to be regarded as an inflection, it has to be applied to several signs. There are also examples of analogue modifications that are not inflections because they are not used systematically. Articulating HAT in a manner that shows that the hat has a large brim (HAT-WITH-BRIM) is an example of this kind of modification. A relatively high share of verbs (around 25 percent) among children using manual signs may – together with adjectives and a modest number of prepositions – contribute to the children's spontaneous production of sentences (Grove, 2019a). In an intervention study involving eight children with intellectual disabilities and limited speech, Rudd and associates (2007) used a matrix design to teach them to modify the verbs WALK, FLY, JUMP and CRAWL with UP, DOWN, FAST and SLOW and to modify the nouns CIRCLE, CHILD, HOUSE and BALL with BIG, SMALL, LOTS and ONE. The children were guided to use the signs to describe pictures and actions with objects that corresponded to the verb and noun modifications. The training was for 30 minutes twice a week for six weeks and, even after this short time, the children learned to contrast many of the meanings of the signs with different modifications, and generalize this to untaught items. The results indicate that teachers might start to include sign modifiers as soon as the individuals have learnt some manual signs that can be modified.

Children using graphic systems with primarily pictographic symbols may be taught similar functions with grammatical symbols, such as *SMALL* and *BIG*, or *FAST* and *SLOW*. The Widgit Symbol System and Blissymbolics have several grammatical indicators that have the same functions as inflections, such as PAST-TIME, FUTURE and PLURAL (see Chapter 1). The Blissymbolics system has indicators that specify word classes. For example, adding ACTION to CYCLE transforms the noun "bicycle" into the verb "to bicycle" (see p. 14). Such grammatical markers are not part of the pictogram and PCS systems, but some individuals have used these systems in similar ways. One young aided communicator spontaneously used the pictogram *HAVE* as a marker of "past time" (Brekke & von Tetzchner, 2003). Other children have used *NO* in an inflectional way by putting *NO* on top of a graphic symbol or a photograph to express negation (see p. 283).

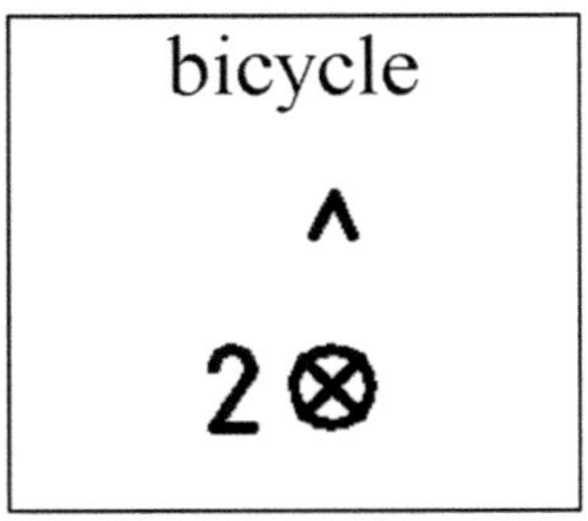

Bliss-words: BICYCLE (noun), BICYCLE (verb)

The Blissymbolics system is mainly used by individuals in the expressive language group who have language comprehension in the typical range and may not be the first system for children who start with graphic communication around the same age as children with typical development begin to speak – around their first birthday. It may be introduced when the child's language comprehension is about the same as a three-year-old with typical development, or earlier with some simple Bliss-words. Studies of children using other symbol systems have found that some preschool-age aided communicators can learn to combine graphic symbols representing content and symbols representing grammatical features of speech, such as possessive function, plural and past tense (Binger, 2008).

To support sentence development, adults should try to use graphic sentences when giving instructions or saying what they are doing, such as *FETCH BOOK* or *TURN-OFF LIGHT*. With a little imagination and knowledge of the individual's interests and likes, this approach may be used in expressive training. The teacher and the individual may take turns at giving and following instructions, so that the teacher sometimes has to fetch the book (or another physically possible action). Such utterances may also be used when talking about events, often in combination with the name of one of the staff members or other residents: PETER GET TRAIN RAILS or MARY FINISH DRINK WATER.

Ready-made sentences

Sometimes the gloss of a graphic symbol is a whole or partial sentence. Electronic communication aids enable users to select one or a few graphic symbols to say ready-made sentences with synthetic speech output. This might seem practical because the communication then bears a closer resemblance to spoken communication and appears to overcome some of the problems created by the lack of self-made sentences. However, ready-made sentences may make communication stereotypical because the sentences are selected rather than constructed. Children need communicative experiences where they can learn to construct sentences that go beyond interactional routines and can relay new content. Thus, as long as children are in an early phase of aided language development, the use of ready-made sentences should be limited. With older and more competent aided communicators, access to a small selection of ready-made sentences, or parts of sentences, may be useful in small talk and contribute to speeding up the conversation (Savolainen et al., 2020).

A major concern with ready-made sentences is that communication partners tend to interpret them in the same way across contexts. Aided communicators have limited possibilities for adapting their meaning to the situation (Jagoe & Smith, 2016). Some ready-made sentences – for example in devices with synthetic speech – may be useful in social situations and situations that call for routine questions or fast comments and are repeated often, such as *'What's your name?'*, *'That is great'*, *'Your turn next'* or *'You misunderstood me'*. Sentences for indicating a particular need for help, such 'Need my medicine' or 'Need new sitting position' may also be practical. Ready-made sentences are less useful when relating an unshared event or expressing thoughts not evident in the situation (see Neuvonen et al., 2022; Smith et al., 2018). When the actual content of the utterance is important in the context, individuals have to construct their own sentences symbol by symbol (Todman et al., 2008). Single symbols may give more communicative flexibility because they can be interpreted in more ways than a sentence. For example, depending on the communicative context, *BOOK* may mean "Give me the book", "There is the book" or "Take the book away". The ready-made device-produced utterance *'Give me the book'* has only one meaning, while BOOK with added GIVE, pointing or MOVE specifies the meaning. Teaching strategies for constructing sentences are mainly based on sequencing individual symbols and ready-made sentences may lead the child to develop strategies that can hinder creative construction of sentences. It may be practical for the child to have some ready-made sentences, but too many sentences may hinder linguistic development. When children do not have individual symbols for constructing sentences, they do not learn to produce sentences independently.

Cognitive effort

Several factors may contribute to the high proportion of single-symbol utterances in the production of children with a good comprehension of spoken language, as well as of children with limited speech comprehension. One important reason is that the operation of many communication aids requires considerable cognitive resources.

Young children with typical development tend to have a fuller knowledge of semantic-syntactic relationships than is realised in their sentences. One reason is that the physical production of utterances – articulation – takes some of the children's cognitive resources. When children struggle with articulation, they have fewer cognitive resources for content. Similarly, when the content is complex, there will be fewer resources for articulation. Children tend to make longer sentences when using familiar words, which may be more automatized, than with more recently acquired vocabulary (Bloom, 1998; Masterson, 1997).

In the course of development, there thus seems to be some trade-off between different aspects of utterance production. For motor-impaired individuals using graphic symbols, the physical aspects of sentence construction may require more cognitive resources than the articulation of individuals using natural speech, and the efforts may be more tiring. It takes longer time to select a graphic symbol than to articulate the corresponding word. The search for each symbol is not automatized like in speech and may also take a larger share of the cognitive resources. It may take considerable resources to maintain an intended message in the mind and construct a longer utterance, and maybe at the same time remember a question or comment posed by the communication partner. The aided communicator has to keep the full construction in mind while navigating for the graphic symbols. If using an electronic device, the symbols selected will remain on a display, but the individual still needs to keep the intended utterance in the mind. With communication boards or books, a conversation place or page may be useful, which can function as a "rehearsal buffer" when the user is constructing utterances.

Language experiences

Individuals in the three main groups differ in their ability to understand spoken language. Some have an age-appropriate understanding of speech; others understand speech only when it is augmented by AAC. Some understand manual signs or graphic symbols by themselves, others understand the signs or symbols only when they are presented together with speech.

For children who understand some speech, one important question is to what extent their mapping of semantic and pragmatic content is the same for graphic symbols as for the written gloss. The general assumption among professionals and other communication partners seems to be that there is a close correspondence. However, children who speak tend to have much more exposure to their own language mode than children using AAC, and they have a much broader repertoire of expressive language than children using manual signs or graphic symbols (see Chapter 7). Children who use AAC need to observe others making sentences in their own expressive language system – with its possibilities and limitations. When the exposure to own language mode is limited, they have to create their own sentence structures – or develop none at all. It is therefore important that, as early as possible, communication partners not only augment their speech with individual key sign or symbols, but use at least two syntactically related manual signs or graphic symbols for each spoken utterance when they augment their speech. Instead of "sign- or symbol-supported speech", communication partners should use "sign- or symbol-sentence-supported speech" (see Chapter 12). Communication partners should be attentive to what semantic elements their spoken sentences contain and try to include most of these elements in the supporting sentences with manual signs or graphic symbols. Together with the Action, the most frequent semantic roles are Agent, Object, Patient and Location (see p. 280).

In addition to providing aided language stimulation (see p. 277), adults who use keyword graphic symbols may expand children's graphic utterances by adding information, changing parts of the utterance or making the content clearer in other ways (Soto et al., 2020). Expansion is a characteristic of child-directed speech, as well as being a common technique for enhancing children's understanding and use of sentences on the basis of their own initiative and language production in speech therapy (Nelson, 1996; Snow & Ferguson, 1977). In typical development, there is an association between the parents' expansion of the child's utterances and the child's mean length of utterance (Che & Brooks, 2021). For young aided communicators, adults' expansions are often part of co-construction where adults recast the child's utterance in speech, like in the examples below from Clarke and associates (2017). The 13-year-old boy (N) is using a communication aid with speech output and is talking with the teacher (T) about a recent trip to the snow with his family.

N: *'Sled'*.
T: *Is that something you did?*
N: "Yes" (nods).
T: *You went on the sled?*
N: "Yes" (nods).

In this situation, the boy contributed only one content word. The teacher could have encouraged the boy to tell more, for example, by using *wh*-questions (*who, where, when* and so on) instead of *yes-no* questions. In the next example, the teacher (T) is talking with a nine-year-old girl (C) during an intervention session.

T: *You wanted to talk about something?*
C: *.C-a-m-p rock,.*
T: *Camp rock, what is camp rock?*
N: *'Is movie.'*
T: *Camp rock, is movie or camp rock is a movie, is a movie?*
N: *'A movie.'*

Moreover, because the aid lexicon is usually limited, adults should take care to expand the child's utterance in such a way that the child will be able to produce all or at least part of the expanded utterance.

C: *BALL*
A: {*THROW BALL I throw the ball to you*}

It is important to distinguish between the spoken interpretations and reformulations of graphic utterances and the expansions of these utterances. The aided communicator may not be able to produce graphic symbols corresponding to all the words of the interpretation, which is why the adult has to articulate this sentence. In the example above, the adult expands the child's *BALL* to *THROW BALL* while saying *I throw the ball to you*. This acknowledges the child's request in the form of a reply, thus avoiding unnecessary and non-functional repetition. Expanding utterances with manual signs and graphic symbols in parallel to spoken sentences also has the advantage that it makes the communication partner aware of the possibilities – and lack of possibilities – that the individual may have to express different semantic elements. The teacher may, for example, find out that she or he has forgotten to provide the individual with vocabulary items for expressing locations like GARDEN or STREET, and spatial relations like BEHIND or IN-FRONT-OF.

Sentences as frames for comprehension

When children with typical development hear a new word in a sentence, they use their knowledge about sentence structure and the familiar words in the sentence as cues for what kind of word the new word might be (Babineau et al., 2020). For example, the usual construction of sentences indicates that if none of the other words are verbs, it is probable that the new word is a verb. This means that the sentence constitutes a *syntactic frame* for understanding new words. Also elements of the situation that the sentence describes or is related to, are cues for the child's interpretation of a new word. The child will know which semantic roles the familiar words are likely to represent and base her or his interpretation on the implicit assumption that the new word represents a semantic role not represented by the other words. In this way, the situation constitutes a *semantic frame* for understanding new words in sentences. Together, the syntactic and the semantic frames and the familiar words in the sentence provide the individual with cues for understanding both new manual signs or graphic symbols, and the meaning of the utterance as a whole. These types of "bootstrap strategies" are assumed to be important in both typical and atypical development (Abend et al., 2017; Morgan & Demuth, 1996). Thus, if individuals are mainly using utterances with single manual signs or graphic symbols, they lose both opportunities to express more complex and specific meanings, and an important tool for acquiring new vocabulary.

In language intervention, strategies based on the idea of syntactic and semantic frames may be combined with aided language stimulation to support the individual's comprehension by presenting new signs or symbols in sentences with otherwise familiar sign or symbol vocabulary. The teacher may, for example, give a boy a choice between BOY GIVE BALL TEACHER and BOY KICK BALL TEACHER to teach him GIVE and KICK when BOY, BALL and TEACHER are known. To further support understanding, the teacher may guide the individual to make sentences with the same items, for example, to instruct the teacher with TEACHER KICK BALL BOY. This strategy builds on knowledge about critical information (see p. 291) and presumes that the teacher has analysed what the child needs to know for attributing the right meaning to a new sign or symbol. The teacher highlights the new sign or symbol by taking care that the child is familiar with the other signs or symbols in the utterance, and that the situation is generally known to the child. The child might need both situational cues and familiar vocabulary to attribute the intended meaning to the new sign or symbol and the sentence as a whole.

The strategies described here are similar to fill-in strategies, but while the aim of the fill-in strategy is to teach the individual to *produce* sentences (see p. 292), the aim of the present strategy is to teach *comprehension* by presenting new signs or symbols in a familiar language frame. They are complementary strategies that both attempt to utilize and promote individuals' understanding of the relations between manual signs or graphic symbols in sentences.

Perspective

Most situations can be perceived from different perspectives. Communication implies choosing one perspective and establishing a shared context (see p. 160). If the individual and the communication partner communicate on the basis of different perspectives, the result may be incorrect interpretations and misunderstandings. One strategy for supporting comprehension of words, signs and symbols is to make explicit the perspective of the utterance that is expressed. For example, when 3- to 4-year-old children with typical development were asked to perform *The cat is bitten by the duck*, the action they performed was the cat biting the duck. This course of event was in accordance with their knowledge of cats and ducks, and the children interpreted the sentence from this perspective. When the experimenter prepared the children's perspective by saying *Bad duck* before presenting the sentence, the children let the duck bite the cat when asked to act out the sentence (MacWhinney, 1982). A similar strategy may be used to provide individuals using AAC with a variety of cues to the meaning of manual signs or graphic symbols. To give guidance on perspective is, to some extent, similar to topicalization. Both represent strategies for directing the individual's contextual frame or context in order to gain a correct interpretation of the message presented.

Variation in language use

Construction of sentences is necessary for making the most out of language in any mode. The principles and strategies presented here represent a basis for promoting the development of sentence constructions with manual signs or graphic symbols. These can be further elaborated to support more versatile and flexible language use in children and adults using AAC. Learning takes time and to prevent the boredom of monotonous expression, it is important not to restrict the individuals 'communication to a small number of topics in a limited number of routine situations. Variability in both input and production supports language learning (Plante et al., 2014; Schiff et al., 2021). This means that both the individuals developing AAC, and their communication partners should vary the form, content, use and context of their sentences.

The typical acquisition of language structure depends on children's observations of the distributional statistics of words and that words are used together in different ways, for a variety of purposes and in different situations (Newport, 2016). Semantic analysis may be a useful tool for assessing the individual's communication and use of signs or symbols as Agents, Actions, Entities, Attributes, Patients and so forth in sentences. Repetitive language situations may reduce the individual's semantic scope and variation in expression, while more varied communication experiences may promote acquisition of new aspects of the language structure. If individuals are only indicating objects and activities they want, or taking part in non-functional training of naming, their further understanding of what language is about and how manual signs or graphic symbols can be used may remain limited. Sentence constructions facilitate the acquisition of lexical items representing other categories than physical objects and actions made by the individuals themselves. In assessments and evaluations of interventions, professionals should always take care to investigate the structures and functions of the individual's utterances in various settings, for example, whether they mainly represent the topic and the communication partner contributes everything else, and if the individual's communication is as varied as might be possible.

For individuals with sufficient comprehension of spoken language, the teacher may use explicit strategies when teaching sentences with manual signs or graphic symbols. For this group, teaching of sentence constructions may be possible in ordinary classrooms as well as in individual training sessions. However, because all language use is embedded in context, a substantial part of the language stimulation should take place outside special training situations (see Chapter 5)

Chapter 10

AAC, participation and activities

Social interaction within activities is a foundation of all aspects of children's development. Language is learned and used in a variety of contexts and language is a way to enter different activities (Ervin-Tripp, 1996; Rowe & Weisleder, 2020). The small and large shared activities of everyday family and community life represent an ecology for learning and enculturation (Dunst et al., 2000; von Tetzchner, 2019a). The types and contents of activities vary with socioeconomic and cultural background, and age-related changes in activities reflect the individual's growth and development (Elkonin, 1971; Veresov, 2006; Weisner, 2002). Disabilities may make participation difficult, and participation in social and societal activities is both a means and a goal of intervention for children and adolescents with disabilities (Imms et al., 2017).

For individuals developing AAC, participation in activities is closely related to the role of context in language comprehension and use (see p. 160). People and things represent action possibilities, including communicative and linguistic actions when the individual is able to communicate and use language in some form (Borghi, 2021). Language use depends on both participation in activities with communication *and* access to language means (von Tetzchner et al., 2018). Participation in age-appropriate activities is therefore a natural framework for supporting communication and language development in all modalities (Clarke et al., 2012).

The content of an individual's activities may to a large extent determine what manual signs or graphic symbols he or she is likely to learn and come to use (Hedvall & Rydeman, 2010). Communication, in play and other leisure activities, represents common grounds that support comprehension and establish a framework for constructing utterances (Bohn & Frank, 2019; Weisberg et al., 2013). Communicative participation in varied situations is therefore an overriding goal of AAC intervention (Batorowicz et al., 2014; Beukelman & Light, 2020).

Individuals who develop AAC need support and training that enable participation in various activities because the adults and peers in their environment rarely use AAC. A relatively large share of their communication may be training or elicited utterances (Barker et al., 2013). Training is important for children developing AAC, but true participation implies the use of communication and language outside training activities.

Deciding activities and choosing objects are usually core elements in the initial of phases of AAC training (see Chapter 6). They support early learning of names of things and activities and promote the individual's development of agency and autonomy (Batorowicz et al., 2016). Making requests and choices is also an important communicative function for adolescents and adults who are using AAC, although it represents only a small part of everyday language use. Therefore, AAC interventions should go beyond choosing activities and focus more on

DOI: 10.4324/9781003387633-11

communicative turn-taking *within* activities. For example, meals represent several opportunities for choice and are commonly used in AAC training, but the mealtime conversations of children with typical development may address a variety of other topics (Ferm et al., 2005; Hu et al., 2019). Children who develop AAC should be guided to use AAC for different communicative purposes within all ordinary activities (and some special ones). This chapter is about activities that may support the use of AAC in communicative interaction beyond choice.

Inclusion is a goal of many AAC interventions, but participatory inclusion does not always imply doing the same as the other participants in an activity (see Chapter 5). A child with limited motor skills may eagerly keep the scores and comment on them, while other children kick the ball. They both take an active part in the game, but in different ways.

Routine activities and variation

Many researchers and practitioners emphasize the function of routines in typical early language development (Bruner, 1983; Peters & Boggs, 1986) and in the development of AAC (e.g., Gevarter et al., 2021; Kaiser & Wright, 2013; Mandak et al., 2017). Routines constitute familiar frameworks that help children to infer the meaning of utterances produced by others and to produce their own utterances. Routines thus represent possibilities for introducing lexical items and sentence constructions and are often used to establish communication with AAC. However, children usually "grow out of" their routines, and language development may not be optimally supported when most communications take place in routine activities and the individual has access to only a limited expressive vocabulary. Too much focus on routine situations may reduce experiences within situations that promote acquisition of new vocabulary. To utilize the language environment in the best possible way, adults should try to create varied situations where conversations are a natural part of the activity (see also Chapter 12).

Children like to engage in household chores and show pleasure or pride in helping adults. These activities may also represent a frame of language development – both vocabulary and sentence formulas (Clegg et al., 2021). Supporting participation in such activities is a natural part of AAC intervention because they represent culturally valued activities. They are common among children with relatively good motor skills, and they can be adapted to children in wheelchairs if the children have good enough fine motor skills. The children may, for example, turn blenders or other technical cooking devices on and off using switches. Children with severe fine motor impairments may use language for action, instructing adults or peers. Although they cannot "help" like children with typical development do, children with limited motor abilities may be equally proud when they instruct the mother and father to clean, bake a cake or do other household chores, using topic boards or reading a recipe with graphic symbols "aloud" with their communication aid (Figure 10.1).

Supporting communicative participation beyond routines may represent new demands on communication partners. It is a goal that both the individual and the communication partner should experience communicative success. When necessary, the situation can be made more transparent for the conversational partner in order to make her or him experience success in conversations involving manual signs or graphic symbols. At the same time, it is important that the situation is not designed in such a way that the contribution of the individual using AAC is hardly needed. For example, parents often use their knowledge about the child to infer or guess what he or she wants. Children with disabilities may take part in only a few activities and their parents are familiar with most of them. It is therefore often easy for the parents to infer their child's wishes without much expressive communication from the child. The parents and the child may experience communicative success, but the conversations may become

Figure 10.1 Children who are motor impaired can "read" the bread recipe and instruct the father in the baking process.

repetitive and monotonous. Hence, not everything that is expressed should be predictable from the context. The individual must have something to communicate that makes a difference and the conversational partner should really want to understand what the individual is communicating. It is a shared communicative responsibility, but initially the partners are the more competent and should make sure the individuals using AAC gets their say. Low partner expectations, and limited communicative responsibility and communication that may make a difference are common barriers to real participation (De Bortoli et al., 2011; Moorcroft et al., 2019; von Tetzchner & Martinsen, 1996). For individuals who have passed the earliest phases of AAC development, it is necessary that the intervention enables varied communication in routine activities as well as more communicative interaction in various activities that go beyond routines.

Play

Play is a core activity in early childhood and is considered important for children's cognitive, linguistic and social development, peer relations, autonomy and self-efficacy (Lillard, 2017; Piaget, 1951; Ridgway & Quiñones, 2020; Vygotsky, 1967). Play may take many forms: sensorimotor play, locomotor play, exercise play, rough-and-tumble play, constructive play and symbolic play, including pretend play. Play is as important for young children with disabilities as for children with typical development (Besio, 2017) but children with physical or cognitive disabilities may spend less time in play than their peers (Barron et al., 2017; Barton, 2015; O'Connor et al., 2021). In interventions for younger children, play is often a goal in itself, but play is also a gateway into the peer culture and social interaction with peers. In AAC interventions, using communication and language within play activities should therefore be a main element (see Chapter 6). In this chapter, constructive play and pretend play are used to illustrate the use of AAC in play.

There are different reasons why individuals using AAC participate less in play than their peers with typical development and guiding of play activities can have different aims in intervention. Interventionists may use *structured play-like activities* to promote particular intervention goals, including motor skills, language skills, social skills and self-regulation (Feleihi et al., 2023; Gevarter et al., 2023a). However, a main characteristic of play is that it has no purpose beyond itself (von Tetzchner, 2019a). Educational play-like activities are thus not really play but positive educational activities that children may find motivating and interesting. An equally important intervention aim is to help children with disabilities to engage in *play for the sake of playing*, particularly with peers (Besio, 2017). In play, children should have the leading role, although adults may introduce play and games and guide the child into new play scenarios. Play interventions often use demonstrations from adults or peers, sometimes also with video (Briet et al., 2023; Hine & Wolery, 2006; Persicke et al., 2023). The borderline between play activities and play-like educational activities can be quite fuzzy. In both activities, participation may support the development of AAC, but it is a different activity when the child is supposed to do or say what the interventionist considers to be the "right" thing.

Early intervention programmes for autistic children that focus on play have found positive effects on communication and language development, including AAC development (Chang et al., 2016; Goods et al., 2013; Papacek et al., 2016). Participation in play activities with conversation may support the development of AAC but AAC may also be a means to support play for children with limited playing skills (von Tetzchner, 1987). However, much of the literature on play intervention for children belonging to the diagnostic groups who may need AAC, hardly mentions a possible need for AAC or how to use play to support the development of alternative means of communication and language (e.g., Barton et al., 2020; Besio et al., 2017; Blanche, 2008).

Children's play will reflect their perceptual, motor and cognitive abilities, as well as their social and linguistic functioning. Disabilities may affect both the form and the function of children's play (Barron et al., 2017; Besio et al., 2017). Much of children's early play involves physical actions and so motor impairments are likely to affect a child's development of play skills (Pfeifer et al., 2011). Children who have poor self-propelled mobility and use of the hands may be unable to perform the actions that are essential to many forms of play and other collaborative activities, because the demands on motor skills are too high. They typically play on their own or together with adults (Skär & Tamm, 2002). Even moderate motor impairments can hinder children's participation in locomotor play. Children with motor impairments understand play but need access to play and opportunities for practising play skills. Symbolic play with objects can be problematic for children with limited use of their hands. However, children in this group do not need to be left out of play activities if they get the necessary help and support from adults and peers (Graham et al., 2014).

Autistic children generally have difficulty understanding other people, imagining and planning the future, and realizing that another person can perceive the world as different from how it actually is (see p. 80). Pretend play with different roles and social interaction appears difficult for this group and a number of studies have shown that they rarely initiate pretend play, even if they are able to perform pretend actions when explicitly asked to do so (Jarrold et al., 1996; Kasari et al., 2013; Lam & Yeung, 2012). Thus, AAC is a means for helping them to understand the function of play and play is used to promote their communication and language. The double challenge involved in play for autistic children who are developing AAC implies that introducing new play activities and new manual signs or graphic symbols at the same time should be avoided as much as possible. Although new forms of pretend play may imply a need for new manual signs or graphic symbols, new forms of play should be introduced with already learnt vocabulary and sentence structures, and new vocabulary and sentence structures should be introduced within the framework of play forms that the individual already is familiar with.

Children with intellectual disabilities typically show a delay in play similar to other areas and need more help than children with typical development to initiate and carry out play activities (Layton et al., 2014; Venuti et al., 2009). Autistic children tend to be particularly delayed in pretend play and may do better in construction play (Papacek et al., 2016). The various kinds of play may support different forms of language use (Chu & Schulz, 2020; Lillard, 2015; Mertala et al., 2016).

Language for action in play

There are many studies addressing adaptation of the physical environment to make access to objects and mobility possible when children's motor disorders prevent them from constructing or performing other play actions with their hands, such as an adult moving the child's hand to push or grasp an object (Barron et al., 2017; Hsieh et al., 2020). Some children learn to operate robots with assistive devices (Bonarini & Besio, 2022; Espin-Tello et al., 2023) but need a communication aid to engage in the play narrative. For children with severe hand motor impairments, language (independent of form) may become their main tool for participation in play. In spite of the fact that they have little or no intelligible speech, language is their best skill, and they may use language creatively to instruct others to do the physical actions needed instead of showing or manipulating things. They can use graphic symbols or written text to instruct peers and adults to perform the actions they themselves are physically unable to perform, like in this example from the Becoming an Aided Communicator study (BAC; Batorowicz et al., 2016). The aided communicator (A) is instructing a peer (P) to dress a doll the same way as another doll that only the aided communicator can see. He is operating a speech-generating device by selecting graphic symbols with two switches.

A: *'Yellow.'*
P: *Is it this yellow shirt?*
A: *Yeah. 'Brown.'*
P: *I am just trying to put his arms in* (puts the shirt on the dolls). *Was it brown pants?*
A: *Yeah.*
P: *There is just a brown bag. There are blue pants. I do not see any brown pants. There are no brown pants. Is this what you mean?* (Picks up a pair of khaki pants).
A: *Yeah. 'Brown.'*

P: (Puts the pants on the doll).
A: *'Brown.'*
P: *Is it a brown bag?*
A: *Yeah.*
P: *How about sweater? There is a green sweater here. It matches* (puts bag across the right way).
A: *'Shoes.'*
P: *What kind of shoes? The only shoes here are these brown shoes. Or maybe these slippers?* (Points to a pair of slippers.)
A: *'Blue.'*
P: *I don't know. Because these are blue, these are half blue and these are sort of blue. What kind?* (Points to different slippers).
A: "Yes" (nods).
P: *There is a hat* (looks at remaining pieces at the table and the aided communicator).
A: "No hat" (looks away).
P: *Boy, this doll looks so cute.*

This conversation illustrates how individuals with severe motor impairments can use language for action and develop personal autonomy in spite of physical limitations and dependence on others to perform the actions. Even if the peer produced longer utterances, the aided communicator had the communicative responsibility and was guiding the peer's actions. There are many ways of using AAC in play beyond choice of play activities and toys, but it is important that toys and other play material are suitable and appeal to the child (O'Connor et al., 2021).

Constructive play

Constructive play is a natural part of children's physical exploration of the world. In addition, constructive play involves creating something, such as building a house with blocks or Lego, or forming a clay figure (Christie & Johnson, 1987). Most kindergartens are well equipped for this type of play. Compared to peers with typical development, children with severe motor impairments and limited use of the hands may be unable to manipulate objects and perform the physical actions needed in constructive play and have fewer opportunities for active exploration of objects (Besio & Amelina, 2017; von Tetzchner & Grove, 2003). For these children, aided communication is an important means for engaging in constructive play. A set of blocks and a small topic board with UP, DOWN, MORE, HIT and FINISH may be useful for giving them a first introduction to constructive play using aided language to instruct a peer or an adult to perform physical play actions, such as building a tower and tearing it down (see Figure 10.2).

Aided constructive play may help children to learn to communicate about objects, forms, colours, spatial relations and so on, like in this conversation from von Tetzchner and Martinsen (1996). George, aged seven years, communicates with eye pointing and dependent scanning. His communication book contains 845 pictograms, drawings and photographs. He and his father were building a house on a square.

F: *We should start with the living room.*
G: "Yes" (eye movement).
F: *Yes. And a sofa there. Sofa. Did you want the living room there?*

Figure 10.2 A young aided communicator instructs a peer to build and tear down a block tower.

G: (Looks at the square and the house).
F: *Or?* (turns the house around).
Here? (turns it again, looks at George).
Here? (points to another room).
There? (points to the last room).
Here? Where do you want the living room? (Tries to follow George's gaze).
G: (Looks at the roof of the house they are building).
F: *Hello.*
G: "Yes" (eye movement).
F: *Here?* (points).
Is it so difficult to make up your mind? Hm?
Should we rebuild the house, or what are you thinking of?
G: "Roof" (looks at the father and quickly up).
F: *Hm. The roof. Should we move the roof? The wall?*
G: "Yes" (eye movements).
F: *Hm. Should we move the wall?*
G: "Yes" (eye movements).
F: *This?* (points). *Should we move it?*
G: "Yes" (eye movements).
F: *Yes* (takes George's hand and moves the wall).
Where should we move it? Just take it away?
(Points at the square) *Over here?* (Puts down the wall) *Like this?*
G: (Looks at the father).

F: *Did you think it was too small?*
G: "Yes" (eye movement).
F: *All the way?* (moves the wall).
G: "Yes" (eye movements).
F: *Yes.*

The conversation above demonstrates the positive potential of AAC in constructive play. However, in this shared aided constructive play, the father was attentive to his son's wishes but maintained the lead and almost all of George's contributions were expressions of agreement. In spite of George's relatively large aid lexicon and his father's sensitive manner, the interaction hardly supported George's language development and exploration of the physical world through constructive play. With quite small changes in interaction strategies, the father could have let George take the lead in the Lego construction, George might have produced more and longer utterances, and the father would have performed the various play actions suggested by George. Parents may need guidance to support their children's development of AAC by allowing them to take the lead (see Chapters 11 and 12).

The same principles may be applied to support more complex joint constructions. As children grow older, the simple elements of early constructive play are gradually replaced by electric train sets, doll houses, complicated Lego structures and model airplanes. Making constructions on a two-dimensional computer screen is not the same as manipulating real objects. Children using AAC should be introduced to gradually more complex play material and engaged in the construction of gradually more complex and comprehensive play narratives (see Chapter 11). Peers may be guided to form more child-based co-constructive play scenarios with children using AAC (see Chapter 12). The constructions may evolve into role play and pretend play (see following section), where dolls living in a house built of blocks do house chores, or puppets eat a clay cake the child has directed a peer to bake. The principles of integrating AAC in advanced play activities are the same as in early play. Topic boards may be useful in the early phases of aided language intervention. However, when the play actions get more complex, a topic board may limit the creativity of both the play and the conversation. Vocabulary items relevant to a particular play scenario should, instead, be added to the child's main communication board or device.

Pretend play

In pretend play, children take on the role of a person or an animal, for example, a nurse, a firefighter or a pirate, or a dog or a lion. They may also use dolls, action figures or other toy figures in this type of play. Pretend play reflects children's imagination but also the basic human tendency to thinking in metaphors (see Fauconnier & Turner, 2002; Lakoff & Johnson, 1980). Pretend play is often social and particularly common when children engage in play with their parents. Language is usually a core element, both to establish roles and engage in play conversations. With increasing age, children become more self-reliant and able to play together on their own (Christie & Johnson, 1987; Pellegrini, 2013). Collaborative play implies complementary roles and tasks and is particularly good for joint involvement of children using AAC and peers (Figure 10.3). For children with motor impairments, AAC is a means to get a role in the play. For autistic children, pretend play may help them understand the world and also, for those who are lacking speech, AAC is a means to take part in this form of the play.

Figure 10.3 Doll play with aided communicator.

Play transcends the here and now and allows individuals using AAC to enter new and blended mental spaces (Turner, 1996) and use vocabulary they might otherwise not perceive or use, for example, names of real or imaginary persons, actions and attributes, for example, doctors, pirates, trolls and hobbits, and jobs, exploratory travels and magic. One mother explained that the best activity for stimulating her daughter's use of the communication device was to engage her in a three-way conversation with an adult and a doll – with all three using the communication device to communicate (McNaughton et al., 2008).

In play activities involving AAC, typical play scenarios with objects like zoos or farms, blocks, vehicles, balls, dolls and housekeeping toys can be varied to stimulate interesting and creative conversations (Barton et al., 2020; Taylor & Iacono, 2003). Even young children and children with intellectual disabilities may engage in pretend play (Barton & Wolery, 2008). In this example, Lisa (L), a two-and-a-half-year-old girl with Down syndrome and the researcher (R) are playing with dolls. Lisa is using manual signs and an electronic device with speech output, and the researcher is speaking and also signing and using the device (Iacono & Duncom, 1995, p. 253).

R: *What is the baby doing?*
L: *'Sleep.'*
R: *Good.* {The baby is sleeping BABY SLEEP}.
'Baby sleep' Baby sleep.

L: '*Baby sleep*.'
L: (Lies down and closes eyes, then sits up) SLEEP.

The play content was appropriate for a well-functioning toddler with Down syndrome. Lisa engaged in the pretend play, spontaneously taking the role as sleeping infant. This excerpt is somewhat repetitive but Lisa's utterances in other conversations around this scenario included LISA GOODNIGHT, TEDDY BABY, HAT ON BABY and LISA FOOT with sign or graphic symbols on the device with speech output. The researcher said good when Lisa answered "sleep" to her question about what the doll was doing. It is possible that the researcher intended to convey that it was good for the doll to sleep, but it seems more likely that the researcher praised Lisa for answering – or for answering correctly. If that was the case, *good* was a meta-comment unrelated to the play conversation. Barton (2016) advises against praising children in play activities because praise may interfere with the flow of the communication and play actions. Reacting to and answering the child's utterances may rather function to expand the play.

SLEEP

Manual sign: SLEEP

PCS: BABY, SLEEP

Essentially, AAC intervention is based on the principle that all children want to communicate, but that some have difficulties understanding the functions of communicative expressions. Establishing play activities may elicit communication engagement in the child. The example below demonstrates the importance of using the apparent interests of the individual.

Hannah is ten years old and motor impaired due to cerebral palsy. She has severe intellectual disabilities and no functional speech. She uses a few manual signs, which are imprecise due to her motor impairments and some vocalizations. The teacher uses a daily schedule with graphic symbols as visual support. Hannah's former teacher had tried to introduce topic boards with graphic symbols, but without success. The new teacher decides to utilize that Hannah likes to play with dolls. In the first play-session, she seems to particularly enjoy washing the doll in the bathtub. The teacher brings a simple topic board with graphic symbols related to doll play, including DRESS, WATER, FEED, BATH and STROLLER, and indicates relevant graphic symbols during the play (Figure 10.3). However, Hannah does not seem to take notice of them. In the second session, the teacher brings the doll and the objects that had been used in the first session with doll play but "forgets" to bring the bathtub. At first, Hannah just looks at the teacher and vocalizes. The teacher asks if Hannah wants to say something and shows her the topic board. Hannah points quickly and repeatedly to BATH and the teacher goes to find the bathtub.

The doll play was an activity Hannah liked, and the teacher's "forgetfulness" seemed to help Hannah realize that she could use graphic symbols to express her wishes – and that symbols make it possible to communicate about things that are not observable in the immediate environment. Graphic symbols are often used for early visual support and if the individual believes that the symbols are only behavioural directions, this may shadow for the communicative use of symbols. It is possible that Hannah associated the graphic symbols with routine activities and did not perceive them as a means for her to make her own wishes known. She therefore paid little attention to them in other situations. The teacher's "forgetfulness" helped Hannah understand one communicative function of the graphic symbols.

It is important that structured play is adapted to the competence of the child. The next example illustrates the use of play with peers to support the development of more advanced language skills.

Marianne is five years and has severe cerebral palsy. She cannot speak but understands many spoken words. She had been taught some manual signs, but her poor motor coordination makes it difficult for others to understand them. Her pointing is relatively precise, and she uses a communication board with graphic symbols. She is attending a mainstream kindergarten, and the teachers use communication in adapted play activities to support her and the other children's language development. "Who" is a critical term in conversations about people but also difficult to learn. During circle time one morning, the teacher introduces a game where one group of children hides a person or a doll under a large rug while another group of children are outside the room. The outside group then enter the room and the teacher points to *QUESTION WHO UNDER RUG* on a large board. The inside group uses graphic symbols to describe or tell something about the person or doll that is under the rug, using a set of graphic symbols: *QUESTION, WHO, WHAT, UNDER, RUG, BOY, GIRL, TROUSERS, T-SHIRT, SWEATER, HAIR* and several colours. They construct sentences like *GIRL BROWN HAIR* or *BOY BLUE TROUSERS*. In the beginning, the children's information has to be elicited by questions from the teacher, including the use of *WHAT*. The peers say the gloss at the same time as they put the graphic symbol on the board. When it is her turn, Marianne indicates the graphic symbol on her communication board and the teacher, or a peer, puts the same symbol on the large board. Marianne and her peers take turns asking and answering, and spontaneously use the same questions as the teacher did when it is their turn to ask, thereby laying a foundation for independent peer conversations. (von Tetzchner et al., 2005)

PCS: WHO, RUG, UNDER

Both Marianne and the peers benefitted from this game. The teachers introduced many other adapted games which supported language learning in Marianne and her peers.

Intervention studies have thus addressed various play skills in young children with disabilities, such as object play and pretend play for children with autism spectrum disorder or intellectual disabilities (Barton et al., 2020). Many of the studies used edible rewards and praise. However, the children may not really have been taught to play but rather to follow instructions to perform certain actions in order to get a reward.

Outdoor play

Much of the play intervention literature is about indoor play. However, children with typical development spend much time at playgrounds in kindergarten and school, in gardens and in play areas in the neighbourhood. Outdoor play may include individual play, like swings, climbing and building, and social play like hide and seek, police and robbers, ball games, pretend play and being explorers.

For children with severe motor disabilities, many forms of outdoor play represent challenges (Therrien et al., 2022). The children's participation may require physical and organizational adaptations, assistive technology or help from adults or peers. For children in this group using aided language, equal participation in ball play may not be possible even with adaptations, but they may do coaching and organization with aided language. Participation in joint constructive play and social play is also possible through language for action, provided the peers are AAC competent and the play environment communicative accessible.

Outdoor play equipment is, in general, physically accessible to autistic children. However, many in this group do not like to engage in new things and may not have tried out swings or other forms of play apparatus (Ripat & Becker, 2012). The outdoor playground represents possibilities for exploration and, with guidance from adults or peers, some autistic children may find that they like the equipment. The use of the apparatus and communication about the actions may also represent a context for acquiring new vocabulary and sentence structures.

Dialogue plans as part of an activity

A script is a representation of what usually happens within a given activity – the sequence of events, what is being said, and so on (Nelson, 2007; Schank & Abelson, 1977). Scripted activities are often used in play interventions, in particular in interventions with pretend play for autistic children (Hart Barnett, 2018). They are also used in communication and language intervention. Making activity scripts may help anticipate vocabulary that individuals using AAC may need (Taylor & Iacono, 2003).

Older children and adults with severe intellectual disabilities may benefit from scripted conversation in activities, for example, activities involving turn-taking regulated with language. For individuals with limited language skills, it may be useful to teach dialogue plans, that is, dialogues written beforehand to be used in a particular activity. This is illustrated in a study involving six individuals with autism spectrum disorder and intellectual disabilities, aged between 8 and 25 years (Sommer et al., 1988). They had little or no speech and had been taught 40–80 manual signs, but they rarely used the signs spontaneously. The aim of the intervention was to guide them to use manual signs in conversations with each other when they were playing quoits. They all enjoyed playing this game but performed without communicating with each other; they were only given directions by the teacher. The dialogue plan below included seven manual signs – YOU, I, WANT, (TO) PLAY, (TO) THROW, MORE and YES.

P1: YOU WANT (TO) PLAY.
P2: I WANT (TO) PLAY.
P1: THROW.
P2: (Throws).
P2: YOU THROW.
P1: (Throws).
P1: YOU THROW.
P2: (Throws).
P2: YOU THROW.
P1: (Throws).
P2: PLAY MORE.
P1: YES.

Manual signs: YOU, PLAY, THROW, YES

The teacher first performed the conversation with each of the participants and then helped them to have the conversation together in pairs. If one of the participants stopped, he or she was reminded of what they were supposed to sign. Two of the individuals learned to use all the elements of the dialogue plan, while the other four individuals used some of the elements. The dialogue was part of a situation in which the individuals generally interacted. The sign sentences added communication elements and fulfilled a functional role. The individuals continued to use some of the signs when they played quoits after the training sessions ended. The two individuals in this study who mastered all the elements of the dialogue plan had previously taken part in a study where they were taught to perform a conversation about orange juice and biscuits. That study included 15 manual signs and three different dialogue plans. They did not do so well, probably because the dialogues were too complex for them and the training period too short (Keogh et al., 1987). This emphasizes the need to adapt the complexity of the activity and the dialogue plan to the abilities of the individuals involved, but also illustrates the cumulative effect of experience and the importance of maintaining activities with dialogue plans over time, when the individuals have limited cognitive resources. Both of the studies mentioned above used dialogue plans adapted to particular activities. However, the aim of dialogue plans is not only that the individuals should learn to use the dialogue elements in a particular activity but that dialogue plans gradually should become more flexible and generalize to other instances and to other types of activities.

From role play to the real world

An increase in the range of communicative actions and the activities that the individual participates in implies more opportunities for language use and an opening up of society for the individual. Ideally, AAC should not only be used at home, at nursery school, school, work and in other familiar situations, but also with unknown people, on the street and in shops, cafes, meeting places, cinemas and so on. However, some individuals may be apprehensive about being exposed to potential partners who are not used to communicating with individuals who use AAC and may be worried about entering new situations. They may need some preparatory training before communicating in new activities. To support the individual's competence and confidence, it may be useful to begin by giving the individual a good overview of the situation and what is likely to happen there, so that he or she can feel more secure. Role play is one way of preparing for new situations and gaining confidence.

> Becky is a nine-year-old girl with cerebral palsy. She has some speech, but it is almost unintelligible. She uses a communication book with 200 graphic symbols. The book contains several pages with different domains (art, snacks, assembly, and so on). Becky often goes to Burger King with her parents but has never ordered anything there herself. First, she and her teacher communicate about what happens at Burger King: One must wait to be served, order exactly what one wants, and pay. Becky and the teacher then make a domain page for Burger King. In the classroom, her class mates make a model of Burger King and one of them plays the role of waiter. When the "waiter" asks what she wants, Becky indicates the items on the Burger King page in the communication book. She also practises telling the waiter whether he has understood her correctly or not. When Becky goes to Burger King with the class mate who played the role of waiter, she gets the hamburger she wants, without any difficulties (adapted from Mills & Higgins, 1984).

PIC: HAMBURGER

Communication within activities may function to disclose possible needs for vocabulary, sentence formation and pragmatic conversational skills.

> Martin is a 12-year-old boy with cerebral palsy. He has no speech but good comprehension of spoken language. He uses an electronic communication device with several thematic pages with graphic symbols and spelling, although his spelling is extremely slow. Martin likes to read books but has never been to the library. As preparation, he and his teacher communicate about the library, how it is there and the process of borrowing books. Martin practises spelling a few sentences that will be useful in the library, such as W-h-e-r-e a-r-e t-h-e b-o-o-k-s a-b-o-u-t l-i-o-n-s? and H-o-w m-a-n-y b-o-o-k-s c-a-n I b-o-r-r-o-w? Then a friend from his class plays the role of librarian. He asks questions and Martin answers. The following day, they go to the library, where Martin easily masters the new situation. He asks for the books he wants and borrows them (adapted from Higgins & Mills, 1986).

Participation in real situations gives people authentic knowledge of the society they live in and is an important part of their enculturation. For individuals who use AAC, many communicative experiences consist of pretend situations. Role play is useful but should mainly be used to prepare the individual using AAC, and not as a replacement for real situations. The aim of the role play is only to make it easier for the individual to begin to participate in real situations. This should be clear from the outset, for both teacher and learner, and real participation should be planned at the same time as the role play is initiated.

Interactive picture book reading

Shared picture book reading is a common activity for young children and their parents. It is believed to support vocabulary development, turn-taking and the growth of knowledge in general. Studies involving children aged one to five years with typical development suggest that interventions with shared picture book reading have a small or moderate positive impact on receptive and expressive language (Dowdall et al., 2020; McNally et al., 2024).

Individuals who develop AAC tend to participate in fewer activities and to have less varied experiences than their peers. Joint book reading may therefore be particularly important for them, as book reading constitutes a basis for communicating about things outside the here and now, and about the actions and feelings of others than the individuals themselves, like in this example.

> Thomas is five years old and has cerebral palsy. He has no speech and uses a communication book with graphic symbols. He likes Gunilla Bergström's story books about the boy Alfons Åberg, who is also five years old. One of Thomas's favourites is the book about Alfons who is unable to go to sleep in the evening. Alfons calls his dad with all kinds of excuses, like that he is thirsty, that they forgot to brush his teeth, that he has to go to the toilet, or that the father has to search in the closet as there is most probably a lion inside. The story ends with the father being so tired that he falls asleep, while searching for Alfons's teddy bear under the sofa in the living room. Finding his father asleep on the living room floor, Alfons crawls into bed and falls asleep. Thomas has a topic table with graphic symbols pertaining to the story. He knows the story so well that he can read the story "aloud" using the graphic symbols on the topic board while his parents point to and comment the pictures in the book. He uses his main communication board to comment on the story.

Figure 10.4 Thomas is using graphic symbols in interactive book reading with the mother, with, among others: *SLEEP, THIRSTY, TOILET, LION, BRUSH-TEETH, TEDDY, LOOK* and *BED*.

Interactive or dialogical picture book reading implies that the child has an active role and engages in conversations about the content during reading (Bedrosian, 1999; Edmister & Wegner, 2015). A primary aim of shared reading in AAC is thus that the reading should be truly shared, meaning that the child should be active and have the lead as much as possible. When possible, the reading should not only be done by the adult. If the individual has learnt to read, he or she can read text "aloud" with manual signs or graphic symbols, or spell it out with an electronic device. Another possibility is to use wordless books (see p. 350) where the individual – alone or together with the teacher – creates the story with manual signs or graphic symbols in a communication book or with a speech-generating device. Another way is to replace the ordinary text with graphic symbols or drawings of manual signs. Cartoons may also be useful for shared reading, as they may contain more interesting and complex stories. It is important that the conversations that are part of the shared book reading represent positive and interesting challenges for the individual. Many children like repetitions of stories but one study of three children using mainly aided communication found that the engagement and interaction tended to increase with one or two repetitions, but decreased if the same story was repeated more times (Edmister & Wegner, 2015). Fortunately, there is a wealth of books that may be used in joint reading.

AAC and participation in social media

Communication via digital media is an important activity and part of participation in modern societal life. Social media include electronic communication between two or more people via smartphones, tablets or computers (Calvert, 2015; O'Keeffe, 2016). Young children, adolescents and adults share everyday experiences and special events through social media and participate in games and exchanges about special interests on the Internet (Haughton et al., 2015; Rideout, 2015; Toh et al., 2019). In the digital age, individuals using AAC want to participate in electronic events and it is a natural intervention aim to help individuals using AAC to participate in digital meeting places (Caron & Light, 2016; Hynan et al., 2015; King et al., 2020). Many electronic communication devices have direct access to the Internet, but it is also possible to communicate with manual signs and non-electronic communication books or boards via a computer and video link. Conversations may use text messages with smartphones (Wepener et al., 2021), a shared screen with graphic symbols or text, or electronic devices with synthetic speech output. It is also possible to have conversations via chat or electronic mail with Bliss-words or other graphic symbols (DeRuyter et al., 2007; Lundälv et al., 2013; Sándor et al., 2002).

Internet use is frequent among individuals who use AAC, although less than among peers with typical development. For individuals with severe motor impairments, the Internet and social media represent important means to achieve greater social and societal participation (Bosse et al., 2020; Hemsley et al., 2017). They provide opportunities for conversations in the form of chatting or electronic mail. There are, however, many reasons for less participation in digital events, including problems with spelling, a limited number of friends to communicate with, lack of support and worries about communicating with strangers. An advantage of electronic meeting places for individuals with severe motor impairment is that dialogues may stretch over time, and they need not communicate quickly. In interviews, adolescent and adult aided communicators with motor impairments relate that they feel less disabled because they can communicate what they want at their own speed and are not dependent on others to interpret for them, as long as the receivers can read or use the same graphic system as themselves (Caron & Light, 2016; Howery, 2018b). This means that professionals should try to adapt communication aids for digital communication.

Common news about sports, politics, music, fashion and small and large events tend to be a starting point for many conversations. In Norway, the School Channel of the commercial television company TV2 includes graphic symbols as an option. This has proven useful for children using AAC for face-to-face communication but also for immigrant children with limited Norwegian language skills. It gives their peers insights into communication with graphic symbols and gives them and the AAC users shared information to discuss. Moreover, many of the terms used will be new to both the AAC users and their peers, and thus represent opportunities for learning and discussing together.

AAC in challenging circumstances

The content in this part raises many issues related to the safety and well-being of individuals with disabilities; issues that would require a book on their own (see Byrne, 2018; Clasby et al., 2022; Lindsey, 2019; Mitra, 2018; Steele, 2020). These few paragraphs only address issues directly related to AAC.

Language is a means for communicating and coping with positive and negative emotional events. Intervention for individuals with disabilities tends to focus on participation in positive activities, but language skills are equally important when individuals encounter challenging circumstances. Individuals who use AAC may experience fires, floods and other natural catastrophes. Disabilities and limited speech do not protect against emotional strain, abuse, pandemics, or wars and other types of unrest. Individuals who use AAC may also experience such conditions. These may put special demands on communication and language skills.

Individuals who use AAC, their families and teachers need to be aware of these kinds of conditions. Individuals using AAC need language means that enable them to relate challenging circumstances and seek comfort, and may need encouragement and guidance in communicating about sadness, pain or abuse.

Providing individuals who use manual signs or graphic symbols with the means they need to communicate about challenging events and emotionally difficult issues is only one side of their communication about such issues. Their messages in manual signs or aided communication must be understood and acknowledged by relevant public services. Several training courses have therefore been developed for those working in health institutions, police stations, fire departments, courts and other public services (Bornman, 2023). These have increased AAC awareness and competence in central public services and the communicative access of individuals using AAC to these services and reduced individuals' vulnerability and risk of abuse (Bornman, 2017; Kryvonogova et al., 2023).

AAC in court

Individuals using AAC may experience sexual harassment, abuse, robbery or other events that may require communication with the police or in court, as a victim or a witness (Bryen & Wickman, 2011). It is important that individuals who use AAC have the means to express different kinds of experiences. They may have a need to describe negative actions that they have experienced or observed in others (Møller & von Tetzchner, 1996). Many people are involved in a court case at some time or have to act as a witness in court, including individuals using AAC (Bornman et al., 2011; Bryen & Wickman, 2011; White et al., 2020, 2021).

Experiencing or being a witness to such events and seeking justice or taking the witness stand requires knowledge about the justice system and the language skills necessary for describing scenes and actions, and reporting potential criminal events (White et al., 2015). Several topic boards have been developed to facilitate giving witness in court (see Figure 10.5) or reporting physical or sexual abuse.

Talking Mats may helpful as part of an approach for making it easier to communicate about difficult issues, which has been used with different groups of people with severe communication and language difficulties (Murphy & Cameron, 2008). A Talking Mat is a display or board which contains three sets of graphic symbols: one set for the user to indicate the topic of the conversation, one set with options for comments, and a visual scale to indicate strengths of feelings.

AAC in hospitals

Many individuals who use AAC have severe medical conditions and are used to spending time in hospitals. They therefore need vocabulary, for example, for body parts, expressing degree of pain, and indicating when the treatment is functioning well (Johnson et al., 2016; Zaylskie et al., 2023). Pandemics may require the use of communication boards and devices in hospitals and a need for vocabulary related to these conditions, such as BREATH, COUGH, HEAVY or TIRED (Altschuler et al., 2021; Garnett et al., 2022). Moreover, AAC users may attend hospital units where the staff are not familiar with AAC. They therefore need strategies for communicating with unfamiliar people in intensive or ordinary care units.

Widgit: BREATH, COUGH, HEAVY, TIRED

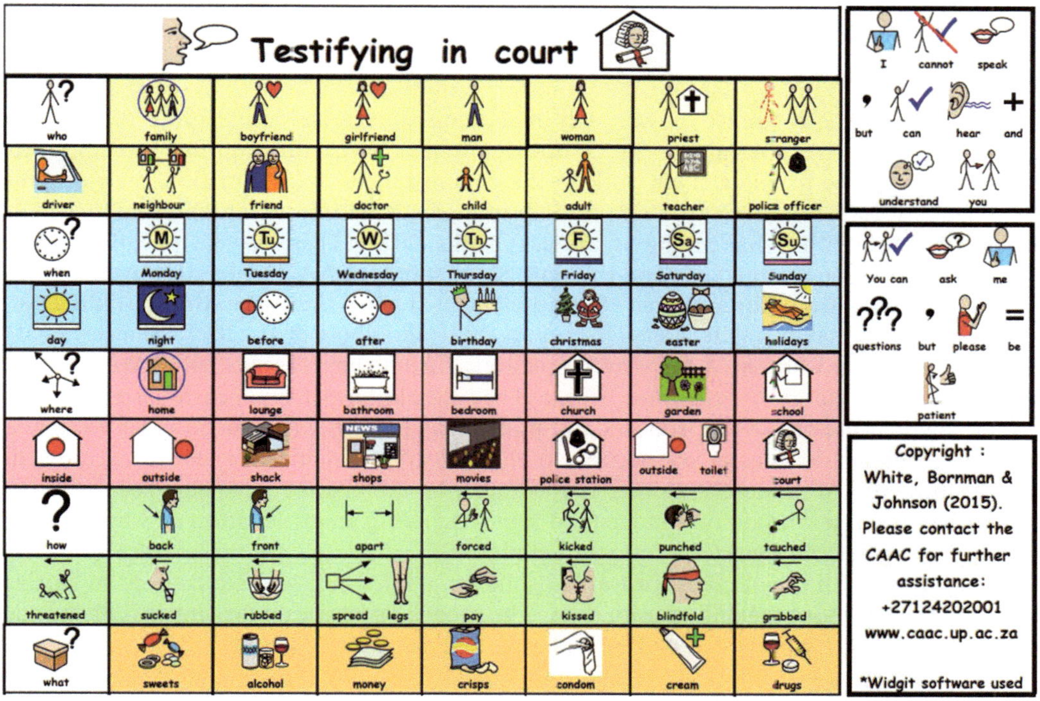

Figure 10.5 Topic board for witnessing in court (from White et al., 2015).

AAC and pandemics

The Covid-19 pandemic had a significant impact on medical, educational and social services for children, adolescents and adults using AAC (Allison & Levac, 2022; Barton-Hulsey et al., 2023). The frequent home-schooling represented challenges for children and adolescents in many countries, and especially for those with disabilities and their families (Fäldt et al., 2022; Mazrekaj & De Witte, 2024). The digital classroom may need special adaptations for the functioning of individuals using communication aids (Biggs et al., 2017). Education may be more arduous for teachers who need to be prepared for extensive use of online communication with students using AAC. Ordinary AAC services were often reduced during the pandemic and, to some extent, replaced with assessment, intervention, guidance and follow up via telecommunication (Pujol et al., 2021; Zhang et al., 2022). This meant that there was an increased use of telepractice. Telepractice strategies were in use prior to the pandemic but many new technological solutions have been suggested following the pandemic (Lohmann et al., 2022; Nader & Erickson, 2023).

An important consequence beyond education itself was the reduced social interaction experienced by most students. All the students had to learn new ways of interacting with teachers and peers, but the consequences were more severe for students who used AAC because they tended to have less social contact outside kindergarten or school (Fäldt et al., 2022). Teachers may need to organize social interaction with classmates for students using AAC when physical meetings in school are reduced.

ACC in unrest and war

Situations with social unrest or war may make communicative access more difficult for individuals using AAC (Armitage, 2022). Interventionists have a difficult time providing services and also have to adapt their work to the circumstances, such as making new graphic symbols or social stories (Gray, 2022) to help individuals with intellectual disabilities cope with air raids and other challenging situations (Chaika, 2023). There may be immediate needs and little or no time for guidance and training. Some standard AAC material related to medical issues should always be available, to be implemented when there is no time to individualize. Adaptations may be made later (Dind et al., 2021; Goldberg et al., 2021; Hemsley et al., 2001). Individuals who use AAC may be separated from their families and have to make themselves understood to unfamiliar people. They should have a small card describing and explaining their use of AAC. Electronic equipment may be vulnerable due to breakdown and lack of repair possibilities or connection to electricity. Communication books and boards may be more robust in such situations. Individuals who use manual signs may need sign dictionaries for people who do not understand signs, including an explanation of why the individual is using manual signs (Kryvonogova et al., 2023).

In situations with social unrest or war, all children, adolescents and adults need to be able to communicate about the difficult situation. The need for new vocabulary items is illustrated in the following story presented by Kryvonogova and associates (2023).

> Anya is three years old. She has used AAC from a very early age, for more than two years. She has an active vocabulary of 30 graphic symbols. When she heard the alarm, Anya began to move chaotically around the apartment, grimacing and waving her hands. The parents realized that her behaviour was due to anxiety. They needed to explain to her what she should do, so she could act in the right way and cope in spite of her repeated anxiety attacks. They introduced three new symbols on her communication board: *ALERT, SHELTER* and *SIREN*. The parents created a social story about how to behave during an air raid alert. Using graphic symbols as key words, they explained that it is necessary to move fast when one hears the siren. They read the social story several times before there was any siren, as well as when there were repeated alarms. After a little while, Anya appeared to understand what she should do in the time of anxiety so it was no longer necessary to follow the social story recipe, and her chaotic behaviour disappeared.

Being able to express both positive and negative thoughts and feelings related to the immediate situation may make the situation more bearable and reduce psychological strain. Knowledge of manual signs or graphic symbols such as AFRAID, PAIN, HEAR, RELIEF, AEROPLANE, BOMB, ESCAPE, PROTECT, RESCUE, WAIT, PEACE and LOVE will be helpful. Individuals with good comprehension of spoken language may take part in selecting the vocabulary. Active participation in their own intervention may contribute positively to the healing progress.

ARASAAC: ALERT, SHELTER, SIREN, BOMB, AFRAID, ESCAPE, PEACE, LOVE

Fortunately, most people are rarely or never involved in this kind of situations. However, they are a part of societal life that individuals using AAC should also be able to communicate about. Knowledge about these kinds of situations and the ability to communicate about them will depend on the cognitive and linguistic abilities of the individual. Children are quite old before they begin to learn how society works (von Tetzchner, 2019a). Learning to communicate about these kinds of situations may have to be through conversations about news stories, narratives and role play.

Chapter 11

Conversational skills and narratives

A conversation may be defined as an exchange of linguistic turns involving two or more persons. It is a basic unit in language use and attainment of understanding through coherent conversations in everyday life is a unique aspect of human communication (Gunaratne et al., 2019). Children learn to use all aspects of language through conversations, and conversational skills are necessary to become a competent language user (Clark, 2018; Veneziano, 2018). Participating in and managing conversations should therefore be the ultimate goal of AAC interventions, but it is also important when the aim is to increase vocabulary, grammatical functions and language creativity. Starting a conversation, maintaining it and ending it are basic conversational skills. Furthermore, taking turns, changing topics, adapting to conversational partners and repairing breakdowns in the conversation caused by misunderstandings are essential conversational skills. Conversation skills emerge as a blend of children's earlier communication skills, concept formation, and aided and non-aided language skills (Veneziano, 2018). Narratives emerge as elaborations of conversational skills (Ervin-Tripp & Küntay, 1997). Narratives should also be an essential part of interventions for individuals who use AAC, to help them get the most out of their alternative language skills. Much of this chapter is about aided communication and graphic systems, but most of the issues also apply to conversations and narratives with manual signs.

In typical early language development, adults structure their conversations with children by guiding and encouraging the children's contributions. In the dialogue below, the adult (A) chains the child's (C) utterances together and into a meaningful entity.

A: *Yesterday you went to…*
C:
A: *You went to Grand…*
C: *To Grandmother.*
A: *And you travelled by…*
C: *Train.*
A: *You travelled together with…*
C: *Mama.*
A: *And…*
C: *Daddy.*
V: *And we ate at Grandmother's. And then you got….*
C: *Pizza and juice and cake.*

DOI: 10.4324/9781003387633-12

Early conversations typically concern things children and adults are doing or have done together. They may be about the food the adult is cooking, a visit to a relative or friend, the child's peers at nursery school, animals on the farm and so on. Many early conversations recur often, and the child gradually learns what to say to the various cue words. Some conversations may be repeated on a daily basis, often starting with eliciting questions like: *What did you do in kindergarten today?* Over time, the children's contributions become more autonomous and less dependent on the adults' help and chaining together (Pan & Snow, 1999).

Conversations enable exchange of information, ideas, viewpoints and emotions, as well as opportunities for influencing and being influenced by others. Conversations may be task oriented, like at school or work, or casual, including small talk, short conversations when people meet incidentally or longer conversations during play or meals (Gilmartin et al., 2018). Conversations may have diverse purposes, such as commenting on things in the present or ongoing events, joking, engaging in conflict or giving advice or instruction (see Table 11.1). Good conversational skills make it easier for an individual to learn from others, as well as to argue for her or his own viewpoints and decisions, to negotiate and to understand others (Veneziano, 2013). An improvement in conversational skills may have a positive influence on the individual's social participation, development of independence and sense of equality.

Users of AAC belonging to all the main language groups (see Chapter 3) may have difficulties acquiring conversational skills. Many are dependent on assistance when engaging in conversations, both when performing daily tasks and during their leisure time. The overall aim is that the individual should engage in conversations for a variety of purposes. However, the considerable differences between these groups in terms of language comprehension, social

Table 11.1 Nine main purposes of conversations (based on Egbert et al., 2021)

1.	Situation-dependent commentary. Occurs when participants in a conversation are commenting on people or objects that are present, or events that are occurring in their shared situational context.
2.	Joking around. Conversation that is intended to be humorous, including both light-hearted and darker humour. It also includes good-humoured banter, teasing and flirting.
3.	Engaging in conflict. Includes disagreement of any type, including light-hearted debate as well as more serious quarrelling.
4.	Figuring things out. Discussion aimed at exploring or considering options or plans, including discussion about how things work and what the best solution to a problem may be.
5.	Sharing feelings and opinions. Discussion about feelings, opinions and beliefs, including the airing of grievances and the sharing of personal perspectives.
6.	Giving advice and instructions. Occurs when one participant offers directions, advice or suggestions to another participant.
7.	Describing or explaining the past. Narrative stories about true events from the past or other references to people or events from the past.
8.	Describing or explaining the future. Descriptions or speculations about future events and intentions, including those that are planned and those that are more hypothetical.
9.	Describing or explaining (time-neutral). Descriptions or explanations about facts, information, people or events where time (past or future) is either irrelevant or unspecified.

skills and interests imply that the intervention aims and the methods utilized to promote their conversational skills will differ. Teachers may videotape conversations to observe the interaction process and gain insights into the competence and contribution of the AAC user in the conversations, as well as their own role as conversational partners.

Conversational skills are best developed through participation in interesting conversations. Interventions for individuals developing AAC should therefore include conversations in training sessions as well as facilitation of conversations with significant people in their environment. Similar to early dialogues in typical language development, the conversational partner may initially take control of the course of the conversation, encourage the individual and help him or her to initiate, reply and continue the dialogue with new turns (Soto et al., 2006, 2020). The help is gradually reduced, although individuals belonging to the alternative language group may require conversational support and guidance for the rest of their lives (see Webster et al., 2016). Structured conversations are also used for teaching vocabulary and grammar (Luckins & Clarke, 2021; Soto & Clarke, 2018). However, including explicit teaching of vocabulary or grammar as part of the conversation may interfere with the flow of the conversation. Teachers should therefore differentiate between conversations that aim to promote communicative problem solving and conversational skills, and structured conversations to promote lexical or grammatical skills. Interventions aimed at conversational skills should guide the individual to manage conversations and learn the roles of a conversational partner. Parents and other significant people may scaffold for the individual and gradually weave new elements into the everyday conversations, particularly elements that may lead to new learning for the individual.

In typical language development, conversations with adults constitute a significant part of the children's enculturation process (Veneziano, 2018). They are occasions for learning the language, concepts and values of the culture. Adults comment on what the children say and do, tell them the names of people, objects and activities, explain how particular objects are used and tell children what they can and cannot do. For adults, the children's contributions to the conversations give insights into their thoughts and feelings, as well as their language competence. Children with severe disorders of language and communication, and children who have difficulty in expressing themselves due to motor impairments, tend to miss out on a great deal of this type of natural learning. Moreover, repetitive conversations may become boring for both the AAC user and the communication partners. A central objective of AAC intervention is therefore that alternative means of communication should give the individual more learning opportunities and access to varied conversations. With better conversational skills children and adults who use AAC will benefit more from social interactions with other people.

Intervention sessions directed at improving conversational skills usually include structured conversations around a particular topic. The planned content will reflect the current educational aims of the teachers. The topics will vary, depending on the interests, general functioning and language competence of the individual. For example, the individual may use new vocabulary introduced in the teaching of flowers or vehicles to engage others in interesting conversations – sometimes to the surprise of the communication partners. Structured conversations are also useful for supporting the family and peers in engaging in communicative interchanges with the individual that go beyond social routines, for example, about recently experienced positive or negative emotional situations. Attempts at longer conversations may utilize topics that both the individual and the communication partners find amusing and interesting, such as sports, politics or movie stars. Peer conversations with self-disclosure are important in the development of friendship relations and self-image (Rotenberg, 1995) among AAC users, too (Østvik et al., 2018; Wickenden, 2011a, b). Conversational training thus has a broad scope, with an emphasis on conversations about topics that may make the individual an attractive communication partner.

Starting, changing and ending conversations

Although the participants in a conversation sometimes talk at the same time and may pay little attention to what others say, most participants manage to join in the conversation. Individuals who are unable to speak, however, must have other ways of attracting the attention of the others to initiate a conversation. If they are able to vocalize, make clicking noises with the tongue, say some words or use a communication device with voice output, this is usually not a major problem. For individuals who are dependent on establishing visual contact without being able to produce a sound, it can be difficult to attract the attention of a potential communication partner. Their attempts at communication may be overlooked when they try to take the initiative. Success depends on the potential conversational partner looking in the right direction. When the individual is responding to an initiative from the communication partner, the situation is different. The person who is taking the initiative is attentive to the individual who is going to answer.

Studies of conversations involving aided communicators find that it is the adults or peers with natural speech who tend to take the initiative to communicate most of the time (Bailey, 2013). Observations of conversations between 2–10-year-old children who used communication aids and their mothers showed that 65 percent of the mothers' utterances and only 8 percent of the children's were initiatives (Pennington & McConachie, 1999, 2001). A case study of a nine-year-old girl showed no initiations or spontaneous (voluntary) turns when she communicated with her teacher and peers (Smith, 1991). In a study of 12 aided communicators aged 7–15 years and their peers using natural speech, the peers took most of the initiative, while the aided communicators responded most (Clarke & Kirton, 2003). In another study of 23 aided communicators aged 6–11 years, only a few spontaneous initiations were observed over 117 hours (Andzik et al., 2016). These results emphasize the individuals' need for training in initiation and other conversational skills, but also the need for communication partner instruction (see Chapter 12).

Moreover, one study found that 20–40 percent of the communicative initiatives of children with motor impairments were overlooked in the classroom (Calculator & Dollaghan, 1982). One reason may be that the initiatives were not expected. Another reason may be that many children with severe motor impairments produce involuntary sounds or movements that people around them have become used to ignoring. Some individuals who struggle with articulating sounds have difficulties when they want to say something important because increased excitement may lead to poorer motor control. If they are not using a device with speech output, they may need some kind of sound device to attract the attention of the person they want to communicate with. A buzzer or a bell can be practical, but a small device with speech output that says '*Hello*' or something similar may be better. It is important that the sound is pleasant and does not annoy people in the environment if the individual often repeats the attention-getting sound. For individuals who use communication aids with speech output, ready-made opening phrases may make it easy to for them begin a conversation, for example: '*Hi, I'd like to talk to you*'. A light touch may also be a way of attracting someone's attention, but this may be awkward if the individual does not know the other person very well.

If the individual initiates the conversation with a word or sentence, these are likely to perceived as the intended content of that conversation. It is not uncommon for aided communicators to apply the same content phrase when initiating conversations. This may lead to repetitive conversations and the individual's regular conversational partners may become bored. It is therefore important that the individual uses different contents when initiating conversations. The teacher may help individuals to develop a small repertoire of conversational starters for different topics or situations.

When conversations are initiated by the conversational partner, he or she will also often decide when the conversation ends. This may happen either sooner or later than the individual might wish. It is not always easy for individuals to withdraw from the conversation or tell the partner that they wish to stop. It is therefore essential that they are given the means and taught strategies for ending a conversation, for example, producing *END CONVERSATION*, NICE TALK TO YOU or a similar phrase. If the individual wants to communicate more when the partner seems to be ending the conversation, he or she should be able to express this, for example, by signing or indicating *SPEAK MORE, NO FINISH*. In addition, DIFFERENT TOPIC or I HAVE SOMETHING TO SAY may be used to indicate a change of subject. These strategies assume that the individual has access to the necessary vocabulary. Many aided communicators have useful lexical items in their communication aid, and if not, they should be provided with the necessary graphic symbols (or manual signs). However, aided communicators may have little experience with ending conversations and need to be guided in how they can use symbols for this function.

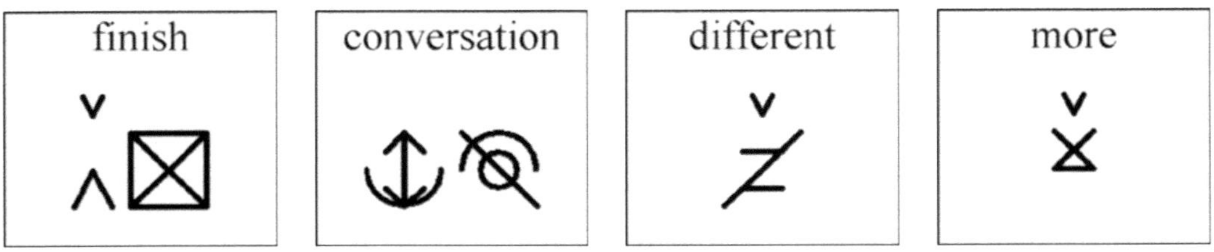

Bliss-words: FINISH, CONVERSATION, DIFFERENT, MORE

Taking turns

To maintain a conversation, an individual must be able to take turns in the conversation but this can be difficult for aided communicators with limited use of the hands. They might lose their turn because they take so long getting started that the conversational partner gets bored and takes over the turn (Howery, 2018a; Smith et al., 2010). In one study, the mothers of preschool-age aided communicators used almost all the opportunities they had to take their turn, while their children used only half of their chances for turns. One reason may have been that the mothers wished to succeed in the observed communication and therefore took the child's turn if the child was slow to answer (Light et al., 1985).

There are different forms of obligatory turns in a conversation, where one conversational partner requires the other to take the next turn. This could be a question, but a comment may also require some response from the other. Most of the obligatory turns of aided communicators are answers to questions, but aided communicators do not always take these obligatory turns (Pennington & McConachie, 1999). One way to change this is to guide the individual to recognize and utilize opportunities for asking questions when they arise in conversations, while communication partners may be advised to wait a little longer before they take over the turn in the conversation (Light et al., 1999).

In conversations involving an aided communicator, there is thus typically an imbalance with regard to how much each of the partners is communicating. The communication partner using natural speech may have much longer exchanges than the aided communicators (Neuvonen et al., 2022a; Smith et al., 2018; von Tetzchner & Martinsen, 1996). Making brief comments while the conversational partner is speaking, for example, in telling funny stories or cracking jokes, may be difficult for individuals who use aided communication (Waller & O'Mara, 2003). The opportunities for aided communicators to engage in many conversations and take their full turns depend on the communication partners' sensitivity and being mindful of not deciding too much of the content of the conversation.

Topic-comment as a conversational strategy

Topic-comment structures are often used in sentence construction (see Chapter 10) and may also be useful in conversations. They represent both a strategy for initiating a conversation or introducing a new subject, and a means of taking control of the content of the conversation, for example, producing FOOTBALL MATCH or NEW MOVIE to start conversations on these topics. It is an economical strategy that enables the use of shorter utterances, making the strategy particularly useful for people who communicate slowly (Woll & Barnett, 1998).

Intervention for individuals who use communication aids is often characterized by a normative attitude and a demand for "correct" language. The use of topic-comment constructions of sentences and conversations tend to differ from the common assumptions of how language should be and break with the normative conception of "correct" language based on the spoken language. However, this may be necessary to ensure aided communicators the most effective participation in conversations when the time for each turn is long. In conversations with people who are unfamiliar with aided communication, it may nonetheless be necessary for aided communicators to adapt linguistically and use more elaborate or "correct" language if they are able to do so, even when this takes a longer time.

Misunderstandings and repairs

Misunderstanding or lack of understanding is common in conversations involving young children (Clark, 2020). Requests for repetitions and other attempts to clarify the meaning during conversations inform speakers that what they said was unclear in some way. In the course of language acquisition, children learn to monitor whether they are understood by the communication partner and to resolve misunderstandings in conversations with adults or peers (Aviezer, 2003; Laakso & Soininen, 2010).

Individuals using aided communication tend to experience more misunderstandings and breakdowns in communication than individuals with typical development (Hjelmquist & Dahlgren Sandberg, 1996; Smith et al., 2018). To make sure that a misunderstanding does not lead to a breakdown of the whole conversation, communicators need strategies for signalling that a misunderstanding has occurred and strategies for resolving the misunderstanding. This often takes the form of negotiations about meaning (Neuvonen et al., 2022c).

The breakdowns may be related to the long time it takes aided communicators with severe motor impairment to express themselves (Howery, 2018a; Smith et al., 2010). Imprecise pointing at a communication board may cause misunderstandings or the articulation of a different utterance than intended on an electronic communication aid. Breakdowns in communication may also be due to problems encountered by individuals when attempting to express themselves with a limited number of graphic symbols or words, like in this example.

> A 12-year-old girl with cerebral palsy used a communication board with Bliss-words. She attended a boarding school and was going home for her Christmas holidays. When she was going to leave, she communicated *MOTHER HOLIDAY BOOK* to the teacher. She refused to leave the school and continued to repeat the same three Bliss-words. After an hour, the teacher realized that the girl wanted to take home the school report card that the teacher had read aloud to her. It said that she had made great progress in class.

From the girl's perspective, all the information was there: the holidays, the mother and a book. She was persistent but did not change her message to make it clearer to the partner.

When they fail in their communicative intention, young children with typical development may make great efforts to make the other understand (Clark, 1992, 2020). Adults use different strategies to help children to repair communication failures due to missing information, such as specific questions (*Is the girl blonde?*) or wh-questions (*What is the colour of the girl's dress?*). They may also use recasts (*I see; the girl's dress is blue*) or more elaboration when guiding the child to provide relevant about information (*You did not mention the colour of the girl's dress. There are two girls, and they have different colours on their dresses*) (Yıldız & Uzundağ, 2022). Questions, recasts and other forms of scaffolding by adult partners, together with their own efforts, may support the children's language learning. However, although toddlers can be persistent in achieving their communicative goals – an object or just getting an answer – repair strategies emerge only gradually in children with typical language development (Lloyd et al., 1995). Before five years of age, children are not very attentive to expressions of confusion or surprise in their conversation partner, which may indicate that she or he has not understood what the child said. Young children also often fail to indicate their own lack of understanding (Garvey, 1977).

The difficulties in conversations involving aided communication mean that managing situations with misunderstandings is a particularly important conversational skill for aided communicators who are using graphic symbols. However, strategies for repairing communication breakdowns appear to develop more slowly in children using communication aids (Cooper et al., 2021; Smith et al., 2018). In the above example, it was the girl's persistence and the teacher's efforts that made it possible for the girl to take home her report card. However, she did not rephrase her utterance, and it seems unlikely that she had received sufficient guidance in how to clarify her communication when it is not understood by the communication partner. Like many other young aided communicators, much of the girl's communication had taken place in educational situations where the adults knew what she was going to say or in routine situations where the message was easy to infer from the situation. Hence, she might rarely have had any need for correcting misunderstandings. Moreover, individuals with limited expressive means sometimes allow misunderstandings to pass because they do not know how to repair or remedy them, or because they would take too long to rectify (von Tetzchner & Martinsen, 1996).

Signed or aided language constructions are not the only cause of communication breakdowns in conversations involving AAC. The AAC users may also have problems understanding what the conversational partner is saying. They therefore need some ways to request clarification, for example, a manual sign or graphic symbol WHAT YOU SAY? or WHAT YOU MEAN?

The ability to manage their own and the communication partners' misunderstandings is important for AAC users' engagement in interesting conversation on an equal footing. In fact, when resolved, misunderstandings may lead to positive learning and enhance language acquisition, because the individual gets to know what was wrong, and what kind of strategies may be applied to make the conversation more successful. Due to the complexities of conversations involving AAC, repair strategies should be an integral and early part of interventions for individuals using AAC. Individuals should be taught repair strategies in line with their comprehension, including how they can make their conversational partners aware that they may have misconstrued or misunderstood what was communicated (Cooper et al., 2021; Møller & von Tetzchner, 1996). The use of clarification questions from individuals using AAC will also function to inform the communication partner what they understand of what has been said. The partners may provide spoken clarifications with simultaneous keyword manual signs or graphic symbols, which, in turn, may promote the aided communicator's acquisition of clarification strategies.

A common strategy among AAC users is to repeat the same utterance. This may be a good strategy if the communication partner was inattentive and did not see the sign or symbol or hear the voice output. However, a repetition might be misunderstood as the beginning of the next utterance and the conversational partner may be uncertain about what the communication is about or whether the utterance is a correction or rephrasing, or the start of a new sentence. Another basic repair strategy is to reformulate the aided utterance by adding or changing graphic symbols, for example, adding YESTERDAY to clarify that an event happened the day before (Møller & von Tetzchner, 1996). The individual can be guided to make the repair more explicit by using manual signs or graphic symbols like MISUNDERSTANDING or MISTAKE. Such items should be included as early as possible in the individual's vocabulary, and individuals should be taught to use the manual sign or graphic symbol to communicate that the other's interpretation or perception of the utterance is incorrect. For aided communicators who use devices with voice output, an utterance such as '*That wasn't exactly what I meant*' may be useful. The information may also be graded: ALMOST RIGHT may indicate that the partner's interpretation is wrong but not totally so, while VERY WRONG might indicate that the interpretation is quite far from the communicator's intention. Individuals should be taught such strategic use of signs or symbol before they get into a habit of repeating signs or symbols when trying to clarify what they intended to communicate. The fact that conversational repairs appear quite early in children with typical development as well as in children with intellectual disabilities (Barstein et al., 2018; Price et al., 2018) indicates that it is possible to teach repair strategies to individuals with intellectual disabilities using AAC.

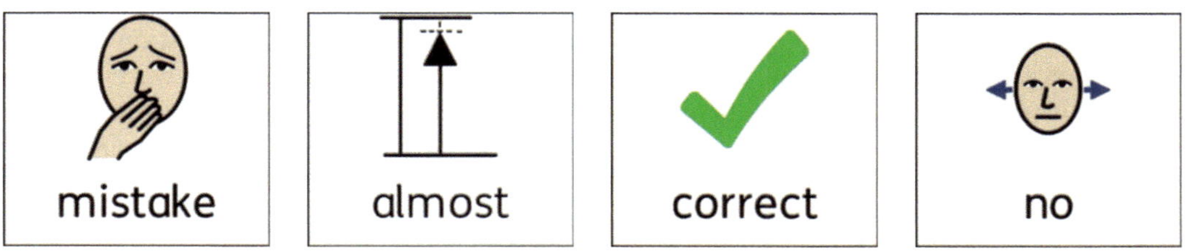

Widgit: MISTAKE, ALMOST, CORRECT, NO

It is important to distinguish between interpretative formulations and corrections or requests for clarification. In educational settings, following guidance from the teacher, young aided communicators may change their utterances to make them grammatically more correct, however, this change is not motivated by partner misunderstanding in the conversation but instead has a formal educational aim (Binger & Light, 2007; Soto et al., 2020). In aided conversations, the partner typically interprets and formulates the utterances of the aided communicator, who then indicates whether the interpretations and formulations are correct. However, people may ask aided communicators to repeat or rephrase a graphic utterance, even when it has been well understood. This is unfortunate when teaching grammar is not the aim of the conversation. A request for repetition usually signals an error, making children vary their answers and make changes in the utterance when this is not needed. Moreover, if children experience corrections as rejections of their attempt to communicate, this may have a negative influence on their language development. True negotiations about meaning, on the other hand, do not seem to make children feel rejected, but rather to influence their language development in a positive manner (Ceci & Bruck, 1993).

The alternative language group

For individuals with limited comprehension of spoken language, most communication intervention is about choices and the here and now. These interactions are often started by the teacher or another adult, and an early aim is to teach the individual useful ways of obtaining the attention of another person and initiating communicative interactions, for example, by moving in front of the other person when signing, bringing the communication book or device or handing over a graphic symbol.

The main objective of intervention for individuals in this group is often to teach them to use manual signs or graphic symbols as a means of obtaining something, and, to a lesser degree, to name an object or activity (see Chapter 6). However, when an individual asks for something and gets it, the dialogue typically consists of two utterances and the communicative interaction comes to an end. The individual (I) is asking for something, and the partner (P) is providing it, like in this example.

I: RAISIN.
P: {YOU RAISIN *You can have a raisin*}.

If the partner starts the dialogue, there may be three turns.

P: {WHAT *What do you want to do?*}
I: OUT WALK
P: {JACKET *Put on your jacket.*}

Some individuals in this group have more fundamental problems of communication and language, but it is still important to try to guide them to engage in somewhat longer conversations. Interventions should seek to break the pattern of mainly request-related conversations, except in situations that should be strictly structured or ritualized. In the example above, the interchange might have continued if there were a question instead of the instruction.

P: {JACKET WHAT CHOOSE *Which jacket do you choose?*}
I: RED
P: {RED NICE *Red is a nice colour.*}

{WHERE GO *Where do you want to go?*}
I: SHOP.

The conversation could go on to making a list of what to buy. During the walk, the teacher could start a conversation by commenting on people, things and events on the way.

Much AAC intervention for individuals with intellectual disabilities tends to focus on school and work-related activities, but individuals should be guided to engage in conversation in all kinds of situations. Communication about earlier experiences the individual had shared with the conversational partner, or perhaps with friends, may become engaging conversations. Photographs taken in familiar or unusual situations are often a good way to begin a longer conversation with individuals belonging to the alternative language group, applying a conversational topic-comment strategy (see p. 289). Modern cell phones make it easy to have photograph of recent events that are relevant to the individual. The photographs function to establish attention on the topic that is discussed in the conversation. They may also support the individual's memory and contribute to maintaining attention on the selected topic. For example, if the individual is interested in animals, topical photographs may show a horse or another animal in various situations: running, eating, lying down, pulling a cart and so forth. The conversation may also be more interesting to the individual when the teacher compares and contrasts pictures of new situations and events with known ones.

It is important to distinguish clearly between photographs that are used to support the topic of the conversation and photographs and graphic symbols that are part of the individual's aid lexicon and have the same function as spoken words in the conversation. When using a photograph to support memory (for example, of a visit to the zoo) and the conversation, the individual should not explain by pointing to the photograph. He or she should be guided to use manual signs or graphic symbols from his or her own communication aid to name people, actions and things or make evaluative comments about the objects, events or scenes in the photograph, for example, FATHER SWIM, MARY FUN, LARGE BALL or WATER COLD. The conversation should not be allowed to turn into a situation where the individual points at the photograph and only the communication partner comments with signs, symbols or speech.

In typical development, there is usually a relationship between conversational skills and other language skills (Clark, 2018; Veneziano, 2018). However, there are no fixed rules as to how many graphic symbols or spoken words the individual must master before the teacher attempts to engage him or her in gradually longer dialogues. It is rather a question of finding suitable topics. Toddlers with typical development may have limited vocabularies, but still take part in simple dialogues with their parents and other adults. Training with dialogues has proven successful with individuals with autism spectrum disorders and intellectual disabilities who had learned 40–80 manual signs or graphic symbols, and was also effective when these were seldom used spontaneously (Sommer et al., 1988). Participation in conversations may contribute to increasing the individual's use of previously learned signs and symbols.

Structured conversation around a topic (p. 190) may be a useful strategy even when the individual's comprehension of spoken language is very limited and the conversational partner has to use the individual's mode of communication (von Tetzchner et al., 2005). Attempts at direct training of conversational skills for individuals in the alternative language group have mixed results. However, there is good reason to try to have structured conversations with individuals who have learned some manual signs or graphic symbols. Although most of their communication may be about needs and wants, individuals with severe intellectual disabilities should also be given opportunities for using AAC for other forms of talk. Conversation about needs or wants may be expanded to include more than the activity or thing, such as DRUM TEACHER, CAR RED, PANDA CUTE or JOHN ORANGE. For some individuals this may not be possible, but it is only known after it has been tried. It is important that people in the environment – in spite of the individuals' challenges – attribute ordinary emotions and relationships to them and take into consideration the need they may have for communicating about such issues.

Intervention for individuals in the alternative language group, often includes structuring and routines (see p. 147). The structure or routine helps the individual to understand what is happening and to infer the meaning of the communication. They also contribute to building up expectations in the individual, which in turn may form a basis for communication. *A plan* is a description of a specific course of events. In a communicative situation with strict structuring, the plan may reflect the routine, general cultural knowledge and cues specific to a conversation. Plans may be designed for promoting conversational skills that are useful in a broader set of situations. Heller and associates (1996) used a plan-like approach to promote social interaction and communication about other things than the work tasks in a sheltered work setting for three adults with intellectual disabilities, hearing loss and no severe motor-impairment. They had vocabularies of about 200 manual signs, but did not use the signs in interactions with co-workers. They were therefore provided with two communication boards with PCS and drawings of manual signs: one with lexical items related to work tasks and one with non-task vocabulary like *HOW-ARE-YOU, FINE, TIRED, SHOPPING, FOOTBALL* and *TELEVISION*. The three adults were given training in how to greet, to answer when they were offered an object, to comment, to converse about a topic, and to close conversations. Following a period with special training sessions, the three individuals were guided to use their new conversation skills with their co-workers at work. The result was that they communicated more about things other than work tasks and took more part in social interactions at work. As part of intervention, the co-workers were taught comprehension and use of relevant manual signs. The intervention thus implied a change in competence for both the three persons and the other people in the environment, and all of them benefitted socially. Moreover, the staff became more aware of their own role as part of the adults' language environment.

The supportive language group

All problems related to communication and language are likely to influence participation in conversations. The first conversations may be rather frustrating experiences for young children with severe articulation problems that make it difficult for their communication partners to understand what they are saying. Conversations tend to come to a standstill. Some children develop a strategy of answering *yes* to all questions, whether they have understood the question or not (Kettner & Carpendale, 2013).

When parents and other significant adults have difficulties understanding a child's speech, they depend mainly on behavioural and situational cues to infer what the child is trying to say (Cress et al., 2013; Mohan et al., 2021). In situations where there are few or no clues to meaning, the adults' comprehension will be limited. For example, parents explain that it is especially difficult for them to understand their child when they are out driving because of the noise. They may try *yes* and *no* answers – in the same way as the children – in the hope that the reply happens to be the correct one. Sometimes their answer is only a vague *Mmm*. Such answers do not encourage continued conversation, and children may give up communicating when they feel that they receive irrelevant or meaningless answers. The adults, in an effort to keep the conversation going when they have not understood what the child is saying, typically take control of the conversation by asking the child questions or just deciding the course of action. This exerts pressure on the child's ability to achieve his or her own communicative goals.

The objective of AAC intervention in the developmental subgroup is to support speech development and make it easier for the children to contribute to conversations, and for others to understand them. The child's use of graphic symbols or manual signs helps conversational partners understand the messages, thereby preventing the conversation coming to a halt or deterring communication partners from their attempts to understand what the child means. This will provide the children with more opportunities for indirect learning and give them greater benefit from communicative interaction with adults and peers (Luckins & Clarke, 2021). Moreover, producing utterances with an AAC mode, including communication devices with speech output, may be faster than the child's unintelligible speech, which helps establish the child as a more equal conversational partner (Lüke, 2014).

Many of the intervention strategies used with the support group are similar not only to those used with individuals in the expressive language group, but also to strategies employed with individuals in the alternative language group, depending on the individual's cognitive functioning and comprehension of spoken language. The emphasis is on structured conversations about defined topics in various settings. The conversations begin by establishing a topic, for example, by saying *What do you think about your bicycle?* or *You know that walk we're going on tomorrow.*

> Robert is eight years old with autism spectrum disorder. He has used graphic symbols and is just beginning to speak. His speech is often difficult to understand, and he continues to support his speech with graphic symbols. He likes to travel by airplanes and ships, and to talk about his trips. The teacher had picked up some brochures from travel agencies and used these as starting points for conversations about planes, ships and things and events associates with planes and ships. Robert maintained this interest over many years and the teacher varied the content of the conversations to teach him about geography, history, physics, mathematics and English as a foreign language.

The communication mode used to establish the topic will depend on the individual's comprehension. To make sure that the individual is attentive, and that the topic has been understood, the teacher may ask the individual to confirm the topic, for example, by signing or indicating BICYCLE or WALK. To make it easier for the teacher to understand the child's communication, she or he may arrange sequences of simple events. This means that the teacher creates *new* situations that are easy to grasp and understand, and where the individual is able to make an independent contribution to the conversation, that is, relay something that he or she has not just told by the teacher to express.

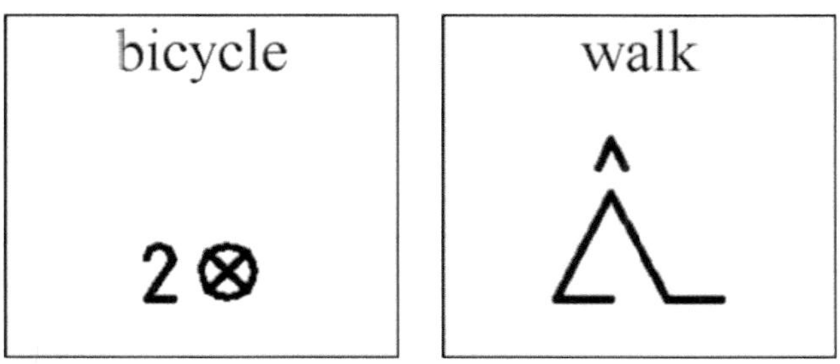

Bliss-words: BICYCLE, WALK

In addition to using manual signs or graphic symbols and establishing a topic of conversation, the intelligibility of the speech of children with articulatory disorders may be improved by designing situations in which the adult has several situational cues for what the child is interested in and often communicates about. Having conversations in varied situations is important and teachers can arrange this in simple ways: a child and an adult may play together with the same toys over several days, while the content of the play differs somewhat (see Chapter 10). Adults are encouraged to engage the child in conversation where the adult is commenting on what the child is doing with the toys and the child is presenting the story content of their play. In such situations, the child is likely to experience that more of what he or she says is understood without having to resort to repeating words that are equally unintelligible, and the adult will gradually become better at recognizing the child's speech and articulation of particular sounds. Conversations may be centred around pictures or toys, but the situation should contribute to making it natural for children to provide information that is unknown to the conversational partner. This is necessary for children to learn when their communication succeeds and when it does not (von Tetzchner, 2018).

An essential element of conversation training is that the individual and the teacher change roles during the conversations. It should not always be the teacher who is asking questions and the individual who is answering. Also the individual should ask for information, encourage activities and so forth. Studies show that children using AAC rarely do this (Pennington & McConachie, 1999, 2001; von Tetzchner & Martinsen, 1996). Because many of their conversations end in a standstill, individuals using AAC typically have little experience of keeping to one topic of conversation over time. This is also true for young children with typical development, although to a lesser degree (Schley & Snow, 1992). It is important to help children using AAC to maintain a topic and follow it up in the conversation. Role play may be useful and fun but should be varied. Even if children often like some repetition, the conversations may become stereotypical and ritualized if the adult initiates the same play and makes the same comments each time. By changing roles, the adult's scaffolding and chaining – which are important initially to keep the conversation going – may gradually be reduced and a larger share of the communicative responsibility may be transferred to the child in a positive manner.

Because the speech of children in the supportive language group is difficult to understand, people around them may assume that the children have nothing of significance to say. Similar attitudes may be found towards individuals in the expressive language group (Smucker et al., 2018; Wickenden, 2011a). An important aim of the conversational intervention is therefore to demonstrate to people in the environment that individuals can engage in interesting conversations when the conversational setting is adapted to their possibilities and constraints. Both the individual's vocabulary of manual signs or graphic symbols and ability to construct sentences are of importance. When people in the environment realize that the individual has interesting things to say, this will increase the informal language learning in situations with social interaction. For the developmental language support group, such learning may be supplemented with more formalized teaching over time.

For some individuals in the supportive language group, for example, children with Down syndrome, the problem of initiating conversations may be related to the fact that they may need a long time to react to what the communication partner is doing and what else is happening in the situation (Schworer et al., 2021; Silverman, 2007). Also with this group, conversational partners may proceed before the child has had a chance to take a turn. The best way of remedying this is to encourage conversational partners to wait a little longer than usual before taking the turn, and let them be convinced by personal experience that this kind of waiting is not in vain (see also p. 178). To ensure positive experiences, the waiting should take place in familiar situations where it is likely that the individual will take the initiative in a conversation. It is important that individuals still continue using AAC to take the initiative when their speech starts to improve. Their speech may remain difficult to understand for a long time, especially for adults and children who do not know the individual so well (Launonen, 2019a).

For individuals who belong to the situational subgroup of the supportive language group, problems with unintelligible speech continue through adolescence and adulthood. They may experience their communication partners pretending that they understand them and answering vaguely or incorrectly to what they say, and communication partners not really listening, but just continuing to talk because they feel awkward when they do not understand what the individual is saying. In order to increase the length of the conversations, the individual can make it easier for the partner to understand by supplementing speech with manual signs, graphic symbols or written words. Individuals who have learned to spell, may support their speech with written letters or letters from the hand alphabet. Children and adults in this group need to learn to evaluate the situation and know when they need to correct a misunderstanding and what they have to do to be understood. Structured conversations in the intervention are important for them to learn how to augment their communication with alternative means. The teacher should create situations where she or he, or another communication partner, does not know what the child is going to say, sometimes not even what the topic is, to give the child experience with both being and not being understood. It may be useful sometimes to bring persons who are less familiar into such situations. They are not used to the child's articulation and the child may therefore have to use AAC more than usual in order to be understood. Another important intervention measure is to inform the individual's usual communication partners about his or her conversation strategies, to ensure that enough feedback is received to know whether he or she has been understood or not. When the individual communicates with unfamiliar or sporadic conversational partners, he or she should try to lead the conversation in such a way that it maximizes the probability of being understood. This requires the training and experience necessary for the individual to feel confident in such situations.

In some schools and small or large institutions, individuals with intellectual disabilities may use AAC almost solely to communicate with staff members (Marková et al., 1992; Meuris et al., 2015). Possible consequences for autonomy and independent mastery are illustrated in a study of a group of adolescents with intellectual disabilities who communicated with manual signs and graphic symbols. Their comprehension of spoken language corresponded to their intellectual abilities. One day, adults helped them to start a simple game and then left the room. After a little while, one of the adolescents went to ask the adults for help with the game. The adolescents appeared unable to continue the game without assistance from adults (Tavares & Peixoto, 2003). When members of the staff are the only communication partners, all the social interactions and communication between the individuals become constrained by the actions and attitudes of the staff (Brewster, 2007). Unlike adolescents with typical development, where conversations replace the play of childhood, conversations may play a lesser role in the friendship relations of augmented speakers (Østvik et al., 2018). Conversational training should therefore aim at promoting skills that enable individuals to communicate with each other, as well as with peers with typical development.

The expressive language group

The gap between comprehension and expression in the expressive language group may imply that the potential for engaging in conversations is not fulfilled. The aim of conversational AAC strategies is to help individuals make contributions to conversations that are more equal to those of their peers. Different factors may contribute to the problems children and adults in the expressive language group have with participating in meaningful conversations. Many individuals in this group have slow language production due to poor manual motor control. Helpers may answer questions and speak for them, rather than allowing them to take the time they need. In interviews, aided communicators mention giving enough time and opportunities for communicating as the most important quality of good communication partners (Clarke et al., 2001; Howery, 2018a; Mendes et al., 2023). There are also individuals in this language group who use manual signs, for example, individuals with Down syndrome or autism spectrum disorders, who understand spoken language but whose speech remains unintelligible (Launonen, 2019a). For both signers and aided communicators, low expectations and little focus on conversational strategies in intervention may contribute to low conversational competence, as well as many experiences of being unsuccessful when communicating with others. However, there is considerable variation within this group. For some, a lack of communicative initiative and a passive communicative style may be the first issues to attend to. For others, slow communication and a lack of adequate strategies are most urgent in the intervention. These problems are intertwined. A good solution requires communicative access in varied situations and that both the individual and the conversational partners learn to interact in new ways (see Chapter 12).

For members of the expressive language group who have a good comprehension of spoken language, the development of conversational skills may be the most important part of their AAC intervention. It may not be the lack of linguistic skills that constrains these aided communicators, but instead, insufficient opportunities to use what they know (von Tetzchner et al., 2018). Communicative experiences with "helpful" dominating communication partners may have played a significant role in their development of a passive communicative style. There also appears to have been a general assumption that aided communicators will engage in the conversations once they are able to use a graphic system and have mastered the communication aid technically (Salminen, 2001). Strategies for initiating and maintaining interesting conversations should therefore have a more prominent place than they presently appear to have in many interventions.

Many in the expressive language group have age-typical or near age-typical comprehension of spoken language, although this is not a requirement for participating in complex conversations. In particular, it is important to attribute normal feelings and relations to AAC users, and to acknowledge their need to communicate about such matters. This is illustrated in the following example from von Tetzchner (2019b).

> Bodil was 43 years old. She was severely intellectually disabled, had no speech, and had acquired a graphic vocabulary of about 150 photographs and pictograms during the last year. Her main interest was people, and her communication aid contained 50 names of people in the form of photographs. Most of the intervention consisted in topical conversations with the teacher. In these conversations, she demonstrated a genuine need for sharing her experiences with others, and for putting into words (in her case, graphic symbols) her own positive or negative emotional encounters with other people, as well as for "presenting" herself.

Other studies have also pointed to the importance of expressive language competence for identity formation among aided communicators (Clarke et al., 2001). According to the assessment, Bodil's language comprehension was in line with her intellectual disabilities. However, there was still a large gap between her comprehension and production, and she therefore belonged to the expressive language group. Moreover, although she was not severely motor impaired, language was her best ability. The fact that she, in the course of one year of intervention with graphic communication, showed both unexpected insights and an ability to formulate messages with graphic symbols emphasizes how important it is that communication intervention for adults with intellectual disabilities, as far as possible, takes place within a conversational frame.

In addition to *conversational strategies*, intervention for promoting better conversational skills in the expressive language group may be divided into *environmental strategies and partner strategies*. Environmental strategies and partner strategies aim at changing the environment in such a way that it increases the individual's participation in ordinary conversations and that the conversational partners adapt to the alternative language mode of the individual. Many of the examples in this section concern individuals with language comprehension that approaches typical functioning, but most of the strategies are possible to adapt to intervention for individuals with different degrees of intellectual disabilities.

Environmental strategies

Many individuals with severe motor impairments have better language skills than motor skills. To utilize this strength, they should therefore spend much of their time in situations with communicative interaction. In reality, however, they tend to participate in relatively few such situations (Pilesjö & Norén, 2017; von Tetzchner et al., 2018). Their conversations may be mainly with professional helpers and much of their communication takes place in routine situations. Communication in routine situations is emphasized in many intervention programmes and routine activities tend to take up a larger part of the day than they do for children without motor impairments. Moreover, parents may tend to communicate in routine situations because they understand their children best in such settings.

When the child is in school, there is usually a need for easy communication about the child's experiences and events during the day that the parents or the school think the home or school should know about. This may be a message booklet that is carried between home and school, or electronically via electronic mail or an app. The communication between school and home ensures that practical information is systematically conveyed between home and school. However, the information often includes events that the individuals themselves may be able to relate, and thus deprives them of potential communicative responsibility. The parents and teachers may use the information in the booklet or app and choose to initiate conversations about topics that are mentioned there, making it difficult for the children to decide what events or experiences they want to recount from home or school. In the next example from von Tetzchner and Martinsen (1996), eight-year-old Henry is severely speech and motor impaired and uses a communication book with 145 pictograms through dependent scanning. His father had just read Henry's message booklet and initiates a conversation about Henry's school day.

F: *Did you learn about any animals today or which animals did you learn about?*
It is in your book, so I know about it.
Which animal did you learn about in school today?

H: *DOG.*
F: *Yes. Dog, yes. Did anybody bring a dog to school today? Who was it? Who brought a dog to school today?*
H: Looks at the table and smiles.
F: *Was it Mary?*
H: "No" (shakes head).
F: *Was it Joan who brought a dog?*
H: "Yes" (nods).
F: *Yes, it was in your book that Joan brought her dog.*

Because the content is known to the father, many of his questions are rhetorical and not genuine. Henry's only contribution is *DOG* and this is already known to the father.

Also, in routine conversations, the adult can infer with great certainty what the answer will be with a minimal contribution from the individual. The result may be that the individual does not learn when his or her utterances contain sufficient information to relay the content he or she intended. This may hinder the individual's pragmatic development and ability to monitor partner understanding and possible needs for repair or elaboration. It is better if the parents just ask for more information or for specific details that may be used in further co-construction. The booklet or electronic communication between home and school is a practical tool. Occasionally, it will also contain information about events that the parents or teachers believe it is important to communicate about with the child. However, in general, individuals using AAC should have as much communicative responsibility as possible and decide for themselves what information they want to relay to others.

This discussion of conversation and information booklets illustrates how important it is that the professionals have a developmental perspective when they adapt the environment to the abilities and limitations of individuals using AAC. Intervention measures rarely last forever. Strategies that were functional in the early phases of AAC intervention may no longer be useful and sometimes function as a straitjacket. This is particularly evident when the focus should be on the individual's conversational skills.

Adolescents with typical language development spend an increasing amount of their time with peers, and conversations take over from play as the preferred activity (von Tetzchner, 2019a). Young aided communicators participate less in conversations than their peers, and their conversations tend to be with adults (Andzik et al., 2016; Wickenden, 2011a). Conversations with peers should therefore be a main focus in interventions for adolescents using aided communication (Smith, 2005b, 2015; see also Chapter 12). Situations where young people interact with adults differ from situations where they interact with one another. Children and adolescents who use communication aids also seem to have different and more varied conversations with their peers than with adults (Brekke & von Tetzchner, 2003), and conversations with peers give the individuals access to the youth culture (Wickenden, 2011a). Professionals should try hard to create activities where young aided communicators can interact directly with peers without the help of an adult, for example, using role play and games. If adults have to be mediators between children who use communication aids, it is important that they function only as interpreters, without trying to influence the messages they relay, like in this example.

A girl and a boy, both using communication boards and a few manual signs, were sitting together with their teacher, who was functioning as a mediator between them. The girl was listing the children she wanted to come for her birthday party, but did not mention the boy, who eagerly communicated that he wanted to come. The teacher relayed his request. The girl indicated *NO* and the teacher relayed this message to the boy without interfering, that is, without attempting to make her change her answer (Soro et al., 1992).

Adults should also refrain from interrupting unnecessarily even if conflicts and arguments arise. Moreover, AAC users should experience such situations and learn how to cope with them. This is illustrated in the next conversation (von Tetzchner et al., 2005). Liv is a three-year-old girl with cerebral palsy. She has no speech and uses a communication aid with pictograms and photographs. She is attending a mainstream kindergarten and is having lunch in the kindergarten.

Liv:	"Finished eating" (turns away when offered food, fruit or drink). (Half a kiwi is left on the plate and Liv stretches her hands towards it).
Teacher:	(Thinks Liv wants the kiwi and peels it, cuts it into pieces with a knife and offers it to Liv).
Liv:	"I don't want it" (turns away).
Teacher:	*You said you wanted {fruit* FRUIT}.
Liv:	*FRUIT* "you" (looks at Tonje, one of the other children).
Tonje:	*No, I don't like kiwi.*
Liv:	*FRUIT* "you" (looks at Tonje).
Tonje:	*I don't want kiwi.*
Liv:	(Starts to look quite upset).
Tonje:	*Ask Elin if she wants kiwi.*
Liv:	*FRUIT* "you"? (looks at Elin).
Elin:	*Yes, thanks.*
Liv:	(Relaxes and offers kiwi to each of the other children at the table).

The teacher did not interfere, and the children sorted out the conflict that arose by themselves. The teacher's restraint and Tonje's suggestion gave Liv an opportunity to realize that there was a possible solution to the situation and to learn what to do from a peer. The other children had been taught about aided communication and were used to communicating with Liv. Information about communication aids and how the individual is using the aid gives peers better insights into the conversational challenges and possibilities of young aided communicators (Beck & Fritz-Verticchio, 2003; Brekke & von Tetzchner, 2003).

Children need relevant experiences if they are going to learn to use language and cope in situations with various emotional aspects, including ordinary conflicts involving peers (Eisenberg et al., 2010; Kurki et al., 2017). Many children who use AAC are sheltered from all potentially negative and challenging situations (von Tetzchner, 2003, 2004). However, by sheltering the children from moderate emotional experiences, adults may in fact shelter them from important opportunities for emotional, social, communicative and cultural learning. One result of this may be poorer emotional self-regulation. Moreover, not being excluded from negative and challenging experiences is likely to imply more varied social participation.

Partner strategies

When an individual uses AAC, this has implications for the functions of communication partners in conversations. In addition to producing their own utterances, the communication partners of aided communicators must often take an active part in articulating what the aided communicator wants to say – hence contributing to the co-construction of the utterances of the aided communicators. If using communication books or boards, the partner may say the gloss and engage in the interpretation of the aided elements as they are presented by the aided communicator. The partners infer the meaning of each element, assemble the elements and may tentatively produce the utterance before the aided communicator has finished constructing the utterance. Conversational partners are thus active participants both when they are speaking for themselves and when they are receiving an aided message (Murray et al., 2018; Smith et al., 2018; Brekke & von Tetzchner, 2003).

The experience and competence of conversational partners vary and can both enhance and hinder the individual's conversational success. Because the conversational partners have a double role, the training of family members, peers and other regular conversational partners is an important element of interventions for providing aided communicators with better opportunities for developing conversational skills (Kent-Walsh & McNaughton, 2005; Starble et al., 2005; see also Chapter 12).

In conversations involving an aided communicator, it is usually the person with natural speech who takes the initiative, chooses the topics and generally controls the conversation. Probably because of the limited expressive means of many aided communicators, this often involves *simplification strategies*, such as limiting suggestions for topics and repeating topics from earlier conversations. The aided communicator's contributions may mainly consist of replies and the conversational partners restrict the number of possible answers by posing a large number of *yes/no* questions. This may make it easier for aided communicators to be part of the conversation, but more difficult for them to introduce other issues and express their own opinions. It is possible that the role as helper misleads the partner into underestimating the aided communicator and not taking into account what the individual actually knows and understands. Such attitudes may be particularly evident among conversational partners who are not aware of their double role in conversations and who fail to acknowledge the communicative achievements of aided communicators, in spite of limited means (Collins & Marková, 1999; Smucker et al., 2018).

Time to say something

Conversations are always stretched out in time, and conversation involving aided communication always take somewhat longer than when both participants use natural speech. This implies a demand for good time-management in both aided communicators and their communication partners. In one study, young aided communicators with good language skills took an average of one minute to name a well-known object with a single graphic symbol. A reference group of peers with typical development needed about one second to say the name of the object (Deliberato et al., 2018). If a conversation has several turns and contains a mutual exchange of information and opinions, the time it takes increases considerably. When aided communicators communicate something that is outside their ordinary routines or conversation topics, it may take a long time before they are understood (Murray et al., 2018; Neuvonen et al., 2022c; Smith et al., 2018). The time-consuming factor may make it difficult for aided communicators to express the things they have on their minds, or the things they believe are important. The result is sometimes that the communication aid is not used (Salminen, 2001).

In spite of the fact that aided communication often takes a long time, aided communicators tend to spend less time in conversations than their peers. Time usage is a main reason for the asymmetrical conversational structure and the strategies generally used by conversational partners. Many conversational partners become impatient and find it difficult to wait (Smith et al., 2010). In one study, the mothers of 3–6-year-old children began to speak 1–2 seconds after they had given the turn to the child (Light et al., 1985). Pauses of more than one second made the mothers start to speak 92.5 percent of the time. The children, who needed more time to produce a graphic utterance, only had enough time to answer *yes/no* questions, which they could do by vocalizing, nodding or shaking the head. The importance of giving the children sufficient time is also demonstrated by the fact that the mother of the child who communicated the most, also waited the longest – sometimes as long as 47 seconds – before she took over the turn. While the average number of communicative initiatives on the part of the children in the course of 20 minutes was 11, this particular child had 45 initiatives. When communication partners are taught structured or expectant waiting, the initiatives of individuals using AAC increase (Flink et al., 2022). Studies show that to be able to control the course of the conversation and contribute to the conversation on a more equal footing, individuals using AAC need conversational skills, and the conversational partners have to restrain themselves from the urge to move the conversation forwards. Only then can slow aided communicators apply their skills and express their ideas, opinions and feelings (Howery, 2018b; Wickenden, 2011b).

Inference and interpretation

Because there is not always complete correspondence between spoken words and manual signs or graphic symbols, the communication partner must, to some extent, infer the meaning of the individual's construction and formulate it for him or her. In order to speed up the conversation, conversational partners may present their interpretations before the aided communicator has indicated all the graphic symbols of the planned utterance. In the excerpt below, adapted from Howery (2018a), Jennifer (J) is severely motor and speech impaired and uses a communication aid with speech output. It is the first day of the school year and the teacher (T) is going to find a desk for Jennifer. Jennifer has started to construct a message. Jennifer's assistant (A) and several children (C) are also present.

T: *How about over there?*
J: *'Michelle.'*
T: *You want to sit by Michelle?*
A: *She sat with Michelle last year.*
J: *'Not.'*
T: *You don't want to sit by Michelle?*
A: (Looks at the teacher and shrugs her shoulders).
J: *'Here.'*
(The bell rings and the rest of the children start coming in).
J: (Continues constructing her message).
T: *Jennifer, maybe for today you can just sit here by the door. Michelle will probably be here soon.*
J: (Continues constructing her message).
T: *Okay, guys, quiet down* (the room is full of the children's excited voices, which made it difficult to hear Jennifer's device).
J: *'Sick.'*

C: *Hey Jen, ya Ms. M is way sick …*
J: *'Michelle not here today she is sick.'*

When many utterances produced by young aided communicators consist of single symbols, this is partly due to the fact that a large part of these utterances are replies to questions (see following section on yes-no questions). However, it may also reflect that the conversational partner starts to make inferences for the whole utterance as soon as the individual has indicated the first symbol. The aim is to speed up the communication, but if the interpretation is not correct, the result can be a longer dialogue, like in the conversation below from Collins (1996). Fay (F) has no useful speech and uses a communication board with 200 Bliss-words. She initiates communication with a carer, Conrad (C).

F: *FATHER. Mmm mmm.*
C: *Wanna tell your father.*
F: *HOLIDAY.*
C: (Looks up at Fay, then down at communication board).
F: *HOLIDAY. Mm mm mm.*
C: *Oh you're going…* (looks down at communication board).
F: "No!" (shakes head and vocalizes).
C: *…on holiday with your father.*
F: (Leans forward over communication board).
C: *Right.* (Leans back a little and says something inaudible).
F: *LIKE.*
C: *You like.*
F: *FATHER. Mmm mmm.*
C: *Your father.*
F: (Moving finger to point to another Bliss-word).
C: *To go on holiday.*
F: "Yes" (nods). *Mm.*
C: *Right.*
C: (Sits back) *You'd like that to happen.*
F: *Mmm.* "Yes" (nods).

Bliss-words: FATHER, HOLIDAY, LIKE

In this type of conversation, conversational partners should not make premature interpretations but wait until they know more elements and are more likely to be able to infer the meaning of the aided construction. Conrad tried to jump ahead and guess the full sentence without sufficient knowledge. When Fay communicated *FATHER*, rather than just acknowledge the meaning of the Bliss-word and wait for the next, Conrad attempted to guess the whole meaning of what Fay was going to communicate, assuming that Fay was the subject and her father the object. When this was rejected by Fay (implicitly through continuing on to *HOLIDAY* and ignoring Conrad's guess), Conrad suggested a second interpretation, again without enough information of what Fay was communicating. This time Conrad thought Fay was continuing a prior conversation by saying something about what she would like to do for her next holiday. In reality, Fay was communicating something quite different: that she would like her father to go on holiday. This illustrates that the conversational partner must be patient and take care to get confirmation of the interpretation in order to ensure that misunderstandings are not being multiplied in the conversation. Seeking confirmation shows that the individual's aided utterances are taken seriously (von Tetzchner & Jensen, 1999). Except for in clear routine situations, the conversational partner should not start guessing early on, but rather seek sufficient clues to infer a probable meaning of the utterance.

This discussion is not meant as an argument against intermediate interpretation as a strategy. Even raw guessing may speed up routine conversations and there are aided communicators who prefer the partner to try to infer the meaning before they have finished constructing the utterance (Midtlin et al., 2015). People who know the user well may be able do it effectively. In less familiar situations, premature guesses may delay or hinder the individual's messages. It is also important that the individual is not too dependent on a competent conversational partner. Aided communicators should also be able to make themselves understood when the conversational partner does not manage to interpret the meaning or when guessing leads them astray.

Yes/no questions

Asking questions is an important conversational skill. However, in conversations involving spoken and aided communication, the aided communicator typically has a responsive role answering questions, while the partner's turns include many *yes/no* questions (Clarke & Kirton, 2003; Soto, 1999). In one study, adult aided communicators produced eight requests and questions and 163 answers, while the speaking partners produced 285 questions and challenges and eight answers (Wexler et al., 1983). One reason may be that many communication partners find that the conversation flows better when they are asking questions that can be answered fast with gestures, than when the individual has to find graphic symbols.

In addition, many adult questions are rhetorical, that is, about something the adult who asks already knows the answer to (von Tetzchner & Martinsen, 1996). Such questions are common in adults' conversations with young children, as well as in teacher–student interactions in school, but not in other conversations involving older children with typical development and adults in other situations. Aided communicators are aware of this and may find the conversation of little interest besides being together with the communication partner. In conversations between young aided communicators and peers with typical development, rhetorical questions are less prominent (Clarke & Wilkinson, 2007). This emphasizes the important role peer conversations may have for children developing aided language.

Another common feature of conversation involving aided communication is that a question may be followed by more specific sub-questions before the individual has been given enough time to answer. In the following example, the teacher (T) begins by asking a question that could have been a good starting point for a conversation with the student (S) (Harris, 1982).

T: *What did you do last night?*
S: (Begins to formulate an answer on the communication board).
T: *Did you go home?*
T: *Did you go to the cinema?*
T: *Did you watch television?*
T: *Did you watch Walt Disney?*
T: *Did your brother come?*

By adding several questions, the teacher ruined the conversation before it had even begun; the student never got to answer any of the questions. This emphasizes the communication partners' need for guidance. Managing conversations is usually a shared responsibility with the communication partners, but asymmetrical power means that the communication partner also has some responsibility for ensuring the contributions of the aided communicator.

A dominant use of *yes/no* questions is particularly detrimental to AAC users because it reduces their opportunities for learning new expressive vocabulary and trying out strategies for constructing more complex messages. In order to increase the aided communicator's contribution to the conversation, the conversational partner should use few *yes/no* questions, except when they are necessary for clarifying the meaning of the aided communicator's utterance, for example, because he or she does not have the graphic symbols needed for expressing what he or she wants to express. When possible, questions should be open, starting with question words like *what, who* and *where*, which prompt other answers than "yes" and "no", but the general aim should be to reduce the number of questions. A focus on strategies that promote the use of longer utterances may also increase the conversational contributions of aided communicators (see Chapter 9).

Partner styles

Many children and adolescents seldom use their communication aid spontaneously (Andzik et al., 2016). To make them use the aid more frequently, teachers and parents often encourage them to use the aid in situations where the individuals have already managed to make themselves understood in other ways (Harris, 1982).

Teacher: *What do you want?*
Student: "Ball" (points to the ball).
T: *No, tell me with your board.*
S: "Ball" (points to the ball again).
T: *How can you tell me with your board.*
S: (Puts head down on lap tray).

Adults should not demand other ways to express something the individual has already communicated effectively – except in educational sessions dedicated to formal training of AAC. Educational interactions have a different aim than ordinary conversations, but AAC training should help individuals to communicate in situations where their existing skills are insufficient, or they feel uncertain. It has little purpose to force individuals to use a communication aid when this is not necessary or functional, in the belief that they will become better at communicating because they are pointing at a graphic symbol instead of at the object. The student in the example above knew the graphic symbol *BALL* but in that situation it was quicker to answer by pointing to a ball. His reaction shows that he experienced the request as unnecessary nagging. Such situations produce negative experiences which may make the individuals less motivated to engage in conversations.

Sometimes communication partners outside educational settings take a teacher role and more or less tell the aided communicator what to do, like in this example from Smith (2003). Yvonne (Y) was six years old with cerebral palsy. She had no intelligible speech and used a communication board with 250 graphic symbols (PCS). Yvonne was participating in a research project. She and the researcher had played with a boat that squirted water without the mother present, and Yvonne's task was to tell her mother (M) what they had done.

M: *Is it a {GIRL girl}?*
Y: "Yes" (nods).
M: *Or a {WOMAN woman}?*
Y: "Yes" (nods).
M: *Which one? {GIRL girl} or {WOMAN woman}? Show me with your finger.*
Y: *GIRL.*
M: *A girl is it?*
Y: "Yes" (nods, laughing).
M: *Right. Did you do? What did you do?*
Y: (Looks to right of her chart).
M: *Uhuh. Excuse me. Verb first* (points to green section of chart).
Y: (Looks to left of the chart) E̲ *ALLGONE.*
M: *All gone. That's the wrong one. You something all gone. Somewhere up here so.*
Y: *OPEN.*
M: *OK, you opened it.*
Y: *PUT.*
M: *Oh, you put. Put what so? Sorry. It's open. I thought it was open you were going to go for. What did you put?*
Y: *WET.*
M: *Wet? Your board is wet alright. But what did you put?*
Y: (Hands out either side, vocalizing).
M: *You have water on the board. Where's your water picture? Your finger* (says something unintelligible). *Where's the water picture?*
Y: *ABC.*
M: *This one? ABC? That's not the water picture. Where's the water picture? You should know it by now. Definitely you know your water picture.*
Y: *WATER.*
M: *That's it. Water. Where did you put the water? Where's the water? Where is the water? Is it on? Upside down?*
Y: *BOAT.*
M: *Excuse me. Wait a minute. You forgot your prepositions again. I told you. You have to use them, I'm afraid.*
Y: *UP.*
M: *Now. Look at your book.*

PCS: ALLGONE, PUT, WET, BOAT

This was not an educational situation. The aim of the research study was to observe how Yvonne would use aided communication to tell the mother what she had played. However, the conversation turned into a kind of lesson where the mother tried to make Yvonne use a particular sentence structure. She told Yvonne to use verbs and prepositions and specified the word order. She asked Yvonne to indicate a specific symbol when she had already understood what Yvonne was saying. The mother told Yvonne which symbols to use and claimed that Yvonne was using wrong graphic symbols before she really knew what Yvonne was telling her about. She did not seem to pay so much attention to the function of Yvonne's communication. Like many other parents and teachers, Yvonne's mother was eager to show the competence of her daughter and focused more on the form of the communication than the content, maybe because the content in many situations is assumed to be known.

The conversation below with Yvonne's father illustrates a more adaptive style where Yvonne has a lead in the co-construction. Yvonne has seen a video of herself while the father was out of the room.

F: *Something in here.*
Y: *I.*
F: *You.*
Y: E.
F: *Yeah?*
Y: (Looks at chart, points).
F: *This one?*
Y: "No" (shakes head).
F: *Which one?*
Y: *GO.*
F: *You go?*
Y: "No" (shakes head).
F: *What, where is it? Down here? This one? You talk?*
Y: "No" (shakes head). *LOOK.*
F: *Look.*
Y: "Yes" (nods).
F: *You look. Don't be tearing.*
Y: *I.*
F: *You look at yourself?*
Y: "Yes" (nods).
F: *You're looking for me?*
Y: *VIDEO.*

F: *Video?*
Y: "Yes" (nods).
F: *Is that it?*
Y: "Yes" (nods).
F: *What?*
Y: (Points to camera).
F: *You look at the video? At yourself?*
Y: "Yes" (nods head).

This is a good example of co-construction. Yvonne and her father collaborated to convey her meaning. He asked for confirmation of each graphic symbol and gave a preliminary interpretation when Yvonne indicated a symbol. But it was Yvonne who was leading the conversation and the construction of her messages.

These two examples illustrate how important the interactional styles of the communication partners may be for the aided communicator's use of conversational skills and what they learn to express. The father's style seemed to give Yvonne opportunities for a larger contribution than in the conversations with her mother and she produced more long graphic sentences with the father than with the mother. Both of the parents wanted Yvonne to succeed in her communication, but the father's style may have been more likely to have a positive influence on her language development.

Because communication partners differ considerably in their use of conversational strategies with individuals who use AAC, it is important to guide significant people in the environment to become good conversational partners (see Chapter 12). However, intervention should also help AAC users to become aware of the common differences in children's and adults' communication styles, as well as in their AAC competence, and how they can take these differences into consideration when interacting with others.

Narratives

In all societies, humans communicate about people and events. The ability to tell others about events or event details that are unknown to them is a core element of human communicative competence. A narrative is a story, a representation of a chain of events in time and space in which people (or other characters) engage in actions and have intentions, motives, interests and emotions (Labov, 1972). Stories are descriptions of real or fictitious events, often personal experiences, with an onset, unfolding and conclusion (Aksu-Koç & Aktan-Erciyes, 2018). Construction of narratives constitutes an important part of children's language development and is a basis for learning about the world and the development of autobiographical memory (Bruner, 1991; Nelson, 2010). Narrative skills are important throughout life when telling others about positive and negative events (see Chapter 10).

Children with typical development start early to share experiences, comment on ongoing events – such as *Daddy car* to say that the father is coming home – and talk about past and future events with the help of parents or other adults. Narratives are a natural extension of these conversations about events and at around three years of age, children begin to tell more coherent stories (Kuntay, 2004; Schick & Melzi, 2010). The story is a special way of thinking about events and mentally representing social and cultural understanding (Bruner, 1986). Becoming familiar with the stories of a society – including gossip – is part of the enculturation process (Foster, 2004; Guendouzi, 2020). With this background, it should always be an aim of AAC intervention to help the individual to communicate about events in the present, the past and the future, to produce gradually longer narratives and to become an autonomous storyteller when possible. The ability to relay narratives that comprise more than one event is a milestone skill that needs to be promoted among individuals using manual signs and graphic symbols. Also individuals with severe intellectual disabilities can develop some narrative skills but may continue to need support (Grove, 2022).

Co-construction is a basic process in the development of narratives in young children with typical development (Jacoby & Ochs, 1995), as well as in scaffolding everyday communication about events and in narrative intervention for children using manual signs or graphic symbols (Grove & Tucker, 2003; Launonen, 2019a; Solomon-Rice & Soto, 2011). Co-construction means that two or more communication partners are contributing elements and sequential order to the narrative. The intervention may include storybook reading and retelling, and the production of personal or fictional stories (Soto et al., 2007).

There are many ways to support narrative production. Interesting picture sequences and videos of events are useful for eliciting and sustaining narratives, including homemade sequences with photographs of the individual and familiar adults and peers. Wordless picture books, like *Frog Where Are You?* are used to stimulate storytelling and literacy in children with typical development (Grolig et al., 2020; Honaker & Miller, 2024; Serafini, 2014). To understand and construct a narrative, the child has to pay attention to details in the pictures. Wordless picture books and cartoons are used in structured narrative training with manual signs or graphic symbols (Soto et al., 2007). They provide opportunities for individuals to be creative and use their expressive means to tell stories, including emotional aspects of the events (Rangel-Rodríguez et al., 2021). However, this material is only a support, and individuals should construct the narrative with their own expressive means – manual signs, graphic symbols, letters, gestures and so on. How the individual approaches communication about fictional or real past events gives parents and teachers insights into the individual's ability to construct narratives, which can be a basis for selecting content material and narrative strategies for the intervention (Adams et al., 2010). The co-construction of narratives with an adult also represents opportunities for individuals to learn about themselves and others (Waller, 2006).

Early teacher-led co-construction

Early narratives tend to be descriptions of something an individual has recently experienced – been part of or observed. Individuals with severe intellectual disabilities may relay important experiences through enactment – by imitating actions from the event they have experienced –but they may also depend on some degree of shared knowledge about the event (Ellis, 2007). Joint storytelling should be adapted to the abilities of the child and the adult. Simple fictional stories may function to engage individuals with limited language skills in joint storytelling (Grove, 2022). Describing the content of photographs may also be a useful start.

> Mari was 16 years old with autism spectrum disorder and severe intellectual disabilities. She had no speech and both formal and informal assessment showed a lack of comprehension of spoken language, and she therefore belonged to the alternative language group. She had a communication book with about 100 graphic symbols and used a few manual signs. For many years, Mari had made clear choices of objects and activities, but her teachers had made no attempts to introduce other language functions. Because it had not been tried,

there was no evidence that she could not learn to recount events, and a new intervention approach was implemented to teach her to describe picture content and events. Mari liked to dress up in funny clothes and a series of photograph were made with her and the teacher dressed in various costumes. For example, there was one photograph of Mari with a witch hat and another photograph with the teacher wearing the hat. Mari was taught to put the name photograph of herself and the pictogram HAT under the photograph of herself with the witch hat and TEACHER and HAT under the photograph of the teacher wearing the hat. Mari clearly enjoyed both looking at the photographs and placing the small descriptive graphic sentences under the photographs.

PIC: GIRL, TEACHER, HAT

The teachers had been satisfied with Mari's clear choice making. Because she showed no comprehension of spoken language, they did not think she could learn other ways to use her signs and symbols, and therefore they did not see any reason to introduce other usages. Mari's performance proved this assumption wrong and her engagement in the picture description activity indicates that it could have been initiated successfully much earlier. This emphasizes the importance of always trying to expand communication functioning, including when children are severely intellectually disabled and have very little comprehension of spoken language.

In joint storytelling, adults expand children's utterances and contribute new elements to the story (Soto et al., 2007). When the individual's vocabulary is limited, the expansion should not contain too many additional elements. Similarly, when new material is introduced for co-constructing a new narrative, the teacher should include mainly manual signs or graphic symbols that are part of the individual's vocabulary. Narratives may also be used to teach vocabulary and sentence structure, but when this is the aim it may be better to use variations of familiar narratives. It may be difficult for individuals with intellectual disabilities to manage both new narrative content and new vocabulary at the same time. According to the "operating principles" of Slobin (1973), it is usually easier for the individual first to express new functions with old forms (existing vocabulary), and to introduce new forms with old (established) communicative functions.

In order to utilize their narrative skills in everyday life, individuals need experience with initiating their own narrative and telling it to somebody who does not know what they are going to tell. If an individual who is using manual signs or graphic symbols is only used to retelling narratives that the communication partners present, and thus know, his or her contributions will be based on the assumption that the content is already known and that there is no need to provide many details (Launonen, 2019b; von Tetzchner, 2018).

The stories of individuals with severe intellectual disabilities may relate to their immediate surroundings and personal experiences, but also tales of fantasy and adventure are central to human communication and culture. Both simple stories like *Three Little Pigs* and classical works like *The Odyssey, The Hobbit* and *Gulliver's Travels* have been adapted to individuals with intellectual disabilities and used in communication intervention (Grove, 1998, 2022).

Intervention aim: from adult-led to self-made narratives

A narrative describes the agents, actions and other elements of the event and evaluates its moral and emotional aspects (Labov, 1972). Self-initiated narration requires some memory, language skills and social understanding (Hudson & Shapiro, 1991). The overall intervention aim is to guide AAC users to produce more parts of the narrative. There are a number of strategies that are useful for supporting storytelling and narrative development in individuals at different stages of narrative development. For AAC users with good comprehension of spoken language and more advanced aided language skills, narrative interventions may utilize open questions (wh-questions) about persons, actions, places, time, intentions and emotions to elicit more elaborations and evaluations of the narrative persons and actions: *Who ran away? – What did the witch do? – Where did the frog go? – When did the boy come? – Why did he take the dog? – How did the frog feel? – What do you think about the dog's behaviour?*

Even when the aided communicator has good comprehension of spoken language, there is a risk that the co-construction with a partner leading the narrative construction can turn into a kind of interrogation with sequences of *yes/no* questions, like in this example from Soto and associates (2006). Heidi (H) is an eight-year-old using aided communication. Her task was to complete a story starter presented by the teacher (T), such as: *Once upon a time there was a princess who lived in a glass castle.*

T: *Okay, you are trying to tell me something about the princess, sings a song with Erica. Are they outside?*
H: "Yes" (nods).
T: *Or are they singing a song about outside?*
H: "No" (shakes head).
T: *Okay, they are outside.*
H: "Yes" (nods).
T: *Of the castle?*
H: "Yes" (nods).
T: *Yes, what are they doing outside, besides singing?*
H: *Ahhh ha ha* (initiates message construction).
T: *You don't know?*
H: "Yes" (nods).

Yes/no questions may be useful for fast clarification and confirmation but in general, they do not contribute to increasing the contributions and narrative development of the individual and should therefore be kept to a minimum (as discussed earlier). The guidelines for narrative support listed in Table 11.2 build on Grove and Tucker (2003). They also list some adult behaviours that may discourage the production of narratives. These include lack of attention to what the individual communicates, direct corrections, such as *That is wrong*, as well as corrections which only require saying something in a different way, and many *yes/no* questions.

Table 11.2 Guidelines for supporting storytelling and narrative development (based on Grove & Tucker, 2003)

1.	Be a role model: tell the individual a personal story in manual signs or graphic symbols and then ask if the individual has had a similar experience.
2.	Expand the topic: help the individual to contribute more to his or her own narrative by asking, for example, *What happened then?* or *How did you feel?*
3.	Use repetition: repeat what the individual has communicated with an expectant intonation, for example, *You fell down?*
4.	Repeat and expand: repeat what the individual communicated and add further information, for example, *You fell down, and you hurt your knee!*
5.	Display communicative attention: show that you are attending keenly, with positive engagement and responsivity.
6.	Use clarifying questions: direct the individual to provide orientations and evaluations.
7.	Be persistent: maintain the individual's attention and encourage contributions to the dialogue.
8.	Take an interest: show interest in the narrative by offering your own contributions in response to what the individual is recounting.
9.	Encourage unshared experience: show interest in what the individual is relating and make a genuine effort to understand what the individual has experienced. Avoid guesses, especially based on routine interactions or premature inferences.
10.	Find new partners: include new people who don't know the individual's experiences.
11.	Offer rich information: show creativity and give rich feedback in such a way that the individual learns possible topics for new stories.

Repetitious feedback, with no expansion and too many prompts for shared experience, when the individual knows that the adult knows the answer, may give the individual little reason to construct a new story. Also, drills where the individual only fills a slot in a statement provided by the adult, like *And then we went to …* may discourage children with relatively good comprehension of spoken language who struggle with narrative development.

The aim of intervention with co-construction is to create opportunities for greater contributions from the individual but many aided communicators – particularly those with severe motor impairments – continue to have a lesser role than they should. The utterances of young aided communicators in the expressive language group may consist of a sequence of individual graphic symbols, as in the example below from von Tetzchner and Martinsen (1996). Eva (E), aged 5 years was using a communication book with 285 pictograms and photographs. She and her mother (M) were communicating about a visit to an aunt.

M: *When we went to Aunt Kari, what did you bring?*
E: *BICYCLE.*
M: *You brought that bicycle when we went to Aunt Kari.*
E: *BICYCLE.* (TO) BICYCLE (lifts the arm up and down, which is a manual home sign for "to bicycle").
M: *Yes, you did bicycle there.*
M: *Mm?*
E: *SANDBOX.*
M: *Were you also in the sandbox?*
E: "Yes" (nods).
M: *Hm.*

E: *SWING.*
M: *And then you used the swing.*
E: "Yes" (nods).
M: *Hm.*
E: *SEESAW.*
M: *And the SEESAW was there. Eva was in a playground when we visited Aunt Kari.*

PIC: BICYCLE, SWING

In this dialogue, Eva indicated *BICYCLE* after the mother's question: *What did you bring?* It was a routine conversation where Eva contributed to the further content of the narrative with the verb *(TO) BICYCLE* and the objects *SANDBOX, SWING* and *SEESAW*. She did not attempt to elaborate these or make any further comments. The visit was shared knowledge and the dialogue a retelling of what Eva and the mother did at that specific visit.

Like Eva, young aided communicators often use a few graphic symbols to direct an adult partner to tell a story about a particular event or aspect of an event, saying something like: "Tell me about X", where X can be a trip, a person, an event and so on. This particular pragmatic use of symbols in co-construction of narratives is called *directive*, because the aided communicators use the graphic symbols to direct the speaking partner towards formulating a narrative about a particular event that they want the partner to tell about on their own behalf. In the example above, the mother elaborated on Eva's single symbol utterances and did not encourage Eva to comment on or expand them, taking that role upon herself.

Ana (A) is eight years old and has with cerebral palsy. She is using natural speech (partly unintelligble) and her electronic communication device with speech output. She is telling her speech and language therapist (S) about her recent birthday party (Solomon-Rice & Soto, 2011).

S: *How were you feeling that day?*
A: *'Nervous.'*
S: *Really* (laughing) *nervous?*
A: "Yes" (nods).
S: *Oh my goodness. Let me write that down* (writing on easel)
S: *That makes me want to ask you a question about nervous.*
You know what question I want to ask?
A: *What?*
S: *Why were you nervous?* (pointing to *WHY* on story grammar map).
Why?

A: *My birthday.*
S: *Because it was your birthday?* (laughing)
Were you nervous because it was your birthday? (writing on the easel)
A: (Vocalizes, unintelligible).
S: *Hmmm?*
A: (Vocalizes, unintelligible).
S: *Ask me with that with your Vantage* (communication device). *Say it with your Vantage.*
A: *'Eleanor.'*
S: *What about Eleanor?*
A: *Coming.*
S: *Oh, Eleanor.*
A: *Coming.*
S: *Coming.*

PIC: FISH, TRIP, FUN

The dialogue above is an instance of communicative externalization, a small personal narrative, where the communication partner did not know what Ana was going to say. It is also co-constructive, because the speech and language therapist commented and asked guiding questions to support Ana's narrative.

To gradually reduce the teacher's part in co-construction and increase the individual's responsibility for the narrative, the intervention may follow a stepwise course with new events and stories, rather than stories from standard storybooks which are told repetitively to young children. The aim is to teach narrative skills, not a particular popular story. That requires variation in content (Plante et al., 2014). The language mode is not important, the individual may use manual signs, graphic symbols or spoken or written words.

1. The teacher presents a photograph depicting a familiar and clear event with persons, animals, objects and actions that are interesting to the individual, such as a birthday party, a bicycle or wheelchair trip, or somebody cooking. The teacher encourages the individual to name or comment on something in the photograph. This may include evaluations like FUNNY, BIG or NICE. The individual should produce more than one utterance, with guidance from the teacher. If this is not possible, the teacher may add one or two elements to the description of the event on the photograph.
2. The teacher shows a small sequence of pictures (2–4) or a short video with an everyday event, for example, somebody baking a cake, or throwing a ball. The content should be adapted to the individual's likely experience and expressive means. The individual is

encouraged to communicate something about the event with manual signs or graphic symbols. The teacher should take the lead but carefully expand and build on any expression the individual may give. *Yes/no* questions may be used for confirmation but should be avoided as much as possible.

3. The teacher tells the individual a story from a book with pictures. Then, they retell the story together. The complexity of the story should be adapted to the individual's expressive means. The teacher will take the lead and give the child opportunities to contribute to the retelling using suggestions and open questions. *Yes/no* questions may be used for confirmation but should be avoided as much as possible.
4. The teacher presents a longer sequence of pictures or a wordless book without saying anything about the content and encourages the individual to tell a story based on the material to the teacher. The individual takes the lead, but the teacher will give support and co-construct when needed.
5. The teacher reads a story to the individual or tells it if it is a wordless picture book, engaging the individual in the reading and telling. Following this, a familiar person who does not know the story is brought in and the individual is asked to retell the story to the person, using the pictures or book. The person can be another teacher, assistant, parent or peer. The individual should take the lead, but the new person may take part in the co-construction, ask for clarifications and details and present suggestions. The teacher will be present and give help if the partner does not understand, or the individual gets stuck.
6. The teacher reads a story to the individual or tells it if it is a wordless picture book, engaging the individual in the reading and telling. The individual retells the story to another teacher, assistant, parent or peer who does not know the story, without supporting pictorial material. The retelling will not be immediate but later in the day, or the next day, in order to make the task less repetitive. The individual should take the lead, but the new person may ask for clarifications and details. The teacher will be present and will give help if the partner does not understand, or the individual gets stuck.
7. The individual tells a story (not read by the teacher) using a sequence of pictures or a wordless book to a person who does not know the story from before. The teacher will be present and will give help if the partner does not understand, or the individual gets stuck.
8. The individual recounts a recent experience or a self-invented fictitious story to another person who does not know about the event or the story, for example, another teacher, an assistant, a parent or a peer. The individual's teacher will be present and help if the partner does not understand, or the individual gets stuck.

These strategies may be supplemented with intermediate steps and variation around these steps, paying attention to the guidelines in Table 11.2. Importantly, the focus should be on the content of the story, not on the child's behaviour. After the narrative session, the teacher should highlight the interesting elements of the story rather than praising the individual for them. However, the teacher may tell the individual that he or she really is a good storyteller at the end of the session (if the session was OK).

Some aided communicators store ready-made stories in their electronic communication aids, but stories tend to be short-lived and may have little function when all the usual communication partners have heard them.

Chapter 12

The language environment

Language development is a social process, and the language environment is where language is both learned and practised. Children engage in social relations and learn the functions of communication and language through their interaction with more competent members of the language community (Bruner, 1983; Nelson, 2007). The quantity and quality of communicative interaction with family members, peers and others will influence children's language development (Rowe & Weisleder, 2020). Conversation always implies some degree of reciprocal adaptation of the communication partners and in interactions involving individuals in the early phases of language development, it is the more competent communication partner who adapts to the one who is learning. This can be observed in child-directed language in early child–adult conversations (Rowe & Snow, 2020) but even four-year-olds speak differently to two-year-olds and to adults (Shatz & Gelman, 1973). The characteristics of child-directed language are also present in the signing of deaf parents to their young children (Holzrichter & Meier, 2000; Masataka, 1992) and in adult gestures to young children (Dunst et al., 2012).

Unlike typical language development, the development of AAC is a planned process that usually involves direct teaching of graphic symbols or manuals signs (see Chapter 6). Teaching is important but AAC training sessions are usually limited in time, scope and variation (Barker et al., 2013; Kleinert et al., 2023). Interventionists may see the child 1–2 hours a couple of times per week, or less, while parents may interact with the child in play and other activities many hours every day (Weisberg & Jones, 2019). Adults and peers in kindergartens also constitute a large part of young children's language environment. The language environment is equally important for children who develop alternative language modes and adaptation of the environment is a natural part of all AAC interventions. The overall aims are to provide the individuals with a means of communication that they can understand and use, *and* to make their language environment communicatively accessible (von Tetzchner & Stadskleiv, 2016). Communicative access means that significant people in the environment understand the individual's expressive language and answer the individual in a language mode that he or she understands. A communicatively accessible language environment means that the child's communication is met with communication, rather than praise or rewards. The language environment should represent opportunities for using AAC and for learning through communicative problem solving. AAC intervention is therefore more than teaching the individual some form of AAC – the wider aim is to create a language environment that supports the individual's communicative problem solving and development and use of AAC. The result of AAC interventions should be that the individual can use AAC for diverse purposes throughout the day *and* is understood by all significant people in the environment.

DOI: 10.4324/9781003387633-13

The development of language requires the use of language with different people and in a variety of situations. The child's spontaneous and active solving of communicative problems and use of language are essential processes in all language development (Tomasello, 2003). Many parents and teachers are strongly engaged in the individual's development of AAC and seek information about what they should do to support the individual's communication in the best possible way (Berenguer et al., 2022; Stadskleiv, 2017). However, when the individual has a comparatively good comprehension of spoken language, people in the environment do not always see the need for learning and using the individual's expressive language mode. The result may be a communicative one-way road in the vocal mode – from the communication partner with natural speech to the individual using AAC – which means that essential environmental elements for supporting the individual's development of AAC are lacking. The individual's own expressive contributions may be reduced when the family or the teachers lack AAC competence (Doak, 2021; Kim et al., 2021; Snell et al., 2008). This may, for instance, be evident in classrooms where teachers have limited experience with AAC and rely mainly on *yes/no* questions. Also care staff working with adults with intellectual disabilities using AAC may lack the skills and understanding of AAC that is needed to engage the adults in reciprocal communication (Bunning, 2018; Møller & von Tetzchner, 1996). It should therefore always be an aim of AAC intervention to go beyond training of the individual to building up AAC competence among people in the individual's social environments, including family members, peers, teachers, other staff and other significant people (Blackstone, 1999; Kent-Walsh & McNaughton, 2005)

Children's production of manual signs or indication of graphic symbols may not be precise. This may be addressed in training sessions, but precision is not important in everyday communication as long as the family and other people in the home environment understand what sign or symbol the child is trying to communicate and are able to infer the intended meaning – at least after some negotiation of meaning. Communication is also the basis of parents' scaffolding in everyday conversations and co-construction of meaning with their child in developing AAC (Jonsson et al., 2011; Neuvonen et al., 2022a).

The main aim of the strategies presented in this chapter is to guide family members, peers, teachers and others to interact with individuals using AAC and help them to create communicative possibilities, and thereby support the individuals' language development, social participation and relationships with adults and peers. It also includes guidance for teachers and others who are communication partners and involved in the everyday training of AAC. The guidance they need will depend on the abilities and challenges of the individual. Involving a minimally verbal autistic child in communicative interaction may require different forms of adaptation than an individual who needs AAC due to severe motor disabilities caused by cerebral palsy. This chapter is thus about intervention measures that help significant people to become competent conversational partners who communicate with the individuals using AAC for diverse purposes and in a variety of situations throughout the day.

Adapting the early and later language environment

Individuals who develop AAC grow up in environments where spoken language is the main mode of communication. They are typically taught basic AAC skills as part of a more comprehensive intervention programme, but this is not sufficient to fully support their development of AAC. Their everyday language environment should include some people who use their language mode and thereby enable observational learning of new vocabulary and sentence structures. Only a very small minority of parents and other significant people have prior experience with AAC. They therefore express a need for help and guidance in making the environment communicatively accessible and adapted to the particular individual's abilities and disabilities, language mode and communication skills (Hanley et al., 2023).

It is a common observation that children tend to use signs less or have less access to graphic symbols outside training sessions (Doak, 2021; von Tetzchner et al., 2018). One reason may be limited communicative access. Many individuals who develop AAC risk becoming communicative under-achievers due to few communicative opportunities (Goldbart & Marshall, 2004). They may not be credited with having anything of interest to communicate (Bird et al., 1989; Mellman et al., 2010), and staff may feel that because of other duties they have too little time to respond to the individuals' initiatives (Fisher et al., 2014; Møller & von Tetzchner, 1996).

Studies show that interventions addressing the AAC competence of the family and other natural communication partners in the environment support the individual's development of the alternative language mode (Hanley et al., 2023; Kent-Walsh et al., 2015; van der Meer et al., 2017). Potential communication partners learn about AAC in general and how individuals with different abilities and challenges develop AAC. It is of special importance that people in the proximal environment become aware of the achievements of individuals using manual signs or graphic symbols and what the individuals are capable of communicating with these means, and how they themselves as communication partners can support the individual's continued language development (von Tetzchner & Stadskleiv, 2016). This information may be provided in AAC courses and through systematic guidance of family members, teachers, peers and other significant people.

The plan for education and support of potential communication partners should have a long-term perspective. Although the communication partners are competent users of spoken language, they may find learning an alternative language mode slow and laborious. This is a transactional process (Sameroff, 2009): the language supportive environment contributes to making the individual a better communicator, this creates new positive educational needs of people in the environment, which increases their positive impact and makes the individual a better communicator, and so forth. This is not a plan for the early phases only; the plan for AAC support may in fact extend into adulthood. Many but not all individuals who continue to use AAC in late childhood and adolescence need manual signs or graphic symbols throughout life (Balandin & Morgan, 2001; Cumley & Stuart, 2005; Webster et al., 2016). A competent language environment is necessary for maintaining the individual's communication and language skills in adulthood, as well as providing new vocabulary and supporting further development of language skills, for example, related to communication at work and other roles of adult life (Bryen, 2008; Hughes et al., 2022; McNaughton et al., 2012).

A major early aim is to make the home communicatively accessible by guiding the sensitivity of parents and other family members and the way they react to and initiate communication with children using AAC. For infants and children with early diagnoses that imply a risk of severe delay or of not developing intelligible speech, professionals may start to introduce the family to AAC as early as when the child is six months old (Launonen, 1996, 2019b; Romski et al., 2015). When possible, the family should be taught comprehension and use of some manual signs or graphic symbols *before* the child is expected to begin paying attention to, and using, signs or graphic symbols. Being ahead of the child means that the parents are ready when the child starts using his or her first manual signs or graphic symbols, and are likely to feel more competent and relaxed, as well as playful and engaged, in early communication with the child (Launonen, 2019b).

Staff and children with typical development in the nursery school that the child developing AAC attends, or will soon attend, are core parts of the early language environment. They may produce keyword manual signs or show keyword graphic symbols together with their speech when the child shows interest in particular objects, activities and events in the environment, and when they are trying to direct the child's attention towards particular people, things or other aspects of the environment. Staff and peers should be taught manual signs or graphic symbols before the child joins the group and hence are prepared to become communication partners (von Tetzchner et al., 2005).

Further environmental adaptations for older children and adults who use AAC will depend on their progress in communication and language development. For individuals with limited comprehension and ability to express themselves, over-interpretation of their actions as communicative may continue to be an important environmental strategy (see p. 172). People in the environment are typically very attentive to the individual's vocalizations but may fail to react to the individual's communicative efforts in other modalities, for example, arm movements or body postures (Snell et al., 2008). Guiding significant people in the environment to interpret or over-interpret the individual's movements, facial expressions or body postures increases the likelihood that the individual will be reacted to, which in turn may promote self-initiated activity and joint attention, but interpretation should be made with care to avoid attributing unfounded intentions to the individual (Dhondt et al., 2023; Grove et al., 1999) (see p. 68).

For children and adults with more advanced AAC competence, people in the environment should get beyond the individual's routines and rather seek opportunities for him or her to engage in gradually more complex conversations with people who understand their communication system and can answer in a mode that they understand (communicative access). Importantly, professionals should make sure that people in the environment are aware of what the individual understands and is able to express and show potential communication partners how they can scaffold the individual's incidental learning in everyday communication situations, without turning all these situations into spontaneous training sessions (see p. 186).

The days of individuals with extensive motor impairments are often filled with fixed routines that leave few opportunities for spontaneous dialogues (von Tetzchner and Grove, 2003). When guiding potential communication partners of these individuals, an important objective is to help them to create varied everyday communication situations, especially communicative situations in which parents and other conversational partners do not know in advance what the individual wants to communicate *and* take the time needed to find out what the individual wants to communicate about (Murray et al., 2018; Wickenden, 2011c).

A common way of creating awareness of graphic symbols among people in the environment is to place graphic symbols as labels on objects in the environment, for example, *TOILET, CHAIR, GLASS, TELEVISION, RADIO* and *BED*. This makes graphic symbols visible in the environment and it may be easier for other people to use keyword graphic symbols and thereby help the individuals to learn the graphic names of things. However, these should not replace the individual's use of his or her own communication aid. Individuals should not point at the graphic symbols placed on things in the environment but on the corresponding symbols in their aids. This adaptation may be useful in the early phases of graphic language development and the graphic symbols used in this manner are typically the ones that the individual is in the process of learning. However, it may also be useful to label cupboards and drawers containing the individual's belongings and other relevant objects. They may become a standard part of the environment and help individuals to keep order and remember where things are. A related strategy is to hang relevant topic boards or individual graphic symbols on the wall, for example, play-related boards or symbols on the wall in the play corner to facilitate more varied communication during play.

The simultaneous use of speech and manual signs or graphic symbols

Most children who use AAC have at least some understanding of spoken language and spoken utterances in the environment are an important source of information of how language is used in different situations. The way the conversational partners take turns and speak will, to a large extent, determine the individual's role in the conversation. They may adapt their speech to both the individual's comprehension of spoken language and his or her mode of expressive communication. *Yes/no* questions often constitute a large part of communication partners' utterances, as they only require the individual to confirm or reject. *Yes/no* questions are an important element in conversations (Hörmeyer & Renner, 2013), but individuals using AAC need a language environment that promotes communicative initiative and more varied language use than answering "yes" or "no" to the partners' questions (see p. 342). They need to observe others using utterances with manual signs or graphic symbols that are not yet part of their vocabulary and to become positively challenged to use a growing number of manual signs or graphic symbols and to produce more varied utterances. Signs and symbols should therefore become a natural part of the language environment. People in the environment should be conscious of their own use of spoken language, with or without simultaneous manual signs or graphic symbols, as well as the need to vary their language, for example, increasing the number of comments and open questions when communicating with individuals using AAC.

Simplified speech may help some individuals understand what is said and make it easier for them to align spoken utterances with the manual signs or graphic symbols used. However, the efficiency of this modification depends both on the individual's comprehension of spoken language and the cues people in the environment use to make the correspondences between signs or symbols and spoken words more understandable. Individuals in the alternative language group may have limited benefit from hearing speech alone. In an optimally adapted language environment for individuals learning AAC, people use the individual's language mode as much as possible when communicating with him or her and they always speak while performing manual signs or indicating graphic symbols. Even if the individual's comprehension of spoken language is very limited or lacking, simultaneous communication may help individuals relate signs or symbols to spoken words if they have an emerging ability to do so (von Tetzchner, 2019b). They need information of how their own language mode is used by others, but speech should never be omitted.

Manual signs

The use of simultaneous speech and sign, often called "total communication", has a long history, especially in the form of keyword signing. People in the environment speak slowly and clearly, accompanying their spoken utterances with manual signs. Studies have found that this contributes to improve the comprehension and use of both spoken words and manual signs (Grove & Launonen, 2019; Rombouts et al., 2017).

Individuals with some intelligible speech may use keyword signs to supplement their speech but as an intervention measure keyword signing is mainly directed at people in the environment (Cologon & Mevawalla, 2018). This is the most common environmental adaptation of the environment for individuals with autism spectrum disorder and intellectual disabilities (Bonvillian, 2019; Launonen, 1996, 2019a, b). If the individual uses simplified signs, people in the environment should use simplified signs as well, including using the signs to represent several related meanings (Bonvillian et al., 2020a, b) (see p. 253). When groups of people in the environment become competent signers and use manual signs in most communications with the individual, and when the individual is present, they create enclaves of signing within the environment of mainly natural speakers. The home, kindergarten, school, day-centre, institution or similarly restricted environments may contain such enclaves. Some individuals need such enclaves throughout life.

In keyword signing accompanying speech, communication partners typically use one or a few manual signs without structural coherence and omit signs for grammatical functions (Grove, 2019a, b). This makes it easier for communication partners with limited sign competence to use manual signs, but this unstructured use of manual signs fails to provide information about even simple sign sentences. Most individuals who develop manual signs are able to learn simple sentence structures with actors, actions and objects, and signed utterances may also include prepositions and time vocabulary. Seeing others use simple sign sentences will promote the individuals' use of sentences and language creativity. More advanced signers should have opportunities to observe more complex sentence structures, as well as the use of signs for more function words once they reach an appropriate linguistic level (see Chapters 8 and 9).

It is usually more difficult to recognize other people's manual signs than to produce signs oneself. Signs produced by the individual in unplanned everyday situations may be particularly difficult to recognize. In teaching situations, the teacher tries to elicit certain signs and usually knows which manual signs the individual is trying to perform and will respond appropriately to the sign, even when it is poorly articulated. In more spontaneous communication, the individual's intention may not be evident, and the same sign may not be understood. The result may be that the individual's signing outside the training situation often fails and leads to frustration. A significant part of manual sign teaching of people in the environment should therefore be aimed at comprehension of signs. A common training strategy is that one person performs manual signs that other potential communication partners have to recognize. Video recordings of an individual's articulation of manual signs may be used to teach staff members how he or she performs the signs. Recognition of signs without extra clues is also good training, that is, video recordings where objects or activities the individual is referring to are not visible, and the sound is turned down so it is impossible to hear what is being said.

Graphic symbols

New graphic symbols may be introduced in teaching sessions, but they should simultaneously be included in the individual's everyday conversations. However, outside training sessions, people in the environment mainly seem to use graphic symbols when telling the individual what to do or presenting a choice. The use of keywords with graphic symbols by people in the environment is rarely reported. Most communication partners do not use a board of their own, or the individual's board, to support the individual's comprehension or to introduce new vocabulary items as part of conversations with aided communicators (Binger & Light, 2007;

Doak, 2021). Most "aided language stimulation" takes place in training situations where the use of graphic symbols is taught and "modelled" (see Chapter 6) and rarely at home (Tegler et al., 2021). One reason for the more frequent use of keyword signing may be that both the individual and people in the environment always have the means to make manual signs – the hands – while communication aids may not be available in many situations, and even when available, it may not be practical for the communication partner to use the aid (Batorowicz et al., 2014; Doak, 2021; von Tetzchner et al., 2018). Availability of the communication aid is necessary for communicative access and the family's and other people's use of aided communication. This can be the communication board or book that functions as a backup in case the electronic device breaks down. The conversation between Bodil and a staff member (see p. 386) illustrates that communication partners can use graphic symbols as keywords and that this may be easier with communication boards or books than with electronic devices (Smith et al., 2010). Note that the aim of communication partners' simultaneous use of speech and graphic symbols as an environmental intervention is not to prompt the child to produce a particular utterance or "model" an utterance the individual should repeat immediately or later, but rather to use their own turns in the conversation to expose the individual to more aided language.

Graphic symbols usually have a written gloss above the symbol so it is not necessary for people in the environment who can read to learn the design of each of the graphic symbols. However, parents and staff members should nonetheless be taught how the graphic system is constructed and the reasons why specific symbols are included in the individual's communication board or device. They should also be taught how each individual uses the graphic system, including the individual's creative use and idiosyncratic combinations (see p. 119). Many aided communicators have poor motor coordination, and it can be difficult to understand where and how they are pointing. Video recording is a useful tool for demonstrating the individual's way of indicating symbols, and thereby reducing the risk that people in the environment misunderstand the message. Staff members may gain insight into the potentials and limitations of the individual's system by communicating with each other using the individual's graphic symbols without speaking.

When communication partners accompany their speech with graphic symbols, even individuals who have limited comprehension of spoken language may increase their understanding, if they are able to do so. In order to promote an individual's understanding of the fact that graphic symbols have corresponding spoken words, people in the environment should therefore use graphic symbols together with speech, whenever this is practical. In this way, the individual may experience the combined graphic symbol and word in different situations and thereby learn that symbol–word correspondences to some extent may depend on the context. For individuals with some understanding of spoken language, the simultaneous use of graphic symbols and speech in the environment may make it easier for them to understand spoken words and develop speech (Sterrett et al., 2023; von Tetzchner, 2019b).

AAC in the family

The family is the centre of most children's lives. Parents and siblings are usually young children's most important communication partners. Parents engage in communication with the child in play and other activities, create communication opportunities and guide the child towards communication and language competence (Adamson et al., 2020; Service et al., 1989). The help adults give children when they attempt to solve problems that they cannot yet solve on their own has been termed "scaffolding" (Belland, 2014; Wood et al., 1976). Scaffolding is based on the idea that children's problem-solving proceeds from doing together, to doing alone, from *interdependence to independence*. The term is often used in education, but language scaffolding was originally used about the informal guidance children get from parents and other competent language users (Shvarts & Bakker, 2019). Communication scaffolding gives young children experiences that help them to solve immediate communicative problems and lays the ground for solving similar problems in the future without needing help. The adult should not solve the task for the child, only give the child just enough help to solve the problem (Bruner, 1983). The child's language development is influenced by the parents' scaffolding skills, sensitivity and responsiveness, their positive reactions to the child's initiations and their use of language in routines and other situations that are familiar to the child (Bruner, 1990).

Children spend much time together with their siblings, often more than with their parents (Howe & Recchia, 2014). Older siblings influence the language use of younger siblings (Bridges & Hoff, 2014) and may also have a positive influence on a sibling's use of AAC (Gatt, 2022). Siblings with and without disabilities generally spend less time together than other siblings, but siblings tend to have a very special role for children with disabilities who may have fewer friends and peer relations (Petalas et al., 2015). The special relationship often lasts throughout life, including when a sibling is using AAC (Dew et al., 2008; Rossetti & Hall, 2015).

Early intervention of communication and language development typically gives parents a prominent role in creating a rich language environment for their child (Adamson et al., 2020; Yoder & McDuffie, 2006). Many studies aim to make parents into AAC trainers (e.g., Anderson et al., 2015; Ganz & Hong, 2014; Gona et al., 2014; Granlund et al., 2008). The parents are taught common training strategies, including some of the strategies mentioned in Chapter 6. Some parents find home training useful, while others find such training assignments stressful (Donato et al., 2018; Goldbart & Marshall, 2004; King et al., 2020). One mother described the many demands she experienced: "I feel like her dietician and her nutritionist, I feel like her therapist, I feel like her teacher. And finally there comes a point where I also want to feel like Mom" (O'Neill & Wilkinson, 2020, p. 249). Moreover, many corrections outside training sessions may not support the individual's language development (Smith, 2003). Typical language development is in many ways "self-corrective" – the child learns implicitly what is correct and incorrect without the adult interrupting the flow of the conversation. Parental feedback seems to relate to communicative success rather than to point out linguistic "errors" of form (Brown & Hanlon, 1970; Nikolaus & Fourtassi, 2023).

The everyday communicative interactions within the family may be even more important for children developing AAC because they tend to have few other regular communication partners. The direct teaching of AAC in school is important, but children who are developing AAC spend more time at home than they do in AAC training (Harrington et al., 2023). Interview studies report that parents express a strong need for gaining AAC competence, for explanations why AAC is needed and for help with engaging in conversations and supporting their child's use of AAC (Fäldt et al., 2020; Launonen, 2003, 2019b; Marshall & Goldbart, 2008). They specifically ask for guidance in how to integrate AAC in the everyday life of the family (Berenguer et al., 2022). Children are more likely to become competent users of manual signs or graphic symbols when family members have been given partner training, understand the functions of AAC and recognize the child's communication efforts in daily activities (Tegler et al., 2021). Young adults who use AAC mention the family as their most important source of support in AAC development and the loss they experience if contact with the family is reduced (Cooper et al., 2009).

A number of approaches to parent guidance exist, such as ComeAlong courses (Fäldt et al., 2020; Jonsson et al., 2011), Aided Language Stimulation (Goosens', 1989), Keyword Signing (Cologon & Mevawalla, 2018), and Improving Partner Applications of Augmentative Communication Techniques, IMPAACT (Timpe et al., 2021). Together they reflect common features as well as the variability that exists in AAC intervention for families. A functional programme should include four main elements:

1 An introduction to AAC; this may be a general course with many attendees.
2 Group sessions involving two or more families, which focus on major issues related to the individuals needing AAC in these families.
3 Individual family sessions with parent–child and sibling interactions with guidance from professionals, often including video recordings, and follow-up discussion.
4 Group meetings where parents share experiences, ideas, challenges and solutions – without being directed by professionals.

Parents should have an active role in decisions about their child's AAC training and this requires that they have relevant knowledge. Professionals should go through the assessment with the parents – the methods used, results, other observations and implications (see Chapter 4). The parents should be informed about the bases of AAC development in general, different modes of AAC, AAC and speech development, and research findings and clinical experiences with the different AAC modes in general and related to the diagnostic group of their child (see Table 12.1). General AAC courses give parents a basis for understanding their child's potential for developing manual signs and graphic symbols. Manual sign courses and courses about technical aspects of electronic communication aids may be necessary elements but they are not sufficient. Parents should learn about the main theoretical assumptions and empirical bases that underlie the training practices. It is especially important to emphasize that AAC will not hinder speech, and that the aim is to enhance speech when speech development is possible for the child (see p. 269). There are many programmes to support children who have siblings with disabilities (Haukeland et al., 2020; Nguyen et al., 2023). Siblings represent an important resource for children developing AAC, but they need some AAC guidance (Gatt, 2022). Older siblings may attend some or all parts of the family programme or they may receive most of their information and guidance from the parents. Siblings may also attend peer programmes (see below).

General courses should be repeated as the individual's needs change over time and there are new developments in AAC interventions or technology. However, a general AAC course for parents and a discussion of intervention and teaching methods will not guarantee that the use of AAC is well implemented in the home. The need for individualized intervention for children with disabilities is generally acknowledged (Kasari et al., 2021; Sevcik et al., 2022) and family programmes should be similarly individualized. Moreover, the best developmental path of AAC for the child may not be found at the first attempt. For example, individuals who did not profit from manual signs may do better with graphic symbols, and individuals who

Table 12.1 Common information in courses about AAC and developmental disorders

Typical and atypical development of communication and language
Communicative access
Terminology: augmentative and alternative communication (AAC)
Manual sign systems, graphic communication systems and tangible symbols
Communication aids and how to make communication folders and books
The technology of communication devices
The diagnostic groups in need of AAC: individuals with motor disorders, autism spectrum disorder, intellectual disabilities, and developmental speech and language disorders
AAC over the life span: use and support for children, adolescents and adults
AAC and speech development
AAC and orthographic writing
Assessment of individuals who may need AAC
Vocabulary development and selection of vocabulary
Sentence construction with AAC
Conversation with AAC
Communication breakdown: misunderstanding, negotiation and repair
A developmental approach to AAC intervention
An individual plan for AAC intervention and use
AAC intervention strategies
Supporting participation in activities
AAC and play
A language-supportive environment for children using AAC
Being a communication partner for individuals using AAC
AAC in the family and everyday life
Scaffolding of AAC in the family
Educational needs of family members
AAC in the classroom: beyond individual training
Making peers AAC competent
Collaboration between the family and kindergarten and school
AAC and life quality within and outside the family
Challenging behaviour and communication
Using AAC: a creative process

have problems with graphic symbols may do better with manual signs (von Tetzchner, 2019b). Many parents have tried several approaches before finding the blend of intervention measures that is right for their child (Sevcik et al., 2022).

Group sessions and individual sessions focus on the family members as communication partners. Useful strategies include role playing and video recordings of communicative interactions (Fäldt et al., 2020; Kim et al., 2021). Parents may observe the teacher interacting with their child using AAC at preschool or school and see how the child indicates graphic symbols or performs manual signs. Home visits where the teacher comments on child–parent and child–sibling interactions are useful not only for the family, but also for the teacher who gets a better impression of communication in the home. Home visits further function to make the intervention better adapted to the child's communication opportunities in the home, and make it more likely that members of the family utilize these opportunities. Home sessions may be repeated regularly to ensure that this part of the language environment is optimally adapted to the individual's skills and abilities all the time.

It is not always necessary to involve professionals in group sessions. Parents who have similar experiences are sometimes the best guides and helpers for each other. Issues from parent-only groups may be followed up in discussions with professionals (Biggs & Hacker, 2021a; O'Neill, 2018).

Parents are an important resource for their children's development of AAC, but professionals sometimes complain that parents represent barriers to AAC intervention, for example, because they are worried that AAC may hinder their child's speech development (Donato et al., 2018). On the other hand, many parents report that they, rather than the professionals, take the lead in implementing and supporting their child's development of AAC (Marshall & Goldbart, 2008; O'Neill & Wilkinson, 2020). AAC courses should take care to acknowledge the efforts of the families and the importance of what they are doing, and emphasize that the results will be worth the parents' efforts. However, courses should also prepare parents for how "impractical" and slow it may be to use AAC, especially for aided communicators with severe motor disabilities.

Most parents need guidance and strategies for making AAC function optimally within the family. For example, parents are often busy with other things when they are speaking to children with typical language development, for example, cooking or doing other house choresores. When the child is using AAC, parents (and others) may have to pause what they are doing to ensure the child's visual attention before they make a manual sign or indicate a graphic symbol. If the child is severely motor impaired and unable to make sounds to attract attention (see p. 111), parents have to look at the child regularly to capture the child's attempts to communicate. They may have to change routine activities to ensure that communication is part of these activities. Parents need continuous support, particularly in the period before the child has started to show some significant achievement (Glacken et al., 2019). When the child utters his or her first spoken words or word-like vocalizations, there is a risk that the family will stop using AAC (see p. 205). The family may need guidance to ensure that family continues to use AAC in the home until the speech is sufficiently developed for all functions (Launonen, 2003, 2019b).

The small group sessions should focus on the communicative possibilities of each child and how parents can best utilize these possibilities. Parents especially need to learn and use strategies that provide their child with opportunities for taking communicative initiative and participating in dialogues with real content. If families are not given sufficient guidance, this may negatively influence the children's communication opportunities and possibilities for participation in activities they like in the home (Doak, 2021). The result may be passivity and lack of social participation.

Margarida had no speech and was unable to produce vocalizations loud enough to be heard by others. Until she was eight years old, she did not have the means to communicate her needs, wants, thoughts and feelings in an efficient manner. When she arrived from school, she was seated on the sofa with the television in front of her, while her parents occupied themselves with their daily duties. Unable to walk and vocalize she could not move away or even change television station of her own volition. The parents said that she loved to watch television because she stayed still for two or three hours without giving them trouble. When a communication board with PCS and Bliss-words was introduced to the whole family, the parents observed that Margarida became more active and assertive, and actively chose television programs and other activities. She used movements to get attention and the communication board to express what she wanted to say (Lourenço et al., 1996).

Parents need AAC guidance, but parents have unique experiences with their child and may have other priorities for communication and activities in everyday life than the professionals, such as enabling the child with motor impairment to sail with a small boat on a nearby lake (Biggs & Hacker, 2021a; Stadskleiv, 2017). AAC intervention programmes are likely to have a greater and more lasting effect when the parents' experiences become part of the shared team knowledge, the family's priorities are included in the communication plan and the family shares "ownership" of the intervention (see p. 109). It is a cooperative effort: parents should be consulted but not given the full responsibility for implementing the intervention measures. The role of parent programmes is first and foremost to help parents to engage in conversations with their child. When the child is severely disabled, this is a demanding enough task in itself: it may take the parents a considerable amount of time and resources to perform such routine activities with the child as dressing, washing and eating (Goldbart & Marshall, 2004). There may be little time left for the parents and the child to engage in play and other pleasant activities together. The parent programme should help parents to engage in joint activities and communication with their child, and make everyday activities and routines as smooth, varied and interesting as possible for both the child using AAC and the parents.

The longer holidays can be a difficult time for children developing AAC and their parents. The parents may find it difficult to fill the days with activities that are meaningful for the child and themselves. The family should be helped to plan communication opportunities for the child during the holidays and decide which new manual signs or graphic symbols they may need during the planned summer activities (see Chapter 8). An AAC camp during the holidays may be an option in some countries, where the child may also meet other children using AAC (Bell, 2018; Berger & Feucht, 2012; Bruno & Trembath, 2006). Siblings also find attending AAC camps useful (Hutchinson et al., 2019). At the same time, holidays may represent a period when the parents and siblings have more time for conversations with the child and experience progress in his or her communicative achievements that may not be evident in the busy everyday life of the family.

It is a necessary part of the family programme that parents are taught the communication system their child is using but professionals sometimes want to spare the parents in the early phases. They suggest starting in kindergarten or school and then introduce AAC into the home after the child has shown some progress. However, by doing this, professionals may in fact "protect" the parents from communicating optimally with their own child. A mother expressed her sentiments in this way:

> I would like to be ahead of him and maybe learn his signs before they start teaching them to him. For example, he now knows colours I don't know the signs for. It is quite silly when he can express things clearly and I don't understand because I don't know the signs. It is not necessary to teach him to communicate when he hasn't got anybody to communicate with.
>
> (von Tetzchner, 1996b)

On the other hand, some parents struggle to find babysitters and spend the only free evening they have each week in order to attend a comprehensive manual sign course. After one year they may have learned several hundred signs. During the same period of time, the child may have learned only 10 or 20 signs. This may not be a bad start for the child, because the acquisition of the first manual signs or graphic symbols (or words) often takes some time (see Chapter 7). However, the parents may be disappointed and feel that this is a poor result of the intervention of which they had such great hopes, and in which they had invested all their free time. The family may rather attend a small course organized by professionals who are teaching individuals with developmental disorders. If the child learns to use ten manual signs and the members of the family know 50 or maybe 100 signs and use them as keywords to accompany their speech, the result will be good in terms of time and energy invested. If the child's sign development turns out to be rapid, this will motivate the family to speed up their learning efforts and get ahead of the child again.

Families of children who learn graphic symbols need thorough guidance in how their child's graphic communication system works. This need for teaching appears obvious with systems like Blissymbolics, but more pictographic systems such as pictograms and PCS also need clear explanations to enable parents to scaffold the child's utterances and use the graphic symbols in an optimal way. It should be emphasized that graphic symbols are not merely a collection of incidental pictures but the child's words which replace or supplement his spoken language – either for the time being or as a permanent alternative to speech. Some parents begin to talk about the image on the graphic symbols that the child is indicating in much the same way as they comment ordinary pictures (Basil, 1992). This undermines the linguistic function the graphic symbols are intended to have. Professionals should therefore not call the child's graphic symbols "pictures" but rather remind the family of the symbols' emerging linguistic functions even in the very early phases of the child's graphic language development. The family should be shown how they can use graphic symbols to comment on ordinary events in photographs or video, such as walking trips, birthdays or other shared family events. It is important that the child uses his or her own words (graphic symbols) to communicate about what is on the photograph, and does not only point to people and things in the photograph and leaves the storytelling to the parent or sibling (see p. 349). This is also a good activity for small group sessions.

It is important that the parents can follow the child's progress. Some manual signs or graphic symbols are introduced first at nursery school or school but should become part of the parents' repertoire as soon as possible – preferably at the same time as they are introduced in the classroom. Similarly, signs or symbols that are first introduced at home should be included in activities at school as soon as possible. Teachers may give the child and parents "communication homework", for example, having a conversation about a particular school subject. However, teachers should not regard AAC at home as simply following up of schoolwork and doing homework. Parents should be encouraged to use new vocabulary in communication with the child beyond the schoolwork and teachers should learn from the successes at home. Professionals should reflect on the home situation and base their help and guidance on knowledge about the home environment and how it can be best adapted to support the child's development of language and communication, while at the same time taking the family's total needs, potentials and limitations into considerations. For example, if parents tend to use manual signs at home while the individual is learning a graphic system at school, signing should also be supported by the school.

When the child's development of AAC is slow, parents may not notice any progress and new skills may not be utilized at home. It is an important part of the follow-up that professionals observe and report the child's progress to the family, both generally and in communication and language. They should point out what difference the child's new manual signs or graphic symbols make – what he or she can express with and without AAC. Communication tasks where the individual communicates about things, photographs or drawings that the individual but not the family member can see, may be useful for demonstrating the individual's – and the family's own – AAC skills and achievements (see p. 255).

Parents are sometimes given communication assignments that are so extensive that they encroach upon all other activities the family enjoys (Goldbart & Marshall, 2004). Moreover, it is not uncommon to hear criticism from professionals who think that the parents are not following up properly (Moorcroft et al., 2019). However, the aim of the family programme is not to turn the home into a classroom. The assignments are the child's homework and teachers should take the family situation into account when giving these assignments. Professionals may forget that while they can leave their work at the office, parents have their responsibilities all the time.

Although it is important that part of the family training takes place in the child's home, AAC courses and workshops where families are together for 1–3 weeks also have advantages. The children and the parents may have slightly different programmes. The children may get intensive AAC training in groups of AAC users, in which the family participates some of the time, to promote engagement in interaction and good communication skills. The parents attend lectures about theoretical and practical issues related to ACC. They participate in discussions about vocabulary selection and the construction of utterances with two or more signs or symbols, role play and other forms of group activities. It is of particular significance that in such workshops, the parents are relieved of their daily duties and have time to focus in-depth on relevant issues. The families get to know each other and may build up a parent network where they exchange experiences, problems and solutions. These kind of courses have been demonstrated to change the communication of both parents and children (Bruno & Dribbon, 1998; Fäldt et al., 2020).

As a group, fathers tend to have somewhat different parenting styles and practices than mothers (Yaffe, 2023), as well as different language directed to children (Hilvert et al., 2023). The involvement of fathers varies, some are more involved in the AAC intervention than the mothers; others are less involved and may not utilize the child's communication skills fully when they communicate with him or her (Biggs & Hacker, 2021b; Mandak et al., 2017; Smith, 2003; Sweeney, 1999). Although parent programmes related to AAC do not tend to focus on gender roles, the parents' sharing of responsibilities may still be encouraged. Professionals may use differences in interests between the father and the mother in a constructive manner to broaden the child's experiences and language learning, for example, by giving a father who is interested in music, dance and sports the task of introducing these activities and related vocabulary to the child using AAC.

Caring for a child who needs AAC usually places a wide range of demands on a family, and these should be assessed when guiding parents. *The Family Resource and Support Guide* (Dunst et al., 1994) may be useful for gaining insight into a family's various resources and needs (see also Sexton & Rush, 2012). *The Family Impact of Assistive Technology Scale for Augmentative and Alternative Communication* (Ryan & Renzoni, 2019) may be used to get an overview of how aided communication intervention influences the everyday life of the family.

Finally, comments from caregivers indicate that the time spent on intervention may be too short, like this mother's comment (Tegler et al., 2021, p. 22).

> It is hard to understand. I have received a lot of information from the speech and language pathologist, but it was hard to understand.

Family AAC support is a long-term job. Parents and siblings need time to learn how the child's AAC system can be used. As the child develops and come to master new communication systems and conversation skills, the family will also have new needs for help and guidance, reflecting the positive development.

AAC and the peer environment

Peers have a prominent place in children's social lives from an early age. Infants are especially attentive to the actions of other infants and children (Bradley et al., 2024). When a young child is sitting by the mother, a nearby one-year-old will look more at the child than at the mother (Lewis et al., 1975). Much of children's learning and meaning-making takes place within peer culture activities, which, to some extent, evolves independently of, but still as part of children's life in society at large. Children's interaction and communication with peers are qualitatively different from those with adults. They offer experiences and natural learning opportunities that relationships with adults cannot provide, including both competition and cooperation (Dunn, 1999; Kemple, 2004). Social power is more equally distributed, although peers may have different roles when interacting. It can be difficult for individuals using AAC to make friends. However, their communication system is also a means to establish peer relations and friendships (Therrien et al., 2023).

Peer relations change with age and development. Joint meaning-making and communication with peers become more important as the child's social world expands; much is taking place within play and other child-led activities (see Chapter 10). In adolescence, conversations take over from play as the leading peer activity. However, children and adolescents using AAC tend to communicate more with adults than with peers (Berenguer et al., 2022). In adulthood, conversation about a variety of topics with peers is an essential part of social life.

There are thus many reasons for supporting peer interaction for children, adolescents and adults who use AAC. The cognitive, linguistic and social abilities of individuals who use AAC differ considerably, and interventions should always aim at establishing a language environment that is adapted to the functioning of the individual. However, rather than introducing the individual to classmates and other peers as "non-speaking" or "an aided communicator", he or she may be introduced as someone who is interested in music, fashion or sports, as a storyteller, as a science fiction nerd and so forth. This increases the likelihood of conversations with peers about joint interests and activities that may lead to friendships (Therrien, 2019; Østvik et al., 2018).

Communication with peers who use their system have been found to have a positive impact on the communication and language development of AAC users (Barker et al., 2013). The aim of peer intervention is to influence the whole peer community, to create a shared competence, increase the peers' understanding of individuals who use AAC and increase peer interactions for individuals using AAC.

Childhood

Peers are an important part of the language environment and an invaluable resource when adapting the early environment of children who are developing AAC (Barker et al., 2013; Fisher & Shogren, 2012; von Tetzchner et al., 2005). Classmates appear to be especially important for children with disabilities in inclusive educational settings, because they tend to have less contact with peers outside school (Batorowicz et al., 2014; Chen et al., 2020; Chung et al., 2012). A number of studies have shown increased communication and more balanced dialogues as a result of peer training (Barker et al., 2013; Chung & Douglas, 2015; Romski & Sevcik, 1996). Studies also find that children with motor disabilities feel less dependent when being helped by other children instead of adults (Madge & Fassam, 1982) and that the continuous presence of adult assistants in inclusive settings may interfere with the children's communication with peers without disabilities (Cole-Lade & Bailey, 2020; Giangreco, 2010).

Children vary in their attitudes towards and interest in their classmate who is using AAC. Some are curious and compassionate and engage in interaction, others are less involved and seldom initiate communication, and some show little understanding of the child using AAC, or are negative (Biggs & Hacker, 2021a, b; Chung & Douglas, 2015). This is the ordinary variation to be expected among children. All should be encouraged to interact with the individual using AAC, but positive engagement only emerges from voluntary involvement. There are usually some children in the class who become the core peer group or friends of the child using AAC. In our experience, age seems to be an important factor for establishing relationships between children using AAC and their peers. In fact, attending an inclusive kindergarten and following the same group of children into mainstream school seems to be the best way to promote long-term peer relations and true inclusion.

The peers' understanding of AAC and their attitude towards the children who are using AAC will influence their interactions. Several studies address factors that may influence the peers' attitudes, for example, whether the individual uses a communication board or an electronic communication device with speech output (Radici et al., 2022; Versteeg, 2020). However, the best way to influence peer attitudes may be to teach them to use manual signs or graphic symbols and give them insights into the efforts and achievements of children using AAC. Much of the information in Table 12.1 may also be presented to peers but in a way that takes the age and abilities of the peers into consideration. Practice is important. One study found that providing information about AAC together with using AAC in role play had a greater positive influence on children's attitudes than information about AAC alone (Beck & Fritz-Verticchio, 2003). The peers' own experience with AAC thus had a positive influence on their attitudes. Guiding them to use AAC is also the best way to make peers competent communication partners. The result may be successful communications that extend beyond short exchanges (Østvik et al., 2018). However, they should be able to communicate together in all sorts of circumstances. For example, the peers need to learn to use series of *yes/no* questions in case the communication aid breaks down and the backup communication book is not available at that time.

Common strategies used to increase the AAC competence of peers are class lessons and class discussions on AAC, peer groups with children using AAC and children using natural speech doing assignments together, and Class Clubs or Circles of Friends Clubs where the AAC user and classmates meet regularly to play games and discuss non-educational topics of common interest (Brekke & von Tetzchner, 2003; Hunt et al., 2002). Studies often instruct peers to prompt and praise the individual's utterances, to use expectant delay and to "model" utterances that the individual might find useful (Chung & Carter, 2013; Ganz & Hong, 2014). Although it is important to give the AAC user enough time, teaching such strategies may make peers more focused on the construction of the individual's utterances than on discussing the topic of the conversation. Instead, shared AAC competence, joint activities involving language and varied conversation should be the main goals in interventions addressing the language environment of peers, as illustrated in the following example.

> Sander is attending an ordinary class in his neighbourhood school. He has cerebral palsy, severe motor impairments, good comprehension of spoken language and no intelligible speech. It was an explicit aim that Sander's communication mode should not be "private" but shared with as many people in his environment as possible. His graphic systems – first pictograms, later Blissymbolics – were included in the class curriculum, so that the whole class became familiar with the systems. Each of the children in the class has made a copy of Sander's Bliss-board. Every time a new subject is introduced in the class, the relevant Bliss-words are explained, and Bliss-words are often used as headings on the blackboard and on posters the children make in group work and hang on the wall. The bliss-boards are also used in a class club with Sander and a few classmates. Through frequent translations to and from Bliss-words, which the classmates find very exciting, they discover both how the Blissymbolics system really works and how difficult it can be to translate spoken sentences into Bliss-words. Sander is the expert, and the other children often ask him when they are uncertain about how to translate a word or phrase. When they are telling jokes with Bliss-words, Sander excels. The use of Bliss-words has become a part of the class culture (Brekke & von Tetzchner, 2003).

Sander's story demonstrates that shared activities involving the use of AAC are core elements of AAC intervention with peers. The positive effects of the many shared activities in the class on peer attitudes are well illustrated by a classmate saying: "Sander is lucky he can talk like this."

A creative way for children using AAC and their peers to investigate the use of AAC together is to produce stories from wordless picture books, such as *Frog, Where Are You?* (Mayer, 1969) or *The Secret Box* (Lehman, 2011). The content of these books may be suitable for most age groups, from age three years to adults. The stories made by individual children or small groups can be presented orally, with manual signs or graphic symbols, or as written text, and the content and the stories may be compared.

Although many pictographic symbols appear easy to understand, they may be misinterpreted by children who cannot read the gloss (Fallon et al., 2003; Smith, 1996). Peers need guidance in using graphic symbols in conversations with the aided communicator, as well as more generally in activities in kindergarten or school. In school, the class may have a graphic symbol lesson once a week and all the children may have to write reports and make presentations with graphic symbols. The fact that graphic symbols are not merely incidental pictures and that their use must be learned is not only negative. It may make the symbols more interesting for the peers and increase the status of the child who is using them. Studies show that all children in a class may benefit from learning graphic symbols. One study found that explanations of the Blissymbolics system made the children aware of the features of different categories (Brekke & von Tetzchner, 2003). This was followed up with similar lessons about the use of letters in orthographic reading and writing.

Growing up with AAC as the main mode of communication influences children's lives in many ways. Books such as *A Voice of Her Own* (Yong & Yong, 2021), *Speechless* (Darbishire, 2018) or *I Talk in Different Ways* (Hartmann, 2022) can give children with typical development insights into the achievements and challenges of children using AAC. The literature about AAC emphasizes the needs peers may have for information about the communication of the child using AAC. However, the routines and everyday life of children using AAC may differ from children with typical development. Children using AAC may also need information about the classmates' interests and activities. Reciprocal exchange of information may contribute to shared insights, a joint society of learners and a child culture, as in the example below from Brekke and von Tetzchner (2003).

> As part of the schoolwork, Sander and the classmates write small scripts about their everyday life (see Figure 12.1). Sander uses Bliss-words while the classmates use orthographic writing. These scripts enable them to share both personal experiences and their perspectives on events all the children in the class have been part of. Through narration, discussion

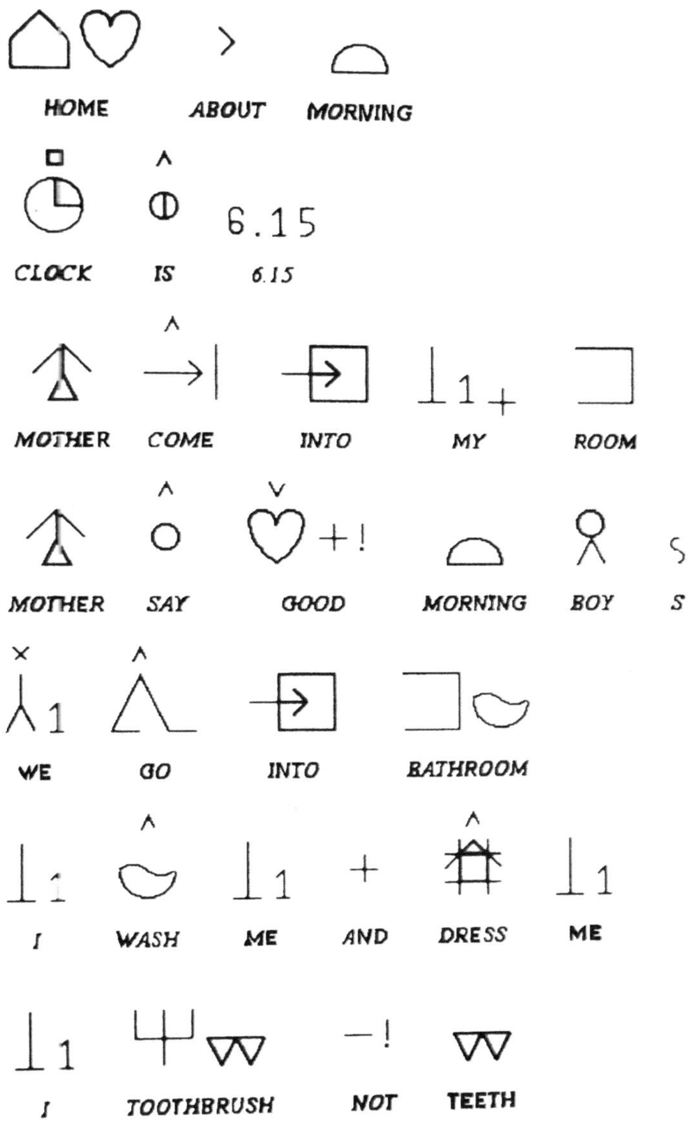

Figure 12.1 Script of everyday life made by Sander in Bliss-words.

> and role play of the events, the children develop a shared understanding of the situations covered by the scripts. The scripts of Sander and the other children in the class, for example, about birthday celebrations, are compared and similarities and differences discussed. Through these conversations, Sander and his classmates gain insights into different perspectives and increase their social knowledge.

It is a general finding that communication partners with natural speech tend to dominate the conversations with children using AAC, but this seems to be less prominent when peers are communication partners (Clarke & Wilkinson, 2009). Moreover, for children using AAC with cognitive development in the typical range, peers may be better informed than adults about the interests and preferences of the AAC users, because these usually correspond to those of peers. This emphasizes the importance of conversations with peers.

The peer environment is significant for children with autism spectrum disorder and intellectual disabilities who use AAC. An important argument for facilitating peer interaction is that peer initiations and reactions to communication attempts from the children using AAC may reduce these children's frustration and anger and increase the number of shared positive experiences. In kindergarten, the staff may use circle time to introduce manual signs and graphic symbols to all the children, thereby making the kindergarten communicatively accessible for children using AAC. The story below illustrates how a communicatively accessible environment supports inclusion (von Tetzchner et al., 2005).

> Ole is a five-year-old autistic boy from a bilingual background. Assessment indicates nonverbal cognitive skills moderately below his age level, while his comprehension of spoken language is comparable to that of an 18-month-old in both languages. He attends a small adapted unit with six autistic children in an ordinary kindergarten. Both the staff and the other children have been taught manual signs and Ole's signs are understood by everybody. Many of the children and the adults are ahead of Ole and use signs he has not yet started to use, thus providing him with opportunities for learning new signs outside his individual sign training with the special teachers. Synne is a five-year-old girl with typical development in the same kindergarten.
>
> | | |
> |---|---|
> | Synne: | (Has brought a doll from home and stands on the floor holding it). |
> | Ole: | (Positions himself in front of Synne) "Borrow" (stretches out the hand but does not seem to remember what else he should do). |
> | Synne: | (Looks at Ole and helps him sign BORROW) *Borrow* {DOLL *doll*}. |
> | Ole: | {BORROW *Borrow*} {DOLL *doll*} (signs and speaks simultaneously with Synne, then smiles and reaches out for the doll). |
> | Synne: | (Gives the doll to Ole). |

Although Ole has some speech, he often seems to depend on manual signs for managing to articulate spoken words. Synne scaffolds Ole's communication by helping him to express in signs what she perceives to be his intention and continues the dialogue by asking him whether he wants to borrow her doll, similar to how she has seen the teacher react in similar situations. Importantly, she stays on topic and does not distract the interaction with praise for communicating or other meta-communicative comments (communication about communication). The two children walk together to the doll corner and Ole puts Synne's doll to bed. Synne finds another doll and starts playing with it: feeding it and putting it to sleep. This continues for a little while, until:

Synne: *Can I have my doll back?* (offers Ole the other doll by holding it out to him).
Ole: "No" (shakes his head).
Synne: {FINISHED *finished*} {BORROW *borrow*}.
Ole: (Gives the doll to Synne and accepts the other doll which he puts in the doll bed).

Manual signs: DOLL, FINISH

The communicative practices of the words and signs "borrow" and "finished" learned through adult guidance seemed to have afforded positive interactions among the children. In AAC intervention, FINISHED is important for regulating own participation in activities and the behaviour of other people, and it was used often by both teachers and children in the kindergarten. In the example above, Synne uses FINISHED in a regulating manner together with BORROW when Ole refuses to give her doll back. This was a significant development. If a similar situation had happened a few months earlier, Ole would probably have tried to take the doll from Synne without asking her for permission and Synne would probably have resisted and started to scream. It is highly unlikely that the interchange would have resulted in joint play. By introducing "borrow" in relation to useful communicative routines and significant child events, the staff promoted the development of both social skills and culturally appropriate knowledge and communication.

It is notable that the communication between Ole and Synne took place without direct guidance or participation from adults. Inclusion is a two-way process: AAC users are members of the community and share ordinary and special experiences with other members. This implies a shared mode of communication. Because AAC users have limited speech, it is the peers who have to learn to understand the individual's manual signs or graphic symbols, as well as to use some of these in their own communication. It is quite common that all the children in a school or kindergarten class learn some manual signs or graphic symbols, which they mainly use to tell individuals using AAC that they are going to eat, go for a walk, and so forth, or to inquire whether they want to do such activities. However, their use of the individual's communication mode should also involve conversations during play and other activities.

Individual differences in communicative style influence conversations and should be taken into account in peer interventions. Many older children in the expressive language group seem to be aware of partner characteristics and adapt their communication to the partner (Mendes et al., 2023). Buzolich and Lunger (1995) asked Vivian, a 12-year-old aided communicator with severe motor impairments to comment on the communication styles of three class mates who were singled out for training as communication partners. The result was that both Vivian and the class mates changed strategies as they became aware of their styles of communication. The communication became more efficient when the partners were better adapted to each other.

Adolescence

Adolescence completes the developmental pathways of childhood and marks out the course for a more autonomous and independent existence (Soenens et al., 2018). Adolescents establish relations that may last a lifetime (von Tetzchner, 2019a). Communication with friends and peers changes during adolescence, reflecting the physical and mental changes taking place in adolescence, identity formation and youth culture. Adolescents spend a lot of time talking together – about people, music, popular culture, fashion, politics, sports, jokes and so forth – and increasing amounts of time in self-disclosure and telling stories about themselves and others in an effort to achieve acknowledgement and emotional support (Nippold et al., 2014). Adolescents' language contains many new words and expressions and contributes to the continuous change in language use in societies (Kirkham & Moore, 2013). Conversations are often embedded in shopping and other leisure activities and interventions aiming to increase peer conversations should therefore seek to engage adolescents using AAC and their peers in joint activities in line with their age and developmental functioning (Figure 12.2). For example, in class, the teacher can organize discussions about particular topics in small groups (Ratcliff & Cress, 1998).

Many of the issues related to peer interventions in childhood also apply to adolescence. The main strategies are the same: providing peers with information about AAC, teaching of manual signs and graphic symbols, promoting competence as communication partner and providing practice in communicating with the individual's system. Due to their disabilities, adolescents who use AAC continue to need various support services and professional carers may be their most frequent communication partners (Holyfield et al., 2017). Adolescence implies new possibilities and demands, whether the individual has intellectual abilities in the

Figure 12.2 Aided communicator shopping with peer.

typical range or intellectual disabilities (Holyfield & Caron, 2019). Shared activities and conversations with peers always represent an entrance to participation in the adolescent community. When intervention in school age has been successful in creating communicative access and peer interaction for children using AAC, the peer guidance and adaptations in adolescence represent a continuation and elaboration of the earlier strategies but with more focus on autonomy and equal footing in peer interactions when the difference in functioning is not too large. This implies that peers should be guided to treat individuals using AAC as equals. Individuals with severe motor disabilities may prefer being helped by peers in many situations but if peers take a model and helper role in conversations, this may influence the content and turntaking of the conversations and interfere with the development of horizontal peer relations (Rossetti & Keenan, 2018). When possible, communication should also include interactions between peers who are using AAC.

The peer language environment and peer interactions are especially important for adolescents using AAC. They want to be perceived as teenagers and share adolescent culture, including use of adolescent language and some youth rebellion against parents and other adults (Wickenden, 2011a, 2015). Although they may still benefit from some direct AAC teaching, interaction with peers should be the main focus of most AAC interventions for this age group. However, access to conversations with peers without adults present may be limited for adolescents using AAC (Biggs et al., 2017; McCarty & Light, 2022). Today, social media is a natural source of social attendance among young people. This involves less time pressure and hence makes social participation more accessible for many aided communicators (Grace et al., 2023; Howery, 2018a). For those who struggle with written language, the change in language use that characterizes adolescence may not be apparent. They may have little experience with telling peers about personal events and feelings or using narration to cope with difficult situations. More interaction with peers during childhood and adolescence may lead to better understanding of personal and social events and positively affect the individual's transition to adulthood and autonomy. Peer interaction in adolescence may function as a bridge to more peer communication in adult life (Smith, 2005b, 2015).

Adulthood

The transition from adolescence to adulthood is a major shift in both typical and atypical development, an extended period sometimes termed "emergent adulthood" (Arnett, 2015). In typical development, it is a transition from dependence to independence, and from mandatory school attendance to personal choices regarding education, occupation and lifestyle, with all the changes in social roles, goals and responsibilities this entails. The social environment of adults includes family, colleagues, acquaintances and friends with whom they communicate regularly, and peer conversations are an essential part of adult life, sometimes in a café (Figure 12.3).

Some individuals use AAC from kindergarten to old age (Parrott, 2016). Adults who use AAC report that their communication systems make them more independent and able to decide for themselves, for example, what clothes they want to buy, what food they want to order or what colour they want to dye their hair (Cooper et al., 2009; Wickenden, 2010). One young man had found that telling other people news about himself and general news from the media helped in establishing relationships with others (Iacono et al., 2013). The reason was probably that potential communication partners realized that he had something to say that they did not know and that he could be an interesting person to communicate with. This demonstrates the importance of enabling real conversations with peers with exchange of

Figure 12.3 Adult using communication aid in cafe with other adults.

information that is unknown to the other. It should have been promoted already in childhood but may have to be repeated with new peers. Interventions should try to counter the risk of peers only taking a helper role and to encourage conversations on an equal footing.

However, the transition to adulthood may be less pronounced for young adults who use AAC than for their peers with typical development and they may experience less autonomy and independence. They may need further AAC intervention because adult life may require new vocabulary (see Chapter 8) and conversational skills (Chapter 11) in formal and informal conversations at work and in other activities. Conversations with classmates may be limited in childhood and adolescence, but school is a social system that represents a natural access to peers. Young adults who leave school usually take different educational and vocational routes and may establish new social networks. For adults using AAC, leaving school tends to imply a reduction in peer contact and many divulge feelings of loneliness (Cooper et al., 2009).

It is therefore an important aim of AAC intervention for adults to maintain their earlier peer relations and promote the establishment of new relations, both with adults with typical functioning and adults with disabilities who do, or do not, use some form of AAC. The peer environment should be inviting both in frequency of opportunities and quality of everyday communication. Instructional programmes directed at adults may make them less dominant as peers and more attentive to initiations and turns by individuals using AAC (Light et al., 1992).

When adult AAC users are interviewed about friendship, they emphasize mutuality, commitment and depth of the relationship, but also shared activities, acceptance of the AAC communication mode and sense of humour – and continued communication over time. They also mention the role of the parents, teachers and professionals in their friendship development (Josol et al., 2023; Therrien, 2019). This implies that supporting and maintaining conversational AAC competence among peers and participation in preferred activities with peers are important for promoting AAC users' language development and their friendships and other peer relations in adult age. Furthermore, communication in romantic and sexual relations may require the addition of new vocabulary items. One young man who had recently fallen in love asked for *MISS, LOVE, KISS* and *HUG* to be put on his communication board (von Tetzchner, 1986). Aided communicators with motor impairments may need to develop special communication strategies that work in intimate situations (Sellwood et al., 2022). Conversations about this may be part of AAC intervention for adolescents and adults.

Which intervention measures may be useful for creating communicative access after the individual has left school depends on the individuals' intellectual abilities and their receptive and expressive language. Some may only need to be introduced to peers who are potential communication partners, others need more help to initiate communication and answer the conversational initiations of peers. The content and strategies will also depend on the abilities of the peers, but studies show that it is possible to increase peer interaction among adults with developmental disorders (Beck et al., 2009). These interventions should give the peers insight into the individual's communication and help them to apply communication strategies that they are able to master. Some individuals are reluctant to use their communication board or device in public, or even to take it along, as they feel others look at them as stupid (Iacono et al., 2013). The use of tablets and smart phones with communication programmes and other commonly used technologies have reduced the stigma related to AAC technology. However, it still emphasizes the need for education not only of significant people in the environment, but also to help aided communicators overcome such negative thoughts and promote the use of the communication aid at work.

The communication aid can be an important tool at work (see Figure 2.9, p. 50). Sheltered work is most common if individuals using AAC find work at all and many of those who have work do not use AAC at work (Bosse & Wilkens, 2016). However, studies also find that autistic individuals using manual signs or graphic symbols who have good use of their hands may enjoy working in shops, cleaning, preparing, packing and loading, as well as serving customers (Lerman, 2023). Having a job and earning money make life fuller for the individual and are a basis for a good working life and self-respect, as well as social interaction with fellow workers. Moreover, many employers share the individual's pride and find that the aided communicator is worth the extra effort needed for an employee using AAC (Richardson et al., 2019).

Adults with autism spectrum disorder and intellectual disabilities who use AAC tend to communicate mainly with family and staff. They may communicate little among themselves even when they spend much time together in day centres and supported housing (Cooper et al., 2009). It is an important objective to promote interaction between individuals with intellectual disability who speak and those who use AAC. Many people with intellectual disabilities using natural speech wish to communicate more with the individuals who use manual signs or graphic symbols and need training to become good communication partners for the individuals. The content of this intervention may be quite similar to other partner programmes but adapted to the peers' abilities and disabilities, and with an emphasis on role play and practical guidance. The peer interventions may lead to a significant expansion of the language environment of the individuals who use AAC. The programmes also signal that the staff values the individuals' ability to express themselves and that they are willing to invest time and resources to promote autonomous and staff-independent use of AAC.

When people in the environment use the individual's communication mode and show that they take it seriously, this is likely to boost his or her status.

> A day centre for people with intellectual disabilities had a youth meeting every week. One young man used manual signs, while the others were able to speak. The young man had a good understanding of spoken language and used about 200 manual signs actively. The other young people at the centre had not been taught signs and therefore had trouble

> understanding him at the meetings. One of the teachers therefore functioned as an interpreter for him, which impressed the other young people. They were very attentive to what he expressed and his esteem in the group was boosted. (Steindal, 1990)

This was a positive solution but in addition, they should have started to teach manual signs to the young people who wanted it, and thereby created a shared mode of communication. A shared mode will also help the individuals using AAC establish new social relations in day centres and sheltered housing that may last for many years. In one study, three individuals with intellectual disabilities asked to learn manual signs to communicate with friends who used this mode of communication (Meuris et al., 2015).

Adults AAC users as role models

Adults are always part of children's language environment. Children with typical language development are surrounded by children, adolescents and adults who are competent users of the language(s) the children are learning. Children who develop AAC seldom meet adults who have the same mode of language as their main means of communication as themselves (von Tetzchner et al., 2018). They may never communicate with or observe adults who engage in conversations using aided communication or manual signs, whom they can learn from and look up to.

When possible, services or parent associations should give children developing manual signs or aided communication possibilities for meeting adults who communicate in a similar way to themselves. Adolescents and adults who use AAC may work as teachers or assistants in kindergartens and school, or have special assignments in the intervention plan, as in the "children's day" below.

> During circle time, the children presented themselves and used aided communication to choose songs to sing and instruments to play. A teenager who used aided communication led the first circle time. She presented a children's story about a cat and dog on a fishing trip that she had written. Thus, in demonstrating the possibilities of aided communication in practice, she was a role model for the preschool children and their parents. (Stadskleiv, 2017, p. 7)

Being a role model does not imply producing utterances for the less competent AAC user to imitate but providing broader insight into the language mode and the life situation as an aided communicator or signer.

Support of educational and other staff

Teachers and other staff in kindergarten, school, institution and work place tend to have a central role in interventions involving AAC. They are also among the most frequent communication partners of children, adolescents and adults using AAC and thus constitute a central part of their everyday language environment. Staff training should include all those who may be in contact with individuals using AAC, including assistants, relief carers and kitchen staff. It is often assistants who have most opportunities to communicate with the individuals. For staff to fulfil their functions as trainers and communication partners in an optimal manner, they may need guidance and support from AAC specialists over longer time.

Supporting AAC in the classroom

Teachers and other staff in kindergarten and school spend much time with children developing AAC. Their observations of communication and language in everyday situations may be as important as the other professionals' observations during assessment and training, including when asking the individual questions during ordinary activities in the classroom (Figure 12.4). Teachers and assistants are often responsible for a major part of the direct AAC training, implementing some of the strategies presented in Chapter 6 (Andzik et al., 2019; Kashinath et al., 2022).

Teacher education, including special education, does not generally prepare teachers for students using AAC. Although the use of AAC has become quite common, many teachers have little knowledge about AAC and limited or no experience with working with students who use AAC, even those who have worked for many years as special education teachers. Some teachers have attended general AAC courses, but many learn about AAC and the student's mode of communication at the same time as they are teaching this mode to the student. Teachers may be positive to having a child using AAC in the class, but their lack of experience and competence may make them uncertain, nervous and overwhelmed (Leatherman & Wegner, 2022). This means that even experienced special educators may need support and guidance from AAC specialists or others who have more experience with AAC than themselves (Aldabas, 2022; Andzik et al., 2019; Da Fonte et al., 2022). Moreover, assistants with little educational background may be assigned training of individuals with severe disabilities, including children and adolescents who use AAC. Their AAC experiences and skills vary but most will need much guidance and help to perform training of AAC.

Figure 12.4 Child with Down syndrome signing by the whiteboard in a general classroom.

Staff members need to be informed about expectations for the individual's communication and language development, but also about the uncertainties behind those expectations. This will help them to be observant, react sensitively in new situations and take note of developments that support the expectations or indicate that they should be revised – in a positive or negative direction. Both the individuals' and the staff's AAC competence and use change over time. An introductory AAC support package may get the teacher started but this is not enough. AAC support should be long-term and changed in line with the individual's development of AAC and other skills and the teacher's corresponding need for support, including updates related to knowledge development within the AAC field (Snodgrass, 2016). Table 12.2 shows some of the information teachers have found important in courses and what they have found missing in their AAC education (Aldabas, 2022; Andzik et al., 2019; Cole-Lade & Bailey, 2020). Senner and Baud (2017) suggest training of school staff consisting of a sequence of five elements: (1) theory/strategy description, (2) demonstration and modelling, (3) practice, (4) feedback, and (5) coaching. The content of the training will depend on the competence of the staff, the abilities of the learners and the relevant communication systems.

Learning the meaning of individual graphic symbols or manual signs is usually the easiest part of AAC training. The staff should learn about the basis for the formation of manual signs, graphic symbols and tangible symbols; the ideas underlying the systems' constructions. They should be introduced to the general principles behind the choice of system and any specific reasons for the choice of the individual's system. However, learning how an alternative means of communication works, and is best taught takes time. It is not enough to teach a few manual signs or demonstrate what graphic symbols look like. Comments from teachers indicate that they are sometimes asked to implement intervention strategies without enough training, like this teacher's remark: "We have often felt a little bit lost concerning this [behaviour chain interruption strategy] and [we] need more education" (Tegler et al., 2021, p. 22).

AAC specialists should inform teachers and assistants about relevant aspects of the individual's assessment and the implications his or her strong and weak sides might have for interactions with him or her. They should not only be taught to implement a particular intervention strategy but also offered an explanation of *why* this strategy is implemented and the

Table 12.2 Information teachers have found important and information they have been missing in their AAC education

General information about AAC and how to implement AAC
The philosophy and objectives of using AAC
Information about systems that are used in the class or institution
How to support the student's use of AAC
How to include the child in the class
How to involve all of the class in AAC
How to prepare the classroom and placement of child in the classroom
How to teach AAC skills
Selection of AAC vocabulary
How to support AAC in conversations
How to use AAC in the general curriculum
How to adapt teaching to AAC
Planning activities for AAC within and outside of the classroom
Information about technology in accordance with the technical development in the field

theoretical foundation of AAC intervention in general. One professional expressed the importance of this kind of training for how she perceived the child using AAC:

> To study the theoretical background and the research on intervention methodologies was essential for me in order to understand the disabled child. It made me regard and treat the child in a totally different way.
>
> (Mendes & Rato, 1996, p. 351)

Everyday use of AAC is important for individuals to achieve the full benefit of AAC intervention and achieve long-term use of AAC. Some programmes focus on supporting and maintaining the individual's development and use of AAC by training staff members in communication with manual signs and graphic symbols (Cole-Lade & Bailey, 2020; Kashinath et al., 2022; Meuris et al., 2015).

Preparation of material, including updating communication books or devices and individual sign and symbol dictionaries, is a necessary element of AAC intervention, often done by the classroom teacher or the special educator. However, it is time-consuming and teachers and others must be allocated enough work hours to do this. Lack of preparation time may be a hindrance to the individual's optimal development of AAC (Andzik et al., 2019; Finke et al., 2009).

Supporting educational staff as communication partners

Communicative access requires partner competence. All the staff in kindergarten and school who are in regular contact with individuals using AAC should be given relevant information and help to develop appropriate communication partner skills. It is crucial that they understand that manual signs and graphic symbols are the individuals' language modes, not only some more or less natural gestures or pictures. When preschool staff are trained to be better communication partners and taught strategies for promoting the use of AAC in ordinary settings, the total communication of the young communicators increases (Kaiser et al., 1993). Because experience using AAC is the foundation of AAC development and opportunities for spontaneous communication may be limited, teachers and assistants should encourage the individual's spontaneous use of AAC and always try to give the individual the attention and time needed.

Supporting AAC training after school

Finishing school does not mean that AAC development or AAC intervention stop. Staff working with adolescents and adults using AAC in day-centres and sheltered houses may also have training tasks related to AAC, for example, to implement AAC for individuals who did not have access to AAC in childhood or continue or refresh earlier interventions. They therefore need guidance in starting up or continuing AAC intervention. This may involve individual training sessions but incidental training or milieu intervention using naturally occurring situations to teach communication with manual signs or graphic symbols may be most relevant.

Staff retire or change jobs and there is therefore a continuous need for staff education and guidance to maintain the intervention measures that are planned. Staff training – and refreshment training – should take place on a regular basis and be aimed at all aspects of AAC intervention. If some of the staff members have received intensive training from external AAC specialists, they should share their knowledge with other members of the staff, thus increasing the total impact of the training on the environment (Granlund et al., 1992). The repetition implied in this will also increase the awareness and thus the competence of staff members who received the intensive training first.

Supporting non-educational staff as communication partners

Staff taking the role of communication partners is important for maintaining adults' communication and use of manual signs or graphic symbols (Andzik & Chung, 2022; Webster et al., 1973, 2016). There is a constant need for staff education and guidance to maintain a communicatively accessible environment throughout the lifespan for individuals using AAC. In one study, eight staff members attended four 2-hour workshops in which they were taught key word signing. Thereafter, the eight members taught the rest of the staff two signs per week, which they subsequently began to use with the adults who were intellectually disabled. Both the individuals and the staff increased their daily use of manual signs (Meuris et al., 2015). A similar organization may be useful when teaching staff partner skills for conversations involving graphic symbols and communication aids.

Staff training should emphasize that AAC is the language mode of the individual and the importance of staff being available for communication and giving priority to communicative interactions over other activities, whenever possible. When staff members show an interest in, and an understanding of, the individual's communication system, this signals a positive attitude to, and respect for, both the communication mode and the individual, that may increase his or her self-esteem. Moreover, if members of staff find use of the individual's AAC system complex, they should say this to the individual and also explain that they admire his or her skills and proficiency in using the system. This may make the individual feel more competent and less frustrated by other people's lack of understanding. It may also provide a good opportunity for the individual to function as a teacher for the staff and for the staff to utilize his or her competence (see p. 137).

Staff members should be regularly informed about how each individual wishes communication to take place, for example, whether they should try to infer the individual's intention and interpret the message before the individual is finished constructing the utterance. Some prefer this, others want the partner to wait until they have completed construction of the utterance. Staff members may need guidance about not taking over the communicative initiative and being sensitive and responsive to an individual's attempts at communicating (see Chapter 11). This implies that staff members are aware of their role as communication partners. Mendes and Rato (1996) implemented a long-term training course including video of interactions between individuals and staff. Two participants reported:

> I started to become aware of all the attempts, ways and possibilities used by the girl to communicate, allowing her time to take her turn, avoiding a situation where her every effort ended with the frustration of being misunderstood.

> The most important factor was the development of my skills as an interlocutor. I learned to observe, to be attentive and to react better to the child's behaviour. I started to adapt my speech to my communication partner (Mendes & Rato, 1996, p. 349).

The training should inform staff about the difficulties that may arise in everyday communication but also prevent them from promoting communication on a level that is too elementary in relation to a particular individual. When staff members know about the problems the individual may encounter, it is easier for them to help him or her overcome such problems. The staff training should thus enable them to help individuals to use their AAC systems as effectively as possible, and thereby make their own and the individual's contributions more equal.

If the people who are responsible for AAC training are part of the ordinary staff, they should function as models for the rest of the staff by showing exemplary communication in unplanned situations involving AAC. For many staff members, using manual signs and graphic symbols is a new experience and observing other staff members engaging in interactions involving AAC may make it easier for them to try using what they are learning.

Authenticity and engagement are important in all conversations, including conversations between aided communicators and partners with natural speech. In the example below, the partner's engagement made the conversation exemplary.

> Bodil is 42 years old. She is intellectually impaired, understands some speech, has no speech and uses a communication board with about 150 lexical items and a few manual signs (see also p. 338). One day, she tells the AAC teacher about a fishing trip the day before, who had been there, and that they had had coffee and cakes. This conversation takes more than half an hour. Later in the day, Bodil and the teachers go to her home for video recording of a conversation with one of the staff members. Bodil immediately indicates *FISHING-TRIP* and begins to recount the trip. The staff member, however, begins talking about a fishing trip they are planning for the following Tuesday. He mentions other people and says they were going to have juice and cakes. They are clearly in disagreement! The staff member insists that his information is correct and that Bodil is wrong. Bodil is the first to realize that they are communicating about two different fishing trips. She begins to smile, signs FUN and points to Tuesday in the calendar, expressing that she is looking forward to the trip (Møller & von Tetzchner, 1996).

During this conversation, which lasted 13 minutes, Bodil produced 17 manual signs and gestures 34 times. She pointed 33 times at 16 graphic symbols on the board and 14 times at eight photographs of people and used the calendar three times. The staff member formulated Bodil's manual and graphic utterances in spoken language, took his own dialogue turns and pointed at the board 14 times, demonstrating that he took the matter seriously and wanted to convince her that she was wrong.

This conversation was important because it demonstrated that Bodil was able to discover such an advanced misunderstanding and repair it. The staff member did not know about the fishing trip Bodil had been to and just assumed that she was in error, or not discussing an actual event. The teacher also thought Bodil might have misunderstood the information about the trip, which, given her limited comprehension of spoken language, did not seem unlikely. However, it was later confirmed by others that Bodil really had been on the fishing trip she described. It was Bodil who first gave evidence of understanding that there were *two* trips. She understood that the staff member held a false belief, and hence showed evidence of mind understanding (see von Tetzchner, 2019a). The incident led to a redefinition of the staff members' views of Bodil, her reflections and abilities. Her status as communicator increased and revealed the need for staff members to gain better insight into her communication and engage in more advanced conversations with her.

A good educational programme helps produce competent staff who understand and master both their work and their role as communication partner, and who, in turn, will constitute an important part of the language environment of individuals in the process of learning and using AAC. Language development never really ceases; languages change over time, and people learn new words and expressions throughout life (Sankoff, 2018, 2019). This means that individuals who are using manual signs or graphic symbols need lifelong support. There will always be changes in staff, implying a need for continuous staff training throughout the lives of people who use manual or graphic communication.

Concluding comments

The overall aim is that individuals who use AAC should be part of mainstream society and participate in smaller and larger social activities and events from their early years to old age. This requires an accessible language environment that adapts and changes with the development of the individual. An accessible language environment for an individual developing AAC may involve many potential communication partners. Partners who are competent enable the individual's acquisition of alternative means of communication and create an environment that allows the individual to use these means. Resources should always be used in the most efficient manner, but it is not an aim that the intervention measures should take as little time as possible. There is a risk that the result will be minimal training and unfulfilled human potential.

There are huge benefits of intervention aimed at making people in the environment competent communication partners, while the consequences may be serious if such intervention is not provided. In fact, without a competent and supportive environment, AAC intervention is likely to fail its objectives. Supporting the AAC competence of the family, peers and staff will always take time and resources, but the resources and time are well spent. The abilities, skills and self-efficacy of individuals using AAC vary, and hence also the content and the nature of their social and societal participation, but an environment that supports individuals who use AAC to develop communication and language skills to their potential will also allow them to live their lives to the fullest.

Glossary

AAC See *augmentative and alternative communication.*

Abstraction A cognitive process that gives rise to a generalized category of something concrete, such as people, objects and events that are associated with less detailed features, aspects or similarities.

Access (in aided communication) The physical manner in which an individual indicates a tangible symbol, a graphic symbol, letter or written word on a communication aid; see *auditory scanning, direct access, eye-gaze access, scanning.*

Aided communication Communicative expressions produced by indicating an expressive item (e.g., letter, graphic symbol, or object) outside of the user.

Aided language Language constructed in a graphic mode, such as graphic symbols or letters, or with tangible symbols; see *graphic symbol, tangible symbol*

Aided language stimulation Communication partners using natural speech producing whole or partial utterances in the language mode of an aided communicator.

Atypical development Course of development that differs significantly from the development of the majority of a population; see *typical development.*

Auditory scanning A communication aid designed so that the vocabulary available for the aided communicator is read out by the electronic device or a communication partner; see *access (in aided communication), partner-assisted scanning, scanning.*

Augmentative and alternative communication (AAC) Non-vocal expressions that replace or supplement the functions of speech.

Automatization Reduced conscious regulation of motor and cognitive processes as a result of repeated execution.

Autonomy Making independent decisions related to life's diverse tasks.

Basic vocabulary A set of lexical items that are regarded as useful in many conversational contexts; see *core vocabulary, fringe vocabulary.*

Challenging behaviour Behaviour perceived as socially unacceptable and challenging by other people, such injury to self or others.

Checklist Questionnaire or interview with specific observational categories, questions or statements answered by an individual, parents or someone who knows the individual well; often used to assess the development of an individual in one or more domains.

Child-directed language Adults' and older children's adaptation of their language form, content and structure when interacting with infants and toddlers.

Communication Intentional conveyance of thoughts, stories, desires, ideas, emotions and so forth, to one or more persons.

Communicative access A language environment where there are people that the individual can learn from, who understand the individual's mode of communication and answer in a way that the individual can understand; see *language environment.*

Communicative competence Abilities and skills necessary for comprehension and production of utterances in a mode that is accessible and available to the individual.

Communicative success An individual's communicative intention is understood by the conversation partner; see *instrumental success*.
Concept Mental *representation* of a category of objects, events, persons, ideas, etc.; see *extension (of a concept)*, *intension (of a concept)*.
Contrast principle The hypothesis that young children assume that every new word has a meaning that is different from the words they have previously learned.
Core vocabulary A set of lexical items of very high frequency in language use; see *basic vocabulary*, *fringe vocabulary*.
Declarative communication Communication with the sole purpose of providing information and directing another person's attention at something, such as a person, an object, or an idea; see *instrumental communication*.
Deictic gesture Pointing gesture; gesture that directs others' attention at something in the environment without naming it; see *symbolic gesture*.
Developmental disorder Disorder that is congenital or appears in infancy or childhood and not caused by external injuries.
Developmental coordination disorder Neurodevelopmental disorder affecting the ability to execute coordinated motor actions; see *dyspraxia*.
Digitized speech Natural speech recorded and stored electronically, sometimes used in voice output communication devices; see *synthetic speech*, *voice blending*.
Direct selection Pointing at, touching or handing over a graphic symbol, letter or word, or pressing a key on a keyboard; see *scanning*.
Disability The difference between an individual's abilities and the demands of the environment.
Dynamic assessment The mapping of children's cognitive abilities by recording how much progress they make in the solution of a certain type of task after having received specific help and training for a given period.
Dynamic display Screen display that changes functionally, similar to changing pages in a communication book.
Dyspraxia Partial or complete inability to perform voluntary movements; see *developmental coordination disorder*.
Enculturation Acquisition of a culture's practices, customs, norms, values, and the like.
Expansion (in language development) Rephrasing what a child is saying, with longer sentence and greater complexity.
Expressive language The language that the individual produces; see *receptive language*.
Extension (of a concept) All actual and possible exemplars encompassed by a concept; see *intension (of a concept)*.
Eye-gaze access Using eye-tracking technology to operate an electronic communication aid or another technological device.
Eye tracking Technology that registers eye-movements.
Figurative language Language that makes use of metaphors or similes to express facts or ideas.
Fine motor skills Skills involved in moving and using the fine muscles of the hands and wrists; see *gross motor skills*.
Formula (in language) Simple utterance construction in early language development.
Fringe vocabulary Lexical items not considered core, consisting mainly of content words: nouns, verbs, adjectives and adverbs; see *basic vocabulary*, *core vocabulary*.
Generalize Perceiving and reacting in the same way to events which are similar in some respects.
Gesture Distinct movement primarily used as a means of communication and interpreted consistently within a social system; see *deictic gesture*, *symbolic gesture*.
Gloss The written word which is part of the *graphic communication symbol*.
Grammar Rules that describe how sentences are formed in a language; includes *morphology* and *syntax*.

Graphic communication symbol Visual symbol consisting of image and *gloss*, usually part of a *graphic communication system.*

Graphic communication system A set of graphic symbols intended to use for everyday communication.

Gross motor skills Movements of the body, arms and legs; see *fine motor skills.*

Habilitation Intervention efforts to improve and support functionality, interaction and quality of life of individuals with congenital or early acquired disabilities.

Hand alphabet Manual forms representing letters of an alphabet.

High-technology communication aid Electronic communication aid, typically based on information technology; see *low-technology communication aid.*

Holophrase Single-word utterance that in early language development functions as an entire sentence.

Horizontal structure (in language) Utterances consisting of several words that all lie within the same intonation contour or aided language construction; see *vertical structure.*

Iconicity Similarity in form between a manual sign or graphic symbol and the form or execution of the thing or event they refer to.

Imitation The deliberate execution of an action that corresponds to an action somebody else has performed.

Individual education plan Plan that describes the content and organization of an individual's education; see *individual habilitation plan.*

Individual habilitation plan Broad plan based on a vision of the individual's future, short-term and long-term intervention goals, and allocation of responsibility for different intervention domains, includes the *individual education plan*; see *habilitation.*

Instrumental communication Communicative action aimed at getting something or making someone else do something specific; see *declarative communication.*

Instrumental success Success in using communication to make someone else to do something specific; see *communicative success.*

Intension (of a concept) The content, all of the attributes embraced by a *concept*; see *extension (of a concept).*

Intentionality Goal-oriented determination; includes a notion of the goal of an action, and emotions and plans related to achieving the goal.

Internalization Process whereby external processes are reconstructed to become internal processes, such as when an individual independently adopts problem-solving strategies he or she has previously used in interaction with others, or attitudes, characteristics and standards of others as their own.

Joint attention Two or more individuals sharing a common focus of attention, while at the same time being aware that the same focus of attention is shared by the other person(s).

Keyword(s) Manual sign(s) or graphic symbol(s) accompanying a spoken utterance, corresponding to the main word(s).

Language act Action performed via a linguistic utterance, such as a greet, question, narrate, promise or command.

Language environment The social environment where language is learnt and practised; see *communicative access.*

Language function The purpose of language; the objective one wants to achieve by conveying something to another person using language, see *pragmatics.*

Learned helplessness The experience of lacking self-determination and the ability to affect one's environment as a result of having experienced situations in which one felt little control; see *self-efficacy.*

Lemma The word form chosen to represent a particular lexeme, for example in a dictionary; see *lexeme, morphology, word class, word family.*

Lexeme A word with its various inflections; see *lemma, morphology, word family.*

Lexical development The development of vocabulary.

Low-technology communication aid Non-electronic, paper-based communication aid; see *high-technology communication aid.*
Manual sign system Visual-manual language system constructed to represent major elements of a spoken language, a form of AAC; see *sign language.*
Mean length of utterance (MLU) Average number of lexical items (or morphemes) per utterance; generally calculated on the basis of 100 utterances, and commonly used to measure young children's level of language proficiency.
Morphology The principles of word formation, including stems and inflections; see *grammar, lexeme, syntax, word class.*
Multilingualism Proficiency in two or more languages, may be practised within the family alone, or between the family and society.
Non-verbal communication Gestures and other behaviours of the face, body, or voice (minus the linguistic content); see *pre-verbal, verbal.*
Object of reference Object or model of object used as a referring symbol; see *tangible symbol.*
Observational learning Learning by observing the behaviour of others and the functions and consequences of their behaviour.
Over-extension Use of a word to instances beyond the category usually referred to; see *under-extension.*
Partner-assisted scanning Access method where the communication partner systematically indicates the graphic symbols, words or letters of the communication aid and the aided communicator accepts or rejects the items indicated by the communication partner; see *access, auditory scanning, scanning.*
Pragmatics (in language) Functions of language in everyday use; see *language function, semantics.*
Prediction (in aided communication) Suggestions provided by an electronic communication device (or a person) to complete a word or sentence that an aided communicator is producing.
Pre-verbal communication Children's communication skills before they begin to comprehend and use language; see *non-verbal, verbal.*
Receptive language The language that the individual understands; see *expressive language.*
Regulating function of language Individuals' use of language to regulate their own behavior.
Representation (mental) An individual's mental storage of understanding and knowledge about the world.
Responsive (caregiver) Providing quick and appropriate responses to an individual's signals and behaviour; see *sensitive (caregiver), signal.*
Scaffolding The external regulation, help and support provided by adults or more experienced peers to children, adapted to their level and allowing them to transcend their independent coping skills and develop new skills and knowledge; see *zone of proximal development.*
Scanning Producing a message with a communication device by moving some kind of marker (e.g., arrow, cursor) to the intended expression (directed scanning), or indicating when the marker is in the location of the intended expression (automatic scanning); see *auditory scanning, direct selection, partner-assisted scanning.*
Screening instrument Brief questionnaire, checklist or test designed to identify individuals who should be examined using more thorough and time-consuming methods.
Self-efficacy The experience of acting and having control over one's own life; belief in one's own ability to deal with different situations and events.
Self-regulation The ability to monitor and adapt one's own thoughts, feelings, reactions and actions in order to cope with the requirements, challenges and opportunities of the environment and be able to achieve one's goals; also referred to as self-control.
Semantic compaction Coding system used in some electronic devices, combining a limited number of graphic symbols to produce pre-made utterances (e.g., Minspeak).
Semantics The branch of linguistics concerned with the meaning of words and phrases.

Sensitive (caregiver) Ability to understand a child's condition, respond quickly and adequately to the child's signals and behaviour, and provide challenges the child is able to master; see *responsive (caregiver), signal.*

Sign language National visual-manual language developed in a deaf community, primarily using movements of the arms, hands and fingers, supported by body movements, mouth movements and facial gestures.

Signal (in early development) Infant actions and expressions without communicative intent used by adults as an indication of the infant's interests, preferences and general well-being.

Speech-generating device Electronic communication aid with synthetic speech output; see *voice output communication aid.*

Standardization (test) Developing administrative guidelines and surveying how the test items are solved in a representative sample of the population targeted by the test; aims to estimate the distribution of scores in a given population.

Successive one-word utterances Utterances during early language development that consist of several thematically related words, but articulated in such a way that the words do not lie within the same intonation contour or utterance construction but have short pauses between them; see *horizontal structure, vertical structure.*

Symbol An entity representing something other than itself, such as a sign, a word, an image or the like.

Symbolic gesture Gesture that specifies or names the thing or category it used to refer to; see *deictic gesture.*

Syntax The grammatical arrangement of words and phrases in a language.

Synthetic speech Artificial speech, produced with software that contains rules for transferring written letters and words to speech, see *digitized speech, text-to-speech, voice blending.*

Tactile sign Manual sign perceived and produced with touch and hand movements.

Tangible communication symbol Material communication symbol, typically made of wood or plastic, may consist of small objects or models of objects; see *object of reference.*

Telegraphic speech Short and incomplete utterances produced in early language development; containing primarily content words.

Test Measurement instrument; a collection of questions or tasks that provide a basis for assessing an individual's performance relative to peers or a specific set of criteria.

Text-to-speech Rules for transferring letters and words of a language to speech; see *synthetic speech, voice blending.*

Time delay Strategy used in AAC intervention and by conversational partners to give the individual time to initiate or answer an utterance.

Typical development Course of development that characterizes the majority of a population; see *atypical development.*

Unaided communication system Language expressions made by the communicator using own body.

Under-extension More limited use of a word than its common meaning indicates; see *over-extension.*

Variation set A series of statements that express the same information in slightly different ways; common in child-directed speech.

Verbal Language in any modality.

Verbal communication Communication with language in any modality.

Vertical structure (in language) Utterance consisting of several items (words, manual signs, graphic symbols) that do not lie within the same intonation contour or utterance construction, but with short pauses between them; see *horizontal structure (in language); successive one-word utterance.*

Visual activity schedule Visual support to help the individual structure and organize an activity or task; see *visual schedule, visual support.*

Visual schedule Visual support to help the individual understand the activities and plan of the day and prepare him or her for the things that will happen; see *visual activity schedule*, *visual support*.
Visual support Visual elements introduced to help the individual in organizing and solving problems and performing activities of daily life; see *visual activity schedule*; *visual schedule*.
Vocal language Language produced with voice or speech.
Voice blending Combining digitized speech of an individual with general synthetic speech; see *digitized speech*, *synthetic speech*.
Voice output communication aid (VOCA) Communication aid with digitized or synthetic speech, see *speech-generating device*.
Word family All variations of a word, with inflections and derivations; see *lemma*, *lexeme*, *morphology*.
Working memory Part of the memory system related to what an individual does while trying to remember something for a short period of time or dealing with a problem.
Zone of developmental maintenance In progressive conditions where the individual is losing skills over time, interdependent mastery maintained with support from others; see *zone of proximal development*.
Zone of proximal development Children's interdependent mastery of skills, that is, in collaboration with more competent individuals within a specific area of knowledge or expertise, as opposed to independent mastery; see *scaffolding*, *zone of developmental maintenance*.

Resources

American Sign Language; Dictionary. https://www.handspeak.com
Aragonese Portal of Augmentative and Alternative Communication (ARASAAC). http://arasaac.org
Autism International Foundation; Non-profit organization supporting services to autistic children throughout the developing world. https://autisminternationalfoundation.org
Blissymbolics Communication International. www.blissymbolics.org
British Sign Language; Dictionary. https://www.signdictionary.co.uk
CanChild; Non-profit research centre located at McMaster University, Canada. https://canchild.ca/en
Cerebral Palsy Foundation. https://www.yourcpf.org
Communication, Access, Literacy and Learning (CALL), Scotland. https://www.symbolsforall.org.uk/home/. Communication Matrix. https://communicationmatrix.org
Communication Matters, UK chapter of ISAAC. https://www.communicationmatters.org.uk
Enable Ireland. https://enableireland.ie
European Academy of Childhood Disability. https://www.eacd.org
Everyone Communicates; Information about AAC Resources. http://www.everyonecommunicates.org
International Association for the Scientific Study of Intellectual and Developmental Disabilities (IASSIDD). https://iassidd.org
International Cerebral Palsy Society. https://www.cpint.org
International Disability Alliance (IDA); Network of organizations of persons with disabilities. https://www.internationaldisabilityalliance.org
International Down Syndrome Society; International network for families with members who have Down syndrome. https://www.ds-int.org
International Society for Augmentative and Alternative Communication (ISAAC). https://www.isaac-online.org
International Society for Autism Research. https://www.autism-insar.org
ISAACAUSTRALIA; Australian chapter of ISAAC. https://isaacaustralia.com
ISAAC-Canada; Canadian chapter of ISAAC. https://isaac-canada.org
ISAAC Singapore; Singapore chapter of ISAAC. http://isaac-singapore.org
Makaton. https://www.makaton.org
Minspeak. https://minspeak.com
MyChild; Provides information about cerebral palsy, aimed at USA. https://www.cerebralpalsy.org
National Disability Services Organization, Ireland. https://www.ndsa.ie
Open AAC Initiative; contains links to various free services. https://www.openaac.org
Pictogram Ideogram Communication (PIC)|. http://www.pictoworld.com
Picture Communication Symbols (PCS) at Tobee Dynavox. https://goboardmaker.com/pages/picture-communication-symbols
Rehabilitation International, Non-profit organization. https://www.riglobal.org
Scope; Disability equality charity. http://www.scope.org.uk/
SignHow, Global sign language dictionary with signs from deaf communities worldwide. https://www.signhow.co

United Cerebral Palsy. https://ucp.org
UNICEF initiative for AAC for children. https://www.unicef.org/innovation/stories/giving-every-child-voice-aac-technology
USSAAC; American chapter of ISAAC. https://ussaac.org
Widgit Symbols. https://www.widgit.com
World Health Organization: International Classification of Diseases, 11th revision. https://icd.who.int/browse11/l-m/en

References

Aasen, G. & Nærland, T. (2014) Enhancing activity by means of tactile symbols: A study of a heterogeneous group of pupils with congenital blindness, intellectual disability and autism spectrum disorder. *Journal of Intellectual Disabilities*, *18*, 61–75.

Abbeduto, L., Thurman, A. J., Bullard, L., Nelson, S. & McDuffie, A. (2019) Genetic syndromes associated with intellectual disabilities. In C. Armstrong and L. Morrow (Eds.), *Handbook of medical neuropsychology: Applications of cognitive neuroscience* (pp. 263–299). New York: Springer.

Abend, O., Kwiatkowski, T., Smith, N. J., Goldwater, S. & Steedman, M. (2017) Bootstrapping language acquisition. *Cognition*, *164*, 116–143.

Achenbach, T. M., Ivanova, M. Y. & Rescorla, L. A. (2017) Empirically based assessment and taxonomy of psychopathology for ages 1½–90+ years: Developmental, multi-informant, and multicultural findings. *Comprehensive Psychiatry*, *79*, 4–18.

Achenbach, T. M. & Rescorla, L. A. (2000) *Manual for the ASEBA preschool forms and profiles*. Burlington, VT: University of Vermont, Research Center for Children, Youth, and Families.

Achenbach, T. M. & Rescorla, L. A. (2001) *Manual for the ASEBA school-age forms and profiles*. Burlington, VT: University of Vermont, Research Center for Children, Youth, and Families.

Achmadi, D., Sigafoos, J., van der Meer, L., Sutherland, D., Lancioni, G. E. et al. (2014) Acquisition, preference, and follow-up data on the use of three AAC options by four boys with developmental disability/delay. *Journal of Developmental and Physical Disabilities*, *26*, 565–583.

Acredolo, L. & Goodwyn, S. (2000) *Baby signs*. London: Vermilion.

Adams, K., Helmbold, B. & Lucky, K. (2010) I tell you a story: Using narrative re-tell to assess AAC competencies. *Presented at 14th International Society of Augmentative and Alternative Communication Conference*, Barcelona, Spain. July 26–29, 2010.

Adamson, L. B. & Dunbar, B. (1991) Communication development of young children with tracheostomies. *Augmentative and Alternative Communication*, *7*, 275–283.

Adamson, L. B., Kaiser, A. P., Tamis-LaMonda, C. S., Owen, M. T. & Dimitrova, N. (2020) The developmental landscape of early parent-focused language intervention. *Early Childhood Research Quarterly*, *50*, 59–67.

Adolph, K. E. & Hoch, J. E. (2019) Motor development: Embodied, embedded, enculturated, and enabling. *Annual Review of Psychology*, *70*, 141–164.

Agirre, E. & Edmonds, P. (Eds.) (2007) *Word sense disambiguation: Algorithms and applications*. New York: Springer.

Ahmmed, A. U., Asif, A. & Winterburn, S. (2022) Visual processing impairment in children with suspected auditory processing disorder: A transdisciplinary dimensional approach to diagnosis. *American Journal of Audiology*, *31*, 268–283.

Ahonniska-Assa, J., Polack, O., Saraf, E., Wine, J., Silberg, T., Nissenkorn, A., & Ben-Zeev, B. (2018) Assessing cognitive functioning in females with Rett syndrome by eye-tracking methodology. *European Journal of Paediatric Neurology*, *22*, 39–45

Aksu-Koç, A. & Erciyes, A. A. (2018) Narrative discourse: Developmental perspectives. In A. Bar-On and D. Ravid (Eds.), *Handbook of communicative disorders: Theoretical, empirical, and applied-linguistic perspectives* (pp. 329–356). Boston, MA: Mouton de Gruyter.

Alant, E., Life, H. & Harty, M. (2005) Comparison of the learnability and retention between Blissymbols and CyberGlyphs. *International Journal of Language and Communication Disorders*, *40*, 151–169.

Alant, E., Zheng, W., Harty, M. & Lloyd, L. (2013) Translucency ratings of Blissymbols over repeated exposures by children with autism. *Augmentative and Alternative Communication*, *29*, 272–283.

Aldabas, R. (2022) Professional training needs for using augmentative and alternative communication in inclusive classrooms: Voices from Saudi Arabia. *Journal of Special Education Technology*, *37*, 163–173.

Alder, E. C. (2017) English and non-English-speaking families utilizing Augmentative and Alternative Communication (AAC) at home. Master Thesis, California State University, East Bay.

Allen, A. A. & Shane, H. C. (2014) Autism spectrum disorders in the era of mobile technologies: Impact on caregivers. *Developmental Neurorehabilitation*, *17*, 110–114.

Allison, K. M. & Levac, D. E. (2022) Impact of the COVID-19 pandemic on therapy service delivery and functioning for school-aged children with disabilities in the United States. *Disability and Health Journal*, *15*, 101266.

Alm, N. & Newell, A. F. (1996) Being an interesting communication partner. In S. von Tetzchner and M. H. Jensen (Eds.), *Augmentative and alternative communication: European perspectives* (pp. 171–181). London: Whurr/Wiley.

Almirall, D., DiStefano, C., Chang, Y. C., Shire, S., Kaiser, A. et al. (2016) Longitudinal effects of adaptive interventions with a speech-generating device in minimally verbal children with ASD. *Journal of Clinical Child and Adolescent Psychology*, *45*, 442–456.

Alt, M. & Plante, E. (2006) Factors that influence lexical and semantic fast mapping of young children with specific language impairment. *Journal of Speech, Language, and Hearing Research*, *49*, 941–954

Altschuler, T., Santiago, R. & Gormley, J. (2021) Ensuring communication access for all during the COVID-19 pandemic and beyond: Supporting patients, providers, and caregivers in hospitals. *Augmentative and Alternative Communication*, *37*, 155–167.

American Psychiatric Association (2013) *Diagnostic and statistical manual of mental disorders*, 5th edition. Arlington, VA: American Psychiatric Association.

Amor, A. M., Hagiwara, M., Shogren, K. A., Thompson, J. R., Verdugo, M. Á. et al. (2019) International perspectives and trends in research on inclusive education: A systematic review. *International Journal of Inclusive Education*, *23*(12), 1277–1295.

An, S., Feng, X., Dai, Y., Bo, H., Wang, X. et al. (2017) Development and evaluation of a speech-generating AAC mobile app for minimally verbal children with autism spectrum disorder in Mainland China. *Molecular Autism*, *8*, 1–12.

Andersen, G. L., Irgens, L. M., Haagaas, I., Skranes, J. S., Meberg, A. E., & Vik, T. (2008) Cerebral palsy in Norway: Prevalence, subtypes and severity. *European Journal of Paediatric Neurology*, *12*, 4–13.

Andersen, G. L., Mjøen, T. R. & Vik, T. (2010) Prevalence of speech problems and the use of augmentative and alternative communication in children with cerebral palsy: A registry-based study in Norway. *Perspectives on Augmentative and Alternative Communication*, *19*, 12–20.

Anderson, D. K., Lord, C., Risi, S., DiLavore, P. S., Shulman, C. et al. (2007) Patterns of growth in verbal abilities among children with autism spectrum disorder. *Journal of Consulting and Clinical Psychology*, *75*, 594–604.

Anderson, K. L., Balandin, S. & Stancliffe, R. J. (2015) Alternative service delivery models for families with a new speech generating device: Perspectives of parents and therapists. *International Journal of Speech-Language Pathology*, *17*, 185–195.

Andzik, N. R. & Chung, Y. C. (2022) Augmentative and alternative communication for adults with complex communication needs: A review of single-case research. *Communication Disorders Quarterly*, *43*, 182–194.

Andzik, N. R., Chung, Y. C., Doneski-Nicol, J. & Dollarhide, C. T. (2019) AAC services in schools: A special educator's perspective. *International Journal of Developmental Disabilities*, *65*, 89–97.

Andzik, N., Chung, Y.-C. & Kranak, M. (2016) Communication opportunities for elementary school students who use augmentative and alternative communication. *Augmentative and Alternative Communication*, *32*, 272–281.

Anglin, J. M. (1993) Knowing versus learning words. *Monographs of the Society for Research in Child Development*, *58*, 10.

Ankenman, K., Elgin, J., Sullivan, K., Vincent, L. & Bernier, R. (2014) Nonverbal and verbal cognitive discrepancy profiles in autism spectrum disorders: Influence of age and gender. *American Journal on Intellectual and Developmental Disabilities*, *119*, 84–99.

Arciuli, J. & Bailey, B. (2021) The promise of comprehensive early reading instruction for children with autism and recommendations for future directions. *Language, Speech, and Hearing Services in Schools*, *52*, 225–238.

Armitage, R. C. (2022) War in Ukraine: Public health, rehabilitation and assistive technologies. *Disability and Rehabilitation: Assistive Technology*, *17*, 989–990.

Armstrong, D. D. (2001) Rett syndrome neuropathology review 2000. *Brain and Development*, *23*, S72–S76.

Arnesen, B. & Wergeland, E. (1994) *VMK – Visuelt manipulativt kommunikasjonssystem*. Porsgrunn: Wabe forlag.

Arnett, J. J. (2015) *Emerging adulthood: The winding road from the late teens through the twenties*, 2nd edition. New York: Oxford University Press.

Arthur, S. M., Creem, A. N., Bahry, S., Cauchi, J. & Leaf, J. B. (2023) Evidence-based interventions to teach social skills. In J. Matson (Ed.), *Handbook of clinical child psychology: Integrating theory and research into practice* (pp. 903–921). Cham, Switzerland: Springer.

Atterström, A., Malmqvist, J., Anderberg, E., & Swärd, A. K. (2023) Experiences about reading and writing development narrated by students with severe speech and physical impairment. *International Journal of Disability, Development and Education*, *70*, 1101–1119.

Aviezer, O. (2003) Bedtime talk of three-year-olds: Collaborative repair of miscommunication. *First Language*, *23*, 117–139.

Babineau, M., Shi, R. & Christophe, A. (2020) 14-month-olds exploit verbs' syntactic contexts to build expectations about novel words. *Infancy*, *25*, 719–733.

Baggetta, P. & Alexander, P. A. (2016) Conceptualization and operationalization of executive function. *Mind, Brain, and Education*, 10, 10–33.

Bailey, P. (2013) The 'Telling Stories' Project: A case series study of narrative interaction between children who use speech generating devices and their educational staff. Doctoral dissertation, University of East Anglia.

Baio, J., Wiggins, L., Christensen, D. L., Maenner, M. J., Daniels, J. et al. (2018) Prevalence of autism spectrum disorder among children aged 8 years—autism and developmental disabilities monitoring network, 11 sites, United States, 2014. *MMWR Surveillance Summaries*, *67*, 1.

Baker, B. L., Marquis, W. A., & Feinfield, K. A. (2016) Early intervention and parent education. In A. Cass et al. (Eds.), *The handbook of intellectual disability and clinical psychology practice* (pp. 311–338). Abingdon, UK: Routledge.

Baker, B. (1982) Minspeak: A semantic compaction system that makes self-expression easier for communicatively disabled individuals. *Byte*, *7*, 186–202.

Baker, B. (1986) Using images to generate speech. *Byte*, *11*, 160–168.

Balandin, S. & Iacono, T. (1998) Topics of meal-break converstaions. *Augmentative and Alternative Communication*, *14*, 131–146.

Balandin, S. & Morgan, J. (2001) Preparing for the future: Aging and alternative and augmentative communication. *Augmentative and Alternative Communication*, *17*, 99–108.

Bambini, V. & Torregrossa, J. (2010) Cognitive categories behind early Topic/Comment structures. In M. Chine (Ed.), *Topic, struttura dell'informazione e acquisizione linguistica* (pp. 35–58). Milan: Franco Angeli.

Bamford, C. K., Masso, S., Baker, E., & Ballard, K. J. (2022) Dynamic assessment for children with communication disorders: A systematic scoping review and framework. *American Journal of Speech-Language Pathology*, *31*, 1878–1893.

Bancroft, S. L., Weiss, J. S., Libby, M. E. & Ahearn, W. H. (2011) A comparison of procedural variations in teaching behavior chains: Manual guidance, trainer completion, and no completion of untrained steps. *Journal of Applied Behavior Analysis*, *44*, 559–569.

Banda, D. R., Grimmett, E. & Hart, S. L. (2009) Activity schedules: Helping students with autism spectrum disorders in general education classrooms manage transition issues. *Teaching Exceptional Children*, *41*, 16–21.

Bandura, A. (1997) *Self-efficacy: The exercise of control*. New York: W. H. Freeman.

Baranello, G., Signorini, S., Tinelli, F., Guzzetta, A., Pagliano, E. et al. (2020) Visual function classification system for children with cerebral palsy: Development and validation. *Developmental Medicine and Child Neurology*, *62*, 104–110.

Barba-Colmenero, F., Robles-Bello, M. A. & Valencia-Naranjo, N. (2024) The relationship between learning potential in preschool children and their cognitive abilities. *Educational Psychology*, *30*. 11–18.

Barker, R. M., Akaba, S., Brady, N. C. & Thiemann-Bourque, K. (2013) Support for AAC use in preschool, and growth in language skills, for young children with developmental disabilities. *Augmentative and Alternative Communication*, *29*, 334–346.

Barker, R. M., Saunders, K. J. & Brady, N. C. (2012) Reading instruction for children who use AAC: Considerations in the pursuit of generalizable results. *Augmentative and Alternative Communication*, *28*, 160–170.

Baron, L. S. & Arbel, Y. (2022) An implicit–explicit framework for intervention methods in developmental language disorder. *American Journal of Speech-Language Pathology*, *31*, 1557–1573.

Barrett, M. J. (1982) The holophrastic hypothesis: Conceptual and empirical issues. *Cognition*, *11*, 47–76.

Barrett, M. J., Harris, M. & Chasin, J. (1991) Early lexical development and maternal speech: A comparison of children's initial and subsequent uses of words. *Journal of Child Language*, *18*, 21–40.

Barron, C., Beckett, A., Coussens, M., Desoete, A., Cannon Jones, N. et al. (2017) *Barriers to play and recreation for children and young people with disabilities: Exploring environmental factors*. Berlin: De Gruyter.

Barstein, J., Martin, G. E., Lee, M. & Losh, M. (2018) A duck wearing boots?! Pragmatic language strategies for repairing communication breakdowns across genetically based neurodevelopmental disabilities. *Journal of Speech, Language, and Hearing Research*, *61*, 1440–1454.

Barton, E. E. (2015) Teaching generalized pretend play and related behaviors to young children with disabilities. *Exceptional Children*, *81*, 489–506.

Barton, E. E. (2016) Critical issues and promising practices for teaching play to young children with disabilities. In B. Reichow et al. (Eds.), *Handbook of early childhood special education* (pp. 267–286). Basel: Springer.

Barton, E. E., Murray, R., O'Flaherty, C., Sweeney, E. M. & Gossett, S. (2020) Teaching object play to young children with disabilities: A systematic review of methods and rigor. *American Journal on Intellectual and Developmental Disabilities*, *125*, 14–36.

Barton, A., Sevcik, R. A. & Romski, M. A. (2006) Exploring visual-graphic symbol acquisition by preschool age children with developmental and language delays. *Augmentative and Alternative Communication*, *22*, 10–20

Barton, E. E. & Wolery, M. (2008) Teaching pretend play to children with disabilities: A review of the literature. *Topics in Early Childhood Special Education*, *28*, 109–125.

Barton-Hulsey, A., Collins, S. C., Therrien, M. C., Biggs, E. E., Romano, M., & Coltellino, B. (2023) Augmentative and alternative communication services during the COVID-19 pandemic: Contextual determinants of the parent–speech-language pathologist partnership. *American Journal of Speech-Language Pathology*, *32*, 2889–2907.

Basil, C. (1989) Personal communication.

Basil, C. (1992) Social interaction and learned helplessness in severely disabled children. *Augmentative and Alternative Communication*, *8*, 188–199.

Basil, C. & Soro-Camats, E. (1996) Supporting graphic language acquisition by a girl with multiple impairments. In S. von Tetzchner and M. H. Jensen (Eds.), *Augmentative and alternative communication: European perspectives* (pp. 270–291). London: Whurr/Wiley.

Bates, E., Bretherton, I & Snyder, L. (1988) *From first words to grammar: Individual differences and dissociable mechanisms*. Cambridge: Cambridge University Press.

Bates, E., Dale, P. S. & Thal, D. (1995) Individual differences and their implications for theories of language development. In P. Fletcher and B. MacWhinney (Eds.), *Handbook of child language* (pp. 96–151) Oxford: Basil Blackwell.

Bates, E. & Goodman, J. C. (1997) On the inseparability of grammar and the lexicon: Evidence from acquisition, aphasia and real-time processing. *Language and cognitive Processes*, *12*, 507–584.

Batorowicz, B., Campbell, C., King, G., von Tetzchner, S. & Missiuna, C. (2014) Social participation of school-aged children who use communication aids: The views of children and parents. *Augmentative and Alternative Communication*, *30*, 237–251.

Batorowicz, B., McDougall, S. & Shepherd, T. A. (2006) AAC and community partnerships: The participation path to community inclusion. *Augmentative and Alternative Communication*, *22*, 178–195.

Batorowicz, B., Stadskleiv, K., Renner, G., Sandberg, A. D. & von Tetzchner, S. (2018) Assessment of aided language comprehension and use in children and adolescents with severe speech and motor impairments. *Augmentative and Alternative Communication*, *34*, 54–67.

Batorowicz, B., Stadskleiv, K., von Tetzchner, S. & Missiuna, C. (2016) Children who use communication aids instructing peer and adult partners during play-based activity. *Augmentative and Alternative Communication*, *32*, 105–119.

Baus, C., Carreiras, M. & Emmorey, K. (2013) When does iconicity in sign language matter? *Language and Cognitive Processes*, *28*, 261–271.

Baxter, S., Enderby, P. Evans, P. & Judge, S. (2012) Barriers and facilitators to the use of high-technology augmentative and alternative communication devices: A systematic review and qualitative synthesis. *International Journal of Language and Communication Disorders*, *47*, 115–129.

Beals, K. P. (2020) Review of «Communication alternatives in autism: Perspectives on typing and spelling approaches for the nonspeaking» by Edlyn Vallejo Peña. *Journal of Evidence-Based Social Work*, *17*, 361–367.

Bean, A., Harris, K., Kim, H., DiGiovine, C. & Sonntag, A. M. (2023) A scoping review of communication outcomes measures in augmentative and alternative communication. *Assistive Technology*, 10.1080/10400435.2023.2251041

Beauchamp, F., Bourke-Taylor, H. & Brown, T. (2018) Therapists' perspectives: Supporting children to use switches and technology for accessing their environment, leisure, and communication. *Journal of Occupational Therapy, Schools, and Early Intervention*, *11*, 133–147.

Beck, A. R. & Fritz-Verticchio, H. (2003) The influence of information and role-playing experiences on children's attitudes toward peers who use AAC. *American Journal of Speech and Language Pathology*, *12*, 51–60.

Beck, A. R., Stoner, J. B. & Dennis, M. L. (2009) An investigation of aided language stimulation: Does it increase AAC use with adults with developmental disabilities and complex communication needs? *Augmentative and Alternative Communication*, *25*, 42–54.

Beck, I. L., McKeown, M. G. & Omanson, R. C. (1987) The effects and uses of diverse vocabulary instructional techniques. In M. G. McKeown and M. E. Curtis (Eds.), *The nature of vocabulary acquisition* (pp. 147–163). Hillsdale, NJ: Lawrence Erlbaum.

Bedrosian, J. (1999) Efficacy research issues in AAC: Interactive storybook reading. *Augmentative and Alternative Communication*, *15*, 45–55.

Beghdadi, M. (2019) Texhnology in education. In S. von Tetzchner et al. (Eds.), *Juvenile neuronal ceroid lipofuscinosis, childhood dementia and education* (pp. 373–398). Trondheim: Snøfugl.

Bekteshi, S., Konings, M., Vanmechelen, I., Deklerck, J., Ortibus, E. et al. (2020) Eye gaze gaming intervention in children with Dyskinetic cerebral palsy: A pilot study of task performance and its relation with dystonia and Choreoathetosis. *Developmental Neurorehabilitation, 23*, 548–556.
Bell, J. L. (2018) KiwiChat Camp: Experiences and perceptions of children with complex communication needs and their family/whānau. Master Thesis, Massey University, Albany, New Zealand.
Belland, B. R. (2014) Scaffolding: Definition, current debates, and future directions. In J. M. Spector et al. (Eds.), *Handbook of research on educational communications and technology* (pp. 505–518). Cham, Switzerland: Springer.
Bello, A., Stefanini, S., Rinaldi, P., Onofrio, D. & Volterra, V. (2020) Gestural symbolic strategies in children with Down syndrome. *Gesture, 19*, 299–334.
Bendel, O. (2019) The synthetization of human voices. *AI and Society, 34*, 83–89.
Bennett, C. R., Bex, P. J., Bauer, C. M. & Merabet, L. B. (2019) The assessment of visual function and functional vision. *Seminars in Pediatric Neurology, 31*, 30–40.
Berenguer, C., Martínez, E. R., De Stasio, S. & Baixauli, I. (2022) Parents' perceptions and experiences with their children's use of augmentative/alternative communication: A systematic review and qualitative meta-synthesis. *International Journal of Environmental Research and Public Health, 19*, 8091.
Berg, Å. & Sørhuglen, M. (1980) *Tegn med psykisk utviklingshemmede*. Breistein, Norway: Vestlandsheimen.
Berg, M. H. (1998) Children's use of pointing cues in aided language intervention. *Presented at The 8th Biennial Conference on Augmentative and Alternative Communication*. Dublin, August 1998.
Berger, R. J. & Feucht, J. (2012) Thank you for your words, Observations from a disability summer camp. *Qualitative Inquiry, 18*, 76–85.
Berger-Sweeney, J. (2011) Cognitive deficits in Rett syndrome: What we know and what we need to know to treat them. *Neurobiology of Learning and Memory, 96*, 637–646.
Berry, D. C. & Dienes, Z. (1993) Towards a working characterisation of implicit learning. In D. C. Berry and Z. Dienes (Eds.), *Implicit learning. Theoretical and empirical issues* (pp. 1–18) Hillsdale, NJ: Lawrence Erlbaum.
Bertenthal, B. I. & Boyer, T. W. (2015) The development of social attention in human infants. In A. Puce and B. I. Bertenthal (Eds.), *The many faces of social attention: Behavioral and neural measures* (pp. 21–65). Cham, Switzerland: Springer.
Besio, S. (2017) The need for play for the sake of play. In S. Besio et al. (Eds.), *Play development in children with disabilities* (pp. 9–52). Berlin: De Gruyter.
Besio, S. & Amelina, N. (2017) Play in children with physical impairment. In S. Besio et al. (Eds.), *Play development in children with disabilities* (pp. 120–136). Berlin: De Gruyter.
Besio, S., Bulgarelli, D. & Stancheva-Popkostadinova, V. (Eds.) (2017) *Play development in children with disabilties*. Berlin: De Gruyter.
Besio, S., Bulgarelli, D. & Stancheva-Popkostadinova, V. (Eds.) (2018) *Evaluation of children's play. Tools and methods*. Warsaw, Poland: De Gruyter.
Beukelman, D. R. & Light, J. C. (2020) *Augmentative and alternative communication. Supporting children an adults with complex communication needs*, 5th edition. Baltimore, MD: Paul H. Brookes.
Beukelman, D. R., Yorkston, K. M., Poblete, M. & Naranjo, C. (1984) Frequency of word occurrence in communication samples produced by adult communication aid users. *Journal of Speech and Hearing Disorders, 49*, 360–367.
Bialystok, E., Hawrylewicz, K., Grundy, J. G. & Chung-Fat-Yim, A. (2022) The swerve: How childhood bilingualism changed from liability to benefit. *Developmental Psychology, 58*, 1429–1440.
Bialystok, E. & Werker, J. F. (2017) The systematic effects of bilingualism on children's development. *Developmental Science, 20*, e12535.
Biggs, E. E., Carter, E. W. & Gustafson, J. (2017) Efficacy of peer support arrangements to increase peer interaction and AAC use. *American Journal on Intellectual and Developmental Disabilities, 122*, 25–48.
Biggs, E. E. & Hacker, R. (2021a) Engaging stakeholders to improve social validity: Intervention priorities for students with complex communication needs. *Augmentative and Alternative Communication, 37*, 25–38.

Biggs, E. E. & Hacker, R. E. (2021b) Ecological systems for students who use AAC: Stakeholders' views on factors impacting intervention and outcomes. *Research and Practice for Persons with Severe Disabilities, 46*, 259–277.

Biklen, D. (1990) Communication unbound: Autism and praxis. *Harvard Educational Review, 60*, 291–315.

Binger, C. (2008) Classroom-based language goals and intervention for children who use AAC: Back to basics. *Perspectives on Augmentative and Alternative Communication, 17*, 20–26.

Binger, C., Kent-Walsh, J., Harrington, N. & Hollerbach, Q. (2020) Tracking early sentence-building progress in graphic symbol communication. *Language, Speech, and Hearing Services in Schools, 51*, 317–328

Binger, C., Kent-Walsh, J. & King, M. (2017) Dynamic assessment for 3- and 4-year-old children who use augmentative and alternative communication: Evaluating expressive syntax. *Journal of Speech, Language, and Hearing Research, 60*, 1946–1958.

Binger, C., Kent-Walsh, J., King, M., & Mansfield, L. (2017a) Early sentence productions of 3- and 4-year-old children who use augmentative and alternative communication. *Journal of Speech, Language, and Hearing Research, 60*, 1930–1945.

Binger, C., Kent-Walsh, J., King, M., Webb, E. & Buenviaje, E. (2017b) Early sentence productions of 5-year-old children who use augmentative and alternative communication. *Communication Disorders Quarterly, 38*, 131–142.

Binger, C. & Light, J. (2007) The effect of aided AAC modeling on the expression of multi-symbol messages by preschoolers who use AAC. *Augmentative and Alternative Communication, 23*, 30–43.

Binger, C. & Light, J. (2008) The morphology and syntax of individuals who use AAC: Research review and implications for effective practice. *Augmentative and Alternative Communication, 24*, 123–138

Binger, C., Renley, N., Babej, E. & Hahs-Vaughn, D. (2021) A survey of school-age children with highly unintelligible speech. *Augmentative and Alternative Communication, 37*, 194–205.

Bird, F., Dores, P. A., Moniz, D. & Robinson, J. (1989) Reducing severe aggressive and self-injurious behaviors with functional communication training, *American Journal on Mental Retardation, 94*, 37–48.

Bishop, D. V. M. (2003) *Test for reception of grammar 2*. London: The Psychological Corporation

Bishop, D. V. M., Snowling, M. J., Thompson, P. A., Greenhalgh, T. & Catalise Consortium. (2016) CATALISE: A multinational and multidisciplinary Delphi consensus study. Identifying language impairments in children. *PLOS One, 11*, e0158753.

Bishop, D. V. M. (2006) What causes specific language impairment in children? *Current Directions in Psychological Science, 15*, 217–221.

Bishop, D. V. M. (2014) Ten questions about terminology for children with unexplained language problems. *International Journal of language and Communication Disorders, 49*, 381–415.

Bishop, D. V. M. (2017) Why is it so hard to reach agreement on terminology? The case of developmental language disorder (DLD) *International Journal of Language and Communication Disorders, 52*, 671–680.

Bishop, K., Rankin, J & Mirenda, P. (1994) Impact of graphic symbol use on reading acquisition. *Augmentative and Alternative Communication, 10*, 113–125.

Bishop, N., Aziz, A. & Barth, C. (2014) Phenotypic variation in autism spectrum disorder: Insights from syndromic forms of Autism. In V- B- Patel, V. R. Preedy and C. R. Martin (Eds.), *Comprehensive guide to autism* (pp. 1715–1736). London: Springer.

Bjerkan, B. (1975) En re-definering av stamming og en analyse av stammingens situasjonsvariabilitet. Thesis, University of Oslo.

Blackstone, S. W. (1999) Circles of communication partners. *Augmentative Communication News, 12*, 1–2.

Blackstone, S. W. & Bruskin, D. M. (1986) *Augmentative communication: An introduction*. Rockville: American Speech-Language Hearing Association.

Blackstone, S. W. & Hunt-Berg, M. (2012) *Social networks: A communication inventory for individuals with complex communication needs and their communication partners*. Verona, Wisconsin: Attainment Company.

Blackstone, S. W., Luo, F., Barker, R. M., Sevcik, R. A., Romski, M., Casella, V., & Roman-Lantzy, C. (2022) Profiles of children with cortical visual impairment who use augmentative and alternative communication: A retrospective examination. *American Journal of Speech-Language Pathology, 31*, 2707–2721.

Blackstone, S. W., Luo, F., Canchola, J., Wilkinson, K. M. & Roman-Lantzy, C. (2021) Children with cortical visual impairment and complex communication needs: Identifying gaps between needs and current practice. *Language, Speech, and Hearing Services in Schools, 52*, 612–629.

Blackstone, S. W., Williams, M. B. & Wilkins, D. P. (2007) Key principles underlying research and practice in AAC. *Augmentative and Alternative Communication, 23*, 191–203.

Blackwell, A. K., Harding, S., Babayiğit, S. & Roulstone, S. (2015) Characteristics of parent–child interactions: A systematic review of studies comparing children with primary language impairment and their typically developing peers. *Communication Disorders Quarterly, 36*, 67–78.

Blair, C. (2016) Executive function and early childhood education. *Current Opinion in Behavioral Sciences, 10*, 102–107.

Blanche, E. I. (2008) Play in children with cerebral palsy: Doing with – not doing to. In L. D. Parham and L. S. Fazio (Eds.), *Play in occupational therapy for children* (pp. 375–393). Saint Louis, MO: Mosby Elsevier.

Blischak, D. M. & McDaniels, M. A. (1995) Effects of picture size and placement on memory for written words. *Journal of Speech and Hearing Research, 38*, 1356–1362.

Bliss, C. (1965) *Semantography (Blissymbolics)* Sydney: Semantography Publications.

Blissymbolics Communication International (2020) *The fundamental rules of Blissymbolics: Creating new Blissymbolics characters and vocabulary*. Uppsala, Sweden: Blissymbolics Communication International.

Bloom, L. (1973) *One word at a time*. The Hague: Mouton.

Bloom, L. (1998) Language acquisition in its developmental context. In W. Damon et al. (Eds.), *Handbook of child psychology*, Volume 2 (pp. 309–420) New York: Wiley.

Bloom, L. & Lahey, M. (1978) *Language development and language disorders*. New York: Wiley.

Bloom, L., Tinker, E. & Margulis, C. (1994) The words children learn: Evidence against a noun bias in childrren's vocabularies. *Cognitive Development, 8*, 431–450.

Bloom, Y. (1990) *Object symbols: A communication option*. North Rocks, Australia: North Rocks Press.

Boers, E., Janssen, M. J., Minnaert, A. E., & Ruijssenaars, W. A. (2013) The application of dynamic assessment in people communicating at a prelinguistic level: A descriptive review of the literature. *International Journal of Disability, Development and Education, 60*, 119–145.

Bohn, M. & Frank, M. C. (2019) The pervasive role of pragmatics in early language. *Annual Review of Developmental Psychology, 1*, 223–249.

Bonarini, A. S. & Besio, S. (2022) *Robot play for all: Developing toys and games for disability*. Cham, Switzerland: Springer.

Bondy, A. (2012) The unusual suspects: Myths and misconceptions associated with PECS. *The Psychological Record, 62*, 789–816.

Bondy, A. S. & Frost, L. A. (1998) The picture exchange communication system. *Seminars in Speech and Language, 19*, 373–424.

Bondy, A. S. & Frost, L. A. (2002) *A picture's worth: PECS and other visual communication strategies in autism*. Bethesda, MD: Woodbine House.

Bonis, S. (2016) Stress and parents of children with autism: A review of literature. *Issues in Mental Health Nursing, 37*, 153–163.

Bonvillian, J. D. (2019) Sign acquisition and development by hearing children with autism spectrum disorders. In N. Grove and K. Launonen (Eds.), *Manual sign acquisition in children with developmental disabilities* (pp. 115–131) New York: Nova.

Bonvillian, J. D. & Blackburn, D. W. (1991) Manual communication and autism: Factors relating to sign language acquisition. In P. Siple and S. D. Fischer (Eds.), *Theoretical issues in sign language research. Volume 2: Psychology* (pp. 255–277). Chicago, IL: Chicago University Press.

Bonvillian, J. D., Kissane Lee, N., Dooley, T. T. & Loncke, F. (2020a) *Simplified aigns: A manual sign-communication system for special populations, Volume 1: Principles, background, and application.* Cambridge, UK: Open Book Publishers.

Bonvillian, J. D., Kissane Lee, N., Dooley, T. T. & Loncke, F. (2020b) *Simplified signs: A manual sign-communication system for special populations, Volume 2: Sign lexicon, descriptions, and memory aids.* Cambridge, UK: Open Book Publishers.

Bonvillian, J. D. & Nelson, K. E. (1976) Sign language acquisition in a mute autistic boy. *Journal of Speech and Hearing Disorders, 41*, 339–347.

Bonvillian, J. D., Nelson, K. E. & Rhyne, J. M. (1981) Sign language and autism. *Journal of Autism and Developmental Disorders, 11*, 125–137.

Bonvillian, J. D., Orlansky, M. D., & Novack, L. L. (1983) Developmental milestones: Sign language acquisition and motor development. *Child Development*, 54, 1435–1445.

Booth, T. (1978) Early receptive language training for the severely and profoundly retarded. *Language, Speech, and Hearing Services in Schools, 9*, 142–150.

Borgestig, M., Rytterström, P., & Hemmingsson, H. (2017) Gaze-based assistive technology used in daily life by children with severe physical impairments–parents' experiences. *Developmental Neurorehabilitation, 20*, 301–308.

Borghi, A. M. (2021) Affordances, context and sociality. *Synthese, 199*, 12485–12515.

Bornman, J., Nelson Bryen, D., Kershaw, P. & Ledwaba, G. (2011) Reducing the risk of being a victim of crime in South Africa: You can tell and be heard! *Augmentative and Alternative Communication, 27*, 117–130.

Bornman, J. (2017) Preventing abuse and providing access to justice for individuals with complex communication needs: The role of augmentative and alternative communication. *Seminars in Speech and Language, 38*, 321–331.

Bornman, J. (2023) The ABC's of AAC training for police officers and legal practitioners: From science to solutions. *Presented at 5th International Conference on Augmentative and Alternative Communication – AAC beyond the AAC system*, Sofia, Bulgaria, November 24–26, 2023.

Bornman, J., Alant, E. & Du Preez, A. (2009) Translucency and learnability of Blissymbols in Setswana-speaking children: An exploration. *Augmentative and Alternative Communication, 25*, 287–298

Bornman, E. Alant, E & Meiring, J. (2001) The use of a digital voice output device to facilitate language development in a child with developmental apraxia of speech: A case study. *Disability and Rehabilitation, 23*, 623–634.

Bornstein, M. H. & Hendricks, C. (2013) Screening for developmental disabilities in developing countries. *Social Science and Medicine, 97*, 307–315.

Bosse, I. K., Renner, G. & Wilkens, L. (2020) Social media and internet use patterns by adolescents with complex communication needs. *Language, Speech, and Hearing Services in Schools, 51*(4), 1024–1036.

Bosse, I. K. & Wilkens, L. (2016) Research and intervention to improve institutional structures for adult aac users. In M. Antona and C. Stephanidis (Eds.), *Universal access in human-computer interaction. Methods, techniques, and best practices* (pp. 161–171). Cham, Switzerland: Springer.

Boster, J. B., Findlen, U. M., Pitt, K. & McCarthy, J. W. (2023) Design of aided augmentative and alternative communication systems for children with vision impairment: Psychoacoustic perspectives. *Augmentative and Alternative Communication, 40*, 57–67.

Bova, A. (2021) Co-construction of argumentative discussions between parents and children during mealtime conversations. A pragma-dialectical analysis. *Learning, Culture and Social Interaction, 29*, 100519.

Bowring, D. L., Totsika, V., Hastings, R. P., Toogood, S. & Griffith, G. M. (2017) Challenging behaviours in adults with an intellectual disability: A total population study and exploration of risk indices. *British Journal of Clinical Psychology, 56*, 16–32.

Boynton, J. (2012) Facilitated Communication—what harm it can do: Confessions of a former facilitator. *Evidence-Based Communication Assessment and Intervention*, *6*, 3–13.

Bradley, B. S., Selby, J. & Stapleton, M. (2024) *Babies in groups: Expanding imaginations*. Oxford, UK: Oxford University Press.

Brady, N. (2000) Improved comprehension of object names folowing voice output communication aid use: Two case studies. *Augmentative and Alternative Communication*, *16*, 197–204.

Braine, M. D., & Bowerman, M. (1976) Children's first word combinations. *Monographs of the Society for Research in Child Development*, *41*, 1–104.

Branson, D. & Demchak, M. (2009) The use of augmentative and alternative communication methods with infants and toddlers with disabilities: A research review. *Augmentative and Alternative Communication*, *25*, 274–286

Brekke, K. M. (2001) *Utvikling av en grafisk kommunikasjonsform*. Stavanger: Senter for atferdsforskning.

Brekke, K. M. & von Tetzchner, S. (2003) Co-construction in graphic language development. In S. von Tetzchner and N. Grove (Eds.), *Augmentative and alternative communication: Developmental issues* (pp. 176–210). London: Whurr/Wiley.

Brewster, S. (2007) Asymmetries of power and competence and implications for AAC: Interaction between adults with severe learning disabilities and their care staff. Dissertation, University of Birmingham.

Bridges, K. & Hoff, E. (2014) Older sibling influences on the language environment and language development of toddlers in bilingual homes. *Applied Psycholinguistics*, *35*, 225–241.

Briet, G., Le Maner-Idrissi, G., Seveno, T., Le Marec, O. & Le Sourn-Bissaoui, S. (2023) Peer mediation in play settings for minimally verbal students with autism spectrum disorder. *Autism and Developmental Language Impairments*, *8*, 23969415231204837

Brij, R. S. (2019) Effects of visual supports with and without systematic instruction on the acquisition of daily living skills for students with autism spectrum disorder and intellectual disability. Dissertation, Flinders University, Australia.

Broberg, M., Ferm, U. & Thunberg, G. (2012) Measuring responsive style in parents who use AAC with their children: Development and evaluation of a new instrument. *Augmentative and Alternative Communication*, *28*, 243–253.

Brock, K. L. & Thomas, E. (2021) The effectiveness of aided aac modeling for Belizean children: A case study. *Perspectives of the ASHA Special Interest Groups*, *6*, 1182–1197.

Brown, A. & Cariveau, T. (2022) A systematic review of simultaneous prompting and prompt delay procedures. *Journal of Behavioral Education*, 10.1007/s10864-022-09481-6

Brown, R. & Hanlon, C. (1970) Derivational complexity and order of acquisition in child speech. In J. R. Hayes (Ed.), *Cognition and the development of language* (pp. 11–53). New York: Wiley.

Bruner, J. S. (1975) The ontogenesis of speech acts. *Journal of Child Language*, *2*, 1–19.

Bruner, J. S. (1983) *Child's talk*. Oxford, UK: Oxford University Press.

Bruner, J. S. (1986) *Actual minds, possible worlds*. Cambridge, MA: Harvard University Press.

Bruner, J. S. (1990) *Acts of meaning*. Cambridge, MA: Harvard University Press.

Bruner, J. S. (1991) The narrative construction of reality. *Critical Inquiry*, *18*, 1–21.

Bruno, J. (2010) *Test of aided-communication symbol performance*. Pittsburgh, PA: Dynavox Mayer Johnson.

Bruno, J. & Dribbon, M. (1998) Outcomes in AAC: Evaluating the effectiveness of a parent training program. *Augmentative and Alternative Communication*, *14*, 59–70.

Bruno, J. & Trembath, D. (2006) Use of aided language stimulation to improve syntactic performance during a weeklong intervention program. *Augmentative and Alternative Communication*, *22*, 300–313.

Bryan, L. C. & Gast, D. L. (2000) Teaching on-task and on-schedule behaviors to high-functioning children with autism via picture activity schedules. *Journal of Autism and Developmental Disorders*, *30*, 553–567.

Bryen, D. N. (2008) Vocabulary to support socially-valued adult roles. *Augmentative and Alternative Communication*, *24*, 294–301.

Bryen, D. N. & Joyce, D. G. (1985) Language intervention with the severely handicapped: A decade of research. *The Journal of Special Education, 19*, 7–39.

Bryen, D. N. & Wickman, C. H. (2011) Ending the silence of people with little or no functional speech: Testifying in court. *Disability Studies Quarterly, 31*(4).

Brysbaert, M., Stevens, M., Mandera, P. & Keuleers, E. (2016) How many words do we know? Practical estimates of vocabulary size dependent on word definition, the degree of language input and the participant's age. *Frontiers in Psychology, 7*, 1116.

Buchholz, M., Holmgren, K. & Ferm, U. (2020) Remote communication for people with disabilities: Support persons' views on benefits, challenges, and suggestions for technology development. *Technology and Disability, 32*, 69–80.

Bulgarelli, D., Corno, F. & De Russis, L. (2018) Collaborative accessible gameplay with one-switch interfaces. In *2018 IEEE Games, Entertainment, Media Conference (GEM) Galway*, Ireland, August 2018 (pp. 95–100).

Bunning, K. (2018) Commentary on "promoting positive communication environments: A service evaluation": The communication partnership as a focus for change. *Tizard Learning Disability Review, 23*, 201–206.

Burkhart, L. J. (1987) *Using computers and speech synthesis to facilitate communicative interaction with young and/or severely handicapped children.* College Park: Burkhart.

Burnley, A., St Clair, M., Bedford, R., Wren, Y. & Dack, C. (2023) Understanding the prevalence and manifestation of anxiety and other socio-emotional and behavioural difficulties in children with developmental language disorder. *Journal of Neurodevelopmental Disorders, 15*, 1–21.

Buzolich, M. J. & Lunger, J. (1995) Empowering system users in peer training. *Augmentative and Alternative Communication, 11*, 37–48.

Byiers, B. J. & Symons, F. J. (2012) Issues in estimating developmental level and cognitive function in Rett syndrome. *International Review of Research in Developmental Disabilities, 43*, 147–185..

Byler, J. K. (1985) The Makaton vocabulary: An analysis based on recent research. *British Journal of Special Education, 12*, 113–129.

Byrne, G. (2018) Prevalence and psychological sequelae of sexual abuse among individuals with an intellectual disability: A review of the recent literature. *Journal of Intellectual Disabilities, 22*, 294–310.

Cairns, P., Power, C., Barlet, M. & Haynes, G. (2019) Future design of accessibility in games: A design vocabulary. *International Journal of Human-Computer Studies, 131*, 64–71.

Calculator, S. (1988) Evaluating the effectiveness of AAC programs for persons with severe handicaps. *Augmentative and Alternative Communication, 4*, 177–179.

Calculator, S. N. (2009) Augmentative and alternative communication (AAC) and inclusive education for students with the most severe disabilities. *International Journal of Inclusive Education, 13*, 93–113.

Calculator, S. & Dollaghan, C. (1982) The use of communication boards in a residential setting: An evaluation. *Journal of Speech and Hearing Disorders, 47*, 281–287.

Calder, S. D., Brennan-Jones, C. G., Robinson, M., Whitehouse, A. & Hill, E. (2022) The prevalence of and potential risk factors for developmental language disorder at 10 years in the Raine Study. *Journal of Paediatrics and Child Health, 58*, 2044–2050.

Calderoni, S. (2023) Sex/gender differences in children with autism spectrum disorder: A brief overview on epidemiology, symptom profile, and neuroanatomy. *Journal of Neuroscience Research, 101*, 739–750.

Calvert, S. L. (2015) Children and digital media. In M. H. Bornstein et al. (Eds.), *Handbook of child psychology and developmental science, Seventh edition, Volume 4: Ecological settings and processes in developmental systems* (pp. 375–415) Hoboken, NJ: Wiley.

Camaioni, L., Perucchini, P., Muratori, F., Parrini, B. & Cesari, A. (2003) The communicative use of pointing in autism: Developmental profile and factors related to change. *European Psychiatry, 18*, 6–12.

Camden, C. & Silva, M. (2021) Pediatric teleheath: Opportunities created by the COVID-19 and suggestions to sustain its use to support families of children with disabilities. *Physical and Occupational Therapy in Pediatrics*, *41*, 1–17.

Cameron, R. J. (1986) *Portage: Pre-schoolers, parents and professionals*. Windsor: NFER-Nelson.

Campos, J., Anderson, D. I., Barbu-Roth, M. A., Hubbard, E. M., Hertenstein, M. J. & Witherington, D. (2000) Travel broadens the mind. *Infancy*, *1*, 149–219.

Cancer, A., Minoliti, R., Crepaldi, M. & Antonietti, A. (2020) Identifying developmental motor difficulties: A review of tests to assess motor coordination in children. *Journal of Functional Morphology and Kinesiology*, *5*, 16.

Capone, N. C. & McGregor, K. K. (2004) Gesture development. *Journal of Speech Language and Hearing Research* 47, 173–186.

Carbone, V. J., Lewis, L., Sweeney-Kerwin, E. J., Dixon, J., Louden, R. & Quinn, S. (2006) A comparison of two approaches for teaching VB functions: Total communication vs. vocal-alone. *The Journal of Speech-Language Pathology and Applied Behavior Analysis*, *1*, 181–192.

Carey, S. (1978) The child as word learner. In M. Halle, J. Bresnan and G. A. Miller (Eds.), *Linguistic theory and psychological reality* (pp. 264–293) Cambridge, MA: MIT Press.

Carlier, M. & Roubertoux, P. L. (2014) Genetic and environmental influences on intellectual disability in childhood. In D. Finkel and C. A. Reynold (Eds.), *Behavior genetics of cognition across the lifespan* (pp. 69–101). New York: Springer.

Carlson, F. (1981) A format for selecting vocabulary for the nonspeaking child. *Language, Speech, and Hearing Services in Schools*, *12*, 240–245.

Carlson, S. M., Zelazo, P. D. & Faja, S. (2013) Executive function. In P. D. Zelazo (Ed.), *The Oxford handbook of developmental psychology: Volume 1. Body and mind* (pp. 706– 742). Oxford, UK: Oxford University Press.

Carnahan, K. D., Arner, M. & Hägglund, G. (2007) Association between gross motor function (GMFCS) and manual ability (MACS) in children with cerebral palsy. A population-based study of 359 children. *BMC Musculoskeletal Disorders*, *8*, 1–7.

Caron, J. G. & Light, J. (2016) Social media has opened a world of open communication: Experiences of adults with cerebral palsy who use augmentative and alternative communication and social media. *Augmentative and Alternative Communication*, *32* 25–40.

Caron, J. G. & Light, J. (2017) Social media experiences of adolescents and young adults with cerebral palsy who use augmentative and alternative communication. *International journal of Speech-Language Pathology*, *19*, 30–42.

Caron, J. G., Light, J. & McNaughton, D. (2023) Effects of adapted letter-sound correspondence instruction with older learners with complex communication needs and autism spectrum disorder. *Augmentative and Alternative Communication*, *39*, 45–59.

Carpenter, M. and Liebal, K. (2011) Joint attention, communication, and knowing together in infancy. In A. Seemann (Ed.), *Joint attention: New developments in psychology, philosophy of mind, and social neuroscience* (pp. 159–181). Cambridge, MA: MIT Press.

Carr, D. & Felce, J. (2007) The effects of PECS teaching to Phase III on the communicative interactions between children with autism and their teachers *Journal of Autism and Developmental Disorders*, 37, 724–737.

Carr, A. & O'Reilly, G. (2016a) Diagnosis, classification and epidemiology. In A. Carr et al. (Eds.), *The handbook of intellectual disability and clinical psychology practice* (pp. 3–44). Hove, UK: Routledge.

Carr, A. & O'Reilly, G. (2016b) Lifespan development and the family lifecycle. In A. Carr et al. (Eds.), *The handbook of intellectual disability and clinical psychology practice* (pp. 45–74). Hove, UK: Routledge.

Carr, E. G., Levin, L., McConnachie, G., Carlson, J. I., Kemp, D. C. & Smith, C. E. (1994) *Communication intervention for problem behavior: A user's guide for producing positive change*. Baltimore, MD: Paul H. Brookes.

Carr, E. G., Reeve, C. E. & Magito-McLaughlin, D. (1996) Contextual influences on problem behavior in people with developmental disabilities. In L. K. Koegel et al. (Eds.), *Positive behavioral support: Including people with difficult behavior in the community* (pp. 403–423). Baltimore. MD: Paul H. Brookes.

Carston, R. (2021) Polysemy: Pragmatics and sense conventions. *Mind and Language*, *36*, 108–133.

Carter, M. & Grunsell, J. (2001) The behavior chain interruption strategy: A review of research and discussion of future directions. *Journal of the Association for Persons with Severe Handicaps*, *26*, 37–49.

Caselli, N. K. & Pyers, J. E. (2017) The road to language learning is not entirely iconic: Iconicity, neighborhood density, and frequency facilitate acquisition of sign language. *Psychological Science*, *28*, 979–987

Caselli, N. K., Lieberman, A. M. & Pyers, J. E. (2020) The ASL-CDI 2.0: An updated, normed adaptation of the MacArthur bates communicative development inventory for American sign language. *Behavior Research Methods*, *52*, 2071–2084.

Casey, L. O. (1978) Development of communicative behavior in autistic children: A parent program using manual signs. *Journal of Autism and Childhood Schizophrenia*, *8*, 45–59.

Cass, H., Reilly, S., Owen, L., Wisbeach, A., Weekes, L. et al. (2003) Findings from a multidisciplinary clinical case series of females with Rett syndrome. *Developmental Medicine and Child Neurology*, *45*, 325–337.

Ceci, S. J. & Bruck, M. (1993) The suggestibility of the child witness: A historical review and synthesis. *Psychological Bulletin*, *113*, 403–439.

Chaika, M. (2023) Working as a therapist while suffering war in Ukraine. *Intervention Journal of Mental Health and Psychosocial Support in Conflict Affected Areas*, *21*, 170–175.

Chan, J. & Nankervis, K. (2014) Stolen voices: Facilitated communication is an abuse of human rights. *Evidence-Based Communication Assessment and Intervention*, *8*, 151–156.

Chandler, D. (2002) *The basics*. London, UK: Routledge.

Chang, E. F. & Anumanchipalli, G. K. (2020) Toward a speech neuroprosthesis. *JAMA*, *323*, 413–414.

Chang, Y. C., Shire, S. Y., Shih, W., Gelfand, C. & Kasari, C. (2016) Preschool deployment of evidence-based social communication intervention: JASPER in the classroom. *Journal of Autism and Developmental Disorders*, *46*, 2211–2223.

Chapman, R. S. & Miller, J. F. (1980) Analyzing language and communication in the child. In R. L. Schiefelbusch (Ed.), *Nonspeech language and communication* (pp. 159–196). Baltimore: University Park Press.

Charman, T., Drew, A., Baird, C. & Baird, G. (2003) Measuring early language development in preschool children with autism spectrum disorder using the MacArthur Communicative Development Inventory (Infant Form) *Journal of Child Language*, *30*(1), 213–236.

Che, E. S. & Brooks, P J. (2021) Maternal repetition and expansion of child utterances at the outset of combinatorial speech promote growth in MLU. In D. Dionne and L.-A. Vidal Covas (Eds.), *Proceedings of the 45th annual Boston University Conference on Language Development* (pp. 120–133). Somerville, MA: Cascadilla Press

Chelly, J., Khelfaoui, M., Francis, F., Chérif, B. & Bienvenu, T. (2006) Genetics and pathophysiology of mental retardation. *European Journal of Human Genetics*, *14*, 701–713.

Chen, C. C., Farmer, T. W., Hamm, J. V., Brooks, D. S., Lee, D. et al. (2020) Emotional and behavioral risk configurations, students with disabilities, and perceptions of the middle school ecology. *Journal of Emotional and Behavioral Disorders*, *28*, 180–192.

Chen, M., Hyppa-Martin, J., Bunnell, H. T., Lilley, J., Foo, C. et al. (2023) Voice banking to support individuals who use speech-generating devices: Development and evaluation of Singaporean-accented English synthetic voices and a Singapore Colloquial English recording inventory. *Augmentative and Alternative Communication*, *39*, 208–218.

Chiang, H.-M. & Kemp, K. (2019) Curriculums. In J. L. Matson (Ed.), *Handbook of intellectual disabilities: Integrating theory, research, and practice* (pp. 775–794). Cham, Swizerland: Springer.

Christie, J. F. & Johnson, E. P. (1987) Reconceptualizing constructive play: A review of the empirical literature. *Merrill-Palmer Quarterly*, *33*, 439–452.

Chu, J. & Schulz, L. E. (2020) Play, curiosity, and cognition. *Annual Review of Developmental Psychology*, *2*, 317–343.

Chung, Y. C. & Carter, E. W. (2013) Promoting peer interactions in inclusive classrooms for students who use speech-generating devices. *Research and Practice for Persons with Severe Disabilities*, *38*, 94–109.

Chung, Y. C., Carter, E. W. & Sisco, L. G. (2012) Social interactions of students with disabilities who use augmentative and alternative communication in inclusive classrooms. *American Journal on Intellectual and Developmental Disabilities*, *117*, 349–367.

Chung, Y. C. & Douglas, K. H. (2015) A peer interaction package for students with autism spectrum disorders who use speech-generating devices. *Journal of Developmental and Physical Disabilities*, *27*, 831–849.

Clark, C. R. (1981) Learning words using traditional orthography and the symbols of Rebus, Bliss and Carrier. *Journal of Speech and Hearing Disorders*, *46*, 191–196.

Clark, E. V. (1992) Conventionality and contrast: Pragmatic principles with lexical consequences. In A. Lehrer and E. F. Kittay (Eds.), *Frames, fields and contrasts* (pp. 171–188). Hove, UK: Lawrence Erlbaum.

Clark, E. V. (2018) Conversation and language acquisition: A pragmatic approach. *Language Learning and Development*, *14*, 170–185.

Clark, E. V. (2020) Perspective-taking and pretend-play: Precursors to figurative language use in young children. *Journal of Pragmatics*, *156*, 100–109.

Clarke, H., McConachie, H., Price, K. & Wood, P. (2001) Views of young people using augmentative and alternative communication systems. *International Journal of Language and Communication Disorders*, *36*, 107–115.

Clarke, M. & Kirton, A. (2003) Patterns of interaction between children with physical disabilities using augmentative and alternative communication and their peers. *Child Language Teaching and Therapy*, *19*, 135–151.

Clarke, M., Newton, C., Petrides, K., Griffiths, T., Lysley, A. & Price, K. (2012) An examination of relations between participation, communication and age in children with complex communication needs. *Augmentative and Alternative Communication*, *28*, 44–51.

Clarke, M. & Wilkinson, R. (2007) Interaction between children with Cerebral Palsy and their peers 1: Organising and understanding VOCA use. *Augmentative and Alternative Communication*, *23*, 336–348.

Clarke, M. & Wilkinson, R. (2009) The collaborative construction of non-serious episodes of interaction by non-speaking children with cerebral palsy and their peers. *Clinical Linguistics and Phonetics*, *23*, 583–597.

Clarke, M. T., Sargent, J., Cooper, R., Aberbach, G., McLaughlin, L. et al. (2022) Development and testing of the eye-pointing classification scale for children with cerebral palsy. *Disability and Rehabilitation*, *44*, 1451–1456.

Clarke, M. T., Soto, G. & Nelson, K. (2017) Language learning, recasts, and interaction involving AAC: Background and potential for intervention. *Augmentative and Alternative Communication*, *33*, 42–50.

Clarke, S., Remington, B. & Light, P. (1986) An evaluation of the relationship between receptive speech skills and expressive signing. *Journal of Applied Behavior Analysis*, *19*, 231–239.

Clasby, B., Mirfin-Veitch, B., Blackett, R., Kedge, S. & Whitehead, E. (2022) Responding to neurodiversity in the courtroom: A brief evaluation of environmental accommodations to increase procedural fairness. *Criminal Behaviour and Mental Health*, *32*, 197–211.

Clegg, J. M., Wen, N. J., DeBaylo, P. H., Alcott, A., Keltner, E. C. & Legare, C. H. (2021) Teaching through collaboration: Flexibility and diversity in caregiver–child interaction across cultures. *Child Development*, *92*, e56–e75.

Clemens, L. F. & Kegel, C. A. (2021) Unique contribution of shared book reading on adult-child language interaction. *Journal of Child Language*, *48*, 373–386.

Clibbens, J. (2001) Signing and lexical development in children with Down syndrome. *Down Syndrome Research and Practice*, *7*, 101–105.

Cognolato, M., Atzori, M. & Müller, H. (2018) Head-mounted eye gaze tracking devices: An overview of modern devices and recent advances. *Journal of Rehabilitation and Assistive Technologies Engineering*, *5*, 1–13.

Cole-Lade, G. M. & Bailey, L. E. (2020) Examining the role of paraeducators when supporting children with complex communication needs: A multiple case study. *Teacher Education and Special Education*, *43*, 144–161.

Collins, B. E. & Neul, J. L. (2022) Rett syndrome and MECP2 duplication syndrome: Disorders of mecp2 dosage. *Neuropsychiatric Disease and Treatment*, 2813–2835.

Collins, S. (1996) Referring expressions in conversations between aided and natural speakers. In S. von Tetzchner and M. H. Jensen (Eds.), *Augmentative and alternative communication: European perspectives* (pp. 89–100). London: Whurr/Wiley.

Collins, S. & Markovà, I. (1999) Interaction between impaired and unimpaired speakers: Intersubjectivity and the interplay of culturally shared and situation specific knowledge. *British Journal of Social Psychology*, *38*, 339–368.

Cologon, K. & Mevawalla, Z. (2018) Increasing inclusion in early childhood: Key Word Sign as a communication partner intervention. *International Journal of Inclusive Education*, *22*(8), 902–920.

Compañ-Rosique, P., Molina-Carmona, R., Gallego-Durán, F., Satorre-Cuerda, R., Villagrá-Arnedo, C. & Llorens-Largo, F. (2019) A guide for making video games accessible to users with cerebral palsy. *Universal Access in the Information Society*, *18*, 565–581.

Connelly, R. (2013) Interpreting test scores. *Institute of Education, Discussion Paper*, 1.

Contaldo, N., Satta, E., Zambon, Y., Paltrinieri, S. & Bertaccini, A. (2016) Development and evaluation of different complex media for phytoplasma isolation and growth. *Journal of Microbiological Methods*, *127*, 105–110.

Conty, L., George, N. & Hietanen, J. K. (2016) Watching eyes effects: When others meet the self. *Consciousness and Cognition*, *45*, 184–197.

Conway, N. (1986) My perceptions of communication aids. *Presented at The 2nd Biennial Conference on Augmentative and Alternative Communication*, Cardiff, 1986.

Cook, A. M., Polgar, J. M. & Encarnação, P. (2020) *Assistive technologies: Principles and practice*, 5th edition. St. Louis, MO: Elsevier.

Cook, J. L., Baruni, R. R. & Lanovaz, M. J. (2023) Noncompliance. In *Handbook of applied behavior analysis for children with autism: Clinical guide to assessment and treatment* (pp. 313–338). Cham, Switzerland: Springer International Publishing.

Cooper, L., Balandin, S. & Trembath, D. (2009) The loneliness experiences of young adults with cerebral palsy who use alternative and augmentative communication. *Augmentative and Alternative Communication*, *25*, 154–164.

Cooper, B., Soto, G. & Clarke, M. T. (2021) Prompting for repair as a language teaching strategy for augmentative and alternative communication. *Augmentative and Alternative Communication*, *37*, 251–260.

Cordier, R., Munro, N., Wilkes-Gillan, S., Speyer, R. & Pearce, W. M. (2014) Reliability and validity of the Pragmatics Observational Measure (POM): A new observational measure of pragmatic language for children. *Research in Developmental Disabilities*, *35*, 1588–1598.

Costigan, F. A. & Light, J. (2010) Effect of seated position on upper-extremity access to augmentative communication for children with cerebral palsy: Preliminary investigation. *American Journal of Occupational Therapy*, *64*, 596–604.

Cott, J. (2008) Critical review: The effect of sign language on speech production in children with developmental disabilities. School of Communication Sciences and Disorders, University of Western Ontario,

Coulmas, F. (2022) *Language, writing, and mobility: A sociological perspective*. Oxford, UK: Oxford University Press.

Creaghe, N., Quinn, S. & Kidd, E. (2021) Symbolic play provides a fertile context for language development. *Infancy, 26*, 980–1010.

Creel, D. J. (2019) Visually evoked potentials. *Handbook of Clinical Neurology, 160*, 501–522.

Creer, S., Cunningham, S., Green, P. & Yamagishi, J. (2013) Building personalised synthetic voices for individuals with severe speech impairment. *Computer Speech and Language, 27*, 1178–1193.

Creer, S., Enderby, P., Judge, S. & John, A. (2016) Prevalence of people who could benefit from augmentative and alternative communication (AAC) in the UK: Determining the need. *International Journal of Language and Communication Disorders, 51*, 639–653.

Cress, C. J., Grabast, J. & Burgers Jerke, K. (2013) Contingent interactions between parents and young children with severe expressive communication impairments. *Communication Disorders Quarterly, 34*, 81–96.

Crossley, R. (1994) *Facilitated communication training*. New York: Teachers College Press.

Crossley, R. & Remington-Gurney, J. (1992) Getting the words out: Facilitated communication training. *Topics in Language Disorders, 12*, 29–45.

Cumley, G. D. & Stuart, S. (2005) The aging process and the affect on successful AAC use. *Perspectives on Augmentative and Alternative Communication, 14*, 22–25.

Cummings, L. (2008) *Clinical linguistics*. Edinburgh: Edinburg University Press.

Cummings, L. (2014) *Pragmatic disorders*. Dordrecht, The Netherlands: Springer.

Cunningham, B. J., Thomas-Stonell, N. & Rosenbaum, P. (2021) Assessing communicative participation in preschool children with the focus on the outcomes of communication under six: A scoping review. *Developmental Medicine and Child Neurology, 63*, 47–53.

Da Fonte, A. Boesch, M. C., DeLuca, E. R., Papp, S. K., Mohler, A. E. et al. (2022) Current preparation status in AAC: Perspectives of special education teachers in the United States. *Augmentative and Alternative Communication, 38*, 29–40.

Dada, S. (2019) A comparison of special education teachers' attitudes toward various augmentative and alternative communication systems. In S. Halder and V. Argyropoulos (Eds.), *Inclusion, equity and access for individuals with disabilities* (pp. 153–178). London: Palgrave Macmillan.

Dada, S. & Alant, E. (2009) The effect of aided language stimulation on vocabulary acquisition of children with little or no functional speech. *American Journal of Speech-Language Pathology, 18*, 50–64.

Dada, S., Flores, C., Bastable, K. & Schlosser, R. W. (2021) The effects of augmentative and alternative communication interventions on the receptive language skills of children with developmental disabilities: A scoping review, *International Journal of Speech-Language Pathology, 23*, 247–257

Dahlgren Sandberg, A. (1996) Literacy abilities in nonvocal children with cerebral palsy. Thesis, Gothenburg University.

Dahlgren Sandberg, A. (2006) Reading and spelling abilities in children with severe speech impairments and cerebral palsy at 6, 9, and 12 years of age in relation to cognitive development: A longitudinal study. *Developmental Medicine and Child Neurology, 48*, 629–634.

Dahlgren Sandberg, A. & Hjelmquist, E. (1996) Sound and silence: Interaction in aided language use. In S. von Tetzchner and M. H. Jensen (Eds.), *Augmentative and alternative communication: European perspectives* (pp. 137–152). London: Whurr/Wiley.

Dahlgren Sandberg, A., Smith, M. & Larsson, M. (2010) An analysis of reading and spelling abilities of children using AAC: Understanding a continuum of competence. *Augmentative and Alternative Communication, 26*, 191–202.

Dai, Y. G., Burke, J. D., Naigles, L., Eigsti, I. M. and Fein, D. A. (2018) Language abilities in monolingual- and bilingual-exposed children with autism or other developmental disorders. *Research in Autism Spectrum Disorders, 55*, 38–49.

Dalhoff, F. (1986) *Forstår han hvad man sier?* Fredrikshavn, DK: Dafolo Forlag.

Darbishire, K. (2018) *Speechless*. London: Stickhouse Publishing.

Dark, L., Brownlie, E. & Bloomberg, K. (2019) Selecting, developing and supporting key word sign vocabularies for children with developmental disabilities. In N. Grove and K. Launonen (Eds.), *Manual sign acquisition in children with developmental disabilities* (pp. 215–245). New York: Nova

Davies, C., Ebbels, S., Nicoll, H., Syrett, K., White, S. & Zuniga-Montanez, C. (2023) Supporting adjective learning by children with developmental language disorder: Enhancing metalinguistic approaches. *International Journal of Language and Communication Disorders*, *58*, 629–650.

Davis, T., Parab, P., May, D. M. & Ruetsch, C. (2023) Characteristics, conditions, and healthcare service utilization patterns of individuals diagnosed with Rett Syndrome: An analysis of administrative claims data. *Future Rare Diseases*, *3*, FRD41.

de Almeida Barbosa, R. T., Bulle de Oliveira, A. S., Ferreira de Lima Antão, J. Y., Crocetta, T. B., Guarnieri, R. et al. (2018) Augmentative and alternative communication in children with Down's syndrome: Aa systematic review. *BMC Pediatrics*, *18*, 160.

De Bortoli, T., Arthur-Kelly, M., Foreman, P., Balandin, S. & Mathisen, B. (2011) Complex contextual influences on the communicative interactions of students with multiple and severe disabilities. *International Journal of Speech-Language Pathology*, *13*, 422–435.

De Houwer, A. (2021) *Bilingual development in childhood*. Cambridge: Cambridge University Press.

de Marchena, A. B., Eigsti, I. M. & Yerys, B. E. (2015) Brief report: Generalization weaknesses in verbally fluent children and adolescents with autism spectrum disorder. *Journal of Autism and Developmental Disorders*, *45*, 3370–3376.

De Simone, C. & Ruggeri, A. (2022) Searching for information, from infancy to adolescence. In I. Cogliati-Dezza et al. (Eds.), *The drive for knowledge: The science of human information-seeking* (pp. 77–97). Cambridge: Cambridge University Press.

De Villiers, T. (2007) Why Peirce matters: The symbol in Deacon's Symbolic Species. *Language Sciences*, *29*, 88–108.

Deacon, J. (1974) *Tongue tied*. London: Spastics Society.

Deacon, T. W. (2011) The symbol concept. In M. Tallerman and K. Gibson (Eds.), *The Oxford handbook of language evolution* (pp. 393–405). Oxford: Oxford University Press.

Deacon, T. W. (2017) Human variability and the origins and evolution of language. In M. Tibayrenc and F. J. Ayala (Eds.), *On human nature: Biology, psychology, ethics, politics, and religion* (pp. 557–564). Cambridge, MA: Elsevier.

Deich, R. F. & Hodges, P. M. (1977) *Language without speech*. London: Souvenir Press.

Delarosa, E., Horner, S., Eisenberg, C., Ball, L., Renzoni, A. M. & Ryan, S. E. (2012) Family impact of assistive technology scale: Development of a measurement scale for parents of children with complex communication needs. *Augmentative and Alternative Communication*, *28*(3), 171–180.

Deliberato, D., Jennische, M., Oxley, J., Nunes, L., Walter, C. et al. (2018) Vocabulary comprehension and strategies in name construction among children using aided communication. *Augmentative and Alternative Communication*, *34*, 16–29.

Dell, A. & Newton, D. (2014) Assistive technology to provide access to the curriculum and increase independence. In L. Florian (Ed.), *The SAGE handbook of special education*, 2nd edition (pp. 703–717). London: SAGE

DeLoache, J. S. (2004) Becoming symbol-minded. *Trends in Cognitive Sciences*, *8*, 66–70.

DeLoache, J. S., Miller, K. F. and Pierroutsakos, S. L. (1998) Reasoning and problem solving. In W. Damon et al. (Eds.), *Handbook of child psychology*, Volume 2 (pp. 801–850). New York: Wiley.

DeMauro, S. B., Wei, J. L. & Lin, R. J. (2016) Perspectives on neonatal and infant tracheostomy. *Seminars in Fetal and Neonatal Medicine*, 21, 285–291.

Denman, D., Speyer, R., Munro, N., Pearce, W. M., Chen, Y. W. & Cordier, R. (2017) Psychometric properties of language assessments for children aged 4–12 years: A systematic review. *Frontiers in Psychology*, *8*, 1515.

Deramore Denver, B., Froude, E., Rosenbaum, P. & Imms, C. (2022) Measure of early vision use: Development of a new assessment tool for children with cerebral palsy. *Disability and Rehabilitation*, *44*, 4055–4065.

DeRosa, N. M., Sullivan, W. E. & Roane, H. S. (2019) Evidence-based treatment. In J. L. Matson (Ed.), *Handbook of intellectual disabilities* (pp. 485–500). Los Angeles, CA: Springer.

Deruyter, F., McNaughton, D., Caves, K., Bryen, D. N. & Williams, M. B. (2007) Enhancing AAC connections with the world. *Augmentative and Alternative Communication, 23*, 258–270.

Deshais, M. A., MacDonald, J. & Quiroz, L. (2022) Generalized imitation and applied behavior analysis. In J. L. Matson and P. Sturmey (Eds.), *Handbook of autism and pervasive developmental disorder: Assessment, diagnosis, and treatment* (pp. 821–844). Cham, Switzerland: Springer.

Dessemontet, R. S., Martinet, C., de Chambrier, A. F., Martini-Willemin, B. M. & Audrin, C. (2019) A meta-analysis on the effectiveness of phonics instruction for teaching decoding skills to students with intellectual disability. *Educational Research Review, 26*, 52–70.

Detheridge, T. & Detheridge, M. (2002) *Literacy through symbols: Improving access for children and adults*, 2nd edition. Abingdon, UK: Routledge

Detheridge, T., Whittle, H. & Detheridge, C. (2002) *The Widgit Rebus Symbol Collection*. London: Widgit.

Dewart, H. & Summers, S. (1995) *Pragmatics profile of everyday communication in children*. Windsor, UK: NFER-NELSON

Dew, A., Balandin, S. & Llewellyn, G. (2008) The psychosocial impact on siblings of people with lifelong physical disability: A review of the literature. *Journal of Developmental and Physical Disabilities, 20*, 485–507

Dhondt, A., Van Keer, I., van der Putten, A. & Maes, B. (2023) Analysis of early expressive communicative behaviour of young children with significant cognitive and motor developmental delays. *British Journal of Learning Disabilities, 51*, 24–37.

DiCarlo, C. F., Stricklin, S., Banajee, M. & Reid, D. H. (2001) Effects of manual signing on communicative verbalizations by toddlers with and without disabilities in inclusive classrooms. *Journal of the Association for Persons with Severe Handicaps, 26*, 120–126.

Didden, R., Sturmey, P., Sigafoos, J., Lang, R., O'Reilly, M. & Lancioni, G. (2012) Nature, prevalence and characteristics of challenging behavior. In J. Matson (Ed.), *Functional assessment for challenging behaviors* (pp. 25–44). New York: Springer.

Dind, A. J., Starr, J. S. & Arora, S. (2021) iPad-based apps to facilitate communication in critically ill patients with impaired ability to communicate: A preclinical analysis. *Indian Journal of Critical Care Medicine, 25*, 1232–1240.

Dixon, L. S. (1981) A functional analysis of photo-object matching skills of severely retarded adolescents. *Journal of Applied Behavior Analysis, 14*, 465–478.

Doak, L. (2021) Rethinking family (dis) engagement with augmentative and alternative communication. *Journal of Research in Special Educational Needs, 21*, 198–210.

Doherty, J. E. (1985) The effect of sign characteristics on sign acquisition and retention: An integrative review of the literature. *Augmentative and Alternative Communication, 1*, 108–121.

Dollaghan, C. (1985) Child meets word: 'Fast mapping' in preschool children. *Journal of Speech, Language, and Hearing Research, 28*, 449–454.

Dombrowski, S. C., McGill, R., Farmer, R. L., Kranzler, J. H. & Canivez, G. L. (2022) Beyond the rhetoric of evidence-based assessment: A framework for critical thinking in clinical practice. *School Psychology Review, 51*, 771–784.

Donato, C., Spencer, E. & Arthur-Kelly, M. (2018) A critical synthesis of barriers and facilitators to the use of AAC by children with autism spectrum disorder and their communication partners. *Augmentative and Alternative Communication, 34*, 242–253.

Doneski-Nicol, J. & Bartz, J. M. (2018) Early literacy and AAC for learners with complex communication needs. In *Autism spectrum disorders: Breakthroughs in research and practice* (pp. 392–427). Hershey, PA: IGI Global.

Doost, H. T. N., Moradi, A. R., Taghavi, M. R., Yule, W. & Dalgleish, T. (1999) The development of a corpus of emotional words produced by children and adolescents. *Personality and Individual Differences, 27*, 433–451.

Douglas, S. N., Meadan, H., Biggs, E. E., Bagawan, A. & Terol, A. K. (2023) Building family capacity: Supporting multiple family members to implement aided language modeling. *Journal of Autism and Developmental Disorders*, *53*, 2587–2599.
Dowdall, N., Melendez-Torres, G. J., Murray, L., Gardner, F., Hartford, L. & Cooper, P. J. (2020) Shared picture book reading interventions for child language development: A systematic review and meta-analysis. *Child Development*, *91*, e383–e399.
Draffan, E. A., Ding, C., Wald, M. & Newman, R. (2020, July) Multilingual symbolic support for low levels of literacy on the web. In *Companion publication of the 12th ACM Conference on Web Science* (pp. 60–63). New York: The Association for Computing Machinery
Drager, K. D. R. (2009) Aided modeling interventions for children with autism spectrum disorders who require AAC. *Perspectives on Augmentative and Alternative Communication*, *18*, 114–120.
Drager, K. D. R., Light, J. C., Carlson, R., D'Silva, K., Larsson, B. et al. (2004) Learning of dynamic display AAC technologies by typically developing 3-year-olds: Effect of different layouts and menu approaches. *Journal of Speech Language Hearing Research*, *47*, 1133–1148.
Drager, K. D. R., Reichle, J. & Pinkoski, C. (2010) Synthesized speech output and children: A scoping review. *American Journal of Speech-Language Pathology*, *19*, 259–273.
Dromi, E. (1993) The mysteries of early lexical development: Underlying cognitive and linguistic pocesses in meaning acquisition. In E. Dromi (Ed.), *Language and cognition: A developmental perspective* (pp. 32–60). Norwood, NJ: Ablex.
Drysdale, H., van der Meer, L. & Kagohara, D. (2015) Children with autism spectrum disorder from bilingual families: A systematic review. *Review Journal of Autism and Developmental Disorders*, *2*, 26–38.
Dugan, L., Campbell, P. H. & Wilcox, M. J. (2006) Decision-making about assistive technology use with infants and toddlers. *Topics in Early Childhood Special Education*, *26*, 25–32.
Dunn, D. M. (2019) *Peabody picture vocabulary test*, 5th edition. Bloomington, MN: NCS Pearson.
Dunn, J. (1999) Siblings, friends, and the development of social understanding. In W. A. Collins and B. Laursen (Eds.), *Relationships as developmental contexts* (pp. 263–279). Mahwah, NJ: Erlbaum.
Dunn, L. M., Dunn, D. M., Sewell, J., Styles, B., Brzyska, B. et al. (2009) *The British picture vocabulary scale*, 3rd edition. London: GL Assessment.
Dunst, C. J., Gorman, E. & Hamby, D. W. (2012) Child-directed motionese with infants and toddlers with and without hearing impairments. *Center for Early Literacy Learning*, *5*(8).
Dunst, C. J., Hamby, D., Trivette, C. M., Raab, M. & Bruder, M. B. (2000) Everyday family and community life and children's naturally occurring learning opportunities. *Journal of Early Intervention*, *23*, 151–164.
Dunst, C. J., Meter, D. & Hamby, D. W. (2011) Influences of sign and oral language interventions on the speech and oral language production of young children with disabilities. *Center for Early Literacy Learning*, *4*, 1–20.
Dunst, C. J., Trivette, C. M. & Deal, A. G. (1994) *Enabling and empowering families*. Cambridge, MA: Brookline books.
Durand, V. M. & Moskowitz, L. J. (2019) The link between problem behavior and communication impairment in persons with developmental disabilities. *Current Developmental Disorders Reports*, *6*, 138–144.
Dylman, A. S., Blomqvist, E. & Champoux-Larsson, M. F. (2020) Reading habits and emotional vocabulary in adolescents. *Educational Psychology*, *40*, 681–694.
Ebbels, S. (2014) Effectiveness of intervention for grammar in school-aged children with primary language impairments: A review of the evidence. *Child Language Teaching and Therapy*, *30*, 7–40.
Eckstein, M. K., Guerra-Carrillo, B., Singley, A. T. M. & Bunge, S. A. (2017) Beyond eye gaze: What else can eyetracking reveal about cognition and cognitive development? *Developmental Cognitive Neuroscience*, *25*, 69–91.
Edman, P. (1991) Relief Bliss: A low tech technique. *Communicating Together*, *9*, 21–22.
Edmister, E. & Wegner, J. (2015) Repeated reading, turn taking, and augmentative and alternative communication (AAC). *International Journal of Disability, Development and Education*, *62*, 319–338.

Edwards, S., Letts, C. & Sinka, I. (2011) *The New Reynell Developmental Language Scales*. London: GL-Assessment.
Egbert, J., Wizner, S., Keller, D., Biber, D., McEnery, T. & Baker, P. (2021) Identifying and describing functional discourse units in the BNC Spoken 2014. *Text and Talk*, *41*, 715–737.
Ego, A., Lidzba, K., Brovedani, P., Belmonti, V., Gonzalez-Monge, S. et al. (2015) Visual–perceptual impairment in children with cerebral palsy: A systematic review. *Developmental Medicine and Child Neurology*, *57*, 46–51.
Ehrhart, F., Sangani, N. B. & Curfs, L. M. (2018) Current developments in the genetics of Rett and Rett-like syndrome. *Current Opinion in Psychiatry*, *31*, 103–108.
Eisenberg, N., Spinrad, T. L. & Eggum, N. D. (2010) Emotion-related self-regulation and its relation to children's maladjustment. *Annual Review of Clinical Psychology*, *6*, 495–525.
Elbro, C., Rasmussen, I. & Spelling, B. (1996) Teaching reading to disabled readers with language disorders: A controlled evaluation of synthetic speech feedback. *Scandinavian Journal of Psychology*, *37*, 140–155.
Elder, C. H. & Haugh, M. (2018) The interactional achievement of speaker meaning: Toward a formal account of conversational inference. *Intercultural Pragmatics*, *15*, 593–625.
Eliasson, A. C., Krumlinde-Sundholm, L., Rösblad, B., Beckung, E., Arner, M. et al. (2006) The Manual Ability Classification System (MACS) for children with cerebral palsy: Scale development and evidence of validity and reliability. *Developmental Medicine and Child Neurology*, *48*, 549–554.
Eliasson, A. C., Ullenhag, A., Wahlström, U. & Krumlinde-Sundholm, L. (2017) Mini-MACS: Development of the manual ability classification system for children younger than 4 years of age with signs of cerebral palsy. *Developmental Medicine and Child Neurology*, *59*, 72–78.
Elkonin, D. B. (1971) Development of speech. In A. V. Zaporozhets and D. B. Elkonin (Eds.), *The psychology of preschool children* (pp. 111–182). Cambridge, MA: MIT Press
Ellawadi, A. B. & Weismer, S. E. (2014) Assessing gestures in young children with autism spectrum disorder. *Journal of Speech, Language, and Hearing Research*, *57*, 524–531.
Ellis, N. C. (2008) The dynamics of second language emergence: Cycles of language use, language change, and language acquisition. *The Modern Language Journal*, *92*, 232–249.
Ellis, N. C. & Ogden, D. C. (2017) Thinking about multiword constructions: Usage-based approaches to acquisition and processing. *Topics in Cognitive Science*, *9*, 604–620.
Ellis, V. (2007) The narrative matrix and wordless narrations: A research note. *Augmentative and Alternative Communication*, *23*, 113–125.
Elman, J. L., Bates, E. A., Johnson, M. H., Karmiloff-Smith, A., Parisi, D. & Plunkett, K. (1996) *Rethinking innateness. A connectionist perspective on development*. London: MIT Press.
Elmquist, M., Simacek, J., Dimian, A. F. & Reichle, J. (2019) Impact of aided AAC interventions on speech comprehension of children with neurodevelopmental disabilities: A critically appraised topic. *Evidence-Based Communication Assessment and Intervention*, *13*, 67–84.
Elsahar, Y., Hu, S., Bouazza-Marouf, K., Kerr, D. & Mansor, A. (2019) Augmentative and alternative communication (AAC) advances: A review of configurations for individuals with a speech disability. *Sensors*, *19*, 1911.
Elsner, B. (2007) Infants' imitation of goal-directed actions: The role of movements and action effects. *Acta Psychologica*, *124*, 44–59.
Elvrum, A. K. G., Beckung, E., Sæther, R., Lydersen, S., Vik, T. & Himmelmann, K. (2017) Bimanual capacity of children with cerebral palsy: Intra-and interrater reliability of a revised edition of the bimanual fine motor function classification. *Physical and Occupational Therapy in Pediatrics*, *37*, 239–251.
Emberti Gialloreti, L., Mazzone, L., Benvenuto, A., Fasano, A., Garcia Alcon, A. et al. (2019) Risk and protective environmental factors associated with autism spectrum disorder: Evidence-based principles and recommendations. *Journal of Clinical Medicine*, *8*, 217.
Emerson, E. & Einfeld, S. (2011) *Challenging behaviour*, 3rd edition. Cambridge: Cambridge University Press.

Emerson, E. & Robertson, J. (2011) The estimated prevalence of visual impairment among people with learning disabilities in the UK. Learning Disabilities Observatory report for RNIB and SeeAbility.

Emmorey, K. & Lane, H, (Eds.) (2000) *The signs of language revisited*. London: Lawrence Erlbaum.

Enns, C., Haug, T., Herman, R., Hoffmeister, R., Mann, W. & McQuarrie, L. (2016) Exploring signed language assessment tools in Europe and North America. In M. Marschark et al. (Eds.), *Diversity in deaf education* (pp. 172–218). New York: Oxford University Press.

Ervin-Tripp, S. M. (1996) Context in language. In D. I. Slobin et al. (Eds.), *Social interaction, social context, and language: Essays in honor of Susan Ervin-Tripp* (pp. 21–36). Mahwah, NJ: Lawrence Erlbaum.

Ervin-Tripp, S. M. & Küntay, A. (1997) The occasioning and structure of conversational stories. In T. Givin (Ed.), *Conversation: Cognitive, communicative and social perspectives* (pp. 133–166). Amsterdam: John Benjamins.

Espín-Tello, S. M., Gardeazabal, X. & Abascal, J. (2023) The use of robots for augmentative manipulation during play activities among children with motor impairment: A scoping review. *Disability and Rehabilitation*, *45*, 896–910.

Fäldt, A., Fabian, H., Thunberg, G. & Lucas, S. (2020) "All of a sudden we noticed a difference at home too": Parents' perception of a parent-focused early communication and AAC intervention for toddlers. *Augmentative and Alternative Communication*, *36*, 143–154.

Fäldt, A., Klint, F., Warner, G. & Sarkadi, A. (2022) Experiences of children with disabilities during the COVID-19 pandemic in Sweden: A qualitative interview study. *BMJ Paediatrics Open*, *6*, e001398.

Fallon, K., Light, J. & Achenbach, A. (2003) The semantic organization patterns of young children: Implications for augmentative and alternative communication. *Augmentative and Alternative Communication*, *19*, 74–85.

Farah, M. J. (2004) *Visual agnosia*. Cambridge, MA: MIT Press.

Fauconnier, G. & Turner, M. (2002) *The way we think: Conceptual blending and the mind's hidden complexities*. New York: Basic Books.

Feallock, B. (1958) Communication boards for the non-vocal individual. *American Journal of Occupational Therapy*, *12*, 60–63.

Felder, F. (2018) The value of inclusion. *Journal of Philosophy of Education*, *52*, 54–70.

Feleihi, S., Abedanzadeh, R. & Saemi, E. (2023) 'Let them play' the effect of active play on motor proficiency and social maturity of children. *Early Child Development and Care*, *193*, 201–210.

Ferguson, C. A. (1978) Learning to pronounce: The earliest stages of phonological development in the child. In F. D. Minifie and L. L. Lloyd (Eds.), *Communicative and cognitive abilities – Early behavioral assessment* (pp. 273–297). Baltimore, MD: University Park Press.

Ferm, U. Ahlsén, E. & Björck-Åkesson, E. (2005) Conversational topics between a child with complex communication needs and her caregiver at mealtime. *Augmentative and Alternative Communication*, *21*, 19–40.

Ferm, U., Amberntson, B. & Thunberg, G. (2001) Development and evaluation of a Minspeak™ application using Blissymbols: Experiences from two case studies. *Augmentative and Alternative Communication*, *17*, 233–244.

Fernández-Batanero, J M., Montenegro-Rueda, M., Fernández-Cerero, J. & García-Martínez, I. (2022) Assistive technology for the inclusion of students with disabilities: A systematic review. *Educational Technology Research and Development*, *70*, 1911–1930.

Ferreira, J., Rönnberg, J., Gustafson, S. & Wengelin, Å. (2007) Reading, why not? Literacy skills in children with motor and speech impairments. *Communication Disorders Quarterly*, *28*, 236–251.

Finke, E. H., Davis, J M., Benedict, M., Goga, L., Kelly, J. et al. (2017) Effects of a least-to-most prompting procedure on multisymbol message production in children with autism spectrum disorder who use augmentative and alternative communication. *American Journal of Speech-Language Pathology*, *26*, 81–98.

Finke, E. H., McNaughton, D. B. & Drager, K. D. R. (2009) "All children can and should have the opportunity to learn": General education teachers' perspectives on including children with autism spectrum disorder who require ACC. *Augmentative and Alternative Communication*, *25*, 110–122.

Fischer, U. (1994) Learning words from context and dictionaries: An experimantal comparison. *Applied Psycholinguistics*, *15*, 551–574.
Fischer, S. D. (2000) More than just handwaving: The mutual contributions of sign language and linguistics. In K. Emmorey and H. Lane (Eds.), *The signs of language revisited* (pp. 173–188). Mahwah, NJ: Lawrence Erlbaum.
Fischer, S. D. (2017) Crosslinguistic variation in sign language syntax. *Annual Review of Linguistics*, *3*, 125–147.
Fisher, K. W. & Shogren, K. A. (2012) Integrating augmentative and alternative communication and peer support for students with disabilities: A social-ecological perspective. *Journal of Special Education Technology*, *27*, 23–39.
Fisher, W. W., Greer, B. D., Querim, A. C. & DeRosa, N. (2014) Decreasing excessive functional communication responses while treating destructive behavior using response restriction. *Research in Developmental Disabilities*, *35*, 2614–2623..
Fiske, S. I., Haddeland, A. L., Skipar, I., Bootsma, J. N., Geytenbeek, J. J. & Stadskleiv, K. (2020) Assessing language comprehension in motor impaired children needing AAC: Validity and reliability of the Norwegian version of the receptive language test C-BiLLT. *Augmentative and Alternative Communication*, *36*, 95–106.
Flack, Z. M., Field, A. P. & Horst, J. S. (2018) The effects of shared storybook reading on word learning: A meta-analysis. *Developmental Psychology*, *54*, 1334–1346.
Fletcher, K. L. & Reese, E. (2005) Picture book reading with young children: A conceptual framework. *Developmental Review*, *25*, 64–103.
Flink, A. R., Åsberg Johnels, J., Broberg, M. & Thunberg, G. (2022) Examining perceptions of a communication course for parents of children with profound intellectual and multiple disabilities. *International Journal of Developmental Disabilities*, *68*, 156–167.
Fluss, J. & Lidzba, K. (2020) Cognitive and academic profiles in children with cerebral palsy: A narrative review. *Annals of Physical and Rehabilitation Medicine*, *63*, 447–456.
Fodstad, J. C., Rojahn, J. & Matson, J. L. (2012) The emergence of challenging behaviors in at-risk toddlers with and without autism spectrum disorder: A cross-sectional study. *Journal of Developmental and Physical Disabilities*, *24*, 217–234.
Foreman, P. & Crews, G. (1998) Using augmentative communication with infants and young children with Down syndrome. *Down Syndrome Research and Practice*, *5*, 16–25.
Foster, E. K. (2004) Research on gossip: Taxonomy, methods, and future directions. *Review of General Psychology*, *8*, 78–99.
Foster-Cohen, S., van Bysterveldt, A. & Papp, V. (2021) The roles of language use and vocabulary size in the emergence of word-combining in children with complex neurodevelopmental disabilities. *Journal of Child Language*, *48*, 202–214.
Foxx, R. M., Kyle, M. S., Faw, G. D. & Bittle, R. G. (1988) Cues-pause-point training and simultaneous communication to teach the use of signed labeling repertoires. *American Journal of Mental Retardation*, *93*, 305–311.
Franklin, K., Mirenda, P. & Phillips, G. (1996) Comparisons of five symbol assessment protocols with nondisabled preschoolers and learners with severe intellectual disabilities. *Augmentative and Alternative Communication*, *12*, 63–77.
Frick, B. J., Bean, A. F. & Sonntag, A. M. (2023) Multicultural considerations in augmentative and alternative communication. *Assistive Technology*, *35*, 435–450.
Fried-Oken, M. & More, L. (1992) Initial vocabulary for nonspeaking preschool children based on developmental and environmental language samples. *Augmentative and Alternative Communication*, *8*, 1–16.
Fristoe, M. & Lloyd, L. L. (1980) Planning an initial expressive sign lexicon for persons with severe communication impairment. *Journal of Speech and Hearing Disorders*, *45*, 170–180.
Fritz, H. L. & Sewell-Roberts, C. (2020) Family stress associated with cerebral palsy. In F. Miller et al. (Eds.), *Cerebral palsy* (pp. 515–545). Cham, Switzerland: Springer.
Frizelle, P., Allenby, R., Hassett, E., Holland, O., Ryan, E. et al. (2023) Embedding key word sign prompts in a shared book reading activity: The impact on communication between children with

Down syndrome and their parents. *International Journal of Language and Communication Disorders, 58*, 1029–1045.

Fu, C., Armstrong, D., Marsh, E., Lieberman, D., Motil, K. et al. (2020) Consensus guidelines on managing Rett syndrome across the lifespan. *BMJ Paediatrics Open, 4*, e000717.

Fuller, D. R. (1997) Initial study into the effects of translucency and complexity on the learning of Blissymbols by children and adults with normal cognitive abilities. *Augmentative and Alternative Communication, 13*, 30–39.

Fuller, D. R. & Lloyd, L. L. (1987) A study of physical and semantic characteristics of a graphic symbol system as predictors of perceived complexity. *Augmentative and Alternative Communication, 3*, 26–35.

Fulwiler, R. L. & Fouts, R. S. (1976) Acquisition of American sign language by a noncommunicating autistic child. *Journal of Autism and Childhood Schizophrenia, 6*, 43–51.

Funayama, M. & Nakajima, A. (2023) Development of self-made gestures as an adaptive strategy for communication in an individual with childhood apraxia of speech. *Cognitive and Behavioral Neurology, 36*, 249–258.

Gangkofer, M. & von Tetzchner, S. (1996) Cleaning-ladies and broken buses. A case study on the development of Blissymbol use. In S. von Tetzchner and M. H. Jensen (Eds.), *Augmentative and alternative communication: European perspectives* (pp. 292–308). London: Whurr/Wiley.

Ganz, J. B. & Hong, E. R. (2014) Naturalistic aided AAC instruction. In J. B. Ganz (Ed.), *Aided augmentative communication for individuals with autism spectrum disorders* (pp. 55–75). New York: Springer.

Ganz, J. B., Simpson, R. & Corbin-Newsome, J. (2008) The impact of the Picture Exchange Communication System on requesting and speech development in preschoolers with autism spectrum disorders and similar characteristics. *Research in Autism Spectrum Disorders, 2*, 157–169.

Garber, N. & Veydt, N. (1990) Rett syndrome: A longitudinal developmental case report. *Journal of Communication Disorders, 23*, 61–75.

García, J. C., Díez, E., Wojcik, D. Z. & Santamaría, M. (2020) Communication support needs in adults with intellectual disabilities and its relation to quality of life. *International Journal of Environmental Research and Public Health, 17*, 7370.

Garcia, L. F., de Oliveira, L. & de Matos, D. (2014) Word and sentence prediction: Using the best of the two worlds to assist AAC users. *Technology and Disability, 26*, 79–91.

Garcia, L. F., de Oliveira, L. C. & de Matos, D. M. (2016) Evaluating pictogram prediction in a location-aware augmentative and alternative communication system. *Assistive Technology, 28*, 83–92.

Garnett, R., Davidson, B. & Eadie, P. (2022) Parent perceptions of a group telepractice communication intervention for autism. *Autism and Developmental Language Impairments*, 10.1177/23969415211070127

Garrett, S. (1986) A case study in tactile Blissymbols. *Communicating Together, 4*, 16.

Garvey, C. (1977) The contingent query: A dependant act in conversation. In M. Lewis and L. A. Rosenblum (Eds.), *Interaction, conversation and the development of language* (pp. 63–93). New York: Wiley.

Gatt, M. (2022) Improving augmentative and alternative communication use between mothers, siblings, and children with communication disabilities. Dissertation, University of Kent, UK.

Georgila, K. (2023) Considerations for child speech synthesis for dialogue systems. *Presented at Language-Based AI Agent Interaction with Children Workshop (AIAIC) – Co-located with IWSDS*, Los Angeles, CA, February 21, 2023.

Geschwind, N. (1972) Language and the brain. *Scientific American, 233*, 76–83.

Gevarter, C., Groll, M., Stone, E. & Medina Najar, A. (2021) A parent-implemented embedded AAC intervention for teaching navigational requests and other communicative functions to children with autism spectrum disorder. *Augmentative and Alternative Communication, 37*, 180–193.

Gevarter, C., Najar, A. M. & Siciliano, M. (2023a) Teaching children with autism to create multi-symbol messages on augmentative alternative communication applications during play. *Advances in Neurodevelopmental Disorders, 7*, 314–328.

Gevarter, C., Prieto, V., Binger, C. & Hartley, M. (2023b) Dynamic assessment of AAC action verb symbols for children with ASD. *Advances in Neurodevelopmental Disorders*, *7*, 329–343.

Geytenbeek, J., Harlaar, L., Stam, M., Ket, H., Becher, J. G. et al. (2010) Utility of language comprehension tests for unintelligible or non-speaking children with cerebral palsy: A systematic review. *Developmental Medicine and Child Neurology*, *52*, e267–e277.

Geytenbeek, J. J., Mokkink, L. B., Knol, D. L., Vermeulen, R. J. & Oostrom, K. J. (2014) Reliability and validity of the C-BiLLT: A new instrument to assess comprehension of spoken language in young children with cerebral palsy and complex communication needs. *Augmentative and Alternative Communication*, *30*, 252–266.

Giangreco, M. F. (2010) Utilization of teacher assistants in inclusive schools: Is it the kind of help that helping is all about?. *European Journal of Special Needs Education*, *25*, 341–345.

Gibbon, F. & Grunwell, P. (1990) Specific developmental language learning disabilities. In P. Grunwell (Ed.), *Developmental speech disorders* (pp. 135–161). Edinburgh: Churchill Livingstone.

Gibson, R. C., Dunlop, M. D., Bouamrane, M. M. & Nayar, R. (2020) Designing clinical AAC tablet applications with adults who have mild intellectual disabilities. *Proceedings of the 2020 CHI Conference on Human Factors in Computing Systems*, Honolulu, HI, 25–30 April 2020 (pp. 1–13).

Gillon, G. T. & Moriarty, B. C. (2007) Childhood apraxia of speech: Children at risk for persistent reading and spelling disorder. *Seminars in Speech and Language*, 28, 48–57.

Gilmartin, E., Saam, C., Vogel, C., Campbell, N. & Wade, V. (2018, July) Just talking-modelling casual conversation. *Proceedings of the 19th Annual SIGdial Meeting on Discourse and Dialogue* (pp. 51–59).

Gioia, G. A., Isquith, P. K., Guy, S. C. & Kenworthy, L. (2000) *BRIEF: Behavior rating inventory of executive function*. Lutz, FL: Psychological Assessment Resources.

Glacken, M., Healy, D., Gilrane, U., Gowan, S. H. M., Dolan, S. et al. (2019) Key word signing: Parents' experiences of an unaided form of augmentative and alternative communication (Lámh). *Journal of Intellectual Disabilities*, *23*, 327–343.

Glenn, S., Cunningham, C., Poole, H., Reeves, D. & Weindling, M. (2009) Maternal parenting stress and its correlates in families with a young child with cerebral palsy. *Child: Care, Health and Development*, *35*, 71–78.

Gohsman, M. K. (2021) Identification of opportunity barriers and supports for individuals using augmentative and alternative communication (AAC) and stakeholders. Dissertation, Old Dominion University, USA.

Goldbart, J. & Marshall, J. (2004) "Pushes and pulls" on the parents of children who use AAC. *Augmentative and Alternative Communication*, *20*, 194–208.

Goldberg, M. A., Hochberg, L. R., Carpenter, D. & Walz, J. M. (2021) Development of a manually operated communication system (MOCS) for patients in intensive care units. *Augmentative and Alternative Communication*, *37*, 261–273.

Goldenberg, E. R., Repetti, R. L. & Sandhofer, C. M. (2022) Contextual variation in language input to children: A naturalistic approach. *Developmental Psychology*, *58*, 1051–1065.

Goldin-Meadow, S. & Alibali, M. W. (2013) Gesture's role in speaking, learning, and creating language. *Annual Review of Psychology*, *64*, 257–283.

Goldin-Meadow, S. (2020) Using gesture to identify and address early concerns about language and pragmatics. *Pediatrics*, *146* (Supplement 3), S278–S283.

Goldman, S., Wang, C., Salgado, M., Greene, P., Kim, M. & Rapin, I. (2009) Motor stereotypies in children with autism and other developmental disorders. *Developmental Medicine and Child Neurology*, *51*, 30–38.

Gona, J. K., Newton, C. R., Hartley, S. & Bunning, K. (2014) A home-based intervention using augmentative and alternative communication (AAC) techniques in rural Kenya: What are the caregivers' experiences?. *Child: Care, Health and Development*, *40*, 29–41.

Gonzalez-Barrero, A. M. & Nadig, A. (2019) Vocabulary and grammatical skills of bilingual children with autism spectrum disorders at school age. *Journal of Autism and Developmental Disorders*, *49*, 3888–3897.

Goods, K. S., Ishijima, E., Chang, Y. C. & Kasari, C. (2013) Preschool based JASPER intervention in minimally verbal children with autism: Pilot RCT. *Journal of Autism and Developmental Disorders*, *43*, 1050–1056.

Goosens', C. A. (1983) The relative iconicity and learnability of verb referents represented in Blissymbolics, Rebus symbols, and manual signs: An investigation with moderately retarded individuals. Dissertation, Purdue University.

Goosens', C. A. (1989) Aided communication intervention before assessment: A case study of a child with cerebral palsy. *Augmentative and Alternative Communication*, *3*, 14–26.

Gorgan, E. M. & Kodak, T. (2019) Comparison of interventions to treat prompt dependence for children with developmental disabilities. *Journal of Applied Behavior Analysis*, *52*, 1049–1063.

Grace, E., Raghavendra, P., McMillan, J. M. & Gunson, J. S. (2019) Exploring participation experiences of youth who use AAC in social media settings: Impact of an e-mentoring intervention. *Augmentative and Alternative Communication*, *35*, 132–141.

Grace, E., Shipman, J., Raghavendra, P. & McMillan, J. M. (2023) "You got an instant conversation": Goal progress and perceptions following an e-mentoring social media intervention for young people who use augmentative and alternative communication. *Journal of Communication Disorders*, *103*, 106328.

Graham, N., Truman, J. & Holgate, H. (2014) An exploratory study: Expanding the concept of play for children with severe cerebral palsy. *British Journal of Occupational Therapy*, *77*, 358–365.

Granlund, M., Björck-Åkesson, E., Wilder, J. & Ylvén, R. (2008) AAC interventions for children in a family environment: Implementing evidence in practice. *Augmentative and Alternative Communication*, *24*, 207–219.

Granlund, M., Terneby, J. & Olsson, C. (1992) Creating communicative opporptunities through a combined in-service training and supervision package. *European Journal of Special Needs Education*, *7*, 229–252.

Gray, C. (2022) Social stories. In N. Grove (Ed.), *Storytelling, special needs and disabilities practical approaches for children and adults*, 2nd edition (pp. 152–158). London: Routledge.

Greenspan, S. & Woods, G. W. (2014) Intellectual disability as a disorder of reasoning and judgement: The gradual move away from intelligence quotient-ceilings. *Current Opinion in Psychiatry*, *27*, 110–116.

Griffith, P. L. & Robinson, J. H. (1980) Influence of iconicity and phonological similarity on sign learning by mentally retarded children. *American journal of Mental Deficiency*, *85*, 291–298.

Griffith, P. L. & Robinson, J. H. (1981) A comparative and normative study of the iconicity of signs rated by three groups. *American Annals of the Deaf*, *126*, 440–449.

Griffiths, P. (1986) Early vocabulary. In P. Fletcher and M. Garman (Eds.), *Language acquisition*, 2nd edition (pp. 279–306). Cambridge: Cambridge University Press.

Griffiths, T. (2020) Access to eye-gaze control technology for children with cerebral palsy. Dissertation, University College London.

Grolig, L., Cohrdes, C., Tiffin-Richards, S. P. & Schroeder, S. (2020) Narrative dialogic reading with wordless picture books: A cluster-randomized intervention study. *Early Childhood Research Quarterly*, *51*, 191–203.

Grosjean, F. (2022) *The mysteries of bilingualism: Unresolved issues*. Hoboken, NJ: John Wiley.

Grosjean, F. (2024) *On bilinguals and bilingualism*. Cambridge, UK: Cambridge University Press.

Grosse, G., Streubel, B., Gunzenhauser, C. & Saalbach, H. (2021) Let's talk about emotions: The development of children's emotion vocabulary from 4 to 11 years of age. *Affective Science*, *2*, 150–162.

Grove, N. (1990) Developing intelligible signs with learning-disabled students: A review of the literature and an assessment procedure. *International Journal of Language and Communication Disorders*, *25*, 265–293.

Grove, N. (1998) *Literature for all*. London: David Fulton.

Grove, N. (2019a) Multi-sign utterances by children with intellectual disabilities: Patterns of use, assessment and intervention. In N. Grove and K. Launonen (Eds.), *Manual sign acquisition in children with developmental disabilities* (pp. 271–292). New York: Nova.

Grove, N. (2019b) Pragmatic skills of key word signers. In N. Grove and K. Launonen (Eds.), *Manual sign acquisition in children with developmental disabilities* (pp. 293–314). New York: Nova.
Grove, N. (2022) *Storytelling, special needs and disabilities*, 2nd edition. Abingdon, UK: Routledge.
Grove, N., Bunning, K., Porter, J. & Olsson, C. (1999) See what I mean: Interpreting the meaning of communication by people with severe and profound intellectual disabilities. *Journal of Applied Research in Intellectual Disabilities*, *12*, 190–203.
Grove, N., Dark, L., Brownlie, E. & Bloomberg, K. (2019) Assessment and intervention for problems in sign production. In N. Grove and K. Launonen (Eds.), *Manual sign acquisition in children with developmental disabilities* (pp. 247–270). New York: Nova.
Grove, N. & Dockrell, J. (2000) Multi-sign combinations by children with intellectual impairments: An analysing of language skills. *Journal of Speech, Language and Hearing Research*, *43*, 309–323.
Grove, N., Dockrell, J. & Woll, B. (1996) The two-word stage in manual signs: Language development in signers with intellectual impairment. In S. von Tetzchner and M. H. Jensen (Eds.), *Augmentative and alternative communication: European perspectives* (pp. 101–118). London: Whurr/Wiley.
Grove, N. & Launonen, K. (Eds.) (2019) *Manual sign acquisition in children with developmental disabilities*. New York: Nova.
Grove, N. & Tucker, S. (2003) Narratives in manual sign by children with intellectual impairments. In S. von Tetzchner and N. Grove (Eds.), *Augmentative and alternative communication: Developmental issues* (pp. 229–255). London, UK: Whurr/Wiley.
Grove, N. & Walker, M. (1990) The Makaton Vocabulary: Using manual signs and graphic symbols to develop interpersonal communication. *Augmentative and Alternative Communication*, *6*, 15–28.
Grove, N. & Woll, B. (2017) Assessing language skills in adult key word signers with intellectual disabilities: Insights from sign linguistics. *Research in Developmental Disabilities*, *62*, 174–183.
Grunér, S., Östberg, P. & Hedenius, M. (2018) The compensatory effect of text-to-speech technology on reading comprehension and reading rate in Swedish schoolchildren with reading disability: The moderating effect of inattention and hyperactivity symptoms differs by grade groups. *Journal of Special Education Technology*, *33*, 98–110.
Gudmundsson, E. & Gretarsson, S. J. (2009) Comparison of mothers' and fathers' ratings of their children's verbal and motor development. *Nordic Psychology*, *61*, 14–25.
Guendouzi, J. (2020) Social functions of gossip in adolescent girl's talk. *Discourse Studies*, *22*, 678–696.
Guillaume, P. (1971) *Imitation in children*. Chicago: Chicago University Press.
Gulsrud, A. C., Hellemann, G. S., Freeman, S. F. & Kasari, C. (2014) Two to ten years: Developmental trajectories of joint attention in children with ASD who received targeted social communication interventions. *Autism Research*, *7*, 207–215.
Gunaratne, C., Senevirathna, C., Jayalath, C., Baral, N., Rand, W. & Garibay, I. (2019) A multi-action cascade model of conversation. *Presented at The 5th International Conference on Computational Social Science*. Amsterdam, The Netherlands, July 17–20, 2019.
Guralnick, M. J. (2005) Inclusion as a core principle in the early intervention system. In M. J. Guralnick (Ed.), *The developmental systems approach to early intervention* (pp. 59–69). Baltimore, MD: Paul H. Brookes.
Guralnick, M. J. (2011) Why early intervention works: A systems perspective. *Infants and Young Children*, *24*, 6–28.
Guralnick, M. J. (2017) Early intervention for children with intellectual disabilities: An update. *Journal of Applied Research in Intellectual Disabilities*, *30*, 211–229.
Gustason, G., Pfetzing, D. & Zawolkow, E. (1980) *Signing excact Engisih*, 3rd edition. Los Alamitos, CA: Modern Signs Press.
Hagberg, B. & Hagberg, G. (1997) Rett syndrome: Epidemiology and geographical variability. *European Child and Adolescent Psychiatry*, *6*(Supplement 1), 5–7.
Hagberg, B. & Skjeldal, O. H. (1994) Rett variant: A suggested model for inclusion criteria. *Pediatric Neurology*, *11*, 5–11.

Hagemoen, M. K., Opsal, K., Hellberg, K., Krabbe, S., Borøy, A. & von Tetzchner, S. (2004) *'Jeg har noe å si!' Strategisk språkbruk hos barn som utvikler alternativ og supplerende kommunikasjon.* Oslo: Oslo National Hospital.

Hagood, M. C. (2002) Critical literacy for whom? *Reading Research and Instruction, 41*, 247–266.

Haley, S. M., Coster, W. J., Dumas, H. M., Fragala-Pinkham, M. A. & Moed, R. (2012) *The pediatric evaluation of disability inventory – Computer adaptive test.* Boston, MA: CRE Care.

Hall, I., Strydom, A., Richards, M., Hardy, R., Bernal, J. & Wadsworth, M. (2005) Social outcomes in adulthood of children with intellectual impairment: Evidence from a birth cohort. *Journal of Intellectual Disability Research, 49*, 171–182.

Hall, D. G. (2009) Proper names in early word learning: Rethinking a theoretical account of lexical development. *Mind and Language, 24*, 404–432.

Hall, J. A., Horgan, T. G. & Murphy, N. A. (2019) Nonverbal communication. *Annual Review of Psychology, 70*, 271–294.

Halle, J. W., Alpert, C. L. & Anderson, S. R. (1984) Natural environment language assessment and intervention with severely impaired preschoolers. *Topics in Early Childhood Special Education, 4*, 36–56.

Hamid, A. & Kristensson, P. O. (2024) 40 years of eye typing: Challenges, gaps, and emergent strategies. In J. Nicholls (Ed.), *Proceedings of the ACM on Human-Computer Interaction, 8 (ETRA)*, Article 222, 1–19.

Hamrick, L. R. (2023) Novel approaches for characterizing social communication and language development of young children with neurogenetic syndromes. *International Review of Research in Developmental Disabilities, 64*, 51–95.

Hancock, T. B., Ledbetter-Cho, K., Howell, A. & Lang, R. (2016) Enhanced milieu teaching. In R. Lang, T. B. Hancock and N. N. Singh (Eds.), *Early intervention for young children with autism spectrum disorder* (pp. 177–218). Cham, Switzerland: Springer.

Hanley, E., Martin, A. M., Dalton, C. & Lehane, E. (2023) Communication partners experiences of communicating with adults with severe/profound intellectual disability through augmentative and alternative communication: A mixed methods systematic review. *Journal of Intellectual Disabilities, 27*, 1107–1134.

Hansen, S. G., Carnett, A. & Tullis, C. A. (2018) Defining early social communication skills: A systematic review and analysis. *Advances in Neurodevelopmental Disorders, 2*, 116–128.

Happé, F. & Frith, U. (Eds.) (2010) *Autism and talent.* Oxford, UK: Oxford University Press.

Happé, F. & Frith, U. (2020) Annual research review: Looking back to look forward – Changes in the concept of autism and implications for future research. *Journal of Child Psychology and Psychiatry, 61*, 218–232.

Happé, F., Ronald, A. & Plomin, R. (2006) Time to give up on a single explanation for autism. *Nature Neuroscience, 9*, 1218–1220.

Haque, S., Vaphiades, M. S. & Lueck, C. J. (2018) The visual agnosias and related disorders. *Journal of Neuro-Ophthalmology, 38*, 379–392.

Harrington, N., Buchanan, C., Kent-Walsh, J. & Binger, C. (2023) Supporting communication and language development in preschool children using AAC. In M. M. Smith (Ed.), *Clinical cases in augmentative and alternative communication* (pp. 42–61). Abingdon, UK: Routledge.

Harris, D. (1982) Communicative interaction processes involving nonvocal physically handicapped children. *Topics in Language Disorders, 2*, 21–37.

Harris, J., Golinkoff, R. & Hirsh-Pasek, K. (2011) Lessons from the crib for the classroom: How children really learn vocabulary. In S. Neuman and D. Dickinson (Eds.), *Handbook of early literacy research*, Volume 3 (pp. 49–65). New York: The Guilford Press.

Harris, M. (1992) *Language experience and early language development: From input to uptake.* London, UK: Erlbaum.

Harris, P. L., Kavanaugh, R. D. & Dowson, L. (1997) The depiction of imaginary transformations: Early comprehension of a symbolic function. *Cognitive Development, 12*, 1–19.

Harrison, P. & Oakland, T. (2015) *Adaptive behavior assessment system*, 3rd edition. Torrance: Western Psychological Services.

Harrison, J. E., Weber, S., Jakob, R. & Chute, C. G. (2021) ICD-11: An international classification of diseases for the twenty-first century. *BMC Medical Informatics and Decision Making*, *21*, 206.

Hart, B. M. & Risley, T. R. (1982) *How to use incidental teaching for elaborating language*. Lawrence, KS: H and H Enterprises.

Hart, S. M., Hill, M. F. & Gaffney, J. S. (2021) Timetabling a transition with dignity: Perspectives of young adults with significant support needs. *Journal of Intellectual and Developmental Disability*, *46*, 227–238.

Hart Barnett, J. (2018) Three evidence-based strategies that support social skills and play among young children with autism spectrum disorders. *Early Childhood Education Journal*, *46*, 665–672.

Hartmann, A. C. (2022) *I talk in different ways*. 4 Little Monkeys.

Hassan, L. (2023) Accessibility of games and game-based applications: A systematic literature review and mapping of future directions. *New Media and Society*, 10.1177/14614448231204020

Hasson, N. & Joffe, V. (2007) The case for dynamic assessment in speech and language therapy. *Child Language Teaching and Therapy*, *23*, 9–25.

Haughton, C., Aiken, M., & Cheevers, C. (2015) Cyber Babies: The impact of emerging technology on the developing infant. *Psychology Research*, *5*, 504–518.

Haukeland, Y. B., Czajkowski, N. O., Fjermestad, K. W., Silverman, W. K., Mossige, S. & Vatne, T. M. (2020) Evaluation of "SIBS", an intervention for siblings and parents of children with chronic disorders. *Journal of Child and Family Studies*, *29*, 2201–2217.

Haupt, E. (2001) The iconicity of selected picture communication symbols for rural Zulu-speaking children. Master thesis, University of Pretoria.

Hawkes, R. (1998) A visual communication-based intervention approach for challenging behaviour. *Presented at The 8th Biennial Conference on Augmentative and Alternative Communication*, Dublin, August 1998.

Hayes, C. (2014) Positive and negative aspects of inclusion services. *Journal of the American Academy of Special Education Professionals*, *5*, 60–65.

Haywood, H. C. & Lidz, C. S. (2006) *Dynamic assessment in practice: Clinical and educational applications*. Cambridge, UK: Cambridge University Press.

Hedvall, P.-O. & Rydeman, B. (2010) An activity systemic approach to augmentative and alternative communication. *Augmentative and Alternative Communication*, *26*, 230–241.

Heikura, U., Linna, S. L., Olsen, P., Hartikainen. A. L., Taanila, A. & Jarvelin, M. R. (2005) Etiological survey on intellectual disability in the northern Finland birth cohort 1986. *American Journal on Mental Retardation*, *110*, 171–180.

Heilmann, J., Weismer, S. E., Evans, J. & Hollar, C. (2005) Utility of the MacArthur-Bates Communicative Development Inventory in identifying language abilities of late-talking and typically developing toddlers. *American Journal of Speech-Language Pathology*, *14*, 40–51.

Heimann, M., Laberg, K. E. & Nordoen, B. (2006) Imitative interaction increases social interest and elicited imitation in non-verbal children with autism. *Infant and Child Development 15*, 297–309.

Heller, K. W., Allgood, M. H., Davis, B., Arnold, S. E., Castelle, M. D. & Taber, T. A. (1996) Promoting ontask-related communication at vocational sites. *Augmentative and Alternative Communication*, *12*, 169–178.

Helverschou, S. B. & Martinsen, H. (2011) Anxiety in people diagnosed with autism and intellectual disability: Recognition and phenomenology. *Research in Autism Spectrum Disorders*, *5*, 377–387.

Heim, M. J. M. & Baker-Mills, A. E. (1996) Early development of symbolic communication and linguistic complexity through augmentative and alternative communication. In S. von Tetzchner and M. H. Jensen (Eds.), *Augmentative and alternative communication: European perspectives* (pp. 232–248). London: Whurr/Wiley.

Hemmingsson, H., Ahlsten, G., Wandin, H., Rytterström, P. & Borgestig, M. (2018) Eye-gaze control technology as early intervention for a non-verbal young child with high spinal cord injury: A case report. *Technologies*, *6*, 12.

Hemmingsson, H. & Borgestig, M. (2020) Usability of eye-gaze controlled computers in Sweden: A total population survey. *International Journal of Environmental Research and Public Health*, *17*, 1639.
Hemsley, B. & Balandin, S. (2014) A metasynthesis of patient-provider communication in hospital for patients with severe communication disabilities: Informing new translational research. *Augmentative and Alternative Communication*, *30*, 329–343.
Hemsley, B., Balandin, S., Palmer, S. & Dann, S. (2017) A call for innovative social media research in the field of augmentative and alternative communication. *Augmentative and Alternative Communication*, *33*, 14–22.
Hemsley, B., Bryant, L., Schlosser, R. W., Shane, H. C., Lang, R. et al. (2018) Systematic review of facilitated communication 2014–2018 finds no new evidence that messages delivered using facilitated communication are authored by the person with disability. *Autism and Developmental Language Impairments*, *3*, 1–8.
Hemsley, B., Sigafoos, J., Balandin, S., Forbes, R., Taylor, C., Green, V. A. & Parmenter, T. (2001) Nursing the patient with severe communication impairment. *Journal of Advanced Nursing*, *35*, 827–835.
Hendriks, P. (2014) *Asymmetries between language production and comprehension*. Dordrecht, Netherlands: Springer.
Henriksen, M. W., Breck, H., von Tetzchner, S., Paus, B., Skjeldal, O. H. & Brodtkorb, E. (2018) Epilepsy in classic Rett syndrome: Course and characteristics in adult age. *Epilepsy Research*, *145*, 134–139.
Henriksen, M. W., Breck, H., von Tetzchner, S., Paus, B. & Skjeldal, O. H. (2020) Medical issues in adults with Rett syndrome–a national survey. *Developmental Neurorehabilitation*, *23*, 106–112.
Herer, G. R. (2012) Intellectual disabilities and hearing loss. *Communication Disorders Quarterly*, *33*, 252–260.
Herman, R., Grove, N. Holmes, S., Morgan, G., Sutherland, H. & Woll, B. (2004) *Assessing British sign language: Production test (narrative skills)*. London: City University Publication.
Herr-Israel, E. & McCune, L. (2011) Successive single-word utterances and use of conversational input: A pre-syntactic route to multiword utterances. *Journal of Child Language*, *38*, 166–180.
Hervás, R., Bautista, S., Méndez, G., Galván, P. & Gervás, P. (2020) Predictive composition of pictogram messages for users with autism. *Journal of Ambient Intelligence and Humanized Computing*, *11*, 5649–5664.
Hesselberg, F. & von Tetzchner, S. (2016) *Pedagogisk-psykologisk arbeid*. Oslo: Gyldendal Akademisk.
Hetzroni, O. E. (2013) Use of technology for literacy acquisition among children with communication difficulties. In A. Shamir & O. Korat (Eds.),*Technology as a support for literacy achievements for children at risk* (pp. 221–234). Dordrecht: Springer.
Hidecker, M. J. C., Paneth, N., Rosenbaum, P. L., Kent, R. D., Lillie, J. et al. (2011) Developing and validating the communication function classification system for individuals with cerebral palsy. *Developmental Medicine and Child Neurology*, *53*, 704–710.
Hidecker, M. J. C., Slaughter, J., Abeysekara, P., Ho, N. T., Dodge, N. et al. (2018) Early predictors and correlates of communication function in children with cerebral palsy. *Journal of Child Neurology*, *33*, 275–285.
Higginbotham, D. J. (2010) Humanizing vox artificialis: The role of speech synthesis in augmentative and alternative communication. In J. Mullennix and S. Stern (Eds.), *Computer synthesized speech technologies: Tools for aiding impairment* (pp. 50–70). Hershey, PA: IGI Global.
Higgins, J. & Mills, J. (1986) Communication training in real environments. In S. W. Blackstone and Bruskin, D. M. (Eds.), *Augmentative communication: An introduction* (pp. 345–352). Rockville: American Speech and Hearing Association.
Hilvert, E., Lorang, E., Maltman, N. & Sterling, A. (2023) Assessing the quantity and quality of language used by mothers and fathers of children with Down syndrome during shared book reading. *Journal of Child Language*, *50*, 778–790.
Hine, J. F. & Wolery, M. (2006) Using point-of-view video modeling to teach play to preschoolers with autism. *Topics in Early Childhood Special Education*, *26*, 83–93.

Hine, N. & Arnott, J. L. (2002) Assistive social interaction for non-speaking people living in the community. In *Proceedings of the ACM SIGCAPH conference on Assistive technologies* (pp. 162–169). New York: ACM Press.

Hitoglou, M., Ververi, A., Antoniadis, A. & Zafeiriou, D. I. (2010) Childhood autism and auditory system abnormalities. *Pediatric Neurology*, *42*, 309–314.

Hjelmquist, E. & Dahlgren Sandberg, A. (1996) Sounds and silence: Interaction in aided language use. In S. von Tetzchner and M. H. Jensen (Eds.), *Augmentative and alternative communication: European perspectives* (pp. 137–152). London: Whurr/Wiley.

Hjelmquist, E., Dahlgren Sandberg, A. & Hedelin, L. (1994) Linguistics, AAC, and metalinguistics in communicatively handicapped adolescents. *Augmentative and Alternative Communication*, *10*, 169–183.

Hodges, L. E., Özçalışkan, Ş. & Williamson, R. (2018) Type of iconicity influences children's comprehension of gesture. *Journal of Experimental Child Psychology*, *166*, 327–339.

Hodges, P. M. & Schwethelm, B. (1984) A comparison of the effectiveness of graphic symbol and manual sign training with profoundly retarded children. *Applied Psycholinguistics*, *5*, 223–253.

Hofmann, V. & Müller, C. M. (2021) Peer influence on aggression at school: How vulnerable are higher risk adolescents? *Journal of Emotional and Behavioral Disorders*, *29*, 83–92.

Hollo, A., Wehby, J. H. & Oliver, R. M. (2014) Unidentified language deficits in children with emotional and behavioral disorders: A meta-analysis. *Exceptional Children*, *80*, 169–186.

Holyfield, C. & Caron, J. (2019) Augmentative and alternative communication technology innovations to build skills and compensate for limitations in adolescent language. *Topics in Language Disorders*, *39*, 350–369.

Holyfield, C., Drager, K. D., Kremkow, J. M. & Light, J. (2017) Systematic review of AAC intervention research for adolescents and adults with autism spectrum disorder. *Augmentative and Alternative Communication*, *33*, 201–212.

Holzrichter, A. S. & Meier, R. P. (2000) Child-directed signing in American Sign Language. In C. Chamberlain et al. (Eds.), *Language acquisition by eye* (pp. 25–40). Mahwah, NJ: Erlbaum.

Honaker, J. D. & Miller, R. T. (2024) Wordless but not silent: Unlocking the power of wordless picture books. *TESOL Journal*, *15*, e721.

Hoppenbrouwers, G., Stewart, H. & Kernot, J. (2014) Assistive technology assessment tools for assessing switch use of children: A systematic review and descriptive analysis. *Technology and Disability*, *26*, 171–185.

Hörmeyer, I. & Renner, G. (2013) Confirming and denying in co-construction processes: A case study of an adult with cerebral palsy and two familiar partners. *Augmentative and Alternative Communication*, *29*, 259–271.

Horn, E. M. & Jones, H. A. (1996) Comparison of two selection techniques used in augmentative and alternative communication. *Augmentative and Alternative Communication*, *12*, 23–31.

Horton, E. L., Renganathan, R., Toth, B. N., Cohen, A. J., Bajcsy, A. V. et al. (2017) A review of principles in design and usability testing of tactile technology for individuals with visual impairments. *Assistive technology*, *29*, 28–36.

Horvath, S. & Arunachalam, S. (2019) Optimal contexts for verb learning. *Perspectives of the ASHA Special Interest Groups*, *4*, 1239–1249.

Hourcade, J., Everhart Pilotte, T., West, E. & Parette, P. (2004) A history of augmentative and alternative communication for individuals with severe and profound disabilities. *Focus on Autism and Other Developmental Disabilities*, *19*, 235–244.

Howe, N. & Recchia, H. (2014) Sibling relationships as a context for learning and development. *Early Education and Development*, *25*, 155–159.

Howery, K. (2018a) Out of time: The experience of speech-generating device users. *Communication Disorders Quarterly*, *40*, 40–49.

Howery, K. (2018b) When my voice is not my voice: Speaking through a speech generating device. *Phenomenology and Practice*, *12*, 4–17.

Howlin, P. A., Gordon, R. K., Pasco, G., Wade, A. & Charman, T. (2007) The effectiveness of picture exchange communication system (PECS) training for teachers of children with autism: A pragmatic, group randomised controlled trial. *Journal of Child Psychology and Psychiatry*, *48*, 473–481.

Hsieh, Y. H., Granlund, M., Odom, S. L., Hwang, A. W. & Hemmingsson, H. (2022) Increasing participation in computer activities using eye-gaze assistive technology for children with complex needs. *Disability and Rehabilitation: Assistive Technology*, *19*, 492–505.

Hsieh, H., Liu, C. & Chen, P. (2020) Lego robots in puppet play for children with cerebral palsy. In M. Antona and C. Stephanidis (Eds.), *Universal access in human-computer interaction: Design approaches and supporting technologies* (pp. 465–476). Thousand Oaks, CA: Springer.

Hu, J., Torr, J., Wei, Y. & Jiang, C. (2019) Mealtime talk as a language learning context: Australian Chinese parents' language use in interactions with their preschool-aged children at the dinner table. *Early Child Development and Care*, *191*, 415–430,

Hudry, K., Leadbitter, K., Temple, K., Slonims, V., McConachie, H. et al. (2010) Preschoolers with autism show greater impairment in receptive compared with expressive language abilities. *International Journal of Language and Communication Disorders*, *45*, 681–690.

Hudson, J. A. & Shapiro, L. R. (1991) From knowing to telling: The development of children's scripts, stories, and personal narratives. In A. McCabe and C. Peterson (Eds.), *Developing narrative structure* (pp. 89–136). London, UK: Lawrence Erlbaum.

Hughes, D. M., Vento-Wilson, M. & Boyd, L. E. (2022) Direct speech-language intervention effects on augmentative and alternative communication system use in adults with developmental disabilities in a naturalistic environment. *American Journal of Speech-Language Pathology*, *31*, 1621–1636.

Hughes, J. R. (2009) Update on autism: A review of 1300 reports published in 2008. *Epilepsy and Behavior*, *16*, 569–589.

Humphreys, G. W. & Riddoch, M. J. (1987) *To see but not to see. A case study of visual agnosia*. London: Lawrence Erlbaum.

Hunnicutt, S. (1984) Bliss symbol-to-speech conversion: "Blisstalk". *Speech Transmission Laboratory Quarterly Progress and Status Report*, *25*, 58–77.

Hunsley, J. & Mash, E. J. (2007) Evidence-based assessment. *Annual Review of Clinical Psychology*, *3*, 29–51.

Hunt, E., Nang, C., Meldrum, S. & Armstrong, E. (2022) Can dynamic assessment identify language disorder in multilingual children? Clinical applications from a systematic review. *Language, Speech, and Hearing Services in Schools*, *53*, 598–625.

Hunt, P., Soto, G., Maier, J., Müller, E. & Goetz, L. (2002) Collaborative teaming to support students with augmentative and alternative communication needs in general education classrooms. *Augmentative and Alternative Communication*, *18*, 20–35.

Hustyi, K. M., Ryan, A. H. & Hall, S. S. (2023) A scoping review of behavioral interventions for promoting social gaze in individuals with autism spectrum disorder and other developmental disabilities. *Research in Autism Spectrum Disorders*, *100*, 102074.

Hutchinson, M., McPhedran, T., Miller, C., Wilson, T., Adams, K. & Pollock, K. (2019) Sibling Perspectives on an AAC camp experience. *Poster presented at The Annual Convention of the American Speech-Language-Hearing Association (ASHA)*, Orlando, FL, November 2019.

Hynan, A., Goldbart, J. & Murray, J. (2015) A grounded theory of Internet and social media use by young people who use augmentative and alternative communication (AAC). *Disability and Rehabilitation*, *37*, 1559–1575.

Hynan, A., Murray, J. & Goldbart, J. (2014) 'Happy and excited': Perceptions of using digital technology and social media by young people who use augmentative and alternative communication. *Child Language Teaching and Therapy*, *30*, 175–186.

Iacono, T., Bould, E., Beadle-Brown, J. & Bigby, C. (2019) An exploration of communication within active support for adults with high and low support needs. *Journal of Applied Research in Intellectual Disabilities*, *32*, 61–70.

Iacono, T. A. & Duncom, J. E. (1995) Comparison of sign alone and in combination with an electronic communication device in early language intervention: Case study. *Augmentative and Alternative Communication*, *11*, 249–259.

Iacono, T., Goldbart, J., Douglas, S. N. & Garcia-Melgar, A. (2022) A scoping review and appraisal of AAC research in inclusive school settings. *Journal of Developmental and Physical Disabilities*, *34*, 963–985.

Iacono, T., Lyon, K., Johnson, H. & West, D. (2013) Experiences of adults with complex communication needs receiving and using low tech AAC: An Australian context. *Disability and Rehabilitation: Assistive Technology*, *8*, 392–401.

Iacono, T., Lyon, K. & West, D. (2011) Non-electronic communication aids for people with complex communication needs. *International Journal of Speech-Language Pathology*, *13*, 399–410.

Iacono, T. A. & Parsons, C. L. (1986) A comparison of techniques for teaching signs to intellectually disabled individuals using an alternating treatment design. *Australian Journal of Human Communication Disorders*, *14*, 23–34.

Im-Bolter, N. & Cohen, N. J. (2007) Language impairment and psychiatric comorbidities. *Pediatric Clinics of North America*, *54*, 525–542.

Imms, C., Granlund, M., Wilson, P. H., Steenbergen, B., Rosenbaum, P. L. & Gordon, A. M. (2017) Participation, both a means and an end: A conceptual analysis of processes and outcomes in childhood disability. *Developmental Medicine and Child Neurology*, *59*, 16–25.

Isaacson, M. D. & Lloyd, L. L. (2015) The potential for developing a tactile communication system based on Blissymbolics. *Developmental Neurorehabilitation*, *18*, 47–58.

Itard, J. M. (1801) *Memoire sur les premier developpments de Victor de L'Aveyron*. Paris: Goujon

Iuzzini-Seigel, J., Moorer, L. & Tamplain, P. (2022) An investigation of developmental coordination disorder characteristics in children with childhood apraxia of speech. *Language, Speech, and Hearing Services in Schools*, *53*, 1006–1021.

Ivy, J. W. & Schreck, K. A. (2016) The efficacy of ABA for individuals with autism across the lifespan. *Current Developmental Disorders Reports*, *3*, 57–66.

Jackson, L., Ryndak, D. & Wehmeyer, M. (2010) The dynamic relationship between context, curriculum, and student learning: A case for inclusive education as a research-based practice. *Research and Practice in Severe Disabilities*, *34*, 175–195.

Jacoby, S. & Ochs, E. (1995) Co-construction: An introduction. *Research on Language and Social Interaction*, *28*, 171–183.

Jagoe, C. & Smith, M. M. (2016) Relevance in the context of multimodality and aided communication. In M. M. Smith and J. Murray (Eds.), *The silent partner? Language, interaction and aided communication* (pp. 229–246). Guildford, UK: J&R Press.

Jakobson, R. (1968) *Child language, aphasia and phonological universals*. Paris: Mouton.

James, S., Ziviani, J. & Boyd, R. (2014) A systematic review of activities of daily living measures for children and adolescents with cerebral palsy. *Developmental Medicine and Child Neurology*, *56*, 233–244.

Janakiefski, L., Tippenhauer, N., Liu, Q., Green, M., Loughmiller, S. & Saylor, M. M. (2022) Gaining access to the unknown: Preschoolers privilege unknown information as the target of their questions about verbs. *Journal of Experimental Child Psychology*, *217*, 105358.

Jarrold, C., Boucher, J. & Smith, P. K. (1996) Generativity deficits in pretend play in autism. *British Journal of Developmental Psychology*, *14*, 275–300.

Jenkinson, R., Milne, E. & Thompson, A. (2020) The relationship between intolerance of uncertainty and anxiety in autism: A systematic literature review and meta-analysis. *Autism*, *24*, 1933–1944.

Jennische, M. (1988) Alternative and augmentative communication routes used by a nonspeaking autistic boy. *Presented at The Bienniel Conference of the International Society for Augmentative and Alternative Communication*, Anaheim, USA, August 1988.

Jennische, M. & Zetterlund, M. (2015) Interpretation and construction of meaning of Bliss-words in children. *Augmentative and Alternative Communication*, *31*, 97–107.

Jimenez-Gomez, C., Haggerty, K. & Topçuoğlu, B. (2021) Wearable activity schedules to promote independence in young children. *Journal of Applied Behavior Analysis*, *54*, 197–216.

Johnson, E., Bornman, J. & Tönsing, K. M. (2016) An exploration of pain-related vocabulary: Implications for AAC use with children. *Augmentative and Alternative Communication*, *32*, 249–260.

Johnson, K. T., Narain, J., Ferguson, C., Picard, R. & Maes, P. (2020) The ECHOS platform to enhance communication for nonverbal children with autism: A case study. *Extended abstracts of the 2020 CHI Conference on Human Factors in Computing Systems*, Honolulu, April 25–30, 2020 (pp. 1–8).

Johnson, R. (1981) *The picture communication symbols*. Solana Beach, CA: Mayer-Johnson.

Johnson, R. (1985) *The picture communication symbols – Book II*. Solana Beach, CA: Mayer-Johnson.

Johnson, R. (1992) *The picture communication symbols – Book III*. Solana Beach, CA: Mayer-Johnson.

Johnson, R. (2001) *The Picture Communication Symbols*. Solana Beach, CA: Mayer-Johnson.

Jones, J. & Stewart, H. (2004) A description of how three occupational therapists train children in using the scanning access technique. *Australian Occupational Therapy Journal*, *51*, 155–165.

Jones, K. (1979) A Rebus system of non-fade visual language. *Child: Care, Health and Development*, *5*, 1–7.

Jones, W., Carr, K. & Klin, A. (2008) Absence of preferential looking to the eyes of approaching adults predicts level of social disability in 2-year-old toddlers with autism spectrum disorder. *Archives of General Psychiatry*, *65*, 946–954.

Jonsson, A., Kristofferssson, L., Ferm, U. & Thunberg, G. (2011) The ComAlong communication boards: Parents' use and experiences of aided language stimulation. *Augmentative and Alternative Communication*, *27*, 103–116.

Jordan, M., Neto, G. N. N., Brito Jr, A. & Nohama, P. (2020) Virtual keyboard with the prediction of words for children with cerebral palsy. *Computer Methods and Programs in Biomedicine*, *192*, 105402.

Josol, C. K., Fisher, M. H. & Athamanah, L. S. (2023) Perspectives of adults without disabilities on their friendships with individuals with intellectual and developmental disabilities. *Journal of Intellectual Disabilities*, *27*, 613–632.

Judge, S., Hawley, M. S., Cunningham, S. & Kirton, A. (2015) What is the potential for context aware communication aids?. *Journal of Medical Engineering and Technology*, *39*, 448–453.

Judge, S., Murray, J., Lynch, Y., Meredith, S., Moulam, L. et al. (2023) Attributes of communication aids as described by those supporting children and young people with AAC. *International Journal of Language and Communication Disorders*, *58*, 910–928.

Kaga, K. (2009) *Central auditory pathway disorders*. Tokyo: Springer.

Kagohara, D. M., van der Meer, L., Achmadi, D., Green, V. A., O'Reilly, M. F. et al. (2012) Teaching picture naming to two adolescents with autism spectrum disorders using systematic instruction and speech-generating devices. *Research in Autism Spectrum Disorders*, *6*, 1224–1233.

Kaiser, A. P. & Roberts, M. Y. (2011) Advances in early communication and language intervention. *Journal of Early Intervention*, *33*(4), 298–309.

Kaiser, A. & Wright, C. (2013) Enhanced milieu teaching: Incorporating AAC into naturalistic teaching with young children and their partners. *Perspectives on Augmentative and Alternative Communication*, *22*, 37–50.

Kaiser, A. P., Ostrosky M. M. & Alpert, C. I. (1993) Training teachers to use environmental and milieu teaching with nonvocal preschool children. *Journal of The Association for Persons with Severe handicaps*, *18*, 188–199.

Kalman, S. J. & Pajor A. (1996) Psychological and sociological aspects of introducing augmantative and alternative communication in Hungary: Tales, facts and numbers. In S. von Tetzchner and M. H. Jensen (Eds.), *Augmentative and alternative communication: European perspectives* (pp. 355–372). London: Whurr/Wiley.

Kan, P. F. & Windsor, J. (2010) Word learning in children with primary language impairment: A meta-analysis. *Journal of Speech, Language, and Hearing Research*, *53*, 739–756

Kanner, L. (1943) Autistic disturbances of affective contact. *The Nervous Child*, *2*, 217–250.

Kanto, L., Syrjälä, H. & Mann, W. (2021) Assessing vocabulary in deaf and hearing children using Finnish Sign Language. *The Journal of Deaf Studies and Deaf Education*, *26*, 147–158.

Karlsson, P., Bech, A., Stone, H., Vale, C., Griffin, S., Monbaliu, E. & Wallen, M. (2019) Eyes on communication: Trialling eye-gaze control technology in young children with dyskinetic cerebral palsy. *Developmental Neurorehabilitation*, *22*, 134–140.

Karlsson, P., Griffiths, T., Clarke, M. T., Monbaliu, E., Himmelmann, K. et al. (2021) Stakeholder consensus for decision making in eye-gaze control technology for children, adolescents and adults with cerebral palsy service provision: Findings from a Delphi study. *BMC Neurology*, *21*, 63.

Kasari, C., Chang, Y. C. & Patterson, S. (2013) Pretending to play or playing to pretend: The case of autism. *American Journal of Play*, *6*, 124–135.

Kasari, C., Freeman, S. & Paparella, T. (2006) Joint attention and symbolic play in young children with autism: A randomized controlled intervention study. *Journal of Child Psychology and Psychiatry*, *47*, 611–620.

Kasari, C., Gulsrud, A. C., Shire, S. Y. & Strawbridge, C. (2021) *The JASPER model for children with autism: Promoting joint attention, symbolic play, engagement, and regulation*. New York: Guilford Press.

Kasari, C. & Smith, T. (2016) Forest for the trees: Evidence-based practices in ASD. *Clinical Psychology: Science and Practice*, *23*, 260–264

Kashinath, S., Dukhovny, E. & Polit, P. (2022) Effects of a coaching intervention on paraeducator use of aided language modeling in classroom settings: A pilot investigation. *Communication Disorders Quarterly*, *44*, 33–44.

Kay-Raining Bird, E., Genesee, F. & Verhoeven, L. (2016) Bilingualism in children with developmental disorders: A narrative review. *Journal of Communication Disorders*, *63*, 1–14.

Kelly, K. R. & Bailey, A. L. (2013) Dual development of conversational and narrative discourse: Mother and child interactions during narrative co-construction. *Merrill-Palmer Quarterly*, *59*, 426–460.

Kelly-Vance, L. & Ryalls, B. O. (2008) Best practices in play assessment and intervention. In A. Thomas and J. Grimes (Eds.), *Best practices in school psychology*, Volume 2 (pp. 549–560). Bethesda, MD: National Association of School Psychologists.

Kemp, N. (2023) Digital communication, texting, and literacy acquisition. In Y. Ye et al. (Eds.), *Routledge international handbook of visual-motor skills, handwriting, and spelling* (pp. 446–457). London: Routledge.

Kemple, K. M. (2004) *Let's be friends: Peer competence and social inclusion in early childhood programs*. New York: Teachers College Press.

Kent, R. D. & Vorperian, H. K. (2013) Speech impairment in down syndrome: A review. *Journal of Speech, Language, and Hearing Research*, *56*, 178–210.

Kent-Walsh, J. & McNaughton, D. (2005) Communication partner instruction in AAC: Present practices and future directions. *Augmentative and Alternative Communication*, *21*, 195–204.

Kent-Walsh, J., Murza, K. A., Malani, M. D. & Binger, C. (2015) Effects of communication partner instruction on the communication of individuals using AAC: A meta-analysis. *Augmentative and Alternative Communication*, *31*, 271–284.

Keogh, D., Whitman, T., Beeman, D., Halligan, K. & Starzynski, T. (1987) Teaching interactive signing in a dialogue situation to mentally retarded individuals. *Research in Developmental Disabilities*, *8*, 39–53.

Kerns, C. M. & Kendall, P. C. (2014): Autism and anxiety: Overlap, similarities and differences. In T. E. Davis et al. (Eds.), *Handbook of autism and anxiety* (pp. 75–89). New York: Springer.

Kessler, B. & Treiman, R. (2015) Writing systems: Their properties and implications for reading. In A. Pollatsek and R. Treiman (Eds.), *The oxford handbook of reading* (pp. 10–25). New York: Oxford University Press.

Kettner, V. A. & Carpendale, J. I. (2013) Developing gestures for no and yes: Head shaking and nodding in infancy. *Gesture*, *13*, 193–209.

Khan, I. J. & Akter, M. S. (2021) Pidgin and creole: Concept, origin and evolution. *British Journal of Arts and Humanities*, *3*, 164–170.

Kidd, E., Donnelly, S. & Christiansen, M. H. (2018) Individual differences in language acquisition and processing. *Trends in Cognitive Sciences*, *22*, 154–169.

Kiernan, C. (1977) Alternatives to speech: A review of research on manual and other forms of communication with the mentally handicapped and other non-communicating populations. *The British Journal of Mental Subnormality*, *23*, 6–28.

Kiernan, C., Reid, B. & Jones, L. (1982) *Signs and symbols*. London: Heinemann.

Kildal, E., Stadskleiv, K., Boysen, E. S., Øderud, T., Dahl, I. L. et al. (2021) Increased heart rate functions as a signal of acute distress in non-communicating persons with intellectual disability. *Scientific Reports*, *11*, 6479.

Kim, S., Park, H., Shin, S., Kim, S., Park, H. & Shin, S. (2021) The effects of parent education on perceptions of augmentative and alternative communication. *Communication Sciences and Disorders*, *26*, 834–846.

Kim, S. H. & Lord, C. (2013) The behavioral manifestations of autism spectrum disorders. In J. D. Buxbaum and P. R. Hof (Eds.), *The neuroscience of autism spectrum disorders* (pp. 25–37). Oxford, UK: Academic Press.

King, M. R., Romski, M. & Sevcik, R. A. (2020) Growing up with AAC in the digital age: A longitudinal profile of communication across contexts from toddler to teen. *Augmentative and Alternative Communication*, *36*, 128–141.

King, M. R. & Soto, G. (2022) Code-switching using aided AAC: Toward an integrated theoretical framework. *Augmentative and Alternative Communication*, *38*, 67–76.

King, M. R., Ward, H., Soto, G. & Barrett, T. S. (2022) Supporting emergent bilinguals who use augmentative and alternative communication and their families: Lessons in telepractice from the COVID-19 pandemic. *American Journal of Speech-Language Pathology*, *31*, 2004–2021.

Kirk, S. A., McCarthy, J. J. & Kirk, W. D. (1968) *The Illinois test of psycholinguistic abilities*, Revised edition. Urbana, IL: University of Illinois Press.

Kirkham, S. & Moore, E. (2013) Adolescence. In J. K. Chambers and N. Schilling (Eds.), *The handbook of language variation and change*, 2nd edition (pp. 277–296). Malden, MA: Wiley-Blackwell.

Kleinert, H. L., Kearns, J., Land, L. A., L. Page, & Kleinert, J. O. R. (2023) Peer-assisted aided AAC modeling for students with complex communication needs. *Teaching Exceptional Children*, *55*, 268–277.

Klima, E. S. & Bellugi, U. (1979) *The signs of language*. Cambridge, MA: Harvard University Press.

Knight, V., Sartini, E. & Spriggs, A. D. (2015) Evaluating visual activity schedules as evidence-based practice for individuals with autism spectrum disorders. *Journal of Autism and Developmental Disorders*, *45*, 157–178.

Koegel, L. K., Ashbaugh, K. & Koegel, R. L. (2016) Pivotal response treatment. In R. Lang et al. (Eds.), *Early intervention for young children with autism spectrum disorder* (pp. 85–112). Cham, Switzerland: Springer.

Koegel, L. K., Bryan, K. M., Su, P., Vaidya, M. & Camarata, S. (2019) Intervention for non-verbal and minimally-verbal individuals with autism: A systematic review. *International Journal of Pediatric Research*, *5*, 1–16.

Koegel, R. L., Koegel, L. K. & Surratt, A. (1992) Language intervention and disruptive behavior in preschool children with autism. *Journal of Autism and Developmental Disorders*, *22*, 141–153.

Kollar, Z. (1999) Growing up with Blissymbols. *Paper at Second Regional Eastern and Central European Conference on AAC*, Prague, Czech Republic, November 11–13, 1999.

Kollinzas, G. (1983) The communication record: Sharing information to promote sign language generalization. *Journal of the Association for Persons with Severe Handicaps*, *8*, 49–55.

Kotrba, A. (2015) *Selective mutism: An assessment and intervention guide for therapists, educators and parents*. Eau Claire, WI: PESI Publishing and Media.

Koyama, T. & Wang, H.-T. (2011) Use of activity schedule to promote independent performance of individuals with autism and other intellectual disabilities: A review. *Research in Developmental Disabilities*, *32*, 2235–2242.

Kraat, A. W. (1985) *Communication interaction between aided and natural speakers: A state of the art report*. Toronto: Canadian Rehabilitation Council for the Disabled.

Kratochwill, T. R. & Shernoff, E. S. (2004) Evidence-based practice: Promoting evidence-based interventions in school psychology. *School Psychology Review*, *33*, 34–48.

Kristensson, P. O., Lilley, J., Black, R. & Waller, A. (2020) A design engineering approach for quantitatively exploring context-aware sentence retrieval for nonspeaking individuals with motor disabilities. *Proceedings of the 2020 CHI Conference on Human Factors in Computing Systems* (Paper 198).

Kristoffersen, J. H. & Troelsgård, T. (2010) Making a dictionary without words: Lemmatization problems in a sign language dictionary. In S. Granger and M. Paquot (Eds.), *eLexicography in the 21st century: New challenges, new Applications* (pp. 165–172). Louvain-la-Neuve, Belgium: Presses Universitaires de Louvaine.

Kristoffersson, E., Dahlgren Sandberg, A. & Holck, P. (2020) Communication ability and communication methods in children with cerebral palsy. *Developmental Medicine and Child Neurology*, *62*, 933–938.

Kron, A. T., Kingsnorth, S., Wright, F. V. & Ryan, S. E. (2018) Construct validity of the family impact of assistive technology scale for augmentative and alternative communication. *Augmentative and Alternative Communication*, *34*, 335–347.

Krstic, S. & Littorin, E. (2014) The iconicity and learnability of Blissymbols: A study of the interpretations of blissymbols by kenyan children with diverse language backgrounds. Thesis, University of Linköping.

Kryvonogova, O., Trapizanova, N., Palamarchuk, D. & von Tetzchner, S. (2023) Augmentative and alternative communication in times of unrest and war: Report from Ukraine. *Poster at 19th Biennial Conference of the International Society for Augmentative and Alternative Communication*, Cancun, Mexico, July 24–27, 2023.

Kuntay, A. C. (2004) Lists as alternative discourse structures to narratives in preschool children's conversations. *Discourse Processes*, *38*, 95–118.

Kurki, K., Järvenoja, H., Järvelä, S. & Mykkänen, A. (2017) Young children's use of emotion and behaviour regulation strategies in socio-emotionally challenging day-care situations. *Early Childhood Research Quarterly*, *41*, 50–62.

Kurmanaviciute, R. & Stadskleiv, K. (2017) Assessment of verbal comprehension and non-verbal reasoning when standard response mode is challenging: A comparison of different response modes and an exploration of their clinical usefulness. *Cogent Psychology*, *4*, 1275416.

Kvale, A. M., Martinsen, H. & Schjølberg, S. (1992) *Miljømessige betingelser for trivsel og læring hos autistiske barn og voksne*. Oslo: Landsforeningen for Autister.

Laakso, M. & Soininen, M. (2010) Mother-initiated repair sequences in interactions of 3-year-old children. *First Language*, *30*, 329–353.

Labov, W. (1972) The transformation of reality in narrative syntax. In W. Labov, *Language in the inner city* (pp. 354–396). Philadelphia, PA: University of Pennsylvania Press.

Lahey, M. & Bloom, L. (1977) Planning a lexicon: Which words to teach first. *Journal of Speech and Hearing Disorders*, *42*, 340–350.

Lai, C. L. E., Lau, Z., Lui, S. S., Lok, E., Tam, V. et al. (2017) Meta-nalysis of neuropsychological measures of executive functioning in children and adolescents with high-functioning autism spectrum disorder. *Autism Research*, *10*, 911–939.

Lakoff, G. & Johnson, M. H. (1980) *Metaphors we live by*. Chicago: Chicago University Press.

Lam, Y. G. & Yeung, S. S. S. (2012) Cognitive deficits and symbolic play in preschoolers with autism. *Research in Autism Spectrum Disorders*, *6*, 560–564.

Lancioni, G. E., Olivetti, M., Singh, N. N., O'Reilly, M., Sigafoos, J. & Alberti, G. (2019) Recent technology-aided programs to support adaptive responses, functional activities, and leisure and communication in people with significant disabilities. *Frontiers in Neurology*, *10*, 643.

Lancioni, G. E., Sigafoos, J., O'Reilly, M. F. & Singh, N. N. (Eds.) (2013) *Assistive technologies. Interventions for individuals with severe/profound and multiple disabilities*. New York: Springer.

Lancioni, G. E., Singh, N. N., O'Reilly, M. F., Green, V. A., Van der Meer, L. et al. (2016) A speech generating device for persons with intellectual and sensory-motor disabilities. *Journal of Developmental and Physical Disabilities*, *28*, 85–98.

Landa, R. J., Gross, A. L., Stuart, E. A. & Faherty, A. (2013) Developmental trajectories in children with and without autism spectrum disorders: The first 3 years. *Child Development*, *84*, 429–442.

Lane, H. (1977) *The wild boy of Aveyron*. London: George Allen and Unwin.

Lang, R., McLay, L. & Rispoli, M. (2023) Advanced language models: Potential to improve augmentative and alternative communication for individuals with intellectual and developmental disabilities. *Advances in Neurodevelopmental Disorders*, *7*, 481–484.

Langarika-Rocafort, A., Mondragon, N. I. & Etxebarrieta, G. R. (2021) A systematic review of research on augmentative and alternative communication interventions for children aged 6–10 in the last decade. *Language, Speech, and Hearing Services in Schools*, *52*, 899–916.

Lanphere, A. & Terlektsi, E. (2023) Communication needs of a deaf child with cerebral palsy and how to support these: A case study. *Deafness and Education International*, *25*, 101–120.

Laubscher, E. & Light, J. (2020) Core vocabulary lists for young children and considerations for early language development: A narrative review. *Augmentative and Alternative Communication*, *36*, 43–53.

Launonen, K. (1996) Enhancing communication skills of children with Down syndrome: Early use of manual signs. In S. von Tetzchner and M. H. Jensen (Eds.), *Augmentative and alternative communication: European perspectives* (pp. 213–231). London: Whurr/Wiley.

Launonen, K. (2003) Manual signing as a tool for communicative interaction and language: The development of children with Down syndrome and their parents. In S. von Tetzchner and N. Grove (Eds.), *Augmentative and alternative communication: Developmental issues* (pp. 83–122). London: Whurr/Wiley.

Launonen, K. (2019a) Sign acquisition in Down syndrome: Longitudinal perspectives. In N. Grove and K. Launonen (Eds.), *Manual sign acquisition in children with developmental disabilities* (pp. 89–113). New York: Nova.

Launonen, K. (2019b) Signing at home. In N. Grove and K. Launonen (Eds.), *Manual sign acquisition in children with developmental disabilities* (pp. 337–358). New York: Nova.

Launonen, K. & Grove, N. (2003) A longitudinal study of sign and speech in a boy with down syndrome. In S. von Tetzchner and N. Grove (Eds.), *Augmentative and alternative communication: Developmental issues* (pp. 123–154). London: Whurr/Wiley.

Lauricella, A. R., Cingel, D. P., Blackwell, C., Wartella, E. & Conway, A. (2014) The mobile generation: Youth and adolescent ownership and use of new media. *Communication Research Reports*, *31*, 357–364.

Lave, J. & Wenger, E. (1991) *Situated learning*. Cambridge: Cambridge University Press.

Lawrence, J. F. & Snow, C. E. (2011) Oral discourse and reading. In M. L. Kamil et al. (Eds.), *Handbook of reading research*, Volume 4 (pp. 320–337). New York: Routledge.

Layton, T., Chuang, M. C. & Hao, G. (2014) Play behaviors in Chinese toddlers with Down Syndrome. *Journal of Psychological Abnormalities in Children*, *3*, 131.

Leach, M. M. & Oakland, T. (2007) Ethics standards impacting test development and use: A review of 31 ethics codes impacting practices in 35 countries. *International Journal of Testing*, *7*, 71–88.

Leatherman, E. M. & Wegner, J. R. (2022) Augmentative and alternative communication in the classroom: Teacher practices and experiences. *Language, Speech, and Hearing Services in Schools*, *53*, 874–893.

Lee, D. Y. (2001) Defining core vocabulary and tracking its distribution across spoken and written genres: Evidence of a gradience of variation from the British National Corpus. *Journal of English Linguistics*, *29*, 250–278.

Lee, E. S., Hwang, E. J., Hur, T. S., Woo, Y. S. & Min, H. K. (2003) A study on the predicate prediction using symbols in augmentative and alternative communication system. In L. Chittaro (Ed.), *Human-computer interaction with mobile devices and services* (pp. 466–470). Berlin: Springer.

Leekam, S. R., Nieto, C., Libby, S. J., Wing, L. & Gould, J. (2007) Describing the sensory abnormalities of children and adults with autism. *Journal of Autism and Developmental Disorders*, *37*, 894–910.

Lehman, B. (2011) *The secret box*. New York: Clarion Books.

Lenneberg, E. H. (1967) *Biological foundations of language*. New York: Wiley.

Leonard, H. & Wen, X. (2002) The epidemiology of mental retardation: Challenges and opportunities in the new millennium. *Mental Retardation and Developmental Disabilities Research Reviews*, *8*, 117–134.

Leonard, L. B. (1981) Facilitating linguistic skills in children with specific language impairment. *Applied Psycholinguistics*, *2*, 89–118.

Leonet, O., Orcasitas-Vicandi, M., Langarika-Rocafort, A., Mondragon, N. I. & Etxebarrieta, G. R. (2022) A systematic review of augmentative and alternative communication interventions for children aged from 0 to 6 years. *Language, Speech, and Hearing Services in Schools*, *53*, 894–920.

Lerman, D. C. (2023) *Neurodevelopmental disabilities and employment: Helping learners prepare for social demands in the workplace*. Abingdon, UK: Routledge.

Lerman, D. C., Valentino, A. L. & Leblanc, L. A. (2016) Discrete trial training. In R. Lang, T. B. Hancock and N. N. Singh (Eds.), *Early intervention for young children with autism spectrum disorder* (pp. 47–83). Cham, Switzerland: Springer.

Lesher, G., Moulton, B. & Higginbotham, D. J. (1998) Techniques for augmenting scanning communication. *Augmentative and Alternative Communication*, *14*, 81–101.

Leung, J. P. (1994) Teaching spontaneous requests to children with autism using a time delay procedure with multi-component toys. *Journal of Behavioral Education*, *4*, 21–31.

Lewis, B. A., Miller, G. J., Iyengar, S. K., Stein, C. & Benchek, P. (2023) Long-term outcomes for individuals with childhood apraxia of speech. *Journal of Speech, Language, and Hearing Research*, 1–17.

Lewis, M. (2008) The emergence of human emotions. In M. Lewis, J. M. Haviland-Jones and L. F. Barrett (Eds.), *Handbook of emotions*, 3rd edition (pp. 304–319). London: Guilford Press.

Lewis, M., Young, G., Brooks, J. & Michalson, L. (1975) The beginning of friendship. In M. Lewis and L. A. Rosenblum (Eds.), *Friendship and peer relations: The origins of behavior* (pp. 27–66). New York: Wiley.

Lewis, S., McGrath, K. & Reuppel, J. (2004) Language identification and language specific letter-to-sound rules. *Colorado Research in Linguistics*, *17*, 1–8.

Liber, D. B., Frea, W. D. & Symon, J. B. (2008) Using time-delay to improve social play skills with peers for children with autism. *Journal of Autism and Developmental Disorders*, *38*, 312–323.

Liberman, A. (1999) The reading researcher and the reading teacher need the right theory of speech. *Scientific Studies of Reading*, *3*, 95–111.

Licence, L., Oliver, C., Moss, J. & Richards, C. (2020) Prevalence and risk-markers of self-harm in autistic children and adults. *Journal of Autism and Developmental Disorders*, *50*, 3561–3574.

Lieberth, A. K. & Gamble, M. E. B. (1991) The role of iconicity in sign language learning by hearing adults. *Journal of Communication Disorders*, *24*, 89–99.

Lifter, K., Mason, E. J., Cannarella, A. M. & Cameron, A. D. (2022) *Developmental play assessment for practitioners (DPA-P) guidebook and training website: Project play*. Abingdin, UK: Routledge.

Light, J., Barwise, A., Gardner, A. M. & Flynn, M. (2021) Personalized early AAC intervention to build language and literacy skills: A case study of a 3-year-old with complex communication needs. *Topics in Language Disorders*, *41*, 209–231.

Light, J. C., Beukelman, D. R. & Reichle, J. (2003) *Communicative competence for individuals who use AAC: From research to effective practice*. Baltimore, MD: Brookes.

Light, J., Binger, C., Agate, T. L. & Ramsay, K. N. (1999) Teaching partner-focused questions to individuals who use augmentative and alternative communication to enhance their communicative competence. *Journal of Speech, Language and Hearing Research*, *42*, 241–255.

Light, J. C., Collier, B. & Parnes, P. (1985) Communicative interaction between young nonspeaking physically disabled children and their primary caregivers. Part I: Discourse patterns. *Augmentative and Alternative Communication*, *1*, 74–83.

Light, J. C., Dattilo, J., English, J., Gutierrez, L. & Hartz, J. (1992) Instructing facilitators to support the communication of people who use augmentative communication systems. *Journal of Speech and Hearing Research*, *35*, 865–875.

Light, J. C. & McNaughton, D. (2012a) Supporting the communication, language, and literacy development of children with complex communication needs: State of the science and future research priorities. *Assistive Technology*, *24*, 34–44,

Light, J. C. & McNaughton, D. (2012b) The changing face of augmentative and alternative communication: Past, present, and future challenges. *Augmentative and Alternative Communication*, *28*, 197–204.

Light, J. C. & McNaughton, D. (2014) Communicative competence for individuals who require augmentative and alternative communication: A new definition for a new era of communication? *Augmentative and Alternative Communication*, *30*, 1–18.

Light, J., Roberts, B., Dimarco, R. & Greiner, N. (1998) Augmentative and alternative communication to suport receptive and expressive communication for people with autism. *Journal of Communication Disorders*, *31*, 153–180.

Lillard, A. S. (2015) The development of play. In L. S. Liben and U. Mueller (Eds.), *Handbook of child psychology and developmental science, Seventh edition, Volume 2: Cognitive processes* (pp. 425–468). New York: Wiley.

Lillard, A. S. (2017) Why do the children (pretend) play? *Trends in Cognitive Sciences*, *11*, 826–834.

Lillehaug, H. A., Klevberg, G. L. & Stadskleiv, K. (2023) Provision of augmentative and alternative communication interventions to Norwegian preschool children with cerebral palsy: Are the right children receiving interventions? *Augmentative and Alternative Communication*, *39*, 219–229.

Lillo-Martin, D. & Henner, J. (2021) Acquisition of sign languages. *Annual Review of Linguistics*, *7*, 395–419.

Lim, N., O'Reilly, M. F., Sigafoos, J., Ledbetter-Cho, K. & Lancioni, G. E. (2019) Should heritage languages be incorporated into interventions for bilingual individuals with neurodevelopmental disorders? A systematic review. *Journal of Autism and Developmental Disorders*, *49*, 887–912.

Lindberg, B. (1987) *Retts syndrom – En kartlegging av psykologiske och pedagogiska erfarenheter i Sverige*. Stockholm: Högskolan för lärarutbildning i Stockholm.

Lindberg, B. (2006) *Understanding Rett syndrome: A practical guide for parents, teachers, and therapists*. Newburyport, MA: Hogrefe Publishing.

Lindsey, J. (2019) Testimonial injustice and vulnerability: A qualitative analysis of participation in the Court of Protection. *Social and Legal Studies*, *28*, 450–469.

Lindström, C. (2019) Contributing to a tactile language: Partners communicative accommodation to a bodily/tactile modality. *Journal of Deafblind Studies on Communication*, *5*, 50–72.

Lloyd, P., Camaioni, L. & Ercolani, P. (1995) Assessing referential communication skills in the primary school years: A comparative study. *British Journal of Developmental Psychology*, *13*, 13–29.

Lock, A. (1980) *The guided reinvention of language*. London: Academic Press

Logan, K., Iacono, T. & Trembath, D. (2017) A systematic review of research into aided AAC to increase social-communication functions in children with autism spectrum disorder. *Augmentative and Alternative Communication*, *33*, 51–64.

Lohmann, M. J., Kappel, A. & Taylor, M. S. (2022) Augmentative and alternative communication and remote learning. *Rural Special Education Quarterly*, *41*, 48–54.

López, S. A., Corno, F. & De Russis, L. (2017) Design and development of one-switch video games for children with severe motor disabilities. *ACM Transactions on Accessible Computing (TACCESS)*, *10*, 1–42.

Lorah, E. R., Holyfield, C., Griffen, B. & Caldwell, N. (2022) A systematic review of evidence-based instruction for individuals with autism using mobile augmentative and alternative communication technology. *Review Journal of Autism and Developmental Disorders*, *11*, 210–224.

Lorang, E., Maltman, N., Venker, C., Eith, A. & Sterling, A. (2022) Speech-language pathologists' practices in augmentative and alternative communication during early intervention. *Augmentative and Alternative Communication, 38*, 41–52.

Lord, C., Bishop, S. & Anderson, D. (2015) Developmental trajectories as autism phenotypes. *American Journal of Medical Genetics Part C: Seminars in Medical Genetics, 169*, 198–208.

Lord, C., Brugha, T. S., Charman, T., Cusack, J., Dumas, G. et al. (2020) Autism spectrum disorder. *Nature Reviews Disease Primers, 6*, 1–23.

Lord, C., Rutter, M., DiLavore, P. C., Risi, S., Gotham, K. & Bishop, S. L. (2012) *Autism diagnostic observation schedule, Second edition (ADOS-2)*. Torrance, CA: Western Psychological Services.

Lotter, V. (1966) Epidemiology of autistic conditions in young children: 1. Prevalence. *Social Psychiatry, 1*, 124–135.

Lourenço, L., Faias, J., Afonso, R., Moreira, A. & Ferreira, J. M. (1996) Improving communication and language skills of children with developmental disorders: Family involvement in graphic language intervention. In S. von Tetzchner and M. H. Jensen (Eds.), *Augmentative and alternative communication: European perspectives* (pp. 309–323). London: Whurr/Wiley.

Lovaas, O. I., Koegel, R. L. & Schreibman, L. (1979) Stimulus overselectivity in autism: A review of research. *Psychological Bulletin, 86*, 1236–1254.

Luchsinger, R. & Arnold, G. E. (Eds.) (1965) *Voice – Speech – Language*. Belmont: Wadsworth.

Luckins, J. M. & Clarke, M. T. (2021) Can conversation-based intervention using speech-generating devices improve language in children with partially intelligible speech? *Communication Disorders Quarterly, 42*, 131–144.

Ludlow, A., Skelly, C. & Rohleder, P. (2012) Challenges faced by parents of children diagnosed with autism spectrum disorder. *Journal of Health Psychology, 17*, 702–711.

Lüke, C. (2014) Impact of speech-generating devices on the language development of a child with childhood apraxia of speech: A case study. *Disability and Rehabilitation: Assistive Technology, 11*, 80–88.

Lund, E. M., Kohlmeier, T. L. & Durán, L. K. (2017) Comparative language development in bilingual and monolingual children with autism spectrum disorder: A systematic review. *Journal of Early Intervention, 39*, 106–124.

Lund, S. K. (2015) Longitudinal studies of aided language development. In S. von Tetzchner and J. Oxley (Eds.), *Processes of aided language development in cognitively high-functioning children and adolescents. Proceedings of a seminar at the Twelfth Biennial Research Symposium of the International Society for Augmentative and Alternative Communication, Lisbon, Portugal, July 25–26, 2014* (pp. 11–17). Toronto: ISAAC.

Lund, S. K. & Light, J. (2006) Long-term outcomes for individuals who use AAC: Part I – what is a "good" outcome? *Augmentative and Alternative Communication, 22*, 284–299.

Lund, S. K. & Light, J. (2007) Long-term outcomes for individuals who use augmentative and alternative communication: Part II – Communicative interaction. *Augmentative and Alternative Communication, 23*, 1–15.

Lund, S. K. & Troha, J. M. (2008) Teaching young people who are blind and have autism to make requests using a variation on the Picture Exchange Communication System with tactile symbols: A preliminary investigation. *Journal of Autism and Developmental Disorders, 38*, 719–730.

Lundälv, M. & Derbring, S. (2012a) Towards general cross-platform CCF based multi-modal language support. In K. Miesenberger et al. (Eds.), *Computers helping People with special needs* (pp. 261–268). Berlin: Springer.

Lundälv, M. & Derbring, S. (2012b) AAC vocabulary standardisation and harmonisation. In K. Miesenberger et al. (Eds.), *Computers helping People with special needs* (pp. 303–310). Berlin: Springer.

Lundälv, M., Derbring, S., Brännström, A., Farre, B. & Nordberg, L. (2013) Inclusive AAC-multi-modal and multilingual language support for all. In P. Encarnaçãc ed et al. (Eds.), *Assistive technology: From research to practice* (pp. 332–339). Berlin: IOS Press.

Luria, A. R. (1969) *The mind of a mnemonist*. London: Jonathan Cape.

Lynch, Y., McCleary, M. & Smith, M. M. (2018) Instructional strategies used in direct AAC interventions with children to support graphic symbol learning: A systematic review. *Child Language Teaching and Therapy*, *34*, 23–36.

MacKay, D., Wills, S. & Waller, A. (2007) Bliss-Dasher – Efficient semantic writing with any muscle. *Paper presented at International Workshop on Blissymbolics*, Dundee, July 2007.

MacWhinney, B. (1982) Basic syntactic processes. In S. Kuczaj (Ed.), *Language development. Volume 1. Syntax and semantics* (pp. 73–136). Hillsdale, New Jersey: Erlbaum.

MacWhinney, B. (2015) Language development. In R. M. Lerner et al. (Eds.), *Handbook of child psychology and developmental science, Seventh edition, Volume 2 Cognitive processes* (pp. 296–338). New York: Wiley.

Madge, N. & Fassam, M. (1982) *Ask the children*. London: Batsford.

Madigan, S., McArthur, B. A., Anhorn, C., Eirich, R. & Christakis, D. A. (2020) Associations between screen use and child language skills: A systematic review and meta-analysis. *JAMA Pediatrics*, *174*, 665–675.

Maharaj, S. C. (1980) *Pictogram ideogram communication*. Regina, Canada: The George Reed Foundation for the Handicapped.

Maharaj, S. C. (2022) *The dignity of symbols*. Available at https://pictoworld.com

Maloney, E. S. & Larrivee, L. S. (2007) Limitations of age-equivalent scores in reporting the results of norm-referenced tests. *Contemporary Issues in Communication Science and Disorders*, *34*, 86–93.

Mandak, K., O'Neill, T., Light, J. & Fosco, G. M. (2017) Bridging the gap from values to actions: A family systems framework for family-centered AAC services. *Augmentative and Alternative Communication*, *33*, 32–41.

Mandak, K., Light, J. & Boyle, S. (2018) The effects of literacy interventions on single-word reading for individuals who use aided AAC: A systematic review. *Augmentative and Alternative Communication*, *34*, 206–218.

Mandy, W. & Lai, M. C. (2016) The role of the environment in the developmental psychopathology of autism spectrum condition. *Journal of Child Psychology and Psychiatry*, *57*, 271–292.

Mann, W. & Haug, T. (2015) New directions in sign language assessment. In M. Marschark and P. E. Spencer (Eds.), *The Oxford handbook of deaf studies in language* (pp. 412–421). New York: Oxford University Press.

Manzoor, M. & Vimarlund, V. (2018) Digital technologies for social inclusion of individuals with disabilities. *Health and Technology*, *8*, 377–390.

Marchman, V. A. & Dale, P. S. (2023) The MacArthur-Bates Communicative Development Inventories: Updates from the CDI Advisory Board. *Frontiers in Psychology*, *14*, 1170303.

Marchman, V. A., Dale, P. S. & Fenson, L. (2023) *The MacArthur-Bates Communicative Development Inventories: User's guide and technical manual*, 3rd edition. Baltimore, MD: Brookes.

Marina, K., Drynan, D. & Tiessen, E. (2012) Evaluation of methods for teaching electronic visual scanning to children with cerebral palsy: Two series of case studies. *Disability and Rehabilitation: Assistive Technology*, *7*, 249–260.

Marková, I., Jahoda, A., Cattermole, M. & Woodward, D. (1992) Living in hospital and hostel: The pattern of interactions of people with learning difficulties. *Journal of Intellectual Disability Research*, *36*, 115–127.

Marschik, P. B., Pini, G., Bartl-Pokorny, K. D., Duckworth, M., Gugatschka, M. et al. (2012) Early speech–language development in females with Rett syndrome: Focusing on the preserved speech variant. *Developmental Medicine and Child Neurology*, *54*, 451–456.

Marshall, J. & Goldbart, J. (2008) 'Communication is everything I think.' Parenting a child who needs Augmentative and Alternative Communication (AAC). *International Journal of Language and Communication Disorders*, *43*, 77–98.

Martinsen, H. and von Tetzchner, S. (1989) Imitation at the onset of speech. In S. von Tetzchner, L. S. Siegel and L. Smith (Eds.), *The social and cognitive aspects of normal and atypical language development* (pp. 51–68). New York: Springer-Verlag.

Marx, O. (1967) The history of biological basis of language. In E. Lenneberg, *Biological foundations of language* (pp. 443–469). New York: Wiley.

Marzano, R. J. (2012) A comprehensive approach to vocabulary instruction. *Voices from the Middle, 20*, 31–35.

Masataka, N. (1992) Motherese in a signed language. *Infant Behavior and Development, 15*, 453–460.

Massé, B., Ba, S. & Horaud, R. (2017) Tracking gaze and visual focus of attention of people involved in social interaction. *IEEE Transactions on Pattern Analysis and Machine Intelligence, 40*, 2711–2724.

Masterson, J. J. (1997) Interrelationships in children's language production. *Topics in Language Disorders, 17*, 11–22.

Masur, E. (1997) Materbnal labelling of novel and familiar obejcts: Implications for children's development of lexical constraints. *Journal of Child Language, 24*, 427–439.

Mathisen, B., Arthur-Kelly, M., Kidd, J. & Nissen, C. (2009) Using MINSPEAK: A case study of a preschool child with complex communication needs. *Disability and Rehabilitation: Assistive Technology, 4*, 376–385.

Mathy-Laikko, P., Iacono, T., Ratcliff, A., Villarruel, F., Yoder, D. & Vanderheiden, G. (1989) Teaching a child with multiple disabilities to use a tactile augmentative communication device. *Augmentative and Alternative Communication, 5*, 249–256.

Mayer, M. (1969) *Frog, where are you?* New York: Dial Press.

Mazrekaj, D. & De Witte, K. (2024) The impact of school closures on learning and mental health of children: Lessons from the COVID-19 pandemic. *Perspectives on Psychological Science, 19*, 686–693.

McCarthy, J. H., Hogan, T. P., Beukelman, D. R. & Schwarz, I. E. (2015) Influence of computerized sounding out on spelling performance for children who do and do not rely on AAC. *Disability and Rehabilitation: Assistive Technology, 10*, 221–230.

McCarty, T. V. & Light, J. C. (2022) Supporting peer interactions for students with complex communication needs in inclusive settings: Paraeducator roles. *Perspectives of the ASHA Special Interest Groups, 7*, 229–244.

McClenny, C. S., Roberts, J. E. & Layton, T. L. (1992) Unexpected events and their effect on children's language. *Child Language Teaching and Therapy, 8*, 229–245.

McCord, M. S. & Soto, G. (2004) Perceptions of AAC: An ethnographic investigation of Mexican-American families. *Augmentative and Alternative Communication, 20*, 209–227.

McDonald, E. T. & Schultz, A. R. (1973) Communication boards for cerebral–palsied children. *Journal of Speech and Hearing Disorders, 38*, 73–88.

McDowell, N. (2023) A review of the literature to inform the development of a practice framework for supporting children with cerebral visual impairment (CVI). *International Journal of Inclusive Education, 27*, 718–738.

McGee, G. G. (2022) Incidental teaching research: Early beginnings through recent innovations. In J. B. Leaf et al. (Red.), *Handbook of applied behavior analysis interventions for autism: Integrating research into practice* (pp. 185–206). Cham, Switzerland: Springer.

McGee, G. G., Morrier, M. J. & Daly, T. (1999) An incidental teaching approach to early intervention for toddlers with autism. *Journal of the Association for Persons with Severe Handicaps, 24*, 133–146.

McGregor, K. K. (2017) Semantics in child language disorders. In R. G. Schwartz (Ed.), *Handbook of child language disorders*, 2nd edition (pp. 392–415). New York: Routledge.

McGrew, J. H., Ruble, L. A. & Smith, I. M. (2016) Autism spectrum disorder and evidence-based practice in psychology. *Clinical Psychology: Science and Practice, 23*, 239–255.

McIntyre, S., Goldsmith, S., Webb, A., Ehlinger, V., Hollung, S. J. et al. (2022) Global prevalence of cerebral palsy: A systematic analysis. *Developmental Medicine and Child Neurology, 64*, 1494–1506.

McKearnan, K. A., Kieckhefer, G. M., Engel, J. M., Jensen, M. P. & Labyak, S. (2004) Pain in children with cerebral palsy: A review. *Journal of Neuroscience Nursing, 36*, 252–259.

Mckinnon, C. T., Meehan, E. M., Harvey, A. R., Antolovich, G. C. & Morgan, P. E. (2019) Prevalence and characteristics of pain in children and young adults with cerebral palsy: A systematic review. *Developmental Medicine and Child Neurology, 61*, 305–314.

McLarty, M. (1997) Putting objects of reference in context. *European Journal of Special Needs Education, 12*, 12–20.
McLay, L., Hansen, S. & Carnett, A. (2019) TEACCH and other structured approaches to teaching. In S. Little and A. Akin Little (Eds.), *Behavioral interventions in schools: Evidence-based positive strategies* (pp. 299–322). Washington: American Psychological Association.
McLay, L., Schäfer, M. C., van der Meer, L., Couper, L., McKenzie, E. et al. (2017) Acquisition, preference and follow-up comparison across three AAC modalities taught to two children with autism spectrum disorder. *International Journal of Disability, Development and Education, 64*, 117–130.
McLay, L., van der Meer, L., Schäfer, M. C., Couper, L., McKenzie, E. et al. (2015) Comparing acquisition, generalization, maintenance, and preference across three AAC options in four children with autism spectrum disorder. *Journal of Developmental and Physical Disabilities, 27*, 323–339.
McLean, L. K., Brady, N. C., McLean, J. E. & Behrens, G. A. (1999) Communication forms and functions of children and adults with severe mental retardation in community and institutional settings. *Journal of Speech, Language, and Hearing Research, 42*, 231–240.
McLeod, S. & Harrison, L. J. (2009) Epidemiology of speech and language impairment in a nationally representative sample of 4- to 5-year-old children. *Journal of Speech, Language, and Hearing Research, 11*, 155–170.
McNally, S., Leech, K. A., Corriveau, K. H. & Daly, M. (2024) Indirect effects of early shared reading and access to books on reading vocabulary in middle childhood. *Scientific Studies of Reading, 28*, 42–59.
McNaughton, D., Bryen, D., Blackstone, S., Williams, M. & Kennedy, P. (2012) Young adults with complex communication needs: Research and development in AAC for a "diverse" population. *Assistive Technology, 24*, 45–53.
McNaughton, D. & Light, J. C. (1989) Teaching facilitators to support the communication skills of an adult with severe cognitive disabilities: A case study. *Augmentative and Alternative Communication, 5*, 35–41.
McNaughton, D. & Light, J. C. (2015) What we write about when we write about AAC: The past 30 years of research and future directions. *Augmentative and Alternative Communication, 31*, 261–270
McNaughton, D., Rackensperger, T., Benedek-Wood, E., Krezman, C., Williams, M. B. & Light, J. C. (2008) "A child needs to be given a chance to succeed": Parents of individuals who use AAC describe the benefits and challenges of learning AAC technologies. *Augmentative and Alternative Communication, 24*, 43–55.
McNaughton, S. (1998) Reading acquisistion of adults with severe congenital speech and physical impairments: Theoretical infrastructure, empirical investigation, educational application. Dissertation, University of Toronto.
McNaughton, S. (2003) Blissymbol learners, their language and their language partners: Development through three decades. In S. von Tetzchner and N. Grove (Eds.), *Augmentative and alternative communication: Developmental issues* (pp. 357–387). London, UK: Whurr/Wiley.
McNaughton, S. (2014) The early years of graphic communication systems – and the many issues still to be understood. In L. Lloyd et al. (Eds.), *Augmentative and alternative communication: Research issues and needs. Proceedings of the 13th Biennial Research Symposium of the International Society for Augmentative and Alternative Communication, Pittsburg, USA, August 3–4, 2012* (pp. 61–66). Toronto: ISAAC.
McNeil, M. R., Ballard, K. J., Duffy, J. R. & Wambaugh, J. (2017) Apraxia of speech theory, assessment, differential diagnosis, and treatment: Past, present, and future. In P. van Lieshout et al. (Eds.), *Speech motor control in normal and disordered speech: Future developments in theory and methodology* (pp. 195–221). Rockville, MD: ASHA Press
Meadan, H., Ostrosky, M. M., Triplett, B., Michna, A. & Fettig, A. (2011) Using visual supports with young children with autism spectrum disorder. *Teaching Exceptional Children, 43*, 28–35.
Mei, C., Reilly, S., Bickerton, M., Mensah, F., Turner, S. et al. (2020) Speech in children with cerebral palsy. *Developmental Medicine and Child Neurology, 62*, 1374–1382.

Mei, C., Reilly, S., Reddihough, D., Mensah, F., Pennington, L. & Morgan, A. (2016) Language outcomes of children with cerebral palsy aged 5 years and 6 years: A population-based study. *Developmental Medicine and Child Neurology, 58*, 605–611.

Meier, R. P. (2019) Acquiering signed languages as first languge: The milestones of acquisition and the form of early signs. In N. Grove and K. Launonen (Eds.). *Manual sign acquisition in children with developmental disabilities* (pp. 59–86). New York: Nova.

Mellman, L. M., DeThorne, L. S. & Hengst, J. A. (2010) "Shhhh! Alex has something to say": AAC-SGD use in the classroom setting. *Perspectives on Augmentative and Alternative Communication, 19*, 108–114.

Melo, C., Ruano, L., Jorge, J., Pinto Ribeiro, T., Oliveira, G. et al. (2020) Prevalence and determinants of motor stereotypies in autism spectrum disorder: A systematic review and meta-analysis. *Autism, 24*, 569–590.

Mendes, E., Batorowicz, B., Jennische, M., Oxley, J., von Tetzchner, S. & Launonen, K. (2023) Uncovering children's views on being an aided communicator. *Presented at 19th Biennial Conference of the International Society for Augmentative and Alternative Communication*, Cancun, Mexico, July 24–27 2023.

Mendes, E. & Rato, J. (1996) From system to communication: Staff training for attitude change. In S. von Tetzchner and M. H. Jensen (Eds.), *Augmentative and alternative communication: European perspectives* (pp. 342–354). London: Whurr/Wiley.

Mertala, P., Karikoski, H., Tähtinen, L. & Sarenius, V. M. (2016) The value of toys: 6–8-year-old children's toy preferences and the functional analysis of popular toys. *International Journal of Play, 5*, 11–27.

Mesibov, G. B. & Shea, V. (2010) The TEACCH program in the era of evidence-based practice. *Journal of Autism and Developmental Disorders, 40*, 570–579.

Mesibov, G. B., Shea, V. & Schopler, E. (2004) *The TEACCH approach to autism spectrum disorders*. New York: Springer.

Meuris, K., Maes, B., De Meyer, A. M. & Zink, I. (2014) Manual signing in adults with intellectual disability: Influence of sign characteristics on functional sign vocabulary. *Journal of Speech, Language, and Hearing Research, 57*, 990–1010.

Meuris, K., Maes, B. & Zink, I. (2015) Teaching adults with intellectual disability manual signs through their support staff: A key word signing program. *American Journal of Speech-Language Pathology, 24*, 545–560.

Midtlin, H. S., Næss, K. A. B., Taxt, T. & Karlsen, A. V. (2015) What communication strategies do AAC users want their communication partners to use? A preliminary study. *Disability and Rehabilitation, 37*, 1260–1267.

Millar, D. C., Light, J. C. & Schlosser, R. W. (2006) The impact of augmentative and alternative communication intervention on the speech production of individuals with developmental disabilities: A research review. *Journal of Speech, Language, and Hearing Research, 49*, 248–264.

Miller, M. S. (1987) Sign iconicity: Single-sign receptive vocabulary skills of nonsigning hearing preeschoolers. *Journal of Communication Disorders, 20*, 359–365.

Mills, J. & Higgins, J. (1984) An environmental approach to delivery of microcomputer-based and other communication systems. *Seminars in Speech and Language, 5*, 35–45.

Milward, S. J. & Carpenter, M. (2018) Joint action and joint attention: Drawing parallels between the literatures. *Social and Personality Psychology Compass, 12*, e12377.

Mishra, A., Ceballos, V., Himmelwright, K., McCabe, S. & Scott, L. (2021) Gesture production in toddlers with autism spectrum disorder. *Journal of Autism and Developmental Disorders, 51*, 1658–1667

Misra, V., Pandey, D. J., Sharma, B. D. & Maheshwari, B. B. (2019) Evaluation of correlation between ocular manifestations and severity of mental retardation. *Journal of Advanced Medical and Dental Sciences Research, 7*, 136–139.

Mitra, S. (2018) *Disability, health and human development*. New York: Plagrave Macmillan.

Mitteer, D. R., Randall, K. R., Van Winkle, L. J. & Greer, B. D. (2020) Incorporating discriminative stimuli into functional communication training with augmentative and alternative communication devices: A tutorial. *Augmentative and Alternative Communication*, *36*, 63–70.
Miyake, A. & Friedman, N. P. (2012) The nature and organization of individual differences in executive functions: Four general conclusions. *Current Directions in Psychological Science*, *21*, 8–14.
Mizuko, M. (1987) Transparency and ease of learning of symbols represented by Blissymbols, PCS, and Picsyms. *Augmentative and Alternative Communication*, *3*, 129–136.
Mohan, M., Bajaj, G., Deshpande, A., Anakkathil Anil, M. & Bhat, J. S. (2021) Child, parent, and play – An insight into these dimensions among children with and without receptive expressive language disorder using video-based analysis. *Psychology Research and Behavior Management*, *14*, 971–985.
Møller, S. & von Tetzchner, S. (1996) Allowing for developmental potential: A case study of intervention change. In S. von Tetzchner and M. H. Jensen (Eds.), *Augmentative and alternative communication: European perspectives* (pp. 249–269). London: Whurr/Wiley.
Molinaro, M., Broman, A. T., Rathouz, P. J. & Hustad, K. C. (2020) Longitudinal development of receptive vocabulary in children with cerebral palsy and anarthria: Use of the MacArthur-Bates CDI. *Developmental Neurorehabilitation*, *23*, 285–293.
Montag, J. L., Jones, M. N. & Smith, L. B. (2018) Quantity and diversity: Simulating early word learning environments. *Cognitive Science*, *42*, 375–412.
Moorcroft, A., Scarinci, N. & Meyer, C. (2019) A systematic review of the barriers and facilitators to the provision and use of low-tech and unaided AAC systems for people with complex communication needs and their families. *Disability and Rehabilitation: Assistive Technology*, *14*, 710–731.
Moorcroft, A., Scarinci, N. & Meyer, C. (2020) 'We were just kind of handed it and then it was smoke bombed by everyone': How do external stakeholders contribute to parent rejection and the abandonment of AAC systems? *International Journal of Language and Communication Disorders*, *55*, 59–69.
Moorcroft, A., Scarinci, N. & Meyer, C. (2021) "I've had a love-hate, I mean mostly hate relationship with these PODD books": Parent perceptions of how they and their child contributed to AAC rejection and abandonment. *Disability and Rehabilitation: Assistive Technology*, *16*, 72–82.
Moore, S. M. & Pérez-Méndez, C. (2006) Working with linguistically diverse families in early intervention: Misconceptions and missed opportunities. *Seminars in Speech and Language*, *27*, 187–198.
Moores, D. F. (2010) The history of language and communication issues in deaf education. In M. Marschark and P. E. Spencer (Eds.), *The Oxford handbook of deaf studies, language, and education*, Volume 2 (pp. 17–30). Oxford, UK: Oxford University Press.
Morel, G. M. & Spector, J. M. (2023) *Foundations of educational technology: Integrative approaches and interdisciplinary perspectives*, 3rd edition. Abingdon, UK: Routledge.
Morgan, J. L. & Demuth, K. (Eds.) (1996) *Signal to syntax: Bootstrapping from speech to grammar in early acquisition*. New York: Psychology Press.
Mphahlele, L. (2020) Context-specific inclusive education: A local perspective on the enterprise. *Educational Research and Reviews*, *15*, 210–213.
Muharib, R. & Alzrayer, N. M. (2018) The use of high-tech speech-generating devices as an evidence-based practice for children with autism spectrum disorders: A meta-analysis. *Review Journal of Autism and Developmental Disorders*, *5*, 43–57.
Mundy, P. & Bullen, J. (2022) The bidirectional social-cognitive mechanisms of the social-attention symptoms of autism. *Frontiers in Psychiatry*, *12*, 752274.
Mundy, P., Delgado, C., Block, J., Venezia, M., Hogan, A. & Seibert, J. (2003a). *Early social communication scales (ESCS)*. Coral Gables, FL: University of Miami.
Mundy, P., Delgado, C., Block, J., Venezia, M., Hogan, A. & Seibert, J. (2003b) *A manual for the abridged early social communication scales*. Coral Gables, FL: University of Miami.
Mundy, P., Sigman, M. & Kasari, C. (1990) A longitudinal study of joint attention and language development in autistic children. *Journal of Autism and Developmental Disorders*, *20*, 115–128.
Murphy, J., & Cameron, L. (2008) The effectiveness of Talking Mats® with people with intellectual disability. *British Journal of Learning Disabilities*, *36*, 232–241.

Murray, J., Lynch, Y., Goldbart, J., Moulam, L., Judge, S. et al. (2020) The decision-making process in recommending electronic communication aids for children and young people who are non-speaking: The I-ASC mixed-methods study. *Health Services and Delivery Research, 8*, 1–158.

Murray, J., Sandberg, A. D., Smith, M. M., Deliberato, D., Stadskleiv, K. & von Tetzchner, S. (2018) Communicating the unknown: Descriptions of pictured scenes and events presented on video by children and adolescents using aided communication and their peers using natural speech. *Augmentative and Alternative Communication, 34*, 30–39.

Murza, K. A., Schwartz, J. B., Hahs-Vaughn, D. L. & Nye, C. (2016) Joint attention interventions for children with autism spectrum disorder: A systematic review and meta-analysis. *International Journal of Language and Communication Disorders, 51*, 236–251.

Musiek, F. E., Chermak, G. D. & Cone, B. (2019) Central deafness: A review of past and current perspectives. *International Journal of Audiology, 58*, 605–617.

Naber, F. B. A., Bakermans-Kranenburg, M. J., van IJzendoorn, M. H., Dietz, C., van Daalen, E. et al. (2008) Joint attention development in toddlers with autism. *European Child and Adolescent Psychiatry, 17*, 143–152.

Nader, D. T. & Erickson, K. A. (2023) Teletherapy, AAC and COVID-19: The experiences of speech language pathologists providing teletherapy during a global pandemic. *Augmentative and Alternative Communication, 39*, 146–156

Nagy, W. E. & Anderson, R. C. (1984) How many words are there in printed school English? *Reading Research Quarterly, 19*, 304–330.

Nagy, W. & Townsend, D. (2012) Words as tools: Learning academic vocabulary as language acquisition. *Reading Research Quarterly, 47*, 91–108.

Naidoo, M. & Singh, S. (2020) A dental communication board as an oral care tool for children with autism spectrum disorder *Journal of Autism and Developmental Disorders, 50*, 3831–3843.

Napier, J. & Leeson, L. (2016) *Sign language in action*. Basingstoke, UK: Palgrave Macmillan.

Naples, A., Tenenbaum, E. J., Jones, R. N., Righi, G., Sheinkopf, S. J. & Eigsti, I. M. (2023) Exploring communicative competence in autistic children who are minimally verbal: The Low Verbal Investigatory Survey for Autism (LVIS). *Autism, 27*, 1391–1406.

Napoli, D. J. (2019) Morphological theory and sign languages. In J. Audring and F. Masini (Eds.), *The Oxford handbook of morphological theory* (pp. 594–614). Oxford, UK: Oxford Univerwsity Press.

Napoli, D. J. & Sutton-Spence, R. (2014) Order of the major constituents in sign languages: Implications for all language. *Frontiers in Psychology, 5*, 376.

Narayanan, U. G., Fehlings, D., Weir, S., Knights, S., Kiran, S. & Campbell, K. (2006) Initial development and validation of the Caregiver Priorities and Child Health Index of Life with Disabilities (CPCHILD). *Developmental Medicine and Child Neurology, 48*, 804–812.

Nation, I. S. P. (2015) Which words do you need? In J. R. Taylor (Ed.) *Handbook of the word* (pp. 568–581). Oxford, UK: Oxford University Press.

Navarro, I. I., Cretcher, S. R., McCarron, A. R., Figueroa, C. & Alt, M. (2020) Using AAC to unlock communicative potential in late-talking toddlers. *Journal of Communication Disorders, 87*, 106025.

Neisworth, J. T. & Bagnato, S. J. (2004) The mismeasure of young children The authentic assessment alternative. *Infants and Young Children, 17*, 198–212.

Nelson, K. E., Camarata, S. M., Welsh, J., Butkovsky, L. & Camarata, M. (1996) Effects of imitative and conversational recasting treatment on the acquisition of grammar in children with specific language impairment and younger language-normal children. *Journal of Speech and Hearing Research, 39*, 850–859.

Nelson, K. (1996) *Language in cognitive development: The emergence of the mediated mind*. Cambridge, MA: Cambridge University Press.

Nelson, K. (2007) *Young minds in social worlds: Experience, meaning and memory*. Cambridge, MA: Cambridge University Press

Nelson, K. (2010) Developmental narratives of the experiencing child. *Child Development Perspectives, 4*, 42–47.

Nelson, K. (2015) Making sense with private speech. *Cognitive Development*, *36*, 171–179.

Nerișanu, R., Nerișanu, R.-A., Maniu, I. & Neamțu, B. (2017) Cerebral palsy and eye-gaze technology. Interaction, perspective and usability. A review. *Acta Medica Transilvanica*, *22*, 59–62.

Neul, J. L., Kaufmann, W. E., Glaze, D. G., Christodoulou, J., Clarke, A. J. et al. (2010) Rett syndrome: Revised diagnostic criteria and nomenclature. *Annals of Neurology*, *68*, 944–950.

Neuvonen, K., Launonen, K., Smith, M., Stadskleiv, K. & von Tetzchner, S. (2022a) Strategies in conveying information about unshared events using aided communication. *Child Language Teaching and Therapy*, *38*, 78–94.

Neuvonen, K. A., Smith, M. M., Launonen, K. & von Tetzchner, S. (2022b) Communication partner strategies in negotiation for meaning in interactions involving aided communication. *Clinical Linguistics and Phonetics*, *37*, 1104–1123.

Neuvonen, K., van Balkom, H., Deliberato, D. & von Tetzchner, S. (2022c) Vocabulary use in aided communication. In S. von Tetzchner and J. Murray (Eds.), *Becoming an Aided Communicator (BAC): Theory, methods, findings and practical implications. Proceedings of a study day, University of Leeds, June 21st 2022* (pp. 21–26). Leeds, UK: Communication Matters.

Newell, A. F., Booth, L. & Beattie, W. (1991) Predictive text entry with PAL and children with learning difficulties. *British Journal of Educational Techneology*, *22*, 23–40.

Newport, E. L. (2016) Statistical language learning: Computational, maturational, and linguistic constraints. *Language and Cognition*, *8*, 447–461.

Newport, E. L., Bavelier, D. & Neville, H. J. (2001) Critical thinking about critical periods: Perspectives on a critical period for language acquisition. In E. Dupoux (Ed., *Language, brain and cognitive development: Essays in honor of Jacques Mehler* (pp. 481–502). Cambridge, MA: MIT Press.

Nguyen, L., Bootsma, J., Ketelaar, M., Di Rezze, B., Jack, S. M. & Gorter, J. W. (2023) Programs to prepare siblings for future roles to support their brother or sister with a neurodevelopmental disability: A scoping review. *Current Developmental Disorders Reports*, *10*, 47–79.

Nigam, R., Schlosser, R. W. & Lloyd, L. L. (2006) Concomitant use of the matrix strategy and the mand-model procedure in teaching graphic symbol combinations. *Augmentative and Alternative Communication*, *22*, 160–177.

Nikolaus, M. & Fourtassi, A. (2023) Communicative feedback in language acquisition. *New Ideas in Psychology*, *68*, 100985.

Nippold, M. A., Frantz-Kaspar, M. W., Cramond, P. M., Kirk, C., Hayward-Mayhew, C. & MacKinnon, M. (2014) Conversational and narrative speaking in adolescents: Examining the use of complex syntax. *Journal of Speech, Language, and Hearing Research*, *57*, 876–886.

Norrelgen, F., Fernell, E., Eriksson, M., Hedvall, Å., Persson, C. et al. (2015) Children with autism spectrum disorders who do not develop phrase speech in the preschool years. *Autism*, *19*, 934–943.

Norrie, C. S., Waller, A. & Hannah, E. F. (2021) Establishing context: AAC device adoption and support in a special-education setting. *ACM Transactions on Computer-Human Interaction*, *28*, 1–30.

Novak, I., Hines, M., Goldsmith, S. & Barclay, R. (2012) Clinical prognostic messages from a systematic review on cerebral palsy. *Pediatrics*, *130*, e1285–1312.

Ntoa, S., Margetis, G., Antona, M. & Stephanidis, C. (2014) Scanning-based interaction techniques for motor impaired users. In G. Kouroupetroglou (Ed.), *Assistive technologies and computer access for motor disabilities* (pp. 57–89). Hershey, PA: IGI Global.

Nunes, D. R. (2008) AAC Interventions for autism: A research summary. *International Journal of Special Education*, *23*, 17–26.

O'Connor, D., Butler, A. & Lynch, H. (2021) Partners in play: Exploring 'playing with'children living with severe physical and intellectual disabilities. *British Journal of Occupational Therapy*, *84*, 694–702.

O'Keeffe, G. S. (2016) Social media: Challenges and concerns for families. *Pediatric Clinics*, *63*, 841–849.

O'Neill, J., Bansal, R., Goh, S., Rodie, M., Sawardekar, S. & Peterson, B. S. (2020) Parsing the heterogeneity of brain metabolic disturbances in autism spectrum disorder. *Biological Psychiatry*, *87*, 174–184.

O'Neill, T. (2018) Perspectives of parents of children with cerebral palsy on the supports, challenges, and realities of integrating AAC into everyday life. Dissertation, Pennsylvania State University.

O'Neill, T., Light, J. & Pope, L. (2018) Effects of interventions that include aided augmentative and alternative communication input on the communication of individuals with complex communication needs: A meta-analysis. *Journal of Speech, Language, and Hearing Research*, *61*, 1743–1765.

O'Neill, T. & Wilkinson, K. M. (2020) Preliminary investigation of the perspectives of parents of children with cerebral palsy on the supports, challenges, and realities of integrating augmentative and alternative communication into everyday life. *American Journal of Speech-Language Pathology*, *29*, 238–254.

O'Neill, Y. V. (1980) *Speech and speech disorders in Western thought before 1600*. London: Greenwood Press.

Oates, A., Bebbington, A., Bourke, J., Girdler, S. & Leonard, H. (2011) Leisure participation for school-aged children with Down syndrome. *Disability and Rehabilitation*, *33*, 1880–1889.

Occhino, C., Anible, B., Wilkinson, E. & Morford, J. P. (2017) Iconicity is in the eye of the beholder: How language experience affects perceived iconicity. *Gesture*, *16*, 100–126.

Olaszi, P., Koutny, I. & Kálmán, S. L. (2002) From bliss symbols to grammatically correct voice output: A communication tool for people with disabilities. *International Journal of Speech Technology*, *5*, 49–56.

Oliver, C. B. & Halle, J. W. (1982) Language training in the everyday environment. *Journal of the Association for the Severely Handicapped*, *8*, 50–62.

Oliver, C., Ellis, K., Agar, G., Bissell, S., Chung, J. C. Y. et al. (2022) Distress and challenging behavior in people with profound or severe intellectual disability and complex needs: Assessment of causes and evaluation of intervention outcomes. *International Review of Research in Developmental Disabilities*, *62*, 109–189.

Oliver, M. (2019) Communication devices and electronic aids to activities of daily living. In J. B. Webster and F. P. Murphy (Eds.), *Atlas of orthoses and assistive devices*, 5th edition (pp. 403–417). Philadelphia, PA: Elsevier.

Olsson, B. & Rett, A. (1987) Autism and Rett syndrome: Behaviourial investigations and differential diagnosis. *Developmental Medicine and Child Neurology*, *29*, 429–441.

Olsson, B. & Rett, A. (1990) A review of the Rett syndrome with a theory of autism. *Brain and Development*, *12*, 11–15.

Oommen, E. R. & McCarthy, J. W. (2015) Simultaneous natural speech and AAC interventions for children with childhood apraxia of speech: Lessons from a speech-language pathologist focus group. *Augmentative and Alternative Communication*, *31*, 63–76.

Orellana, C. I., Wada, R. & Gillam, R. B. (2019) The use of dynamic assessment for the diagnosis of language disorders in bilingual children: A meta-analysis. *American Journal of Speech-Language Pathology*, *28*, 1298–1317.

Ortega, G. (2017) Iconicity and sign lexical acquisition: A review. *Frontiers in Psychology*, *8*, 1280.

Ortibus, E., Fazzi, E. & Dale, N. (2019) Cerebral visual impairment and clinical assessment: The European perspective. *Seminars in Pediatric Neurology*, 31, 15–24.

Østvik, J., Balandin, S. & Ytterhus, B. (2018) Interactional facilitators and barriers to social relationships between students who use AAC and fellow students. *Society, Health and Vulnerability*, *9*, 1438692.

Ottem, E. (2001) Use of pictographic-articulatory symbols to promote alphabetic reading in a language-impaired boy: Case study. *Augmentative and Alternative Communication*, *17*, 52–60.

Osguthorpe, R. T. & Chang, L. L. (1987) Computerized symbol processors for individuals with severe communication disabilities. *Journal of Special Education Technology*, *8*, 43–54.

Oxley, J. D. & von Tetzchner, S. (1999) Reflections on the development of alternative language forms. In F. T. Loncke et al. (Eds.), *Augmentative and alternative communication: New directions in research and practice* (pp. 62–74). London: Whurr/Wiley.

Paget, R., Gorman, P. & Paget, P. (1976) *The Paget Gorman sign system*, 6th edition. London: Association for Experiment in Deaf Education.

Palfreman, J. (2012) The dark legacy of FC. *Evidence-Based Communication Assessment and Intervention, 6*, 14–17.
Palisano, R. J., Rosenbaum, P., Bartlett, D. & Livingston, M. H. (2008) Content validity of the expanded and revised Gross Motor Function Classification System. *Developmental Medicine and Child Neurology, 50*, 744–750.
Palisano, R., Rosenbaum, P., Walter, S., Russell, D., Wood, E. & Galuppi, B. (1997) Development and reliability of a system to classify gross motor function in children with cerebral palsy. *Developmental Medicine and Child Neurology, 39*, 214–223.
Pan, B. A. & Snow, C. E. (1999) The development of conversational and discourse skills. In M. Barrett (Ed.), *Development of language* (pp. 229–249). Hove, UK: Psychology Press.
Paolieri, D. & Marful, A. (2018) Norms for a pictographic system: The Aragonese portal of augmentative/alternative communication (ARASAAC) system. *Frontiers in Psychology, 9*, 2538.
Papacek, A. M., Chai, Z. & Green, K. B. (2016) Play and social interaction strategies for young children with autism spectrum disorder in inclusive preschool settings. *Young Exceptional Children, 19*, 3–17.
Parette, H. P., Boeckmann, N. M. & Hourcade, J. J. (2008) Use of writing with symbols 2000 software to facilitate emergent literacy development. *Early Childhood Education Journal, 36*, 161–170.
Park, I. & Kim, Y. R. (2018) Effects of TEACCH structured teaching on independent work skills among individuals with severe disabilities. *Education and Training in Autism and Developmental Disabilities, 53*, 343–352.
Park, K. (1997) How do objects become object of reference? *British Journal of Special Education, 24*, 103–114.
Parrott, L. (2016) Communication participation of adults who are lifelong aided communicators. In M. M. Smith and J. Murray (Eds.), *The silent partner? Language, interaction and aided communication* (pp. 247–267). Guildford, UK: J&R Press.
Partey, F. A., Addo-Danquah, R. G., Bonku, L. K. & Sarfo-Adu, K. (2018) Investigating unconventional abbreviations in SMS texts. *International Journal of Applied Linguistics and English Literature, 7*, 25–32.
Paul, R. & Elwood, T. J. (1991) Maternal linguistic input to toddlers with slow expressive language development. *Journal of Speech, Language, and Hearing Research, 34*, 982–988.
Paul, R. (1997) Facilitating transitions in language development for children using AAC. *Augmentative and Alternative Communication, 13*, 141–148.
Paul, R. (2020) Language disorders. In A. Gallagher et al. (Eds.), *Handbook of clinical neurology*, Volume 174 (pp. 21–35). Amsterdam: Elsevier.
Paulson, A. & Vargus-Adams, J. (2017) Overview of four functional classification systems commonly used in cerebral palsy. *Children, 4*, 30.
Pecukonis, M., Skwerer, D. P., Eggleston, B., Meyer, S. & Tager-Flusberg, H. (2019) Concurrent social communication predictors of expressive language in minimally verbal children and adolescents with autism spectrum disorder. *Journal of Autism and Developmental Disorders, 49*, 3767–3785.
Pellegrini, A. D. (2013) Play. In P. D. Zelazo (Ed.), *Oxford handbook of developmental psychology, Volume 2: Self and other* (pp. 276–298). New York: Oxford University Press.
Peña, E. V. (Ed.) (2019) *Communication alternatives in autism: Perspectives on typing and spelling approaches for the nonspeaking*. Jefferson, NC: McFarland.
Pennington, B. F. (2015) Atypical cognitive development. In R. M. Lerner et al. (Eds.) *Handbook of child psychology and Developmental Science, Seventh edition, Volume 2: Cognitive Processes* (pp. 995–1037). New York: Wiley.
Pennington, L. & McConachie, H. (1999) Mother–child interaction revisited: Communication with non-speaking physically disabled children. *International Journal of Language and Communication Disorders, 34*, 391–416.
Pennington, L. & McConachie, H. (2001) Interaction between children with cerebral palsy and their mothers: The effects of speech intelligibility. *International Journal of Language and Communication Disorders, 36*, 371–393.

Pennington, L., Virella, D., Mjøen, T., da Graça Andrada, M., Murray, J. et al. (2013) Development of The Viking Speech Scale to classify the speech of children with cerebral palsy. *Research in Developmental Disabilities*, *34*, 3202–3210.

Percy, A. K., Lane, J., Annese, F., Warren, H., Skinner, S. A. & Neul, J. L. (2018) When Rett syndrome is due to genes other than MECP2. *Translational Science of Rare Diseases*, *3*, 49–53.

Pereira, J. A., de Medeiros, S., Zanchettin, C. & Fidalgo, R. D. N. (2022) Pictogram prediction in alternative communication boards: A mapping study. In *Anais do III Simpósio Brasileiro de Informática na Educação* (pp. 705–717). Porto Alegere, Brazil: SBC.

Pérez-Pereira, M. & Conti-Ramsden, G. (1999) *Language development and social interaction in blind children*. Hove, UK: Psychology Press.

Pérez-Pereira, M. & Conti-Ramsden, G. (2020) *Language development and social interaction in blind children*, Classic edition. Abingdon, UK: Routledge.

Perfect, E., Hoskin, E., Noyek, S. & Davies, T. C. (2020) A systematic review investigating outcome measures and uptake barriers when children and youth with complex disabilities use eye gaze assistive technology. *Developmental Neurorehabilitation*, *23*, 145–159.

Perfetti, C. A., & Dunlap, S (2008) Learning to read: General principles and writing system variations. In K. Koda and A. M. Zehler (Eds.), *Learning to read across languages* (pp. 13–38). Abingdon, UK: Routledge.

Perone, S. & Simmering, V. R. (2017) Applications of dynamic systems theory to cognition and development: New frontiers. *Advances in Child Development and Behavior*, *52*, 43–80.

Persicke, A., Meshes, E., Najdowski, A. C. & Moon, E. I. (2023) Teaching play skills. In J. L. Matson (Ed.), *Handbook of applied behavior analysis: Integrating research into practice* (pp. 963–977). Cham, Switzerland: Springer.

Persico, A. M. & Napolioni, V. (2013) Autism genetics. *Behavioral Brain Research*, *251*, 95–112.

Petalas, M. A., Hastings, R. P., Nash, S. & Duff, S. (2015) Typicality and subtle difference in sibling relationships: Experiences of adolescents with autism. *Journal of Child and Family Studies*, *24*, 38–49.

Peters, A. M. (1995) Strategies in the acquisition of syntax. In P. Fletcher and B. MacWhinney (Eds), *The handbook of child language* (pp. 462–482). Oxford, UK: Basil Blackwell.

Peters, A. M. & Boggs, S. T. (1986) Interactional routines as cultural influences on language acquisition. In B. Schieffelin and E. Ochs (Eds.), *Language socialization across cultures* (pp. 80–96). Cambridge: Cambridge University Press.

Peters, B., Eddy, B., Galvin-McLaughlin, D., Betz, G., Oken, B. & Fried-Oken, M. (2022) A systematic review of research on augmentative and alternative communication brain-computer interface systems for individuals with disabilities. *Frontiers in Human Neuroscience*, *16*, 952380.

Peters, N. A. & Kirstein, I J. (1978) A communication system for nonoral handicapped children. *Rehabilitation Psychology*, *25*, 213–219.

Petersen, J. M., Marinova-Todd, S. H. & Mirenda, P. (2012) An exploratory study of lexical skills in bilingual children with autism spectrum disorder. *Journal of Autism and Developmental Disorders*, *42*, 1499–1503.

Pfeifer, L. I., Pacciulio, A. M., Santos, C. A. D., Santos, J. L. D. & Stagnitti, K. E. (2011) Pretend play of children with cerebral palsy. *Physical and Occupational Therapy in Pediatrics*, *31*, 390–402.

Phillips, W., Gómez, J. C., Baron-Cohen, S., Laá, V. & Rivière, A. (1995) Treating people as objects, agents, or "subjects": How young children with and without autism make requests. *Journal of Child Psychology and Psychiatry*, *36*, 1383–1398.

Piaget, J. (1950) *The psychology of the child*. London: Routledge and Kegan Paul.

Piaget, J. (1951) *Play, dreams and imitation in childhood*. London: Heineman.

Piaget, J. & Inhelder, B. (1969) *The psychology of the child*. London: Routledge and Kegan Paul.

Piantadosi, S. T., Tily, H. & Gibson, E. (2012) The communicative function of ambiguity in language. *Cognition*, *122*, 280–291.

Pickett, E., Pullara, O., O'Grady, J. & Gordon, B. (2009) Speech acquisition in older nonverbal individuals with autism: A review of features, methods, and prognosis. *Cognitive and Behavioral Neurology*, *22*, 1–21.

Picton, T. W. (2010) *Human auditory evoked potentials*. Abingdon, UK: Plural Publishing.

Pilesjö, M. S. & Norén, N. (2017) Teaching communication aid use in everyday conversation. *Child Language Teaching and Therapy*, *33*, 241–253.

Pinkoski-Ball, C., Reichle, J. & Munson, B. (2012) Synthesized speech intelligibility and early preschool-age children: Comparing accuracy for single-word repetition with repeated exposure. *American Journal of Speech-Language Pathology*, *21*, 293–301,

Pirila, S., van der Meere, J., Pentikainen, T., Ruusu-Niemi, P., Korpela, R. & Kilpinen, J. (2007) Language and motor speech skills in children with cerebral palsy. *Journal of Communication Disorders*, *40*, 116–128.

Pizzuto, E. & Volterra, V. (2000) Iconicity and transparency in sign languages: A cross-linguistic cross-cultural view. In K. Emmorey and H. Lane (Eds.), *The signs of language revisited* (pp. 261–286). Mahwah, NJ: Lawrence Erlbaum.

Plante, E., Ogilvie, T., Vance, R., Aguilar, J. M., Dailey, N. S. et al. (2014) Variability in the language input to children enhances learning in a treatment context. *American Journal of Speech-Language Pathology*, *23*, 530–545.

Ploog, B. O. (2010) Stimulus overselectivity four decades later: A review of the literature and its implications for current research in autism spectrum disorder. *Journal of Autism and Developmental Disorders*, *40*, 1332–1349.

Pohodich, A. E. & Zoghbi, H. Y. (2015) Rett syndrome: Disruption of epigenetic control of postnatal neurological functions. *Human Molecular Genetics*, *24*, R10–R16.

Porter, G. & Cafiero, J. M. (2009) Pragmatic organization dynamic display (PODD) communication books: A promising practice for individuals with autism spectrum disorders. *Perspectives on Augmentative and Alternative Communication*, *18*, 121–129.

Potharaju, N. R. (2022) Excessive crying in children with cerebral palsy and communication deficits. *Neurology*, *11*, 25–44.

Poulin-Dubois, D. & Graham, S. A. (1994) Infant categorization and early object–word meaning. In A. Vyt et al. (Eds.), *Early child development in the French tradition: Contributions from current research* (pp. 207–225). Hillsdale, NJ: Erlbaum.

Presson, A. P., Partyka, G., Jensen, K. M., Devine, O. J., Rasmussen, S. A. et al. (2013) Current estimate of Down syndrome population prevalence in the United States. *The Journal of Pediatrics*, *163*, 1163–1168.

Price, J. R., Vizoso, A., Ellerbee, T., Roberts, J. E. & Sideris, J. (2018) Communication breakdowns and repair strategies of children with Down syndrome. *Advances in Neurodevelopmental Disorders*, *2*, 16–24.

Prizant, B. (2009) Treatment options and parent choice: Is ABA the only way? *Autism Spectrum Quarterly, Spring*, 28–31.

Pujol, C. L., Nevares, A. & Schladant, M. (2021) Increasing access to augmentative and alternative communication services for people with complex communication needs during Covid-19 and beyond. *Developmental Disabilities Network Journal*, *1*, 170–191.

Pullin, G. & Hennig, S. (2015) 17 ways to say yes: Toward nuanced tone of voice in AAC and speech technology. *Augmentative and Alternative Communication*, *31*, 170–180

Purwowibowo, P., Hendrijanto, K. & Trihartono, A. (2018) Total communication learning model: Using pictures, writing and reading to increase language capacity for deaf children. *Advances in Social Science, Education and Humanities Research*, *307*, 99–102.

Quinto-Pozos, D. & Adam, R. (2020) Language contact considering sign language. In A. P. Grant (Ed.), *The Oxford handbook of language contact* (pp. 679–693). Oxford, UK: Oxford University Press.

Qvortrup, A. & Qvortrup, L. (2018) Inclusion: Dimensions of inclusion in education. *International Journal of Inclusive Education*, *22*, 803–817,

Radhakrishnan, S., Gerow, S. & Weston, R. (2020) Resurgence of challenging behavior following functional communication training for children with disabilities: A literature review. *Journal of Developmental and Physical Disabilities*, *32*, 213–239.

Radici, E., Heboyan, V., Mantovani, F. & De Leo, G. (2022) Attitudes and perceived communicative competence: The impact of different AAC means of communication among Italian teenagers. *International Journal of Disability, Development and Education*, *69*, 976–986.

Raghavendra, P. & Fristoe, M. (1990) "A spinach with a V on it": What 3-year-olds see in standard and enhanced Blissymbols. *Journal of Speech and Hearing Disorders*, *55*, 149–159.

Raghavendra, P. & Fristoe, M. (1995) "No shoes; they walked away?": Effects of enhancement on learning and using Blissymbols by normal 3-year-old children. *Journal of Speech and Hearing Research*, *38*, 174–188.

Ramer, A. (1976) Syntactic styles in emerging language. *Journal of Child Language*, *3*, 49–62.

Rangel-Rodríguez, G. A., Badia, M. & Blanch, S. (2021) Encouraging emotional conversations in children with complex communication needs: An observational case study. *Frontiers in Psychology*, *12*, 2225.

Rankin, J. L., Harwood, K. & Mirenda, P. (1994) Influence of graphic symbol use on reading cmprehension. *Augmentative and Alternative Communication*, *10*, 269–281.

Rapin, I., Dunn, M. A., Allen, D. A., Stevens, M. C. & Fein, D. (2009) Subtypes of language disorders in school-age children with autism. *Developmental Neuropsychology*, *34*, 66–84.

Rapp, J. T., Cook, J. L., Nuta, R., Balagot, C., Crouchman, K. et al. (2019) Further evaluation of a practitioner model for increasing eye contact in children with autism. *Behavior Modification*, *43*, 389–412.

Ratcliff, A. E. (1994) Comparison of realtive demands implicated in direct selection and scanning: Considerations from normal children. *Augmentative and Alternative Communication*, *10*, 67–74.

Ratcliff, A. E. & Cress, C. J. (1998) Guidelines for enhancing reciprocal peer communication with adolescents who use augmentative/alternative communication. *Journal of Children's Communication Development*, *20*, 25–35.

Rebuschat, P. (Ed.) (2015) *Implicit and explicit learning of languages*. Amsterdam: John Benjamins.

Reetzke, R., Zou, X., Sheng, L. & Katsos, N. (2015) Communicative development in bilingually exposed Chinese children with autism spectrum disorders. *Journal of Speech, Language, and Hearing Research*, *58*, 813–825.

Reichle, J., O'Neill, R. E. & Johnston, S. S. (2021) Advances in AAC intervention: Some contributions related to applied behavior analysis. *Augmentative and Alternative Communication*, *37*, 206–216.

Reichle, J. & Ward, M. (1985) Teaching discriminative use of an encoding electronic communication device and Signing Exact English to a moderately handicapped child. *Language, Speech, and Hearing Services in Schools*, *16*, 58–63.

Renieri, A., Mari, F., Mencarelli, M. A., Scala, E., Ariani, F. et al. (2009) Diagnostic criteria for the Zappella variant of Rett syndrome (the preserved speech variant). *Brain and Development*, *31*, 208–216.

Renner, G. (2014) Semiotic aspects of graphic signs in general and blissymbolics specifically. In L. L. Lloyd et al. (Eds.), *Augmentative and alternative communication: Research issues and needs. Proceedings of the 13th Biennial Research Symposium of the International Society for Augmentative and Alternative Communication, Pittsburg, USA, August 3–4, 2012* (pp. 77–90). Toronto: ISAAC.

Resch, J. A., Mireles, G., Benz, M. R., Grenwelge, C., Peterson, R. & Zhang, D. (2010) Giving parents a voice: A qualitative study of the challenges experienced by parents of children with disabilities. *Rehabilitation Psychology*, *55*, 139–150.

Rescorla, L. A., Ginzburg, S., Achenbach, T. M., Ivanova, M. Y., Almqvist, F. et al. (2013) Cross-informant agreement between parent-reported and adolescent self-reported problems in 25 societies. *Journal of Clinical Child and Adolescent Psychology*, *42*, 262–273.

Rescorla, L. A. & Schwartz, E. (1990) Outcome of toddlers with specific expressive language delay. *Applied Psycholinguistics*, *11*, 393–407.

Reyes-Martín, J., Simó-Pinatella, D. & Font-Roura, J. (2022) Assessment of challenging behavior exhibited by people with intellectual and developmental disabilities: A systematic review. *International Journal of Environmental Research and Public Health*, *19*, 8701.

Richardson, L., McCoy, A. & McNaughton, D. (2019) "He's worth the extra work": The employment experiences of adults with ASD who use augmentative and alternative communication (AAC) as reported by adults with ASD, family members, and employers. *Work*, *62*, 205–219.

Riddoch, M. J. & Humphreys, G. W. (2003) Visual agnosia. *Neurologic Clinics*, *21*, 501–520.

Rideout, V. (2015) *The common sense census: Media use by tweens and teens*. San Francisco, CA: Common Sense Media.

Ridgway, A. & Quiñones, G. (2020) *Peer play and relationships in early childhood: International research perspectives*. Cham, Switzerland: Springer.

Rinaldi, P. & Caselli, C. (2009) Lexical and grammatical abilities in deaf Italian preschoolers: The role of duration of formal language experience. *Journal of Deaf Studies and Deaf Education*, *14*, 63–75.

Rinaldi, R., Batselé, E. & Haelewyck, M. C. (2022) Attachment and challenging behaviors in adults with intellectual disability: A scoping review. *Journal of Mental Health Research in Intellectual Disabilities*, *15*, 197–216.

Ripat, J. & Becker, P. (2012) Playground usability: What do playground users say? *Occupational Therapy International*, *19*, 144–153.

Robertson, C. E. & Baron-Cohen, S. (2017) Sensory perception in autism. *Nature Reviews Neuroscience*, *18*, 671–684.

Roche, L., Sigafoos, J., Lancioni, G. E., O'Reilly, M. F., Green, V. A. et al. (2014) Tangible symbols as an AAC option for individuals with developmental disabilities: A systematic review of intervention studies. *Augmentative and Alternative Communication*, *30*, 28–39.

Rodríguez-Ortiz, I. R., Pérez, M., Valmaseda, M., Cantillo, C., Díez, M. A. et al. (2020) A Spanish Sign Language (LSE) adaptation of the Communicative Development Inventories. *Journal of Deaf Studies and Deaf Education*, *25*, 105–114.

Rogoff, B. Matusov, E. & White, C. (1996) Models of teaching and learning: Participation in a community of learners. In D. R. Olson and N. Torrance (Eds.), *The handbook of education and human development* (pp. 373–398). Oxford, UK: Blackwell.

Roman-Lantzy, C. (2007) *Cortical visual impairment. An approach to assessment and intervention*. New York: American Foundation for the Blind.

Rombouts, E., Maes, B. & Zink, I. (2017) Maintenance of key word signing in adults with intellectual disabilities: Novel signed turns facilitated by partners' consistent input and sign imitation. *Augmentative and Alternative Communication*, *33*, 121–130.

Rombouts, E., Maessen, B., Maes, B. & Zink, I. (2020) Key word signing has higher iconicity than sign language. *Journal of Speech, Language, and Hearing Research*, *63*, 2418–2424.

Rombouts, E., Sheehy, K., Buchanan-Mellon, J. & Grove, N. (2019) Signing in school. In N. Grove and K. Launonen (Eds.), *Manual sign acquisition in children with developmental disabilities* (pp. 359–377). New York: Nova.

Romski, M. A. & Ruder, K. F. (1984) Effect of speech and speech and sign instruction on oral language learning and generalization of action+object combinations by Down's syndrome children. *Journal of Speech and Hearing Research*, *49*, 293–302.

Romski, M. A. & Sevcik, R. A. (1996) *Breaking the speech barrier*. Baltimore: Paul H. Brookes.

Romski, M. & Sevcik, R. A. (2005) Augmentative communication and early intervention: Myths and realities. *Infants and Young Children*, *18*, 174–185.

Romski, M., Sevcik, R. A., Adamson, L. B., Cheslock, M., Smith, A. et al. (2010) Randomized comparison of augmented and nonaugmented language interventions for toddlers with developmental delays and their parents. *Journal of Speech, Language, and Hearing Research*, *53*, 350–364.

Romski, M., Sevcik, R. A., Barton-Hulsey, A. & Whitmore, A. S. (2015) Early intervention and AAC: What a difference 30 years makes. *Augmentative and Alternative Communication*, *31*, 181–202.

Romski, M. A., Sevcik, R. A. & Fonseca, A. H. (2003) Augmentative and alternative communication for persons with mental retardation. In L. Abbeduto (Ed.), *Language and communication in mental retardation* (pp. 255–280). Boston, MA: Academic Press.

Romski, M. A., Sevcik, R. A. & Pate, J. L. (1988) Establishment of symbolic communication in persons with severe retardation. *Journal of Speech and Hearing Disorders, 53*, 94–107.

Rondal, J. A. (2009) Spoken language in persons with Down syndrome: A life-span perspective. *International Journal of Early Childhood Special Education, 1*, 138–163.

Rosch, E. (1978) Principles of categorization. In E. Rosch and B. B. Lloyd (Eds.), *Cognition and categorization* (pp. 27–48). Hillsdalle, New Jersey: Lawrence Eaarlbaum.

Rose, S. A., Djukic, A., Jankowski, J. J., Feldman, J. F., Fishman, I. & Valicenti-Mcdermott, M. (2013) Rett syndrome: An eye-tracking study of attention and recognition memory. *Developmental Medicine and Child Neurology, 55*, 364–371.

Rosen, N. E., Lord, C. & Volkmar, F. R. (2021) The diagnosis of autism: From Kanner to DSM-III to DSM-5 and beyond. *Journal of Autism and Developmental Disorders, 51*, 4253–4270.

Rosenbaum, P., Eliasson, A. C., Hidecker, M. J. C. & Palisano, R. J. (2014) Classification in childhood disability: Focusing on function in the 21st century. *Journal of Child Neurology, 29*, 1036–1045.

Rosenbaum, P., Paneth, N., Leviton, A., Goldstein, M., Bax, M. et al. (2007) A report: The definition and classification of cerebral palsy April 2006. *Developmental Medicine and Child Neurolology, 49* (Supplement 109), 8–14.

Rossetti, Z. & Hall, S. (2015) Adult sibling relationships with brothers and sisters with severe disabilities. *Research and Practice for Persons with Severe Disabilities, 40*, 120–137.

Rossetti, Z. & Keenan, J. (2018) The nature of friendship between students with and without severe disabilities. *Remedial and Special Education, 39*, 195–210.

Rotenberg, K. J. (1995) Moral development and children's differential disclosure to adults versus peers. In K. J. Rotenberg (Ed.), *Disclosure processes in children and adolescents* (pp. 135–147). Cambridge, UK: Cambridge University Press.

Roth, T. L. & Sweatt, J. D. (2011) Annual research review: Epigenetic mechanisms and environmental shaping of the brain during sensitive periods of development. *Journal of Child Psychology and Psychiatry, 52*, 398–408.

Roth, R. M., Isquith, P. K. & Gioia, G. A. (2013) Assessment of executive functioning using the Behavior Rating Inventory of Executive Function (BRIEF). In S. Goldstein and J. A. Naglieri (Eds.), *Handbook of executive functioning* (pp. 301–331). New York: Springer.

Rowe, M. L., Levine, S. C., Fisher, J. A. & Goldin-Meadow, S. (2009) Does linguistic input play the same role in language learning for children with and without early brain injury? *Developmental Psychology, 45*, 90–102.

Rowe, M. L. & Snow, C. (2020) Analyzing input quality along three dimensions: Interactive, linguistic and conceptual. *Journal of Child Language, 47*, 5–21.

Rowe, M. L. & Weisleder, A. (2020) Language development in context. *Annual Review of Developmental Psychology, 2*, 201–223.

Rowland, C. (2004a) *Communication Matrix*, Revised edition. Portland, OR: Oregon Health and Science University.

Rowland, C. (2004b) *Communication Matrix… Especially for Parents*. Portland, OR: Oregon Health and Science University.

Rowland, C. & Schweigert, P. (2000) Tangible symbols, tangible outcomes. *Augmentative and Alternative Communication, 16*, 61–78.

Rowland, C. & Schweigert, P. (2003) Cognitive skills and AAC. In J. C. Light et al. (Eds.), *Communicative competence for individuals who use AAC* (pp. 241–276). Baltimore, MD: Brookes.

Roy, B. C., Frank, M. C., DeCamp, P., Miller, M. & Roy, D. (2015) Predicting the birth of a spoken word. *Proceedings of the National Academy of Sciences, 112*, 12663–12668.

Roy, P. & Chiat, S. (2022) Design of spoken language tests for hearing L1 children. In T. Haug et al. (Eds.), *The handbook of language assessment across modalities* (pp. 15–27). Oxford, UK: Oxford University Press.

Rudd, H., Grove, N. & Pring, T. (2007) Teaching productive sign modifications to children with intellectual disabilities. *Augmentative and Alternative Communication, 23*, 154–163.

Ruppar, A. L., Dymond, S. K. & Gaffney, J. S. (2011) Teachers' perspectives on literacy instruction for students with severe disabilities who use augmentative and alternative communication. *Research and Practice for Persons with Severe Disabilities*, *36*, 100–111.

Rutherford, M., Baxter, J., Grayson, Z., Johnston, L. & O'Hare, A. (2020a) Visual supports at home and in the community for individuals with autism spectrum disorders: A scoping review. *Autism*, *24*, 447–469.

Rutherford, M., Lahood-Kullberg, B., Baxter, J., Johnston, L. & Cebula, K. (2020b) Pupils' views on visual timetables and labels in mainstream primary classrooms. *Good Autism Practice*, *21*, 11–22.

Rutter, M., Bailey, A. & Lord, C. (2003) SCQ. *The Social Communication Questionnaire*. Torrance, CA: Western Psychological Services.

Ryan, J. (1977) The silence of stupidity. In J. Morton and J. C. Marshall (Eds.), *Psycholinguistic series, Volume 1. Developmental and pathological* (pp. 99–124). London: Elek Science.

Ryan, S. E. & Renzoni, A. M. (2019) *Family Impact of Assistive Technology Scale for Augmentative and Alternative Communication (FIATS-AAC), manual, Volume 2.0*. Toronto: Holland-Bloorview Kids Rehabilitation Hospital.

Ryan, S. E., Shepherd, T. A. & Renzoni, A. M. (2019) *Family Impact of Assistive Technology Scale for Augmentative and Alternative Communication. FIATS-AAC manual, Version 2.0*. Available at: https://www.hollandbloorview.ca/research-education/bloorview-research-institute/outcome-measures/family-impact-assistive-technology

Ryan, S. E., Shepherd, T. A., Renzoni, A. M., Servais, M., Kingsnorth, S. et al. (2018) Responsiveness of a parent-reported outcome measure to evaluate AAC interventions for children and youth with complex communication needs. *Augmentative and Alternative Communication*, *34*, 348–358.

Rytterström, P., Borgestig, M. & Hemmingsson, H. (2016) Teachers' experiences of using eye gaze-controlled computers for pupils with severe motor impairments and without speech. *European Journal of Special Needs Education*, *31*, 506–519.

Sacks, O. (1987) *The man who mistook his wife for a hat*. Cambridge: MIT Press.

Sacks, O. (1996) *The island of the colour-blind*. London, UK: Pan Macmillan.

Saito, Y. & Turnbull, A. (2007) Augmentative and alternative communication practice in the pursuit of family quality of life: A review of the literature. *Research and Practice for Persons with Severe Disabilities*, *32*, 50–65

Salisbury, J. R. (2022) Investigating bilingual AAC practices in bilingual communities. Masters Thesis, University of Massachusetts, Amherst.

Salminen, A.-L. (2001) *Daily life with computer augmented communication*. Helsinki: Stakes National Research and Development Centre for Welfare and Health.

Sameroff, A. J. (Ed.) (2009) *The transactional model of development: How children and contexts shape each other*. Washington, DC: American Psychological Association.

Sameroff, A. J. (2010) A unified theory of development: A dialectic integration of nature and nurture. *Child Development*, *81*, 6–22.

Sameroff, A. J. & Fiese, B. H. (2000) Transactional regulation: The developmental ecology of early intervention. In J. P. Shonkoff and S. J. Meisels (Eds.), *Handbook of early childhood intervention*, 2nd edition (pp. 135–159).

Samuelson, L. K. & McMurray, B. (2017) What does it take to learn a word? *Wiley Interdisciplinary Reviews: Cognitive Science*, *8*, e1421.

Sandhofer, C. & Schonberg, C. (2020) Multiple examples support children's word learning: The roles of aggregation, decontextualization, and memory dynamics. In J. B. Childers (Ed.), *Language and concept acquisition from infancy through childhood: Learning from multiple exemplars* (pp. 159–178). Cham, Switzerland: Springer.

Sandler, W. (2017) The challenge of sign language phonology. *Annual Review of Linguistics*, *3*, 43–63.

Sandler, W. & Lillo-Martin, D. (2017) Sign languages. In M. Aronoff and J. Rees-Miller (Eds.), *The handbook of linguistics*, 2nd edition (pp. 371–396). Chichester, UK: John Wiley.

Sándor, N., Várady, G., Szalmás, A., Sik-Lányi, C. & Kálmán, Z. (2002) Electronic usage of Bliss symbols. In P. Sharkey et al. (Eds.), *Proceedings of the 4th International Conference on Disability, Virtual Reality and Associated Technologies, Veszprém, Hungary, September 18–20 2002* (pp. 33–38). Reading, UK: University of Reading.

Sandweiss, A. J., Brandt, V. L. & Zoghbi, H. Y. (2020) Advances in understanding of Rett syndrome and MECP2 duplication syndrome: Prospects for future therapies. *The Lancet Neurology, 19*, 689–698.

Sankoff, G. (2018) Language change across the lifespan. *Annual Review of Linguistics, 4*, 297–316.

Sankoff, G. (2019) Language change across the lifespan: Three trajectory types. *Language, 95*, 197–229.

Sargent, J., Clarke, M., Price, K., Griffiths, T. & Swettenham, J. (2013) Use of eye-pointing by children with cerebral palsy: What are we looking at? *International Journal of Language and Communication Disorders, 48*, 477–485.

Sarriá, E., Gómez, J. C. & Tamarit, J. (1996) Joint attention and alternative language intervention in autism: Implications of theory for practice. In S. von Tetzchner and M. H. Jensen (Eds.), *Augmentative and alternative communication: European perspectives* (pp. 49–64). London, UK: Whurr/Wiley.

Savaldi-Harussi, G. Lustigman, L. & Soto, G. (2019) The emergence of clause construction in children who use speech generating devices. *Augmentative and Alternative Communication, 35*, 109–119.

Savaldi-Harussi, G. & Soto, G. (2018) Early verbal categories and inflections in children who use speech-generating devices. *Augmentative and Alternative Communication, 34*, 194–205.

Savatt, J. M. & Myers, S. M. (2021) Genetic testing in neurodevelopmental disorders. *Frontiers in Pediatrics, 9*, 526779.

Savolainen, I., Klippi, A., Tykkyläinen, T., Higginbotham, J. & Launonen, K. (2020) The structure of participants' turn-transition practices in aided conversations that use speech-output technologies. *Augmentative and Alternative Communication*, 36, 18–30.

Schaeffer, B., Raphael, A. & Kollinzas, G. (1994) *Signed speech for nonverbal students*. Seattle, WA: Educational Achievement Systems.

Schaeffer, J., Abd El-Raziq, M., Castroviejo, E., Durrleman, S., Ferré, S. et al. (2023) Language in autism: Domains, profiles and co-occurring conditions. *Journal of Neural Transmission, 130*, 433–457.

Schaffer, H. R. (1989) Language development in context. In S. von Tetzchner et al. (Eds.), *The social and cognitive aspects of normal and atypical language development* (pp. 1–22). New York: Springer.

Schalock, R. L., Luckasson, R. & Tassé, M. J. (2021) *Intellectual disability: Definition, diagnosis, classification, and systems of supports*, 12th edition. Washington, DC: American Association on Intellectual and Developmental Disabilities.

Schank, R. C. & Abelson, R. P. (1977) *Scripts, plans, goals, and understanding*. Hillsdale, NJ: Lawrence Erlbaum.

Schick, A. & Melzi, G. (2010) The development of children's oral narratives across contexts. *Early Education and Development, 21*, 293–317.

Schiff, R., Ashkenazi, P., Kahta, S. & Sasson, A. (2021) Stimulus variation-based training enhances artificial grammar learning. *Acta Psychologica, 214*, 103252.

Schiørbeck, H. & Stadskleiv, K. (2008) Utredning og tiltak ved kognitive vansker. In S. von Tetzchner et al. (Eds.), *Habilitering: Tverrfaglig arbeid for mennesker med utviklingsmessige funksjonshemninger* (pp. 239–290). Oslo: Gyldendal Akademisk

Schjølberg, S. (1984) Forståeligheten av talen til barn med språkvansker. Thesis, University of Oslo.

Schley, S. & Snow, C. E. (1992) The conversational skills of school aged children. *Social Development, 1*, 18–35.

Schlosser, R. W. (1997a) Nomenclature of category levels in graphic symbols, Part I: Is a flower a flower a flower? *Augmentative and Alternative Communication, 13*, 4–13.

Schlosser, R. W. (1997b) Nomenclature of category levels in graphic symbols, Part II: The role of similarity in categorization. *Augmentative and Alternative Communication, 13*, 14–29.

Schlosser, R. W., Balandin, S., Hemsley, B., Iacono, T. Probst, P. & von Tetzchner, S. (2014) Facilitated communication and authorship: A systematic review. *Augmentative and Alternative Communication, 30*, 359–368.
Schlosser, R. W. & Blischak, D. M. (2001) Is there a role for speech output in interventions for persons with autism? A review. *Focus on Autism and other Developmental Disabilities, 16*, 170–178.
Schlosser, R. W. & Koul, R. K. (2015) Speech output technologies in interventions for individuals with autism spectrum disorders: A scoping review. *Augmentative and Alternative Communication, 31*, 285–309.
Schlosser, R. W. & Lee, D. (2000) Promoting generalization and maintenance in augmentative and alternative communication: A meta-analysis of 20 years of effectiveness research. *Augmentative and Alternative Communication, 16*, 208–226.
Schlosser, R. W. & Lloyd, L. L. (1997) Effects of paired-associate learning versus symbol explanations on Blissymbol comprehension and production. *Augmentative and Alternative Communication, 13*, 226–238.
Schlosser, R. W. & Raghavendra. P. (2004) Evidence-based practice in augmentative and alternative communication. *Augmentative and Alternative Communication, 20*, 1–21,
Schlosser, R. W. & Sigafoos, J. (2009) Navigating evidence-based information sources in augmentative and alternative communication. *Augmentative and Alternative Communication, 25*, 225–235.
Schlosser, R. W. & Wendt, O. (2008) Effects of augmentative and alternative communication intervention on speech production in children with autism: A systematic review. *American Journal of Speech-Language Pathology, 17*, 212–230.
Schmidt, A., de Oliveira Franco, M. G., dos Santos Lotério, L. & Gomes, G. F. (2016) Learning name-object relations after a single exclusion trial in 18-to 48-month-old children. *The Psychological Record, 66*, 53–63.
Schneider, W., Niklas, F. & Schmiedeler, S. (2014) Intellectual development from early childhood to early adulthood: The impact of early IQ differences on stability and change over time. *Learning and Individual Differences, 32*, 156–162.
Schopler, E., Lansing, M. D., Reichler, R. J. & Marcus, L. M. (2005) *Psychoeducational Profile*, 3rd edition. Austin, TX: Pro-ed.
Schreibman, L., Dawson, G., Stahmer, A. C., Landa, R., Rogers, S. J. et al. (2015) Naturalistic developmental behavioral interventions: Empirically validated treatments for autism spectrum disorder. *Journal of Autism and Developmental Disorders, 45*, 2411–2428.
Schulerud, A. (2002) *Bridge over troubled water – Utvikling av lesekunnskap med alternativ og supplerende kommunikasjon som språklig grunnlag*. Skien: Habiliteringstjenesten.
Schwartz, I. S., Garfinkle, A. N. & Bauer, J. (1998) The Picture Exchange Communication System: Communicative outcomes for young children with disabilities. *Topics in Early Childhood Special Education, 18*, 144–159.
Schwartz, J. B. & Nye, C. (2006) A systematic review, synthesis, and evaluation of the evidence for teaching sign language to children with autism. *EBP Briefs, 1*, 1–17.
Schworer, E. K., Fidler, D. J. & Daunhauer, L. A. (2021) Early regulatory skills and social communication development in infants with Down syndrome. *Brain Sciences, 11*, 208.
Scollon, R. (1976) *Conversations with a one year old.* Honolulu: University of Hawaii Press.
Scope (2008) *No voice, no choice: Professional experiences of the provision and support of alternative and augmentative communication (AAC).* London: Scope.
Scott, S. & Beidel, D. C. (2011) Selective mutism: An update and suggestions for future research. *Current Psychiatry Reports, 13*, 251–257.
Scott, J. A. & Henner, J. (2021) Second verse, same as the first: On the use of signing systems in modern interventions for deaf and hard of hearing children in the USA. *Deafness and Education International, 23*, 123–141,
Seal, B. C. & DePaolis, R. A. (2014) Manual activity and onset of first words in babies exposed and not exposed to baby signing. *Sign Language Studies, 14*, 444–465.

Seifer, R., Sameroff, A., Dickstein, S., Schiller, M. & Hayden, L. C. (2004) Your own children are special: Clues to the sources of reporting bias in temperament assessments. *Infant Behavior and Development*, *27*, 323–341.
Seligman, M. E. (1972) Learned helplessness. *Annual Review of Medicine*, *23*, 407–412.
Seligman, M. E. & Darling, R. B. (2007) *Ordinary families, special children: A systems approach to childhood disability*, 3rd edition. London: Guilford Press.
Sellers, D., Mandy, A., Pennington, L., Hankins, M. & Morris, C. (2014) Development and reliability of a system to classify the eating and drinking ability of people with cerebral palsy. *Developmental Medicine and Child Neurology*, *56*, 245–251.
Sellers, D., Pennington, L., Bryant, E., Benfer, K., Weir, K. et al. (2022) Mini-EDACS: Development of the Eating and Drinking Ability Classification System for young children with cerebral palsy. *Developmental Medicine and Child Neurology*, *64*, 897–906.
Sellwood, D., Raghavendra, P. & Walker, R. (2022) Facilitators and barriers to developing romantic and sexual relationships: Lived experiences of people with complex communication needs. *Augmentative and Alternative Communication*, *38*, 1–14.
Senner, J. E. & Baud, M. R. (2017) The use of an eight-step instructional model to train school staff in partner-augmented input. *Communication Disorders Quarterly*, *38*, 89–95.
Sennott, S. C., Akagi, L., Lee, M. & Rhodes, A. (2019) AAC and artificial intelligence (AI). *Topics in Language Disorders*, *39*, 389–403.
Sennott, S. C., Light, J. C. & McNaughton, D. (2016) AAC modeling intervention research review. *Research and Practice for Persons with Severe Disabilities*, *41*, 101–115.
Sennott, S. C. & Mason, L. H. (2016) AAC modeling with the iPad during shared storybook reading pilot study. *Communication Disorders Quarterly*, *37*, 242–254.
Serafini, F. (2014) Exploring wordless picture books. *The Reading Teacher*, *68*, 24–26.
Serna, R. W. & Carlin, M. T. (2001) Guiding visual attention in individuals with mental retardation. *International Review of Research in Mental Retardation*, 24, 321–357.
Service, V., Lock, A. & Chandler, P. (1989) Individual differences in early communicative development: A social constructivist perspective. In S. von Tetzchner et al. (Eds.), *The social and cognitive aspects of normal and atypical language development* (pp. 23–49). New York: Springer.
Sevcik, R. A., Barton-Hulsey, A., Bruce, S., Goldman, A., Ogletree, B. T. et al. (2022) It's never too late: Debunking myths about communication and adults with severe disabilities. *Intellectual and Developmental Disabilities*, *60*, 416–425.
Sevcik, R. A., Barton-Hulsey, A., Walters, C. & Romski, M. (2019) Reading interventions for individuals with intellectual and developmental disabilities: A review. *International Review of Research in Developmental Disabilities*, *57*, 81–118.
Sexton, S. & Rush, D. (2012) The family resource support guide. *CASEtools*, *6*, 1–14.
Shablack, H., & Lindquist, K. A. (2019) The role of language in emotional development. In V. LoBue et al. (Eds.), *Handbook of emotional development* (pp. 451–478). Cham, Switzerland: Springer.
Shadiev, R. & Yang, M. (2020) Review of studies on technology-enhanced language learning and teaching. *Sustainability*, *12*, 524.
Shane, H. C. & Bashir, A. S (1981) Election criteria for the adoption of an augmentative communication system: Preliminary considerations. *Journal of Speech and Hearing Disorders*, *45*, 408–414.
Shanmugarajah, K., Rosenbaum, P., Zubairi, M. & Di Rezze, B. (2021) A narrative review of function-focused measures for children with neurodevelopmental disorders. *Frontiers in Rehabilitation Sciences*, *2*, 709978.
Sharpe, P. A. (1992) Comparative effects of bilateral hand splints and an elbow orthosis on stereotypic hand movements and toy play in two children with Rett syndrome. *American Journal of Occupational Therapy*, *46*, 134–140.
Shatz, M. & Gelman, R. (1973) The development of communication skills: Modification in the speech of young children as a function of the listener. *Monographs of the Society for Research in Child Development*, *38*.

Shenouda, J., Barrett, E., Davidow, A. L., Sidwell, K., Lescott, C. et al. (2023) Prevalence and disparities in the detection of autism without intellectual disability. *Pediatrics*, *151*, e2022056594.

Shepherd, G. (1977) Social skills training: The generalization problem. *Behavior Therapy*, *8*. 1008–1009.

Shepherd, T. A., Campbell, K. A., Renzoni, A. M. & Sloan, N. (2009) Reliability of speech generating devices: A 5-year review. *Augmentative and Alternative Communication*, *25*, 145–153.

Shepherd, T. A. & Haaf, R. G. (1995) Comparison of two training methods in the learning and generalization of Blissymbolics. studies. *Augmentative and Alternative Communication*, *11*, 154–164.

Sherman, E., Tan. J. E. & Hrabok, M. (2022) *A compendium of neuropsychological tests: Fundamentals of neuropsychological assessment and test reviews for clinical practice*, 4th edition. Oxford, UK: Oxford University Press.

Shore, B. J., Allar, B. G., Miller, P. E., Matheney, T. H., Snyder, B. D. & Fragala-Pinkham, M. (2019) Measuring the reliability and construct validity of the Pediatric Evaluation of Disability Inventory – Computer Adaptive Test (PEDI-CAT) in children with cerebral palsy. *Archives of Physical Medicine and Rehabilitation*, *100*, 45–51.

Shriberg, L. D., Kwiatkowski, J. & Mabie, H. L. (2019) Estimates of the prevalence of motor speech disorders in children with idiopathic speech delay. *Clinical Linguistics and Phonetics*, *33*, 679–706.

Shvarts, A. & Bakker, A. (2019) The early history of the scaffolding metaphor: Bernstein, Luria, Vygotsky, and before. *Mind, Culture, and Activity*, *26*, 4–23.

Sidener, T. M., Shabani, D. B., Carr, J. E. & Roland, J. P. (2006) An evaluation of strategies to maintain mands at practical levels. *Research in Developmental Disabilities*, *27*, 632–644.

Sigafoos, J., Didden, R., Schlosser, R., Green, V. A., O'Reilly, M. F. & Lancioni, G. E. (2008) A review of intervention studies on teaching AAC to individuals who are deaf and blind. *Journal of developmental and Physical Disabilities*, *20*, 71–99.

Sigafoos, J., Kagohara, D., van der Meer, L., Green, V. A., O'Reilly, M. F. et al. (2011) Communication assessment for individuals with Rett syndrome: A systematic review. *Research in Autism Spectrum Disorders*, *5*, 692–700.

Sigafoos, J., O'Reilly, M. F., Lancioni, G. E., Zhang, D. & Marschik, P. B. (2022) The Inventory of Potential Communicative Acts (IPCA): Narrative review of reliability, validity, and clinical utility. *Evidence-Based Communication Assessment and Intervention*, *16*, 105–122.

Sigafoos, J., Roche, L., O'Reilly, M. F. & Lancioni, G. E. (2021) Persistence of primitive reflexes in developmental disorders. *Current Developmental Disorders Reports*, *8*, 98–105.

Sigafoos, J., Roche, L., O'Reilly, M. F., Lancioni, G. E. & Marschik, P. B. (2023) Updated systematic-narrative review on communication intervention in Rett Syndrome: 2010–2022. *Augmentative and Alternative Communication*, *39*, 241–255.

Sigafoos, J., van der Meer, L., Schlosser, R., Lancioni, E. G., O'Reilly, M. F. & Green, V. A. (2016) Augmentative and alternative communication (AAC) in intellectual and developmental disabilities. In J. K. Luiselli and A. J. Fischer (Eds.), *Computer-assisted and web-based innovations in psychology, special education, and health* (pp. 255–285). New York: Academic Press.

Sigafoos, J., Woodyatt, G., Keen, D., Tait, K., Tucker, M. et al. (2000) Identifying potential communicative acts in children with developmental and physical disabilities. *Communication Disorders Quarterly*, *21*, 77–86.

Sigman, M. & McGovern, C. W. (2005) Improvement in cognitive and language skills from preschool to adolescence in autism. *Journal of Autism and Developmental Disorders*, *35*, 15–23.

Silverman, W. (2007) Down syndrome: Cognitive phenotype. *Mental Retardation and Developmental Disabilities Research Reviews*, *13*, 228–236.

Simacek, J., Reichle, J & McComas, J. J. (2016) Communication intervention to teach requesting through aided AAC for two learners with Rett syndrome. *Journal of Developmental and Physical Disabilities*, *28*, 59–81.

Simcock, G. & Deloache, J. S. (2006) Get the Picture? The effects of iconicity on toddlers' re-enactment from picture books. *Developmental Psychology*, *42*, 1352–1357.

Simunovic, M. P. (2010) Colour vision deficiency. *Eye*, *24*, 747–755.

Sireci, S. G. & O'Riordan, M. (2020) Comparability issues in assessing individuals with disabilities. In A. Berman et al. (Eds.), *Comparability issues in large-scale assessment* (pp. 177–204). Washington, DC: National Academy of Education Press

Skär, L. & Tamm, M. (2002) Disability and social network. A comparison between children and adolescents with and without restricted mobility. *Scandinavian Journal of Disability Research*, *4*, 118–137.

Skinner, B. F. (1957) *Verbal behavior*. New York: Appleton-Century-Crofts.

Slobin, D. I. (1973) Cognitive prerequisites for development of grammar. In C. A. Ferguson and D. I. Slobin (Eds.), *Studies of child language development* (pp. 175–208). New York: Holt, Rinehart and Winston.

Slone, L. K., Abney, D. H., Borjon, J. I., Chen, C. H., Franchak, J. M. et al. (2018) Gaze in action: Head-mounted eye tracking of children's dynamic visual attention during naturalistic behavior. *JoVE Journal of Visualized Experiments*, *141*, e58496.

Smith, A. L. & Hustad, K. C. (2015) AAC and early intervention for children with cerebral palsy: Parent perceptions and child risk factors. *Augmentative and Alternative Communication*, *31*, 336–350.

Smith, L. & von Tetzchner, S. (1986) Communicative, sensorimotor, and language skills of young children with Down syndrome. *American Journal of Mental Deficiency*, *91*, 57–66.

Smith, M. M. (1991) Assessment of interaction patterns and AAC use: A case study. *Journal of Clinical Speech and Language Studies*, *1*, 76–102.

Smith, M. M. (1996) The medium or the message: A study of speaking children using communication boards. In S. von Tetzchner and M. H. Jensen (Eds.), *Augmentative and alternative communication: European perspectives* (pp. 119–136) London: Whurr.

Smith, M. M. (2003) Environmental influences on aided language development: The role of parental adaptation. In S. von Tetzchner and N. Grove (Eds.), *Augmentative and alternative communication; Developmental issues* (pp. 155–175). London, UK: Whurr/Wiley.

Smith, M. M. (2005a) *Literacy and augmentative and alternative communication*. London: Academic Press.

Smith, M. M. (2005b) The dual challenges of aided communication and adolescence. *Augmentative and Alternative Communication*, *21*, 67–79.

Smith, M. M. (2014) Supporting vocabulary development in children who use augmentative and alternative communication. *Journal of the Speech-Language-Hearing Association of Taiwan*, *33*, 35–59.

Smith, M. M. (2015) Language development of individuals who require aided communication: Reflections on state of the science and future research directions. *Augmentative and Alternative Communication*, *31*, 215 –233.

Smith, M. M. (2016) Evidence for impact and impact of evidence. *Augmentative and Alternative Communication*, *32*, 227–232

Smith, M. M. (2019) Innovations for supporting communication: Opportunities and challenges for people with complex communication needs. *Folia Phoniatrica et Logopaedica*, *71*, 156–167.

Smith, M. M., Batorowicz, B., Dahlgren Sandberg, A., Murray, A., Stadskleiv, K. et al. (2018) Constructing narratives to describe video events using aided communication. *Augmentative and Alternative Communication*, *34*, 40–53.

Smith, M. M. & Grove, N. (1999) The bimodal situation of children learning language using manual and graphic signs. In F. T. Loncke et al. (Eds.), *Augmentative and alternative communication: New directions in research and practice* (pp. 8–30). London: Whurr/Wiley.

Smith, M. M., Manduchi, B., Burke, É., Carroll, R., McCallion, P. & McCarron, M. (2020) Communication difficulties in adults with Intellectual Disability: Results from a national cross-sectional study. *Research in Developmental Disabilities*, *97*, 103557.

Smith, M. M., Murray, J., von Tetzchner, S. & Langan, P. (2010) A tale of transitions: The challenges of integrating speech synthesis in aided communication. In J. Mullennix and S. Stern (Eds.), *Computer synthesized speech technologies: Tools for aiding impairment* (pp. 234–256). Hershey, PA: IGI Global.

Smith-Lewis, M. (1994) Discontinuity in the development of aided augmentative and alternative communication systems. *Augmentative and Alternative Communication, 10*, 14–26.

Smucker, L. M., McCarthy, J. W., Benigno, J. P. & Boster, J. B. (2018) Personal contact through personal narratives: Attitudes of fifth-grade children toward children who use augmentative and alternative communication. *Journal of Advances in Education Research, 3*, 148–157.

Snell, M. E., Chen, L. Y., Allaire, J. H. & Park, E. (2008) Communication breakdown at home and at school in young children with cerebral palsy and severe disabilities. *Research and Practice for Persons with Severe Disabilities, 33*, 25–36.

Snodgrass, M. R. (2016) Supporting a school team in planning and implementing AAC for a child with intellectual disability. Dissertation, University of Illinois at Urbana Champaign, USA.

Snodgrass, M. R., Stoner, J. B. & Angell, M. E. (2013) Teaching conceptually referenced core vocabulary for initial augmentative and alternative communication. *Augmentative and Alternative Communication, 29*, 322–333.

Snow, C. E. & Ferguson, C. A. (Eds.) (1977) *Talking to children*. Cambridge, UK: Cambridge University Press.

Snowling, M. J. & Hulme, C. (2021) Reading disorders revisited – The critical importance of oral language. *Journal of Child Psychology and Psychiatry, 62*, 635–653.

Soenens, B., Vansteenkiste, M. & Van Petegem, S. (Eds.) (2018) *Autonomy in adolescent development: Towards conceptual clarity*. Abingdon, UK: Routledge.

Solomon-Rice, P. & Soto, G. (2011) Co-construction as a facilitative factor in supporting the personal narratives of children who use augmentative and alternative communication. *Communication Disorders Quarterly, 32*, 70–82.

Sommer, K. S., Whitman, T. L. & Keogh, D. A. (1988) Teaching severely retarded persons to sign interactively through the use of a behavioral script. *Research in Developmental Disabilities, 9*, 291–304.

Sorell, J. (2015) Word frquencies. In J. R. Taylor (Ed.), *Handbook of the word* (pp. 68–88). Oxford, UK: Oxford University Press..

Soro, E., Basil, C. & von Tetzchner, S. (1992) Teaching initial communication and language skills to AAC users. Part 1: Children and adolescents with impairment of language comprehension and expression. *Video presented at Fifth Biennial Conference on Augmentative and Alternative Communication*, Philadelphia, PA, August 1992.

Soto, G. (1999) Understanding the impact of graphic sign use on the message structure. In F. T. Loncke et al. (Eds.), *Augmentative and alternative communication: New directions in research and practice* (pp. 40–48). London, England: Whurr\Wiley.

Soto, G. & Clarke, M. T. (2017) Effects of a conversation-based intervention on the linguistic skills of children with motor speech disorders who use augmentative and alternative communication. *Journal of Speech, Language, and Hearing Research, 60*, 1980–1998.

Soto, G. & Clarke, M. T. (2018) Conversation-based intervention for adolescents using augmentative and alternative communication. *Augmentative and Alternative Communication, 34*, 180–193.

Soto, G., Clarke, M. T., Nelson, K., Starowicz, R. & Savaldi-Harussi, G. (2020) Recast type, repair, and acquisition in AAC mediated interaction. *Journal of Child Language, 47*, 250–264.

Soto, G. & Cooper, B. (2021) An early Spanish vocabulary for children who use AAC: Developmental and linguistic considerations. *Augmentative and Alternative Communication, 37*, 64–74.

Soto, G., Hartmann, E. & Wilkins, D. (2006) Exploring the elements of narrative that emerge in the interactions between an 8-year-old child who uses a device and her teacher. *Augmentative and Alternative Communication, 22*, 231–241.

Soto, G., Müller, E., Hunt, P. & Goetz, L. (2001) Critical issues in the inclusion of students who use augmentative and alternative communication: An educational team perspective. *Augmentative and Alternative Communication, 17*, 62–72.

Soto, G. & Seligman-Wine, J. (2003) Child-driven development of graphic communication: A case study. In S. von Tetzchner and N. Grove (Eds.), *Augmentative and alternative communication: Developmental issues* (pp. 211–228). London, UK: Whurr/Wiley.

Soto, G. & Yu, B. (2014) Considerations for the provision of services to bilingual children who use augmentative and alternative communication. *Augmentative and Alternative Communication, 30*, 83–92,

Soto, G., Yu, B. & Henneberry, S. (2007) Supporting the development of narrative skills of an eight-year old child who uses an augmentative and alternative communication device. *Child Language Teaching and Therapy, 23*, 27–45.

South, M. & Rodgers, J. (2017) Sensory, emotional and cognitive contributions to anxiety in autism spectrum disorders. *Frontiers in Human Neuroscience, 11*, 20.

Sparrow, S. S., Cicchetti, D V. & Saulnier, C. A. (2016) *Vineland adaptive behavior scales*, 3rd edition. San Antonio, TX: Pearson.

Spriggs, A. D., Mims, P. J., van Dijk, W. & Knight, V. F. (2017) Examination of the evidence base for using visual activity schedules with students with intellectual disability. *The Journal of Special Education, 51*, 14–26.

St Clair, M. C., Pickles, A., Durkin, K. & Conti-Ramsden, G. (2011) A longitudinal study of behavioral, emotional and social difficulties in individuals with a history of specific language impairment (SLI). *Journal of Communication Disorders, 44*, 186–199.

Stadskleiv, K. (2015) Assessment of cognitive processes in aided communicators. In S. von Tetzchner and Judith D. Oxley (Eds.), *Processes of aided language development in cognitively high-functioning children and adolescents. Proceedings of the Twelfth Biennial Research Symposium of the International Society for Augmentative and Alternative Communication, Lisbon, Portugal, August 25–26, 2014* (pp. 87–99). Toronto: ISAAC.

Stadskleiv, K. (2017) Experiences from a support group for families of preschool children in the expressive AAC user group. *Augmentative and Alternative Communication, 33*, 3–13.

Stadskleiv, K. (2020) Cognitive functioning in children with cerebral palsy. *Developmental Medicine and Child Neurology, 62*, 283–289.

Stadskleiv, K., Batorowicz, B., Massaro, M., van Balkom, H. & von Tetzchner, S. (2018a) Visual-spatial cognition in children using aided communication. *Augmentative and Alternative Communication, 34*, 68–78.

Stadskleiv, K., Jahnsen, R., Andersen, G. L. & von Tetzchner, S. (2018b) Neuropsychological profiles of children with cerebral palsy. *Developmental Neurorehabilitation, 21*, 108–120.

Stadskleiv, K., van Balkom, H. & von Tetzchner, S. (2022) Cognition and assessment. In S. von Tetzchner and J. Murray (Eds.), *Becoming an Aided Communicator (BAC): Theory, methods, findings and practical implications. Proceedings of a study day, University of Leeds, June 21st 2022* (pp. 10–20). Leeds, UK: Communication Matters.

Stadskleiv, K., von Tetzchner, S., Batorowicz, B., van Balkom, H., Dahlgren Sandberg, A. & Renner, G. (2014) Investigating executive functions in children with severe speech and movement disorders using structured tasks. *Frontiers in Psychology*, 5, 992.

Stancliffe, R. J., Larson, S., Auerbach, K., Engler, J., Taub, S. & Lakin, K. C. (2010) Individuals with intellectual disabilities and augmentative and alternative communication: Analysis of survey data on uptake of aided AAC, and loneliness experiences. *Augmentative and Alternative Communication, 26*, 87–96.

Standart, S. & Couteur, A. L. (2003) The quiet child: A literature review of selective mutism. *Child and Adolescent Mental Health, 8*, 154–160.

Starble, A., Hutchins, T., Favro, M., Prelock, P. & Bitner, B. (2005) Family-centered intervention and satisfaction with AAC device training. *Communication Disorders Quarterly, 27*, 47–54.

Stauter, D. W., Myers, S. R. & Classen, A. I. (2017) Literacy instruction for young children with severe speech and physical impairments: A systematic review. *Journal of Occupational Therapy, Schools, and Early Intervention, 10*, 389–407,

Stauter, D. W., Prehn, J., Peters, M., Jeffries, L. M., Sylvester, L. et al. (2019) Assistive technology for literacy in students with physical disabilities: A systematic review. *Journal of Special Education Technology, 34*, 284–292.

Steele, L. (2020) *Disability, criminal justice and law: Reconsidering court diversion*. Abingdon, UK: Routledge.

Steenbuch, R. (1957) *Jeg lever også*. Oslo: Land og Kirke.

Steffenburg, H., Steffenburg, S., Gillberg, C. & Billstedt, E. (2018) Children with autism spectrum disorders and selective mutism. *Neuropsychiatric Disease and Treatment*, *14*, 1163–1169.

Steindal, K. (1990) Personal communication.

Steinhausen, H. C., Wachter, M., Laimböck, K. & Metzke, C. W. (2006) A long-term outcome study of selective mutism in childhood. *Journal of Child Psychology and Psychiatry*, *47*, 751–756.

Stenberg, N., Bresnahan, M., Gunnes, N., Hirtz, D., Hornig, M. et al. (2014) Identifying children with autism spectrum disorder at 18 months in a general population sample. *Paediatric and Perinatal Epidemiology*, *28*, 255–262.

Stenberg, N., Schjølberg, S., Shic, F., Volkmar, F., Øyen, A. S. et al. (2021) Functional outcomes of children identified early in the developmental period as at risk for ASD utilizing the The Norwegian Mother, Father and Child Cohort Study (MoBa). *Journal of Autism and Developmental Disorders*, *51*, 922–932.

Stephenson, J. (2009a) Iconicity in the development of picture skills: Typical development and implications for individuals with severe intellectual disabilities. *Augmentative and Alternative Communication*, *25*, 187–201.

Stephenson, J. (2009b) Picture-book reading as an intervention to teach the use of line drawings for communication with students with severe intellectual disabilities. *Augmentative and Alternative Communication*, *25*, 202–214.

Stephenson, J. (2009c) Recognition and Use of Line Drawings by Children with Severe Intellectual Disabilities: The Effects of Color and Outline Shape. *Augmentative and Alternative Communication*, *25*, 55–67.

Stephenson, J. & Linfoot, K. (1996) Pictures as communication symbols for students with severe disability. *Augmentative and Alternative Communication*, *12*, 244–255.

Steriadis, C. E. & Constantinou, P. (2003) Designing human-computer interfaces for quadriplegic people. *ACM Transactions on Computer-Human Interaction*, *10*, 87–118.

Sterrett, K., Holbrook A., Landa, R., Kaiser, A. & Kasari, C. (2023) The effect of responsiveness to speech-generating device input on spoken language in children with autism spectrum disorder who are minimally verbal. *Augmentative and Alternative Communication*, *39*, 23–32.

Stokes, T. F., Baer, D. M. & Jackson, R. L. (1974) Programming the generalization of a greeting response in four retarded children. *Journal of Applied Behavior Analysis*, *7*, 599–610.

Stuart, S., Beukelman D. & King, J. (1997) Vocabulary use during extended conversations by two cohorts of older adults. *Augmentative and Alternative Communication*, *13*, 40–47.

Su, P. L., Castle, G. & Camarata, S. (2019) Cross-modal generalization of receptive and expressive vocabulary in children with autism spectrum disorder. *Autism and Developmental Language Impairments*, *4*, 1–18.

Suggate, S., Schaughency, E., McAnally, H. & Reese, E. (2018) From infancy to adolescence: The longitudinal links between vocabulary, early literacy skills, oral narrative, and reading comprehension. *Cognitive Development*, *47*, 82–95.

Sundqvist, A. & Rönnberg, J. (2010) A qualitative analysis of email interactions of children using augmentative and alternative communication. *Augmentative and Alternative Communication*, *26*, 255–266.

Sutton, A., Morford, J. P. & Gallagher, T. M. (2004) Production and comprehension of graphic symbol utterances expressing complex propositions by adults who use augmentative and alternative communication systems. *Applied Psycholinguistics*, *25*, 349–371.

Sweeney, L. A. (1999) Moving forward with families: Perspectives on augmentative and alternative communication research and practice. In F. T. Loncke et al. (Eds.), *Augmentative and alternative communication: New directions in research and practice* (pp. 231–254). London: Whurr/Wiley.

Tager-Flusberg, H. & Kasari, C. (2013) Minimally verbal school-aged children with autism spectrum disorder: The neglected end of the spectrum. *Autism Research, 6*, 468–478.
Takesian, A. E. & Hensch, T. K. (2013) Balancing plasticity/stability across brain development. *Progress in Brain Research, 207*, 3–34.
Tan, C. D. (2018) "I'm a normal autistic person, not an abnormal neurotypical": Autism spectrum disorder diagnosis as biographical illumination. *Social Science and Medicine, 197*, 161–167.
Tan, X. Y., Trembath, D., Bloomberg, K., Iacono, T. & Caithness, T. (2014) Acquisition and generalization of key word signing by three children with autism. *Developmental Neurorehabilitation, 17*, 125–136.
Tardif, T., Fletcher, P., Liang, W., Zhang, Z., Kaciroti, N. & Marchman, V. A. (2008) Baby's first 10 words. *Developmental Psychology, 44*, 929–938.
Tarquinio, D. C., Hou, W., Neul, J. L., Lane, J. B., Barnes, K. V. et al. (2015) Age of diagnosis in Rett syndrome: Patterns of recognition among diagnosticians and risk factors for late diagnosis. *Pediatric Neurology, 52*, 585–591.
Tavares, L. & Peixoto, A. (2003) Late development of independent conversation skills with manual and graphic signs through joint activities. In S. von Tetzchner and N. Grove (Eds.), *Augmentative and alternative communication: Developmental issues* (pp. 272–286). London: Whurr/Wiley.
Taylor, R. & Iacono, T. (2003) AAC and scripting activities to facilitate communication and play. *Advances in Speech-Language Pathology, 5*, 79–93.
Tegler, H. (2020) Social interaction involving nonspeaking children with severe cerebral palsy and intellectual disability. The role of communication partners and speechgenerating devices. Dissertation, Upsalla University.
Tegler, H., Pless, M., Blom Johansson, M. & Sonnander, K. (2021) Caregivers', teachers', and assistants' use and learning of partner strategies in communication using high-tech speech-generating devices with children with severe cerebral palsy. *Assistive Technology, 33*, 17–25.
Terband, H., Maassen, B. & Maas, E. (2019) A psycholinguistic framework for diagnosis and treatment planning of developmental speech disorders. *Folia Phoniatrica et Logopaedica, 71*, 216–227.
Thapar, A., Cooper, M. & Rutter, M. (2017) Neurodevelopmental disorders. *The Lancet Psychiatry, 4*, 339–346.
Theakston, A. & Lieven, E. (2017) Multiunit sequences in first language acquisition. *Topics in Cognitive Science, 9*, 588–603.
Therrien, M. C. S. (2019) Perspectives and experiences of adults who use AAC on making and keeping friends, *Augmentative and Alternative Communication, 35*, 205–216,
Therrien, M. C., Barton-Hulsey, A. & Wong, S. (2022) A scoping review of the playground experiences of children with AAC needs. *Augmentative and Alternative Communication, 38*, 245–255.
Therrien, M., Rossetti, Z. & Østvik, J. (2023) Augmentative and alternative communication and friendships: Considerations for speech-language pathologists. *Perspectives of the ASHA Special Interest Groups, 8*, 151–163.
Thomas, M. S., Alfageme, O. O., D'Souza, H., Patkee, P. A., Rutherford, M. A. et al. (2020) A multilevel developmental approach to exploring individual differences in Down syndrome: Genes, brain, behaviour, and environment. *Research in Developmental Disabilities, 104*, 103638.
Thomas-Stonell, N. L., Cunningham, B. J., Robertson, B. & Rosenbaum, P. (2020) *The Focus on the Outcomes of Communication Under Six (FOCUS) manual*, 2nd edition. Toronto: CanChild.
Thurman, A. J., Bullard, L., Kelly, L., Wong, C., Nguyen, V. et al. (2022) Defining expressive language benchmarks for children with Down syndrome. *Brain Sciences, 12*, 743.
Timpe, E. M., Kent-Walsh, J., Binger, C., Hahs-Vaughn, D., Harrington, N. & Schwartz, J. B. (2021) Using the ImPAACT program with preschoolers with Down syndrome: A hybrid service-delivery model. *Augmentative and Alternative Communication, 37*, 113–128.
Tincani, M. (2004) Comparing the picture exchange communication system and sign language training for children with autism. *Focus on Autism and other Developmental Disabilities, 19*, 152–163.

Tincani, M., Crozier, S. & Alazetta, L. (2006) The picture exchange communication system: Effects on manding and speech development for school-aged children with autism. *Education and Training in Developmental Disabilities, 41*, 177–184.

Todd, J. T. (2012) The moral obligation to be empirical: Comments on Boynton's Facilitated communication – what harm it can do: Confessions of a former "facilitator". *Evidence-Based Communication Assessment and Intervention, 6*, 36–57.

Todman, J., Alm, N., Higginbotham, J. & File, P. (2008) Whole utterance approaches in AAC. *Augmentative and Alternative Communication, 24*, 235–254.

Toffalini, E., Giofrè, D. & Cornoldi, C. (2017) Strengths and weaknesses in the intellectual profile of different subtypes of specific learning disorder: A study on 1,049 diagnosed children. *Clinical Psychological Science, 5*, 402–409.

Toh, S. H., Howie, E. K., Coenen, P., & Straker, L. M. (2019) "From the moment I wake up I will use it… every day, very hour": A qualitative study on the patterns of adolescents' mobile touch screen device use from adolescent and parent perspectives. *BMC Pediatrics, 19*, 1–16.

Tomasello, M. (1992) *First verbs: A case study of early grammatical development*. Cambridge: Cambridge University Press.

Tomasello, M. (2003) *Constructing a language. A usage-based theory of language acquisition*. London, UK: Harvard University Press.

Tomasello, M. (2005) "Cultural constraints on grammar and cognition in Piraha: Another look at the design features of human language": Comment. *Current Anthropology, 46*, 640–641.

Tomasello, M. (2006) Acquiring linguistic constructions. In W. Damon et al. (Eds.), *Handbook of child psychology, Sixth edition, Volume 2: Cognition, perception and language* (pp. 371–384). New York: Wiley.

Tomasello, M. (2009a) *Why we cooperate*. London: MIT Press.

Tomasello, M. (2009b) The usage-based theory of language acquisition. In E. L. Bavin (Ed.), *The Cambridge handbook of child language* (pp. 69–87). Cambridge, UK: Cambridge University Press.

Tomasello, M. (2016) The ontogeny of cultural learning. *Current Opinion in Psychology, 8*, 1–4.

Tomasello, M. (2019) *Becoming human: A theory of ontogeny*. Cambridge, MA: Harvard University Press.

Tomasello, M. (2020) The adaptive origins of uniquely human sociality. *Philosophical Transactions of the Royal Society B, 375*, 20190493.

Tomasello, M., Carpenter, M., Call, J., Behne, T. & Moll, H. (2005) Understanding and sharing intentions: The origins of cultural cognition. *Behavioral and Brain Sciences, 28*, 675–691.

Tomasello, M., Carpenter, M. & Lizskowski, U. (2007) A new look at infant pointing. *Child Development, 78*, 705–722.

Tönsing, K. M. (2012) Using a matrix strategy to teach graphic symbol combinations to children with limited speech during shared storybook reading. Dissertation, University of Pretoria.

Tönsing, K. M. (2016) Supporting the production of graphic symbol combinations by children with limited speech: A comparison of two AAC systems. *Journal of Developmental and Physical Disabilities, 28*, 5–29.

Tönsing, K. M., Bartram, J., Morwane, R. E. & Waller, A. (2024a) Designing electronic graphic symbol-based AAC systems: A scoping review. Part 1: System description. *Disability and Rehabilitation: Assistive Technology, 19*, 1079–1091.

Tönsing, K. M., Bartram, J., Morwane, R. R. & Waller, A. (2024b) Designing electronic graphic symbol-based AAC systems: A scoping review. Part 2: Application of human-centred design. *Disability and Rehabilitation: Assistive Technology, 19*, 1092–1102.

Tönsing, K. M., Dada, S. & Alant, E. (2014) Teaching graphic symbol combinations to children with limited speech during shared story reading. *Augmentative and Alternative Communication, 30*, 279–297.

Tönsing, K. M. & Soto, G. (2020) Multilingualism and augmentative and alternative communication: Examining language ideology and resulting practices. *Augmentative and Alternative Communication, 36*, 190–201.

Topper, S. T. (1975) Gesture language for a non-verbal severely retarded male. *Mental Retardation, 13*, 30–31.

Tøssebro, A.-G., von Tetzchner, S., Christal, A., McElrone, D., Siggs, M., Oxley, J. D. & Cameron, J. (2019) Communication and language in education and intervention for children and adults with juvenile neuronal ceroid lipofuscinosis. In S. von Tetzchner et al. (Eds.), *Juvenile neuronal ceroid lipofuscinosis, childhood dementia and education* (pp. 231–256). Trondheim: Snøfugl Forlag.

Trasher, K. & Bray, N. (1984) Effects of iconicity, taction, and training technique on the initial acquisition of manual signing by the mentally retarded. *Presented at The 17th Annual Gatinburg Conference on Research in Mental Retardation*, Gatinburg, 1984.

Treviranus, J. & Roberts, V. (2003) Supporting competent motor control of AAC systems. In J. Light et al. (Eds.), *Communicative competence for individuals who use AAC* (pp. 107–145). Baltimore, MD: Brookes

Tribushinina, E., Van Den Bergh, H., Kilani-Schoch, M., Aksu-Koç, A., Dabašinskienė, I. et al. (2013) The role of explicit contrast in adjective acquisition: A cross-linguistic longitudinal study of adjective production in spontaneous child speech and parental input. *First Language, 33*, 594–616.

Trief, E., Bruce, S. M., Cascella, P. W. & Ivy, S. (2009) The development of a universal tangible symbol system. *Journal of Visual Impairment and Blindness, 103*, 425–430.

Trief, E., Cascella, P. W. & Bruce, S. M. (2013) A field study of a standardized tangible symbol system for learners who are visually impaired and have multiple disabilities. *Journal of Visual Impairment and Blindness, 107*, 180–191.

Troseth, G. L., Pierroutsakos, S. L. & DeLoache, J. S. (2004) From the innocent to the intelligent eye: The early development of pictorial competence. *Advances in Child Development and Behavior, 32*, 1–35.

Trott, S. & Bergen, B. (2020) Why do human languages have homophones?. *Cognition, 205*, 104449.

Trudeau, N., Sutton, A., Morford, J. P., Côte-Giroux, P., Pauze, A.-M. & Vallée, V. (2010) Strategies in construction and interpretation of graphic-symbol sequences by individuals who use AAC systems. *Augmentative and Alternative Communication, 26*, 299–312.

Trudeau, N., Cleave, P. & Woelk, E. (2003) Using augmentative and alternative communication approaches to promote participation of preschoolers during book reading: A pilot study. *Child Language Teaching and Therapy, 19*, 181–210.

Tsibidaki, A. (2020) Family functioning and strengths in families raising a child with cerebral palsy. *Research in Developmental Disabilities, 106*, 103767.

Tungate, A. S. & Conners, F. A. (2021) Executive function in Down syndrome: A meta-analysis. *Research in Developmental Disabilities, 108*, 103802.

Turner, M. (1996) *The literary mind: The origins of thought and language*. New York: Oxford University Press.

Tzuriel, D. (2021) *Mediated learning and cognitive modifiability*. New York: Springer.

Uchino, J., Suzuki, M., Hoshino, K., Nomura, Y. & Segawa, M. (2001) Development of language in Rett syndrome. *Brain and Development, 23*, S233–S235.

Unicode Consortium (2020) *The Unicode Standard Version 13.0 – Core Specification*. Mountain View, CA: Unicode Consortium.

Urbanowicz, A., Ciccone, N., Girdler, S., Leonard, H. & Downs, J. (2018) Choice making in Rett syndrome: A descriptive study using video data. *Disability and Rehabilitation, 40*, 813–819.

Vaivre-Douret, L., Lalanne, C. & Golse, B. (2016) Developmental coordination disorder, an umbrella term for motor impairments in children: Nature and co-morbid disorders. *Frontiers in Psychology, 7*, 502.

Valencia, S., Cave, R., Kallarackal, K., Seaver, K., Terry, M. & Kane, S. K. (2023) "The less I type, the better": How AI language models can enhance or impede communication for AAC users. In S. Schmidt et al. (Eds.), *Proceedings of the 2023 CHI Conference on Human Factors in Computing Systems, Hamburg, Germany, April 23–28, 2023* (Article 830, pp. 1–14). New York: Association for Computing Macheney.

Valencia-Naranjo, N. & Robles-Bello, M. A. (2020) Dynamic assessment in preschoolers with Down syndrome and nonspecific intellectual disability. *Psicología Educativa*, *26*, 101–107.

Valera-Pozo, M., Adrover-Roig, D., Pérez-Castelló, J. A., Sanchez-Azanza, V. A. & Aguilar-Mediavilla, E. (2020) Behavioral, emotional and school adjustment in adolescents with and without developmental language disorder (DLD) is related to family involvement. *International Journal of Environmental Research and Public Health*, *17*, 1949.

Valle, C. L., Chenausky, K. & Tager-Flusberg, H. (2021) How do minimally verbal children and adolescents with autism spectrum disorder use communicative gestures to complement their spoken language abilities? *Autism and Developmental Language Impairments*, *6*, 23969415211035065.

Van Daal, J., Verhoeven, L. & Van Balkom, H. (2007) Behaviour problems in children with language impairment. *Journal of Child Psychology and Psychiatry*, *48*, 1139–1147.

van der Mark, E. J., Conradie, I., Dedding, C. W. & Broerse, J. E. (2017) How poverty shapes caring for a disabled child: A narrative literature review. *Journal of International Development*, *29*, 1187–1206.

van der Meer, L., Matthews, T., Ogilvie, E., Berry, A., Waddington, H. et al. (2017) Training direct-care staff to provide communication intervention to adults with intellectual disability: A systematic review. *American Journal of Speech-Language Pathology*, *26*, 1279–1295.

van der Meer, L., Sigafoos, J., Sutherland, D., McLay, L., Lang, R. et al. (2014) Preference-enhanced communication intervention and development of social communicative functions in a child with autism spectrum disorder. *Clinical Case Studies*, *13*, 282–295.

van der Merwe, E. & Alant, E. (2004) Associations with Minspeak icons. *Journal of Communication Disorders*, *37*, 255–274.

van Oosterom, J. & Devereux, K. (1985) *Learning with Rebus glossary*. Back Hill, UK: Earo, The Resource Centre.

van Riper, M. (2007) Families of children with Down syndrome: Responding to "a change in plans" with resilience. *Journal of Pediatric Nursing*, *22*, 116–128.

van Tilborg, A. & Deckers, S. J. R. M. (2016) Vocabulary selection in AAC: Application of core vocabulary in atypical populations. *Perspectives of the ASHA Special Interest Groups*, *1*, 125–138.

Vanderheiden, G. C. (2002) A journey through early augmentative communication and computer access. *Journal of Rehabilitation Research and Development*, *39*, 39–53.

Veneziano, E. (2013) A cognitive-pragmatic model for the change from single-word to multiword speech: A constructivist approach. *Journal of Pragmatics*, *56*, 133–150.

Veneziano, E. (2018) Learning conversational skills and learning from conversation. In A. Bar-On and D. Ravid (Eds.), *Handbook of communication disorders: Theoretical, empirical, and applied linguistic perspectives* (pp. 311–328). Berlin: De Gruyter Mouton.

Venkatagiri, H. S. (2010) Digital speech technology: An overview. In J. Mullennix and S. Stern (Eds.), *Computer synthesized speech technologies: Tools for aiding impairments* (pp. 28–49). Hershey, NY: Medical Information Science Reference.

Venuti, P., De Falco, S., Esposito, G. & Bornstein, M. H. (2009) Mother–child play: Children with Down syndrome and typical development. *American Journal on Intellectual and Developmental Disabilities*, *114*, 274–288.

Veresov, N. (2006) Leading activity in developmental psychology: Concept and principle. *Journal of Russian and East European Psychology*, *44*, 7–25.

Versteeg, A. (2020) *Peer attitudes toward a school aged AAC user: Does use of high vs low tech device matter?* London, University of Western Ontario.

Vertanen, K., Trinh, H., Waller, A., Hanson, V. L. & Kristensson, P. O. (2012) Applying prediction techniques to phoneme-based AAC systems. In *Proceedings of the Third Workshop on Speech and Language Processing for Assistive Technologies, Montreal, Canada, June 7–8, 2012* (pp. 19–27). Kerrville, TX: Association for Computational Linguistics.

Vessoyan, K., Smart, E., Steckle, G. & McKillop, M. (2023) A scoping review of eye tracking technology for communication: Current progress and next steps. *Current Developmental Disorders Reports*, *10*, 20–39.

Vihman, M. M. (2018) First word learning. In S. A. Rueschemeyer and M. Gareth Gaskell (Eds.), *The Oxford handbook of psycholinguistics*, 2nd edition (pp. 714–736). Oxford, UK: Oxford University Press

Viljoen, E., Bornman, J., Wiles, L. & Tönsing, K. M. (2017) Police officer disability sensitivity training: A systematic review. *The Police Journal, 90*, 143–159.

Vilvarajan, S., McDonald, M., Douglas, L., Newham, J., Kirkland, R. et al. (2023) Multidisciplinary management of Rett syndrome: Twenty years' experience. *Genes, 14*, 1607.

Vinkel, M. N., Rackauskaite, G. & Finnerup, N. B. (2022) Classification of pain in children with cerebral palsy. *Developmental Medicine and Child Neurology, 64*, 447–452.

Vissers, L. E., Gilissen, C. & Veltman, J. A. (2016) Genetic studies in intellectual disability and related disorders. *Nature Reviews Genetics, 17*, 9–18.

Vivanti, G., Duncan, E., Dawson, G. & Rogers, S. J. (2017) *Implementing the group-based Early Start Denver Model for preschoolers with autism*. Cham, Switzerland: Springer.

Volkmar, F. R. & McPartland, J. C. (2014) From Kanner to DSM-5: Autism as an evolving diagnostic concept. *Annual Review of Clinical Psychology, 10*, 193–212.

von Tetzchner, S. (1984a) Facilitation of early speech development in a dysphatic child by use of signed Norwegian. *Scandinavian Journal of Psychology, 25*, 265–275.

von Tetzchner, S. (1984b) Tegnspråksopplæring med psykotiske/autistiske barn: Teori, metode og en kasusbeskrivelse. *Tidsskrift for Norsk Psykologforening, 21*, 3–15.

von Tetzchner, S. (1985) Words and chips – pragmatics and pidginization of computer-aided communication. *Child Language Teaching and Therapy, 1*, 295–305.

von Tetzchner, S. (1986) Samtaler om kommunikasjon. *CP-Bladet, 32* (3), 17–20.

von Tetzchner, S. (1987) Hjulpet lek. *CP-Bladet, 33* (4), 12–13.

von Tetzchner, S. (1990) Tilbakeblikk. *CP-Bladet, 36* (4), 5–9.

von Tetzchner, S. (1996a) Facilitated, automatic and false communication: Current issues in the use of facilitating techniques. *European Journal of Special Needs Education, 11*, 151–166.

von Tetzchner, S. (1996b) The contexts of early aided language acquisition. *Presented at The 7th Biennial Conference of the International Society for Augmentative and Alternative Communication*, Vancouver, August 1996.

von Tetzchner, S. (1997a) The use of graphic language intervention among young children in Norway. *European Journal of Disorders of Communication, 32*, 217–234.

von Tetzchner, S. (1997b) Communication skills of females with Rett syndrome. *European Child and Adolescent Psychiatry, 6* (Supplement 1), 33–37.

von Tetzchner, S. (1997c) Historical issues in intervention research: Hidden knowledge and facilitating techniques in Denmark. *European Journal of Disorders of Communication, 32*, 1–18.

von Tetzchner, S. (2003) *Utfordrende atferd for mennesker med lærehemning*. Oslo: Gyldendal Akademisk.

von Tetzchner, S. (2004) Early intervention and prevention of challenging behaviour in children with learning disabilities. *Perspectives in Education, 22*, 85–100.

von Tetzchner, S. (2006) Communication impairments in girls with Rett syndrome. *Invited presentation in Autism Affinity Distinguished Lecture Serie, Center for Autism Research and Treatment, University of California*, Los Angeles, December 1 2006.

von Tetzchner, S. (2010) Why reading is difficult for children with motor impairments: On motor theories of speech perception, analysis by synthesis, embodied cognition and mirror neurons. *Presented at The 14th Biennial Conference of the International Society for Augmentative and Alternative Communication*, Barcelona, Spain, August 26–31 2010.

von Tetzchner, S. (2012) Understanding facilitated communication: Lessons from a former facilitator – Comments on Boynton, 2012. *Evidence Based Communication Assessment and Intervention, 6*, 28–35.

von Tetzchner, S. (2015) The semiotics of aided language development. *Cognitive Development, 36*, 180–190.

von Tetzchner, S. (2018) Introduction to the special issue on aided language processes, development, and use: An international perspective. *Augmentative and Alternative Communication, 34*, 1–15.

von Tetzchner, S. (2019a) *Child and adolescent psychology: Typical and atypical development*. Abingdon, UK: Routledge.

von Tetzchner, S. (2019b) Manual signs and graphic symbols as complementary forms of augmentative and alternative communication. In N. Grove and K. Launonen (Eds.), *Manual sign acquisition in children with developmental disabilities* (pp. 195–212). New York: Nova.

von Tetzchner, S. (2021a) Challenging behaviors: Processes, prevention and intervention. In S. von Tetzchner et al. (Eds.), *Development, assessment and intervention of autism spectrum disorders in childhood: International and Chinese* perspectives (pp. 351–375). Beijing, China: Guangming Daily Press

von Tetzchner, S. (2021b) Becoming an aided communicator (BAC): Basic ideas and aims. *Presented at Communication Matters Virtual Conference*, Leeds, UK, September 13–17, 2021.

von Tetzchner, S. & Basil, C. (2011) Terminology and notation in written representations of conversations with augmentative and alternative communication. *Augmentative and Alternative Communication, 27*, 141–149.

von Tetzchner, S., Brekke, K. M., Sjøthun, B. & Grindheim, E. (2005) Constructing preschool communities of learners that afford alternative communication. *Augmentative and Alternatve Communication, 21*, 82–100.

von Tetzchner, S. & Grove, N. (2003) The development of alternative language forms. In S. von Tetzchner and N. Grove (Eds.), *Augmentative and alternative communication: Developmental issues* (pp. 1–27) London, UK: Whurr/Wiley.

von Tetzchner, S., Jacobsen, K. H., Smith, L., Skjeldal, O. H., Heiberg, A. & Fagan, J. F. (1996) Vision, cognition and developmental characteristics of girls and women with Rett syndrome. *Developmental Medicine and Child Neurology, 38*, 212–225.

von Tetzchner, S. & Jensen, K. (1999) Communicating with people who have severe communication impairment: Ethical considerations. *International Journal of Disability, Development and Education, 46*, 453–462.

von Tetzchner, S. & Jensen, M. H. (1996) Introduction. In S. von Tetzchner and M. H. Jensen (Eds.), *Augmentative and alternative communication: European perspectives* (pp. 1–18). London: Whurr/Wiley.

von Tetzchner, S., Launonen, K., Batorowicz, B., Nunes, L., Walter, C. et al. (2018) Communication aid provision and use among children and adolescents developing aided communication: An international survey. *Augmentative and Alternative Communication, 34*, 79–91.

von Tetzchner, S., Lippe-Holstein, J. & Haugen, P. K. (2019) Behavioral and emotional reactions to a difficult life situation. In S. von Tetzchner et al. (Eds.), *Juvenile neuronal ceroid lipofuscinosis, childhood dementia and education* (pp. 519–534). Trondheim: Snøfugl Forlag

von Tetzchner, S. & Martinsen, H. (1996) Words and strategies: Communicating with young children who use aided language. In S. von Tetzchner and M. H. Jensen (Eds.), *Augmentative and alternative communication: European perspectives* (pp. 65–88). London: Whurr/Wiley.

von Tetzchner, S. & Øien, I. (1989) *Rett syndrom: Forløp og tiltak. Video*. Oslo: Norsk forening for Rett syndrom.

von Tetzchner, S., Øvreeide, K. D., Jørgensen, K. K., Ormhaug, B. M., Oxholm, B. & Warme, R. (2004) Acquisition of graphic communication by a young girl without comprehension of spoken language. *Disability and Rehabilitation, 26*, 1335–1346.

von Tetzchner, S. & Oxley, J. (2013) Introduction to Blissymbol research and practice issues. In L. L. Lloyd et al. (Eds.), *Augmentative and alternative communication research issues and needs. Proceedings of the 2012 ISAAC Research Symposium* (pp. 53–60). Toronto: ISAAC.

von Tetzchner, S., Rogne, S. O. & Lilleeng, M. K. (1997) Literacy intervention for a deaf child with severe reading disorders. *Journal of Literacy Research, 29*, 25–46.

von Tetzchner, S. & Sedberg, T. (2005) Young blind children in activities with joint attention. *Presented at X. International Conference for the Study of Child Language*, Berlin, Germany, July 25–29 2005.

von Tetzchner, S. & Stadskleiv, K. (2016) Constructing a language in alternative forms. In M. M. Smith and J. Murray (Eds.), *The silent partner? Language, interaction and aided communication* (pp. 17–34). Guildford, UK: J&R Press.

von Tetzchner, S., Torjussen, K., Carlin, P. E. & Smith, L. (2002) Cross-modal matching of object pictures with natural sounds and word forms in girls with Rett syndrome. In *Proceedings of the Joint Conference of the IX International Congress for the Study of Child Language and the Symposium of Research in Child Language Disorders, Madison, July 2002* (pp. 129–130). Madison, Wisconsin: University of Madison.

Vygotsky, L. (1962) *Thought and language*. Cambridge, MA: MIT Press.

Vygotsky, L. S. (1967) Play and its role in the mental development of the child. *Soviet Psychology, 5*, 6–18.

Wagner, K. R. (1985) How much do children say in a day? *Journal of Child Language, 12*, 475–487.

Walker, J. F. & Archibald, L. M. (2006) Articulation rate in preschool children: A 3-year longitudinal study. *International Journal of Language and Communication Disorders, 41*, 541–565.

Walker, M. (1976) *Language programmes for use with the revised Makaton vocabulary*. Surrey, UK: M. Walker.

Walker, M., Mitha, S. & Riddington, C. (2019) Cultural issues in developing and using signs within the Makaton Language programme in different countries. In N. Grove and K. Launonen (Eds.), *Manual sign acquisition in children with developmental disabilities* (pp. 391–408). New York: Nova.

Waller, A. (2006) Communication access to conversational narrative. *Topics in Language Disorders, 26*, 221–239.

Waller, A. and O'Mara, D. (2003) Augmentative and alternative communication and the development of personal story telling. In S. von Tetzchner and N. Grove (Eds.), *Augmentative and alternative communication: Developmental issues* (pp. 256–271). London, UK: Whurr/Wiley.

Walter, C., Stadskleiv, K., Murray, J. & von Tetzchner, S. (2022) After BAC – Participants' reflections on involvement in research. In S. von Tetzchner and J. Murray (Eds.), *Becoming an Aided Communicator (BAC): Theory, methods, findings and practical implications. Proceedings of a study day, University of Leeds, June 21st 2022* (pp. 46–50). Leeds, UK: Communication Matters.

Wandin, H. (2020) Symbol-based communication intervention for individuals with Rett syndrome: Current practices, assessment of visual attention, and communication partner strategies, Dissertation, Upsalla University, Sweden.

Warburg, M. (2001) Visual impairment in adult people with intellectual disability: Literature review. *Journal of Intellectual Disability Research, 45*, 424–438

Warren, S. F. & Kaiser, A. P. (1986) Incidental teaching: A critical review. *Journal of Speech and Hearing Disorders, 51*, 291–299.

Watson, L. R., Crais, E. R., Baranek, G. T., Dykstra, J. R. & Wilson, K. P. (2013) Communicative gesture use in infants with and without autism: A retrospective home video study. *American Journal of Speech-Language Pathology, 22*, 25–39.

Watson, M. M. & Lof, G. L. (2008, November) Epilogue: What we know about nonspeech oral motor exercises. *Seminars in Speech and Language, 29*, 339–344.

Watters, R. G. Wheeler, L. J. & Watters, W. E. (1981) The realtive efficiency of two orders for training autistic children in the expressive and receptive use of manual signs. *Journal of Communication Disorders, 14*, 273–285.

Webster, C. D., Fruchter, D., Dean, J., Konstantareas, M. M. & Sloman, L. (2016) Lessons that linger: A 40-year follow-along note about a boy with autism taught to communicate by gestures when aged six. *Journal of Autism and Developmental Disorders, 46*, 2561–2564.

Webster, C. D., McPherson, H. M., Sloman, L., Evans, M. A., & Kuchar, E. (1973) Communicating with an autistic boy by gestures. *Journal of Autism and Childhood Schizophrenia, 3*, 337–346.

Weierink, L., Vermeulen, R. J. & Boyd, R. N. (2013) Brain structure and executive functions in children with cerebral palsy: A systematic review. *Research in Developmental Disabilities, 34*, 1678–1688.

Weindrich, D., Jennen-Steinmetz, C., Laucht, M., Esser, G. & Schmidt, M. H. (2000) Epidemiology and prognosis of specific disorders of language and scholastic skills. *European Child and Adolescent Psychiatry*, *9*, 186–194.

Weisberg, D. S., Zosh, J. M., Hirsh-Pasek, K. & Golinkoff, R. M. (2013) Talking it up: Play, language development, and the role of adult support. *American Journal of Play*, *6*, 39–54.

Weisberg, H. R. & Jones, E. A. (2019) Individualizing intervention to teach joint attention, requesting, and social referencing to children with autism. *Behavior Analysis in Practice*, *12*, 105–123.

Weisner, T. S. (2002) Ecocultural understanding of children's developmental pathways. *Human Development*, *45*, 275–281.

Wellnitz, S. A., Kästel, I., Vllasaliu, L., Cholemkery, H., Freitag, C. M. & Bast, N. (2021) The Revised Children's Communication Checklist-2 (CCC-R): Factor structure and psychometric evaluation. *Autism Research*, *14*, 759–772.

Wells, G. (2009) *The meaning makers: Learning to talk and talking to learn*. Bristol, UK: Multilingual Matters.

Wepener, C., Johnson, E. & Bornman, J. (2021) Text messaging "Helps Me to Chat": Exploring the interactional aspects of text messaging using mobile phones for youth with complex communication needs. *Augmentative and Alternative Communication*, *37*, 75–86.

Werker, J. F. (2018a) Perceptual beginnings to language acquisition. *Applied Psycholinguistics*, *39*, 703–728.

Werker, J. F. (2018b) Speech perception, word learning, and language acquisition in infancy: The voyage continues. *Applied Psycholinguistics*, *39*, 769–777.

Westley, M. B. (2018) Creating and evaluating New Zealand-accented synthesised voices using model talker voice banking technology. Thesis, University of Canterbury,

Wetherby, A. M. & Prizant, B. M. (2002) *Communication and Symbolic Behavior Scales: Developmental Profile (1st normed edition)*. Baltimore, MD: Paul H. Brookes.

Wexler, K., Blau, A., Leslie, S. & Dore, J. (1983) *Conversational interaction of nonspeaking cerebral palsied individuals and their speaking partners, with and without augmentative communication aids*. New York: Helen Hayes Hospital.

Whalen, C. & Schreibman, L. (2003) Joint attention training for children with autism using behavior modification procedures. *Journal of Child Psychology and Psychiatry*, *44*, 456–468.

White, R. M., Bornman, J. & Johnson, E. (2015) Testifying in court as a victim of crime for persons with little or no functional speech: Vocabulary implications. *Child Abuse Research: A South African Journal*, *16*, 1–14.

White, R. M., Bornman, J., Johnson, E. & Msipa, D. (2021) Court accommodations for persons with severe communication disabilities: A legal scoping review. *Psychology, Public Policy, and Law*, *27*, 399–420.

White, R. M., Bornman, J., Johnson, E., Tewson, K. & Van Niekerk, J. (2020) Transformative equality: Court accommodations for South African citizens with severe communication disabilities. *African Journal of Disability*, *9*, 1–12.

Whitman, T. L., O'Callaghan, M. & Sommer, K. (1997) Emotion and mental retardation. In W. E. MacLean (Ed.), *Ellis' handbook of mental deficiency, psychological theory and research*, 3rd edition (pp. 77–98). Mahwah, NJ: Lawrence Erlbaum.

Wickenden, M. (2010) Talk to me as a teenage girl: An anthropological study of identity and lifeworlds with teenage AAC users. *Communication Matters*, *24* (3), 4–8.

Wickenden, M. (2011c) Whose voice is that?: Issues of identity, voice and representation arising in an ethnographic study of the lives of disabled teenagers who use augmentative and alternative communication (AAC). *Disability studies quarterly*, *31*, 4.

Wickenden, M. (2011a) «Talk to me as a teenager»: Experiences of friendship for disabled teenagers who have little or no speech. *Childhoods Today*, *5*, 1–35.

Wickenden, M. (2011b) Talking to teenagers: Using anthropological methods to explore identity and the lifeworlds of young people who use AAC. *Communication Disorders Quarterly*, *32*, 151–163.

Wickenden, M. (2015) The life worlds of adolescent aided communicators. In S. von Tetzchner and J. D. Oxley (Eds.), *Processes of aided language development in cognitively high-functioning children and adolescents. Proceedings of the 2014 ISAAC Research Symposium* (pp. 33–45). Toronto: ISAAC.
Wilkinson, K. M., Light, J. & Drager, K. (2012) Considerations for the composition of visual scene displays: Potential contributions of information from visual and cognitive sciences. *Augmentative and Alternative Communication*, *28*, 137–147.
Wilkinson, K. M., Romski, M. A. & Sevcik, R. A. (1994) Emergence of visual-graphic symbol combinations by youth with moderate or severe mental retardation. *Journal of Speech and Hearing Research*, *37*, 883–895.
Wilkinson, K. M., Rosenquist, C. & McIlvane, W. J. (2009) Exclusion learning and emergent symbolic category formation in individuals with severe language impairments and intellectual disabilities. *The Psychological Record*, *59*, 187–205.
Willinger, U., Brunner, E., Diendorfer-Radner, G., Sams, J., Sirsch, U. & Eisenwort, B. (2003) Behaviour in children with language development disorders. *The Canadian Journal of Psychiatry*, *48*, 607–614.
Willoughby, L., Iwasaki, S., Bartlett, M. & Manns, H. (2018) Tactile sign languages. In J.-O. Östman and J. Verschueren (Eds.), *Handbook of pragmatics* (pp. 239–258). Amsterdam: John Benjamins.
Wilson, K. D. (1980) Selection of a core lexicon for use with graphic communicative systems. *Journal of Childhool Communication Disorders*, *4*, 111–123.
Witkowski, D. & Baker, B. (2012) Addressing the content vocabulary with core: Theory and practice for nonliterate or emerging literate students. *Perspectives on Augmentative and Alternative Communication*, *21*, 74–81.
Wolff, N., Stroth, S., Kamp-Becker, I., Roepke, S. & Roessner, V. (2022) Autism spectrum disorder and IQ – A complex interplay *Frontiers in Psychiatry*, *13*, 856084.
Woll, B. & Barnett, S. (1998) Toward a spsiolinguistic perspective on augmentative and alternative communication. *Augmentative and Alternative Communication*, *14*, 200–211.
Wood, D., Bruner, J. S. & Ross, G. (1976) The role of tutoring in problem solving. *Journal of Child Psychology and Psychiatry*, *17*, 89–100.
Woodward, J. & Ferretti, R. (2014) The evolving use of technology in special education: Is 'effectiveness' the right question?. In L. Florian (Ed.), *The SAGE handbook of special education*, Volume 2 (pp. 731–747). London: SAGE
Woodward, A. L. & Markman, L. (1998) Early word learning. In W. Damon et al. (Eds.), *Handbook of child psychology, Fifth edition. Volume 2: Cognition, perception and language* (pp. 371–420). New York: Wiley.
Woodyatt, G. C. & Ozanne, A. E. (1992) Communication abilities in a case of Rett syndrome. *Journal of Intellectual Disability Research*, *36*, 83–92.
Woodyatt, G. C. & Ozanne, A. E. (1993) A longitudinal study of communication behaviours in children with Rett syndrome. *Journal of Intellectual Disability Research*, *37*, 419–435.
Woolfe, T., Herman, R., Roy, P. & Woll, B. (2010) Early vocabulary development in deaf native signers: A British Sign Language adaptation of the communicative development inventories. *Journal of Child Psychology and Psychiatry*, *51*, 322–331.
World Health Organization (2022) *International Classification of Diseases Eleventh Revision (ICD-11)*. Geneva: World Health Organization.
Wren, Y., Miller, L. L., Peters, T. J., Emond, A. & Roulstone, S. (2016) Prevalence and predictors of persistent speech sound disorder at eight years old: Findings from a population cohort study. *Journal of Speech, Language, and Hearing Research*, *59*, 647–673.
Wren, Y., Pagnamenta, E., Peters, T. J., Emond, A., Northstone, K., Miller, L. L. & Roulstone, S. (2021) Educational outcomes associated with persistent speech disorder. *International Journal of Language and Communication Disorders*, *56*, 299–312.
Wright, C. A., Kaiser, A. P., Reikowsky, D. I. & Roberts, M. Y. (2013) Effects of a naturalistic sign intervention on expressive language of toddlers with Down syndrome. *Journal of Speech, Language, and Hearing Research*, *56*, 994–1008.

Wu, D., Wolff, J. J., Ravi, S., Elison, J. T., Estes, A. et al. (2024) Infants who develop autism show smaller inventories of deictic and symbolic gestures at 12 months of age. *Autism Research, 17*, 838–851.

Yaffe, Y. (2023) Systematic review of the differences between mothers and fathers in parenting styles and practices. *Current Psychology, 42*, 16011–16024.

Yang, D., Sidman, J. & Bushnell, E. W. (2010) Beyond the information given: Infants' transfer of actions learned through imitation. *Journal of Experimental Child Psychology, 106*, 62–81.

Yıldız, E. & Uzundağ, B. A. (2022) Mothers' descriptions of referents are related to children's communicative competence. *Cognitive Development, 64*, 101258.

Yin Foo, R., Guppy, M. & Johnston, L. M. (2013) Intelligence assessments for children with cerebral palsy: A systematic review. *Developmental Medicine and Child Neurology, 55*, 911–918.

Yoder, P. & McDuffie, A. (2006) Teaching young children with autism to talk. *Seminars in Speech and Language*, 27, 161–172.

Yong, S. & Yong, L. (2021) *A voice of her own*. Singapore: Yong.

Yorke, A. M., Caron, J. G., Pukys, N., Sternad, E., Grecol, C. & Shermak, C. (2021) Foundational reading interventions adapted for individuals who require augmentative and alternative communication (AAC): A systematic review of the research. *Journal of Developmental and Physical Disabilities, 33*, 537–582.

Yorkston, K. M., Honsinger, M. J., Dowden, P. A. & Marriner, N. (1989) Vocabulary selection: A case report. *Augmentative and Alternative Communication, 5*, 101–109.

Youngstrom, E. A., Van Meter, A., Frazier, T. W., Hunsley, J., Prinstein, M. J. et al. (2017) Evidence-based assessment as an integrative model for applying psychological science to guide the voyage of treatment. *Clinical Psychology: Science and Practice, 24*, 331–363.

Yu, B. (2013) Issues in bilingualism and heritage language maintenance: Perspectives of minority-language mothers of children with autism spectrum disorders. *American Journal of Speech-Language Pathology, 22*, 10–24.

Yu, B. (2016) Bilingualism as conceptualized and bilingualism as lived: A critical examination of the monolingual socialization of a child with autism in a bilingual family. *Journal of Autism and Developmental Disorders, 46*, 424–435.

Zambrana, I. M., Pons, F., Eadie, P. & Ystrom, E. (2014) Trajectories of language delay from age 3 to 5: Persistence, recovery and late onset. *International Journal of Language and Communication Disorders, 49*, 304–316.

Zangari, C., Lloyd, L. L. & Vicker, B. (1994) Augmentative and alternative communication: An historic perspective. *Augmentative and Alternative Communication, 10*, 27–59.

Zaylskie, L. E., Biggs, E. E., Minchin, K. J. & Abel, Z. K. (2023) Nurse perspectives on supporting children and youth who use augmentative and alternative communication (AAC) in the pediatric intensive care unit. *Augmentative and Alternative Communication*, 10.1080/07434618.2023.2284269

Zeidan, J., Fombonne, E., Scorah, J., Ibrahim, A., Durkin, M. S. et al. (2022) Global prevalence of autism: A systematic review update. *Autism Research, 15*, 778–790.

Zhang, S., Hao, Y., Feng, Y. & Lee, N. Y. (2022) COVID-19 pandemic impacts on children with developmental disabilities: Service disruption, transition to telehealth, and child wellbeing. *International Journal of Environmental Research and Public Health, 19*, 3259.

Zimmerman, K. N., Ledford, J. R., Gagnon, K. L. & Martin, J. L. (2020) Social stories and visual supports interventions for students at risk for emotional and behavioral disorders. *Behavioral Disorders, 45*, 207–223.

Zirpoli, T. J. & Bell, R. Q. (1987) Unresponsiveness in children with severe disabilities: Potential effects on parent-child interactions. *The Exceptional Child, 34*, 31–40.

Index

Pages in *italics* refer to figures and pages in **bold** refer to tables.